THE BOOK

Peugeot 406
Service and Repair Manual

Peter T Gill and A K Legg LAE MIMI

Models covered

(3982 - 384)

Peugeot 406 Saloon and Estate models with normally-aspirated four-cylinder petrol engines and turbo-Diesel engines, including special/limited editions;

1761cc, 1749cc & 1997cc petrol engines
1997cc & 2179cc turbo-Diesel engines

Does not cover 1998cc (petrol) Turbo, 1997cc direct injection (HPi) petrol, 2230cc (4 cyl) or 2946cc (V6) engines
Does not cover Coupe

70003563588X

A book in the **Haynes Service and Repair Manual Series**

ISBN **1 85960 982 1**

British Library Cataloguing in Publication Data
A catalogue record for this book is available from the British Library.

ABCDE
FGHIJ
KLM

Printed in the USA

Haynes Publishing
Sparkford, Yeovil, Somerset BA22 7JJ, England

Haynes North America, Inc
861 Lawrence Drive, Newbury Park, California 91320, USA

Editions Haynes
4, Rue de l'Abreuvoir
92415 COURBEVOIE CEDEX, France

Haynes Publishing Nordiska AB
Box 1504, 751 45 UPPSALA, Sverige

Contents

LIVING WITH YOUR PEUGEOT 406

Safety first!	Page	**0•5**
Introduction	Page	**0•6**

Roadside repairs

Introduction	Page	**0•7**
If your car won't start	Page	**0•7**
Jump starting	Page	**0•8**
Wheel changing	Page	**0•9**
Identifying leaks	Page	**0•10**
Towing	Page	**0•10**

Weekly checks

Introduction	Page	**0•11**
Underbonnet check points	Page	**0•11**
Engine oil level	Page	**0•12**
Coolant level	Page	**0•13**
Brake and clutch fluid level	Page	**0•13**
Tyre condition and pressure	Page	**0•14**
Power steering fluid level	Page	**0•15**
Washer fluid level	Page	**0•15**
Wiper blades	Page	**0•16**
Battery	Page	**0•16**
Bulbs and fuses	Page	**0•17**

Lubricants and fluids

	Page	**0•18**

Tyre pressures

	Page	**0•18**

MAINTENANCE

Routine maintenance and servicing

Petrol engine

Maintenance schedule	Page	**1A•3**
Maintenance procedures	Page	**1A•5**

Diesel engine

Maintenance schedule	Page	**1B•3**
Maintenance procedures	Page	**1B•5**

Contents

REPAIRS & OVERHAUL

Engine and associated systems

XU petrol engine in-car repair procedures	Page	2A•1
EW series petrol engine in-car repair procedures	Page	2B•1
Diesel engine in-car repair procedures	Page	2C•1
Engine removal and overhaul procedures	Page	2D•1
Cooling, heating and ventilation systems	Page	3•1
Fuel and exhaust system – petrol models	Page	4A•1
Fuel and exhaust system – diesel models	Page	4B•1
Emission systems	Page	4C•1
Starting and charging systems	Page	5A•1
Ignition system (petrol models)	Page	5B•1
Preheating system (diesel models)	Page	5C•1

Transmission

Clutch	Page	6•1
Manual transmission	Page	7A•1
Automatic transmission	Page	7B•1
Driveshafts	Page	8•1

Brakes and suspension

Braking system	Page	9•1
Suspension and steering	Page	10•1

Body equipment

Bodywork and fittings	Page	11•1
Body electrical system	Page	12•1

Wiring diagrams

	Page	12•24

REFERENCE

Dimensions and weights	Page	REF•1
Conversion factors	Page	REF•2
Buying spare parts	Page	REF•3
Vehicle identification numbers	Page	REF•4
General repair procedures	Page	REF•5
Jacking and vehicle support	Page	REF•6
Disconnecting the battery	Page	REF•7
Tools and working facilities	Page	REF•8
MOT test checks	Page	REF•10
Fault finding	Page	REF•14
Glossary of technical terms	Page	REF•25

Index

	Page	REF•30

Advanced driving

Many people see the words 'advanced driving' and believe that it won't interest them or that it is a style of driving beyond their own abilities. Nothing could be further from the truth. Advanced driving is straightforward safe, sensible driving - the sort of driving we should all do every time we get behind the wheel.

An average of 10 people are killed every day on UK roads and 870 more are injured, some seriously. Lives are ruined daily, usually because somebody did something stupid. Something like 95% of all accidents are due to human error, mostly driver failure. Sometimes we make genuine mistakes - everyone does. Sometimes we have lapses of concentration. Sometimes we deliberately take risks.

For many people, the process of 'learning to drive' doesn't go much further than learning how to pass the driving test because of a common belief that good drivers are made by 'experience'.

Learning to drive by 'experience' teaches three driving skills:

☐ Quick reactions. (Whoops, that was close!)
☐ Good handling skills. (Horn, swerve, brake, horn).
☐ Reliance on vehicle technology. (Great stuff this ABS, stop in no distance even in the wet...)

Drivers whose skills are 'experience based' generally have a lot of near misses and the odd accident. The results can be seen every day in our courts and our hospital casualty departments.

Advanced drivers have learnt to control the risks by controlling the position and speed of their vehicle. They avoid accidents and near misses, even if the drivers around them make mistakes.

The key skills of advanced driving are **concentration,** effective all-round **observation, anticipation** and **planning.** When **good vehicle handling** is added to these skills, all driving situations can be approached and negotiated in a safe, methodical way, leaving nothing to chance.

Concentration means applying your mind to safe driving, completely excluding anything that's not relevant. Driving is usually the most dangerous activity that most of us undertake in our daily routines. It deserves our full attention.

Observation means not just looking, but seeing and seeking out the information found in the driving environment.

Anticipation means asking yourself what is happening, what you can reasonably expect to happen and what could happen unexpectedly. (One of the commonest words used in compiling accident reports is 'suddenly'.)

Planning is the link between seeing something and taking the appropriate action. For many drivers, planning is the missing link.

If you want to become a safer and more skilful driver and you want to enjoy your driving more, contact the Institute of Advanced Motorists on 0208 994 4403 or write to IAM House, Chiswick High Road, London W4 4HS for an information pack.

Working on your car can be dangerous. This page shows just some of the potential risks and hazards, with the aim of creating a safety-conscious attitude.

General hazards

Scalding

• Don't remove the radiator or expansion tank cap while the engine is hot.
• Engine oil, automatic transmission fluid or power steering fluid may also be dangerously hot if the engine has recently been running.

Burning

• Beware of burns from the exhaust system and from any part of the engine. Brake discs and drums can also be extremely hot immediately after use.

Crushing

• When working under or near a raised vehicle, always supplement the jack with axle stands, or use drive-on ramps. *Never venture under a car which is only supported by a jack.*
• Take care if loosening or tightening high-torque nuts when the vehicle is on stands. Initial loosening and final tightening should be done with the wheels on the ground.

Fire

• Fuel is highly flammable; fuel vapour is explosive.
• Don't let fuel spill onto a hot engine.
• Do not smoke or allow naked lights (including pilot lights) anywhere near a vehicle being worked on. Also beware of creating sparks (electrically or by use of tools).
• Fuel vapour is heavier than air, so don't work on the fuel system with the vehicle over an inspection pit.
• Another cause of fire is an electrical overload or short-circuit. Take care when repairing or modifying the vehicle wiring.
• Keep a fire extinguisher handy, of a type suitable for use on fuel and electrical fires.

Electric shock

• Ignition HT voltage can be dangerous, especially to people with heart problems or a pacemaker. Don't work on or near the ignition system with the engine running or the ignition switched on.

• Mains voltage is also dangerous. Make sure that any mains-operated equipment is correctly earthed. Mains power points should be protected by a residual current device (RCD) circuit breaker.

Fume or gas intoxication

• Exhaust fumes are poisonous; they often contain carbon monoxide, which is rapidly fatal if inhaled. Never run the engine in a confined space such as a garage with the doors shut.
• Fuel vapour is also poisonous, as are the vapours from some cleaning solvents and paint thinners.

Poisonous or irritant substances

• Avoid skin contact with battery acid and with any fuel, fluid or lubricant, especially antifreeze, brake hydraulic fluid and Diesel fuel. Don't syphon them by mouth. If such a substance is swallowed or gets into the eyes, seek medical advice.
• Prolonged contact with used engine oil can cause skin cancer. Wear gloves or use a barrier cream if necessary. Change out of oil-soaked clothes and do not keep oily rags in your pocket.
• Air conditioning refrigerant forms a poisonous gas if exposed to a naked flame (including a cigarette). It can also cause skin burns on contact.

Asbestos

• Asbestos dust can cause cancer if inhaled or swallowed. Asbestos may be found in gaskets and in brake and clutch linings. When dealing with such components it is safest to assume that they contain asbestos.

Special hazards

Hydrofluoric acid

• This extremely corrosive acid is formed when certain types of synthetic rubber, found in some O-rings, oil seals, fuel hoses etc, are exposed to temperatures above 400°C. The rubber changes into a charred or sticky substance containing the acid. *Once formed, the acid remains dangerous for years. If it gets onto the skin, it may be necessary to amputate the limb concerned.*
• When dealing with a vehicle which has suffered a fire, or with components salvaged from such a vehicle, wear protective gloves and discard them after use.

The battery

• Batteries contain sulphuric acid, which attacks clothing, eyes and skin. Take care when topping-up or carrying the battery.
• The hydrogen gas given off by the battery is highly explosive. Never cause a spark or allow a naked light nearby. Be careful when connecting and disconnecting battery chargers or jump leads.

Air bags

• Air bags can cause injury if they go off accidentally. Take care when removing the steering wheel and/or facia. Special storage instructions may apply.

Diesel injection equipment

• Diesel injection pumps supply fuel at very high pressure. Take care when working on the fuel injectors and fuel pipes.

⚠ *Warning: Never expose the hands, face or any other part of the body to injector spray; the fuel can penetrate the skin with potentially fatal results.*

Remember...

DO

• Do use eye protection when using power tools, and when working under the vehicle.

• Do wear gloves or use barrier cream to protect your hands when necessary.

• Do get someone to check periodically that all is well when working alone on the vehicle.

• Do keep loose clothing and long hair well out of the way of moving mechanical parts.

• Do remove rings, wristwatch etc, before working on the vehicle – especially the electrical system.

• Do ensure that any lifting or jacking equipment has a safe working load rating adequate for the job.

DON'T

• Don't attempt to lift a heavy component which may be beyond your capability – get assistance.

• Don't rush to finish a job, or take unverified short cuts.

• Don't use ill-fitting tools which may slip and cause injury.

• Don't leave tools or parts lying around where someone can trip over them. Mop up oil and fuel spills at once.

• Don't allow children or pets to play in or near a vehicle being worked on.

The engine is mounted transversely at the front of vehicle, with the transmission mounted on its left-hand end. All engines are fitted with a manual transmission as standard (an automatic transmission is available on certain engines).

All models have fully-independent front and rear suspension arrangements incorporating shock absorbers and coil springs.

A wide range of standard and optional equipment is available within the range to suit most tastes, including central locking, electric windows and front and side airbags. An air conditioning system is available on all models.

Provided that regular servicing is carried out in accordance with the manufacturer's recommendations, the vehicle should prove reliable and very economical. The engine compartment is well-designed, and most of the items requiring frequent attention are easily accessible.

Your Peugeot 406 manual

The aim of this manual is to help you get the best value from your vehicle. It can do so in several ways. It can help you decide what work must be done (even should you choose to get it done by a garage). It will also provide information on routine maintenance and servicing, and give a logical course of action and diagnosis when random faults occur. However, it is hoped that you will use the manual by tackling the work yourself. On simpler jobs it may even be quicker than booking the car into a garage and going there twice, to leave and collect it. Perhaps most important, a lot of money can be saved by avoiding the costs a garage must charge to cover its labour and overheads.

The manual has drawings and descriptions to show the function of the various components so that their layout can be understood. Tasks are described and photographed in a clear step-by-step sequence.

References to the 'left' and 'right' of the vehicle are in the sense of a person in the driver's seat facing forward.

The Peugeot 406 Saloon was introduced into the UK in early 1996. At its launch, the 406 was offered with a choice of 1.6 (1580cc – not available in the UK), 1.8 (1761cc) and 2.0 litre (1998cc) petrol engines or a 1.9 litre (1905cc) turbo diesel engine. In the summer of 1996, a 2.0 litre petrol turbo model was introduced, also a new 2.1 litre (2088cc) turbo diesel engine was introduced into the range with the new diesel engine being a 12-valve version of the XUD engine which has also been used in other Peugeot/Citroën vehicles. In early 1997, Peugeot introduced an Estate model, and also introduced the V6 petrol engine into the range.

This manual covers the facelifted models

introduced in March 1999 which were available with the 1.8 litre (1761cc) petrol engine used in the earlier models. New engines include 1.8 litre (1749cc) and the 2.0 litre (1997cc) petrol engines. The new diesel engines are 2.0 litre (1997cc) and 2.2 litre (2179cc).

The engines fitted to the facelift 406 range are all versions of the well-proven units which have appeared in many Peugeot/Citroën vehicles over the years. The engines are based from the XU engine series, the petrol engines are of four-cylinder double overhead camshaft design. The 2.0 litre diesel engine is a single overhead camshaft 8-valve unit and the 2.2 litre diesel is a double overhead camshaft 16-valve unit.

Acknowledgements

Thanks are due to Draper tools Limited, who provided some of the workshop tools, and to all those people at Sparkford who helped in the production of this manual.

The following pages are intended to help in dealing with common roadside emergencies and breakdowns. You will find more detailed fault finding information at the back of the manual, and repair information in the main chapters.

If your car won't start and the starter motor doesn't turn

☐ If it's a model with automatic transmission, make sure the selector is in P or N.
☐ Open the bonnet and make sure that the battery terminals are clean and tight.
☐ Switch on the headlights and try to start the engine. If the headlights go very dim when you're trying to start, the battery is probably flat. Get out of trouble by jump starting (see next page) using a friend's car.

If your car won't start even though the starter motor turns as normal

☐ Is there fuel in the tank?
☐ Is there moisture on electrical components under the bonnet? Switch off the ignition, then wipe off any obvious dampness with a dry cloth. Spray a water-repellent aerosol product (WD-40 or equivalent) on ignition and fuel system electrical connectors like those shown in the photos. Pay special attention to the ignition coil wiring connector and HT leads. (Note that Diesel engines don't normally suffer from damp.)

A Remove the plastic cover and check the condition and security of the battery connections.

B Check that the fuel/ignition system (as applicable) wiring connectors are securely connected (2.0 litre petrol model shown).

C Check that the alternator wiring connectors are securely connected.

Check that electrical connections are secure (with the ignition switched off) and spray them with a water dispersant spray like WD40 if you suspect a problem due to damp

D Check that all fuses are still in good condition and none have blown.

E Check that the fuel cut-off switch (where fitted) has not been activated.

Jump starting

When jump-starting a car using a booster battery, observe the following precautions:

✔ Before connecting the booster battery, make sure that the ignition is switched off.

✔ Ensure that all electrical equipment (lights, heater, wipers, etc) is switched off.

✔ Take note of any special precautions printed on the battery case.

✔ Make sure that the booster battery is the same voltage as the discharged one in the vehicle.

✔ If the battery is being jump-started from the battery in another vehicle, the two vehicles MUST NOT TOUCH each other.

✔ Make sure that the transmission is in neutral (or PARK, in the case of automatic transmission).

 HAYNES HiNT *Jump starting will get you out of trouble, but you must correct whatever made the battery go flat in the first place. There are three possibilities:*

1 *The battery has been drained by repeated attempts to start, or by leaving the lights on.*

2 *The charging system is not working properly (alternator drivebelt slack or broken, alternator wiring fault or alternator itself faulty).*

3 *The battery itself is at fault (electrolyte low, or battery worn out).*

1 Connect one end of the red jump lead to the positive (+) terminal of the flat battery

2 Connect the other end of the red lead to the positive (+) terminal of the booster battery.

3 Connect one end of the black jump lead to the negative (-) terminal of the booster battery

4 Connect the other end of the black jump lead to a bolt or bracket on the engine block, well away from the battery, on the vehicle to be started.

5 Make sure that the jump leads will not come into contact with the fan, drive-belts or other moving parts of the engine.

6 Start the engine using the booster battery and run it at idle speed. Switch on the lights, rear window demister and heater blower motor, then disconnect the jump leads in the reverse order of connection. Turn off the lights etc.

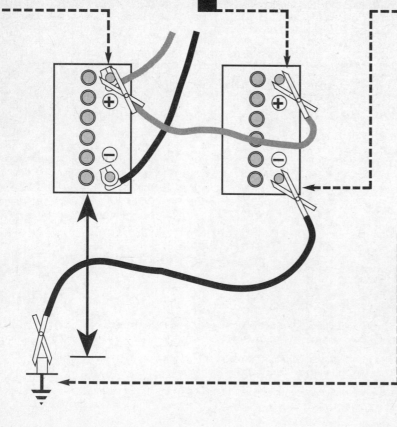

Wheel changing

⚠️ *Warning: Do not change a wheel in a situation where you risk being hit by another vehicle. On busy roads, try to stop in a lay-by or a gateway. Be wary of passing traffic while changing the wheel - it is easy to become distracted by the job in hand.*

Preparation

- ☐ When a puncture occurs, stop as soon as it is safe to do so.
- ☐ Park on firm level ground, if possible, and well out of the way of other traffic.
- ☐ Use hazard warning lights if necessary.

- ☐ If you have one, use a warning triangle to alert other drivers of your presence.
- ☐ Apply the handbrake and engage first or reverse gear (or Park on models with automatic transmission).

- ☐ Chock the wheel diagonally opposite the one being removed – a couple of large stones will do for this.
- ☐ If the ground is soft, use a flat piece of wood to spread the load under the jack.

Changing the wheel

1 The spare wheel and tools are stored in the luggage compartment. Lift up the carpet/rear family seat (as applicable) and remove the tool kit and jack from the centre of the spare wheel. Unscrew the retainer and remove the spare wheel.

2 Remove the wheel trim/hub cap (as applicable).

3 On models where anti-theft wheel bolts are fitted, pull off the plastic cover then unscrew the anti-theft bolt using the special socket provided.

4 With the vehicle on the ground, slacken each wheel bolt by half a turn. On models with alloy wheels, use the special tool to undo the locking wheel nuts.

5 Make sure the jack is located on firm ground, and engage the jack head correctly with the sill. Then raise the jack until the wheel is raised clear of the ground.

6 Unscrew the wheel bolts and remove the wheel. Fit the spare wheel and screw in the bolts. Lightly tighten the bolts with the wheelbrace then lower the car to the ground.

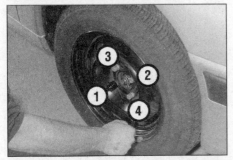

7 Securely tighten the wheel bolts in a diagonal sequence then refit the wheel trim/hub cap/wheel bolt covers (as applicable). Stow the punctured wheel and tools back in the boot, and secure them in position.

Finally...

- ☐ Remove the wheel chocks.
- ☐ Check the tyre pressure on the wheel just fitted. If it is low, or if you don't have a pressure gauge with you, drive slowly to the nearest garage and inflate the tyre to the right pressure.
- ☐ The wheel bolts should be slackened and retightened to the specified torque at the earliest possible opportunity (see Chapter 1A or 1B).
- ☐ Have the damaged tyre or wheel repaired as soon as possible.

Identifying leaks

Puddles on the garage floor or drive, or obvious wetness under the bonnet or underneath the car, suggest a leak that needs investigating. It can sometimes be difficult to decide where the leak is coming from, especially if the engine bay is very dirty already. Leaking oil or fluid can also be blown rearwards by the passage of air under the car, giving a false impression of where the problem lies.

 Warning: Most automotive oils and fluids are poisonous. Wash them off skin, and change out of contaminated clothing, without delay.

HAYNES HINT *The smell of a fluid leaking from the car may provide a clue to what's leaking. Some fluids are distinctively coloured. It may help to clean the car carefully and to park it over some clean paper overnight as an aid to locating the source of the leak.*
Remember that some leaks may only occur while the engine is running.

Sump oil

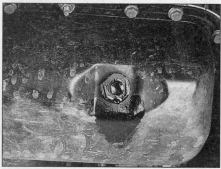

Engine oil may leak from the drain plug...

Oil from filter

...or from the base of the oil filter.

Gearbox oil

Gearbox oil can leak from the seals at the inboard ends of the driveshafts.

Antifreeze

Leaking antifreeze often leaves a crystalline deposit like this.

Brake fluid

A leak occurring at a wheel is almost certainly brake fluid.

Power steering fluid

Power steering fluid may leak from the pipe connectors on the steering rack.

Towing

When all else fails, you may find yourself having to get a tow home – or of course you may be helping somebody else. Long-distance recovery should only be done by a garage or breakdown service. For shorter distances, DIY towing using another car is easy enough, but observe the following points:

☐ Use a proper tow-rope – they are not expensive. The vehicle being towed must display an ON TOW sign in its rear window.
☐ Always turn the ignition key to the 'on' position when the vehicle is being towed, so that the steering lock is released, and that the direction indicator and brake lights will work.

☐ The towing eye is supplied in the vehicle toolkit which is stored in the luggage compartment with the spare wheel (see *Wheel changing*). To fit the eye, unclip the access cover from the relevant bumper and screw the eye firmly into position.
☐ Before being towed, release the handbrake and select neutral on the transmission.
Caution: On models with automatic transmission, do not tow the car at speeds in excess of 45 mph (75 kmh) or for a distance of greater than 60 miles (100 km). If towing speed/distance are to exceed these limits, then the car must be towed with its front wheels off the ground.

☐ Note that greater-than-usual pedal pressure will be required to operate the brakes, since the vacuum servo unit is only operational with the engine running.
☐ On models with power steering, greater-than-usual steering effort will also be required.
☐ The driver of the car being towed must keep the tow-rope taut at all times to avoid snatching.
☐ Make sure that both drivers know the route before setting off.
☐ Only drive at moderate speeds and keep the distance towed to a minimum. Drive smoothly and allow plenty of time for slowing down at junctions.

Introduction

There are some very simple checks which need only take a few minutes to carry out, but which could save you a lot of inconvenience and expense.

These *Weekly checks* require no great skill or special tools, and the small amount of time they take to perform could prove to be very well spent, for example;

☐ Keeping an eye on tyre condition and pressures, will not only help to stop them wearing out prematurely, but could also save your life.

☐ Many breakdowns are caused by electrical problems. Battery-related faults are particularly common, and a quick check on a regular basis will often prevent the majority of these.

☐ If your car develops a brake fluid leak, the first time you might know about it is when your brakes don't work properly. Checking the level regularly will give advance warning of this kind of problem.

☐ If the oil or coolant levels run low, the cost of repairing any engine damage will be far greater than fixing the leak, for example.

Underbonnet check points

◄ 2.0 litre petrol (1.8 litre similar)

A *Engine oil level dipstick*

B *Engine oil filler cap*

C *Coolant expansion tank*

D *Brake fluid reservoir*

E *Screen washer fluid reservoir*

F *Power steering fluid reservoir*

G *Battery*

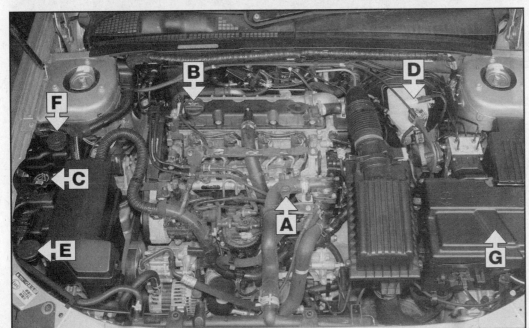

◄ 2.0 litre Diesel

A *Engine oil level dipstick*

B *Engine oil filler cap*

C *Coolant expansion tank*

D *Brake fluid reservoir*

E *Screen washer fluid reservoir*

F *Power steering fluid reservoir*

G *Battery*

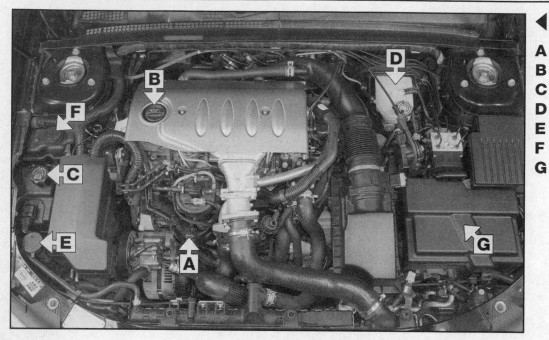

◄ **2.2 litre Diesel**

A *Engine oil level dipstick*

B *Engine oil filler cap*

C *Coolant expansion tank*

D *Brake fluid reservoir*

E *Screen washer fluid reservoir*

F *Power steering fluid reservoir*

G *Battery*

Engine oil level

Before you start

✔ Make sure that your car is on level ground.

✔ Check the oil level before the car is driven, or at least 5 minutes after the engine has been switched off.

 HAYNES HINT *If the oil is checked immediately after driving the vehicle, some of the oil will remain in the upper engine components, resulting in an inaccurate reading on the dipstick.*

The correct oil

Modern engines place great demands on their oil. It is very important that the correct oil for your car is used (See 'Lubricants and fluids').

Car Care

● If you have to add oil frequently, you should check whether you have any leaks. Place some clean paper under the car overnight, and check for stains in the morning. If there are no leaks, the engine may be burning oil.

● Always maintain the level between the upper and lower dipstick marks (see photo 3). If the level is too low severe engine damage may occur. Oil seal failure may result if the engine is overfilled by adding too much oil.

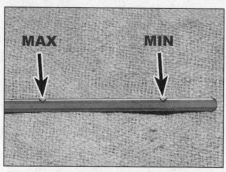

1 The dipstick is located at the front of the engine (see *Underbonnet check points* for exact location); The dipstick is often brightly-coloured or has a picture of an oil can on the top for easy identification. Withdraw the dipstick.

3 Note the oil level on the end of the dipstick, which should be between the upper (MAX) mark and lower (MIN) mark. Approximately 1.0 litre of oil will raise the level from the lower mark to the upper mark.

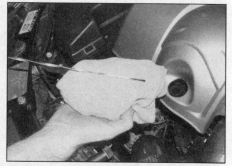

2 Using a clean rag or paper towel remove all oil from the dipstick. Insert the clean dipstick into the tube as far as it will go, then withdraw it again.

4 Oil is added through the filler cap. Unscrew the cap and top-up the level; a funnel may help to reduce spillage. Add the oil slowly, checking the level on the dipstick often. Don't overfill (see *Car care*).

Coolant level

Warning: DO NOT attempt to remove the expansion tank pressure cap when the engine is hot, as there is a very great risk of scalding. Do not leave open containers of coolant about, as it is poisonous.

Car Care

● Adding coolant should not be necessary on a regular basis. If frequent topping-up is required, it is likely there is a leak. Check the radiator, all hoses and joint faces for signs of staining or wetness, and rectify as necessary.

● It is important that antifreeze is used in the cooling system all year round, not just during the winter months. Don't top-up with water alone, as the antifreeze will become too diluted.

1 The coolant level must be checked with the engine cold. Remove the pressure cap (see *Warning*) from the expansion tank which is located on the right-hand side of the engine compartment.

2 The coolant level should be between the MAX and MIN marks on the expansion tank neck insert. The MIN mark is the thin bar at the base of the neck and the MAX mark is the slot approximately halfway up the neck.

3 If topping-up is necessary, add a mixture of water and antifreeze to the expansion tank until the coolant level is between the level marks. Once the level is correct, securely refit the cap.

Brake and clutch fluid level

Warning:
● *Brake fluid can harm your eyes and damage painted surfaces, so use extreme caution when handling and pouring it.*

● *Do not use fluid that has been standing open for some time, as it absorbs moisture from the air, which can cause a dangerous loss of braking effectiveness.*

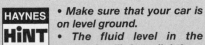

HAYNES HiNT • *Make sure that your car is on level ground.*
• *The fluid level in the reservoir will drop slightly as the brake pads wear down, but the fluid level must never be allowed to drop below the DANGER mark.*

Safety First!

● If the reservoir requires repeated topping-up this is an indication of a fluid leak somewhere in the system, which should be investigated immediately.

● If a leak is suspected, the car should not be driven until the braking system has been checked. Never take any risks where brakes are concerned.

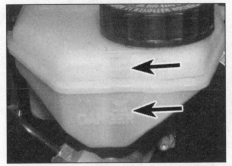

1 The upper (MAX) and lower (DANGER) fluid level markings are on the side of the reservoir, which is located in the left-hand rear corner of the engine compartment. The fluid level must always be kept between these two marks.

2 If topping-up is necessary, first wipe clean the area around the filler cap with a clean cloth, then unscrew the cap and remove it along with the rubber diaphragm.

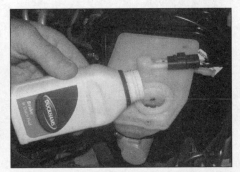

3 Carefully add fluid, avoiding spilling it on the surrounding paintwork. Use only the specified hydraulic fluid. After filling the correct level, refit the cap and diaphragm and tighten it securely. Wipe off any spilt fluid.

Tyre condition and pressure

It is very important that tyres are in good condition, and at the correct pressure - having a tyre failure at any speed is highly dangerous. Tyre wear is influenced by driving style - harsh braking and acceleration, or fast cornering, will all produce more rapid tyre wear. As a general rule, the front tyres wear out faster than the rears. Interchanging the tyres from front to rear ("rotating" the tyres) may result in more even wear. However, if this is completely effective, you may have the expense of replacing all four tyres at once! Remove any nails or stones embedded in the tread before they penetrate the tyre to cause deflation. If removal of a nail does reveal that the tyre has been punctured, refit the nail so that its point of penetration is marked. Then immediately change the wheel, and have the tyre repaired by a tyre dealer.

Regularly check the tyres for damage in the form of cuts or bulges, especially in the sidewalls. Periodically remove the wheels, and clean any dirt or mud from the inside and outside surfaces. Examine the wheel rims for signs of rusting, corrosion or other damage. Light alloy wheels are easily damaged by "kerbing" whilst parking; steel wheels may also become dented or buckled. A new wheel is very often the only way to overcome severe damage.

New tyres should be balanced when they are fitted, but it may become necessary to re-balance them as they wear, or if the balance weights fitted to the wheel rim should fall off. Unbalanced tyres will wear more quickly, as will the steering and suspension components. Wheel imbalance is normally signified by vibration, particularly at a certain speed (typically around 50 mph). If this vibration is felt only through the steering, then it is likely that just the front wheels need balancing. If, however, the vibration is felt through the whole car, the rear wheels could be out of balance. Wheel balancing should be carried out by a tyre dealer or garage.

1 *Tread Depth - visual check*
The original tyres have tread wear safety bands (B), which will appear when the tread depth reaches approximately 1.6 mm. The band positions are indicated by a triangular mark on the tyre sidewall (A).

2 *Tread Depth - manual check*
Alternatively, tread wear can be monitored with a simple, inexpensive device known as a tread depth indicator gauge.

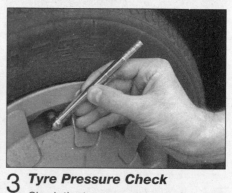

3 *Tyre Pressure Check*
Check the tyre pressures regularly with the tyres cold. Do not adjust the tyre pressures immediately after the vehicle has been used, or an inaccurate setting will result.

Tyre tread wear patterns

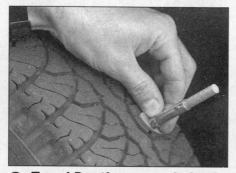

Shoulder Wear

Underinflation (wear on both sides)
Under-inflation will cause overheating of the tyre, because the tyre will flex too much, and the tread will not sit correctly on the road surface. This will cause a loss of grip and excessive wear, not to mention the danger of sudden tyre failure due to heat build-up.
Check and adjust pressures
Incorrect wheel camber (wear on one side)
Repair or renew suspension parts
Hard cornering
Reduce speed!

Centre Wear

Overinflation
Over-inflation will cause rapid wear of the centre part of the tyre tread, coupled with reduced grip, harsher ride, and the danger of shock damage occurring in the tyre casing.
Check and adjust pressures

If you sometimes have to inflate your car's tyres to the higher pressures specified for maximum load or sustained high speed, don't forget to reduce the pressures to normal afterwards.

Uneven Wear

Front tyres may wear unevenly as a result of wheel misalignment. Most tyre dealers and garages can check and adjust the wheel alignment (or "tracking") for a modest charge.
Incorrect camber or castor
Repair or renew suspension parts
Malfunctioning suspension
Repair or renew suspension parts
Unbalanced wheel
Balance tyres
Incorrect toe setting
Adjust front wheel alignment
Note: *The feathered edge of the tread which typifies toe wear is best checked by feel.*

Power steering fluid level

Before you start:
✔ Park the vehicle on level ground.
✔ Set the steering wheel straight-ahead.
✔ The engine should be turned off.

 For the check to be accurate, the steering must not be turned once the engine has been stopped.

Safety First!
● The need for frequent topping-up indicates a leak, which should be investigated immediately.

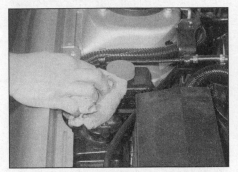

1 The power steering fluid level is checked in the fluid reservoir on the right-hand side of the engine compartment. With the engine cold, wipe clean the area around the reservoir cap.

2 Unscrew the reservoir cap, and check the fluid level is up to the upper (MAXI) level indicators which is visible inside the reservoir.

3 Top-up the reservoir with the specified type of the fluid. Once the level is between the level marks, securely refit the reservoir cap. Do not overfill the reservoir.

Screen washer fluid level

Screenwash additives not only keep the winscreen clean during foul weather, they also prevent the washer system freezing in cold weather - which is when you are likely to need it most. Don't top up using plain water as the screenwash will become too diluted, and will freeze during cold weather. *On no account use coolant antifreeze in the washer system - this could discolour or damage paintwork.*

1 The washer fluid reservoir is located in the right-hand front corner of the engine compartment. To check the fluid level, open the cap and look down the filler neck.

2 If topping-up is necessary, add water and a screenwash additive in the quantities recommended on the bottle.

Wiper blades

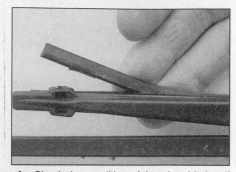

1 Check the condition of the wiper blades: if they are cracked or show signs of deterioration, or if the glass swept area is smeared, renew them. For maximum clarity of vision, wiper blades should be renewed annually.

2 To remove a windscreen wiper blade, lift the arm locking clip then raise the wiper arm slightly away from the screen.

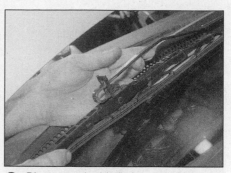

3 Disengage the blade from the wiper arm and remove it from the vehicle, taking care not to allow the arm to damage the windscreen.

Battery

Caution: Before carrying out any work on the vehicle battery, read the precautions given in 'Safety first' at the start of this manual.

✔ Make sure that the battery tray is in good condition, and that the clamp is tight. Corrosion on the tray, retaining clamp and the battery itself can be removed with a solution of water and baking soda. Thoroughly rinse all cleaned areas with water. Any metal parts damaged by corrosion should be covered with a zinc-based primer, then painted.

✔ Periodically (approximately every three months), check the charge condition of the battery as described in Chapter 5A.

✔ If the battery is flat, and you need to jump start your vehicle, see *Roadside Repairs*.

1 Remove the plastic cover to gain access to the battery, which is located at the front left-hand corner of the engine compartment. The exterior of the battery should be inspected periodically for damage such as a cracked case or cover.

2 Check the battery lead clamps for tightness to ensure good electrical connections, and check the leads for signs of damage.

Battery corrosion can be kept to a minimum by applying a layer of petroleum jelly to the clamps and terminals after they are reconnected.

3 If corrosion (white, fluffy deposits) is evident, remove the cables from the battery terminals, clean them with a small wire brush, then refit them. Automotive stores sell a tool for cleaning the battery post . . .

4 . . . as well as the battery cable clamps

Bulbs and fuses

✔ Check all external lights and the horn. Refer to the appropriate Sections of Chapter 12 for details if any of the circuits are found to be inoperative.

✔ Visually check all accessible wiring connectors, harnesses and retaining clips for security, and for signs of chafing or damage.

HAYNES HINT *If you need to check your brake lights and indicators unaided, back up to a wall or garage door and operate the lights. The reflected light should show if they are working properly.*

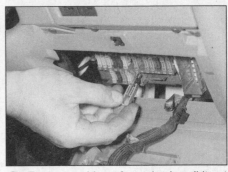

1 If a single indicator light, stop-light, sidelight or headlight has failed, it is likely that a bulb has blown, and will need to be renewed. Refer to Chapter 12 for details. If both stop-lights have failed, it is possible that the switch has failed (see Chapter 9).

2 If more than one indicator light or tail light has failed, it is likely that either a fuse has blown or that there is a fault in the circuit (see Chapter 12). The fuses are located behind the cover on the driver's side lower facia panel, release the three retaining clips and lower the cover. Additional fuses and relays are located in the left-hand side of the engine compartment fusebox.

3 To renew a blown fuse, simply pull it out and fit a new fuse of the correct rating (see Chapter 12). If the fuse blows again, it is important that you find out why – a complete checking procedure is given in Chapter 12.

Lubricants and fluids

Engine (petrol) . . . . Multigrade engine oil to specification ACEA A3 or API SH/SJ
(Duckhams QXR Premium Petrol Engine Oil)

Engine (diesel) . . . . Multigrade engine oil to specification ACEA B3 or API CD/CF
(Duckhams QXR Premium Diesel Engine Oil)

Cooling system . . . . Procor TM108/Glysantin G33 or Revkogel 2000 antifreeze

Manual transmission . . . . ESSO gear oil BV – SAE 75W-80W to API GL5 specification
(Duckhams Hypoid PT 75w-80w)

Automatic transmission . . . . ESSO LT71141 Automatic Transmission Fluid

Braking and clutch system . . . . Hydraulic fluid to DOT 4
(Duckhams Universal Brake & Clutch Fluid)

Power steering . . . . ESSO ATF D or Automatic Transmission Fluid Dexron IID
(Duckhams ATF Autotrans III)

Choosing your engine oil

Engines need oil, not only to lubricate moving parts and minimise wear, but also to maximise power output and to improve fuel economy. By introducing a simplified and improved range of engine oils, Duckhams has taken away the confusion and made it easier for you to choose the right oil for your engine.

HOW ENGINE OIL WORKS

• *Beating friction*

Without oil, the moving surfaces inside your engine will rub together, heat up and melt, quickly causing the engine to seize. Engine oil creates a film which separates these moving parts, preventing wear and heat build-up.

• *Cooling hot-spots*

Temperatures inside the engine can exceed 1000° C. The engine oil circulates and acts as a coolant, transferring heat from the hot-spots to the sump.

• *Cleaning the engine internally*

Good quality engine oils clean the inside of your engine, collecting and dispersing combustion deposits and controlling them until they are trapped by the oil filter or flushed out at oil change.

OIL CARE - FOLLOW THE CODE

To handle and dispose of used engine oil safely, always:

OIL BANK LINE
0800 66 33 66
www.oilbankline.org.uk

• **Avoid skin contact with used engine oil.** Repeated or prolonged contact can be harmful.
• **Dispose of used oil and empty packs in a responsible manner in an authorised disposal site.** Call 0800 663366 to find the one nearest to you. Never tip oil down drains or onto the ground.

DUCKHAMS ENGINE OILS

For the driver who demands a premium quality oil for complete reassurance, we recommend synthetic formula **Duckhams QXR Premium Engine Oils**.
For the driver who requires a straight-forward quality engine oil, we recommend **Duckhams Hypergrade Engine Oils**.

For further information and advice, call the Duckhams UK Helpline on 0800 212988.

Tyre pressures (cold)

Note 1: *The make of tyres, the sizes and the pressures for each specific vehicle are given on a label attached to the driver's door A-pillar (see illustration). On models with a space-saver spare wheel (family estates), a separate pressure is given for the spare tyre, and care must be taken not to misread the sticker; the space-saver wheel is inflated to a lot higher pressure than the standard tyres (typically 60 psi). On models with a space-saver spare wheel, note that the spare is for temporary use only; whilst the spare is fitted, the vehicle should not be driven at speeds in excess of 50 mph (80 kmh).*

Note 2: *Pressures on the label apply to original-equipment tyres listed, and may vary if any other make or type of tyre is fitted; check with the tyre manufacturer or supplier for correct pressures if necessary.*

Note 3: *Tyre pressures must always be checked with the tyres cold to ensure accuracy.*

Saloon models (typical)	Front (psi)	Rear (psi)
195/65 R15 tyres	33	33
205/60 R15 tyres	35	35
Estate models (typical)		
195/65 R15 tyres	33	35
205/60 R15 tyres	35	35

Chapter 1 Part A:
Routine maintenance & servicing – petrol models

Contents

Air filter element renewal	17
Automatic transmission fluid level check	4
Auxiliary drivebelt check and renewal	15
Brake fluid renewal	21
Clutch operation check	7
Coolant renewal	23
Driveshaft gaiter check	8
Engine oil and filter renewal	3
Front brake pad check	11
Fuel filter renewal	18
General information	1
Handbrake check	13
Hinge and lock lubrication	10
Hose and fluid leak check	5
Manual transmission oil level check	19
Pollen filter renewal	6
Rear brake pad check	12
Rear brake shoe check	20
Regular maintenance	2
Road test	14
Spark plug renewal and ignition system check	16
Steering and suspension component check	9
Timing belt renewal	22

Degrees of difficulty

Easy, suitable for novice with little experience	**Fairly easy,** suitable for beginner with some experience	**Fairly difficult,** suitable for competent DIY mechanic	**Difficult,** suitable for experienced DIY mechanic	**Very difficult,** suitable for expert DIY or professional

Lubricants and fluids
Refer to *Weekly checks* on page 0•18

Capacities

Engine oil (including oil filter)
1.8 litre engine:

1749cc	4.25 litres	
1761cc:	**Yellow dipstick**	**Orange dipstick**
Models with air conditioning	4.50 litres	4.25 litres
Models without air conditioning	5.00 litres	4.75 litres
2.0 litre engine	4.25 litres	

Cooling system
All engines (approximate) .... 8.8 litres

Transmission
Manual transmission (approximate) .... 1.9 litres
Automatic transmissions:
  4HP20:
    Drain and refill .... 3.0 litres
    Total capacity (including torque converter) .... 8.0 litres
  AL4:
    Drain and refill .... 4.5 litres
    Total capacity (including torque converter) .... 6.0 litres

Fuel tank .... 70 litres

Cooling system
Antifreeze mixture:
  50% antifreeze .... Protection down to −37°C
  55% antifreeze .... Protection down to −45°C
Note: *Refer to antifreeze manufacturer for latest recommendations.*

Ignition system
Spark plugs:
  XU engines .... Bosch FR8 LDC or Eyquem RFC 42 LZ2E
  EW engines .... Bosch FR8ME, Sagem RFN52HZ or Eyquem RFC 52 LZDP
Electrode gap* .... 0.9 mm
*The spark plug gap quoted is that recommended by Bosch/Sagem/Eyquem for their specified plug listed above. If spark plugs of any other type
are to be fitted, refer to their manufacturer's recommendations.*

Brakes
Brake pad friction material minimum thickness .... 2.0 mm
Brake shoe friction material minimum thickness .... 1.5 mm

Tyre pressures
See end of *Weekly checks* on page 0•18

Torque wrench settings

	Nm	lbf ft
Auxiliary drivebelt tensioner pulley	20	15
Auxiliary drivebelt guide pulley	35	26
Manual transmission filler/level plug	20	15
Spark plugs	25	18
Roadwheel bolts	90	66

The maintenance intervals in this manual are provided with the assumption that you, not the dealer, will be carrying out the work. These are the minimum maintenance intervals recommended by us for vehicles driven daily.

If you wish to keep your vehicle in peak condition at all times, you may wish to perform some of these procedures more often. We encourage frequent maintenance, because it enhances the efficiency, performance and resale value of your vehicle.

When the vehicle is new, it should be serviced by a factory-authorised dealer service department, in order to preserve the factory warranty.

Weekly, or every 250 miles (400 km)
☐ Refer to *Weekly checks*

Every 6000 miles (10 000 km) or 6 months – whichever comes first
☐ Renew the engine oil and filter (Section 3)

Note: *Frequent oil and filter changes are good for the engine. We recommend changing the oil at the mileage specified here, or at least twice a year if the mileage covered is a less.*

Every 12000 miles (20 000 km) or 12 months – whichever comes first
☐ Check the automatic transmission (4HP20 type) fluid level, and top up if necessary (Section 4)
☐ Check all underbonnet components and hoses for fluid leaks (Section 5)
☐ Check the pollen filter (where fitted) (Section 6)
☐ Check the operation of the clutch (Section 7)
☐ Check the condition of the driveshaft rubber gaiters (Section 8)
☐ Check the steering and suspension components for condition and security (Section 9)
☐ Lubricate all hinges and locks (Section 10)

Every 18 000 miles (30 000 km)
In addition to all the items listed above, carry out the following:
☐ Check the condition of the front brake pads, and renew if necessary (Section 11)
☐ Check the condition of the rear brake pads and renew if necessary – rear disc brake models (Section 12)
☐ Check the operation of the handbrake (Section 13)
☐ Carry out a road test (Section 14)
☐ Check the condition of the auxiliary drivebelt, and renew if necessary (Section 15)

Every 18 000 miles (30 000 km) or 2 years, whichever comes first
☐ Renew the 4HP20 automatic transmission fluid (Chapter 7B)

Every 36 000 miles (60 000 km)
In addition to all the items listed above, carry out the following:
☐ Renew the spark plugs (Section 16)
☐ Renew the air filter (Section 17)
☐ Renew the fuel filter (Section 18)
☐ Check the manual transmission oil level, and top-up if necessary (Section 19)
☐ Check the automatic transmission (AL4 type) fluid level, and top up if necessary (Section 4)
☐ Check the condition of the rear brake shoes and renew if necessary – rear drum brake models (Section 20)

Every 36 000 miles (60 000 km) or 2 years, whichever comes first
☐ Renew the brake fluid (Section 21)

Note: *A hydraulic clutch shares its fluid reservoir with the braking system, and may also need to be bled.*

Every 72 000 miles (120 000 km)
In addition to all the items listed above, carry out the following:
☐ Renew the timing belt (Section 22)

Note: *It is strongly recommended that the timing belt renewal interval is halved to 36 000 miles (60 000 km) on vehicles which are subjected to intensive use, ie. mainly short journeys or a lot of stop-start driving. The actual belt renewal interval is therefore very much up to the individual owner, but bear in mind that severe engine damage will result if the belt breaks.*

Every 72 000 miles (120 000 km) or 5 years, whichever comes first
☐ Renew the coolant (Section 23)

Underbonnet view of a 2.0 litre model

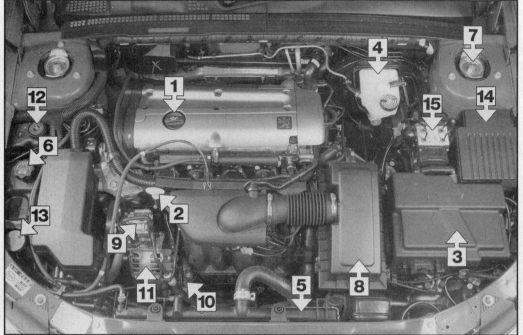

1 Engine oil filler cap
2 Engine oil level dipstick
3 Battery
4 Brake fluid reservoir
5 Radiator
6 Coolant expansion tank
7 Suspension strut upper mounting
8 Air filter housing
9 Power steering pump
10 Air conditioning compressor
11 Alternator
12 Power steering fluid reservoir
13 Washer fluid reservoir
14 Fuse/relay box
15 Anti-lock braking system (ABS) hydraulic unit

Front underbody view

1 Engine oil drain plug
2 Air conditioning compressor
3 Driveshaft intermediate bearing
4 Brake caliper
5 Front suspension lower arm
6 Track rod
7 Front suspension anti-roll bar

Rear underbody view

1 Fuel tank
2 Rear suspension trailing arm
3 Handbrake cable
4 Brake caliper
5 Rear suspension lower arm
6 Rear suspension track arm

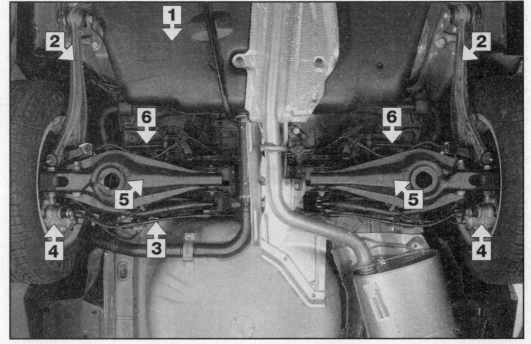

Maintenance procedures

1 General information

1 This Chapter is designed to help the home mechanic maintain his/her vehicle for safety, economy, long life and peak performance.
2 The Chapter contains a master maintenance schedule, followed by Sections dealing specifically with each task in the schedule. Visual checks, adjustments, component renewal and other helpful items are included. Refer to the accompanying illustrations of the engine compartment and the underside of the vehicle for the locations of the various components.
3 Servicing your vehicle in accordance with the mileage/time maintenance schedule and the following Sections will provide a planned maintenance programme, which should result in a long and reliable service life. This is a comprehensive plan, so maintaining some items but not others at the specified service intervals, will not produce the same results.
4 As you service your vehicle, you will discover that many of the procedures can – and should – be grouped together, because of the particular procedure being performed, or because of the proximity of two otherwise-unrelated components to one another. For example, if the vehicle is raised for any reason, the exhaust can be inspected at the same time as the suspension and steering components.
5 The first step in this maintenance pro-gramme is to prepare yourself before the actual work begins. Read through all the Sections relevant to the work to be carried out, then make a list and gather all the parts and tools required. If a problem is encountered, seek advice from a parts specialist, or a dealer service department.

2 Regular maintenance

1 If, from the time the vehicle is new, the routine maintenance schedule is followed closely, and frequent checks are made of fluid levels and high-wear items, as suggested throughout this manual, the engine will be kept in relatively good running condition, and the need for additional work will be minimised.
2 It is possible that there will be times when the engine is running poorly due to the lack of regular maintenance. This is even more likely if a used vehicle, which has not received regular and frequent maintenance checks, is purchased. In such cases, additional work may need to be carried out, outside of the regular maintenance intervals.
3 If engine wear is suspected, a compression test (refer to Chapter 2A or 2B) will provide

valuable information regarding the overall performance of the main internal components. Such a test can be used as a basis to decide on the extent of the work to be carried out. If, for example, a compression test indicates serious internal engine wear, conventional maintenance as described in this Chapter will not greatly improve the performance of the engine, and may prove a waste of time and money, unless extensive overhaul work is carried out first.

4 The following series of operations are those often required to improve the performance of a generally poor-running engine:

Primary operations

a) Clean, inspect and test the battery (refer to 'Weekly checks').
b) Check all the engine-related fluids (refer to 'Weekly checks').
c) Check the condition and tension of the auxiliary drivebelt (Section 15).
d) Renew the spark plugs (Section 16).
e) Check the condition of the air filter, and renew if necessary (Section 17).
f) Renew the fuel filter (Section 18).
g) Check the condition of all hoses, and check for fluid leaks (Section 5).

5 If these operations do not prove effective, carry out the following secondary operations:

Secondary operations

All items listed under *Primary operations*, plus the following:

a) Check the charging system (refer to Chapter 5A).
b) Check the ignition system (refer to Chapter 5B).
c) Check the fuel system (refer to Chapter 4A).
d) Renew the ignition HT leads – where fitted (Section 16).

Every 6000 miles (10 000 km) or 6 months

3 Engine oil and filter renewal

Note: *A suitable square-section wrench may be required to undo the sump drain plug on some models. These wrenches can be obtained from most motor factors or your Peugeot dealer.*

1 Frequent oil and filter changes are the most important preventative maintenance procedures which can be undertaken by the DIY owner. As engine oil ages, it becomes diluted and contaminated, which leads to premature engine wear.

2 Before starting this procedure, gather together all the necessary tools and materials. Also make sure that you have plenty of clean rags and newspapers handy, to mop up any spills. Ideally, the engine oil should be warm, as it will drain better, and more built-up sludge will be removed with it. Take care, however, not to touch the exhaust or any other hot parts of the engine when working under the vehicle. To avoid any possibility of scalding, and to protect yourself from possible skin irritants and other harmful contaminants in used engine oils, it is advisable to wear gloves when carrying out this work. Access to the underside of the vehicle will be greatly improved if it can be raised on a lift, driven onto ramps, or jacked up and supported on axle stands. Whichever method is chosen, make sure that the vehicle remains level, or if it is at an angle, that the drain plug is at the lowest point. Where fitted, remove the splash guard from under the engine.

3 Slacken the drain plug about half a turn. Position the draining container under the drain plug, then remove the plug completely. If possible, try to keep the plug pressed into the sump while unscrewing it by hand the last couple of turns **(see Haynes Hint)**. Recover the sealing ring from the drain plug.

4 Allow some time for the old oil to drain, noting that it may be necessary to reposition the container as the oil flow slows to a trickle.

5 After all the oil has drained, wipe off the drain plug with a clean rag, and fit a new sealing washer. Clean the area around the drain plug opening, and refit the plug. Tighten the plug securely.

6 If the filter is also to be renewed, move the container into position under the oil filter, which is located on the front side of the cylinder block.

7 Using an oil filter removal tool if necessary, slacken the filter initially, then unscrew it by hand the rest of the way **(see illustration)**. Empty the oil in the old filter into the container.

8 Use a clean rag to remove all oil, dirt and sludge from the filter sealing area on the engine. Check the old filter to make sure that the rubber sealing ring hasn't stuck to the engine. If it has, carefully remove it.

9 Apply a light coating of clean engine oil to the sealing ring on the new filter, then screw it into position on the engine. Tighten the filter firmly by hand only – **do not** use any tools. Where necessary, refit the splash guard under the engine.

10 Remove the old oil and all tools from under the car, then lower the car to the ground (if applicable).

11 Remove the dipstick, then unscrew the oil filler cap from the cylinder head cover, or from the top of the filler tube on the front side of the cylinder block, as applicable. Fill the engine, using the correct grade and type of oil (*see Weekly checks*). An oil can spout or funnel may help to reduce spillage. Pour in half the specified quantity of oil first, then wait a few minutes for the oil to fall to the sump. Continue adding oil a small quantity at a time until the level is up to the lower mark on the dipstick. Adding approximately 1.0 litre will bring the level up to the upper mark on the dipstick. Refit the filler cap.

12 Start the engine and run it for a few minutes; check for leaks around the oil filter seal and the sump drain plug. Note that there may be a delay of a few seconds before the oil pressure warning light goes out when the engine is first started, as the oil circulates through the engine oil galleries and the new oil filter (where fitted) before the pressure builds-up.

13 Switch off the engine, and wait a few minutes for the oil to settle in the sump once more. With the new oil circulated and the filter completely full, recheck the level on the dipstick, and add more oil as necessary.

14 Dispose of the used engine oil safely, with reference to *General Repair Procedures*.

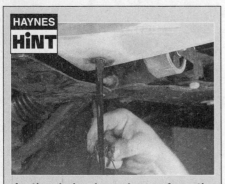

HAYNES HiNT

As the drain plug releases from the threads, move it away sharply so the stream of oil issuing from the sump runs into the container, not up your sleeve.

3.7 Using an oil filter removal tool to slacken the oil filter

Every 12 000 miles (20 000 km) or 12 months

4 Automatic transmission fluid level check

Note: *The AL4 transmission is identified by having the Park Lock facility.*

4HP20 transmission

1 Take the vehicle on a moderate journey (at least 30 minutes), to warm the transmission up to normal operating temperature, then park the vehicle on level ground. Leave the engine idling, apply the handbrake fully, and move the selector lever to the P (Park) position. The fluid level is checked using the dipstick located at the front of the engine compartment, directly in front of the engine unit **(see illustration)**. The dipstick top is brightly-coloured for easy identification.

2 With the engine idling and the footbrake applied, move the selector lever through all gear positions, stopping briefly in each position, then return the selector lever to the P position. Withdraw the dipstick from the tube, and wipe all the fluid from its end with a clean rag or paper towel. Insert the clean dipstick back into the tube as far as it will go, then withdraw it once more. Note the fluid level on the end of the dipstick. The fluid level should be between the two upper marks on the dipstick (the marks located on either side of the number 80) **(see illustration)**.

3 If topping-up is necessary, add the required quantity of the specified fluid to the transmission via the dipstick tube. Use a funnel with a fine-mesh gauze, to avoid spillage, and to ensure that no foreign matter enters the transmission. **Note:** *Never overfill the transmission so that the fluid level is above the upper mark.*

4 After topping-up, take the vehicle on a short run to distribute the fresh fluid, then recheck the level, topping-up if necessary.

5 Always maintain the level between the two upper dipstick marks. If the level is allowed to fall below the lower mark, fluid starvation may result, which could lead to severe transmission damage.

6 Frequent need for topping-up indicates that there is a leak, which should be found and corrected before it becomes serious.

AL4 transmission

7 Take the vehicle on a moderate journey (at least 30 minutes), to warm the transmission up to normal operating temperature, then park the vehicle on level ground.

8 With the engine switched off, the oil level is checked by removing the oil filler and oil level plugs from the transmission housing.

9 Remove the air cleaner air inlet duct as described in Chapter 4A.

10 To improve access to the oil level plug, which is on the base of the transmission housing, it may be preferable to jack up the front and rear of the car, and support it on axle stands (see *Jacking and vehicle support*); it is essential that the car is kept level for the check to be accurate. Remove the engine undertray for access to the plug.

11 Using a square-section wrench, remove the oil filler plug from the top of the transmission housing **(see illustration)**, and add 0.5 litres of the specified oil. As access to the filler plug is limited, Peugeot mechanics use a filling bottle with a length of small-bore hose attached. The end of the hose is inserted into the filler orifice and the bottle (filled with the specified oil) is then suspended from the bonnet. A suitable alternative could easily be made up from, for example, a clean plastic drinks bottle with the base cut off and with a hose attached to the cap.

12 With the handbrake and footbrake firmly applied, start the engine and move the selector through all available positions several times. Finally, select P, and leave the engine running.

13 Working under the car, place a suitable container underneath the transmission, then remove the oil level plug **(see illustration)**. This is the smaller hex-head bolt inside the larger hex-headed transmission drain plug – do not loosen the larger, outer plug with the

4.1 Withdrawing the automatic transmission dipstick – 4HP20 transmission

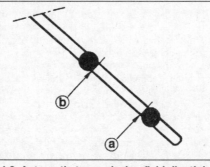

4.2 Automatic transmission fluid dipstick lower (a) and upper (b) fluid level markings

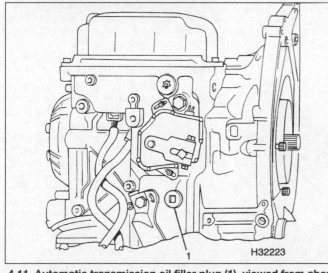

4.11 Automatic transmission oil filler plug (1), viewed from above – AL4 transmission

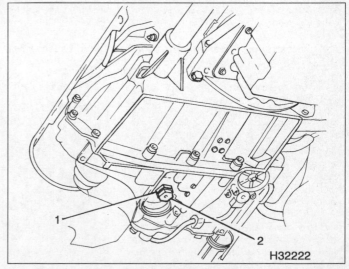

4.13 Automatic transmission oil level plug (2) is located inside the drain plug (1) – AL4 transmission

engine running, or the transmission oil will run out, resulting in transmission damage.

14 If the level is correct, oil will run from the level plug in a steady stream, quickly reducing to a sequence of drips. In theory, the amount of oil lost when the plug is removed should be the same as, or less than, the 0.5 litres just added. When the dripping stops, refit the level plug.

15 If little or no oil emerges, refit the level plug, then switch off the engine. Repeat paragraphs 11 to 14 until the level is correct.

16 On completion, tighten the filler and level plugs to the specified torque (Chapter 7B), then refit the engine undertray and air inlet duct.

17 Frequent need for topping-up indicates that there is a leak, which should be found and corrected before it becomes serious.

5 Hose and fluid leak check

Cooling system

⚠️ **Warning: Refer to the safety information given in 'Safety First!' and Chapter 3 before disturbing any of the cooling system components.**

1 Carefully check the radiator and heater coolant hoses along their entire length. Renew any hose which is cracked, swollen or which shows signs of deterioration. Cracks will show up better if the hose is squeezed. Pay close attention to the clips that secure the hoses to the cooling system components. Hose clips that have been over-tightened can pinch and puncture hoses, resulting in cooling system leaks.

2 Inspect all the cooling system components (hoses, joint faces, etc) for leaks. Where any problems of this nature are found on system components, renew the component or gasket with reference to Chapter 3 **(see Haynes Hint)**.

Fuel

⚠️ **Warning: Refer to the safety information given in 'Safety First!' and Chapter 4A before disturbing any of the fuel system components.**

3 Petrol leaks are difficult to pinpoint, unless the leakage is significant and hence easily visible. Fuel tends to evaporate quickly once it comes into contact with air, especially in a hot engine bay. Small drips can disappear before you get a chance to identify the point of leakage. If you suspect that there is a fuel leak from the area of the engine bay, leave the vehicle overnight then start the engine from cold, with the bonnet open. Metal components tend to shrink when they are cold, and rubber seals and hoses tend to harden, so any leaks will be more apparent whilst the engine is warming-up from a cold start.

4 Check all fuel lines at their connections to the fuel rail, fuel pressure regulator and fuel filter. Examine each rubber fuel hose along its length for splits or cracks. Check for leakage from the crimped joints between rubber and metal fuel lines. Examine the unions between the metal fuel lines and the fuel filter housing. Also check the area around the fuel injectors for signs of O-ring leakage.

5 To identify fuel leaks between the fuel tank and the engine bay, the vehicle should raised and securely supported on axle stands. Inspect the petrol tank and filler neck for punctures, cracks and other damage. The connection between the filler neck and tank is especially critical. Sometimes a rubber filler neck or connecting hose will leak due to loose retaining clamps or deteriorated rubber.

6 Carefully check all rubber hoses and metal fuel lines leading away from the petrol tank. Check for loose connections, deteriorated hoses, kinked lines, and other damage. Pay particular attention to the vent pipes and hoses, which often loop up around the filler neck and can become blocked or kinked, making tank filling difficult. Follow the fuel supply and return lines to the front of the vehicle, carefully inspecting them all the way for signs of damage or corrosion. Renew damaged sections as necessary.

Engine oil

7 Inspect the area around the camshaft cover, cylinder head, oil filter and sump joint faces. Bear in mind that, over a period of time, some very slight seepage from these areas is to be expected – what you are really looking for is any indication of a serious leak caused by gasket failure. Engine oil seeping from the base of the timing belt cover or the transmission bellhousing may be an indication of crankshaft or transmission input shaft oil seal failure. Should a leak be found, renew the failed gasket or oil seal by referring to the appropriate Chapters in this manual.

Automatic transmission fluid

8 Where applicable, check the hoses leading to the transmission fluid cooler at the front of the engine bay for leakage. Look for deterioration caused by corrosion and damage from grounding, or debris thrown up

A leak in the cooling system will usually show-up as white- or rust-coloured deposits on the area adjoining the leak.

from the road surface. Automatic transmission fluid is a thin oil and is usually red in colour.

Power assisted steering fluid

9 Examine the hose running between the fluid reservoir and the power steering pump, and the return hose running from the steering rack to the fluid reservoir. Also examine the high pressure supply hose between the pump and the steering rack.

10 Where applicable, check the hoses leading to the PAS fluid cooler at the front of the engine bay. Look for deterioration caused by corrosion and damage from grounding, or debris thrown up from the road surface.

11 Pay particular attention to crimped unions, and the area surrounding the hoses that are secured with adjustable worm drive clips. Like automatic transmission fluid, PAS fluid is a thin oil, and is usually red in colour.

Air conditioning refrigerant

⚠️ **Warning: Refer to the safety information given in 'Safety First!' and Chapter 3, regarding the dangers of disturbing any of the air conditioning system components.**

12 The air conditioning system is filled with a liquid refrigerant, which is retained under high pressure. If the air conditioning system is opened and depressurised without the aid of specialised equipment, the refrigerant will immediately turn into gas and escape into the atmosphere. If the liquid comes into contact with your skin, it can cause severe frostbite. In addition, the refrigerant contains substances which are environmentally damaging; for this reason, it should not be allowed to escape into the atmosphere.

13 Any suspected air conditioning system leaks should be immediately referred to a Peugeot dealer or air conditioning specialist. Leakage will be shown up as a steady drop in the level of refrigerant in the system.

14 Note that water may drip from the condenser drain pipe, underneath the car, immediately after the air conditioning system has been in use. This is normal, and should not be cause for concern.

Brake (and clutch) fluid

⚠️ **Warning: Refer to the safety information given in 'Safety First!' and Chapter 9, regarding the dangers of handling brake fluid.**

15 With reference to Chapter 9, examine the area surrounding the brake pipe unions at the master cylinder for signs of leakage. Check the area around the base of fluid reservoir, for signs of leakage caused by seal failure. Also examine the brake pipe unions at the ABS hydraulic unit.

16 If fluid loss is evident, but the leak cannot be pinpointed in the engine bay, the brake calipers and under body brake lines and should be carefully checked with the vehicle raised and supported on axle stands. Leakage of fluid from the braking system is serious fault that must be rectified immediately.

17 On models with a hydraulically-operated clutch, refer to Chapter 6 and check for leakage around the hydraulic fluid line connections to the clutch master cylinder at the bulkhead, and to the clutch slave cylinder, bolted to the side of the transmission bell housing.

18 Brake/clutch hydraulic fluid is a toxic substance with a watery consistency. New fluid is almost colourless, but it becomes darker with age and use.

Unidentified fluid leaks

19 If there are signs that a fluid of some description is leaking from the vehicle, but you cannot identify the type of fluid or its exact origin, park the vehicle overnight and slide a large piece of card underneath it. Providing that the card is positioned in roughly the right location, even the smallest leak will show up on the card. Not only will this help you to pinpoint the exact location of the leak, it should be easier to identify the fluid from its colour. Bear in mind, though, that the leak may only be occurring when the engine is running!

Vacuum hoses

20 Although the braking system is hydraulically-operated, the brake servo unit amplifies the effort you apply at the brake pedal, by making use of the vacuum in the inlet manifold, generated by the engine. Vacuum is ported to the servo by means of a large-bore hose. Any leaks that develop in this hose will reduce the effectiveness of the braking system.

21 In addition, many of the underbonnet components, particularly the emission control components, are driven by vacuum supplied from the inlet manifold via narrow-bore hoses. A leak in a vacuum hose means that air is being drawn into the hose (rather than escaping from it) and this makes leakage very difficult to detect. One method is to use an old length of vacuum hose as a kind of stethoscope – hold one end close to (but not in) your ear and use the other end to probe the area around the suspected leak. When the end of the hose is directly over a vacuum leak, a hissing sound will be heard clearly through the hose. Care must be taken to avoid contacting hot or moving components, as the engine must be running, when testing in this manner. Renew any vacuum hoses that are found to be defective.

6 Pollen filter renewal

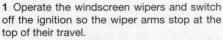

1 Operate the windscreen wipers and switch off the ignition so the wiper arms stop at the top of their travel.

2 Unscrew the retaining nut then unclip and remove the passenger side plastic inlet vent cover from the base of the windscreen **(see illustration)**.

6.2 Undo the retaining nut and remove the passenger side plastic inlet vent cover . . .

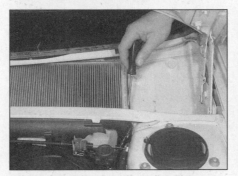

6.4a Carefully ease the pollen filter out from its housing . . .

3 Unclip the passenger side inlet vent panel and remove the panel from beneath the windscreen to gain access to the pollen filter **(see illustration)**.

4 Ease the pollen filter out of its housing and remove it from the vehicle **(see illustrations)**.

5 Check the condition of the filter, if it is dirty, renew the filter.

6 Wipe clean the housing then install the filter, making sure it is clipped securely in position.

7 Clip the vent panel into position, making sure it is correctly engaged with the driver's side panel, then refit the vent cover and retaining nut.

8 Switch the ignition back on and return the wiper arm to the at rest position.

7 Clutch operation check

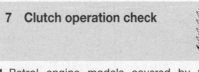

1 Petrol engine models covered by this manual are equipped with either a cable-operated, or hydraulically operated self-adjusting clutch mechanism which is virtually maintenance-free.

2 The only maintenance necessary is to check that the clutch pedal moves smoothly and easily through its full travel, and that the clutch itself functions correctly, with no trace of slip or drag.

3 The hydraulic fluid uses the same reservoir as the brakes, check the fluid level as described in the relevant Chapter. (Note that

6.3 . . . then unclip the inlet vent panel from the vehicle

6.4b . . . and remove it from the vehicle

some early models had a hydraulically-operated clutch mechanism which was a completely sealed assembly. Checking or topping-up of the hydraulic fluid level on this system is not possible.)

4 If any problems are experienced, refer to Chapter 6 for further details.

8 Driveshaft gaiter check

1 With the vehicle raised and securely supported on axle stands, turn the steering to full left or right lock, then slowly rotate the roadwheel. Inspect the outer constant velocity (CV) joint rubber gaiters, squeezing the gaiters to open out the folds **(see illustration)**. Check for signs of cracking, splits or deterioration of the rubber, which may allow the grease to

8.1 Checking a driveshaft gaiter for damage

9.2 Checking a steering gear gaiter for damage

9.4 Check for wear in the hub bearings by grasping the wheel and trying to rock it

escape, or water and grit to enter. Also check the security and condition of the retaining clips. Repeat these checks on the inner CV joints. If any damage or deterioration is found, the gaiters should be renewed (Chapter 8).

2 At the same time, check the general condition of the CV joints themselves by first holding the driveshaft and attempting to rotate the wheel. Repeat this check whilst holding the inner joint and attempting to rotate the driveshaft. Any appreciable movement indicates wear in the CV joints, wear in the driveshaft splines, or a loose driveshaft retaining nut.

9 Steering and suspension component check

Front suspension/steering

1 Raise the front of the vehicle, and securely support it on axle stands.

2 Visually inspect the balljoint dust covers and the steering rack-and-pinion gaiters for splits, chafing or deterioration **(see illustration)**. Any wear of these components will cause loss of lubricant, together with dirt and water entry, resulting in rapid deterioration of the balljoints or steering gear.

3 Check the power steering fluid hoses for chafing or deterioration, and the pipe and hose unions for fluid leaks. Also check for signs of fluid leakage under pressure from the steering gear rubber gaiters, which would indicate failed fluid seals within the steering gear.

4 Grasp the roadwheel at the 12 o'clock and 6 o'clock positions, and try to rock it **(see illustration)**. Very slight free play may be felt, but if the movement is appreciable, further investigation is necessary to determine the source. Continue rocking the wheel while an assistant depresses the footbrake. If the movement is now eliminated or significantly reduced, it is likely that the hub bearings are at fault. If the free play is still evident with the footbrake depressed, then there is wear in the suspension joints or mountings.

5 Now grasp the wheel at the 9 o'clock and 3 o'clock positions, and try to rock it as before. Any movement felt now may again be caused by wear in the hub bearings or the steering track rod balljoints. If the inner or outer balljoint is worn, the visual movement will be obvious.

6 Using a large screwdriver or flat bar, check for wear in the suspension mounting bushes by levering between the relevant suspension component and its attachment point. Some movement is to be expected as the mountings are made of rubber, but excessive wear should be obvious. Also check the condition of any visible rubber bushes, looking for splits,

cracks or contamination of the rubber.

7 With the car standing on its wheels, have an assistant turn the steering wheel back-and-forth about an eighth of a turn each way. There should be very little, if any, lost movement between the steering wheel and roadwheels. If this is not the case, closely observe the joints and mountings previously described, but in addition, check the steering column universal joints for wear, and the rack-and-pinion steering gear itself.

Strut/shock absorber check

8 Check for any signs of fluid leakage around the suspension strut/shock absorber body, or from the rubber gaiter around the piston rod. Should any fluid be noticed, the suspension strut/shock absorber is defective internally, and should be renewed. **Note:** *Suspension struts/shock absorbers should always be renewed in pairs on the same axle, or the handling of the vehicle will be impaired.*

9 The efficiency of the suspension strut/shock absorber may be checked by bouncing the vehicle at each corner. Generally speaking, the body will return to its normal position and stop after being depressed. If it rises and returns on a rebound, the suspension strut/shock absorber is probably suspect. Examine also the suspension strut/shock absorber upper and lower mountings for any signs of wear.

10 Hinge and lock lubrication

1 Lubricate the hinges of the bonnet, doors and tailgate with a light general-purpose oil. Similarly, lubricate all latches, locks and lock strikers. At the same time, check the security and operation of all the locks, adjusting them if necessary (see Chapter 11).

2 Lightly lubricate the bonnet release mechanism and cable with a suitable grease.

Every 18 000 miles (30 000 km)

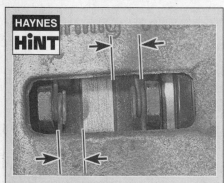

For a quick check, the thickness of the friction material on each brake pad can be measured through the aperture in the caliper body.

11 Front brake pad check

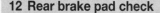

1 Firmly apply the handbrake, then jack up the front of the car and support it securely on axle stands. Remove the front roadwheels.

2 For a comprehensive check, the brake pads should be removed and cleaned. The operation of the caliper can then also be checked, and the condition of the brake disc itself can be fully examined on both sides. Refer to Chapter 9 for further information **(see Haynes Hint)**.

3 If any pad's friction material is worn to the specified thickness or less, *all four pads must be renewed as a set.* **Note**: *If any pad is approaching the minimum thickness, consider*

renewal as a precautionary measure in case the pads wear out before the next service.

12 Rear brake pad check

1 Chock the front wheels, then jack up the rear of the vehicle and support it on axle stands. Remove the rear roadwheels.

2 For a quick check, the thickness of friction material remaining on each brake pad can be measured through the top of the caliper body. If any pad's friction material is worn to the specified thickness or less, all four pads must be renewed as a set.

3 For a comprehensive check, the brake pads should be removed and cleaned. This will

permit the operation of the caliper to be checked, and the condition of the brake disc itself to be fully examined on both sides. Refer to Chapter 9 for further information.

4 If any pad's friction material is worn to the specified thickness or less, *all four pads must be renewed as a set*. Note: *If any pad is approaching the minimum thickness, consider renewal as a precautionary measure in case the pads wear out before the next service.*

13 Handbrake check
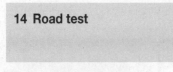

1 Check and, if necessary, adjust the handbrake (see Chapter 9). Check that the handbrake cables are free to move easily and lubricate all exposed linkages/cable pivots.

14 Road test

Instruments and electrical equipment

1 Check the operation of all instruments and electrical equipment.
2 Make sure all instruments read correctly, and switch on all electrical equipment in turn, to check that it functions properly.

Steering and suspension

3 Check for any abnormalities in the steering, suspension, handling or road 'feel'.
4 Drive the vehicle, and check that there are no unusual vibrations or noises.
5 Check that the steering feels positive, with no excessive 'sloppiness', or roughness, and check for any suspension noises when cornering and driving over bumps.

Drivetrain

6 Check the performance of the engine, clutch (where applicable), gearbox/transmission and driveshafts.
7 Listen for any unusual noises from the engine, clutch and gearbox/transmission.
8 Make sure that the engine runs smoothly when idling, and that there is no hesitation when accelerating.
9 Check that, where applicable, the clutch action is smooth and progressive, that the drive is taken up smoothly, and that the pedal travel is not excessive. Also listen for any noises when the clutch pedal is depressed.
10 On manual gearbox models, check that all gears can be engaged smoothly without noise, and that the gear lever action is smooth and not abnormally vague or 'notchy'.
11 On automatic transmission models, make sure that all gearchanges occur smoothly, without snatching, and without an increase in engine speed between changes. Check that all the gear positions can be selected with the

vehicle at rest. If any problems are found, they should be referred to a Peugeot dealer.

Braking system

12 Make sure that the vehicle does not pull to one side when braking, and that the wheels do not lock when braking hard.
13 Check that there is no vibration through the steering when braking.
14 Check that the handbrake operates correctly without excessive movement of the lever, and that it holds the vehicle stationary on a slope.
15 Test the operation of the brake servo unit as follows. With the engine off, depress the footbrake four or five times to exhaust the vacuum. Hold the brake pedal depressed, then start the engine. As the engine starts, there should be a noticeable 'give' in the brake pedal as vacuum builds-up. Allow the engine to run for at least two minutes, and then switch it off. If the brake pedal is depressed now, it should be possible to detect a hiss from the servo as the pedal is depressed. After about four or five applications, no further hissing should be heard, and the pedal should feel much harder.

15 Auxiliary drivebelt check and renewal

Note: *Depending on model and equipment fitted, access to the auxiliary drivebelt can be extremely limited. Where necessary, greater working clearance can be gained by removing the fuel injection/ignition electronic control unit (ECU) and its mounting box (Chapter 4A).*
Note: *On models with a manually-adjusted drivebelt, Peugeot specify the use of a special electronic tool (SEEM C105.5) to correctly set the drivebelt tension. If access to this equipment cannot be obtained, an approximate setting can be achieved using the method*

described below. If this method is used, the tension should be checked using the special electronic tool at the earliest opportunity.

1 All models are equipped with a single poly-V type, multi-ribbed auxiliary drivebelt. The belt tension is adjusted manually on models without air conditioning, and automatically, by means of a spring-loaded tensioner, on models with air conditioning.

Drivebelt condition

2 Apply the handbrake, then jack up the front of the car and support it on axle stands. Remove the right-hand front roadwheel.
3 Release the screws and clips and remove the wheelarch liner from under the right-hand front wing for access to the crankshaft pulley bolt. Where fitted, also remove the splash guard from under the front of the engine.
4 Using a suitable socket and bar fitted to the crankshaft pulley bolt, rotate the crankshaft so that the entire length of the drivebelt can be examined. Examine the drivebelt for cracks, splitting, fraying or damage. Check also for signs of glazing (shiny patches) and for separation of the belt plies. Renew the belt if worn or damaged.
5 If the condition of the belt is satisfactory, on models without air conditioning, check the drivebelt tension as described below. On models with air conditioning, there is no need to check the drivebelt tension.

Removal

6 If not already done, proceed as described in paragraphs 2 and 3.
7 Disconnect the battery negative lead.
8 On models with a manually-adjusted drivebelt, slacken the two bolts securing the tensioning pulley assembly to the engine (see illustration). Rotate the adjuster bolt to move the tensioner pulley away from the drivebelt until there is sufficient slack for the drivebelt to be removed from the pulleys.

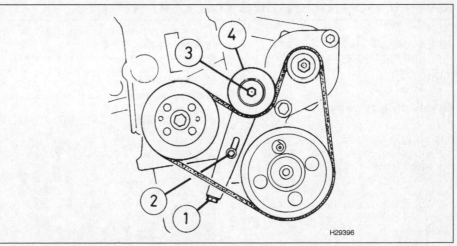

15.8 Auxiliary drivebelt manual adjustment (1.8 litre XU engine, without air conditioning)

1 Adjuster bolt
2 Tensioning pulley assembly lower securing bolt
3 Tensioning pulley assembly upper retaining bolt
4 Tensioning pulley

9 On models with automatic (spring-loaded) adjusted drivebelt, move the tensioner pulley away from the drivebelt, using a spanner on the tensioner roller retaining nut. Rotate the tensioner roller anti-clockwise away from the belt **Note:** *The tensioner roller retaining nut has a left-hand thread, so it will not loosen when releasing the tension on the belt.* Once the tensioner is released, disengage the drivebelt from all the pulleys, noting its correct routing. Remove the drivebelt from the engine **(see illustration)**.

Refitting

10 Fit the drivebelt around the pulleys:
a) *Tensioner pulley.*
b) *Crankshaft.*
c) *Power steering pump.*
d) *Alternator.*
e) *Idler pulley (where applicable).*
f) *Air conditioning compressor (where applicable).*

11 Ensure that the ribs on the belt are correctly engaged with the grooves in the pulleys, and that the drivebelt is correctly routed.

Tensioning

Manual adjuster

12 If not already done, proceed as described in paragraphs 2 and 3.
13 After refitting, take all the slack out of the belt by turning the tensioner pulley adjuster bolt, then tension the belt as follows.
14 Correct tensioning of the drivebelt will ensure that it has a long life. A belt which is too slack will slip and perhaps squeal. Beware, however, of overtightening, as this can cause wear in the alternator bearings.
15 The belt should be tensioned so that, under firm thumb pressure, there is about 5.0 mm of

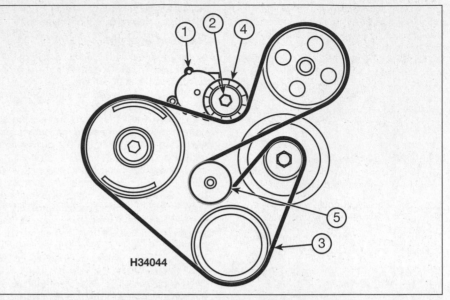

15.9 Auxiliary drivebelt automatic adjustment (EW engines, models with air conditioning)

1 *Tensioning pulley assembly*
2 *Tensioner roller retaining nut (**left-hand thread**)*
3 *Auxiliary drivebelt*
4 *Tensioner roller*
5 *Idler roller*

free movement at the mid-point between the pulleys on the longest belt run.
16 To adjust the tension, with the two tensioner pulley assembly retaining bolts slackened, rotate the adjuster bolt until the correct tension is achieved. Once the belt is correctly tensioned, rotate the crankshaft four complete revolutions in the normal direction of rotation and recheck the tension.
17 When the belt is correctly tensioned, tighten the tensioner pulley assembly retaining bolts to the specified torque, then reconnect the battery negative lead.
18 Refit the wheelarch liner and, where fitted,

the engine splash guard. Refit the roadwheel, and lower the car to the ground.

Automatic adjuster

19 Where necessary, securely tighten the automatic tensioner mounting bolts to the specified torque.
20 The tensioner is spring-loaded, when the tensioner is released it will automatically tension the belt.
21 Reconnect the battery negative lead.
22 Refit the wheelarch liner and, where fitted, the engine splash guard. Refit the roadwheel, and lower the vehicle to the ground.

Every 36 000 miles (60 000 km)

16	Spark plug renewal and ignition system check

Spark plug renewal

1 The correct functioning of the spark plugs is vital for the correct running and efficiency of the engine. It is essential that the plugs fitted are appropriate for the engine (a suitable type is specified at the beginning of this Chapter). If this type is used, and the engine is in good condition, the spark plugs should not need attention between scheduled renewal intervals.
2 Spark plug cleaning is rarely necessary, and should not be attempted unless specialised equipment is available, as damage can easily be caused to the firing ends.

3 To gain access to the spark plugs, the ignition coil unit fitted in the centre of the cylinder head cover must first be removed. Disconnect the wiring connector at the left-hand end of the coil unit, then undo the six retaining bolts and lift the coil unit upwards,

16.3 Ignition coil unit wiring connector (arrowed)

off the spark plugs and from its location in the cylinder head cover **(see illustration)**.
4 On certain models, to improve access to some of the plugs, it may be necessary to remove the air inlet ducting (refer to Chapter 4A for further information).
5 It is advisable to remove the dirt from the spark plug recesses, using a clean brush, vacuum cleaner or compressed air before removing the plugs, to prevent dirt dropping into the cylinders.
6 Unscrew the plugs using a spark plug spanner, suitable box spanner, or a deep socket and extension bar **(see illustration)**. Keep the socket aligned with the spark plug – if it is forcibly moved to one side, the ceramic insulator may be broken off. As each plug is removed, examine it as follows.
7 Examination of the spark plugs will give a good indication of the condition of the engine. If the insulator nose of the spark plug is clean and white, with no deposits, this is indicative

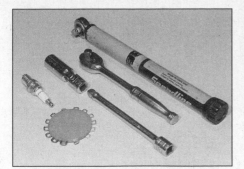

16.6 Tools required for spark plug removal, gap adjustment and refitting

16.10 Measuring the spark plug gap with a wire gauge

16.11 Measuring the spark plug gap with a feeler blade

of a weak mixture. It could also indicate that the plug is too 'hot' for the engine (a hot plug transfers heat away from the electrode slowly, a cold plug transfers heat away quickly). If this condition is apparent, either correct the mixture setting (where possible), or ensure that the correct grade of plug is fitted.

8 If the tip and insulator nose are covered with hard black-looking deposits, then this is indicative that the mixture is too rich. Should the plug be black and oily, then it is likely that the engine is fairly worn, as well as the mixture being too rich.

9 If the insulator nose is covered with light tan to greyish-brown deposits, then the mixture is correct, and it is likely that the engine is in good condition.

10 The spark plug electrode gap is of considerable importance as, if it is too large or too small, the size of the spark and its efficiency will be seriously impaired. The gap should be set to the value given in the Specifications at the beginning of this Chapter **(see illustration)**.

11 To set it, measure the gap with a feeler blade. If necessary, bend the outer plug electrode open or closed until the correct gap is achieved **(see illustration)**. The centre electrode should never be bent, as this may crack the insulator and cause plug failure, if nothing worse.

12 Special spark plug electrode gap adjusting tools are available from most motor accessory shops.

13 Before fitting the spark plugs, check that the threaded connector sleeves (on top of the plug) are tight, and that the plug exterior

surfaces and threads are clean. Apply a smear of copper-based anti-seize compound to the plug threads **(see Haynes Hint)**.

14 Once the plug begins to screw in correctly, remove the rubber hose (if used), and tighten the plug to the specified torque using the spark plug socket and a torque wrench. Refit the remaining spark plugs in the same manner.

15 Refit the ignition coil unit to the head cover. Refit the retaining bolts, tightening them securely, then reconnect the coil unit wiring connectors.

Ignition system check

16 Check that all the primary (LT) circuit wiring connectors are clean and free of corrosion.

17 Ensure that the any wiring is marked accordingly, before removing them, to avoid confusion when refitting.

18 Check inside the end fitting for signs of corrosion, which will look like a white crusty powder. Push the end fitting back onto the spark plug, ensuring that it is a tight fit on the plug.

19 Using a clean rag, wipe the entire length of wiring or leads to remove any built-up dirt and grease. Once clean, check for burns, cracks and other damage.

17 Air filter element renewal

1 Slacken the retaining clip and disconnect

HAYNES HINT

It's often difficult to insert spark plugs into their holes without cross-threading them. To avoid this possibility, fit a short piece of rubber hose over the end of the spark plug. The flexible hose acts as a universal joint, to help align the plug with the plug hole. Should the plug begin to cross-thread, the hose will slip on the spark plug, preventing thread damage.

the inlet duct from the air filter housing top **(see illustration)**.

2 Where applicable, unclip any wiring or cables from the air filter housing, then undo the screws in the air filter housing and lift off the top **(see illustrations)**.

3 Lift out the filter element and wipe clean the lower housing body and top **(see illustration)**.

4 Place the new element in position in the lower housing body. Refit the filter housing top, securing it in position with its retaining screws.

17.1 Slacken the retaining clip (arrowed) and disconnect the inlet duct from the air filter housing top

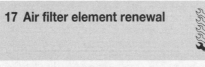

17.2a Unclip any cables/wiring from the air filter housing . . .

17.2b . . . then undo the four screws (one arrowed) securing the top to the housing body . . .

17.3 . . . and withdraw the air filter element

5 Reconnect the inlet duct to the lid, and securely tighten its retaining clip. Secure any cables and wiring that has been unclipped from the air filter housing on removal.

18 Fuel filter renewal

⚠ **Warning: Before carrying out the following operation, refer to the precautions given in 'Safety first!' at the beginning of this manual, and follow them implicitly. Petrol is a highly-dangerous and volatile liquid, and the precautions necessary when handling it cannot be overstressed.**

1 The fuel filter is located beneath the right-hand side of the vehicle, adjacent to the fuel tank **(see illustration)**. To gain access to the filter, chock the front wheels, then jack up the rear of the car and support it on axle stands.

2 Clamp the fuel inlet hose on the tank side of the filter. Bearing in mind the information given in the relevant Part of Chapter 4A on depressurising the fuel system, disconnect the quick-release fuel hose connections and remove the fuel hoses from the filter. Be prepared for fuel spillage.

3 Pull the upper end of the filter retaining strap upward to disengage it from the slot in the retaining bracket, move the strap aside and remove the filter.

4 Dispose of the old filter safely; it will be highly-inflammable, and may explode if thrown on a fire.

5 Locate the new filter in position and secure it with the retaining strap. Make sure that the lug on the strap fully engages with the slot in the retaining bracket.

6 Connect the fuel hoses to the filter and remove the hose clamp.

7 Start the engine, and check the filter hose connections for leaks. Lower the vehicle to the ground on completion.

19 Manual transmission oil level check

Note: *A new sealing washer will be required for the transmission filler/level plug, when refitting.*

1 Jack up the front and rear of the car and securely support it on axle stands so that it remains level. If the car has been recently driven, wait at least 5 minutes after the engine has been switched off. If the oil level is checked immediately after driving the car, some of the oil will remain distributed around the transmission components, resulting in an inaccurate level reading.

2 Remove the left-hand front roadwheel then release the screws and clips and remove the wheelarch liner from under the wing for access to the filler/level plug.

3 Wipe clean the area around the filler/level plug, which is the largest bolt among those securing the end cover to the transmission. Unscrew the plug and clean it; discard the sealing washer **(see illustrations)**.

4 The oil level should reach the lower edge of the filler/level hole. A certain amount of oil will have gathered behind the filler/level plug, and will trickle out when it is removed; this does *not* necessarily indicate that the level is correct. To ensure that a true level is established, wait until the initial trickle has stopped, then add oil as necessary until a trickle of new oil can be seen emerging **(see illustration)**. The level will be correct when the flow ceases; use only good-quality oil of the specified type.

5 Refilling the transmission is an awkward operation; above all, allow plenty of time for the oil level to settle properly before

18.1 The fuel filter is situated underneath the right-hand side of the vehicle, adjacent to the fuel tank

checking it. If a large amount had to be added to the transmission, or if a large amount flowed out on checking the level, refit the filler/level plug and take the vehicle on a short journey. With the new oil distributed fully around the transmission components, recheck the level after allowing time for it to settle again.

6 If the transmission has been overfilled so that oil flows out as soon as the filler/level plug is removed, first check that the car is completely level (front-to-rear and side-to-side). Allow any surplus oil to drain off into a suitable container.

7 When the level is correct, fit a new sealing washer to the filler/level plug. Tighten the plug to the specified torque wrench setting. Wash off any spilt oil. Refit the wheelarch liner, and secure it in position with its retaining screws and clips. Refit the roadwheel.

8 Frequent need for topping-up indicates a leak, which should be found and corrected before it becomes serious.

20 Rear brake shoe check

1 Remove the rear brake drums and check the brake shoes for signs of wear or contamination. At the same time, also check the wheel cylinders for signs of leakage and the brake drums for signs of wear. Refer to the relevant Sections of Chapter 9 for further information.

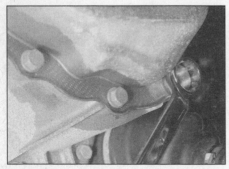

19.3a Use a spanner to loosen the manual transmission filler/level plug . . .

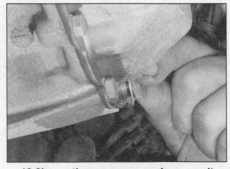

19.3b . . . then unscrew and remove it

19.4 Topping-up the transmission oil level

Every 36 000 miles (60 000 km) or 2 years

21 Brake fluid renewal

⚠️ **Warning: Brake hydraulic fluid can harm your eyes and damage painted surfaces, so use extreme caution when handling and pouring it. Do not use fluid that has been standing open for some time, as it absorbs moisture from the air. Excess moisture can cause a dangerous loss of braking effectiveness.**

Note: *A hydraulic clutch shares its fluid reservoir with the braking system, and may also need to be bled (see Chapter 6).*

1 The procedure is similar to that for the bleeding of the hydraulic system as described in Chapter 9, except that the brake fluid reservoir should be emptied by syphoning, using a clean poultry baster or similar before starting, and allowance should be made for the old fluid to be expelled when bleeding a section of the circuit.

2 Working as described in Chapter 9, open the first bleed screw in the sequence, and pump the brake pedal gently until nearly all the old fluid has been emptied from the master cylinder reservoir.

HAYNES HiNT *Old brake fluid is invariably much darker in colour than the new, making it easy to distinguish the two.*

3 Top-up to the MAX level with new fluid, and continue pumping until only the new fluid remains in the reservoir, and new fluid can be seen emerging from the bleed screw. Tighten the screw, and top the reservoir level up to the MAX level line.

4 Work through all the remaining bleed screws in the sequence until new fluid can be seen at all of them. Be careful to keep the master cylinder reservoir topped-up to above the MIN/DANGER level at all times, or air may enter the system and greatly increase the length of the task.

5 When the operation is complete, check that all bleed screws are securely tightened, and that their dust caps are refitted. Wash off all traces of spilt fluid, and recheck the master cylinder reservoir fluid level.

6 Check the operation of the brakes before taking the car on the road.

Every 72 000 miles (120 000 km)

22 Timing belt renewal

Refer to the relevant Part of Chapter 2.

Every 72 000 miles (120 000 km) or 5 years

23 Coolant renewal

Cooling system draining

⚠️ **Warning: Wait until the engine is cold before starting this procedure. Do not allow antifreeze to come in contact with your skin, or with the painted surfaces of the vehicle. Rinse off spills immediately with plenty of water. Never leave antifreeze lying around in an open container, or in a puddle in the driveway or on the garage floor. Children and pets are attracted by its sweet smell, but antifreeze can be fatal if ingested.**

1 With the engine completely cold, remove the expansion tank filler cap. Turn the cap anti-clockwise until it reaches the first stop. Wait until any pressure remaining in the system is released, then push the cap down, turn it anti-clockwise to the second stop, and lift it off.

2 Remove the splash guard under the engine, where fitted, then position a suitable container beneath the coolant drain outlet at the lower left-hand side of the radiator.

3 Where fitted, loosen the drain plug (there is no need to remove it completely) and allow the coolant to drain into the container. If desired, a length of tubing can be fitted to the drain outlet to direct the flow of coolant during draining **(see illustration)**.

4 To assist draining, open the cooling system bleed screws. These are located in the heater matrix outlet hose union (to improve access, it may be located in an extension hose) on the engine compartment bulkhead, and on the top of the thermostat housing **(see illustrations)**. On some models, there may also be a bleed screw in the top left-hand end of the radiator.

5 When the flow of coolant stops, reposition the container below the cylinder block drain plug.

6 Remove the drain plug, and allow the coolant to drain into the container.

7 If the coolant has been drained for a reason

23.3 Tubing (1) attached to the radiator drain outlet and coolant drain plug (2)

23.4a Heater hose bleed screw (arrowed) . . .

23.4b . . . and thermostat housing bleed screw (arrowed)

Cut the bottom off an old antifreeze container to make a 'header tank' for use when refilling the cooling system. The seal at the point arrowed should be as tight as possible – use an O-ring if available, or seal the joint by some other means.

other than renewal, then provided it is clean and less than two years old, it can be re-used, though this is not recommended.

8 Refit the radiator and cylinder block drain plugs on completion of draining.

Cooling system flushing

9 If coolant renewal has been neglected, or if the antifreeze mixture has become diluted, then in time, the cooling system may gradually lose efficiency, as the coolant passages become restricted due to rust, scale deposits, and other sediment. The cooling system efficiency can be restored by flushing the system clean.

10 The radiator should be flushed independently of the engine, to avoid contamination.

Radiator flushing

11 To flush the radiator, first tighten the radiator drain plug, and the radiator bleed screw, where applicable.

12 Disconnect the top and bottom hoses and any other relevant hoses from the radiator, with reference to Chapter 3.

13 Insert a garden hose into the radiator top inlet. Direct a flow of clean water through the radiator, and continue flushing until clean water emerges from the radiator bottom outlet.

14 If after a reasonable period, the water still does not run clear, the radiator can be flushed with a good proprietary cleaning agent. It is important that their manufacturer's instructions are followed carefully. If the contamination is particularly bad, insert the hose in the radiator bottom outlet, and reverse-flush the radiator.

Engine flushing

15 To flush the engine, first refit the cylinder block drain plug, and tighten the cooling system bleed screws.

16 Remove the thermostat (see Chapter 3), then temporarily refit the thermostat cover.

17 With the top and bottom hoses disconnected from the radiator, insert a garden hose into the radiator top hose. Direct a clean flow of water through the engine, and continue flushing until clean water emerges from the radiator bottom hose.

18 On completion of flushing, refit the thermostat and reconnect the hoses with reference to Chapter 3.

Cooling system filling

19 Before attempting to fill the cooling system, make sure that all hoses and clips are in good condition, and that the clips are tight. Note that an antifreeze mixture must be used all year round, to prevent corrosion of the engine components (see following sub-Section). Also check that the radiator and cylinder block drain plugs are in place and tight.

20 Remove the expansion tank filler cap.

21 Open all the cooling system bleed screws (see paragraph 4).

22 Some of the cooling system hoses are positioned at a higher level than the top of the radiator expansion tank. It is therefore necessary to use a 'header tank' when refilling the cooling system, to reduce the possibility of air being trapped in the system. Although Peugeot dealers use a special header tank, the same effect can be achieved by using a suitable bottle, with a seal between the bottle and the expansion tank **(see Haynes Hint)**.

23 Fit the 'header tank' to the expansion tank and slowly fill the system. Coolant will emerge from each of the bleed screws in turn, starting with the lowest screw. As soon as coolant free from air bubbles emerges from the lowest screw, tighten that screw, and watch the next bleed screw in the system. Repeat the procedure until the coolant is emerging from the highest bleed screw in the cooling system and all bleed screws are securely tightened.

24 Ensure that the header tank is full (at least 0.5 litres of coolant). Start the engine, and run it at a fast idle speed (do not exceed 2000 rpm) until the cooling fan cuts in, and then cuts out. Stop the engine. **Note:** *Take great care not to scald yourself with the hot coolant during this operation.*

25 Allow the engine to cool, then remove the header tank.

26 When the engine has cooled, check the coolant level as described in *Weekly checks*. Top-up the level if necessary, and refit the expansion tank cap. Where applicable, refit the splash guard under the engine.

Antifreeze mixture

27 The antifreeze should always be renewed at the specified intervals. This is necessary not only to maintain the antifreeze properties, but also to prevent corrosion which would otherwise occur as the corrosion inhibitors become progressively less effective.

28 Always use an ethylene-glycol based antifreeze which is suitable for use in mixed-metal cooling systems. The quantity of antifreeze and levels of protection are indicated in the Specifications.

29 Before adding antifreeze, the cooling system should be completely drained, preferably flushed, and all hoses checked for condition and security.

30 After filling with antifreeze, a label should be attached to the expansion tank, stating the type and concentration of antifreeze used, and the date installed. Any subsequent topping-up should be made with the same type and concentration of antifreeze.

31 Do not use engine antifreeze in the washer system, as it will cause damage to the vehicle paintwork. A screenwash additive should be added to the washer system in the quantities stated on the bottle.

Chapter 1 Part B:
Routine maintenance & servicing – diesel models

Contents

Air filter element renewal	16	Hinge and lock lubrication	9
Automatic transmission fluid level check	7	Hose and fluid leak check	5
Auxiliary drivebelt check and renewal	15	Manual transmission oil level check	18
Brake fluid renewal	20	Particulate emission system check	21
Clutch operation check	6	Pollen filter check	10
Coolant renewal	23	Rear brake pad check	12
Engine oil and filter renewal	3	Rear brake shoe check	19
Front brake pad check	11	Regular maintenance	2
Fuel filter renewal	17	Road test	14
Fuel filter water draining	4	Steering, suspension and driveshaft gaiter check	8
General information	1	Timing belt renewal	22
Handbrake check	13		

Degrees of difficulty

Easy, suitable for novice with little experience		**Fairly easy,** suitable for beginner with some experience		**Fairly difficult,** suitable for competent DIY mechanic		**Difficult,** suitable for experienced DIY mechanic		**Very difficult,** suitable for expert DIY or professional	

Lubricants and fluids

Refer to *Weekly checks* on page 0•18

Capacities

Engine oil (including oil filter)

2.0 litre engines	4.5 litres
2.2 litre engine	4.75 litres

Cooling system

All engines (approximate)	8.8 litres

Transmission

Manual transmission (approximate)	1.9 litres
Automatic transmissions:	
4HP20:	
Drain and refill	3.0 litres
Total capacity (including torque converter)	8.0 litres
AL4:	
Drain and refill	4.5 litres
Total capacity (including torque converter)	6.0 litres
Fuel tank	70 litres

Cooling system

Antifreeze mixture:

50% antifreeze	Protection down to –37°C
55% antifreeze	Protection down to –45°C

Note: *Refer to antifreeze manufacturer for latest recommendations.*

Brakes

Brake pad friction material minimum thickness	2.0 mm
Brake shoe friction material minimum thickness	1.5 mm

Tyre pressures

See end of *Weekly checks* on page 0•18

Torque wrench settings

	Nm	lbf ft
Auxiliary drivebelt eccentric tensioner roller bolt	44	32
Manual transmission filler/level plug	20	15
Roadwheel bolts	90	66

The maintenance intervals in this manual are provided with the assumption that you, not the dealer, will be carrying out the work. These are the minimum maintenance intervals recommended by us for vehicles driven daily.

If you wish to keep your vehicle in peak condition at all times, you may wish to perform some of these procedures more often. We encourage frequent maintenance, because it enhances the efficiency, performance and resale value of your vehicle.

When the vehicle is new, it should be serviced by a factory-authorised dealer service department, in order to preserve the factory warranty.

Weekly, or every 250 miles (400 km)
☐ Refer to *Weekly checks*

Every 6000 miles (10 000 km) or 12 months – whichever comes first
In addition to all the items listed above, carry out the following:
☐ Renew the engine oil and filter (Section 3)
Note: *Peugeot recommend that the engine oil and filter are changed every 10 000 miles (16 000 km) or 2 years. However, oil and filter changes are good for the engine and we recommend that the oil and filter are renewed more frequently, especially if the vehicle is used on a lot of short journeys.*
☐ Drain any water from the fuel filter (Section 4)
☐ Check all underbonnet components and hoses for fluid leaks (Section 5)
☐ Check the operation of the clutch (Section 6)
☐ Check the automatic transmission (4HP20 type) fluid level, and top up if necessary (Section 7)
☐ Check the steering, suspension and driveshaft rubber gaiters for condition and security (Section 8)
☐ Lubricate all hinges and locks (Section 9)
☐ Check the pollen filter (where fitted) (Section 10)

Every 12 000 miles (20 000 km)
In addition to all the items listed above, carry out the following:
☐ Check the condition of the front brake pads, and renew if necessary (Section 11)
☐ Check the condition of the rear brake pads, and renew if necessary – rear bisc brake models (Section 12)
☐ Check the operation of the handbrake (Section 13)
☐ Carry out a road test (Section 14)
☐ Check the condition of the auxiliary drivebelt, and renew if necessary (Section 15)

Every 24 000 miles (40 000 km)
In addition to all the items listed above, carry out the following:
☐ Renew the air filter (Section 16)
☐ Renew the fuel filter (Section 17)

Every 36 000 miles (60 000 km)
In addition to all the items listed above, carry out the following:
☐ Check the manual transmission oil level, and top-up if necessary (Section 18)
☐ Check the automatic transmission (AL4 type) fluid level, and top up if necessary (Section 7)
☐ Check the condition of the rear brake shoes and renew if necessary – rear drum brake models (Section 19)

Every 36 000 miles (60 000 km) or 2 years, whichever comes sooner
☐ Renew the brake fluid (Section 20)

Note: *A hydraulic clutch shares its fluid reservoir with the braking system, and may also need to be bled.*

Every 48 000 miles (80 000 km)
☐ Check the particulate emission system (where fitted) (Section 21)

Every 72 000 miles (120 000 km)
In addition to all the items listed above, carry out the following:
☐ Renew the timing belt (Section 22)

Note: *It is strongly recommended that the timing belt renewal interval is halved to 36 000 miles (60 000 km) on vehicles which are subjected to intensive use, ie, mainly short journeys or a lot of stop-start driving. The actual belt renewal interval is therefore very much up to the individual owner, but bear in mind that severe engine damage will result if the belt breaks.*

Every 72 000 miles (120 000 km) or 5 years, whichever comes sooner
☐ Renew the coolant (Section 23)

Underbonnet view of a 2.2 litre model

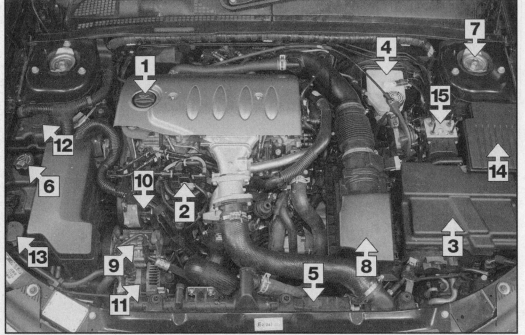

1. Engine oil filler cap/dipstick
2. Fuel filter housing
3. Battery
4. Brake fluid reservoir
5. Radiator
6. Coolant expansion tank
7. Suspension strut upper mounting
8. Air filter housing
9. Power steering pump
10. Injection pump
11. Alternator
12. Power steering fluid reservoir
13. Washer fluid reservoir
14. Fuse/relay box
15. Anti-lock braking system (ABS) hydraulic unit

Front underbody view

1. Engine oil drain plug
2. Air conditioning compressor
3. Driveshaft intermediate bearing
4. Brake caliper
5. Front suspension lower arm
6. Track rod
7. Front suspension anti-roll bar

Rear underbody view

1 Fuel tank
2 Rear suspension trailing arm
3 Handbrake cable
4 Brake caliper
5 Rear suspension lower arm
6 Rear suspension track arm

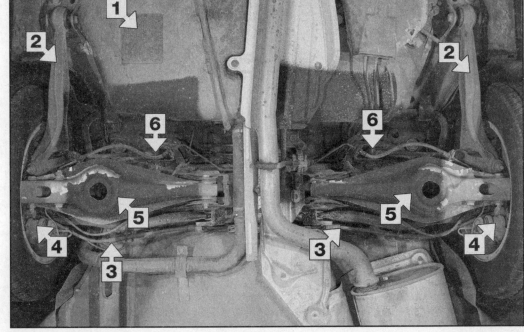

Maintenance procedures

1 General information

This Chapter is designed to help the home mechanic maintain his/her vehicle for safety, economy, long life and peak performance.

The Chapter contains a master maintenance schedule, followed by Sections dealing specifically with each task in the schedule. Visual checks, adjustments, component renewal and other helpful items are included. Refer to the accompanying illustrations of the engine compartment and the underside of the vehicle for the locations of the various components.

Servicing your vehicle in accordance with the mileage/time maintenance schedule and the following Sections will provide a planned maintenance programme, which should result in a long and reliable service life. This is a comprehensive plan, so maintaining some items but not others at the specified service intervals, will not produce the same results.

As you service your vehicle, you will discover that many of the procedures can – and should – be grouped together, because of the particular procedure being performed, or because of the proximity of two otherwise-unrelated components to one another. For example, if the vehicle is raised for any reason, the exhaust can be inspected at the same time as the suspension and steering components.

The first step in this maintenance programme is to prepare yourself before the actual work begins. Read through all the Sections relevant to the work to be carried out, then make a list and gather all the parts and tools required. If a problem is encountered, seek advice from a parts specialist, or a dealer service department.

2 Regular maintenance

1 If, from the time the vehicle is new, the routine maintenance schedule is followed closely, and frequent checks are made of fluid levels and high-wear Items, as suggested throughout this manual, the engine will be kept in relatively good running condition, and the need for additional work will be minimised.

2 It is possible that there will be times when the engine is running poorly due to the lack of regular maintenance. This is even more likely if a used vehicle, which has not received regular and frequent maintenance checks, is purchased. In such cases, additional work may need to be carried out, outside of the regular maintenance intervals.

3 If engine wear is suspected, a compression test (refer to Chapter 2C) will provide valuable information regarding the overall performance of the main internal components. Such a test can be used as a basis to decide on the extent of the work to be carried out. If, for example, a compression test indicates serious internal engine wear, conventional maintenance as described in this Chapter will not greatly improve the performance of the engine, and may prove a waste of time and money, unless extensive overhaul work is carried out first.

4 The following series of operations are those most often required to improve the performance of a generally poor-running engine:

Primary operations

a) Clean, inspect and test the battery (refer to 'Weekly checks').
b) Check all the engine-related fluids (refer to 'Weekly checks').
c) Check the condition and tension of the auxiliary drivebelt (Section 15).
d) Check the condition of the air filter, and renew if necessary (Section 16).
e) Check the condition of all hoses, and check for fluid leaks (Section 5).
f) Renew the fuel filter (Section 17).

5 If the above operations do not prove fully effective, carry out the following secondary operations:

Secondary operations

All items listed under Primary operations, plus the following:

a) Check the charging system (refer to Chapter 5A).
b) Check the preheating system (refer to Chapter 5C).
c) Check the fuel system (refer to Chapter 4B).

Every 6 000 miles (10 000 km) or 12 months

3 Engine oil and filter renewal

1 Frequent oil and filter changes are the most important preventative maintenance procedures which can be undertaken by the DIY owner. As engine oil ages, it becomes diluted and contaminated, which leads to premature engine wear.

2 Before starting this procedure, gather together all the necessary tools and materials. Also make sure that you have plenty of clean rags and newspapers handy, to mop up any spills. Ideally, the engine oil should be warm, as it will drain better, and more built-up sludge will be removed with it. Take care, however, not to touch the exhaust or any other hot parts of the engine when working under the vehicle. To avoid any possibility of scalding, and to protect yourself from possible skin irritants and other harmful contaminants in used engine oils, it is advisable to wear gloves when carrying out this work. Access to the underside of the vehicle will be greatly improved if it can be raised on a lift, driven onto ramps, or jacked up and supported on axle stands. Whichever

3.3 Engine oil sump drain plug (arrowed)

As the drain plug releases from the threads, move it away sharply so the stream of oil issuing from the sump runs into the container, not up your sleeve.

method is chosen, make sure that the vehicle remains level, or if it is at an angle, that the drain plug is at the lowest point. Where fitted, remove the splash guard from under the engine.

3 Slacken the drain plug about half a turn, position the draining container under the drain plug, then remove the plug completely**(see illustration)**. If possible, try to keep the plug pressed into the sump while unscrewing it by hand the last couple of turns **(see Haynes Hint)**. Recover the sealing ring from the drain plug.

4 Allow some time for the old oil to drain, noting that it may be necessary to reposition the container as the oil flow slows to a trickle.

5 After all the oil has drained, wipe off the drain plug with a clean rag, and fit a new sealing washer. Clean the area around the drain plug opening, and refit the plug. Tighten the plug securely.

6 If the filter is also to be renewed, move the container into position under the oil filter, which is located on the front side of the cylinder block.

7 Using an oil filter removal tool if necessary, slacken the filter initially, then unscrew it by hand the rest of the way **(see illustration)**. Empty the oil in the old filter into the container.

8 Use a clean rag to remove all oil, dirt and sludge from the filter sealing area on the engine. Check the old filter to make sure that the rubber sealing ring hasn't stuck to the engine. If it has, carefully remove it.

9 Apply a light coating of clean engine oil to the sealing ring on the new filter, then screw it into position on the engine. Tighten the filter firmly by hand only – **do not** use any tools. Where necessary, refit the splash guard under the engine.

10 Remove the old oil and all tools from under the car, then lower the car to the ground (if applicable).

11 Remove the dipstick, then unscrew the oil filler cap from the top of the filler tube on the front side of the cylinder block. Fill the engine,

using the correct grade and type of oil (*see Weekly checks*). An oil can spout or funnel may help to reduce spillage. Pour in half the specified quantity of oil first, then wait a few minutes for the oil to fall to the sump. Continue adding oil a small quantity at a time until the level is up to the lower mark on the dipstick. Adding approximately 1.0 litre will bring the level up to the upper mark on the dipstick. Refit the filler cap.

12 Start the engine and run it for a few minutes; check for leaks around the oil filter seal and the sump drain plug. Note that there may be a delay of a few seconds before the oil pressure warning light goes out when the engine is first started, as the oil circulates through the engine oil galleries and the new oil filter (where fitted) before the pressure builds-up.

13 Switch off the engine, and wait a few minutes for the oil to settle in the sump once more. With the new oil circulated and the filter completely full, recheck the level on the dipstick, and add more oil as necessary.

14 Dispose of the used engine oil safely, with reference to *General Repair Procedures*.

4 Fuel filter water draining

1 A water drain plug and tube are provided at the base of the fuel filter housing.

2 Place a suitable container beneath the drain tube, and cover the surrounding area with rags. Take care not to allow fuel to enter the transmission bellhousing which is just below.

3 Open the drain plug by turning it anti-clockwise. Allow fuel and water to drain until fuel which is free from water, emerges from the end of the tube **(see illustration)**. Close the drain plug.

4 Dispose of the drained fuel safely.

5 Start the engine. If difficulty is experienced, bleed the fuel system (Chapter 4B).

3.7 Using an oil filter removal tool to slacken the oil filter

4.3 Fuel filter water drain plug location (arrowed) – 2.0 litre

5 Hose and fluid leak check

Cooling system

⚠️ **Warning: Refer to the safety information given in 'Safety first!' and Chapter 3 before disturbing any of the cooling system components.**

1 Carefully check the radiator and heater coolant hoses along their entire length. Renew any hose which is cracked, swollen or which shows signs of deterioration. Cracks will show up better if the hose is squeezed. Pay close attention to the clips that secure the hoses to the cooling system components. Hose clips that have been over-tightened can pinch and puncture hoses, resulting in cooling system leaks.

2 Inspect all the cooling system components (hoses, joint faces, etc) for leaks. Where any problems of this nature are found on system components, renew the component or gasket with reference to Chapter 3.

3 A leak from the cooling system will usually show up as white or rust-coloured deposits, on the area surrounding the leak **(see Haynes Hint)**.

Fuel

⚠️ **Warning: Refer to the safety information given in 'Safety first!' and Chapter 4B before disturbing any of the fuel system components.**

4 Check all fuel lines at their connections to the injection pump, injectors and fuel filter housing.

5 Examine each fuel hose/pipe along its length for splits or cracks. Check for leakage from the union nuts and examine the unions between the metal fuel lines and the fuel filter housing. Also check the area around the fuel injectors for signs of leakage.

6 To identify fuel leaks between the fuel tank and the engine bay, the vehicle should raised and securely supported on axle stands. Inspect the fuel tank and filler neck for punctures, cracks and other damage. The connection between the filler neck and tank is especially critical. Sometimes a rubber filler neck or connecting hose will leak due to loose retaining clamps or deteriorated rubber.

7 Carefully check all rubber hoses and metal fuel lines leading away from the fuel tank. Check for loose connections, deteriorated hoses, kinked lines, and other damage. Pay particular attention to the vent pipes and hoses, which often loop up around the filler neck and can become blocked or kinked, making tank filling difficult. Follow the fuel supply and return lines to the front of the vehicle, carefully inspecting them all the way for signs of damage or corrosion. Renew damaged sections as necessary.

Engine oil

8 Inspect the area around the camshaft cover, cylinder head, oil filter and sump joint faces. Bear in mind that, over a period of time, some very slight seepage from these areas is to be expected – what you are really looking for is any indication of a serious leak caused by gasket failure. Engine oil seeping from the base of the timing belt cover or the transmission bellhousing may be an indication of crankshaft or input shaft oil seal failure. Should a leak be found, renew the failed gasket or oil seal by referring to the appropriate Chapters in this manual.

Power assisted steering fluid

9 Examine the hose running between the fluid reservoir and the power steering pump, and the return hose running from the steering rack to the fluid reservoir. Also examine the high pressure supply hose between the pump and the steering rack.

10 Where applicable, check the hoses leading to the PAS fluid cooler at the front of the engine bay. Look for deterioration caused by corrosion and damage from grounding, or debris thrown up from the road surface.

11 Pay particular attention to crimped unions, and the area surrounding the hoses that are secured with adjustable worm drive clips. PAS fluid is a thin oil, and is usually red in colour.

Air conditioning refrigerant

⚠️ **Warning: Refer to the safety information given in 'Safety first!' and Chapter 3, regarding the dangers of disturbing any of the air conditioning system components.**

12 The air conditioning system is filled with a liquid refrigerant, which is retained under high pressure. If the air conditioning system is opened and depressurised without the aid of specialised equipment, the refrigerant will immediately turn into gas and escape into the atmosphere. If the liquid comes into contact with your skin, it can cause severe frostbite. In addition, the refrigerant contains substances which are environmentally damaging; for this reason, it should not be allowed to escape into the atmosphere.

13 Any suspected air conditioning system leaks should be immediately referred to a Peugeot dealer or air conditioning specialist. Leakage will be shown up as a steady drop in the level of refrigerant in the system.

14 Note that water may drip from the condenser drain pipe, underneath the car, immediately after the air conditioning system has been in use. This is normal, and should not be cause for concern.

Brake (and clutch) fluid

⚠️ **Warning: Refer to the safety information given in 'Safety first!' and Chapter 9, regarding the dangers of handling brake fluid.**

15 With reference to Chapter 9, examine the

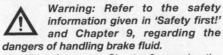
A leak in the cooling system will usually show-up as white- or rust-coloured deposits on the area adjoining the leak.

area surrounding the brake pipe unions at the master cylinder for signs of leakage. Check the area around the base of fluid reservoir, for signs of leakage caused by seal failure. Also examine the brake pipe unions at the ABS hydraulic unit.

16 If fluid loss is evident, but the leak cannot be pinpointed in the engine bay, the brake calipers and underbody brake lines and should be carefully checked with the vehicle raised and supported on axle stands. Leakage of fluid from the braking system is serious fault that must be rectified immediately.

17 Refer to Chapter 6 and check for leakage around the hydraulic fluid line connections to the clutch master cylinder at the bulkhead, and to the clutch slave cylinder, bolted to the side of the transmission bellhousing.

18 Brake/clutch hydraulic fluid is a toxic substance with a watery consistency. New fluid is almost colourless, but it becomes darker with age and use.

Unidentified fluid leaks

19 If there are signs that a fluid of some description is leaking from the vehicle, but you cannot identify the type of fluid or its exact origin, park the vehicle overnight and slide a large piece of card underneath it. Providing that the card is positioned in roughly in the right location, even the smallest leak will show up on the card. Not only will this help you to pinpoint the exact location of the leak, it should be easier to identify the fluid from its colour. Bear in mind, though, that the leak may only be occurring when the engine is running!

Vacuum hoses

20 Although the braking system is hydraulically-operated, the brake servo unit amplifies the effort you apply at the brake pedal, by making use of the vacuum created by the pump (see Chapter 9). Vacuum is ported to the servo by means of a large-bore hose. Any leaks that develop in this hose will reduce the effectiveness of the braking system.

21 In addition, many of the underbonnet components, particularly the emission control components, are driven by vacuum supplied

7.1 Withdrawing the automatic transmission dipstick – 4HP20 transmission

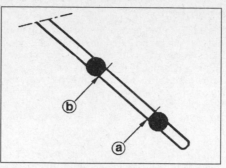

7.2 Automatic transmission fluid dipstick lower (a) and upper (b) fluid level markings

from the vacuum pump via narrow-bore hoses. A leak in a vacuum hose means that air is being drawn into the hose (rather than escaping from it) and this makes leakage very difficult to detect. One method is to use an old length of vacuum hose as a kind of stethoscope – hold one end close to (but not in) your ear and use the other end to probe the area around the suspected leak. When the end of the hose is directly over a vacuum leak, a hissing sound will be heard clearly through the hose. Care must be taken to avoid contacting hot or moving components, as the engine must be running, when testing in this manner. Renew any vacuum hoses that are found to be defective.

6 Clutch operation check

1 Diesel engine models covered by this manual are equipped with a hydraulically operated self-adjusting clutch mechanism

which is virtually maintenance-free.
2 The only maintenance necessary is to check that the clutch pedal moves smoothly and easily through its full travel, and that the clutch itself functions correctly, with no trace of slip or drag.
3 If any problems are experienced, refer to Chapter 6 for further details.

7 Automatic transmission fluid level check

Note: *The AL4 transmission is identified by having the Park Lock facility.*

4HP20 transmission

1 Take the vehicle on a moderate journey (at least 30 minutes), to warm the transmission up to normal operating temperature, then park the vehicle on level ground. Leave the engine idling, apply the handbrake fully, and move the selector lever to the P (Park) position. The fluid level is checked using the dipstick

located at the front of the engine compartment, directly in front of the engine unit **(see illustration)**. The dipstick top is brightly-coloured for easy identification.
2 With the engine idling and the footbrake applied, move the selector lever through all gear positions, stopping briefly in each position, then return the selector lever to the P position. Withdraw the dipstick from the tube, and wipe all the fluid from its end with a clean rag or paper towel. Insert the clean dipstick back into the tube as far as it will go, then withdraw it once more. Note the fluid level on the end of the dipstick. The fluid level should be between the two upper marks on the dipstick (the marks located on either side of the number 80) **(see illustration)**.
3 If topping-up is necessary, add the required quantity of the specified fluid to the transmission via the dipstick tube. Use a funnel with a fine-mesh gauze, to avoid spillage, and to ensure that no foreign matter enters the transmission. **Note:** *Never overfill the transmission so that the fluid level is above the upper mark.*
4 After topping-up, take the vehicle on a short run to distribute the fresh fluid, then recheck the level, topping-up if necessary.
5 Always maintain the level between the two upper dipstick marks. If the level is allowed to fall below the lower mark, fluid starvation may result, which could lead to severe transmission damage.
6 Frequent need for topping-up indicates that there is a leak, which should be found and corrected before it becomes serious.

AL4 transmission

7 Take the vehicle on a moderate journey (at least 30 minutes), to warm the transmission up to normal operating temperature, then park the vehicle on level ground.
8 With the engine switched off, the oil level is checked by removing the oil filler and oil level plugs from the transmission housing.
9 Remove the air cleaner air inlet duct as described in Chapter 4B.
10 To improve access to the oil level plug, which is on the base of the transmission housing, it may be preferable to jack up the front and rear of the car, and support it on axle stands (see *Jacking and vehicle support*); it is essential that the car is kept level for the check to be accurate. Remove the engine undertray for access to the plug.
11 Using a square-section wrench, remove the oil filler plug from the top of the transmission housing **(see illustration)**, and add 0.5 litres of the specified oil. As access to the filler plug is limited, Peugeot mechanics use a filling bottle with a length of small-bore hose attached. The end of the hose is inserted into the filler orifice and the bottle (filled with the specified oil) is then suspended from the bonnet. A suitable alternative could easily be made up from, for example, a clean plastic drinks bottle with the base cut off and with a hose attached to the cap.

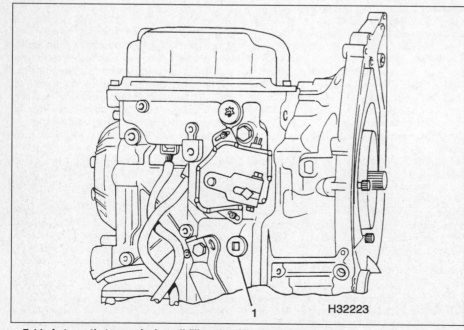

7.11 Automatic transmission oil filler plug (1), viewed from above – AL4 transmission

H32223

12 With the handbrake and footbrake firmly applied, start the engine and move the selector through all available positions several times. Finally, select P, and leave the engine running.

13 Working under the car, place a suitable container underneath the transmission, then remove the oil level plug **(see illustration)**. This is the smaller hex-head bolt inside the larger hex-headed transmission drain plug – do not loosen the larger, outer plug with the engine running, or the transmission oil will run out, resulting in transmission damage.

14 If the level is correct, oil will run from the level plug in a steady stream, quickly reducing to a sequence of drips. In theory, the amount of oil lost when the plug is removed should be the same as, or less than, the 0.5 litres just added. When the dripping stops, refit the level plug.

15 If little or no oil emerges, refit the level plug, then switch off the engine. Repeat paragraphs 11 to 14 until the level is correct.

16 On completion, tighten the filler and level plugs to the specified torque (Chapter 7B), then refit the engine undertray and air inlet duct.

17 Frequent need for topping-up indicates that there is a leak, which should be found and corrected before it becomes serious.

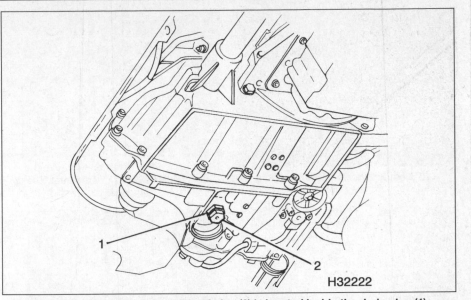

7.13 Automatic transmission oil level plug (2) is located inside the drain plug (1) – AL4 transmission

8 Steering, suspension and driveshaft gaiter check

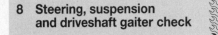

Front suspension/steering

1 Raise the front of the vehicle, and securely support it on axle stands.

2 Visually inspect the balljoint dust covers and the steering rack-and-pinion gaiters for splits, chafing or deterioration **(see illustration)**. Any wear of these components will cause loss of lubricant, together with dirt and water entry, resulting in rapid deterioration of the balljoints or steering gear.

3 Check the power steering fluid hoses for chafing or deterioration, and the pipe and hose unions for fluid leaks. Also check for signs of fluid leakage under pressure from the steering gear rubber gaiters, which would indicate failed fluid seals within the steering gear.

4 Grasp the roadwheel at the 12 o'clock and 6 o'clock positions, and try to rock it **(see illustration)**. Very slight free play may be felt, but if the movement is appreciable, further investigation is necessary to determine the source. Continue rocking the wheel while an assistant depresses the footbrake. If the movement is now eliminated or significantly reduced, it is likely that the hub bearings are at fault. If the free play is still evident with the footbrake depressed, then there is wear in the suspension joints or mountings.

5 Now grasp the wheel at the 9 o'clock and 3 o'clock positions, and try to rock it as before. Any movement felt now may again be caused by wear in the hub bearings or the steering track rod balljoints. If the inner or outer balljoint is worn, the visual movement will be obvious.

6 Using a large screwdriver or flat bar, check for wear in the suspension mounting bushes by levering between the relevant suspension component and its attachment point. Some movement is to be expected as the mountings are made of rubber, but excessive wear should be obvious. Also check the condition of any visible rubber bushes, looking for splits, cracks or contamination of the rubber.

7 With the car standing on its wheels, have an assistant turn the steering wheel back-and-forth about an eighth of a turn each way. There should be very little, if any, lost movement between the steering wheel and roadwheels. If this is not the case, closely observe the joints and mountings previously described, but in addition, check the steering column universal joints for wear, and the rack-and-pinion steering gear itself.

Strut/shock absorber

8 Check for any signs of fluid leakage around the suspension strut/shock absorber body, or from the rubber gaiter around the piston rod. Should any fluid be noticed, the suspension strut/shock absorber is defective internally, and should be renewed. **Note:** *Suspension struts/shock absorbers should always be renewed in pairs on the same axle.*

9 The efficiency of the suspension strut/shock absorber may be checked by bouncing the vehicle at each corner. Generally speaking, the body will return to its normal position and stop after being depressed. If it rises and returns on a rebound, the suspension strut/shock absorber is probably suspect. Examine also the suspension strut/shock absorber upper and lower mountings for any signs of wear.

Driveshaft gaiter check

10 With the vehicle raised and securely supported on axle stands, turn the steering to full left or right lock, then slowly rotate the roadwheel. Inspect the outer constant velocity (CV) joint rubber gaiters, squeezing the gaiters to open out the folds **(see illustration)**. Check for signs of cracking, splits or deterioration of the rubber, which may allow the grease to

8.2 Checking a steering gear gaiter for damage

8.4 Check for wear in the hub bearings by grasping the wheel and trying to rock it

8.10 Checking a driveshaft gaiter for damage

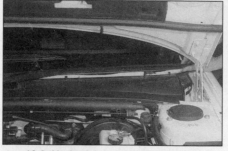

10.2 Undo the nut and remove the passenger side half of the intake vent cover . . .

10.3 . . . then unclip the intake vent panel from the vehicle

escape, or water and grit to enter. Also check the security and condition of the retaining clips. Repeat these checks on the inner CV joints. If any damage or deterioration is found, the gaiters should be renewed (see Chapter 8).

11 At the same time, check the general condition of the CV joints themselves by first holding the driveshaft and attempting to rotate the wheel. Repeat this check whilst holding the inner joint and attempting to rotate the driveshaft. Any appreciable movement indicates wear in the CV joints, wear in the driveshaft splines, or a loose driveshaft retaining nut.

10.4a Carefully ease the pollen filter out from its housing . . .

10.4b . . . and remove it from the vehicle

9 Hinge and lock lubrication

1 Lubricate the hinges of the bonnet, doors and tailgate with a light general-purpose oil. Similarly, lubricate all latches, locks and lock strikers – don't overdo it, or it will get on your clothes as you get in! At the same time, check the security and operation of all the locks, adjusting them if necessary (see Chapter 11).
2 Lightly lubricate the bonnet release mechanism and cable with a suitable grease.

10 Pollen filter check

1 Operate the windscreen wipers and switch off the ignition so the wiper arms stop at the top of their travel.
2 Unscrew the retaining nut then unclip and remove the passenger side plastic intake vent cover from the base of the windscreen (**see illustration**).
3 Unclip the passenger side intake vent panel and remove the panel from beneath the

windscreen to gain access to the pollen filter (**see illustration**).
4 Ease the pollen filter out of its housing and remove it from the vehicle (**see illustrations**).
5 Check the condition of the filter, if it is dirty, renew the filter.
6 Wipe clean the housing then install the new filter (if required), making sure it is clipped securely in position.
7 Clip the vent panel into position, making sure it is correctly engaged with the driver's side panel, then refit the vent cover and retaining nut.
8 Switch the ignition back on and return the wiper arm to the 'at rest' position.

Every 12 000 miles (20 000 km)

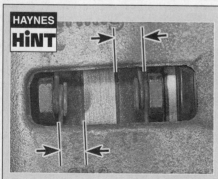

HAYNES HINT

For a quick check, the thickness of the friction material on each brake pad can be measured through the aperture in the caliper body.

11 Front brake pad check

1 Firmly apply the handbrake, then jack up the front of the car and support it securely on axle stands. Remove the front roadwheels.
2 For a comprehensive check, the brake pads should be removed and cleaned. The operation of the caliper can then also be checked, and the condition of the brake disc itself can be fully examined on both sides. Refer to Chapter 9 for further information (**see Haynes Hint**).
3 If any pad's friction material is worn to the specified thickness or less, *all four pads must be renewed as a set*. **Note**: *If any pad is approaching the minimum thickness, consider*

renewal as a precautionary measure in case the pads wear out before the next service.

12 Rear brake pad check

1 Chock the front wheels, then jack up the rear of the vehicle and support it on axle stands. Remove the rear road wheels.
2 For a quick check, the thickness of friction material remaining on each brake pad can be measured through the top of the caliper body.
3 For a comprehensive check, the brake pads should be removed and cleaned. This will permit the operation of the caliper to be checked, and the condition of the brake disc

itself to be fully examined on both sides. Refer to Chapter 9 for further information.

4 If any pad's friction material is worn to the specified thickness or less, *all four pads must be renewed as a set*. **Note**: *If any pad is approaching the minimum thickness, consider renewal as a precautionary measure in case the pads wear out before the next service.*

13 Handbrake check

1 Check and, if necessary, adjust the handbrake (see Chapter 9). Check that the handbrake cables are free to move easily and lubricate all exposed linkages/cable pivots.

14 Road test

Instruments and electrical equipment

1 Check the operation of all instruments and electrical equipment.
2 Make sure that all instruments read correctly, and switch on all electrical equipment in turn, to check that it functions properly.

Steering and suspension

3 Check for any abnormalities in the steering, suspension, handling or road 'feel'.
4 Drive the vehicle, and check that there are no unusual vibrations or noises.
5 Check that the steering feels positive, with no excessive 'sloppiness', or roughness, and check for any suspension noises when cornering and driving over bumps.

Drivetrain

6 Check the performance of the engine, clutch, transmission and driveshafts.
7 Listen for any unusual noises from the engine, clutch and transmission.
8 Make sure that the engine runs smoothly when idling, and that there is no hesitation when accelerating.
9 Check that the clutch action is smooth and progressive, that the drive is taken up smoothly, and that the pedal travel is not excessive. Also listen for any noises when the clutch pedal is depressed.
10 Check that all gears can be engaged smoothly without noise, and that the gear lever action is smooth and not abnormally vague or 'notchy'.

Braking system

11 Make sure that the vehicle does not pull to one side when braking, and that the wheels do not lock when braking hard.
12 Check that there is no vibration through the steering when braking.
13 Check that the handbrake operates

correctly without excessive movement of the lever, and that it holds the vehicle stationary on a slope.
14 Test the operation of the brake servo unit as follows. With the engine off, depress the footbrake four or five times to exhaust the vacuum. Hold the brake pedal depressed, then start the engine. As the engine starts, there should be a noticeable 'give' in the brake pedal as vacuum builds-up. Allow the engine to run for at least two minutes, and then switch it off. If the brake pedal is depressed now, it should be possible to detect a hiss from the servo as the pedal is depressed. After about four or five applications, no further hissing should be heard, and the pedal should feel considerably harder.

15 Auxiliary drivebelt check and renewal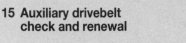

Note: *Depending on model and equipment fitted, access to the auxiliary drivebelt can be extremely limited. Where necessary, greater working clearance can be gained by removing the diesel injection electronic control unit (ECU) and its mounting box as described in Chapter 4B, Section 13.*
Note: *Refer to Chapter 2C for information on engine identification.*

1 All models are equipped with a single poly-V type, multi-ribbed auxiliary drivebelt. The belt tension is adjusted automatically by means of a spring-loaded tensioner. On 2.0 litre engines with a new drivebelt being fitted, an initial setting procedure has to be carried out as described below.

Checking condition

2 Apply the handbrake, then jack up the front of the car and support it on axle stands. Remove the right-hand front roadwheel.
3 Release the screws and clips and remove the wheelarch liner from under the right-hand front wing for access to the crankshaft pulley

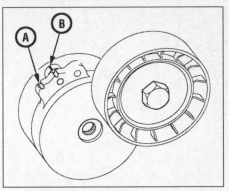

15.5 When groove (A) on the automatic tensioner lines up with the mark (B) on the mounting bracket the belt requires renewing

bolt. Where fitted, also remove the splash guard from under the front of the engine.
4 Using a suitable socket and bar fitted to the crankshaft pulley bolt, rotate the crankshaft so that the entire length of the drivebelt can be examined. Examine the drivebelt for cracks, splitting, fraying or damage. Check also for signs of glazing (shiny patches) and for separation of the belt plies. Renew the belt if worn or damaged.
5 The automatic tensioner has markings on the casing to show when the belt is need of renewal **(see illustration)**.

Removal (all models)

6 If not already done, proceed as described in paragraphs 2 and 3.
7 Disconnect the battery negative lead *(refer to Disconnecting the battery in the Reference Section of this manual).*
8 Using a suitable spanner engaged with the hexagonal stud in the centre of the automatic tensioner pulley, move the pulley towards the rear of the car to release the tension on the drivebelt, then slip the belt off the pulleys **(see illustration)**. Note that considerable effort will be needed to move the pulley against spring tension.

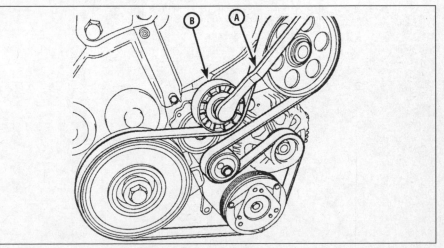

15.8 Move the spanner (A) anti-clockwise to release the tension roller (B) from the drivebelt – 2.0 litre

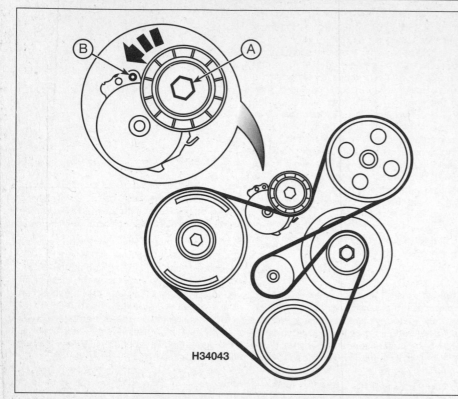

15.9 On 2.2 litre engines, turn tension roller stud (A) anti-clockwise until hole (B) is aligned, then insert the locking tool . . .

15.13 . . . on 2.0 litre engines align the hole (arrowed) to insert the locking tool

Refitting and tensioning

2.2 litre

9 Using the spanner on the hexagonal stud of the automatic tensioner pulley, move the pulley to the rear of the car until the hole in the pulley arm is aligned with the hole in the mounting bracket. When the holes are aligned, slide a suitable locking tool (a bolt or length of bar of approximately 4.0 mm diameter) through the hole in the arm and into the mounting bracket (see illustration). It is useful to have a small mirror available to enable the alignment of the locking holes to be more easily seen in the limited space available.

10 Fit the belt around the pulleys, ensuring that the ribs on the belt are correctly engaged with the grooves in the pulleys, and the drivebelt is correctly routed.

11 Using the spanner on the hexagonal stud of the automatic tensioner pulley, take the tension up in the pulley and remove the locking tool from the tensioner housing.

Release the pressure on the spanner so that the automatic tensioner takes up the slack in the drivebelt.

12 On completion, reconnect the battery negative lead, refit the wheelarch liner and, where fitted, the engine splash guard. Refit the roadwheel, and lower the vehicle to the ground.

2.0 litre – used drivebelt

13 Proceed as described in paragraphs 9 to 12, except the locking tool fits into a different alignment hole in the automatic tensioner pulley mounting bracket (see illustration).

2.0 litre – new drivebelt

14 Using the spanner on the hexagonal stud of the automatic tensioner pulley, move the pulley to the rear of the car until the hole in the pulley arm is aligned with the hole in the mounting bracket. When the holes are aligned, slide a suitable locking tool (a bolt or length of bar of approximately 4.0 mm diameter) through the hole in the arm and into the mounting bracket (see illustration). It is useful to have a small mirror available to enable the alignment of the locking holes to be more easily seen in the limited space available.

15 Working under the wheelarch, slacken the retaining bolt located in the eccentric roller (see illustration).

15.14 Turn the tension roller and insert the 4.0mm locking tool – 2.2 litre

15.15 Slacken the retaining bolt (arrowed) located in the eccentric tensioner pulley – 2.0 litre

16 Ensure that the new belt supplied is correct. Fit the belt around the pulleys, ensuring that the ribs on the belt are correctly engaged with the grooves in the pulleys, and the drivebelt is correctly routed.

17 Turn the eccentric roller to apply tension to the drivebelt, until the load is released from the locking tool in the automatic tensioner **(see illustration)**. Without altering the position of the eccentric roller, tighten its retaining bolt to the specified torque.

18 Remove the locking tool from the automatic tensioner, then rotate the crankshaft through four complete revolutions in the normal direction of rotation.

19 Check that the holes in the automatic adjuster and the mounting bracket are still aligned, and that it is now possible to insert a setting tool of 2.0 mm diameter through both holes. If the setting tool will not slide in easily, slacken the eccentric roller retaining bolt and repeat the entire tensioning procedure.

20 On completion, reconnect the battery negative lead, refit the wheelarch liner and, where fitted, the engine splash guard. Refit the roadwheel, and lower the vehicle to the ground.

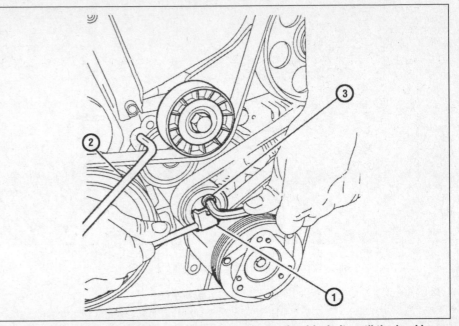

15.17 Turn the eccentric roller (1) to apply tension to the drivebelt, until the load is released from the locking tool (2) in the automatic tensioner, then tighten bolt (3) – 2.0 litre

Every 24 000 miles (40 000 km)

16 Air filter element renewal

1 Undo the screws securing the top to the air filter housing body, lift the top up and withdraw the filter element **(see illustrations)**.

2 If required, slacken the clip and disconnect the intake duct from the filter housing top to give better access to the filter housing body **(see illustration)**.

3 Where applicable, release any wiring or coolant hoses from their retaining clips on the air filter housing top.

4 Wipe clean the housing body and top.

5 Place the new element in position in the housing body. Refit the filter housing top, securing it in position with its retaining screws.

6 Refit any wiring or coolant hoses (where applicable) to their locating clips in the air filter housing, then reconnect the intake duct and securely tighten its retaining clip.

17 Fuel filter renewal

Removal

Note: *Check with your dealer for the availability of fuel filter/housing before removal. On some models the fuel filter/housing may come as a complete assembly.*

1 Remove the engine top cover, then the fuel filter is located in a plastic housing at the front of the engine.

2 Position a suitable container under the end of the fuel filter drain hose. Open the drain screw on the front of the filter housing and allow the fuel to drain completely (see Section 4 in this Chapter).

3 Where applicable, disconnect the wiring connector from the top of the fuel filter **(see illustration)**.

16.1a Undo the screws (arrowed) securing the top of the air filter housing body . . .

16.1b . . . then lift the top and withdraw the filter element

16.2 Slacken the clip (arrowed) and disconnect the intake duct from the air filter housing top

17.3 Disconnect the wiring connector from the fuel filter housing – 2.2 litre

17.5a Remove the fuel filter housing cover, then remove the metal sealing ring and O-ring . . .

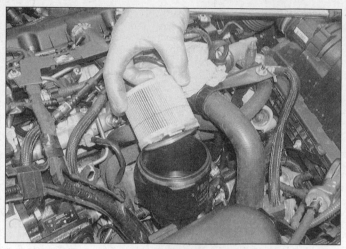

17.5b . . . and lift out the filter from the housing

4 Disconnect the fuel lines from the top of the fuel filter housing by releasing the quick-release fittings using a small screwdriver. Move them to one side, covering the ends of the fuel lines to prevent dirt entry.
5 Where applicable, unscrew the top of the fuel filter and lift the filter from the housing **(see illustrations)**.
6 To remove the complete fuel filter housing, undo the two retaining bolts and remove the assembly from the vehicle **(see illustration)**.

Refitting

7 Refitting is a reversal of removal. Where applicable, place the new filter in the housing, making sure that a new seal is used before refitting the top to the filter housing.
8 Refit the filter housing assembly, close the fuel filter drain screw and prime the fuel system (see Chapter 4B).

17.6 Undo the two retaining bolts (arrowed) and lift the assembly from the engine

Every 36 000 miles (60 000 km)

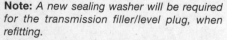

18 Manual transmission oil level check

Note: *A new sealing washer will be required for the transmission filler/level plug, when refitting.*

1 Jack up the front and rear of the car and securely support it on axle stands so that it remains level. If the car has been recently driven, wait at least 5 minutes after the engine has been switched off. If the oil level is checked immediately after driving the car, some of the oil will remain distributed around the transmission components, resulting in an inaccurate level reading.
2 On 2.0 litre models, remove the left-hand front roadwheel then release the screws and clips and remove the wheelarch liner from under the wing for access to the filler/level plug.

3 On 2.2 litre models, remove the splash guard from under the engine.
4 Wipe clean the area around the filler/level plug. On 2.0 litre models the filler/level plug is the largest bolt among those securing the end cover to the transmission; on 2.2 litre models the filler/level plug is located on the rear face of the differential housing. Unscrew the plug and clean it; discard the sealing washer **(see illustrations)**.
5 The oil level should reach the lower edge of

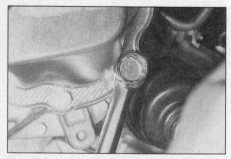

18.4a Use a spanner to remove the manual transmission filler/level plug – 2.0 litre

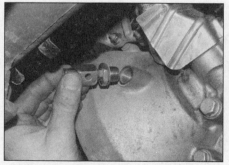

18.4b Manual transmission filler/level plug . . .

18.4c . . . and drain plug (arrowed) – 2.2 litre

the filler/level hole. A certain amount of oil will have gathered behind the filler/level plug, and will trickle out when it is removed; this does *not* necessarily indicate that the level is correct. To ensure that a true level is established, wait until the initial trickle has stopped, then add oil as necessary until a trickle of new oil can be seen emerging **(see illustration)**. The level will be correct when the flow ceases; use only good-quality oil of the specified type.

6 Refilling the transmission is an awkward operation; above all, allow plenty of time for the oil level to settle properly before checking it. If a large amount had to be added to the transmission, or if a large amount flowed out on checking the level, refit the filler/level plug and take the vehicle on a short journey. With the new oil distributed fully around the transmission components, recheck the level after allowing time for it to settle again.

7 If the transmission has been overfilled so

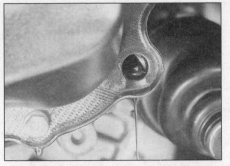

18.5 Oil level is correct when the oil stops flowing out of the filler/level hole

that oil flows out as soon as the filler/level plug is removed, first check that the car is completely level (front-to-rear and side-to-side). Allow any surplus oil to drain off into a suitable container.

8 When the level is correct, fit a new sealing washer to the filler/level plug. Tighten the plug to the specified torque wrench setting. Wash off any spilt oil. Refit the wheelarch liner or splash guard, and secure it in position with its retaining screws and clips. Refit the roadwheel (if removed) then lower the car to the ground.

9 Frequent need for topping-up indicates a leak, which should be found and corrected before it becomes serious.

19 Rear brake shoe check

1 Remove the rear brake drums and check the brake shoes for signs of wear or contamination. At the same time, also check the wheel cylinders for signs of leakage and the brake drums for signs of wear. Refer to the relevant Sections of Chapter 9 for further information.

Every 36 000 miles (60 000 km) or 2 years

20 Brake fluid renewal

⚠ *Warning: Brake hydraulic fluid can harm your eyes and damage painted surfaces, so use extreme caution when handling and pouring it. Do not use fluid that has been standing open for some time, as it absorbs moisture from the air. Excess moisture can cause a dangerous loss of braking effectiveness.*

Note: A hydraulic clutch shares its fluid reservoir with the braking system, and may also need to be bled (see Chapter 6).

1 The procedure is similar to that for the bleeding of the hydraulic system as described

in Chapter 9, except that the brake fluid reservoir should be emptied by syphoning, using a clean poultry baster or similar before starting, and allowance should be made for the old fluid to be expelled when bleeding a section of the circuit.

2 Working as described in Chapter 9, open the first bleed screw in the sequence, and pump the brake pedal gently until nearly all the old fluid has been emptied from the master cylinder reservoir.

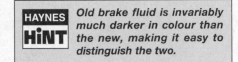

HAYNES HiNT *Old brake fluid is invariably much darker in colour than the new, making it easy to distinguish the two.*

3 Top-up to the MAX level with new fluid, and

continue pumping until only the new fluid remains in the reservoir, and new fluid can be seen emerging from the bleed screw. Tighten the screw, and top the reservoir level up to the MAX level line.

4 Work through all the remaining bleed screws in the sequence until new fluid can be seen at all of them. Be careful to keep the master cylinder reservoir topped-up to above the MIN/DANGER level at all times, or air may enter the system and greatly increase the length of the task.

5 When the operation is complete, check that all bleed screws are securely tightened, and that their dust caps are refitted. Wash off all traces of spilt fluid, and recheck the master cylinder reservoir fluid level.

6 Check the operation of the brakes before taking the car on the road.

Every 48 000 miles (80 000 km)

21 Particulate emission system check

1 Cleaning the filter and topping-up the fuel additive is a dealer-only task, as special tools are required (see Chapter 4C, Section 1).

Every 72 000 miles (120 000 km)

22 Timing belt renewal

Refer to Chapter 2C.

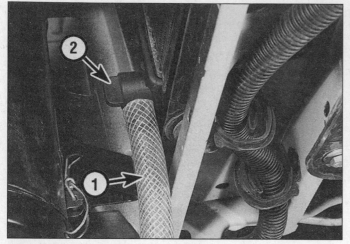

23.3 Tubing (1) attached to the radiator drain outlet and coolant drain plug (2)

23.4a Heater hose bleed screw (arrowed) in the heater matrix outlet hose . . .

Every 72 000 miles (120 000km) or 5 years

23 Coolant renewal

Cooling system draining

⚠ *Warning: Wait until the engine is cold before starting this procedure. Do not allow antifreeze to come in contact with your skin, or with the painted surfaces of the vehicle. Rinse off spills immediately with plenty of water. Never leave antifreeze lying around in an open container, or in a puddle in the driveway or on the garage floor. Children and pets are attracted by its sweet smell, but antifreeze can be fatal if ingested.*

1 With the engine completely cold, remove the expansion tank filler cap. Turn the cap anti-clockwise until it reaches the first stop. Wait until any pressure remaining in the system is released, then push the cap down, turn it anti-clockwise to the second stop, and lift it off.

2 Position a suitable container beneath the coolant drain outlet at the lower left-hand side of the radiator.

3 Where fitted, loosen the drain plug (there is no need to remove it completely) and allow the coolant to drain into the container. If desired, a length of tubing can be fitted to the drain outlet to direct the flow of coolant during draining **(see illustration)**.

4 To assist draining, open the cooling system bleed screws. These are located in the heater matrix outlet hose on the engine compartment bulkhead, in the extension hose (clipped to the rear of the cylinder head) from the thermostat housing and in the coolant bypass hose, depending on model **(see illustrations)**. There may also be a bleed screw in the top left-hand end of the radiator.

5 When the flow of coolant stops, reposition the container below the cylinder block drain plug, located at the rear of the cylinder block.

6 Remove the drain plug, and allow the coolant to drain into the container.

7 If the coolant has been drained for a reason other than renewal, then provided it is clean and less than five years old, it can be re-used, though this is not recommended.

8 Refit the radiator and cylinder block drain plugs on completion of draining.

Cooling system flushing

9 If coolant renewal has been neglected, or if the antifreeze mixture has become diluted, then in time, the cooling system may gradually lose efficiency, as the coolant passages become restricted due to rust, scale deposits, and other sediment. The cooling system efficiency can be restored by flushing the system clean.

10 The radiator should be flushed independently of the engine, to avoid unnecessary contamination.

Radiator flushing

11 To flush the radiator, first tighten the radiator drain plug, and the radiator bleed screw, where applicable.

12 Disconnect the top and bottom hoses and any other relevant hoses from the radiator, with reference to Chapter 3.

13 Insert a garden hose into the radiator top inlet. Direct a flow of clean water through the radiator, and continue flushing until clean water emerges from the radiator bottom outlet.

14 If after a reasonable period, the water still does not run clear, the radiator can be flushed with a good proprietary cleaning agent. It is important that their manufacturer's instructions are followed carefully. If the contamination is particularly bad, insert the hose in the radiator bottom outlet, and reverse-flush the radiator.

Engine flushing

15 To flush the engine, first refit the cylinder block drain plug, and tighten the cooling system bleed screws.

16 Remove the thermostat as described in Chapter 3, then temporarily refit the thermostat cover.

17 With the top and bottom hoses disconnected from the radiator, insert a garden hose into the radiator top hose. Direct a clean flow of water through the engine, and continue flushing until clean water emerges from the radiator bottom hose.

18 On completion of flushing, refit the thermostat and reconnect the hoses with reference to Chapter 3.

Cooling system filling

19 Before attempting to fill the cooling system, make sure that all hoses and clips are in good condition, and that the clips are tight. Note that an antifreeze mixture must be used all year round, to prevent corrosion of the engine components (see following sub-Section). Also check that the radiator and

23.4b . . . and in the thermostat housing (arrowed)

cylinder block drain plugs are in place and tight.

20 Remove the expansion tank filler cap.

21 Open all the cooling system bleed screws (see paragraph 4).

22 Some of the cooling system hoses are positioned at a higher level than the top of the radiator expansion tank. It is therefore necessary to use a 'header tank' when refilling the cooling system, to reduce the possibility of air being trapped in the system. Although Peugeot dealers use a special header tank, the same effect can be achieved by using a suitable bottle, with a seal between the bottle and the expansion tank **(see Haynes Hint)**.

23 Fit the 'header tank' to the expansion tank and slowly fill the system. Coolant will emerge from each of the bleed screws in turn, starting with the lowest screw. As soon as coolant free from air bubbles emerges from the lowest screw, tighten that screw, and watch the next bleed screw in the system. Repeat the procedure until the coolant is emerging from the highest bleed screw in the cooling system and all bleed screws are securely tightened.

24 Ensure that the 'header tank' is full (at least 0.5 litres of coolant). Start the engine, and run it at a fast idle speed (do not exceed 2000 rpm) until the cooling fan cuts in, and then cuts out. Stop the engine. **Note:** *Take great care not to scald yourself with the hot coolant during this operation.*

25 Allow the engine to cool, then remove the 'header tank'.

26 When the engine has cooled, check the coolant level as described in *Weekly checks*. Top-up the level if necessary, and refit the expansion tank cap.

Antifreeze mixture

27 The antifreeze should always be renewed at the specified intervals. This is necessary not only to maintain the antifreeze properties, but also to prevent corrosion which would otherwise occur as the corrosion inhibitors become progressively less effective.

28 Always use an ethylene-glycol based antifreeze which is suitable for use in mixed-metal cooling systems. The quantity of antifreeze and levels of protection are indicated in the Specifications.

29 Before adding antifreeze, the cooling system should be completely drained, preferably flushed, and all hoses checked for condition and security.

30 After filling with antifreeze, a label should be attached to the expansion tank, stating the type and concentration of antifreeze used, and the date installed. Any subsequent

Cut the bottom off an old antifreeze container to make a 'header tank' for use when refilling the cooling system. The seal at the point arrowed should be as tight as possible – use an O-ring if available, or seal the joint by some other means.

topping-up should be made with the same type and concentration of antifreeze.

31 Do not use engine antifreeze in the washer system, as it will cause damage to the vehicle paintwork. A screen wash additive should be added to the washer system in the quantities stated on the bottle.

Notes

Chapter 2 Part A:
XU petrol engine in-car repair procedures

Contents

Camshaft oil seals – renewal 9
Camshafts and followers – removal, inspection and refitting 10
Compression test – description and interpretation 2
Crankshaft oil seals – renewal 15
Crankshaft pulley – removal and refitting 5
Cylinder head – removal and refitting 11
Cylinder head covers – removal and refitting 4
Engine assembly/valve timing holes – general information and
   usage 3
Engine oil and filter renewal ....See Chapter 1A
Engine oil level check ....See Weekly Checks

Engine/transmission mountings – inspection and renewal 17
Flywheel/driveplate – removal, inspection and refitting 16
General information 1
Oil cooler – removal and refitting 14
Oil pump – removal, inspection and refitting 13
Sump – removal and refitting 12
Timing belt – general information, removal and refitting 7
Timing belt covers – removal and refitting 6
Timing belt tensioner and sprockets – removal, inspection and
   refitting 8

Degrees of difficulty

Easy, suitable for novice with little experience	**Fairly easy,** suitable for beginner with some experience	**Fairly difficult,** suitable for competent DIY mechanic	**Difficult,** suitable for experienced DIY mechanic	**Very difficult,** suitable for expert DIY or professional

Specifications

Engine (general)

Capacity .... 1.8 litre (1761 cc)
Designation XU7
Engine code * .... LFY (XU7 JP4/Z/L/L3)
Bore .... 83.00 mm
Stroke .... 81.40 mm
Direction of crankshaft rotation .... Clockwise (viewed from the right-hand side of vehicle)
No 1 cylinder location .... At the transmission end of block
Compression ratio .... 10.4 : 1

* The engine code is stamped on a plate attached to the front left-hand end of the cylinder block. This is the code most often used by Peugeot. The code given in brackets is the factory identification number, and is not often referred to by Peugeot or this manual.

Camshaft

Drive .... Toothed belt
No of bearings 5

Lubrication system

Oil pump type .... Gear-type, chain-driven off the crankshaft right-hand end
Minimum oil pressure at 80°C .... 5.3 bars (approximate) at 4000 rpm
Oil pressure warning switch operating pressure .... 0.5 bars

Torque wrench settings

	Nm	lbf ft
Big-end bearing cap nuts:		
Stage 1	20	15
Stage 2	Angle-tighten a further 70°	
Camshaft bearing housings:		
Stage 1	5	4
Stage 2	10	7
Camshaft sprocket hub-to-camshaft retaining bolts	75	55
Camshaft sprocket-to-hub retaining bolts	10	7
Crankshaft pulley retaining bolt	130	96
Cylinder head bolts (up to VIN No 80800000):		
Stage 1	60	44
Stage 2 – a to c on bolt 1, then bolt 2, etc:		
a	Slacken fully	
b	20	15
c	Angle-tighten a further 107°	
Stage 3	Angle-tighten a further 100°	
Stage 4	Angle-tighten a further 100°	
Cylinder head bolts (from VIN No 80800001):		
Stage 1	20	15
Stage 2	45	33
Stage 3	Angle-tighten a further 270°	
Cylinder head cover bolts (see illustration 4.10):		
All bolts except Nos 4', 5', 12 and 13	13	10
Bolts 4' and 5'	2	1
Bolts 12 and 13	15	11
Engine-to-transmission fixing bolts	45	33
Flywheel/driveplate retaining bolts	50	37
Left-hand engine/transmission mounting:		
Centre nut	65	48
Mounting bracket to body	30	22
Mounting stud bracket to transmission	60	44
Mounting stud to transmission	60	44
Rubber mounting-to-bracket bolts	30	22
Lower engine movement limiter to driveshaft bearing housing	50	37
Lower engine movement limiter to subframe	85	62
Main bearing cap bolts:		
Bearing bolts	54	40
Side securing bolts	23	17
Oil pump retaining bolts	16	12
Oil seal carrier bolts	16	12
Piston oil jet spray tube bolt	10	7
Right-hand engine/transmission mounting:		
Mounting bracket-to-engine bolts	60	44
Mounting bracket-to-engine nuts	45	33
Mounting bracket-to-rubber mounting nut	45	33
Rubber mounting-to-body nut	40	29
Upper engine movement limiter bolts	50	37
Sump retaining bolts	16	12
Timing belt cover bolts	8	6
Timing belt idler bolt	37	27
Timing belt tensioner bolt	21	16

1 General information

How to use this Chapter

This Part of Chapter 2 describes those repair procedures that can reasonably be carried out on the engine, while it remains in the car. If the engine has been removed from the car and is being dismantled as described in Part D, any preliminary dismantling procedures can be ignored.

Note that, while it may be possible physically to overhaul items such as the piston/connecting rod assemblies while the engine is in the car, such tasks are not usually carried out as separate operations. Usually, several additional procedures (not to mention the cleaning of components and oil ways) have to be carried out. For this reason, all such tasks are classed as major overhaul procedures, and are described in Part D of this Chapter.

Part D describes the removal of the engine/transmission unit from the vehicle, and the full overhaul procedures that can then be carried out.

XU series engine

The engine is of the in-line four-cylinder type, mounted transversely at the front of the car. The clutch and transmission are attached to its left-hand end.

The crankshaft runs in five main bearings. Thrust washers are fitted to No 2 main bearing cap, to control crankshaft endfloat.

The connecting rods rotate on horizontally-split bearing shells at their big-ends. The pistons are attached to the connecting rods by gudgeon pins. The gudgeon pins are an interference fit in the connecting rod small-end eyes. The aluminium alloy pistons are fitted with three piston rings – two compression rings and an oil control ring.

The cast aluminium alloy cylinder block incorporates 'wet' liners, and the bores have renewable cast-iron liners that are located from the top of the cylinder block. Sealing O-rings are fitted at the base of each liner, to prevent the escape of coolant into the sump.

The camshafts, driven by a toothed timing belt, operate sixteen valves via followers located beneath each cam lobe. The valve clearances are self-adjusting by means of hydraulic tappets fitted to the cam followers. The camshaft runs in bearing caps which are bolted to the top of the cylinder head. The inlet and exhaust valves are each closed by coil springs, and operate in guides pressed into the cylinder head. Both the valve seats and guides can be renewed separately if worn.

The coolant pump is also driven by the timing belt, and is located in the right-hand end of the cylinder block.

Lubrication is by means of an oil pump which is driven by a chain and sprocket off the crankshaft right-hand end. It draws oil through a strainer located in the sump, and then forces it through an externally-mounted filter into galleries in the cylinder block/crankcase. From there, the oil is distributed to the crankshaft main bearings and camshaft. The big-end bearings are supplied with oil by internal drillings in the crankshaft; the camshaft bearings also receive a pressurised supply. The camshaft lobes and valves are lubricated by splash, as are all other engine components. An oil cooler is fitted to certain models to keep the oil temperature constant under severe operating conditions – it is mounted behind the oil filter. The oil cooler is supplied with coolant from the engine cooling system.

Throughout the manual, it is often necessary to identify the engines not only by their cubic capacity, but also by their engine code. The engine code consists of three letters (eg, LFY). The code is stamped directly onto the front face of the cylinder block, on the machined surface located just to the left of the oil filter (next to the crankcase vent hose union).

Repair operations possible with the engine in the car

The following work can be carried out with the engine in the car:

a) Compression pressure – testing.
b) Cylinder head cover – removal and refitting.
c) Crankshaft pulley – removal and refitting.
d) Timing belt covers – removal and refitting.
e) Timing belt – removal, refitting and adjustment.
f) Timing belt tensioner and sprockets – removal and refitting.
g) Camshaft oil seals – renewal.
h) Camshafts and followers – removal, inspection and refitting.
i) Cylinder head – removal and refitting.
j) Cylinder head and pistons – decarbonising.
k) Sump – removal and refitting.
l) Oil pump – removal, overhaul and refitting.
m) Crankshaft oil seals – renewal.
n) Engine/transmission mountings – inspection and renewal.
o) Flywheel/driveplate – removal, inspection and refitting.
p) Oil cooler – removal and refitting

2 Compression test – description and interpretation

1 When engine performance is down, or if misfiring occurs which cannot be attributed to the ignition or fuel systems, a compression test can provide diagnostic clues as to the engine's condition. If the test is performed regularly, it can give warning of trouble before any other symptoms become apparent.

2 The engine must be fully warmed-up to normal operating temperature, the battery must be fully charged, and all the spark plugs must be removed (Chapter 1A). The aid of an assistant will also be required.

3 Disable the fuel system by disconnecting the wiring connectors from the fuel injectors, referring to Chapter 4A, Section 13, for further information.

4 Fit a compression tester to the No 1 cylinder spark plug hole – the type of tester which screws into the plug thread is to be preferred.

5 Have the assistant hold the throttle wide open, and crank the engine on the starter motor; after one or two revolutions, the compression pressure should build up to a maximum figure, and then stabilise. Record the highest reading obtained.

6 Repeat the test on the remaining cylinders, recording the pressure in each.

7 All cylinders should produce very similar pressures; a difference of more than 2 bars between any two cylinders indicates a fault. Note that the compression should build-up quickly in a healthy engine; low compression on the first stroke, followed by gradually-increasing pressure on successive strokes, indicates worn piston rings. A low compression reading on the first stroke, which does not build-up during successive strokes, indicates leaking valves or a blown head gasket (a cracked head could also be the cause). Deposits on the undersides of the valve heads can also cause low compression.

8 Although Peugeot do not specify exact compression pressures, as a guide, any cylinder pressure of below 10 bars can be considered as less than healthy. Refer to a Peugeot dealer or other specialist if in doubt as to whether a particular pressure reading is acceptable.

9 If the pressure in any cylinder is low, carry out the following test to isolate the cause. Introduce a teaspoonful of clean oil into that cylinder through its spark plug hole, and repeat the test.

10 If the addition of oil temporarily improves the compression pressure, this indicates that bore or piston wear is responsible for the pressure loss. No improvement suggests that leaking or burnt valves, or a blown head gasket, may be to blame.

11 A low reading from two adjacent cylinders is almost certainly due to the head gasket having blown between them; the presence of coolant in the engine oil will confirm this.

12 If one cylinder is about 20 percent lower than the others and the engine has a slightly rough idle, a worn camshaft lobe could be the cause.

13 If the compression reading is unusually high, the combustion chambers are probably coated with carbon deposits. If this is the case, the cylinder head should be removed and decarbonised.

14 On completion of the test, refit the spark plugs and reconnect the wiring.

3 Engine assembly/ valve timing holes – general information and usage

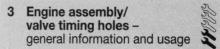

Note: *Do not attempt to rotate the engine whilst the crankshaft/camshaft are locked in position. If the engine is to be left in this state for a long period of time, it is a good idea to place suitable warning notices inside the vehicle, and in the engine compartment. This will reduce the possibility of the engine being accidentally cranked on the starter motor, which is likely to cause damage with the locking pins in place.*

1 Timing holes are drilled in the camshaft sprockets and crankshaft pulley. The holes are used to align the crankshaft and camshaft, to prevent the possibility of the valves contacting the pistons when refitting the cylinder head, or when refitting the timing belt. When the holes are aligned with their corresponding holes in the cylinder head and cylinder block (as appropriate), suitable diameter pins can be inserted to lock both the camshaft and crankshaft in position. Proceed as follows:

2 Remove the timing belt upper cover with reference to Section 6.

3 Jack up the front of the car and support it on axle stands. Remove the right-hand front roadwheel.

4 From underneath the front of the car, unscrew the bolts and prise out the clips securing the plastic cover to the inner wing valance. Remove the cover to gain access to the crankshaft pulley bolt. The crankshaft can then be turned using a suitable socket and extension bar fitted to the pulley bolt. Note that the crankshaft must always be turned in a clockwise direction (viewed from the right-hand side of the vehicle).

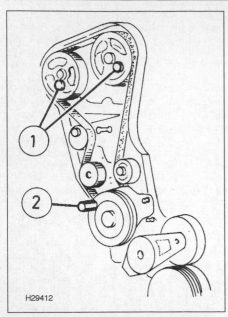

3.7 Camshaft sprocket timing holes (1) and crankshaft pulley timing hole (2) locked with suitable timing pins

5 Rotate the crankshaft pulley until the timing holes in both camshafts are aligned with their corresponding holes in the cylinder head. The holes are aligned when the inlet camshaft sprocket hole is in approximately the 5 o'clock position and the exhaust camshaft sprocket hole is in approximately the 7 o'clock position, when viewed from the right-hand end of the engine.

6 With the camshaft sprocket holes correctly positioned, insert a 6 mm diameter bolt or drill through the timing hole in the crankshaft pulley, and locate it in the corresponding hole in the end of the engine. Note that the hole size may vary according to the type of pulley fitted and auxiliary drivebelt arrangement. If the bolt or drill is not a snug fit, try a larger size until a good fit is achieved in both the pulley and cylinder block.

7 With the crankshaft locked in position, insert a suitable bolt or drill through the timing hole in each camshaft sprocket and locate it in the cylinder head **(see illustration)**.

8 The crankshaft and camshafts are now locked in position, preventing rotation.

4 Cylinder head covers – removal and refitting

Removal

1 Disconnect the battery negative lead (refer to *Disconnecting the battery* at the end of this manual).

2 Remove the fuel rail and fuel injectors as described in Chapter 4A, Section 13.

3 Disconnect the wiring connector at the left-hand end of the ignition coil unit, located in the centre of the cylinder head covers. Undo the six retaining bolts and lift the coil unit upwards, off the spark plugs and from its location between the cylinder head covers.

4 Slacken the retaining clips, and disconnect the breather hoses from the front left-hand side of the front cover. Where the original crimped-type Peugeot hose clips are still fitted, cut them off and discard them; use standard worm-drive hose clips on refitting.

5 Working in a spiral sequence starting from the outside and working inwards, progressively slacken, then remove the retaining bolts of each cylinder head cover, noting the correct fitted position of any brackets or clips.

6 Lift off each cover in turn and remove it along with its rubber seal.

Refitting

7 Clean the cylinder head and cover mating surfaces, and remove all traces of oil.

8 Lubricate the new rubber seals with grease, then locate them in the grooves of each cover, ensuring they are correctly located.

9 Carefully refit the cylinder head covers to the engine, taking great care not to displace the rubber seals.

10 Check that the seal is correctly located, then refit the cover retaining nuts and, working in the sequence shown, tighten them evenly and progressively to the specified torque **(see illustration)**.

11 Reconnect the breather hoses to the front cover and securely tighten the retaining clips.

12 Refit the ignition coil unit between the cylinder head covers. Refit the retaining bolts, tightening them securely, then reconnect the coil unit wiring connectors.

13 Refer to Chapter 4A and refit the fuel rail and fuel injectors.

14 Reconnect the battery negative terminal. On completion, start the engine and check the fuel hose unions for signs of leakage.

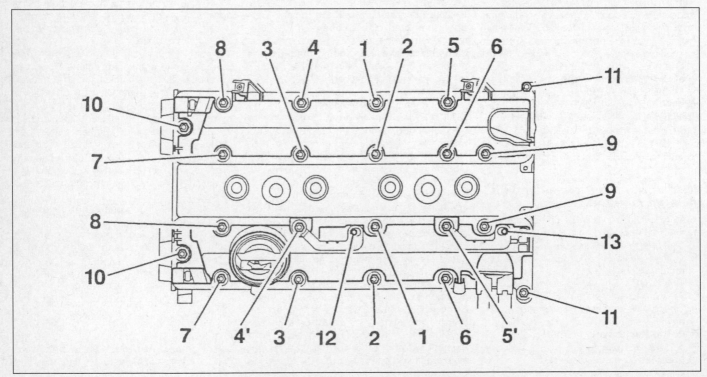

4.10 Cylinder head cover nut tightening sequence

5 Crankshaft pulley –
removal and refitting

Removal

1 Remove the auxiliary drivebelt (Chapter 1A).
2 To prevent the crankshaft turning whilst the pulley retaining bolt is being slackened on manual transmission models, select 4th gear and have an assistant apply the brakes firmly. On automatic transmission models it will be necessary to remove the starter motor (Chapter 5A) and lock the driveplate with a suitable tool. If the engine has been removed from the vehicle, lock the flywheel ring gear using the arrangement shown **(see illustration)**. *Do not* attempt to lock the pulley by inserting a bolt/drill through the timing hole. If the locking pin is in position, temporarily remove it prior to slackening the pulley bolt, then refit it once the bolt has been slackened.
3 Unscrew the retaining bolt and washer, then slide the pulley off the end of the crankshaft **(see illustration)**. If the pulley locating roll pin or Woodruff key (as applicable) is a loose fit, remove it and store it with the pulley for safe-keeping. If the pulley is a tight fit, it can be drawn off the crankshaft using a suitable puller.

Refitting

4 Ensure that the Woodruff key is correctly located in its crankshaft groove, or that the roll pin is in position (as applicable). Refit the pulley to the end of the crankshaft, aligning its locating groove or hole with the Woodruff key or pin.
5 Thoroughly clean the threads of the pulley retaining bolt, then apply a coat of locking compound to the bolt threads. Peugeot recommend the use of Loctite Frenetanche (available from your Peugeot dealer); in the absence of this, any good-quality locking compound may be used.
6 Refit the crankshaft pulley retaining bolt and washer. Tighten the bolt to the specified torque, preventing the crankshaft from turning using the method employed on removal.
7 Refit and tension the auxiliary drivebelt as described in Chapter 1A.

6 Timing belt covers –
removal and refitting

Removal

Upper (outer) cover

1 Undo the upper and lower retaining bolts securing the outer cover to the inner cover. Slide the cover retaining clip upwards to release it from its fasteners.

5.2 Use a fabricated tool like this one to lock the flywheel ring gear and prevent the crankshaft rotation

2 Ease the outer cover upwards and away from the engine, freeing it from its lower locations.

Lower cover

3 Remove the crankshaft pulley as described in Section 5.
4 Remove the upper (outer) cover as described above.
5 Slacken and remove the three retaining bolts, then remove the lower timing belt cover from the engine. Note that on some models it may be necessary to unbolt the auxiliary drivebelt tensioner assembly and remove it from the engine in order to allow the cover to be removed.

Upper (inner) cover

6 Remove the timing belt as described in Section 7.
7 Remove both camshaft sprockets as described in Section 8.
8 Remove the six bolts securing the cover to the side of the cylinder head, and remove the cover from the engine.

Refitting

9 Refitting is a reversal of the relevant removal procedure, ensuring that each cover section is correctly located, and that the cover retaining nuts and/or bolts are securely tightened to the specified torque, where given.

5.3 Removing the crankshaft pulley from the end of the crankshaft

7 Timing belt –
general information, removal and refitting

Note: *Peugeot specify the use of a special electronic tool (SEEM C105.5) to correctly set the timing belt tension.*

General information

1 The timing belt drives the camshafts and coolant pump from a toothed sprocket on the end of the crankshaft. If the belt breaks or slips in service, the pistons are likely to hit the valve heads, resulting in extensive (and expensive) damage.
2 The timing belt should be renewed at the specified intervals (see Chapter 1A), or earlier if it is contaminated with oil, or if it is at all noisy in operation (a 'scraping' noise due to uneven wear).
3 If the timing belt is being removed, it is a wise precaution to check the condition of the coolant pump at the same time (check for signs of coolant leakage). This may avoid the need to remove the timing belt again at a later stage, should the coolant pump fail.
4 Two types of timing belt tensioner pulley may be encountered. On early engines a manual tensioner pulley is used, and the belt tension must be set using an electronic tension checking tool. On later engines (from approximately mid-1999) a dynamic tensioner pulley is used which automatically adjusts the belt tension.
5 On engines with a manual tensioner pulley, Peugeot specify the use of an electronic belt tension checking tool to correctly set the timing belt tension. The following procedure assumes that this equipment (or suitable alternative equipment calibrated to display belt tension in SEEM units) is available. Accurate tensioning of the timing belt is essential, and if the electronic equipment is not available, it is recommended that the work is entrusted to a Peugeot dealer or suitably-equipped garage.

Removal

6 Disconnect the battery negative terminal (refer to *Disconnecting the battery* in the Reference Section of this manual).
7 Remove the auxiliary drivebelt as described in Chapter 1A. Where applicable, unbolt and remove the auxiliary drivebelt tensioner.
8 Move the engine wiring harness and relevant hoses clear of the working area as necessary. This will entail the disconnection of certain connectors, and the removal of the harness from various cable clips and supports. Label any disconnected wiring and components as an aid to refitting.
9 Remove the timing belt upper (outer) cover as described in Section 6.
10 Determine the type of timing belt tensioner pulley fitted then proceed as described in the appropriate following sub-sections **(see illustrations overleaf)**.

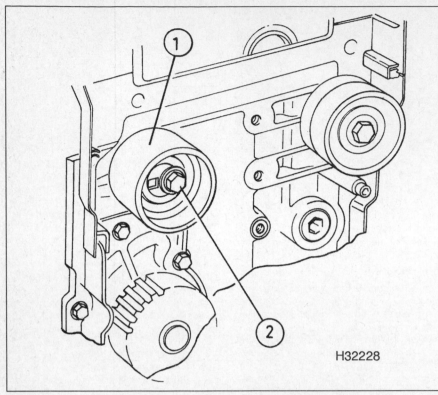

7.10a Early type manual timing belt tensioner pulley

1 Manual tensioner pulley   *2 Retaining bolt*

7.10b Later type dynamic timing belt tensioner pulley

1 Dynamic tensioner pulley   *2 Retaining bolt*

Manual tensioner pulley

11 To improve access, refer to Section 17 and remove the engine right-hand mounting. This is not essential, but it does make several of the timing belt components much easier to remove with the engine in the car.

12 Align the engine assembly/valve timing holes as described in Section 3, and lock the camshaft sprocket hubs in position. *Do not attempt to rotate the engine whilst the locking tools are in place.*

13 Remove the crankshaft pulley as described in Section 5.

14 Unbolt and remove the timing belt lower cover (refer to Section 6 if necessary).

15 Loosen the timing belt tensioner pulley retaining bolt **(see illustration)**. Allow the pulley to pivot in a clockwise direction, to relieve the tension from the timing belt. Retighten the tensioner pulley retaining bolt to secure it in the slackened position.

16 If the timing belt is to be re-used, use white paint or chalk to mark the direction of rotation on the belt (if markings do not already exist), then slip the belt off the sprockets **(see illustration)**. Note that the crankshaft must not be rotated whilst the belt is removed.

17 Check the timing belt carefully for any signs of uneven wear, splitting, or oil contamination. Pay particular attention to the roots of the teeth. Renew it if there is the slightest doubt about its condition. If the engine is undergoing an overhaul, and has covered more than 36 000 miles (60 000 km) with the existing belt fitted, renew the belt as a matter of course, regardless of its apparent

7.15 Loosen the manual timing belt tensioner retaining bolt . . .

7.16 . . . and slip the timing belt off the sprockets

condition. The cost of a new belt is nothing compared with the cost of repairs, should the belt break in service. If signs of oil contamination are found, trace the source of the oil leak and rectify it. Wash down the engine timing belt area and all related components, to remove all traces of oil.

Dynamic tensioner pulley

18 To improve access, refer to Section 17 and remove the engine right-hand mounting. This is not essential, but it does make several of the timing belt components much easier to remove with the engine in the car.

19 Align the engine assembly/valve timing holes as described in Section 3, and lock the camshaft sprocket hubs in position. *Do not attempt to rotate the engine whilst the locking tools are in position.*

20 Remove the crankshaft pulley as described in Section 5.

21 Unbolt and remove the timing belt lower cover (refer to Section 6 if necessary).

22 Slacken the camshaft sprocket centre retaining bolt on each camshaft. To prevent the sprockets rotating as the bolts are slackened, a sprocket holding tool will be required. In the absence of the special Peugeot tool, an acceptable substitute can be fabricated at home **(see Tool Tip in Section 8).** *Do not attempt to use only the sprocket hub locking tools inserted in the engine assembly/valve timing holes to prevent the sprockets from rotating whilst the bolts are slackened.*

23 Slacken the timing belt tensioner pulley retaining bolt and insert a suitable Allen key into the hexagonal hole on the front face of the tensioner pulley.

24 Using the Allen key, turn the tensioner pulley anti-clockwise (as viewed from the right-hand side of the car) until the index pointer is below the reference hole **(see illustration)**. Insert a small drill bit or short length of welding rod into the reference hole to retain the index pointer in this position.

25 Now turn the tensioner pulley clockwise until the hexagonal Allen key hole is positioned approximately adjacent to the upper edge of the coolant pump flange. Tighten the tensioner pulley retaining bolt to retain the pulley in this position.

26 If the timing belt is to be re-used, use white paint or chalk to mark the direction of rotation on the belt (if markings do not already exist), then slip the belt off the sprockets. Note that the crankshaft must not be rotated whilst the belt is removed.

27 Check the timing belt carefully for any signs of uneven wear, splitting, or oil contamination. Pay particular attention to the roots of the teeth. Renew it if there is the slightest doubt about its condition. If the engine is undergoing an overhaul, and has covered more than 36 000 miles (60 000 km) with the existing belt fitted, renew the belt as a matter of course, regardless of its apparent condition. The cost of a new belt is nothing compared with the cost of repairs, should the

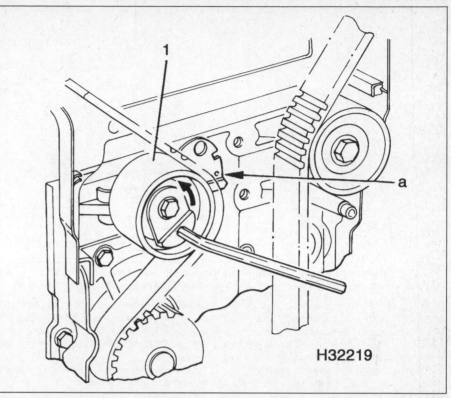

7.24 Rotate the dynamic tensioner pulley (1) anti-clockwise until the index pointer is below the reference hole (a)

belt break in service. If signs of oil contamination are found, trace the source of the oil leak and rectify it. Wash down the engine timing belt area and all related components, to remove all traces of oil.
Refitting and tensioning

Manual tensioner pulley

28 Before refitting, thoroughly clean the timing belt sprockets. Check that the tensioner and idler pulleys rotate freely, without any sign of roughness. If necessary, renew the pulleys as described in Section 8.

29 Ensure that the camshaft sprocket hub locking tools are still in position. Temporarily refit the crankshaft pulley, insert the locking tool through the pulley timing hole to ensure that the crankshaft is still correctly positioned, then remove the pulley.

30 Without removing the locking tools, on early engines, slacken the six camshaft sprocket retaining bolts (three on each sprocket). On later engines, only the single bolt securing each camshaft sprocket need be slackened. Check that both sprockets are free to turn within the limits of their elongated bolt holes, or that the protruding lug on single-bolt sprockets can move within its limits **(see illustrations)**. To prevent the single-bolt sprockets rotating as the bolts are slackened, a sprocket holding tool will be required. In the absence of the special Peugeot tool, an acceptable substitute can be fabricated at home **(see Tool Tip in Section 8)**. *Do not attempt to use only the sprocket hub locking*

tools to prevent the sprockets from rotating whilst the bolts are slackened.

31 Tighten the camshaft sprocket retaining bolts finger-tight, then slacken them all by one sixth of a turn.

32 Again without removing the locking tools, turn each camshaft sprocket clockwise until the protruding lug reaches the end of its travel.

33 Ensuring that any arrows on the belt are pointing in the direction of rotation (clockwise when viewed from the right-hand end of the engine), manoeuvre the timing belt into position on the exhaust camshaft sprocket. Retain the belt on the sprocket using a cable tie.

34 With the sprockets still positioned fully clockwise as far as they will go, feed the belt over the inlet camshaft sprocket, keeping it tight on its top run.

7.30a Slacken the camshaft sprocket retaining bolts (arrowed)

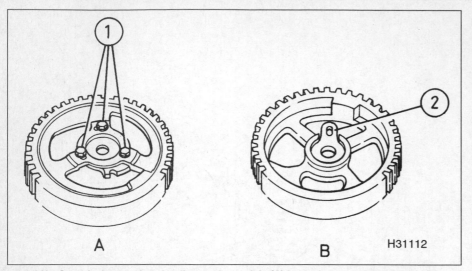

7.30b **Camshaft sprocket details – early models (A) have three retaining bolts (1) in elongated slots, while later models (B) have a single bolt and a protruding lug (2)**

35 Engage the belt around the idler pulley, crankshaft sprocket, coolant pump sprocket and finally around the tensioner pulley.

36 Fit the sensor head of the electronic belt tension measuring equipment to the 'front run' of the timing belt, approximately midway between the idler pulley and crankshaft sprocket.

37 Slacken the tensioner pulley retaining bolt and insert a short length of 8.0 mm square bar into the square hole on the front face of the tensioner pulley **(see Tool Tip)**.

38 Using the square bar and a spanner, pivot the tensioner pulley anti-clockwise until an initial setting of 55 SEEM units is displayed on the tension measuring equipment. Hold the tensioner pulley in that position and retighten the retaining bolt.

39 Check that the sprockets have not been turned so far that the retaining bolts are at the end of their slots, or that the protruding lug on

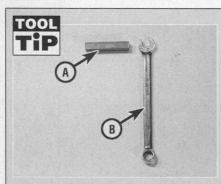

single-bolt sprockets is at the end of its travel. If either condition is evident, repeat the refitting operation. If all is satisfactory, tighten the sprocket retaining bolts to the specified torque.

40 Remove the belt tension measuring equipment, the crankshaft and camshaft locking tools, and the cable tie used to retain the belt on the exhaust camshaft sprocket.

41 Refit the timing belt lower cover and the crankshaft pulley.

42 Rotate the crankshaft through six complete rotations in a clockwise direction (viewed from the right-hand end of the engine). Realign the engine assembly/valve timing holes and refit the crankshaft pulley and camshaft sprocket hub locking tools.

43 Slacken the camshaft sprocket retaining bolts, retighten them finger-tight, then slacken them all by one sixth of a turn.

44 Slacken the tensioner pulley retaining bolt once more. Refit the belt tension measuring equipment to the front run of the belt, and turn the tensioner pulley to give a final setting of 35 SEEM units on the tensioning gauge. Hold the tensioner pulley in this position and tighten the retaining bolt to the specified torque. Remove the tension measuring equipment.

45 Retighten all sprocket retaining bolts to the specified torque.

46 The belt tension must now be checked as follows. Remove the locking tools, then rotate the crankshaft once again through two complete rotations in a clockwise direction. Realign the engine assembly/valve timing holes and refit the crankshaft pulley and camshaft sprocket hub locking tools.

47 Slacken the camshaft sprocket retaining bolts, then retighten them to the specified torque.

48 Remove the camshaft and crankshaft locking tools. Turn the crankshaft approximately one quarter of a turn in the normal direction of rotation, until the locking tool hole

in the crankshaft pulley is aligned with the timing belt lower cover front retaining bolt. It is important that this position is achieved ONLY by turning the engine forwards (ie, clockwise) – if the engine is turned back at all to achieve alignment, the belt tension check will not be valid.

49 In this position, refit the tension measuring equipment to the front run of the belt, and check that the reading is between 32 and 40 SEEM units. If not, the entire belt tensioning procedure must be repeated from the start.

50 Once the belt tension has been correctly set, refit the engine right-hand mounting components (if removed) as described in Section 17.

51 Refit the timing belt upper (outer) cover.

52 Reconnect any hoses and wiring disturbed for access.

53 Refit the auxiliary drivebelt tensioner then refit and tension the drivebelt with reference to Chapter 1A.

54 Reconnect the battery negative terminal.

Dynamic tensioner pulley

55 Before refitting, thoroughly clean the timing belt sprockets. Check that the tensioner and idler pulleys rotate freely, without any sign of roughness. If necessary, renew the pulleys as described in Section 8.

56 Ensure that the camshaft sprocket hub locking tools are still in position. Temporarily refit the crankshaft pulley, insert the locking tool through the pulley timing hole to ensure that the crankshaft is still correctly positioned, then remove the pulley.

57 With the camshaft sprocket retaining bolts still slackened, turn each camshaft sprocket clockwise to the end of its travel. Tighten the sprocket retaining bolts slightly to hold the sprockets in this position.

58 Ensuring that any arrows on the belt are pointing in the direction of rotation (clockwise when viewed from the right-hand end of the engine), manoeuvre the timing belt into position on the exhaust camshaft sprocket. Retain the belt on the sprocket using a cable tie.

59 With the sprockets still positioned fully clockwise as far as they will go, feed the belt over the inlet camshaft sprocket, keeping it tight on its top run.

60 Engage the belt around the idler pulley, crankshaft sprocket, coolant pump sprocket and finally around the tensioner pulley.

61 With the timing belt in position, slacken the camshaft sprocket retaining bolts once more.

62 Remove the drill bit or welding rod from the reference hole in the tensioner pulley.

63 Slacken the tensioner pulley retaining bolt and turn the tensioner pulley, by means of the Allen key, so that the index pointer is positioned in its maximum position (ie, below the reference hole). Hold the tensioner in this position and tighten the retaining bolt.

64 Hold the camshaft sprockets with the tool used during removal, and tighten the sprocket centre retaining bolts to the specified torque.

65 Refit the timing belt lower cover and the crankshaft pulley. Remove the cable tie used to retain the belt on the exhaust sprocket.

66 Remove the locking tools and rotate the crankshaft through four complete rotations in a clockwise direction (viewed from the right-hand end of the engine). Realign the engine assembly/valve timing holes and refit the crankshaft pulley and camshaft sprocket hub locking tools.

67 Hold the camshaft sprockets with the tool used during removal, and once again slacken the sprocket centre retaining bolts.

68 Hold the tensioner pulley in position by means of the Allen key and slacken the tensioner pulley retaining bolt. Turn the tensioner clockwise until the index pointer is aligned with the slot in the centre of the index plate, then tighten the retaining bolt to the specified torque **(see illustration)**.

69 Hold the camshaft sprockets and tighten the sprocket centre retaining bolts to the specified torque.

70 Remove the locking tools and rotate the crankshaft through two complete rotations in a clockwise direction (viewed from the right-hand end of the engine). Realign the engine assembly/valve timing holes and refit the crankshaft pulley and camshaft sprocket hub locking tools.

71 Check that the index pointer on the tensioner pulley is still aligned with the slot in the centre of the index plate. If not, repeat the procedure from paragraph 66 to 70.

72 Once the belt tension has been correctly set, refit the engine right-hand mounting components (if removed) as described in Section 17.

73 Refit the timing belt upper (outer) cover.

74 Reconnect any hoses and wiring disturbed for access.

75 Refit the auxiliary drivebelt tensioner then refit and tension the drivebelt with reference to Chapter 1A.

76 Reconnect the battery negative terminal.

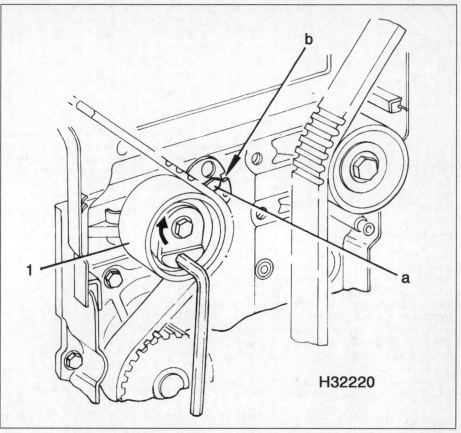

H32220

7.68 Turn the dynamic tensioner pulley (1) clockwise until the index pointer (a) is aligned with the slot (b) in the index plate

---

8 Timing belt tensioner and sprockets – removal, inspection and refitting

Note: *This Section describes the removal and refitting of the components concerned as individual operations – if more than one is to be removed at the same time, start by removing the timing belt as described in Section 7; remove the actual component as described below, ignoring the preliminary dismantling steps.*

Removal

Camshaft sprocket

1 Remove the timing belt from around the sprocket as described in Section 7.

2 Remove the relevant sprocket hub locking tool, then slacken the sprocket centre retaining bolt. To prevent the sprocket rotating as the bolt is slackened, a sprocket holding tool will

be required. In the absence of the special Peugeot tool an acceptable substitute can be fabricated at home **(see Tool Tip)**. Do not attempt to use the engine assembly/valve timing hole locking tool to prevent the sprocket from rotating whilst the bolt is slackened.

3 Remove the previously-slackened hub retaining bolt, and withdraw the relevant sprocket and hub from the end of the camshaft. Suitably mark the sprockets and hubs 'inlet' and/or 'exhaust' as they are removed (although in fact they are identical).

Crankshaft sprocket

4 Remove the timing belt from around the sprocket as described in Section 7.

5 Slide the crankshaft sprocket off the end of the crankshaft. Remove the Woodruff key from the crankshaft, and store it with the sprocket for safe-keeping. Where necessary, also slide the spacer (where fitted) off the end of the crankshaft.

6 Examine the crankshaft oil seal for signs of oil leakage and, if necessary, renew it as described in Section 15.

Tensioner and idler pulleys

7 Remove the timing belt from around the sprocket as described in Section 7.

8 Undo the tensioner and idler pulley retaining bolts and remove the relevant pulley from the engine. On engines with a dynamic

tensioner pulley, recover the small drill bit or welding rod inserted in the reference hole as the assembly is removed.

Inspection

9 Clean the camshaft/crankshaft sprockets thoroughly, and renew any that show signs of wear, damage or cracks.

10 Clean the tensioner/idler pulleys but do not use any strong solvent which may enter the pulley bearings. Check that the pulleys rotate freely, with no sign of stiffness or free play. Renew them if there is any doubt about

HAYNES HINT

Using a home-made tool to retain the camshaft sprocket whilst the sprocket retaining bolt is tightened.

their condition, or if there are any obvious signs of wear or damage.

Refitting

Camshaft sprockets

11 Engage the sprocket hub with the camshaft. Ensure that the correct hub is fitted to the relevant camshaft according to the identification made on removal.

12 Position the relevant sprocket on the hub and refit the sprocket retaining bolt and washer. Tighten the retaining bolt just tight enough to hold the sprocket/hub in place at this stage.

13 Turn the hub so that the locking tool can be engaged.

14 Refit and tension the timing belt as described in Section 7.

Crankshaft sprocket

15 Slide the spacer (where fitted) into position, taking great care not to damage the crankshaft oil seal, and refit the Woodruff key to its slot in the crankshaft end.

16 Slide on the crankshaft sprocket, aligning its slot with the Woodruff key.

17 Temporarily refit the crankshaft pulley, and insert the locking tool through the pulley timing hole, to ensure that the crankshaft is still correctly positioned.

18 Remove the crankshaft pulley, then refit and tension the timing belt as described in Section 7.

Tensioner and idler pulleys

19 Refit the tensioner and idler pulleys and secure with the retaining bolts. On engines with a dynamic tensioner pulley, ensure that the pulley body correctly engages with the projection on the cylinder block, and position the index pointer as described in Section 7.

20 Relocate and tension the timing belt as described in Section 7.

9 Camshaft oil seals – renewal

Note: *If the camshaft oil seal is to be renewed with the timing belt still in place, check first that the belt is free from oil contamination. (Renew the belt as a matter of course if signs of oil contamination are found; see Section 7.) Cover the belt, to protect it from contamination by oil, while work is in progress. If the timing belt is removed, ensure that all traces of oil are removed from the area before the belt is refitted.*

1 Remove the camshaft sprockets and hubs as described in Section 8.

2 Punch or drill two small holes opposite each other in the oil seal. Screw a self-tapping screw into each, and pull on the screws with pliers to extract the seal.

3 Clean the seal housing, and polish off any burrs or raised edges, which may have caused the seal to fail in the first place.

4 Lubricate the lips of the new seal with clean engine oil, and drive it into position until it seats on its locating shoulder. Use a suitable tubular drift, such as a socket, which bears only on the hard outer edge of the seal. Take care not to damage the seal lips during fitting. Note that the seal lips should face inwards.

5 Refit the camshaft sprockets and hubs as described in Section 8.

10 Camshafts and followers – removal, inspection and refitting

Removal

1 Disconnect the battery negative lead (refer to *Disconnecting the battery* at the end of this manual).

2 Remove both cylinder head covers as described in Section 4.

3 Refer to Section 8 and remove both camshaft sprockets together with their hubs, and also remove the timing belt tensioner pulley.

4 Remove the timing belt upper (inner) cover as described in Section 6.

5 Progressively slacken, by a few turn at a time, the twelve bolts securing each camshaft bearing housing to the cylinder head. Release the bearing housings from their dowels and cylinder head locations. When each housing is free, remove the bolts and washers completely, and lift off the bearing housings.

6 As both camshafts are identical, suitably mark them inlet and exhaust, or front and rear before removal.

7 Tilt the camshafts by pressing them down at their transmission end to release the centralising bearing at the timing belt end. Carefully lift the camshafts up and out of their locations and slide the oil seal off each camshaft end.

8 Obtain sixteen small, clean plastic containers, and number them inlet 1 to 8 and exhaust 1 to 8; alternatively, divide a larger container into sixteen compartments and number each compartment accordingly. Using a rubber sucker, withdraw each hydraulic tappet in turn, and place it in its respective container. Do not interchange the tappets, or the rate of wear will be much-increased.

Inspection

9 Examine the camshaft bearing surfaces and cam lobes for signs of wear ridges and scoring. Renew the camshaft if any of these conditions are apparent. Examine the condition of the bearing surfaces, both on the camshaft journals and in the cylinder head/bearing caps. If the head bearing surfaces are worn excessively, the cylinder head will need to be renewed. If suitable measuring equipment is available, camshaft bearing journal wear can be checked by direct measurement (where the necessary specifications have been quoted by Peugeot), noting that No 1 journal is at the transmission end of the head.

10 Examine the cam follower/hydraulic tappet bearing surfaces which contact the camshaft lobes for wear ridges and scoring. Renew any follower/tappet on which these conditions are apparent. If a follower/tappet bearing surface is badly scored, also examine the corresponding lobe on the camshaft for wear, as it is likely that both will be worn. Renew worn components as necessary.

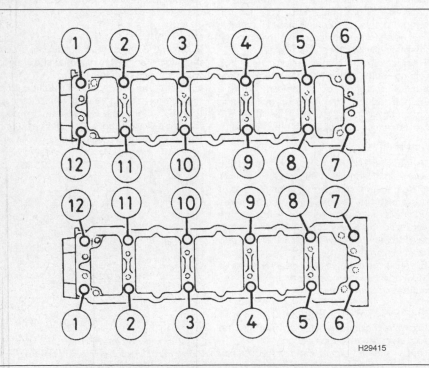

10.17 Camshaft bearing housing retaining bolt tightening sequence

Refitting

11 Before refitting, remove all traces of oil from the bearing housing retaining bolt holes in the cylinder head, using a clean rag. Also ensure that both the cylinder head and bearing housing mating faces are clean and free from oil.

12 Liberally oil the cylinder head hydraulic tappet bores and the tappets. Carefully refit the tappets to the cylinder head, ensuring that each tappet is refitted to its original bore. Some care will be required to enter the tappets squarely into their bores. Check that each tappet rotates freely in its bore.

13 Liberally oil the camshaft bearings in the cylinder head and the camshaft lobes, then refit the camshafts to the cylinder head. Turn the camshafts so that the groove at the timing belt end of the exhaust camshaft is positioned at 12 o'clock, and the groove at the timing belt end of the inlet camshaft groove is positioned at 11 o'clock.

14 Ensure that the four locating dowels are in position, one at each corner of the cylinder head.

15 Apply a bead of silicone-based jointing compound around the perimeter of the mating faces and around the retaining bolt hole locations.

16 Liberally oil the camshaft bearings and carefully locate the bearing housings over the camshafts. Refit the retaining bolts ensuring that each has a washer under its head.

17 Working in the order shown, progressively tighten the bearing housing retaining bolts to the Stage 1 torque setting then to the Stage 2 setting **(see illustration opposite)**.

18 Refit the timing belt upper (inner) cover as described in Section 6.

19 Refit the timing belt tensioner pulley as described in Section 8.

20 Refit the cylinder head covers as described in Section 4.

21 Fit new camshaft oil seals using the information given in Section 9, then refit the camshaft sprockets and hubs as described in Section 8.

---

11 Cylinder head – removal and refitting

Removal

1 Disconnect the battery negative lead (refer to *Disconnecting the battery* at the end of this manual).

2 Drain the cooling system as described in Chapter 1A. For improved access, remove the bonnet as described in Chapter 11.

3 Align the engine assembly/valve timing holes as described in Section 3, locking both the camshaft sprockets and crankshaft pulley in position. *Do not* attempt to rotate the engine whilst the pins are in position.

4 Remove the air cleaner assembly and intake ducting as described in Chapter 4A.

5 Remove the cylinder head covers as described in Section 4.

6 Remove the inlet manifold as described in Chapter 4A.

7 Working as described in Chapter 4A, disconnect the exhaust system front pipe from the manifold. Where necessary, disconnect or release the lambda sensor wiring, so that it is not strained by the weight of the exhaust.

8 Disconnect the radiator hose from the coolant outlet elbow.

9 Disconnect all remaining vacuum/breather hoses, and all electrical connector plugs from the cylinder head.

10 Release the timing belt tensioner and disengage the timing belt from the camshaft sprocket as described in Section 7.

11 Working in the *reverse* of the sequence shown in paragraph 28, progressively slacken the ten cylinder head bolts by half a turn at a time, until all bolts can be unscrewed by hand. Remove the bolts along with their washers. **Note:** *Washers are not fitted to later engines.*

12 With all the cylinder head bolts removed, the joint between the cylinder head and gasket and the cylinder block/crankcase must now be broken. On wet-liner engines, there is a risk of coolant and foreign matter leaking into the sump if the cylinder head is lifted carelessly. If care is not taken and the liners are moved, there is also a possibility of the bottom seals being disturbed, causing leakage after refitting the head.

13 To break the joint, obtain two L-shaped metal bars which fit into the cylinder head bolt holes, and gently 'rock' the cylinder head free towards the front of the car. *Do not* try to swivel the head on the cylinder block/crankcase; it is located by dowels.

14 When the joint is broken, lift the cylinder head away. Seek assistance if possible, as it is a heavy assembly. Remove the gasket from the top of the block, noting the two locating dowels. If the locating dowels are a loose fit, remove them and store them with the head for safe-keeping. Do not discard the gasket; it will be needed for identification purposes.

15 The XU7 engine described in this Chapter is fitted with wet-liners, therefore *do not* attempt to turn the crankshaft with the cylinder head removed, otherwise the liners may be displaced. Operations that require the crankshaft to be turned (eg, cleaning the piston crowns), should only be carried out once the cylinder liners are firmly clamped in position. In the absence of the special Peugeot liner clamps, the liners can be clamped in position as follows. Use large flat washers positioned underneath suitable-length bolts, or temporarily refit the original head bolts, with suitable spacers fitted to their shanks **(see illustration)**.

16 If the cylinder head is to be dismantled for overhaul, remove the camshafts as described in Section 10, then refer to Part D of this Chapter.

Preparation for refitting

17 The mating faces of the cylinder head and cylinder block/crankcase must be perfectly clean before refitting the head. Use a hard plastic or wooden scraper to remove all traces of gasket and carbon; also clean the piston crowns (refer to paragraph 15 before turning the engine). Take particular care as the soft aluminium alloy is easily damaged. Make sure that the carbon is not allowed to enter the oil and water passages – this is particularly important for the lubrication system, as carbon could block the oil supply to the engine's components. Using adhesive tape and paper, seal the water, oil and bolt holes in the cylinder block/crankcase. To prevent carbon entering the gap between the pistons and bores, smear a little grease in the gap. After cleaning each piston, use a small brush to remove all traces of grease and carbon from the gap, then wipe away the remainder with a clean rag. Clean all the pistons in the same way.

18 Check the mating surfaces of the cylinder block/crankcase and the cylinder head for nicks, deep scratches and other damage. If slight, they may be removed carefully with a file, but if excessive, machining may be the only alternative to renewal. If warpage of the cylinder head gasket surface is suspected, use a straight-edge to check it for distortion. Refer to Part D of this Chapter if necessary.

19 Check the cylinder liner protrusion as described in Part D of this Chapter.

20 When purchasing a new cylinder head gasket, it is essential that a gasket of the correct thickness is obtained. On some models only one thickness of gasket is available, so this is not a problem. However on other models, there are two different thicknesses available – the standard gasket which is fitted at the factory, and a slightly thicker 'repair' gasket (+ 0.2 mm), for use once the head gasket face has been machined. If the cylinder head has been machined, it should have the letter R stamped adjacent to the No 3 exhaust port, and the gasket should also have the letter R stamped adjacent to No 3 cylinder on its front upper face. The gaskets can also be identified as described in the following paragraph, using the cut-outs on the left-hand end of the gasket.

11.15 Cylinder liners clamped in position using suitable bolts and large flat washers

21 With the gasket fitted the correct way up on the cylinder block, there will be either a single hole, or a series of holes, punched in the tab on the left-hand end of the gasket. The standard (1.2 mm) gasket has only one hole punched in it; the slightly thicker (1.4 mm) gasket has either two or three holes punched in it, depending on its manufacturer. Identify the gasket type, and ensure that the new gasket obtained is of the correct thickness. Note that modifications to the cylinder head gasket material, type, and manufacturer are constantly taking place; seek the advice of a Peugeot dealer as to the latest recommendations.

22 Check the condition of the cylinder head bolts, and particularly their threads, whenever they are removed. Wash the bolts in a suitable solvent, and wipe them dry. Check each bolt for any sign of visible wear or damage, renewing them if necessary. Measure the length of each bolt (without the washer fitted) from the underside of its head to the end of the bolt. If all bolts are less than 160 mm, they may be re-used. However, if any one bolt is longer than the specified length, *all* of the bolts should be renewed as a complete set. Considering the stress which the cylinder head bolts are under, it is highly recommended that they are renewed, regardless of their apparent condition.

Refitting

23 Wipe clean the mating surfaces of the cylinder head and cylinder block/crankcase. Check that the two locating dowels are in position at each end of the cylinder block/crankcase surface. Where applicable, remove the cylinder liner clamps.

24 Position a new gasket on the cylinder block/crankcase surface, ensuring that its identification holes or the projecting tongue are at the left-hand end of the gasket.

25 Check that the crankshaft pulley and camshaft sprocket are still locked in position with their respective pins. With the aid of an assistant, carefully refit the cylinder head assembly to the block, aligning it with the locating dowels.

26 Apply a smear of grease to the threads, and to the underside of the heads, of the cylinder head bolts. Peugeot recommend the use of Molykote G Rapid Plus (available from your Peugeot dealer); in the absence of the specified grease, any good-quality high-melting-point grease may be used.

27 Carefully enter each bolt (and washer where applicable) into its relevant hole (*do not drop it in*) and screw it in finger-tight.

28 Working progressively and in the sequence shown (**see illustration**), tighten the cylinder head bolts, to their Stage 1 torque setting.

29 Stage 2 torque setting on early models is in three steps on each bolt in turn (see Specifications). On later models the Stage 2 torque wrench setting is more straightforward.

30 With all the bolts tightened to their Stage 2 setting, working again in the specified sequence, angle-tighten the bolts through the specified Stage 3 angle, using a socket and extension bar. It is recommended that an angle-measuring gauge is used during this stage of tightening, to ensure accuracy. If a gauge is not available, use white paint to make alignment marks between the bolt head and cylinder head prior to tightening; the marks can then be used to check that the bolt has rotated sufficiently. Early models also have a Stage 4 angle.

31 Refit the timing belt to the camshaft sprocket as described in Section 8, and tension the belt as described in Section 7.

32 The remainder of the refitting procedure is a reversal of removal, noting the following points:

a) *Ensure that all wiring is correctly routed, and that all connectors are securely reconnected to the correct components.*

b) *Ensure that the coolant hoses are correctly reconnected, and that their retaining clips are securely tightened.*

c) *Ensure that all vacuum/breather hoses are correctly reconnected.*

d) *Refit the cylinder head covers as described in Section 4.*

e) *Reconnect the exhaust system to the manifold, refit the air cleaner housing and ducts, and adjust the accelerator cable, as described in Chapter 4A. If the manifolds were removed, refit these as described in Chapter 4A.*

f) *On completion, refill the cooling system as described in Chapter 1A, and reconnect the battery.*

12 Sump – removal and refitting

Removal

1 Disconnect the battery negative terminal.

2 Chock the rear wheels, jack up the front of the vehicle and support it on axle stands.

3 Drain the engine oil as described in Chapter 1A, then clean and refit the engine oil drain plug, tightening it securely. If the engine is nearing its service interval when the oil and filter are due for renewal, it is recommended that the filter is also removed, and a new one fitted. After reassembly, the engine can then be refilled with fresh oil. Refer to Chapter 1A for further information.

4 Where necessary, disconnect the wiring connector from the oil temperature sender unit, which is screwed into the sump.

5 Remove the auxiliary drivebelt as described in Chapter 1A.

6 On models with air conditioning, where the compressor is located on the side of the sump, unbolt the compressor and position it clear of the sump. Support the weight of the compressor by tying it to the vehicle, to prevent any excess strain being placed on the compressor lines. *Do not* disconnect the refrigerant lines from the compressor (refer to the warnings given in Chapter 3).

7 Progressively slacken and remove all the sump retaining bolts. Since the sump bolts vary in length, remove each bolt in turn, and store it in its correct fitted order by pushing it through a clearly-marked cardboard template. This will avoid the possibility of installing the bolts in the wrong locations on refitting.

8 Break the joint by striking the sump with the palm of your hand. Lower the sump, and withdraw it from underneath the vehicle. Remove the gasket (where fitted), and discard it; a new one must be used on refitting. While the sump is removed, take the opportunity to check the oil pump pick-up/strainer for signs of clogging or splitting. If necessary, remove the pump as described in Section 13, and clean or renew the strainer.

9 On some models, a large spacer plate is fitted between the sump and the base of the cylinder block/crankcase. If this plate is fitted, undo the two retaining screws from diagonally-opposite corners of the plate. Remove the plate from the base of the engine, noting which way round it is fitted.

Refitting

10 Clean all traces of sealant/gasket from the mating surfaces of the cylinder block/crankcase and sump, then use a clean rag to wipe out the sump and the engine's interior.

11 Where a spacer plate is fitted, remove all traces of sealant/gasket from the spacer plate, then apply a thin coating of suitable sealant to the plate upper mating surface. Offer up the plate to the base of the cylinder block/crankcase, and securely tighten its retaining screws.

12 On models where the sump was fitted without a gasket, ensure that the sump mating surfaces are clean and dry, then apply a thin coating of suitable sealant to the sump mating surface.

13 On models where the sump was fitted with a gasket, ensure that all traces of the old gasket have been removed, and that the sump mating surfaces are clean and dry. Position the new gasket on the top of the sump, using a dab of grease to hold it in position.

14 Offer up the sump to the cylinder block/

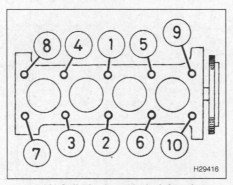

11.28 Cylinder head bolt tightening sequence

crankcase. Refit its retaining bolts, ensuring that each is screwed into its original location. Tighten the bolts evenly and progressively to the specified torque setting.

15 On models with air conditioning, refit the compressor to the side of the sump and tighten the bolts.

16 Refit the auxiliary drivebelt (see Chapter 1A) and the pressure regulator accumulator.

17 Reconnect the wiring connector to the oil temperature sensor (where fitted).

18 Lower the vehicle to the ground, then refill the engine with oil as described in Chapter 1A and reconnect the battery negative terminal.

13.3 Removing the oil pump

13.5a Remove the oil pump cover retaining bolts . . .

13 Oil pump –
removal, inspection and refitting

Removal

1 Remove the sump (see Section 12).

2 Undo the two retaining screws, and slide the sprocket cover off the front of the oil pump.

3 Slacken and remove the three bolts securing the oil pump to the base of the cylinder block/crankcase. Disengage the pump sprocket from the chain, and remove the oil pump **(see illustration)**. Where necessary, also remove the spacer plate which is fitted behind the oil pump.

Inspection

4 Examine the oil pump sprocket for signs of damage and wear, such as chipped or missing teeth. If the sprocket is worn, the pump assembly must be renewed, since the sprocket is not available separately. It is also recommended that the chain and drive sprocket, fitted to the crankshaft, be renewed at the same time. To renew the chain and drive sprocket, first remove the crankshaft timing belt sprocket as described in Section 8. Unbolt the oil seal carrier from the cylinder block. The sprocket, spacer (where fitted) and chain can then be slid off the end of the crankshaft.

5 Slacken and remove the bolts (along with the baffle plate, where fitted) securing the strainer cover to the pump body. Lift off the strainer cover, and take off the relief valve piston and spring, noting which way round they are fitted **(see illustrations)**.

6 Examine the pump rotors and body for signs of wear ridges or scoring. If worn, the complete pump assembly must be renewed.

7 Examine the relief valve piston for signs of wear or damage, and renew if necessary. The condition of the relief valve spring can only be measured by comparing it with a new one; if there is any doubt about its condition, it should also be renewed. Both the piston and spring are available individually.

8 Thoroughly clean the oil pump strainer with a suitable solvent, and check it for signs of clogging or splitting. If the strainer is damaged, the strainer and cover assembly must be renewed.

13.5b . . . then lift off the cover and remove the spring . . .

9 Locate the relief valve spring and piston in the strainer cover. Refit the cover to the pump body, aligning the relief valve piston with its bore in the pump. Refit the baffle plate (where fitted) and the cover retaining bolts, and tighten them securely.

Refitting

10 Offer up the spacer plate (where fitted), then locate the pump sprocket with its drive chain. Seat the pump on the base of the cylinder block/crankcase. Refit the pump retaining bolts, and tighten them to the specified torque setting.

11 Where necessary, slide the sprocket cover into position on the pump. Refit its retaining bolts, tightening them securely.

12 Refit the sump as described in Section 12.

13 Before starting the engine, prime the oil pump as follows. Disconnect the fuel injector wiring connectors, then spin the engine on the

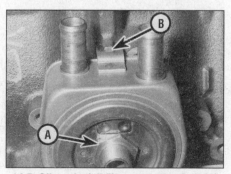

14.5 Oil cooler/oil filter mounting bolt (A) and locating notch (B)

13.5c . . . and the relief valve piston, noting which way round it is fitted

starter until the oil pressure light goes out. Reconnect the injector wiring on completion.

14 Oil cooler –
removal and refitting

Removal

1 Firmly apply the handbrake, then jack up the front of the vehicle and support it on axle stands.

2 Drain the cooling system as described in Chapter 1A. Alternatively, clamp the oil cooler coolant hoses directly above the cooler, and be prepared for some coolant loss as the hoses are disconnected.

3 Position a suitable container beneath the oil filter. Unscrew the filter using an oil filter removal tool if necessary, and drain the oil into the container. If the oil filter is damaged or distorted during removal, it must be renewed. Given the low cost of a new oil filter relative to the cost of repairing the damage which could result if a re-used filter springs a leak, it is probably a good idea to renew the filter in any case.

4 Release the hose clips, and disconnect the coolant hoses from the oil cooler.

5 Unscrew the oil cooler/oil filter mounting bolt from the cylinder block, and withdraw the cooler. Note the locating notch in the cooler flange, which fits over the lug on the cylinder block **(see illustration)**. Discard the oil cooler sealing ring; a new one must be used on refitting.

16.10 If the new flywheel bolt threads are not supplied with their threads precoated, apply a locking compound to them . . .

Refitting

6 Fit a new sealing ring to the recess in the rear of the cooler, then offer the cooler to the cylinder block.

7 Ensure that the locating notch in the cooler flange is correctly engaged with the lug on the cylinder block, then refit the mounting bolt and tighten it securely.

8 Fit the oil filter, then lower the vehicle to the ground. Top-up the engine oil level as described in *Weekly Checks*.

9 Refill or top-up the cooling system as described in Chapter 1A or *Weekly Checks* (as applicable). Start the engine, and check the oil cooler for signs of leakage.

15 Crankshaft oil seals – renewal

Right-hand oil seal

1 Remove the crankshaft sprocket and (where fitted) spacer, referring to Section 8. Secure the timing belt clear of the working area, so that it cannot be contaminated with oil. Make a note of the correct fitted depth of the seal in its housing.

2 Punch or drill two small holes opposite each other in the seal. Screw a self-tapping screw into each, and pull on the screws with pliers to extract the seal. Alternatively, the seal can be levered out of position. Use a flat-bladed screwdriver, and take great care not to

16.12 . . . then refit the flywheel, and tighten the bolts to the specified torque

damage the crankshaft shoulder or seal housing.

3 Clean the seal housing, and polish off any burrs or raised edges, which may have caused the seal to fail in the first place.

4 Lubricate the lips of the new seal with clean engine oil, and carefully locate the seal on the end of the crankshaft. Note that its sealing lip must be facing inwards. Take care not to damage the seal lips during fitting.

5 Fit the new seal using a suitable tubular drift, such as a socket, which bears only on the hard outer edge of the seal. Tap the seal into position, to the same depth in the housing as the original was prior to removal.

6 Wash off any traces of oil, then refit the crankshaft sprocket as described in Section 8.

Left-hand oil seal

7 Remove the flywheel/driveplate as described in Section 16. Make a note of the correct fitted depth of the seal in its housing.

8 Punch or drill two small holes opposite each other in the seal. Screw a self-tapping screw into each, and pull on the screws with pliers to extract the seal.

9 Clean the seal housing, and polish off any burrs or raised edges, which may have caused the seal to fail in the first place.

10 Lubricate the lips of the new seal with clean engine oil, and carefully locate the seal on the end of the crankshaft.

11 Fit the new seal using a suitable tubular drift, which bears only on the hard outer edge of the seal. Drive the seal into position, to the same depth in the housing as the original was prior to removal.

12 Wash off any traces of oil, then refit the flywheel/driveplate as described in Section 16.

16 Flywheel/driveplate – removal, inspection and refitting

Removal

Flywheel

1 Remove the transmission as described in Chapter 7A, then remove the clutch assembly as described in Chapter 6.

2 Prevent the flywheel from turning by locking the ring gear teeth with a similar arrangement to that described in Section 5. Alternatively, bolt a strap between the flywheel and the cylinder block/crankcase. *Do not* attempt to lock the flywheel in position using the crankshaft pulley locking pin described in Section 3.

3 Slacken and remove the flywheel retaining bolts, and remove the flywheel from the end of the crankshaft. Be careful not to drop it; it is heavy. If the flywheel locating dowel is a loose fit in the crankshaft end, remove it and store it with the flywheel for safe-keeping. Discard the flywheel bolts; new ones must be used on refitting.

Driveplate

4 Remove the transmission as described in Chapter 7B. Lock the driveplate as described in paragraph 2. Mark the relationship between the torque converter plate and the driveplate, and slacken all the driveplate retaining bolts.

5 Remove the retaining bolts, along with the torque converter plate and (where fitted) the two shims (one fitted on each side of the torque converter plate). Note that the shims are of different thickness, the thicker one being on the outside of the torque converter plate. Discard the driveplate retaining bolts; new ones must be used on refitting.

6 Remove the driveplate from the end of the crankshaft. If the locating dowel is a loose fit in the crankshaft end, remove it and store it with the driveplate for safe-keeping.

Inspection

7 On models with manual transmission, examine the flywheel for scoring of the clutch face, and for wear or chipping of the ring gear teeth. If the clutch face is scored, the flywheel may be surface-ground, but renewal is preferable. Seek the advice of a Peugeot dealer or engine reconditioning specialist to see if machining is possible. If the ring gear is worn or damaged, the flywheel must be renewed, as it is not possible to renew the ring gear separately.

8 On models with automatic transmission, check the torque converter driveplate carefully for signs of distortion. Look for any hairline cracks around the bolt holes or radiating outwards from the centre, and inspect the ring gear teeth for signs of wear or chipping. If any sign of wear or damage is found, the driveplate must be renewed.

Refitting

Flywheel

9 Clean the mating surfaces of the flywheel and crankshaft. Remove any remaining locking compound from the threads of the crankshaft holes, using the correct-size tap, if available.

> **HAYNES HiNT**
>
> *If a suitable tap is not available, cut two slots into the threads of one of the old flywheel bolts and use the bolt to remove the locking compound from the threads.*

10 If the new flywheel retaining bolts are not supplied with their threads already precoated, apply a suitable thread-locking compound to the threads of each bolt **(see illustration)**.

11 Ensure the locating dowel is in position. Offer up the flywheel, locating it on the dowel, and fit the new retaining bolts.

12 Lock the flywheel using the method employed on dismantling, and tighten the retaining bolts to the specified torque **(see illustration)**.

13 Refit the clutch as described in Chapter 6. Remove the flywheel locking tool, and refit the transmission as described in Chapter 7A.

Driveplate

14 Carry out the operations described above in paragraphs 9 and 10, substituting 'driveplate' for all references to the flywheel.
15 Locate the driveplate on its locating dowel.
16 Offer up the torque converter plate, with the thinner shim positioned behind the plate and the thicker shim on the outside, and align the marks made prior to removal.
17 Fit the new retaining bolts, then lock the driveplate using the method employed on dismantling. Tighten the retaining bolts to the specified torque wrench setting.
18 Remove the driveplate locking tool, and refit the transmission as described in Chapter 7B.

17 Engine/transmission mountings – inspection and renewal

Inspection

1 If improved access is required, raise the front of the car and support it securely on axle stands.
2 Check the mounting rubber to see if it is cracked, hardened or separated from the metal at any point; renew the mounting if any such damage or deterioration is evident.
3 Check that all the mounting's fasteners are securely tightened; use a torque wrench to check if possible.
4 Using a large screwdriver or a crowbar, check for wear in the mounting by carefully levering against it to check for free play. Where this is not possible, enlist the aid of an assistant to move the engine/transmission unit back-and-forth, or from side-to-side, while you watch the mounting. While some free play is to be expected even from new components, excessive wear should be obvious. If excessive free play is found, check first that the fasteners are correctly secured, then renew any worn components as described below.

Renewal

Right-hand mounting

5 Disconnect the battery negative terminal. Release all the relevant hoses and wiring from their retaining clips. Place the hoses/wiring clear of the mounting so that the removal procedure is not hindered.
6 Place a jack beneath the engine, with a block of wood on the jack head. Raise the jack until it is supporting the weight of the engine.
7 Slacken and remove the two nuts and two bolts securing the right-hand engine/transmission mounting bracket to the engine. Remove the single nut securing the bracket to the mounting rubber.
8 Undo the bolt securing the upper engine movement limiter to the right-hand mounting bracket, and the four bolts securing the movement limiter mounting bracket to the body. Lift away the right-hand mounting bracket and the movement limiter assembly.
9 Lift the rubber buffer plate off the mounting rubber stud, then unscrew the mounting rubber from the body and remove it from the vehicle. If necessary, the mounting bracket can be unbolted and removed from the front of the cylinder block.
10 Check all components carefully for signs of wear or damage, and renew as necessary.
11 On reassembly, screw the mounting rubber into the vehicle body, and tighten it securely. Refit the mounting bracket to the front of the cylinder head, and securely tighten its retaining bolts.
12 Refit the engine movement limiter assembly to the engine mounting bracket and to the body and tighten the bolts to the specified torque.
13 Refit the rubber buffer plate to the mounting rubber stud, and install the mounting bracket.
14 Tighten the mounting bracket retaining nuts to the specified torque setting. Remove the jack from underneath the engine and reconnect the battery.

Left-hand mounting

15 Remove the air cleaner assembly, as described in Chapter 4A.
16 Place a jack beneath the transmission, with a block of wood on the jack head. Raise the jack until it is supporting the weight of the transmission.

17 Slacken and remove the centre nut and washer from the left-hand mounting, then undo the nuts securing the mounting in position and remove it from the engine compartment.
18 If necessary, slide the spacer (where fitted) off the mounting stud, then unscrew the stud from the top of the transmission housing, and remove it along with its washer. If the mounting stud is tight, a universal stud extractor can be used to unscrew it.
19 Check all components carefully for signs of wear or damage, and renew as necessary.
20 Clean the threads of the mounting stud, and apply a coat of thread-locking compound to its threads. Refit the stud and washer to the top of the transmission, and tighten it to the specified torque setting.
21 Slide the spacer (where fitted) onto the mounting stud, then refit the rubber mounting. Tighten both the mounting-to-body bolts and the mounting centre nut to their specified torque settings, and remove the jack from underneath the transmission.
22 Refit the air cleaner assembly, then refit the battery as described in Chapter 5A.

Lower engine movement limiter

23 If not already done, chock the rear wheels, then jack up the front of the vehicle and support it securely on axle stands.
24 Unscrew and remove the bolt securing the movement limiter link to the driveshaft intermediate bearing housing.
25 Remove the bolt securing the link to the subframe. Withdraw the link.
26 To remove the intermediate bearing housing assembly it will first be necessary to remove the right-hand driveshaft as described in Chapter 8.
27 With the driveshaft removed, undo the retaining bolts and remove the bearing housing from the rear of the cylinder block.
28 Check carefully for signs of wear or damage on all components, and renew them where necessary.
29 On reassembly, fit the bearing housing assembly to the rear of the cylinder block, and tighten its retaining bolts securely. Refit the driveshaft as described in Chapter 8.
30 Refit the movement limiter link, and tighten both its bolts to their specified torque settings.
31 Lower the vehicle to the ground.

Notes

Chapter 2 Part B:
EW series petrol engine in-car repair procedures

Contents

Camshaft oil seals – renewal 9
Camshafts and followers – removal, inspection and refitting 10
Compression test – description and interpretation 2
Crankshaft oil seals – renewal 14
Crankshaft pulley – removal and refitting 5
Cylinder head – removal and refitting 11
Cylinder head covers – removal and refitting 4
Engine assembly/valve timing holes – general information and
   usage 3
Engine oil and filter renewal .... See Chapter 1A

Engine oil level check .... See Weekly Checks
Engine/transmission mountings – inspection and renewal 16
Flywheel/driveplate – removal, inspection and refitting 15
General information 1
Oil pump – removal, inspection and refitting 13
Sump – removal and refitting 12
Timing belt – general information, removal and refitting 7
Timing belt covers – removal and refitting 6
Timing belt tensioners, sprockets and pulleys – removal, inspection
   and refitting 8

Degrees of difficulty

Easy, suitable for novice with little experience	🔧	**Fairly easy,** suitable for beginner with some experience	🔧	**Fairly difficult,** suitable for competent DIY mechanic	🔧	**Difficult,** suitable for experienced DIY mechanic	🔧	**Very difficult,** suitable for expert DIY or professional	🔧

Specifications

Engine (general)

Designation:
1.8 litre (1749 cc engine)	EW7J4 L4
2.0 litre (1997 cc engine)	EW10J4 KL3
2.0 litre (1997 cc engine)	EW10J4 IFL5

Engine codes*:
1.8 litre engine (EW7J4 L4)	6FZ
2.0 litre engine (EW10J4 KL3)	RFR
2.0 litre engine (EW10J4 IFL5)	RFN

Bore:
1.8 litre engine	82.70 mm
2.0 litre engine	85.00 mm

Stroke:
1.8 litre engine	81.40 mm
2.0 litre engine	88.00 mm
Direction of crankshaft rotation	Clockwise (viewed from the right-hand side of vehicle)
No 1 cylinder location	At the transmission end of block
Compression ratio	10.8 : 1

The engine code is stamped on a plate attached to the front right-hand end of the cylinder block, below the right-hand branch of the exhaust manifold. The code is the first 3-digits on the first line, and this is the code most often used by Peugeot.

Camshaft

Drive	Toothed belt
No of bearings	5

Camshaft bearing journal diameter:

Journal A:
Nominal	28.00 –0.020, –0.041 mm
Oversize	28.50 –0.020, –0.041 mm

Journal B:
Nominal	28.50 –0.020, –0.041 mm
Oversize	29.00 –0.020, –0.041 mm

Journal C:
Nominal	29.00 –0.020, –0.041 mm
Oversize	29.50 –0.020, –0.041 mm

Journal D:
Nominal	29.50 –0.020, –0.041 mm
Oversize	30.00 –0.020, –0.041 mm

Journal E:
Nominal	30.00 –0.020, –0.041 mm
Oversize	30.50 –0.020, –0.041 mm

Cylinder head bearing journal diameter:

Journal A:
Nominal	30.00 +0.033, +0 mm
Oversize	30.50 +0.033, +0 mm

Journal B:
Nominal	29.50 +0.033, +0 mm
Oversize	30.00 +0.033, +0 mm

Journal C:
Nominal	29.00 +0.033, +0 mm
Oversize	29.50 +0.033, +0 mm

Journal D:
Nominal	28.50 +0.033, +0 mm
Oversize	29.00 +0.033, +0 mm

Journal E:
Nominal	28.00 +0.033, +0 mm
Oversize	28.50 +0.033, +0 mm

Lubrication system

Oil pump type	Crescent-type driven directly from crankshaft

Minimum oil pressure at 80°C:
1000 rpm	1.5 bars
3000 rpm	5.0 bars
Oil pressure warning switch operating pressure	0.5 bars

Torque wrench settings

	Nm	lbf ft
Big-end bearing bolts:		
Stage 1	10	7
Stage 2	Slacken each bolt 180°	
Stage 3	23	17
Stage 4	Angle-tighten a further 46° ± 5°	
Camshaft bearing housings	9	7
Camshaft sprocket/hub-to-camshaft retaining bolts	75	55
Camshaft sprocket-to-hub retaining bolts	9	7
Crankshaft pulley retaining bolt (with gold washer):		
Stage 1	40	30
Stage 2	Angle-tighten a further 53°	
Crankshaft pulley retaining bolt (with metallic washer):		
Stage 1	40	30
Stage 2	Angle-tighten a further 40°	
Crankshaft sprocket centre bolt:		
Stage 1	40	30
Stage 2	Angle tighten a further 53°	
Cylinder head bolts:		
Stage 1	15	11
Stage 2	50	37
Stage 3	Slacken each bolt 360°	
Stage 4	20	15
Stage 5	Angle-tighten through a further 285° (using max 2 steps per bolt)	

Torque wrench settings (continued)

	Nm	lbf ft
Cylinder head cover bolts:		
Stage 1	5	4
Stage 2	11	8
Engine-to-transmission fixing bolts	45	33
Flywheel/driveplate retaining bolts (new):		
Stage 1	25	18
Stage 2	Slacken fully	
Stage 3	8	6
Stage 4	20	15
Stage 5	Angle-tighten a further 21° ± 3°	
Left-hand engine/transmission mounting:		
Mounting bracket-to-body bolts	22	16
Mounting bracket-to-transmission bolts	60	44
Rubber mounting centre nut	65	48
Rubber mounting-to-bracket nuts	22	16
Main bearing cap housing:		
Stage 1 – 11.0 mm diameter bolts	10	7
Stage 2 – 6.0 mm diameter bolts	2	1
Stage 3 – 11.0 mm diameter bolts	Slacken fully	
Stage 4 – 11.0 mm diameter bolts	10	7
Stage 5 – 11.0 mm diameter bolts	Angle-tighten a further 70° ± 5°	
Stage 6 – 6.0 mm diameter bolts	10	7
Oil pump-to-engine bolts:		
Stage 1	7	5
Stage 2	9	7
Rear engine/transmission mounting:		
Connecting link-to-mounting bracket bolt	55	41
Connecting link-to-subframe bolt	55	41
Mounting bracket-to-cylinder block bolts	45	33
Right-hand engine/transmission mounting:		
Rubber mounting centre nut	45	33
Rubber mounting to body	22	16
Upper mounting bracket-to-lower (engine) bracket nuts	61	45
Sump retaining bolts	8	6
Timing belt tensioner pulley bolt	21	16
Timing belt idler pulley bolt:		
Stage 1	15	11
Stage 2	37	27

1 General information

How to use this Chapter

This Part of Chapter 2 describes those repair procedures that can reasonably be carried out on the engine, while it remains in the car. If the engine has been removed from the car and is being dismantled as described in Part D, any preliminary dismantling procedures can be ignored.

Note that, while it may be possible physically to overhaul items such as the piston/ connecting rod assemblies while the engine is in the car, such tasks are not usually carried out as separate operations. Usually, several additional procedures (not to mention the cleaning of components and oil ways) have to be carried out. For this reason, all such tasks are classed as major overhaul procedures, and are described in Part D of this Chapter.

Part D describes the removal of the engine/ transmission unit from the vehicle, and the full overhaul procedures that can then be carried out.

EW series engine

The engine is of in-line four-cylinder, double-overhead camshaft, 16-valve type, mounted transversely at the front of the car. The engine is inclined rearwards by 17°, and the clutch and transmission are attached to its left-hand end.

The engine is of conventional 'dry-liner' type, and the cylinder block is cast in aluminium.

The crankshaft runs in five main bearings. Thrust washers are fitted to No 2 main bearing cap, to control crankshaft endfloat.

The connecting rods rotate on horizontally-split bearing shells at their big-ends. The pistons are attached to the connecting rods by gudgeon pins. The gudgeon pins are an interference fit in the connecting rod small-end eyes. The aluminium alloy pistons are fitted with three piston rings – two compression rings and an oil control ring.

The camshafts are driven by a toothed timing belt, and operate sixteen valves by followers located beneath each cam lobe. The valve clearances are self-adjusting by means of hydraulic tappets fitted to the cam followers. The camshaft runs in bearing cap housings which are bolted to the top of the cylinder head. The inlet and exhaust valves are each closed by coil springs, and operate in guides pressed into the cylinder head. Both the valve seats and guides can be renewed separately if worn.

The coolant pump is driven by the timing belt and located in the right-hand end of the cylinder block.

Lubrication is by means of an oil pump driven off the crankshaft right-hand end. It draws oil through a strainer located in the sump, and then forces it through an externally-mounted filter into galleries in the cylinder block/crankcase. From there, the oil is distributed to the crankshaft (main bearings) and camshaft. The big-end bearings are supplied with oil via internal drillings in the crankshaft; the camshaft bearings also receive a pressurised supply. The camshaft lobes and valves are lubricated by splash, as are all other engine components.

Throughout the manual, it is often necessary to identify the engines not only by their cubic capacity, but also by their engine code. The engine code consists of three digits (eg, 6FZ). The code is stamped on a plate attached to the front, left-hand end of the cylinder block, or stamped directly onto the front face of the

3.5 8.0 mm diameter drill bit inserted through the crankshaft sprocket end plate timing hole, and engaged in the corresponding hole in the oil pump housing

cylinder block, on the machined surface located just to the left of the oil filter (next to the crankcase vent hose union).

Repair operations possible with the engine in the car

The following work can be carried out with the engine in the car:

a) Compression pressure – testing.
b) Cylinder head covers – removal and refitting.
c) Crankshaft pulley – removal and refitting.
d) Timing belt covers – removal and refitting.
e) Timing belt – removal, refitting and adjustment.
f) Timing belt tensioner and sprockets – removal and refitting.
g) Camshaft oil seals – renewal.
h) Camshafts and followers – removal, inspection and refitting.
i) Cylinder head – removal and refitting.
j) Cylinder head and pistons – decarbonising.
k) Sump – removal and refitting.
l) Oil pump – removal, overhaul and refitting.
m) Crankshaft oil seals – renewal.
n) Engine/transmission mountings – inspection and renewal.
o) Flywheel/driveplate – removal, inspection and refitting.

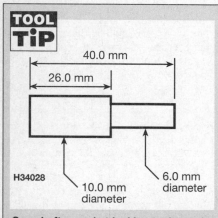

TOOL TiP

40.0 mm

26.0 mm

H34028   10.0 mm diameter   6.0 mm diameter

Camshaft sprocket locking tools can be made from 10.0 mm diameter steel bar, fabricated to the dimensions shown.

---

2 Compression test – description and interpretation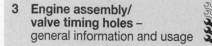

1 When engine performance is down, or if misfiring occurs which cannot be attributed to the ignition or fuel systems, a compression test can provide diagnostic clues as to the engine's condition. If the test is performed regularly, it can give warning of trouble before any other symptoms become apparent.

2 The engine must be fully warmed-up to normal operating temperature, the battery must be fully charged, and all the spark plugs must be removed (Chapter 1A). The aid of an assistant will also be required.

3 Disable the fuel system by disconnecting the wiring connectors from the fuel injectors, referring to Chapter 4A, Section 13, for further information.

4 Fit a compression tester to the No 1 cylinder spark plug hole – the type of tester which screws into the plug thread is to be preferred.

5 Have the assistant hold the throttle wide open, and crank the engine on the starter motor; after one or two revolutions, the compression pressure should build up to a maximum figure, and then stabilise. Record the highest reading obtained.

6 Repeat the test on the remaining cylinders, recording the pressure in each.

7 All cylinders should produce very similar pressures; a difference of more than 2 bars between any two cylinders indicates a fault. Note that the compression should build-up quickly in a healthy engine; low compression on the first stroke, followed by gradually-increasing pressure on successive strokes, indicates worn piston rings. A low compression reading on the first stroke, which does not build-up during successive strokes, indicates leaking valves or a blown head gasket (a cracked head could also be the cause). Deposits on the undersides of the valve heads can also cause low compression.

8 Although Peugeot do not specify exact compression pressures, as a guide, any cylinder pressure of below 10 bars can be considered as less than healthy. Refer to a Peugeot dealer or other specialist if in doubt as to whether a particular pressure reading is acceptable.

9 If the pressure in any cylinder is low, carry out the following test to isolate the cause. Introduce a teaspoonful of clean oil into that cylinder through its spark plug hole, and repeat the test.

10 If the addition of oil temporarily improves the compression pressure, this indicates that bore or piston wear is responsible for the pressure loss. No improvement suggests that leaking or burnt valves, or a blown head gasket, may be to blame.

11 A low reading from two adjacent cylinders is almost certainly due to the head gasket having blown between them; the presence of coolant in the engine oil will confirm this.

---

12 If one cylinder is about 20 percent lower than the others and the engine has a slightly rough idle, a worn camshaft lobe could be the cause.

13 On completion of the test, refit the spark plugs and reconnect the wiring.

3 Engine assembly/ valve timing holes – general information and usage

Note: Do not attempt to rotate the engine whilst the crankshaft/camshaft are locked in position. If the engine is to be left in this state for a long period of time, it is a good idea to place suitable warning notices inside the vehicle, and in the engine compartment. This will reduce the possibility of the engine being accidentally cranked on the starter motor, which is likely to cause damage with the locking pins in place.

1 Timing holes are drilled in the crankshaft sprocket end plate and in the two camshaft sprockets. The holes are used to ensure that the crankshaft and camshafts are correctly positioned when assembling the engine (to prevent the possibility of the valves contacting the pistons when refitting the cylinder head), or refitting the timing belt. When the timing holes are aligned with corresponding holes in the cylinder head and oil pump housing, suitable diameter pins or bolts can be inserted to lock both the camshafts and crankshaft in position, preventing them from rotating. To set the engine in the timing position, proceed as follows.

2 Remove the crankshaft pulley as described in Section 5.

3 Remove the timing belt upper (outer) and lower covers as described in Section 6.

4 Using a socket and extension bar fitted to the crankshaft sprocket centre bolt, turn the crankshaft in the normal direction of rotation until the timing holes in both camshaft sprockets are aligned with their corresponding holes in the cylinder head. The holes are aligned when the inlet camshaft sprocket hole is in approximately the 5 o'clock position and the exhaust camshaft sprocket hole is in approximately the 7 o'clock position, when viewed from the right-hand end of the engine. Use a small mirror to accurately observe the position of the holes.

5 With the camshaft sprocket holes correctly positioned, insert an 8.0 mm diameter drill bit or bolt through the timing hole in the crankshaft sprocket end plate, and locate it in the corresponding hole in the oil pump housing (see illustration). Note: It may be found that an 8.0 mm drill is too large, in which case a 5/16 in drill may be required.

6 The camshaft sprockets can now be locked in position using the Peugeot camshaft setting rods, or suitable home-made alternatives (see Tool Tip). With the crankshaft locked in position, insert the Peugeot special tools, or alternatives, through the timing hole in each camshaft sprocket and locate it in the corresponding hole in the cylinder head (see illustration).

3.6 Camshaft sprocket locking tools inserted through the timing hole in each sprocket

4.1a Disconnect the crankcase breather hose from the rear cylinder head cover

4.1b Disconnect the camshaft position sensor wiring connector . . .

7 The crankshaft and camshafts are now locked in position, preventing rotation. In this position the crankshaft is at 90° BTDC and all the pistons are positioned half-way down their cylinder bores.

4 Cylinder head covers – removal and refitting

Removal

1 If the covers are being removed for major dismantling, disconnect the battery negative lead (refer to *Disconnecting the battery* at the end of this manual) and remove the engine cover. Remove the crankcase ventilation hose and camshaft position sensor from the rear cylinder head cover **(see illustrations)**.

2 Progressively unscrew the bolts securing the cylinder head covers to the cylinder head. The bolts must be unscrewed in a spiral sequence starting from the outside.

3 Remove the cylinder head covers and gaskets **(see illustrations)**. Unless they are obviously damaged, do not attempt to remove the rubber gaskets from the covers.

Refitting

4 Thoroughly clean the surfaces of the covers

4.1c . . . then undo the bolt and remove the sensor from the rear cylinder head cover

and cylinder head.

5 If necessary, fit new gaskets and locate the covers on the head **(see illustration)**. Insert the retaining bolts and finger-tighten them.

6 Progressively tighten the bolts to the Stage 1 torque, in sequence **(see illustration)**, then tighten them to the Stage 2 torque.

7 Check the condition of the O-ring seal on the camshaft position sensor and renew the seal if it is in any way suspect.

8 Refit the camshaft position sensor and secure with the retaining bolt. Reconnect the sensor wiring connector.

9 Reconnect the breather hose to the rear cover.

4.3a Undo the retaining bolts and lift off the front . . .

4.3b . . . and rear cylinder head covers

4.5 Locate the cylinder head cover seal in the groove, ensuring that it is fully seated along its entire length

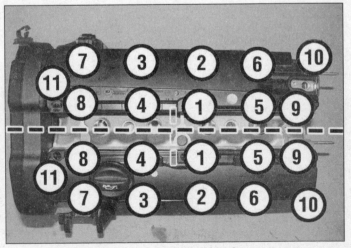

4.6 Cylinder head cover bolt tightening sequence

5.3a Undo the four crankshaft pulley retaining bolts . . .

5.3b . . . and remove the pulley from the crankshaft sprocket end plate

5 Crankshaft pulley – removal and refitting

Removal

1 Remove the auxiliary drivebelt (Chapter 1A).
2 To prevent the crankshaft turning whilst the pulley retaining bolt is being slackened on manual transmission models, select 4th gear and have an assistant apply the brakes firmly. On automatic transmission models it will be necessary to remove the starter motor (Chapter 5A) and lock the driveplate with a suitable tool. If the engine has been removed from the vehicle, lock the flywheel ring gear as

described in Section 8. *Do not* attempt to lock the pulley by inserting a bolt/drill through the timing hole. If the locking pin is in position, temporarily remove it prior to slackening the pulley bolt, then refit it once the bolt has been slackened.
3 Undo the four crankshaft pulley retaining bolts and remove the pulley from the crankshaft sprocket end plate **(see illustrations)**.

Refitting

4 Locate the pulley on the crankshaft sprocket end plate, refit the four retaining bolts and tighten them to the specified torque and angle.
5 Refit and tension the auxiliary drivebelt as described in Chapter 1A.

6 Timing belt covers – removal and refitting

Removal

Upper (outer) cover

1 Undo the upper and lower retaining bolts securing the outer cover to the inner cover **(see illustration)**. Slide the cover retaining clip upwards to release it from its fasteners.
2 Ease the outer cover upwards and away from the engine, freeing it from its lower locations **(see illustration)**.

Lower cover

3 Remove the crankshaft pulley as described in Section 5.
4 Remove the upper (outer) cover as described above.
5 Slacken and remove the three retaining bolts, then remove the lower timing belt cover from the engine **(see illustrations)**. Note that on some models it may be necessary to unbolt the auxiliary drivebelt tensioner assembly and remove it from the engine in order to allow the cover to be removed.

Upper (inner) cover

6 Remove the timing belt as described in Section 7.
7 Remove both camshaft sprockets as described in Section 8.
8 Remove the bolts securing the cover to the side of the cylinder head, and remove the cover from the engine **(see illustration)**.

Refitting

9 Refitting is a reversal of the relevant removal procedure, ensuring that each cover section is correctly located, and that the cover retaining nuts and/or bolts are securely tightened to the specified torque. When refitting the upper (inner) cover, apply thread locking compound to the retaining bolts.

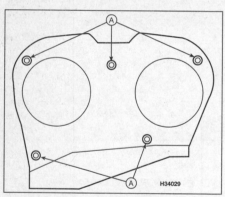

6.1 Undo the upper timing belt cover retaining bolts (A) . . .

6.2 . . . and withdraw the cover from the cylinder head

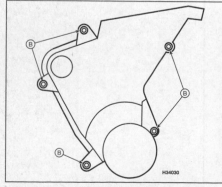

6.5a Undo the lower timing belt cover retaining bolts (B) . . .

6.5b . . . and manipulate the cover up and out from between the engine and bulkhead

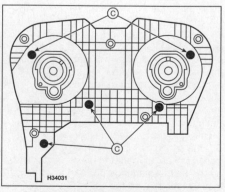

6.8 Upper (inner) timing belt cover retaining bolts (C)

7 Timing belt –
general information, removal and refitting

Note: *From September 2000, modified camshaft sprockets were fitted. In particular, the exhaust camshaft pinion was fitted with a damper, and sprocket hubs were discontinued.*

General information

1 The timing belt drives the camshafts and coolant pump from a toothed sprocket on the end of the crankshaft. If the belt breaks or slips in service, the pistons are likely to hit the valve heads, resulting in extensive (and expensive) damage.

2 The timing belt should be renewed at the specified intervals (see Chapter 1A), or earlier if it is contaminated with oil, or if it is at all noisy in operation (a 'scraping' noise due to uneven wear).

3 If the timing belt is being removed, it is a wise precaution to check the condition of the coolant pump at the same time (check for signs of coolant leakage). This may avoid the need to remove the timing belt again at a later stage, should the coolant pump fail.

4 The crankshaft sprocket is a two-piece assembly consisting of the toothed sprocket itself and an outer end plate. The end plate is locked to the crankshaft by means of a conventional Woodruff key. When the sprocket retaining bolt is slackened, the sprocket is free to turn on the crankshaft within the limits afforded by an additional keyway within the end plate. When the sprocket retaining bolt is tightened the complete assembly is locked to the crankshaft. This arrangement allows accurate tensioning of the timing belt when refitting, provided that the procedures contained in this Section are strictly adhered to.

Removal

5 Disconnect the battery negative terminal (refer to *Disconnecting the battery* in the Reference Chapter).

6 Remove the upper (outer) and lower timing belt covers as described in Section 6.

7 Align the engine assembly/valve timing holes as described in Section 3, and lock the crankshaft sprocket and camshaft sprockets in position. *Do not* attempt to rotate the engine whilst the locking tools are in position.

8 Loosen the timing belt tensioner pulley retaining bolt. Using an Allen key in the hole provided on the front of the pulley, rotate the pulley in a clockwise direction, to relieve the tension from the timing belt **(see illustration)**. Retighten the tensioner pulley retaining bolt to secure it in the slackened position.

9 If the timing belt is to be re-used, use white paint or chalk to mark the direction of rotation on the belt (if markings do not already exist), then slip the belt off the sprockets and pulleys **(see illustration)**. Note that the crankshaft must not be rotated whilst the belt is removed.

7.8 Using an Allen key in the hole (arrowed) on the tensioner pulley, rotate the pulley clockwise to relieve the tension from the timing belt

10 Check the timing belt carefully for any signs of uneven wear, splitting, or oil contamination. Pay particular attention to the roots of the teeth. Renew it if there is the slightest doubt about its condition. If the engine is undergoing an overhaul, it is advisable to renew the belt as a matter of course, regardless of its apparent condition. The cost of a new belt is nothing compared with the cost of repairs, should the belt break in service. If signs of oil contamination are found, trace the source of the oil leak and rectify it. Wash down the engine timing belt area and all related components, to remove all traces of oil.

Refitting

11 Before refitting, thoroughly clean the timing belt sprockets. Check that the tensioner and idler pulleys rotate freely, without any sign of roughness. If necessary, renew the relevant pulley as described in Section 8.

Sprocket with hubs

12 Without removing the locking pins, slacken the six camshaft sprocket retaining bolts (three on each sprocket). Check that both sprockets are free to turn within the limits of their elongated bolt holes.

13 Tighten the six camshaft sprocket

7.9 With the tensioner released, slip the timing belt off the sprockets and pulleys

retaining bolts finger tight, then slacken them all by one sixth of a turn.

14 Turn each sprocket clockwise to the ends of their retaining bolt slots.

15 With the timing belt engaged with the crankshaft sprocket, keep it tight on its front run and engage it with the front idler pulley then up and into engagement with the inlet camshaft sprocket. If the belt teeth are not aligned with the sprocket teeth, carefully turn the inlet camshaft sprocket anti-clockwise until the belt engages. **Note:** *It is important that the pulley is not turned anti-clockwise more than 1 tooth.*

16 Keeping the belt tight, feed the belt over the exhaust camshaft sprocket and again if necessary, turn the exhaust camshaft sprocket anti-clockwise until the belt engages. **Note:** *It is important that the pulley is not turned anti-clockwise more than 1 tooth.*

17 While still keeping the belt tight, feed it over the rear tensioner pulley and finally around the coolant pump.

18 Refit the tensioner roller and engage the roller bracket with the rib on the block. Turn the tensioner lightly anti-clockwise to tension the belt, then finger-tighten the tensioner retaining bolt to retain the tensioner.

19 The tensioner pulley must now be turned anti-clockwise until the pointer is positioned as shown **(see illustration)**. Use a suitable Allen key in the tensioner hub to do this. Hold

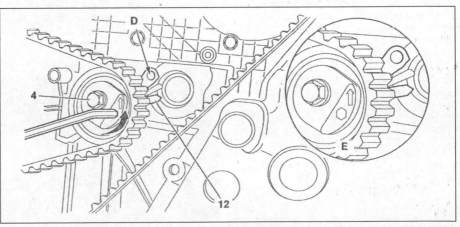

7.19 Turn the tensioner pulley anti-clockwise until the pointer (12) is in the position E

4 Retaining bolt   *D Tensioner roller bracket setting hole*

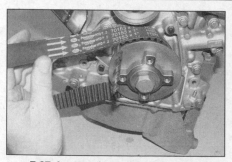

7.27 Locate the timing belt on the crankshaft sprocket, with the arrows on the belt pointing in the direction of rotation

7.28a Retain the belt on the crankshaft sprocket and feed it over the idler pulley . . .

7.28b . . . inlet camshaft sprocket . . .

7.28c exhaust camshaft sprocket . . .

7.28d . . . coolant pump and tensioner pulley

7.30a Using an Allen key, turn the tensioner pulley anti-clockwise . . .

the tensioner in this position and tighten the retaining bolt to the specified torque.

20 Remove one retaining bolt from each camshaft sprocket and check that the sprockets are not at the end of their retaining bolt slots. If they are, repeat the refitting operation. If all is satisfactory, refit the two removed bolts, and tighten all six sprocket retaining bolts to the specified torque.

21 Remove the locking pins, then rotate the crankshaft through six complete rotations in a clockwise direction (viewed from the right-hand end of the engine). Do not turn the crankshaft anti-clockwise.

22 Insert Peugeot setting tool 0189-K or a suitable rod through the hole in the tensioner roller bracket, then loosen the tensioner bolt

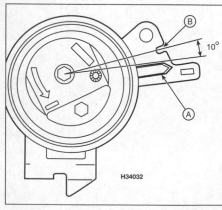

7.30b . . . until the upper edge of the index pointer (A) is positioned approximately 10° past the slot (B) in the backing plate

and use the Allen key to turn the tensioner hub clockwise until the control lever just touches the rod. This allows the pointer to move to its nominal position next to the setting tool. Hold the tensioner in this position and tighten the retaining bolt to the specified torque.

23 Re-align the timing holes and insert the camshaft sprocket and crankshaft locking pins. If the camshaft sprocket holes do not align exactly, temporarily loosen the 6 bolts securing the sprockets to the hubs, insert the pins, then tighten the bolts to the specified torque.

24 Remove one retaining bolt from each camshaft sprocket and check that the sprockets are not at the end of their retaining bolt slots. If they are, repeat the refitting operation. If all is satisfactory, refit the two removed bolts, and tighten all six sprocket retaining bolts to the specified torque.

7.31 Now rotate the pulley clockwise until the index pointer is exactly aligned with the slot in the backing plate

25 Remove the camshaft and crankshaft locking tools.

Fixed sprockets (without hubs)

26 Ensure that the crankshaft and camshaft sprocket locking tools are still in position.

27 Locate the timing belt on the crankshaft sprocket, ensuring that any arrows on the belt are pointing in the direction of rotation (clockwise when viewed from the right-hand end of the engine) **(see illustration)**.

28 Retain the timing belt on the crankshaft sprocket then, keeping it taut, feed the belt over the remaining sprockets and pulleys in the following order **(see illustrations)**:

a) Idler pulley.
b) Inlet camshaft.
c) Exhaust camshaft.
d) Coolant pump.
e) Tensioner pulley.

29 Remove the locking tool from the exhaust camshaft sprocket.

30 Slacken the tensioner pulley retaining bolt and turn the tensioner pulley hub anti-clockwise, by means of the Allen key, so that the upper edge of the index pointer is positioned approximately 10° clockwise past the slot in the backing plate **(see illustrations)**. Note that if the index pointer will not attain a position of at least 10° past the backing plate slot, then the tensioner pulley, or both the tensioner pulley and the timing belt must be renewed.

31 Now rotate the tensioner pulley hub clockwise until the index pointer is exactly aligned with the slot in the backing plate **(see illustration)**. Hold the pulley in this position and tighten the retaining bolt to the specified torque. With the timing belt tensioned and the tensioner pulley retaining bolt tightened, the Allen key slot in the pulley should be below the cylinder head gasket level. If this is not the case, then the tensioner pulley, or both the tensioner pulley and the timing belt must be renewed.

32 Remove the remaining camshaft and crankshaft locking tools and rotate the crankshaft through ten complete rotations in a clockwise direction (viewed from the right-hand end of the engine). Realign the engine assembly/valve timing holes and refit the inlet camshaft sprocket locking tool.

33 Check that the tensioner pulley index pointer is still aligned with the slot in the backing plate. If not repeat the tensioning operation.

34 With the inlet camshaft sprocket locking tool in place, it should now also be possible to fit the crankshaft sprocket locking tool. If so, continue with the refitting procedure. If the crankshaft sprocket locking tool will not engage, then the crankshaft sprocket end plate must be repositioned as follows.

35 Slacken the crankshaft sprocket retaining bolt while holding the sprocket end plate stationary using Peugeot special tool 6310-T or a suitable home-made alternative **(see Tool Tip in Section 8)**. *Do not* attempt to use only the sprocket locking tools inserted in the engine assembly/valve timing holes to prevent rotation whilst the bolt is slackened.

36 With the sprocket retaining bolt slackened, turn the end plate until the sprocket locking tool can be fully inserted through the end plate and into the hole in the oil pump housing.

37 Hold the end plate with the holding tool and tighten the sprocket retaining bolt to the

TOOL TIP

To make a sprocket holding tool, obtain two lengths of steel strip about 6 mm thick by about 30 mm wide or similar, one 600 mm long, the other 200 mm long (all dimensions approximate). Bolt the two strips together to form a forked end, leaving the bolt slack so that the shorter strip can pivot freely. At the other end of each 'prong' of the fork, drill a suitable hole and fit a nut and bolt to engage with the spokes or holes in the sprocket. The same tool can be used to hold both the camshaft sprocket and crankshaft sprocket.

7.37a Hold the crankshaft sprocket end plate with the holding tool and tighten the retaining bolt to the specified torque . . .

specified torque, then through the specified angle **(see illustrations)**.

All engines

38 Refit the lower and upper (outer) timing belt covers as described in Section 6.

39 Refit the crankshaft pulley as described in Section 5.

40 Refit the upper timing belt cover and tighten the bolts.

41 Refit the auxiliary drivebelt with reference to Chapter 1A.

42 Refit the right-hand front wheelarch liner.

43 Refit the roadwheel and lower the vehicle to the ground.

44 Reconnect the battery negative terminal.

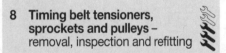

8 Timing belt tensioners, sprockets and pulleys – removal, inspection and refitting

Note: *From September 2000, modified camshaft sprockets were fitted. In particular, the exhaust camshaft pinion was fitted with a damper, and sprocket hubs were discontinued.*

Removal

1 Remove the timing belt as described in Section 7.

Camshaft sprockets with hubs

2 To remove a camshaft sprocket (and where applicable, the hub), first remove the timing locking pin, then use a suitable retaining tool in the sprocket holes to hold it stationary. In the absence of the special Peugeot tool, an acceptable substitute can be fabricated at home **(see Tool Tip)**. *Do not* attempt to use the sprocket locking pin to prevent the sprocket from rotating whilst the bolt is slackened. With the sprocket held stationary, unscrew the bolt securing the sprocket hub to the camshaft.

3 Remove the sprocket/hub from the camshaft, noting that the tag engages with the cut-out in the end of the camshaft. If necessary, unbolt the sprocket from the hub.

Fixed camshaft sprockets (no hubs)

4 The camshafts must now be prevented from rotating to allow the sprocket retaining bolts to be slackened. If working on the exhaust camshaft sprocket, it will be necessary to

7.37b . . . then through the specified angle

remove the rear cylinder head cover (see Section 4) to allow a spanner to be engaged with a square section of the camshaft, provided for this purpose. This is because the sprocket contains a rubber vibration damper incorporated into the sprocket hub. If the sprocket itself is held as the bolt is slackened, the rubber hub will be damaged. The inlet camshaft sprocket is conventional and can be held using Peugeot tool 6016-T, or an acceptable substitute can be fabricated at home **(see Tool Tip above)**. Alternatively, remove the front cylinder head cover and hold the camshaft with a spanner as described for the exhaust camshaft. *Do not* attempt to use the engine assembly/valve timing hole locking tools to prevent the sprockets from rotating whilst the bolts are slackened.

5 Remove the engine assembly/valve timing hole locking tool from the relevant sprocket, then slacken the centre retaining bolt. If a spanner is being used to prevent camshaft rotation, the spanner should be engaged with the square section of the camshaft adjacent to No 8 cam lobe **(see illustration)**.

6 Remove the previously slackened sprocket retaining bolt and washer, and withdraw the relevant sprocket from the end of the camshaft **(see illustrations)**.

Crankshaft sprocket

7 With the crankshaft pulley removed from the flange on the front of the crankshaft, remove the timing locking pin. **Note:** *Do not use the pin to lock the crankshaft when loosening the crankshaft pulley bolt.*

8.5 The camshafts can be held with a spanner engaged with the square section adjacent to No 8 cam lobe

8.6a Remove the previously slackened sprocket retaining bolt and washer . . .

8.6b . . . and withdraw the relevant sprocket from the end of the camshaft

8.8a Hold the crankshaft sprocket end plate with the home-made tool while the retaining bolt is slackened

8.8b Withdraw the crankshaft sprocket end plate . . .

8.8c . . . and the sprocket itself

8.9 Remove the Woodruff key from the end of the crankshaft

8 The flywheel must now be locked. To do this, remove the starter motor and have an assistant insert a wide-bladed screwdriver between the teeth of the ring gear and the transmission casing. Unscrew and remove the bolt and washer, and remove the crankshaft sprocket and flange from the end of the crankshaft. Alternatively a home-made tool may be used as shown (see illustrations).

9 Remove the Woodruff key from the crankshaft, and store it with the sprocket for safe-keeping (see illustration). Where necessary, also slide the spacer (where fitted) off the end of the crankshaft.

10 Examine the crankshaft oil seal for signs of oil leakage and, if necessary, renew it as described in Section 14.

Tensioner and idler pulleys

11 Unscrew the retaining bolts from the tensioner and idler pulleys, then remove the pulleys from the engine (see illustrations). Note that the tensioner roller bracket locates over the rib on the cylinder block.

Inspection

12 Clean the camshaft/crankshaft sprockets thoroughly, and renew any that show signs of wear, damage or cracks. Where applicable, check the condition of the rubber vibration damper in the exhaust camshaft sprocket and renew the sprocket if there is any sign of deterioration of the rubber.

13 Clean the tensioner/idler pulleys but do not use any strong solvent which may enter the pulley bearings. Check that the pulleys rotate freely, with no sign of stiffness or free play. Renew them if there is any doubt about their condition, or if there are any obvious signs of wear or damage.

Refitting

Camshaft sprockets with hubs

15 Refit the sprocket/hub to the camshaft and engage the tag with the cut-out in the end of the camshaft.

16 Insert the retaining bolt and tighten it to the specified torque while holding the sprocket/hub stationary with the tool used for removal.

17 Refit the timing belt and adjust its tension as described in Section 7.

Fixed camshaft sprockets (no hubs)

17 Locate the relevant sprocket on the end of the camshaft, engaging the lug in the sprocket hub with the slot in the end of the camshaft.

18 Refit the sprocket retaining bolt and washer, and tighten it to the specified torque. Prevent the sprocket from turning as the bolt is tightened using the method employed for removal.

19 Realign the hole in the camshaft sprocket with the corresponding hole in the cylinder head, and refit the locking tool. Check that the crankshaft pulley locking tool is still in position.

20 Where removed, refit the cylinder head cover(s) as described in Section 4.

21 Refit and tension the timing belt as described in Section 7.

Crankshaft sprocket

22 Where fitted, refit the spacer, then locate the Woodruff key in the crankshaft groove, making sure that it is parallel with the surface of the crankshaft.

8.11a Removing the timing belt tensioner pulley . . .

8.11b . . . and idler pulley

8.27 Ensure that the slot (arrowed) on the tensioner pulley body engages with the web on the cylinder block when refitting

9.3 Using pliers and a self-tapping screw to extract the inlet camshaft oil seal

9.5 Locate the new seal in position with the seal lips facing inwards

23 Locate the sprocket and flange onto the end of the crankshaft and engage the groove with the Woodruff key.

24 Apply locking fluid to the threads of the crankshaft pulley bolt then insert it together with the washer and screw it in finger-tight.

25 Hold the crankshaft stationary with the method used for removal, then tighten the bolt to the specified torque.

26 Refit and tension the timing belt as described in Section 7.

Tensioner and idler pulleys

27 Locate the tensioner pulley on the engine, making sure that the roller bracket engages over the rib on the cylinder block (see illustration). Insert the bolt and finger-tighten it at this stage.

28 Locate the idler pulley on the engine, insert the bolt, and tighten it to the specified torque and angle.

29 Refit and tension the timing belt as described in Section 7.

9 Camshaft oil seals – renewal

1 Remove the camshaft sprockets and hubs (where applicable) as described in Section 8.

2 Note the fitted depth of the oil seals as a guide to fitting the new ones.

3 Punch or drill two small holes opposite each other in the oil seal. Screw a self-tapping screw into each, and pull on the screws with pliers to extract the seal (see illustration).

4 Clean the seal housing, and polish off any burrs or raised edges, which may have caused the seal to fail in the first place.

5 Lubricate the lips of the new seal with clean engine oil, and drive it into position until it seats on its locating shoulder (see illustration). Use a suitable tubular drift, such as a socket, which bears only on the hard outer edge of the seal. Take care not to damage the seal lips during fitting. Note that the seal lips should face inwards. If available, use the Peugeot tool No 0189-D1/D2.

6 Refit the camshaft sprockets as described in Section 8.

10 Camshafts and followers – removal, inspection and refitting

Removal

1 Remove the timing belt as described in Section 7.

2 Progressively unscrew the bolts securing the cylinder head covers to the cylinder head. The bolts must be unscrewed in a spiral sequence starting from the outside.

3 Remove the cylinder head covers and gaskets.

4 Refer to Section 8 and remove both camshaft sprockets.

5 Unbolt and remove the inner timing cover from the cylinder head. At this stage, note the fitted depth of the oil seals as a guide to fitting new seals during reassembly.

6 Evenly and progressively slacken the

camshaft bearing housing retaining bolts by one turn at a time, in a spiral sequence, starting from the outside. This will relieve the valve spring pressure on the bearing housing gradually and evenly. Once the pressure has been relieved, the bolts can be fully unscrewed together with their washers.

7 Lift the camshaft bearing housings from the cylinder head, noting that the housings are located on dowels (see illustration).

8 Identify each camshaft for position – the exhaust camshaft is at the rear and the inlet camshaft is at the front of the cylinder head. Also note the TDC position of each camshaft for correct refitting.

9 Remove the camshafts by pressing on their transmission ends to release the opposite ends from the bearings. Withdraw the camshafts from the cylinder head and slide the oil seals from their timing ends (see illustration).

10 Obtain sixteen small, clean plastic containers, and number them inlet 1 to 8 and exhaust 1 to 8; alternatively, divide a larger container into sixteen compartments and number each compartment accordingly. Using a rubber sucker, withdraw each hydraulic tappet in turn, and place it in its respective container (see illustration). Do not interchange the tappets, or the rate of wear will be much-increased.

Inspection

11 Examine the camshaft bearing surfaces and cam lobes for signs of wear ridges and scoring. Renew the camshaft if any of these conditions are apparent. Examine the condition of the bearing surfaces, both on the

10.7 Progressively slacken and remove the retaining bolts, then lift off camshaft bearing cap housing(s)

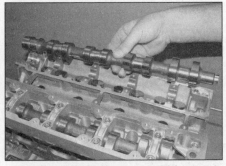

10.9 Carefully lift the camshaft(s) up and out of their locations

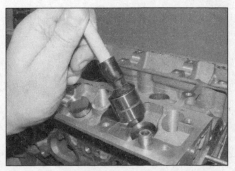

10.10 Use a rubber sucker to withdraw the hydraulic tappets

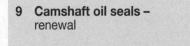

10.14a Lubricate the hydraulic tappet bores and the tappets . . .

10.14b . . . then refit the tappets ensuring that each is refitted to its original bore

10.15 Liberally oil the camshaft bearings and lobes, then lay the camshafts in the cylinder head

camshaft journals and in the cylinder head and bearing housing. If the head bearing surfaces are worn excessively, the cylinder head will need to be renewed. If suitable measuring equipment is available, camshaft bearing journal wear can be checked by direct measurement, noting that No 1 journal is at the transmission end of the head.

12 Examine the hydraulic tappet bearing surfaces which contact the camshaft lobes for wear ridges and scoring. Renew any tappet where these conditions are apparent. If a tappet bearing surface is badly scored, also examine the corresponding lobe on the camshaft for wear, as it is likely that both will be worn. Renew worn components as necessary.

Refitting

13 Before commencing refitting, remove all traces of oil from the bearing housing retaining bolt holes in the cylinder head, using a clean rag. Also ensure that both the cylinder head and bearing housing mating faces are clean and free from oil.

14 Liberally oil the cylinder head hydraulic tappet bores and the tappets. Carefully refit the tappets to the cylinder head, ensuring that each tappet is refitted to its original bore **(see illustrations)**. Some care will be required to enter the tappets squarely into their bores. Check that each tappet rotates freely in its bore.

15 Liberally oil the camshaft bearings in the cylinder head and the camshaft lobes, then

refit the camshafts to the cylinder head in their previously noted positions **(see illustration)**. Note that the exhaust camshaft has a sensor ring on its left-hand end and must be fitted at the rear of the cylinder head.

16 Ensure that the four locating dowels are in position, one at each corner of the cylinder head.

17 Apply a bead of silicone-based jointing compound (Peugeot Silicone Categorie 2) around the perimeter of the mating faces and around the retaining bolt hole locations **(see illustration)**.

18 Liberally oil the camshaft bearings and carefully locate the bearing housings over the camshafts. Refit the retaining bolts ensuring that each has a washer under its head **(see illustration)**. Note that the bearing housing with the sensor hole is located over the exhaust camshaft. Initially finger-tighten the bolts.

19 Progressively tighten the bearing housing retaining bolts to the specified torque, in the order given in Section 4. It is suggested that the bolts are initially tightened to 5 Nm (4 lbf ft), then tightened to their final torque.

20 Refit the inner timing cover to the cylinder head and tighten the retaining bolts securely.

21 Clean the jointing compound from the oil seal seatings in the cylinder head and camshaft housing.

22 Fit new oil seals with reference to Section 9.

23 Refit the sprockets to the camshafts with reference to Section 8.

24 Refit the cylinder head covers together with new gaskets, with reference to Section 4.

25 Refit the timing belt with reference to Section 7.

---

11 Cylinder head – removal and refitting

Removal

1 Disconnect the battery negative lead (refer to *Disconnecting the battery* at the end of this manual).

2 Apply the handbrake, then jack up the front of the vehicle and support it on axle stands (see *Jacking and vehicle support*). Remove the engine compartment undertray where fitted. For improved access, remove the bonnet as described in Chapter 11.

3 Drain the cooling system as described in Chapter 1A.

4 Unbolt the exhaust downpipe from the exhaust manifold on the rear of the engine with reference to Chapter 4A.

5 Unbolt the top cover from the engine.

6 Release the fuel pressure from the fuel system by placing cloth rags around and over the Shrader valve on the fuel rail, and depressing the valve core.

7 Disconnect the fuel supply pipe from the fuel rail.

8 Remove the timing belt as described in Section 7.

9 Remove the timing belt tensioner roller as described in Section 8.

10 Remove the air cleaner and intake pipe with reference to Chapter 4A.

11 Remove the engine oil dipstick from its tube, then remove the tube itself from the block.

12 Disconnect the crankcase breather hose from the camshaft cover. Also disconnect the air inlet hose from the secondary air injection valve at the left-hand end of the cylinder head **(see illustration)**.

13 Remove the coolant hose from the thermostat housing on the left-hand end of the cylinder head.

14 Disconnect the wiring from the left-hand end of the ignition coil module **(see illustration)**.

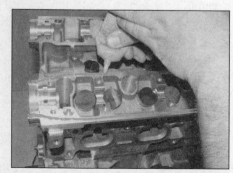

10.17 Apply a bead of anaerobic jointing compound around the perimeter of the cylinder head mating faces

10.18 Carefully locate the bearing cap housings over the camshafts

11.12 Disconnect the air inlet hose from the secondary air injection valve

11.14 Disconnect the wiring connector from the ignition coil unit

11.16a Disconnect the wiring connectors from the EGR valve . . .

11.16b . . . and coolant temperature sensor

11.20 Disconnect the two heater hose from the heater matrix pipes

11.22 Undo the wiring harness support bracket nuts, release the cable ties and clips then move the bracket, wiring harness and hoses clear of the cylinder head

15 Disconnect the wiring from the fuel injectors, charcoal canister electrovalve and air pressure sensor.

16 Disconnect the wiring from the EGR valve and temperature sensor at the left-hand front of the cylinder head **(see illustrations)**.

17 Remove the camshaft position sensor from the left-hand end of the exhaust camshaft cover.

18 Remove the ignition coil module from the top of the cylinder head with reference to Chapter 5B.

19 Unscrew the bolts/nuts securing the inlet manifold to the front of the cylinder head, then support the manifold away from the cylinder head.

20 Loosen the clips and disconnect the heater matrix hoses **(see illustration)**.

21 Remove both cylinder head covers and gaskets with reference to Section 4.

22 Unbolt the wiring harness bracket from the cylinder head outlet housing, and position it to one side **(see illustration)**.

23 Release the clips and disconnect the hoses from the cylinder head outlet housing. Where the original spring-type hose clips are fitted, use a pair of grips to release them.

24 At the rear of the outlet housing, unscrew the bolt and remove the retaining fork **(see illustration)**, then disconnect the hoses.

25 Unscrew the bolt securing the right-hand engine mounting to the cylinder head **(see illustration)**. Do not unscrew the lower bolts securing the mounting to the cylinder block.

26 Undo the bolt securing the lower (engine) mounting bracket to the cylinder head. Ensure that the bolt is fully unscrewed but note that there is insufficient clearance to completely remove the bolt from its location.

27 Using a Torx key socket and working in

the *reverse* of the tightening sequence (see paragraph 41), progressively slacken the ten cylinder head bolts by half a turn at a time, until all bolts can be unscrewed by hand. Recover the washers where fitted.

28 With all the cylinder head bolts removed, the joint between the cylinder head and gasket and the cylinder block/crankcase must now be broken. To break the joint, obtain two L-shaped metal bars which fit into the cylinder head bolt holes, and gently 'rock' the cylinder head free towards the front of the car. *Do not* try to swivel the head on the cylinder block/crankcase; it is located by dowels. When the joint is broken, lift the cylinder head away. Use a hoist or seek assistance if possible, as it is a heavy assembly **(see illustration)**. Remove the gasket from the top

11.24 Remove the bolt and horseshoe-shaped clamp plate securing the coolant pipe to the coolant outlet housing

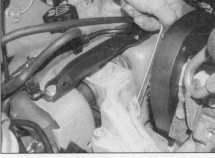

11.25 Undo the bolt securing the lower (engine) mounting bracket to the cylinder head

11.28 Removing the cylinder head from the block

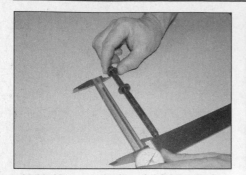

11.33 Measure the length of the cylinder head bolts from the underside of the head to the end of the bolt

11.35a Check that the cylinder head locating dowels (arrowed) are in position in the block . . .

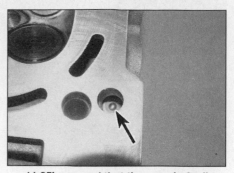

11.35b . . . and that the camshaft oil supply non-return valve (arrowed) is in place in the cylinder head

of the block, noting the two locating dowels. If the locating dowels are a loose fit, remove them and store them with the head for safe-keeping. Do not discard the gasket; it will be needed for identification purposes. During removal, check that the camshaft oil supply non-return valve (located in the underside of the cylinder head at the timing belt end) does not drop out; it is easily lost if it does.

29 If the cylinder head is to be dismantled for overhaul, remove the camshafts as described in Section 10, then refer to Part D of this Chapter. Also remove the rigid pipe from the outlet housing.

Preparation for refitting

30 The mating faces of the cylinder head and cylinder block/crankcase must be perfectly clean before refitting the head. Use a hard plastic or wooden scraper to remove all traces of gasket and carbon and also clean the piston crowns. Make sure that the carbon is not allowed to enter the oil and water passages – this is particularly important for the lubrication system, as carbon could block the oil supply to the engine's components. Using adhesive tape and paper, seal the water, oil and bolt holes in the cylinder block/crankcase. To prevent carbon entering the gap between the pistons and bores, smear a little grease in the gap. After cleaning each piston, use a small brush to remove all traces of grease and carbon from the gap, then wipe away the remainder with a clean rag. Clean all the pistons in the same way.

31 Check the mating surfaces of the cylinder block/crankcase and the cylinder head for nicks, deep scratches and other damage. If slight, they may be removed carefully with a file, but if excessive, machining may be the only alternative to renewal. If warpage of the cylinder head gasket surface is suspected, use a straight-edge to check it for distortion. Refer to Part D of this Chapter if necessary.

32 Obtain a new cylinder head gasket before starting the refitting procedure. At the time of writing, there are two different thicknesses available – the standard gasket which is fitted at the factory, and a slightly thicker 'repair' gasket (+0.3 mm), for use once the head gasket face has been machined. If the cylinder head has been machined, it should be marked '–0.3' on the upper corner, on the inlet manifold side, at the timing belt end. Note that modifications to the cylinder head gasket material, type, and manufacturer are constantly taking place; seek the advice of a Peugeot dealer as to the latest recommendations.

33 Check the condition of the cylinder head bolts, and particularly their threads, whenever they are removed. Wash the bolts in a suitable solvent, and wipe them dry. Check each bolt for any sign of visible wear or damage, renewing them if necessary. Measure the length of each bolt from the underside of its head to the end of the bolt **(see illustration)**. Two different lengths of cylinder head bolts may be encountered according to the date of manufacture of the engine. Early engines were fitted with bolts 127.5 mm in length, whereas

on later engines the length was increased to 144.5 mm. The bolts may be re-used if their length does not exceed the following dimensions.

Early engines	129.0 mm
Later engines	147.0 mm

If any one bolt is longer than the specified length, *all* of the bolts should be renewed as a complete set. Considering the stress which the cylinder head bolts are under, it is highly recommended that they are renewed, regardless of their apparent condition. Also check that the thickness of the head bolt washers is 4.00 ± 0.2 mm.

Refitting

34 Where removed, refit the camshafts, and the rigid pipe to the outlet housing on the cylinder head.

35 Wipe clean the mating surfaces of the cylinder head and cylinder block/crankcase. Check that the two locating dowels are in position at each end of the cylinder block/crankcase surface. Check also that the camshaft oil supply non-return valve is in place in the oil feed bore at the timing belt end of the cylinder head **(see illustrations)**.

36 Position a new gasket on the cylinder block/crankcase surface, ensuring that the TOP mark is uppermost and at the front of the block **(see illustration)**.

37 Check that the crankshaft pulley and camshaft sprockets are still at their TDC positions.

38 With the aid of an assistant, carefully lower the cylinder head assembly onto the block, aligning it with the locating dowels.

39 Apply a smear of grease to the threads, and to the underside of the heads, of the cylinder head bolts. Peugeot recommend the use of Molykote G Rapid Plus (available from your Peugeot dealer); in the absence of the specified grease, any good-quality high-melting-point grease may be used.

40 Carefully enter each bolt and washer into its relevant hole (*do not drop it in*) then screw them in finger-tight.

41 Working progressively and in the sequence shown **(see illustration)**, tighten the cylinder head bolts to their Stage 1 torque setting.

11.36 Position the cylinder head gasket with the word TOP uppermost and toward the oil filter side of the block

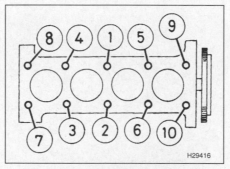

11.41 Cylinder head bolt tightening sequence

H29416

42 Once all the bolts have been tightened to their Stage 1 torque setting, proceed to tighten them through the remaining stages as given in the Specifications. When carrying out Stage 3, slacken each bolt 1 turn working in the reverse of the tightening sequence. It is recommended that an angle-measuring gauge is used for the angle-tightening stages, however, if a gauge is not available, use white paint to make alignment marks between the bolt head and cylinder head prior to tightening; the marks can then by used to check that the bolt has rotated sufficiently. Where a maximum of 2 steps is given for angle-tightening, each step must be completed in one movement without stopping.

43 The remainder of the refitting procedure is a reversal of removal, referring to the relevant Chapters or Sections as required. On completion, refill the cooling system as described in Chapter 1A. Initialise the engine management ECU as follows. Start the engine and run to normal temperature. Carry out a road test during which the following procedure should be made. Engage third gear and stabilise the engine at 1000 rpm. Now accelerate fully to 3500 rpm.

12 Sump – removal and refitting

Removal

1 Disconnect the battery negative lead (refer to *Disconnecting the battery* at the end of this manual).

2 Apply the handbrake, then jack up the front of the vehicle and support it on axle stands (see *Jacking and vehicle support*). Where applicable, remove the engine undertray.

3 Drain the engine oil then clean and refit the engine oil drain plug, tightening it securely. If the engine is nearing its service interval when the oil and filter are due for renewal, it is recommended that the filter is also removed, and a new one fitted. After reassembly, the engine can then be refilled with fresh oil. Refer to Chapter 1A for further information.

4 Withdraw the engine oil dipstick from the guide tube.

5 Undo the bolt securing the upper end of the dipstick guide tube to the ancillary components mounting bracket. Undo the bolt securing the base of the guide tube to the sump and remove the guide tube **(see illustration)**. Collect the two O-rings from the base of the guide tube, noting that new O-rings will be required for refitting.

6 Where applicable, move the power steering pipe supports from the sump. Also disconnect the wiring from the oil temperature sender unit.

7 Progressively slacken and remove all the sump retaining bolts. Since there are nineteen

12.5 Undo the upper and lower retaining bolts and remove the dipstick guide tube

12.8b Crankcase splash plate retaining bolt locations (arrowed)

25.0 mm bolts and seven 110.0 mm bolts, remove each bolt in turn, and store it in its correct fitted order by pushing it through a clearly-marked cardboard template. This will avoid the possibility of installing the bolts in the wrong locations on refitting.

8 Break the joint by striking the sump with the palm of your hand. Lower the sump, and withdraw it from underneath the vehicle. While the sump is removed, take the opportunity to check the oil pump pick-up/strainer for signs of clogging or splitting. If necessary, remove the pump as described in Section 13, and clean or renew the strainer. Also unbolt the oil baffle plate from the bottom of the main bearing ladder, noting which way round it is fitted **(see illustrations)**. Note that the sump is located on a dowel.

Refitting

9 Where removed, refit the baffle plate to the

12.8a Oil pump pick-up tube retaining nuts and retaining bolt locations (arrowed)

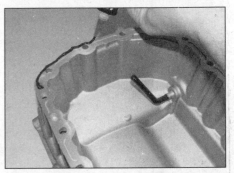

12.12 Apply a thin bead of RTV sealant to the sump mating surface

main bearing ladder and tighten the bolts securely.

10 Where removed, refit the oil pump and pick-up/strainer with reference to Section 13.

11 Clean all traces of sealant/gasket from the mating surfaces of the main bearing ladder and sump, then use a clean rag to wipe out the sump and the engine's interior.

12 Ensure that the sump mating surfaces are clean and dry, then apply a thin coating of suitable sealant to the sump mating surface **(see illustration)**.

13 Check that the location dowel is in place, then refit the sump onto the main bearing ladder and insert the bolts and finger-tighten them at this stage, so that it is still possible to move the sump. Make sure the bolts are refitted in their correct locations **(see illustrations)**.

14 Using a straight-edge, align the flywheel end of the sump with the main bearing ladder

12.13a Four of the long sump retaining bolts are fitted at the transmission end . . .

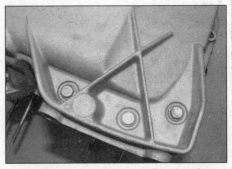

12.13b . . . and three are fitted at the timing belt end on the oil filter side

12.14 Use a straight-edge to ensure that the rear faces of the cylinder block and sump are flush

13.3 Oil pump housing retaining bolt locations (arrowed)

13.4a Slide the oil pump drive collar off the crankshaft . . .

and cylinder block, then progressively tighten the sump bolts to the specified torque **(see illustration)**.

15 Check that the oil drain plug is tightened securely, then refit the engine undertray and lower the vehicle to the ground.

16 Reconnect the battery negative lead.

17 Refill the engine with oil as described in Chapter 1A.

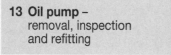

13 Oil pump –
removal, inspection and refitting

Removal

1 Remove the timing belt and crankshaft sprocket as described in Sections 7 and 8.

2 Remove the sump and oil pump pick-up/strainer as described in Section 12.

3 Unscrew the nine bolts securing the oil pump to the main bearing ladder and cylinder block, then withdraw the oil pump over the nose of the crankshaft **(see illustration)**. Note it is located on dowels, and therefore it may be necessary to carefully prise it away to release it.

4 Slide the oil pump drive collar off the end of the crankshaft and collect the O-ring located behind the collar **(see illustrations)**.

5 With the oil pump removed, note the fitted depth of the crankshaft oil seal, then drive it from the oil pump housing. A new oil seal must be obtained for refitting.

Inspection

6 At the time of writing, checking specifications for the oil pump were not available, however, if the oil pump is to be re-used, the internal gears should be cleaned. To do this, unbolt the cover, then mark the gears for location and remove them **(see**

illustrations). Clean the gears and inspect them for damage and excessive wear.

7 Lubricate the gears with oil, then refit them in their locations noted during removal. Refit the cover and tighten the bolts securely.

8 Thoroughly clean the oil pump strainer with a suitable solvent, and check it for signs of clogging or splitting. If the strainer is damaged, the strainer and cover assembly must be renewed.

Refitting

9 Clean the mating surfaces of the oil pump and main bearing ladder/cylinder block. heck that the locating dowels are in position on the pump flange then locate a new O-ring over the oil pump outlet stub **(see illustration)**.

10 Apply a thin coating of suitable sealant to the mating face of the oil pump housing **(see illustration)**.

11 Prime the oil pump by injecting clean

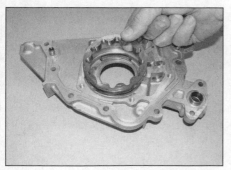

13.4b . . . and collect the O-ring located behind the collar

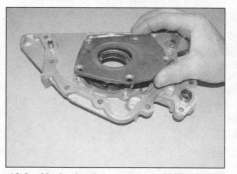

13.6a Undo the five screws and lift off the oil pump rear cover

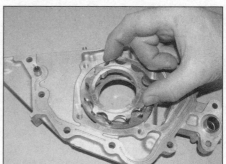

13.6b Remove the inner rotor . . .

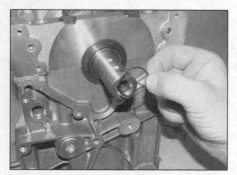

13.6c . . . and outer rotor from the pump housing

13.9 Locate a new O-ring over the oil pump outlet stub

13.10 Apply a thin bead of RTV sealant to the oil pump mating surface

engine oil into the outlet stub, then place the pump in position on the cylinder block, engaging the locating dowels.

12 Apply thread locking compound to the threads of the nine oil pump retaining bolts, then refit the bolts and tighten them to the specified torque.

13 Position a new oil pump drive collar O-ring on the end of the crankshaft **(see illustration)**.

14 Lubricate the sealing lips of the new crankshaft right-hand oil seal and carefully fit the seal over the oil pump drive collar **(see illustrations)**. Note that the open part of the seal must be towards the shoulder of the drive collar.

15 Slide the drive collar over the end of the crankshaft and engage it with the oil pump inner rotor **(see illustration)**. As the collar engages with the pump inner rotor, push the oil seal initially into place in the oil pump housing. Tap the seal fully into position using a suitable drift.

16 Refit the pick-up/strainer, sump and crankshaft sprocket as described in Section 12, and the timing belt as described in Sections 7 and 8.

17 Before starting the engine, prime the oil pump as follows. Disconnect the fuel injector wiring connectors, then spin the engine on the starter until the oil pressure light goes out. Reconnect the injector wiring on completion.

13.13 Position a new oil pump drive collar O-ring on the end of the crankshaft

13.14a Lubricate the sealing lips of the new crankshaft right-hand oil seal . . .

13.14b . . . and carefully fit the seal over the oil pump drive collar

13.15 Slide the drive collar onto the crankshaft and engage it with the oil pump inner rotor

14 Crankshaft oil seals – renewal

Right-hand oil seal

1 Remove the crankshaft sprocket and (where fitted) spacer, referring to Section 8. Secure the timing belt clear of the working area, so that it cannot be contaminated with oil. Make a note of the correct fitted depth of the seal in its housing.

2 Punch or drill two small holes opposite each other in the seal. Screw a self-tapping screw into each, and pull on the screws with pliers to extract the seal. Alternatively, the seal can be levered out of position. Use a flat-bladed screwdriver, and take great care not to damage the crankshaft shoulder or seal housing.

3 Clean the seal housing, and polish off any

burrs or raised edges, which may have caused the seal to fail in the first place.

4 Lubricate the lips of the new seal with clean engine oil, and carefully locate the seal on the end of the crankshaft. Note that its sealing lip must be facing inwards. Take care not to damage the seal lips during fitting.

5 Fit the new seal using a suitable tubular drift, such as a socket, which bears only on the hard outer edge of the seal. Tap the seal into position, to the same depth in the housing as the original was prior to removal **(see illustration)**.

6 Wash off any traces of oil, then refit the crankshaft sprocket as described in Section 8.

Left-hand oil seal

7 Remove the flywheel/driveplate as described in Section 15. Make a note of the correct fitted depth of the seal in its housing.

8 Punch or drill two small holes opposite

each other in the seal. Screw a self-tapping screw into each, and pull on the screws with pliers to extract the seal.

9 Clean the seal housing, and polish off any burrs or raised edges, which may have caused the seal to fail in the first place.

10 Lubricate the lips of the new seal with clean engine oil, and carefully locate the seal on the end of the crankshaft. The new seal will normally be supplied with a plastic fitting sleeve to protect the seal lips as the seal is fitted. If so, lubricate the fitting sleeve and locate it over the end of the crankshaft **(see illustration)**.

11 Lubricate the lips of the new seal with clean engine oil, and carefully locate the seal over the fitting sleeve and onto the end of the crankshaft **(see illustration)**. Drive the seal into position, to the same depth in the housing as the original was prior to removal.

12 Wash off any traces of oil, then refit the flywheel/driveplate as described in Section 15.

14.5 Tap the crankshaft right-hand oil seal into position using a suitable drift

14.10 Lubricate the crankshaft left-hand oil seal fitting sleeve and locate it over the end of the crankshaft

14.11 Locate the oil seal over the fitting sleeve and onto the end of the crankshaft

15 Flywheel/driveplate – removal, inspection and refitting

Removal

Flywheel

1 Remove the transmission as described in Chapter 7A, then remove the clutch assembly as described in Chapter 6.

2 Prevent the flywheel from turning by locking the ring gear teeth with a similar arrangement to that shown in illustration 8.8a. Alternatively, bolt a strap between the flywheel and the cylinder block/crankcase. *Do not* attempt to lock the flywheel in position using the crankshaft pulley locking pin described in Section 3.

3 Slacken and remove the flywheel retaining bolts, and remove the flywheel from the end of the crankshaft. Be careful not to drop it; it is heavy. If the flywheel locating dowel is a loose fit in the crankshaft end, remove it and store it with the flywheel for safe-keeping. Discard the flywheel bolts; new ones must be used on refitting.

Driveplate

4 Remove the transmission as described in Chapter 7B. Lock the driveplate as described in paragraph 2. Mark the relationship between the torque converter plate and the driveplate, and slacken all the driveplate retaining bolts.

5 Remove the retaining bolts, along with the torque converter plate and (where fitted) the two shims (one fitted on each side of the torque converter plate). Note that the shims are of different thickness, the thicker one being on the outside of the torque converter plate. Discard the driveplate retaining bolts; new ones must be used on refitting.

6 Remove the driveplate from the end of the crankshaft. If the locating dowel is a loose fit in the crankshaft end, remove it and store it with the driveplate for safe-keeping.

Inspection

7 On models with manual transmission, examine the flywheel for scoring of the clutch face, and for wear or chipping of the ring gear teeth. If the clutch face is scored, the flywheel may be surface-ground, but renewal is preferable. Seek the advice of a Peugeot dealer or engine reconditioning specialist to see if machining is possible. If the ring gear is worn or damaged, the flywheel must be renewed, as it is not possible to renew the ring gear separately.

8 On models with automatic transmission, check the torque converter driveplate carefully for signs of distortion. Look for any hairline cracks around the bolt holes or radiating outwards from the centre, and inspect the ring gear teeth for signs of wear or chipping. If any sign of wear or damage is found, the driveplate must be renewed.

Refitting

Flywheel

9 Clean the mating surfaces of the flywheel and crankshaft. Remove any remaining locking compound from the threads of the crankshaft holes, using the correct-size tap, if available.

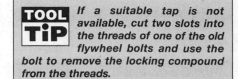

TOOL TiP *If a suitable tap is not available, cut two slots into the threads of one of the old flywheel bolts and use the bolt to remove the locking compound from the threads.*

10 If the new flywheel retaining bolts are not supplied with their threads already precoated, apply a suitable thread-locking compound to the threads of each bolt.

11 Ensure the locating dowel is in position. Offer up the flywheel, locating it on the dowel, and fit the new retaining bolts.

12 Lock the flywheel using the method employed on dismantling, and tighten the retaining bolts to the specified torque and angle.

13 Refit the clutch as described in Chapter 6. Remove the flywheel locking tool, and refit the transmission as described in Chapter 7A.

Driveplate

14 Carry out the operations described above in paragraphs 9 and 10, substituting 'driveplate' for all references to the flywheel.

15 Locate the driveplate on its locating dowel.

16 Offer up the torque converter plate, with the thinner shim positioned behind the plate and the thicker shim on the outside, and align the marks made prior to removal.

17 Fit the new retaining bolts, then lock the driveplate using the method employed on dismantling. Tighten the retaining bolts to the specified torque wrench setting and angle.

18 Remove the driveplate locking tool, and refit the transmission as described in Chapter 7B.

16 Engine/transmission mountings – inspection and renewal

Inspection

1 If improved access is required, raise the front of the car and support it securely on axle stands.

2 Check the mounting rubber to see if it is cracked, hardened or separated from the metal at any point; renew the mounting if any such damage or deterioration is evident.

3 Check that all the mounting's fasteners are securely tightened; use a torque wrench to check if possible.

4 Using a large screwdriver or a crowbar, check for wear in the mounting by carefully levering against it to check for free play.

Where this is not possible, enlist the aid of an assistant to move the engine/transmission unit back-and-forth, or from side-to-side, while you watch the mounting. While some free play is to be expected even from new components, excessive wear should be obvious. If excessive free play is found, check first that the fasteners are correctly secured, then renew any worn components as described below.

Renewal

Right-hand mounting

5 Disconnect the battery negative lead (refer to *Disconnecting the battery* at the end of this manual). Release all the relevant hoses and wiring from their retaining clips. Place the hoses/wiring clear of the mounting so that the removal procedure is not hindered.

6 Place a jack beneath the engine, with a block of wood on the jack head. Raise the jack until it is supporting the weight of the engine.

7 Slacken and remove the two nuts and two bolts securing the right-hand engine/transmission mounting bracket to the engine. Remove the single nut securing the bracket to the mounting rubber.

8 Undo the bolt securing the upper engine movement limiter to the right-hand mounting bracket, and the four bolts securing the movement limiter mounting bracket to the body. Lift away the right-hand mounting bracket and the movement limiter assembly.

9 Lift the rubber buffer plate off the mounting rubber stud, then unscrew the mounting rubber from the body and remove it from the vehicle. If necessary, the mounting bracket can be unbolted and removed from the front of the cylinder block.

10 Check all components carefully for signs of wear or damage, and renew as necessary.

11 On reassembly, screw the mounting rubber into the vehicle body, and tighten it securely. Refit the mounting bracket to the front of the cylinder head, and securely tighten its retaining bolts.

12 Refit the engine movement limiter assembly to the engine mounting bracket and to the body and tighten the bolts securely.

13 Refit the rubber buffer plate to the mounting rubber stud, and install the mounting bracket.

14 Tighten the mounting bracket retaining nuts to the specified torque setting. Remove the jack from underneath the engine and reconnect the battery.

Left-hand mounting

15 Remove the air cleaner assembly, as described in Chapter 4A.

16 Place a jack beneath the transmission, with a block of wood on the jack head. Raise the jack until it is supporting the weight of the transmission.

17 Slacken and remove the centre nut and washer from the left-hand mounting, then undo the nuts securing the mounting in position and remove it from the engine compartment **(see illustration)**.

18 If necessary, slide the spacer (where fitted) off the mounting stud, then unscrew the stud from the top of the transmission housing, and remove it along with its washer. If the mounting stud is tight, a universal stud extractor can be used to unscrew it.

19 Check all components carefully for signs of wear or damage, and renew as necessary.

20 Clean the threads of the mounting stud, and apply a coat of thread-locking compound to its threads. Refit the stud and washer to the top of the transmission, and tighten it securely.

21 Slide the spacer (where fitted) onto the mounting stud, then refit the rubber mounting. Tighten both the mounting-to-body bolts and the mounting centre nut to their specified torque settings, and remove the jack from underneath the transmission.

22 Refit the air cleaner assembly as described in Chapter 4A.

Lower engine movement limiter

23 If not already done, chock the rear wheels, then jack up the front of the vehicle and support it securely on axle stands.

16.17 Left-hand engine mounting

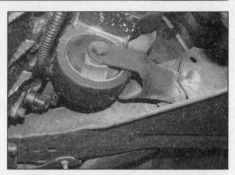

16.24 Lower engine movement limiter

24 Unscrew and remove the bolt securing the movement limiter link to the driveshaft intermediate bearing housing **(see illustration)**.

25 Remove the bolt securing the link to the subframe. Withdraw the link.

26 To remove the intermediate bearing housing assembly it will first be necessary to remove the right-hand driveshaft as described in Chapter 8.

27 With the driveshaft removed, undo the retaining bolts and remove the bearing

housing from the rear of the cylinder block.

28 Check carefully for signs of wear or damage on all components, and renew them where necessary.

29 On reassembly, fit the bearing housing assembly to the rear of the cylinder block, and tighten its retaining bolts securely. Refit the driveshaft as described in Chapter 8.

30 Refit the movement limiter link, and tighten both its bolts to their specified torque settings.

31 Lower the vehicle to the ground.

Chapter 2 Part C:
Diesel engine in-car repair procedures

Contents

Camshaft(s), rocker arms and hydraulic tappets – removal, inspection and refitting 9
Compression and leakdown tests – description and interpretation . 2
Crankshaft pulley – removal and refitting 5
Cylinder head – removal and refitting 10
Cylinder head cover – removal and refitting 4
Engine assembly/valve timing holes – general information and usage 3
Engine oil and filter renewal . . . . See Chapter 1B
Engine oil level check . . . . See Weekly checks
Engine/transmission mountings – inspection and renewal 17
Flywheel/driveplate – removal, inspection and refitting 16
General information 1
Oil cooler – removal and refitting 13
Oil level, temperature and pressure sensors – general 15
Oil pump – removal, inspection and refitting 12
Oil seals – renewal 14
Sump – removal and refitting 11
Timing belt – removal, inspection, refitting and tensioning 7
Timing belt covers – removal and refitting 6
Timing belt sprockets and tensioner – removal and refitting 8

Degrees of difficulty

Easy, suitable for novice with little experience		**Fairly easy,** suitable for beginner with some experience		**Fairly difficult,** suitable for competent DIY mechanic		**Difficult,** suitable for experienced DIY mechanic		**Very difficult,** suitable for expert DIY or professional	

Specifications

General

Designation:

2.0 litre (1997 cc engine)	DW10TD
2.0 litre (1997 cc engine)	DW10ATED
2.2 litre (2179 cc engine)	DW12TED4

Engine codes*:

2.0 litre engine	RHY (DW10TD/L3)
2.0 litre engine	RHZ (DW10ATED/L3)
2.2 litre engine	4HX (DW12TED4/L4)

Bore:

2.0 litre engine	85.00 mm
2.2 litre engine	85.00 mm

Stroke:

2.0 litre engine	88.00 mm
2.2 litre engine	96.00 mm
Direction of crankshaft rotation	Clockwise (viewed from the right-hand side of vehicle)
No 1 cylinder location	At the transmission end of block

Compression ratio:

2.0 litre engine	17.6 : 1
2.2 litre engine	18.0 : 1

* The engine code is stamped on a plate attached to the front of the cylinder block, next to the oil filter

Compression pressures (engine hot, at cranking speed)

Normal	25 to 30 bars (363 to 435 psi)
Minimum	18 bars (261 psi)
Maximum difference between any two cylinders	5 bars (73 psi)

Timing belt

	2.0 litre engine	2.2 litre engine
Tension setting (see text – Section 7):		
Initial setting	98 ± 2 SEEM units	106 ± 2 SEEM units
Final setting	54 ± 3 SEEM units	51 ± 3 SEEM units

Camshaft(s)

Drive	Toothed belt
No of bearings per camshaft	6
Endfloat (bearing No 3)	0.07 to 0.168 mm

Lubrication system

Oil pump type	Gear-type, chain-driven off the crankshaft right-hand end
Minimum oil pressure at 80°C	4.0 bars at 4000 rpm, 2.0 bars at 2000 rpm
Oil pressure warning switch operating pressure	0.8 bars

Torque wrench settings

	Nm	lbf ft
2.0 litre engine		
Big-end bearing cap nuts*:		
Stage 1	20	15
Stage 2	Angle-tighten a further 70°	
Camshaft bearing housing bolts	10	7
Camshaft sprocket hub-to-camshaft bolts	43	32
Camshaft sprocket-to-hub bolts	20	15
Clutch bellhousing closure plate	18	13
Coolant outlet manifold:		
Stage 1 – studs	25	18
Stage 2 – stud nuts	20	15
Stage 3 – 3 bolts	20	15
Crankshaft pulley bolt:		
Stage 1	50	37
Stage 2	Angle-tighten a further 62°	
Crankshaft right-hand oil seal housing bolts	14	10
Cylinder head bolts:		
Stage 1	22	16
Stage 2	60	44
Stage 3	Slacken 180° in reverse sequence	
Stage 4	60	44
Stage 5	Angle-tighten a further 220° ± 5°	
Cylinder head cover bolts	10	7
Engine-to-transmission fixing bolts	45	33
Flywheel/driveplate bolts*	50	37
High-pressure fuel pump sprocket nut	50	37
Left-hand engine/transmission mounting:		
Rubber mounting-to-body bolts	21	15
Mounting bracket-to-transmission bolts	50	37
Rubber mounting centre nut	65	48
Main bearing cap bolts:		
Stage 1	25	18
Stage 2	Angle-tighten a further 60°	
Oil pump mounting bolts	18	13
Piston oil jet spray tube bolt	10	7
Rear engine torque reaction link bolts:		
Link to engine	50	37
Link to body	60	44
Mounting assembly-to-block bolts	45	33
Rear engine/transmission mounting:		
Connecting link-to-mounting assembly nut/bolt	45	33
Connecting link-to-subframe nut/bolt	45	33
Right-hand engine mounting:		
Mounting to body and engine lower mounting bracket	45	33
Lower mounting bracket to cylinder head:		
Uppermost	45	
Lower	20	
Right-hand engine torque reaction link bolts	45	33
Sump bolts	16	12
Timing belt idler roller bolt	25	18
Timing belt tensioner	23	17

New nuts/bolts must be used.

Torque wrench settings (continued)

	Nm	lbf ft
2.2 litre engines (where different to 2.0 litre engine)		
Big-end bearing cap nuts:		
Stage 1	10	7
Stage 2	Slacken by 180°	
Stage 3	23	17
Stage 4	Angle-tighten a further 45° ± 5°	
Camshaft bearing housing:		
Stage 1 – studs	10	7
Stage 2 – bolts	5	4
Stage 3 – bolts	10	7
Crankshaft pulley bolt:		
Stage 1	70	52
Stage 2	Angle-tighten a further 82°	
Cylinder head cover:		
Stage 1	5	
Stage 2	10	7
Exhaust manifold:		
Stage 1	15	11
Stage 2	30	22
Flywheel:		
Stage 1	15	11
Stage 2	47	35
Hub-mounted pulley	20	15
Lower cylinder block:		
Stage 1	10	7
Stage 2	16	12
Main bearing cap:		
Stage 1	25	18
Stage 2	Angle-tighten a further 60° ± 5°	
Oil cooler	58	43
Oil pump:		
Stage 1	7	5
Stage 2	9	7
Piston skirt spray jets	10	7
Right-hand engine mounting:		
Stage 1	10	7
Stage 2 – 8.0 mm diameter bolts	20	15
Stage 3 – 10.0 mm diameter bolts	45	33
Timing belt guide roller:		
Stage 1	15	11
Stage 2	43	32
Timing belt tensioner roller	25	18
Turbocharger lubrication pipe:		
Engine side	30	22
Turbocharger side	20	15

1 General information

How to use this Chapter

This Part of Chapter 2 describes the repair procedures that can reasonably be carried out on the engine while it remains in the vehicle. If the engine has been removed from the vehicle and is being dismantled as described in Part D, any preliminary dismantling procedures can be ignored.

Note that, while it may be possible physically to overhaul items such as the piston/connecting rod assemblies while the engine is in the car, such tasks are not usually carried out as separate operations. Usually, several additional procedures are required (not to mention the cleaning of components and oil ways); for this reason, all such tasks are classed as major overhaul procedures, and are described in Part D of this Chapter. .

Part D describes the removal of the engine/ transmission from the car, and the full overhaul procedures that can then be carried out.

DW series engine

The DW series engine is a relatively new power unit based on the well-proven XUD series engine which has appeared in many Peugeot and Citroën vehicles. In particular, the cylinder block components are very similar to the XUD, however, the remainder of the engine has been completely redesigned. The DW10 engine is of single overhead camshaft design, but the DW12 engine is of double overhead camshaft, 16-valve design.

The turbocharged, four-cylinder engine is mounted transversely, with the transmission mounted on the left-hand side.

On the 2.0 litre DW10 engine, a toothed timing belt drives the camshaft, high-pressure fuel pump and coolant pump. The camshaft operates the inlet and exhaust valves via rocker arms which are supported at their pivot ends by hydraulic self-adjusting tappets. The camshaft is supported by six bearings machined directly in the cylinder head and camshaft bearing housing.

On the 2.2 litre DW12 engine, a toothed timing belt drives the exhaust camshaft, high-pressure fuel pump and coolant pump, and the inlet camshaft is driven by chain from the right-hand end of the exhaust camshaft. A hydraulic tensioner controls the tension of the camshaft chain; it incorporates an internal valve which retains pressure when the engine is stopped.

On both engines, the high-pressure fuel pump supplies fuel to the fuel rail, and subsequently to the electronically-controlled injectors which inject the fuel direct into the combustion chambers. This design differs from the previous type where an injection pump supplies the fuel at high-pressure to each injector. The earlier, conventional type injection pump required fine calibration and timing, and these functions are now completed by the high-pressure pump, electronic injectors and engine management ECU.

On the 2.2 litre DW12 engine, the cylinder head incorporates inlet ducts which are designed to apply 'swirl' to the inlet air as it enters the combustion chambers; in addition 'swirl' control butterflies are fitted in the head to provide variable a 'swirl' action according to operating conditions. One inlet valve in each cylinder is supplied with air through a short inlet duct, and the second inlet valve is supplied with air through a long inlet duct, controlled by the 'swirl' butterflies.

The crankshaft runs in five main bearings of the usual shell type. Endfloat is controlled by thrust washers either side of No 2 main bearing.

The 2.2 litre DW12 engine is equipped with two balance shafts which are located beneath the crankshaft, and are rotated by a large gear on the crankshaft engaged with the rearmost balance shaft. The front balance shaft is geared to the rear shaft and therefore rotates in the opposite direction.

The pistons are selected to be of matching weight, and incorporate fully-floating gudgeon pins retained by circlips.

The oil pump is chain-driven from the right-hand end of the crankshaft and an oil cooler is fitted to all engines.

Throughout the manual, it is often necessary to identify the engines not only by their cubic capacity, but also by their engine code. The engine code, consists of three letters (eg, DW10). The code is stamped on a plate attached to the front of the cylinder block.

Repair operations precaution

The engine is a complex unit with numerous accessories and ancillary components. The design of the engine compartment is such that every conceivable space has been utilised, and access to virtually all of the engine components is extremely limited. In many cases, ancillary components will have to be removed, or moved to one side, and wiring, pipes and hoses will have to be disconnected or removed from various cable clips and support brackets.

When working on this engine, read through the entire procedure first, look at the car and engine at the same time, and establish whether you have the necessary tools, equipment, skill and patience to proceed. Allow considerable time for any operation, and be prepared for the unexpected. Any

major work on these engines is not for the faint-hearted!

Because of the limited access, many of the engine photographs appearing in this Chapter were, by necessity, taken with the engine removed from the vehicle.

⚠️ **Warning: It is essential to observe strict precautions when working on the fuel system components of the engine, particularly the high-pressure side of the system. Before carrying out any engine operations that entail working on, or near, any part of the fuel system, refer to the special information given in Chapter 4B, Section 2.**

Repair operations possible with the engine in the vehicle

a) Compression pressure – testing.
b) Cylinder head cover(s) – removal and refitting.
c) Crankshaft pulley – removal and refitting.
d) Timing belt covers – removal and refitting.
e) Timing belt – removal, refitting and adjustment.
f) Timing belt tensioner and sprockets – removal and refitting.
g) Camshaft oil seal – renewal.
h) Camshaft, rocker arms and hydraulic tappets – removal, inspection and refitting.
i) Sump – removal and refitting.
j) Oil pump – removal and refitting.
k) Crankshaft oil seals – renewal.
l) Engine/transmission mountings – inspection and renewal.
m) Flywheel/driveplate – removal, inspection and refitting.

2 Compression and leakdown tests – description and interpretation

Compression test

Note: *A compression tester specifically designed for diesel engines must be used for this test.*

1 When engine performance is down, or if misfiring occurs which cannot be attributed to the fuel system, a compression test can provide diagnostic clues as to the engine's condition. If the test is performed regularly, it can give warning of trouble before any other symptoms become apparent.

2 A compression tester specifically intended for diesel engines must be used, because of the higher pressures involved. The tester is connected to an adapter which screws into the glow plug or injector hole. On these engines, an adapter suitable for use in the glow plug holes will be required, so as not to disturb the fuel system components. It is unlikely to be worthwhile buying such a tester for occasional use, but it may be possible to borrow or hire one – if not, have the test performed by a garage.

3 Unless specific instructions to the contrary are supplied with the tester, observe the following points:

a) *The battery must be in a good state of charge, the air filter must be clean, and the engine should be at normal operating temperature.*
b) *All the glow plugs should be removed as described in Chapter 5C before starting the test.*
c) *The wiring connector on the engine management system ECU (located in the plastic box behind the battery) must be disconnected.*

4 The compression pressures measured are not so important as the balance between cylinders. Values are given in the Specifications.

5 The cause of poor compression is less easy to establish on a diesel engine than on a petrol one. The effect of introducing oil into the cylinders ('wet' testing) is not conclusive, because there is a risk that the oil will sit in the swirl chamber or in the recess on the piston crown instead of passing to the rings. However, the following can be used as a rough guide to diagnosis.

6 All cylinders should produce very similar pressures; any difference greater than that specified indicates the existence of a fault. Note that the compression should build-up quickly in a healthy engine; low compression on the first stroke, followed by gradually-increasing pressure on successive strokes, indicates worn piston rings. A low compression reading on the first stroke, which does not build-up during successive strokes, indicates leaking valves or a blown head gasket (a cracked head could also be the cause). Deposits on the undersides of the valve heads can also cause low compression.

7 A low reading from two adjacent cylinders is almost certainly due to the head gasket having blown between them; the presence of coolant in the engine oil will confirm this.

8 If the compression reading is unusually high, the cylinder head surfaces, valves and pistons are probably coated with carbon deposits. If this is the case, the cylinder head should be removed and decarbonised (see Part D).

Leakdown test

9 A leakdown test measures the rate at which compressed air fed into the cylinder is lost. It is an alternative to a compression test, and in many ways it is better, since the escaping air provides easy identification of where pressure loss is occurring (piston rings, valves or head gasket).

10 The equipment needed for leakdown testing is unlikely to be available to the home mechanic. If poor compression is suspected, have the test performed by a suitably-equipped garage.

3 Engine assembly/valve timing holes – general information and usage

General

Note: *Do not attempt to rotate the engine whilst the crankshaft and camshaft are locked in position. If the engine is to be left in this state for a long period of time, it is a good idea to place suitable warning notices inside the vehicle, and in the engine compartment. This will reduce the possibility of the engine being accidentally cranked on the starter motor, which is likely to cause damage with the locking pins in place.*

1 Timing holes or slots are located only in the flywheel/driveplate and camshaft sprocket hub. The holes/slots are used to align the crank-shaft and camshaft at the TDC position for Nos 1 and 4 pistons. This will ensure that the valve timing is maintained during operations that require removal and refitting of the timing belt. When the holes/slots are aligned with their corresponding holes in the cylinder block and cylinder head, suitable diameter bolts/pins can be inserted to lock the crankshaft and camshaft in position, preventing rotation. Note: With the timing holes aligned, No 4 piston is at TDC on its compression stroke.

2 Note that the HDi type fuel system used on these engines does not have a conventional diesel injection pump, but instead uses a high-pressure fuel pump that does not have to be timed. The alignment of the fuel pump sprocket (and hence the fuel pump itself) with respect to crankshaft and camshaft position, is therefore irrelevant.

3 To align the engine assembly/valve timing holes, proceed as follows.

4 Remove the upper and intermediate timing belt covers.

5 Apply the handbrake, then jack up the front of the vehicle and support it on axle stands (see *Jacking and vehicle support*). Remove the right-hand front roadwheel.

6 To gain access to the crankshaft pulley, to enable the engine to be turned, the wheelarch plastic liner must be removed. The liner is

3.7a Use a mirror to observe the camshaft sprocket hub timing slot (DW10 engine)

secured by various screws and clips under the wheelarch. Release all the fasteners, and remove liner from under the front wing. Where necessary, unclip the coolant hoses from under the wing to improve access further. The crank-shaft can then be turned using a suitable socket and extension bar fitted to the pulley bolt.

7 Turn the crankshaft until the timing slot in the camshaft sprocket hub is aligned with the corresponding hole in the cylinder head. Note that the crankshaft must always be turned in a clockwise direction (viewed from the right-hand side of vehicle). Use a small mirror so that the position of the sprocket hub timing slot can be observed **(see illustrations)**. When the slot is aligned with the corresponding hole in the cylinder head, the engine is positioned at TDC for Nos 1 and 4 pistons. Note: Make sure that the centre part of the slot is aligned with the hole in the cylinder head, as it is possible to incorrectly align the area to each side of the slot.

8 Insert an 8 mm diameter bolt, rod or drill through the hole in the left-hand flange of the cylinder block by the starter motor; if necessary, carefully turn the crankshaft either way until the rod enters the timing hole in the flywheel/driveplate **(see illustrations)**.

9 Insert an 8 mm bolt, rod or drill through the hole in the camshaft sprocket hub and into engagement with the cylinder head **(see illustration)**. Note that the TDC hole is located at the 8 o'clock position on the DW10 engine, whereas on the DW12 engine it is located at the 4 o'clock position.

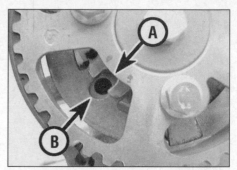

3.7b Camshaft sprocket hub timing slot (A) aligned with the cylinder head timing hole (B) (DW10 engine)

10 The crankshaft and camshaft are now locked in position, preventing unnecessary rotation.

4 Cylinder head cover – removal and refitting

Removal

1 Remove the engine top cover(s).

2 On the DW10 engine, remove the timing belt upper cover. On the DW12 engine, remove the bolt securing the upper timing cover to the top cover.

3 As applicable, slacken or release the clips securing the crankcase ventilation hoses to the cylinder cover and disconnect the hoses.

4 On the DW10 engine, undo the bolts and move the engine cover and cable guide support bracket clear of the right-hand end of the cylinder head cover.

5 Disconnect the camshaft position sensor wiring connector.

6 Release the wiring harness from the clip on the cylinder head cover and move the harness to one side.

7 Progressively unscrew the bolts securing the cylinder head cover to the camshaft carrier or inlet manifold (as applicable) and collect the washers. Carefully lift off the cover taking care not to damage the camshaft position sensor as the cover is removed. Recover the seal from the cover.

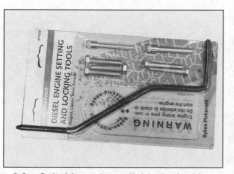

3.8a Suitable tools available for locking the engine in the TDC position

3.8b Rod (arrowed) inserted through the cylinder block into the flywheel timing hole (DW12 engine)

3.9 Insert an 8 mm bolt (arrowed) through the sprocket timing slot and into the cylinder head to lock the camshaft (DW10 engine)

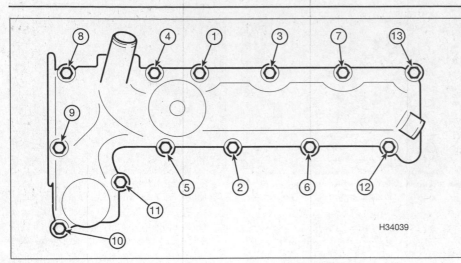

H34039

4.8 Cylinder head cover bolt tightening sequence (DW12 engine)

Refitting

8 Refitting is a reversal of removal, bearing in mind the following points:

a) Examine the cover seal for signs of damage and deterioration, and renew if necessary.

b) Tighten the cylinder head cover bolts to the specified torque in the order shown **(see illustration)**.

c) Before refitting the timing belt upper cover, adjust the camshaft position sensor air gap as described in Chapter 4B, Section 13.

5 Crankshaft pulley – removal and refitting

Removal

1 Remove the auxiliary drivebelt as described in Chapter 1B. Turn the tensioner anti-clockwise and insert a pin or drill to hold it away from the drivebelt **(see illustration)**.

2 To prevent crankshaft turning whilst the pulley retaining bolt is being slackened on manual transmission models, select top gear and have an assistant apply the brakes firmly.

Alternatively, the flywheel/driveplate ring gear can be locked using a suitable tool made from steel angle **(see illustration)**. Remove the cover plate from the base of the transmission bellhousing and bolt the tool to the bellhousing flange so it engages with the ring gear teeth. *Do not* attempt to lock the pulley by inserting a bolt/drill through the timing hole. If the timing hole bolt/drill is in position from a previous operation, temporarily remove it prior to slackening the pulley bolt, then refit it once the bolt has been slackened.

3 Using a suitable socket and extension bar, unscrew the retaining bolt, remove the washer, then slide the pulley off the end of the crankshaft **(see illustration)**. If the pulley is tight fit, it can be drawn off the crankshaft using a suitable puller. If a puller is being used, refit the pulley retaining bolt without the washer, to avoid damaging the crankshaft as the puller is tightened.

4 If the pulley locating Woodruff key is a loose fit, remove it and store it with the pulley for safe-keeping.

Refitting

5 Ensure that the Woodruff key is correctly located in its crankshaft groove, then refit the pulley to the end of the crankshaft.

6 Thoroughly clean the threads of the pulley retaining bolt, then apply a coat of locking compound to the bolt threads. Peugeot recommend the use of Loctite (available from your Peugeot dealer); in the absence of this, any good-quality locking compound may be used.

7 Refit the crankshaft pulley retaining bolt and

5.1 Turn the tensioner anti-clockwise and insert a pin or drill to hold it away from the drivebelt

5.2 Use a fabricated tool similar to this to lock the flywheel ring gear and prevent crankshaft rotation

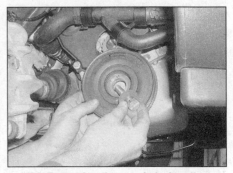

5.3 Removing the crankshaft pulley (DW10 engine)

5.7a Refit the crankshaft pulley retaining bolt after applying locking compound to the threads (DW10 engine)

5.7b Tighten the pulley bolt to the specified Stage 1 torque . . .

5.7c . . . then through the specified Stage 2 angle (DW10 engine)

6.2 Disconnect the fuel supply and return hose quick-release fittings (DW10 engine)

6.3 Release the two fuel hoses from the retaining clips on the timing belt upper cover (DW10 engine)

6.5 Bolt securing the upper cover to the cylinder head cover (DW12 engine)

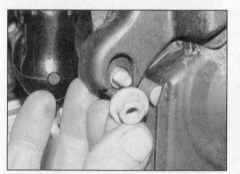

6.7 Removing the lower nut from the stud (DW12 engine)

6.8 Removing the central bolt (DW12 engine)

6.9 Removing the timing belt upper cover . . .

washer. Tighten the bolt to the specified torque, then through the specified angle, preventing the crankshaft from turning using the method employed on removal (see illustrations).

8 Refit and tension the auxiliary drivebelt as described in Chapter 1B.

 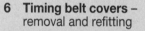

6 Timing belt covers – removal and refitting

⚠️ **Warning: Refer to the pre-cautionary information contained in Section 1 before proceeding.**

Note: *Access to the timing belt covers may be improved by first removing the right-hand engine mounting (see Section 17).*

Removal

Upper cover

1 Disconnect the battery negative lead (refer to *Disconnecting the battery* at the end of this manual).

2 At the connections above the fuel pump, disconnect the fuel supply and return hose quick-release fittings using a small screwdriver to release the locking clip (see illustration). Cover the open unions to prevent dirt entry, using small plastic bags, or fingers cut from clean rubber gloves.

3 Release the two hoses from the retaining clips on the upper timing belt cover and move them to one side (see illustration).

4 Release the EGR solenoid valve vacuum hose from the clip on the upper cover.

5 Undo the bolt securing the upper cover to the cylinder head cover (see illustration).

6 Undo the upper bolt on the edge of the cover nearest to the engine compartment bulkhead.

7 Undo the lower bolt/nut on the bulkhead side of the cover, at the join between the upper and lower covers (see illustration). Note that this bolt/stud also retains the coolant pump. Where a bolt is fitted, to avoid coolant leakage after the upper cover is removed, refit the bolt fitted with a 17.0 mm spacer, and tighten it securely.

8 Undo the remaining bolt in the centre of the cover (see illustration).

9 Disengage the upper cover from the intermediate cover and manipulate the upper cover from its location (see illustration).

Intermediate cover

10 Remove the upper cover as described previously.

6.12 . . . intermediate cover . . .

11 Undo the upper bolt on the top edge of the intermediate cover.

12 Undo the two remaining bolts at the join between the intermediate cover and lower cover, then manipulate the intermediate cover from its location (see illustration).

Lower cover

13 Remove the upper and intermediate covers as described previously.

14 Remove the crankshaft pulley as described in Section 5.

15 Undo the two remaining bolts on the edge of the cover, one on either side of the crankshaft pulley location.

16 Lift the cover off the front of the engine (see illustration).

Refitting

17 Refitting of all the covers is a reversal of the relevant removal procedure, ensuring that

6.16 . . . and lower cover (DW12 engine)

7.7 Removing the front wheelarch liner

7.8 Removing the auxiliary drivebelt

7.9 Removing the turbocharger air inlet pipe

each cover section is correctly located, and that the cover retaining bolts are securely tightened. Ensure that all disturbed hoses are reconnected and retained by their relevant clips.

7 Timing belt – removal, inspection, refitting and tensioning

Note: *Peugeot specify the use of an electronic belt tension checking tool (SEEM CTG 105.M) to correctly set the timing belt tension. The following procedure assumes that this equipment (or suitable alternative equipment calibrated to display belt tension in SEEM units) is available. Accurate tensioning of the timing belt is essential, and if the electronic equipment is not available, it is recommended that the work is entrusted to a Peugeot dealer or suitably-equipped garage.*

General

1 The timing belt drives the camshaft(s), high-pressure fuel pump, and coolant pump from a toothed sprocket on the end of the crankshaft. If the belt breaks or slips in service, the pistons are likely to hit the valve heads, resulting in expensive damage.

2 The timing belt should be renewed at the specified intervals, or earlier if it is contaminated with oil, or at all noisy in operation (a 'scraping' noise due to uneven wear).

3 If the timing belt is being removed, it is a wise precaution to check the condition of the coolant pump at the same time (check for signs of coolant leakage). This may avoid the need to remove the timing belt again at a later stage, should the coolant pump fail.

Removal

4 Apply the handbrake, then jack up the front of the vehicle and support it on axle stands (see *Jacking and vehicle support*). Remove the front right-hand roadwheel.

5 Disconnect the battery negative lead (refer to *Disconnecting the battery* at the end of this manual).

6 Refer to Chapter 4B and remove the complete exhaust system.

Caution: If the exhaust system is not removed, the front pipe flexible section will be damaged when the right-hand engine mounting is detached.

7 Remove the front right-hand wheelarch liner **(see illustration)**.

8 Remove the auxiliary drivebelt as described in Chapter 1B **(see illustration)**.

9 Remove the turbocharger air inlet pipe **(see illustration)**.

10 Unbolt the closure plate from the bottom of the clutch housing

11 Using a suitable tool, lock the flywheel/driveplate, then loosen the crankshaft pulley bolt. Peugeot technicians use a tool which engages the teeth of the starter ring gear and is bolted to the clutch bellhousing. A similar tool may be made out of a length of angle-iron, bent to engage the teeth, or alternatively an assistant may restrain the starter ring gear with a wide-blade screwdriver.

12 Unscrew and remove the crankshaft

pulley bolt, then remove the pulley from the crankshaft **(see illustrations)**. If it is tight, refit the bolt without its washer, leaving sufficient room to release the pulley. Using a puller, remove the pulley from the front of the crankshaft.

13 Unbolt and remove the engine rear torque reaction link.

14 An 8.0 mm diameter flywheel/driveplate locking pin is now required, and may be obtained from a Peugeot dealer or car accessory shop. Note that the locking pin for the DW10TD is different to the pin for DW10ATED and DW12TED4 engines. The pin for the DW10ATED and DW12TED4 engines incorporates a retaining coil spring.

15 Temporarily refit the crankshaft pulley bolt, then turn the engine until the TDC hole in the flywheel/driveplate is aligned with the hole in the front (DW10) or rear (DW12) engine flange (next to the transmission bellhousing). Insert the locking pin to lock the engine.

16 Remove the engine top cover(s).

17 Remove the engine management ECU (see Chapter 4B, Section 13) and the housing from the front right-hand corner of the engine compartment.

18 Unbolt and remove the right-hand engine mounting torque reaction link. The engine will still be supported by the bracket on the rubber mounting. Note that the mounting bracket is slotted so the front bolt need only be loosened **(see illustrations)**.

19 Disconnect the fuel supply and return hoses from the fuel rail, then tape over or plug the hoses and rail to prevent entry of dust and dirt.

7.12a Unscrew the crankshaft pulley bolt . . .

7.12b . . . then remove the pulley

7.18a Unscrew the bolts . . .

7.18b . . . and remove the right-hand engine mounting torque reaction link

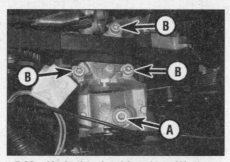

7.22a Undo the shouldered nut (A), then unscrew the Torx bolts (B) from the engine . . .

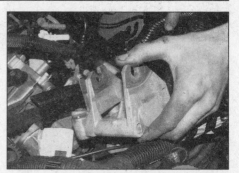

7.22b . . . and remove the right-hand mounting bracket

7.23a Release the wiring loom . . .

7.23b . . . then unbolt the upper . . .

7.23c . . . intermediate . . .

20 The engine must now be supported while the right-hand engine mounting bracket is removed. To do this, either use a trolley jack and block of wood beneath the sump, or an engine lifting hoist. Whichever method is

7.23d . . . and lower timing covers

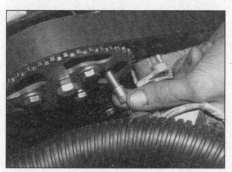

7.24 Inserting the TDC pin through the camshaft sprocket hole (DW12 engine)

used, make sure the engine is adequately supported.
21 As a precaution against damage to the radiator, place a card or piece of hardboard over it on the engine side.
22 Unscrew the shouldered nut securing the right-hand engine mounting bracket to the flexible rubber mounting, then unbolt the bracket from the engine (**see illustrations**). Note that the bracket is located on the engine with two dowels.
23 Release the wiring loom support from the upper timing cover, then unbolt and remove

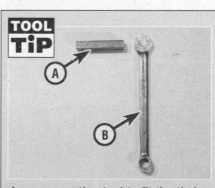

TOOL TIP

A square section tool to fit the timing belt tensioner pulley can be made from a length of standard 10 mm door handle rod (A), obtained from a DIY shop, and then cut to size. Once the rod has been fitted to the tensioner, the timing belt can be tensioned by turning the rod with an 10 mm spanner (B).

the upper, intermediate and lower timing covers (**see illustrations**).
24 Insert a suitable drill or metal dowel through the TDC hole in the camshaft sprocket flange, and into the cylinder head (**see illustration**). Note on the DW10 engine the hole is positioned at 8 o'clock but on the DW12 engine it is at the 4 o'clock position.
25 Loosen the bolt on the tensioner roller, and turn the tensioner clockwise to release the tension on the timing belt. If available, use a 10 mm square drive extension in the hole provided, to turn the tensioner bracket against the spring tension (**see Tool Tip**). Retighten the bolt sufficiently to hold the tensioner in its released position; do not fully tighten the bolt in this position.
26 Mark the timing belt with an arrow to indicate its running direction, if it is to be re-used. Remove the belt from the sprockets (**see illustrations**).

7.26a Removing the timing belt (DW10 engine)

7.26b Removing the timing belt (DW12 engine)

7.29 Slacken the three camshaft sprocket-to-sprocket hub retaining bolts (DW10 engine)

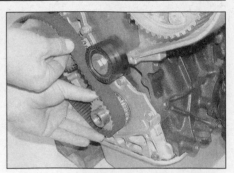

7.31a Retain the timing belt on the crankshaft sprocket and feed it around the idler roller . . .

7.31b . . . high-pressure fuel pump sprocket . . .

7.31c . . . camshaft sprocket . . .

7.31d . . . coolant pump and tensioner pulley (DW10 engine)

Inspection

27 Check the timing belt carefully for any signs of uneven wear, splits or oil contamination. Pay particular attention to the roots of the teeth. Renew it if there is the slightest doubt about its condition. If the engine is undergoing an overhaul, and has covered more than 36 000 miles (60 000 km) with the existing belt fitted, renew the belt as a matter of course, regardless of its apparent condition. The cost of a new belt is nothing compared with the cost of repairs, should the belt break in service. If signs of oil contamination are found, trace the source of the oil leak and rectify it. Wash down the engine timing belt area and all related components, to remove all traces of oil. Check that the tensioner and idler pulleys rotate freely without any sign of roughness, and also check that the coolant pump pulley rotates freely. If necessary, renew these items.

Refitting and tensioning

28 Commence refitting by ensuring that the TDC timing pins are still in position correctly.
29 Loosen the three bolts securing the camshaft sprocket to the camshaft, so that the sprocket can be turned on its hub (see illustration). To do this, either use a tool engaged with the holes in the sprocket, or alternatively, hold the sprocket with an old timing belt.
30 Finger-tighten the sprocket bolts, then slacken each bolt by one sixth of a turn. Turn the sprocket clockwise to the end of the slots.
31 Locate the timing belt on the crankshaft pulley splines, then, keeping it taut, locate it around the idler pulley and onto the high-pressure pump pulley (see illustrations). If refitting the old belt, make sure that the direction arrow is pointing in the normal rotation of the engine. Peugeot technicians

use a plastic clip to retain the belt on the crankshaft pulley; if necessary, use a plastic cable tie to hold it.
32 Locate the belt onto the camshaft pulley splines. If the teeth do not align correctly, turn the camshaft sprocket slightly anti-clockwise until the belt engages. **Note:** *Do not turn the pulley anti-clockwise more than one tooth space.*
33 Continue to locate the belt onto the tensioner pulley and coolant pump splines, then loosen the bolt and turn the tensioner *anti-clockwise* to tension the belt moderately. Pretighten the bolt to 1.0 Nm, then remove the holding clip or cable tie.
34 A timing belt tension setting tool is now required to apply the correct tension. A tool which checks SEEM units is necessary, and should be fitted to the belt run between the camshaft sprocket and high-pressure pump sprocket.
35 Loosen the bolt, then turn the tensioner *anti-clockwise* until 98.0 ± 2.0 SEEM units (DW10 engine) or 106 ± 2.0 SEEM units (DW12 engine) is read on the tool (see illustrations). At this point, tighten the tensioner bolt to the specified torque. **Note:** *In our workshops, it was found impossible to achieve the specified SEEM units on the DW12 engine, as there was insufficient movement of the tensioner. We therefore set it to the maximum possible, before the tensioner reached the apex of its movement.*
36 Temporarily remove one of the three bolts securing the sprocket to the camshaft, and check that the bolts are not at the anti-

7.35a Pivot the tensioner pulley anti-clockwise, then tighten the retaining bolt . . .

7.35b . . . when the specified tension value is shown on the tensioning measuring equipment

clockwise limit of their slots. If they are, repeat the refitting procedure.

37 Tighten the camshaft sprocket bolts to the specified torque.

38 Remove the crankshaft and camshaft TDC setting pins. Also remove the tensioning tool.

39 Turn the engine clockwise 8 times. Do not turn the engine anti-clockwise during this operation.

40 Refit the crankshaft and camshaft TDC setting pins.

41 Loosen the camshaft sprocket bolts again, then finger-tighten them, and loosen each by one sixth of a turn.

42 Refit the tensioning tool midway between the camshaft and high-pressure pump sprocket.

43 Loosen the tensioner bolt, then turn the tensioner anti-clockwise until the tool reads 54.0 ± 2.0 SEEM units (DW10 engine) or 51.0 ± 3.0 SEEM units (DW12 engine). With the tensioner held in this position, tighten the bolt to the specified torque. It is important to apply the correct tension to the timing belt, otherwise the belt may be noisy in operation, or worse still, may break.

44 Tighten the camshaft sprocket bolts to the specified torque.

45 Remove the tensioning tool to release its internal forces, then refit it and check the tension of the belt is between 51.0 and 57.0 SEEM units (DW10 engine) or between 48.0 and 54.0 SEEM units (DW12 engine). If necessary, repeat the tensioning procedure.

46 Remove the tensioning tool and TDC setting pins.

47 Turn the engine clockwise 2 times. Do not turn the engine anti-clockwise during this operation.

48 Refit the crankshaft and camshaft TDC setting/locking pins.

49 Visually check that the offset between the camshaft hub hole and the corresponding setting hole does not exceed 1.0 mm.

50 Remove the TDC setting/locking pins.

51 Refit the lower, intermediate and upper timing covers.

52 Refit the right-hand engine mounting and torque reaction link, tightening the bolts to the specified torque.

53 Remove the protective card from the radiator and also remove the trolley jack from beneath the engine.

54 Reconnect the fuel supply and return hoses to the fuel rail.

55 Refit the ECU control unit housing.

56 Refit the engine management ECU and the engine top cover.

57 Refit the engine rear torque reaction link and tighten the bolts to the specified torque.

58 Locate the crankshaft pulley on the front of the crankshaft.

59 Before refitting the crankshaft pulley bolt, it is recommended that both the threads of the bolt and crankshaft and cleaned of any remaining locking fluid. With the threads clean, apply fresh locking fluid to the bolt threads.

60 Lock the flywheel/driveplate using the method used for removal, then insert the crankshaft pulley bolt and tighten it to its Stage 1 torque. Using an angle-tightening tool, tighten the bolt to the Stage 2 setting. Using the torque wrench, check that the bolt is tightened to at least 195 Nm (144 lbf ft).

61 Refit the closure plate to the bottom of the clutch housing and tighten the bolts securely.

62 Refit the turbocharger pipe.

63 Refit the auxiliary drivebelt with reference to Chapter 1B.

64 Refit the front right-hand wheelarch liner.

65 Refit the exhaust system. Check the mountings and if necessary renew them.

66 Reconnect the battery negative lead (refer to *Disconnecting the battery* at the end of this manual).

67 Refit the roadwheel and lower the vehicle to the ground.

8 Timing belt sprockets and tensioner – removal and refitting

Camshaft sprocket

Removal

1 Remove the crankshaft pulley as described in Section 5. Refit the pulley retaining bolt to allow the engine to be turned in subsequent operations.

2 Remove the upper, intermediate and lower timing belt covers as described in Section 6.

3 Align the engine assembly/valve timing holes as described in Section 3, and lock the camshaft sprocket hub and flywheel/driveplate in position.

4 Loosen the timing belt tensioner pulley retaining bolt. Allow the pulley to pivot in a clockwise direction, to relieve the tension from the timing belt. Retighten the tensioner pulley retaining bolt to secure it in the slackened position.

5 Disengage the timing belt from the camshaft sprocket and position it clear, taking care not to bend or twist the belt sharply.

6 Remove the locking tool from the camshaft sprocket hub. Slacken the sprocket hub retaining bolt, and the three sprocket-to-hub retaining bolts. To prevent the camshaft rotating as the bolts are slackened, a sprocket holding tool will be required. In the absence of the special Peugeot tool, an acceptable substitute can be fabricated at home (see **Tool Tip 1**). *Do not* attempt to use the engine assembly/valve timing locking tool to prevent the sprocket from rotating whilst the bolt is slackened.

7 Remove the sprocket hub retaining bolt and washer, and slide the sprocket and hub off the end of the camshaft **(see illustration)**. If the Woodruff key is a loose fit in the camshaft, remove it for safe-keeping. Examine the camshaft oil seal for signs of oil leakage and, if necessary, renew it as described in Section 14.

Tool Tip 1: *A sprocket holding tool can be made from two lengths of steel strip bolted together to form a forked end. Bend the ends of the strip through 90° to form the fork 'prongs'.*

8 If necessary, the sprocket can be separated from the hub after removing the three retaining bolts.

9 Clean the camshaft sprocket thoroughly, and renew it if there are any signs of wear, damage or cracks.

Refitting

10 If removed, refit the sprocket to the hub and secure with the three retaining bolts, tightened finger tight only at this stage.

11 Where applicable, refit the Woodruff key to the end of the camshaft, then refit the camshaft sprocket and hub.

12 Refit the sprocket hub retaining bolt and washer. Tighten the bolt to the specified torque, preventing the camshaft from turning as during removal.

13 Align the engine assembly/valve timing slot in the camshaft sprocket hub with the hole in the cylinder head and refit the 8 mm bolt to lock the camshaft in position.

14 Fit the timing belt around the pump sprocket and camshaft sprocket, and tension the timing belt as described in Section 7.

Crankshaft sprocket

Removal

15 Align the engine assembly/valve timing holes as described in Section 3, but do not lock the camshaft sprocket hub or flywheel/driveplate in position at this stage.

8.7 Removing the camshaft sprocket hub (DW12 engine)

8.21a Slide the crankshaft sprocket off the end of the crankshaft . . .

16 Remove the crankshaft pulley as described in Section 5. Refit the pulley retaining bolt to allow the engine to be turned in subsequent operations.

17 Remove the timing belt upper, intermediate and lower covers as described in Section 6.

18 Check that the engine assembly/valve timing holes are still aligned as described in Section 3, and lock the camshaft sprocket hub and flywheel/driveplate in position.

19 Loosen the timing belt tensioner pulley retaining bolt. Allow the pulley to pivot in a clockwise direction, to relieve the tension from the timing belt. Retighten the tensioner pulley retaining bolt to secure it in the slackened position.

20 Disengage the timing belt from the crankshaft sprocket and position it clear, taking care not to bend or twist the belt sharply.

21 Slide the sprocket off the end of the crankshaft and collect the Woodruff key **(see illustrations)**.

22 Examine the crankshaft oil seal for signs of oil leakage and, if necessary, renew it as described in Section 14.

23 Clean the crankshaft sprocket thoroughly, and renew it if there are any signs of wear, damage or cracks.

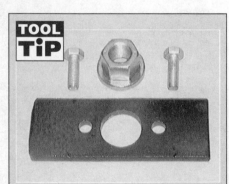

TOOL TiP

Tool Tip 2: Make a sprocket releasing tool from a short strip of steel. Drill two holes in the strip to correspond with the two holes in the sprocket. Drill a third hole just large enough to accept the flats of the sprocket retaining nut.

8.21b . . . and collect the Woodruff key (DW10 engine)

Refitting

24 Refit the Woodruff key to the end of the crankshaft, then refit the crankshaft sprocket (with the flange nearest the cylinder block).

25 Fit the timing belt around the crankshaft sprocket, and tension the timing belt as described in Section 7.

Fuel pump sprocket

Removal

26 Remove the crankshaft pulley as described in Section 5. Refit the pulley retaining bolt to allow the engine to be turned in subsequent operations.

27 Remove the upper, intermediate and lower timing belt covers as described in Section 6.

28 Align the engine assembly/valve timing holes as described in Section 3, and lock the camshaft sprocket hub and flywheel/driveplate in position.

29 Loosen the timing belt tensioner pulley retaining bolt. Allow the pulley to pivot in a clockwise direction, to relieve the tension from the timing belt. Retighten the tensioner pulley retaining bolt to secure it in the slackened position.

30 Disengage the timing belt from the high-pressure fuel pump sprocket and position it clear, taking care not to bend or twist the belt sharply.

31 Using a suitable socket, undo the pump sprocket retaining nut. The sprocket can be held stationary as the nut is slackened using a suitable forked tool engaged with the holes in the sprocket **(see Tool Tip 1)**.

8.33 Using the home-made tools to remove the fuel pump sprocket (DW10 engine)

32 The pump sprocket is a taper fit on the pump shaft and it will be necessary to make up another tool to release it from the taper **(see Tool Tip 2)**.

33 Partially unscrew the sprocket retaining nut, fit the home-made tool, and secure it to the sprocket with two suitable bolts. Prevent the sprocket from rotating as before, and unscrew the sprocket retaining nut **(see illustration)**. The nut will bear against the tool as it is undone, forcing the sprocket off the shaft taper. Once the taper is released, remove the tool, unscrew the nut fully, and remove the sprocket from the pump shaft.

34 Clean the sprocket thoroughly, and renew it if there are any signs of wear, damage or cracks.

Refitting

35 Refit the pump sprocket and retaining nut, and tighten the nut to the specified torque. Prevent the sprocket rotating as the nut is tightened using the sprocket holding tool.

36 Fit the timing belt around the pump sprocket, and tension the timing belt as described in Section 7.

Coolant pump sprocket

37 The coolant pump sprocket is integral with the pump, and cannot be removed.

Tensioner pulley

Removal

38 Remove the upper and intermediate timing belt covers as described in Section 6.

39 Align the engine assembly/valve timing holes as described in Section 3, and lock the camshaft sprocket hub and flywheel/driveplate in position.

40 Loosen the timing belt tensioner pulley retaining bolt. Allow the pulley to pivot in a clockwise direction, to relieve the tension from the timing belt.

41 Remove the tensioner pulley retaining bolt, and slide the pulley off its mounting stud.

42 Clean the tensioner pulley, but do not use any strong solvent which may enter the pulley bearings. Check that the pulley rotates freely, with no sign of stiffness or free play. Renew the pulley if there is any doubt about its condition, or if there are any obvious signs of wear or damage.

43 Examine the pulley mounting stud for signs of damage and if necessary, renew it.

Refitting

44 Refit the tensioner pulley to its mounting stud, and fit the retaining bolt.

45 Fit the timing belt around the pulley, and tension the timing belt as described in Section 7.

Idler roller

Removal

46 Remove the crankshaft pulley as described in Section 5. Refit the pulley retaining bolt to allow the engine to be turned in subsequent operations.

9.14 Remove the camshaft bearing housing from the cylinder head . . .

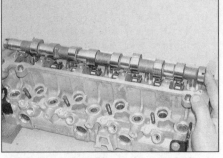

9.15 . . . then lift out the camshaft (DW10 engine)

9.17 Lift out the rocker arms . . .

47 Remove the upper, intermediate and lower timing belt covers as described in Section 6.

48 Align the engine assembly/valve timing holes as described in Section 3, and lock the camshaft sprocket hub and flywheel/driveplate in position.

49 Loosen the timing belt tensioner pulley retaining bolt. Allow the pulley to pivot in a clockwise direction, to relieve the tension from the timing belt. Retighten the tensioner pulley retaining bolt to secure it in the slackened position.

50 Undo the retaining bolt and withdraw the idler roller from the engine.

51 Clean the idler roller, but do not use any strong solvent which may enter the bearings. Check that the roller rotates freely, with no sign of stiffness or free play. Renew the idler roller if there is any doubt about its condition, or if there are any obvious signs of wear or damage.

Refitting

52 Locate the idler roller on the engine, and fit the retaining bolt. Tighten the bolt to the specified torque.

53 Fit the timing belt around the idler roller, and tension the timing belt as described in Section 7.

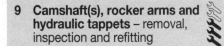

9 Camshaft(s), rocker arms and hydraulic tappets – removal, inspection and refitting

Removal

1 Remove the engine top cover.

2 Remove the air cleaner assembly and air inlet duct as described in Chapter 4B.

3 On the DW10ATED engine, remove the intercooler air duct from the left-hand end of the cylinder head.

4 Remove the timing belt as described in Section 7.

5 Refit the right-hand engine mounting, but only tighten the bolts moderately; this will keep the engine supported during the camshaft removal.

6 Disconnect the crankcase ventilation hose from the cylinder head cover.

7 Disconnect the wiring from the camshaft position sensor on the timing end of the cover.

8 Unbolt and remove the timing cover bracket.

9 Hold the camshaft sprocket stationary, then unscrew and remove the sprocket centre bolt and withdraw the sprocket.

2.0 litre (DW10) engine

10 Working in a spiral fashion starting at the left-hand end and finishing in the middle, progressively unscrew the bolts securing the cover to the camshaft bearing housing (refer to Section 4). Withdraw the cover.

11 Disconnect the vacuum pipe from the brake vacuum pump on the left-hand end of the cylinder head.

12 Remove the vacuum pump from the cylinder head with reference to Chapter 9.

13 Progressively loosen the camshaft bearing cap housing bolts until they can be removed.

14 Withdraw the bearing cap housing from the cylinder head. The housing is likely to be initially tight to release as it is located by two dowels on the forward facing side of the cylinder head. If necessary, very carefully prise up the housing using a screwdriver inserted in the slotted lug adjacent to each dowel location. Once the bearing housing is free, lift it squarely from the cylinder head (**see illustration**). The camshaft will rise up slightly under the pressure of the valve springs – be careful it doesn't tilt and jam in the cylinder head or bearing housing section.

15 Carefully lift the camshaft from its location and remove the oil seal (**see illustration**). Discard the seal, a new one should be used on refitting.

16 Obtain eight small, clean plastic containers, and number them 1 to 8; alternatively, divide a larger container into eight compartments.

17 Lift out each rocker arm and release it from the spring clip on the tappet. Place the rocker arms in their respective positions in the box or containers (**see illustration**).

18 A compartmentalised container filled with engine oil is now required to retain the hydraulic tappets while they are removed from the cylinder head. Using a rubber sucker, withdraw each hydraulic follower and place it in the container, keeping them each identified for correct refitting (**see illustrations**). The tappets must be totally submerged in the oil to prevent air entering them.

2.2 litre (DW12) engine

19 Remove the injectors as described in Chapter 4B. This work includes removing the pipes from the high-pressure fuel common rail. Plug the injector holes to prevent dropping any item into the combustion chambers.

20 Progressively loosen the bolts securing the cylinder head cover to the camshaft bearing housing. Withdraw the cover.

21 Disconnect the vacuum pipe from the brake vacuum pump on the left-hand end of the cylinder head.

22 Remove the vacuum pump from the cylinder head with reference to Chapter 9.

23 Progressively loosen the camshaft bearing cap housing bolts and studs until they can be removed. Note the location of the studs.

9.18a . . . followed by the hydraulic tappets . . .

9.18b . . . and place all the components in their respective positions in a box

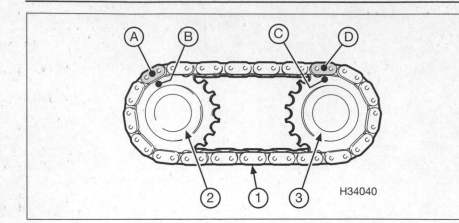

9.26a Camshaft chain timing marks (DW12 engine)

1 Chain	A Exhaust camshaft mark on chain
2 Exhaust camshaft	B Exhaust camshaft mark on tooth
3 Inlet camshaft	C Inlet camshaft mark on tooth
	D Inlet camshaft mark on chain

9.26b The timing mark is highlighted on the camshaft tooth

24 Unbolt and remove the camshaft hydraulic chain tensioner. **Note:** *Do not separate the pad from the tensioner, as the sealing lip will be damaged – use a cable tie to hold the spring-tensioned pad in the body. On later models, it is possible to insert a 1.5 mm diameter pin through the body and pad of the tensioner to hold all of the components together.*

25 Withdraw the bearing cap housing from the cylinder head. The housing is likely to be initially tight to release as it is located by dowels. If necessary, very carefully prise up the housing using a screwdriver inserted in the slotted lug adjacent to each dowel location. Once the bearing housing is free, lift it squarely from the cylinder head. The camshaft will rise up slightly under the pressure of the valve springs – be careful it doesn't tilt and jam in the cylinder head or bearing housing section.

26 Check that the camshafts and chain are marked in relation to each other – the chain should have two black or copper links which align with marks on the teeth. If necessary, mark the chain and teeth with dabs of paint. The marks on the teeth are the most important as they determine the valve timing, however the

chain links can be marked as they are 7 links (inclusive) apart **(see illustrations)**.

27 Simultaneously, lift the camshafts and chain from the cylinder head. Release the camshafts from the chain.

28 Obtain sixteen small, clean plastic containers, and number them 1 to 16; alternatively, divide a larger container into sixteen compartments.

29 Lift out each rocker arm and release it from the spring clip on the tappet. Place the rocker arms in their respective positions in the box or containers.

30 A compartmentalised container filled with engine oil is now required to retain the hydraulic tappets while they are removed from the cylinder head. Using a rubber sucker, withdraw each hydraulic follower and place it in the container, keeping them each identified for correct refitting. The tappets must be totally submerged in the oil to prevent air entering them.

Inspection

31 Inspect the cam lobes and the camshaft bearing journals for scoring or other visible evidence of wear. Once the surface hardening of the cam lobes has been eroded, wear will occur at an accelerated rate. **Note:** *If these symptoms are visible on the tips of the camshaft lobes, check the corresponding rocker arm, as it will probably be worn as well.*

32 Examine the condition of the bearing surfaces in the cylinder head and camshaft bearing housing. If wear is evident, the cylinder head and bearing housing will both have to be renewed, as they are a matched assembly.

33 Inspect the rocker arms and tappets for scuffing, cracking or other damage and renew any components as necessary. Also check the condition of the tappet bores in the cylinder head. As with the camshafts, any wear in this area will necessitate cylinder head renewal.

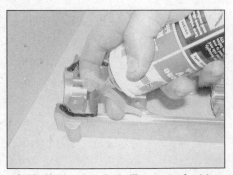

9.43 Apply a bead of silicone sealant to the mating face of the camshaft bearing housing (DW10 engine)

Refitting

34 Thoroughly clean the sealant from the mating surfaces of the cylinder head and camshaft bearing housing. Use a suitable liquid gasket dissolving agent (available from Peugeot dealers) together with a soft putty knife; do not use a metal scraper or the faces will be damaged. As there is no conventional gasket used, the cleanliness of the mating faces is of the utmost importance.

35 Clean off any oil, dirt or grease from both components and dry with a clean lint-free cloth. Ensure that all the oil ways are completely clean.

36 To prevent any possibility of the valves contacting the pistons as the camshaft is refitted, remove the locking pin/drill from the flywheel/driveplate and turn the crankshaft a quarter turn in the *opposite* direction to normal rotation (ie, anti-clockwise) to position all the pistons at mid-stroke.

37 Liberally lubricate the hydraulic tappet bores in the cylinder head with clean engine oil.

38 Insert the hydraulic tappets into their original bores in the cylinder head unless they have been renewed.

39 Lubricate the rocker arms and place them over their respective tappets and valve stems. Ensure that the ends of the rocker arms engage with the spring clips on the tappets.

40 Lubricate the camshaft bearing journals in the cylinder head sparingly with oil, taking care not to allow the oil to spill over onto the camshaft bearing housing contact areas.

2.0 litre (DW10) engine

41 Lay the camshaft in the cylinder head and position it so that the engine assembly/valve timing slot in the sprocket hub is approximately aligned with the timing hole in the cylinder head.

42 Ensure that the mating faces of the cylinder head and camshaft bearing housing are clean and free of any oil or grease.

43 Sparingly apply a bead of silicone sealant to the mating face of the camshaft bearing housing, taking care not to allow the product to contaminate the camshaft bearing journal areas **(see illustration)**.

44 Locate the bearing housing over the camshaft and into position on the cylinder head.

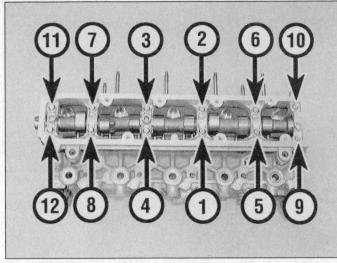

9.45 Camshaft bearing housing bolt tightening sequence (DW10 engine)

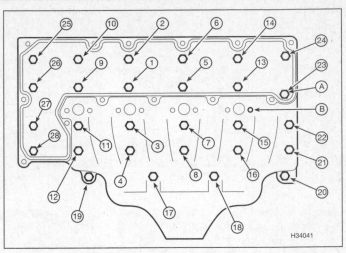

9.51 Camshaft bearing housing bolt tightening sequence (DW12 engine)

A Bolt   *B Stud*

45 Insert all the bearing housing retaining bolts and *progressively* tighten them to the specified torque, in the sequence shown **(see illustration)**.

46 Refit the cylinder head cover as described in Section 4.

2.2 litre (DW12) engine

47 Engage the camshafts with the chain, making sure that the coloured links are aligned with the marked teeth, then lower them in position. The longer exhaust camshaft must go at the rear of the cylinder head.

48 Ensure that the mating faces of the cylinder head and camshaft bearing housing are clean and free of any oil or grease.

49 Sparingly apply a bead of silicone sealant to the mating face of the camshaft bearing housing, taking care not to allow the product to contaminate the camshaft bearing journal areas.

50 Locate the bearing housing over the camshafts and into position on the cylinder head.

51 Insert the bolts and studs in their correct positions, then *progressively* tighten them to the specified torque, in the sequence shown **(see illustration)**. The studs (for the injectors) must be tightened first, then the remaining bolts tightened in two stages.

52 Refit the camshaft chain tensioner and tighten the bolts securely. On later models, remove the pin to release the pad onto the chain.

53 Refit the cylinder head cover as described in Section 4.

54 Refit the injectors with reference to Chapter 4B.

All engines

55 Refit the brake vacuum pump and reconnect the vacuum pipe with reference to Chapter 9.

56 Smear the lips of the new oil seal with clean engine oil and fit it over the camshaft,

9.56a Locate a new oil seal over the camshaft, with its sealing lip facing inwards . . .

making sure its sealing lip is facing inwards. Press the seal into position until it is flush with the end face of the cylinder head. Use a suitable bolt (screwed into the end of the camshaft), washers and a tube or socket to press the seal into position **(see illustrations)**.

57 Make sure that the sprocket hub timing slot is aligned with the corresponding cut-out in the cylinder head.

58 Turn the crankshaft a quarter turn in the normal direction of rotation so that pistons 1 and 4 are again at TDC.

10.1a Depress the centre pin to remove the liner fixings

9.56b . . . then use a bolt and socket or similar arrangement to press the seal into place (DW10 engine)

59 Refit the camshaft sprocket as described in Section 8.

60 Refit the flywheel/driveplate and camshaft TDC locking pins.

61 Refit the timing belt as described in Section 7.

10 Cylinder head –
removal and refitting

Note: *This is an involved procedure, and it is suggested that the Section is read thoroughly before starting work. To aid refitting, make notes on the locations of all relevant brackets and the routing of hoses and cables before removal.*

Removal

1 Apply the handbrake, then jack up the front of the vehicle and support it on axle stands (see *Jacking and vehicle support*). Remove the front right-hand roadwheel, the front wheelarch liner **(see illustrations)**, and where applicable the engine undertray.

2 Disconnect the battery negative lead (refer

10.1b Removing the front wheelarch liner

10.2a Remove the battery cover . . .

10.2b . . . and disconnect the negative lead

10.3 Removing the engine top covers

10.4a Removing the inlet ducts from the front inlet elbow . . .

10.4b . . . and throttle housing

to *Disconnecting the battery* at the end of this manual) **(see illustrations)**.

3 Remove the engine top cover(s) **(see illustration)**, then drain the cooling system as described in Chapter 1B. For improved

access, remove the bonnet as described in Chapter 11.

4 Remove the air cleaner assembly, airflow meter and inlet air ducts as described in Chapter 4B. On the DW12 engine, unclip and

remove the inlet ducts from the throttle body, then remove the throttle body from the inlet manifold/camshaft cap housing with reference to Chapter 4B **(see illustrations)**.

5 Disconnect the quick-release fittings and

10.5a Disconnect the fuel hoses at the fuel filter . . .

10.5b . . . front of the engine . . .

10.5c . . . and bulkhead . . .

10.5d . . . then unclip and remove the fuel hoses

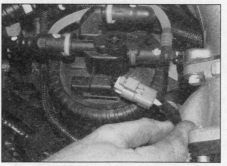

10.6a Disconnect the wiring . . .

10.6b . . . then unscrew the bolts . . .

10.6c . . . and remove the fuel filter . . .

10.6d . . . and mounting bracket

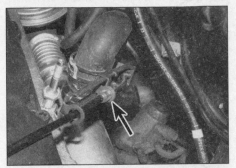

10.7a Using the special tool to remove the spring-type hose clips

10.7b Unscrew the mounting bolt . . .

10.7c . . . disconnect the hoses . . .

10.7d . . . then unbolt and remove the EGR valve assembly . . .

10.7e . . . and recover the gaskets

10.9 Disconnecting the shunt/wiring from the glow plugs

remove the fuel supply and return hoses from the fuel filter. If necessary, disconnect the hoses from the pipes at the bulkhead, then unclip and remove them **(see illustrations)**. Tape over or plug the hose ends and filter ports.

6 Disconnect the wiring then unbolt and remove the fuel filter together with its mounting bracket **(see illustrations)**.
7 On the DW12 engine, release the clips and disconnect the hoses from the EGR valve and

heat exchanger, then unbolt and remove the EGR valve from the inlet and exhaust manifolds and remove it together with the exchanger as an assembly. Recover the gaskets from the manifolds. The original hose clips are of the single spring type and are best removed using a hand-operated tool, however, grips can be used instead **(see illustrations)**.
8 Disconnect the wiring from the injectors and move the harness to one side.
9 Disconnect the wiring/shunt from the glow plugs and position away from the cylinder head **(see illustration)**, then remove the glow plugs with reference to Chapter 5C.
10 Disconnect and remove the crankcase ventilation hose(s) from the cylinder head **(see illustrations)**.
11 Remove the brake vacuum pump from the left-hand side of the cylinder head as described in Chapter 9 **(see illustrations)**.

10.10a Disconnecting the crankcase ventilation hose from the separator . . .

10.10b . . . and valve cover

10.11a Undo the bolts . . .

10.11b . . . and remove the brake vacuum pump from the cylinder head

10.12 Removing the camshaft position sensor

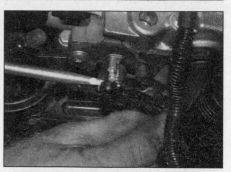

10.15a Use a screwdriver to prise the fitting from the butterfly control rod . . .

10.15b . . . then remove the 'swirl control' diaphragm and electrovalve

10.16a Unscrew the nuts . . .

10.16b . . . then remove the studs from the coolant outlet manifold

12 Disconnect the wiring from the camshaft position sensor then undo the screw and remove the sensor **(see illustration)**. Check that all relevant wiring is disconnected from the sensors on the cylinder head, then move the wiring harness to one side.

13 On the DW10 engine, unbolt and remove the bracket located over the high-pressure fuel pump.

14 On the DW10 engine, unscrew the bolts securing the oil level dipstick tube to the cylinder head.

15 On the DW12 engine, remove the 'swirl control' diaphragm and electrovalve **(see illustrations)**.

16 Unscrew the nuts on the two studs securing the coolant outlet manifold to the left-hand end of the cylinder head, then unscrew and remove the studs. Use a stud extractor or alternatively tighten two nuts together on the stud before unscrewing it. Note the location of brackets on the studs for correct refitting **(see illustrations)**.

17 Without disconnecting the hoses, unscrew the mounting bolts and move the coolant outlet manifold away from the left-hand end of the cylinder head **(see illustrations)**. If necessary, tie it to one side. Recover the seal.

18 Remove the timing belt as described in Section 7. Note that this work includes removing the auxiliary drivebelt, the crankshaft pulley, supporting the engine then removing the right-hand engine mounting.

19 Unscrew and remove the two bolts securing the right-hand engine mounting to the cylinder head **(see illustrations)**. Now temporarily refit the right-hand mounting onto the engine bracket and slightly tighten the bolts to hold the engine while the cylinder head is being removed. The engine support can now be removed.

20 Clean the area around the fuel supply and return line union connections to the high-pressure fuel pump, common rail and injectors. Unscrew the union nuts and remove the fuel lines. Tape over or plug the apertures in the pump, rail, lines and injectors to prevent entry of dust and dirt.

10.17a Unscrew the bolts . . .

10.17b . . . and move the coolant outlet manifold away from the left-hand end of the cylinder head

10.19a Unscrew and remove the two bolts securing the right-hand engine mounting to the cylinder head

10.19b View of the two bolts with the engine removed

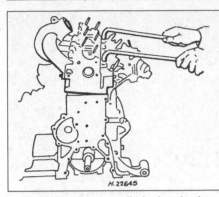

10.28 Freeing the cylinder head using angled rods

Caution: Do not attempt to unscrew the union adapters from the common rail or high-pressure fuel pump.

21 Remove the injectors from the cylinder head with reference to Chapter 4B.

22 At this stage, the manufacturers state that the turbocharger should be removed, however, this includes the removal of the front suspension subframe. On the DW12 diesel engine project car, we found that it was possible to unbolt the turbocharger from the exhaust manifold flange (2 nuts from underneath, 1 nut from above, and 1 horizontal mounting bolt) and leave the turbocharger attached to the exhaust system. The exhaust manifold can then be removed after the cylinder head is removed from the block. If necessary, the turbocharger can be disconnected from the exhaust downpipe, then tied to the rear of the engine compartment.

DW10 engine

23 Remove the camshaft sprocket with reference to Section 8.

24 Working in a spiral fashion starting at the left-hand end and finishing in the middle, progressively unscrew the bolts securing the cover to the cylinder head. Withdraw the cover.

25 Unbolt the bracket from the left-hand end of the head, near the lifting eye.

26 Progressively slacken the cylinder head bolts, in the reverse order to that shown for tightening **(see illustration 10.62)**. A Torx socket will be required for this.

27 When all the bolts are loose, unscrew

10.31 Removing the cover from the camshaft bearing cap housing (DW12 engine)

10.32b ... then unbolt and remove the sprocket ...

them fully and remove them from the cylinder head.

28 Release the cylinder head from the cylinder block and location dowels by rocking it. The Peugeot tool for doing this consists simply of two metal rods with 90-degree angled ends **(see illustration)**. Do not prise between the mating faces of the cylinder head and block, as this may damage the gasket faces.

29 Lift the cylinder head from the block, and recover the gasket.

30 If necessary, remove the inlet and exhaust manifolds with reference to Chapter 4B.

DW12 engine

31 Progressively unscrew the screws securing the cover to the camshaft bearing cap housing. Remove the cover and recover the gasket from the retaining groove **(see illustration)**.

32 Hold the camshaft sprocket stationary

10.32a Loosen the exhaust camshaft sprocket centre bolt ...

10.32c ... followed by the hub (DW12 engine)

using a suitable tool, then loosen the centre bolt from the exhaust camshaft sprocket hub. Unscrew the three screws and remove the sprocket from the hub, then unscrew the centre bolt and remove the hub from the camshaft **(see illustrations)**. **Note:** *Take care not to damage the camshaft position sensor pick-up with the tool.*

33 Unbolt the chain tensioner from the camshaft bearing cap housing and recover the spring **(see illustration)**.

34 Note the fitted position of the exhaust camshaft oil seal in the camshaft bearing cap housing, then progressively unscrew the 28 screws securing the camshaft bearing cap housing to the cylinder head in the reverse order to that given for fitting in Section 9 **(see illustration)**.

35 Using two injector mounting nuts tightened against each other, unscrew and remove the injector retaining studs **(see illustration)**.

10.33 Removing the chain tensioner (DW12 engine)

10.34 Remove the camshaft bearing cap housing retaining screws ...

10.35 ... then remove the injector retaining studs ...

10.36a . . . carefully lever with a screwdriver . . .

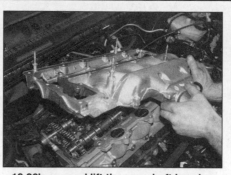

10.36b . . . and lift the camshaft bearing cap housing from the cylinder head (DW12 engine)

10.38 Removing the inlet and exhaust camshafts together with the chain (DW12 engine)

36 Carefully lift the camshaft bearing cap housing from the cylinder head, making sure that the camshafts remain in the head. If necessary, use a screwdriver on the special lug to carefully lever up the housing (see illustrations). Tap the camshafts down with the handle of a hammer if they remain in the camshaft bearing cap housing.

37 Check that the TDC marks are on the inlet and exhaust camshaft sprockets. The tops of two of the sprockets are marked with white paint, however the bright-links on the chain will not necessarily be aligned with the marks. Note that the timing can be set-up when the camshafts are refitted, because the TDC marks are positioned at a 7 link distance (inclusive) from each other. The sprocket hub is splined to the exhaust camshaft, therefore the timing can be set on refitting.

38 Carefully lift the inlet and exhaust camshafts from the cylinder head together with the chain (see illustration), then remove the oil seal from the end of the exhaust camshaft. Separate the chain from the camshafts.

39 Have ready a suitable container to put the hydraulic tappets and rockers in, so that they are identified for position for correct refitting. The tappets must be kept submersed in engine oil until they are refitted. Carefully remove the rockers and tappets and position them in the container (see illustration).

40 Progressively slacken the cylinder head bolts, in the reverse order to that shown for tightening (see illustration 10.62). A Torx socket will be required for this.

41 When all the bolts are loose, unscrew them fully and remove them from the cylinder head (see illustration).

42 Release the cylinder head from the cylinder block and location dowels by rocking it. The Peugeot tool for doing this consists simply of two metal rods with 90-degree angled ends (see illustration 10.28). Do not prise between the mating faces of the cylinder head and block, as this may damage the gasket faces.

43 Lift the cylinder head from the block, and recover the gasket (see illustration). It is quite heavy, and the help of an assistant is recommended.

44 If necessary, remove the exhaust manifold from the cylinder head with reference to Chapter 4B.

Preparation for refitting

45 The mating faces of the cylinder head and cylinder block must be perfectly clean before refitting the head. Peugeot recommend the use of a scouring agent for this purpose, but acceptable results can be achieved by using a hard plastic or wood scraper to remove all traces of gasket and carbon. The same method can be used to clean the piston crowns. Take particular care to avoid scoring or gouging the cylinder head/cylinder block mating surfaces during the cleaning operations, as aluminium alloy is easily damaged. Make sure that the carbon is not allowed to enter the oil and water passages – this is particularly important for the lubrication system, as carbon could block the oil supply

to the engine's components. Using adhesive tape and paper, seal the water, oil and bolt holes in the cylinder block. To prevent carbon entering the gap between the pistons and bores, smear a little grease in the gap. After cleaning each piston, use a small brush to remove all traces of grease and carbon from the gap, then wipe away the remainder with a clean rag.

46 Check the mating surfaces of the cylinder block and the cylinder head for nicks, deep scratches and other damage. If slight, they may be removed carefully with a file, but if excessive, machining may be the only alternative to renewal. If warpage of the cylinder head gasket surface is suspected, use a straight-edge to check it for distortion. Refer to Part D of this Chapter if necessary.

47 Thoroughly clean the threads of the cylinder head bolt holes in the cylinder block. Ensure that the bolts run freely in their threads, and that all traces of oil and water are removed from each bolt hole.

Gasket selection

48 Remove the crankshaft TDC timing pin, then turn the crankshaft until pistons 1 and 4 are at TDC. Position a dial test indicator (dial gauge) on the cylinder block adjacent to the rear of No 1 piston, and zero it on the block face. Transfer the probe to the crown of No 1 piston (10.0 mm in from the rear edge), then slowly turn the crankshaft back-and-forth past TDC, noting the highest reading on the indicator. Record this reading as protrusion A.

49 Repeat the check described in para-

10.39 Removing the rockers and hydraulic tappets (DW12 engine)

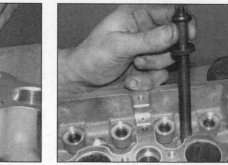

10.41 Remove the cylinder head bolts . . .

10.43 . . . and lift the cylinder head from the block (DW12 engine)

graph 48, this time 10.0 mm in from the front edge of the No 1 piston crown. Record this reading as protrusion B.

50 Add protrusion A to protrusion B, then divide the result by 2 to obtain an average reading for piston No 1.

51 Repeat the procedure described in paragraphs 48 to 50 on piston 4, then turn the crankshaft through 180° and carry out the procedure on the piston Nos 2 and 3 **(see illustration)**. Check that there is a maximum difference of 0.07 mm protrusion between any two pistons.

52 If a dial test indicator is not available, piston protrusion may be measured using a straight-edge and feeler blades or Vernier calipers. However, this is much less accurate, and cannot therefore be recommended.

53 Note the greatest piston protrusion measurement, and use this to determine the correct cylinder head gasket from the following table. The series of up to five (DW10) or four (DW12) notches/holes on the side of the gasket are used for thickness identification. Note on the DW12 engine, the identification holes are on the edge furthest from the cylinders; the single hole nearest the cylinders is for engine identification **(see illustrations)**.

DW10 engine

Piston protrusion	Gasket identification
0.470 to 0.604 mm	1 notch
0.605 to 0.654 mm	2 notches
0.655 to 0.704 mm	3 notches
0.705 to 0.754 mm	4 notches
0.755 to 0.830 mm	5 notches

DW12 engine

Piston protrusion	Gasket identification
0.550 to 0.600 mm	1 hole
0.610 to 0.650 mm	2 holes
0.660 to 0.700 mm	3 holes
0.710 to 0.750 mm	4 holes

Head bolt examination

54 Carefully examine the cylinder head bolts for signs of damage to the threads or head, and for any sign of corrosion. If the bolts are in a satisfactory condition, measure the length of each bolt from the underside of the head, to the end of the shank. The bolts may be re-used providing that the measured length does not exceed 133.3 mm on the DW10 engine, or 134.5 mm on the DW12 engine **(see illustration)**. **Note:** *Considering the stress to which the cylinder head bolts are subjected, it is highly recommended that they are all renewed, regardless of their apparent condition.*

Refitting

55 Turn the crankshaft and position Nos 1 and 4 pistons at TDC, then turn the crankshaft a quarter turn (90°) anti-clockwise.

56 Thoroughly clean the surfaces of the cylinder head and block.

57 Make sure that the locating dowels are in place, then fit the correct gasket the right way round on the cylinder block, with the

10.51 Measuring piston protrusion

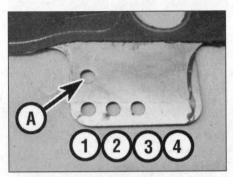

10.53b Cylinder head gasket markings

A   Engine identification
1 to 4 Thickness identification holes

identification notches toward the fuel pump side of the engine **(see illustration)**.

DW10 engine

58 If necessary, refit the inlet and exhaust manifolds with reference to Chapter 4B.

59 Check that the camshaft TDC timing pin is in position, then carefully lower the cylinder head onto the gasket and block, making sure that it locates correctly onto the dowels.

60 Apply a smear of grease to the threads, and to the underside of the heads, of the cylinder head bolts. Peugeot recommend the use of Molykote G Rapid Plus (available from your Peugeot dealer); in the absence of the specified grease, any good-quality high-melting-point grease may be used.

61 Carefully insert the cylinder head bolts into their holes (*do not drop them in*) and initially finger-tighten them.

10.57 Locating the head gasket on the dowels

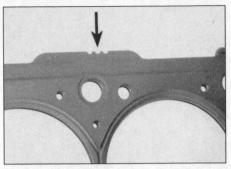

10.53a Cylinder head gasket thickness identification notches (DW10 engine)

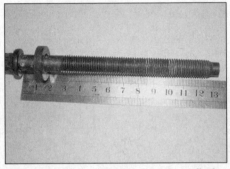

10.54 Measuring the length of the cylinder head bolts

62 Working progressively and in the sequence shown, tighten the cylinder head bolts to their Stage 1 torque setting, using a torque wrench and suitable socket **(see illustration)**.

63 Once all the bolts have been tightened to their Stage 1 torque setting, working again in the specified sequence, tighten each bolt to the specified Stage 2 setting. Working in the reverse order to tightening, loosen all of the bolts by 1 turn. Now tighten them to the Stage 4 setting in their correct order. Finally, angle-tighten the bolts through the specified Stage 5 angle. It is recommended that an angle-measuring gauge is used during this stage of tightening, to ensure accuracy. **Note:** *Retightening of the cylinder head bolts after running the engine is not required.*

64 Refit the cylinder head cover with reference to Section 4, and the camshaft sprocket with reference to Section 8.

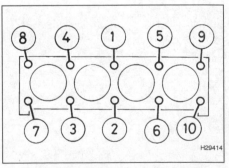

10.62 Cylinder head bolt tightening sequence

10.70 Angle-tightening the cylinder head bolts

10.73 Lower the camshafts onto the cylinder head . . .

10.74 . . . then locate a new oil seal on the exhaust camshaft

DW12 engine

65 If removed, refit the exhaust manifold to the cylinder head with reference to Chapter 4B.

66 Carefully lower the cylinder head onto the gasket and block, making sure that it locates correctly onto the dowels.

67 Apply a smear of grease to the threads, and to the underside of the heads, of the cylinder head bolts. Peugeot recommend the use of Molykote G Rapid Plus (available from your Peugeot dealer); in the absence of the specified grease, any good-quality high-melting-point grease may be used.

68 Carefully insert the cylinder head bolts into their holes (do not drop them in) and initially finger-tighten them.

69 Working progressively and in the sequence shown (see illustration 10.62), tighten the cylinder head bolts to their Stage 1

torque setting, using a torque wrench and suitable socket.

70 Once all the bolts have been tightened to their Stage 1 torque setting, working again in the specified sequence, tighten each bolt to the specified Stage 2 setting. Working in the reverse order to tightening, loosen all of the bolts by 1 turn. Now tighten the bolts to the Stage 4 setting in the correct order. Finally, angle-tighten the bolts through the specified Stage 5 angle. It is recommended that an angle-measuring gauge is used during this stage of tightening, to ensure accuracy (see illustration). Note: Retightening of the cylinder head bolts after running the engine is not required.

71 Refit the hydraulic tappets and rockers in their correct positions in the cylinder head

72 Locate the exhaust and inlet camshafts in the chain so that the TDC marks on the

sprockets are 7 links apart (see illustration 9.26).

73 Carefully lower the camshafts onto the cylinder head and onto the rockers (see illustration). Check that the timing marks are still aligned.

74 Locate a new oil seal on the exhaust camshaft in the position noted on removal of the old seal (see illustration).

75 Locate the hub on the exhaust camshaft and refit the centre bolt, then locate the sprocket on the hub and insert the three retaining bolts.

76 Using the TDC timing pin, peg the camshaft hub to the cylinder head.

77 Clean the surfaces of the camshaft bearing cap housing and cylinder head, then apply Locktite 518 or a suitable sealant to the mating surface of the bearing cap housing. Locate the bearing cap housing in position onto the camshafts (see illustrations).

78 Insert the injector retaining studs and the 28 screws in the housing and initially hand-tighten them.

79 Progressively tighten the studs and screws to the specified torque in the sequence shown (see illustration).

80 Assemble the chain tensioner plunger and spring into its body, then refit the assembly and tighten the bolts to the specified torque (see illustrations).

81 Hold the camshaft sprocket stationary and tighten the centre bolt to the specified torque. Leave the 3 sprocket bolts loose at this stage.

82 Fit a new gasket to the groove in the

10.77a Apply the sealant . . .

10.77b . . . and locate the bearing housing in position

10.79 Inserting the bearing housing retaining bolts

10.80a Assemble the chain tensioner . . .

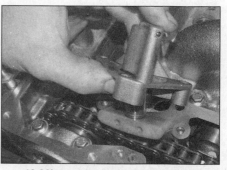

10.80b . . . then refit the assembly

camshaft cover, then refit the cover to the bearing cap housing. Progressively tighten the bolts to the specified torque in the sequence given **(see illustrations)**.

83 Check that the oil seal is correctly fitted to the exhaust camshaft with reference to Section 14.

All models

84 Turn the crankshaft clockwise to its TDC position, with Nos 1 and 4 pistons at TDC, and insert the timing pin (see Section 3).

85 Refit the turbocharger with reference to Chapter 4B.

86 Refit the injectors with reference to Chapter 4B.

87 Refit the fuel supply and return lines. **Note:** *Peugeot recommend that the lines are renewed each time they are removed.*

88 Take the weight of the engine (using the method used during timing belt removal), then unbolt the right-hand engine mounting from the engine bracket. Apply locking fluid to the threads of the uppermost bolt securing the mounting to the cylinder head, then insert it and tighten to the specified torque. Insert the remaining bolt and tighten to the specified torque.

89 Refit the timing belt, crankshaft pulley and auxiliary drivebelt with reference to Section 7, then refit the upper section of the right-hand engine mounting and tighten the bolts to the specified torque. Remove the engine support.

90 Clean the mating surfaces, then refit the coolant outlet manifold together with a new seal and tighten the bolts. Apply thread locking fluid to the threads of the studs, then insert them and tighten to the specified torque.

91 On the DW10 engine, refit the oil level dipstick tube and the bracket over the high-pressure pump.

92 On the DW12 engine, refit the 'swirl control' diaphragm and electrovalve.

93 Refit the camshaft position sensor, then reconnect the wiring. Check and if necessary adjust the air gap with reference to Chapter 4B.

94 Refit the brake vacuum pump with reference to Chapter 9.

95 Reconnect the crankcase ventilation hose(s).

96 Refit the glow plugs and wiring with reference to Chapter 5C.

97 Reconnect the wiring to the injectors.

98 Refit the EGR valve and heat exchanger together with new gaskets, and tighten the bolts securely.

99 Refit the fuel filter and mounting bracket.

100 Refit the fuel supply and return lines.

101 On the DW12 engine, refit the throttle body with reference to Chapter 4B.

102 Refit the air cleaner assembly, airflow meter and inlet air ducts with reference to Chapter 4B.

103 Refit the right-hand front wheelarch liner and roadwheel and lower the car to the ground.

104 Reconnect the battery negative lead, then fill and bleed the cooling system with reference to Chapter 1B.

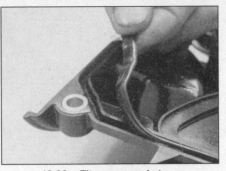

10.82a Fit a new gasket . . .

10.82b . . . then refit the camshaft cover

105 Refit the engine top covers, and the bonnet if removed.

106 Start the engine and run to normal temperature. Carry out a road test during which the following procedure should be made. Engage third gear and stabilise the engine at 1000 rpm. Now accelerate fully to 3500 rpm.

107 Check the engine for leaks.

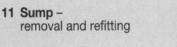

11 Sump – removal and refitting

Removal

1 Disconnect the battery negative lead (refer to *Disconnecting the battery* at the end of this manual).

2 Drain the engine oil, then clean and refit the engine oil drain plug, tightening it securely. If the engine is nearing its service interval when the oil and filter are due for renewal, it is recommended that the filter is also removed, and a new one fitted. After reassembly, the engine can then be refilled with fresh oil. Refer to Chapter 1B for further information.

3 Apply the handbrake, then jack up the front of the vehicle and support it on axle stands (see *Jacking and vehicle support*).

4 On models with air conditioning, where the compressor is mounted onto the side of the sump, remove the drivebelt as described in Chapter 1B. Unbolt the compressor, and position it clear of the sump. Support the weight of the compressor by tying it to the vehicle, to prevent any excess strain being placed on the compressor lines. *Do not* disconnect the

refrigerant lines from the compressor (refer to the warnings given in Chapter 3).

5 Where necessary, disconnect the wiring connector from the oil temperature sender unit, which is screwed into the sump.

6 Progressively slacken and remove all the sump retaining bolts. Since the sump bolts vary in length, remove each bolt in turn, and store it in its correct fitted order by pushing it through a clearly-marked cardboard template. This will avoid the possibility of installing the bolts in the wrong locations on refitting.

7 Try to break the joint by striking the sump with the palm of your hand, then lower and withdraw the sump from under the car. If the sump is stuck (which is quite likely) use a putty knife or similar, carefully inserted between the sump and block. Ease the knife along the joint until the sump is released. While the sump is removed, take the opportunity to check the oil pump pick-up/strainer for signs of clogging or splitting. If necessary, remove the pump as described in Section 12, and clean or renew the strainer. Note that on later models, the oil dipstick tube extends to the bottom of the sump in order to allow the oil to sucked out of the tube using special equipment **(see illustration)**.

Refitting

8 Clean all traces of sealant/gasket from the mating surfaces of the cylinder block/crankcase and sump, then use a clean rag to wipe out the sump and the engine's interior.

9 On engines where the sump was fitted without a gasket, ensure that the sump mating surfaces are clean and dry, then apply a thin coating of suitable sealant to the sump or crankcase mating surface **(see illustration)**.

11.7 On later models the dipstick tube extends to the bottom of the sump

11.9 Apply sealant to the crankcase mating surface

10 Offer up the sump to the cylinder block/crankcase. Refit its retaining bolts, ensuring that each is screwed into its original location. Tighten the bolts evenly and progressively to the specified torque setting. Note the concealed bolts at one end of the sump (see illustrations).

11 Where necessary, align the air conditioning compressor with its mountings on the sump, and insert the retaining bolts. Securely tighten the compressor retaining bolts, then refit the drivebelt as described in Chapter 1B.

12 Reconnect the wiring connector to the oil temperature sensor (where fitted).

13 Lower the vehicle to the ground, then refill the engine with oil as described in Chapter 1B.

11.10a Fitting the sump

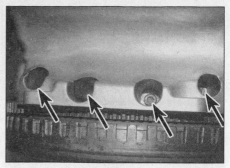
11.10b Concealed bolts at one end of the sump

| 12 Oil pump – |
| removal, inspection |
| and refitting |

Removal

1 Remove the sump as described in Section 11.

2 Unscrew and remove the bolts securing the oil pump to the base of the cylinder block/crankcase/balance shaft housing.

3 Disengage the pump sprocket from the chain, and remove the oil pump (see illustrations). Where necessary, also remove the spacer plate which is fitted behind the oil pump.

Inspection

4 Examine the oil pump sprocket for signs of damage and wear, such as chipped or missing teeth. If the sprocket is worn, the pump assembly must be renewed, since the sprocket is not available separately. It is also recommended that the chain and drive sprocket, fitted to the crankshaft, be renewed at the same time. To renew the chain and drive sprocket, first remove the crankshaft timing belt sprocket, then unbolt the oil seal carrier from the cylinder block. The sprocket, spacer (where fitted) and chain can then be slid off the end of the crankshaft.

5 Unscrew and remove the bolts (along with the baffle plate, where fitted) securing the strainer cover to the pump body. Lift off the strainer cover, and take off the relief valve piston and spring, noting which way round they are fitted (see illustrations).

6 Examine the pump rotors and body for signs of wear ridges or scoring. If worn, the complete pump assembly must be renewed.

7 Examine the relief valve piston for signs of wear or damage, and renew if necessary. The condition of the relief valve spring can only be measured by comparing it with a new one; if there is any doubt about its condition, it should also be renewed. Both the piston and spring are available individually.

8 Thoroughly clean the oil pump strainer with a suitable solvent, and check it for signs of clogging or splitting. If the strainer is damaged, the strainer and cover assembly must be renewed.

9 Locate the relief valve spring and piston in the strainer cover. Refit the cover to the pump body, aligning the relief valve piston with its bore in the pump. Refit the baffle plate (where fitted) and the cover retaining bolts, and tighten them securely.

10 Prime the pump by filling it with clean engine oil before refitting.

Refitting

11 Offer up the spacer plate (where fitted); then engage the pump sprocket with its drive chain, and seat the pump on the base of the cylinder block/crankcase. Refit the pump retaining bolts, and tighten them to the specified torque setting and angle, where necessary.

12 Refit the sump as described in Section 11.

12.3b . . . and on the DW12 engine

12.3a Removing the oil pump on the DW10 engine . . .

12.5a Remove the oil pump cover bolts . . .

12.5b . . . then lift off the cover and remove the spring . . .

12.5c . . . and relief valve piston, noting which way round it is fitted

13 Oil cooler – removal and refitting

Removal

1 Apply the handbrake, then jack up the front of the vehicle and support it on axle stands (see *Jacking and vehicle support*).

2 Drain the cooling system as described in Chapter 1B. Alternatively, clamp the oil cooler coolant hoses directly above the cooler, and be prepared for some coolant loss as the hoses are disconnected.

3 Position a suitable container beneath the oil filter on the front of the engine. Unscrew the filter using an oil filter removal tool if necessary, and drain the oil into the container. If the oil filter is damaged or distorted during removal, it must be renewed. Given the low cost of a new oil filter relative to the cost of repairing the damage which could result if a re-used filter leaks, it is probably a good idea to renew the filter in any case.

4 Release the hose clips, and disconnect the coolant hoses from the oil cooler.

5 Unscrew the oil cooler/oil filter mounting bolt/stud from the cylinder block, and withdraw the cooler. Note the locating notch in the cooler flange, which fits over the lug on the cylinder block **(see illustration)**. Discard the oil cooler sealing ring; a new one must be used on refitting.

Refitting

6 Fit a new sealing ring to the recess in the rear of the cooler, then offer the cooler to the cylinder block.

7 Ensure that the locating notch in the cooler flange is correctly engaged with the lug on the cylinder block. Apply locking fluid to the threads of the mounting bolt/stud, then insert it through the oil cooler and tighten to the specified torque (where given).

8 Fit the oil filter, then lower the vehicle to the ground. Top-up the engine oil level as described in *Weekly Checks*.

9 Refill or top-up the cooling system as described in Chapter 1B or *Weekly Checks* (as applicable). Start the engine, and check the oil cooler for signs of leakage.

14 Oil seals – renewal

Crankshaft

Right-hand oil seal

1 Remove the crankshaft sprocket as described in Section 8.

2 Measure and note the fitted depth of the oil seal.

3 Pull the oil seal from the housing using a hooked instrument. Alternatively, drill a small

13.5 Oil cooler/oil filter mounting bolt A) and locating notch (B)

hole in the oil seal, and use a self-tapping screw and a pair of pliers to remove it **(see illustration)**.

4 Clean the oil seal housing and the crankshaft sealing surface.

5 Dip the new oil seal in clean engine oil, and press it into the housing (open end first) to the previously-noted depth, using a suitable tube or socket. A piece of thin plastic or tape wound around the front of the crankshaft is useful to prevent damage to the oil seal as it is fitted.

6 Where applicable, remove the plastic or tape from the end of the crankshaft.

7 Refit the timing belt crankshaft sprocket as described in Section 8.

Left-hand oil seal

8 Remove the flywheel/driveplate, as described in Section 16.

9 Proceed as described in paragraphs 2 to 6,

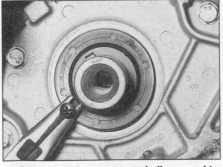

14.3 Self-tapping screw and pliers used to remove the crankshaft right-hand oil seal

14.12b . . . and remove the camshaft oil seal

noting that when fitted, the outer lip of the oil seal must point outwards; if it is pointing inwards, use a piece of bent wire to pull it out. Take care not to damage the oil seal.

10 Refit the flywheel/driveplate, as described in Section 15.

Camshaft

Right-hand oil seal

11 Remove the camshaft sprocket (and hub where applicable) as described in Section 8. In principle there is no need to remove the timing belt completely, but remember that if the belt has been contaminated with oil, it must be renewed.

12 Pull the oil seal from the housing using a hooked instrument. Alternatively, drill a small hole in the oil seal and use a self-tapping screw and a pair of pliers to remove it **(see illustrations)**.

13 Clean the oil seal housing and the camshaft sealing surface.

14 Smear the new oil seal with clean engine oil, then fit it over the end of the camshaft, open end first **(see illustration)**. A piece of thin plastic or tape wound around the front of the camshaft is useful to prevent damage to the oil seal as it is fitted.

15 Press the seal into the housing until it is flush with the end face of the cylinder head. Use an M10 bolt (screwed into the end of the camshaft), washers and a suitable tube or socket to press the seal into position **(see illustration)**.

16 Refit the camshaft sprocket (and hub where applicable) as described in Section 8.

14.12a Use a hooked tool (or self-tapping screw and pliers) to prise out . . .

14.14 Locate the new oil seal in the cylinder head

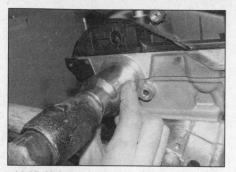

14.15 Using a socket to drive the new oil seal into position

17 Where necessary, fit a new timing belt with reference to Section 7.

Left-hand oil seal

18 No oil seal is fitted to the left-hand end of the camshaft. The sealing is provided by an O-ring fitted to the end plate flange. The O-ring can be renewed after unbolting the plate from the cylinder head.

15 Oil level, temperature and pressure sensors – general

Refer to Chapter 5A for details.

16 Flywheel/driveplate – removal, inspection and refitting

Removal

Flywheel

1 Remove the transmission as described in Chapter 7A, then remove the clutch assembly as described in Chapter 6.

2 Prevent the flywheel from turning by locking the ring gear teeth (see illustration 5.2). Alternatively, bolt a strap between the flywheel and the cylinder block/crankcase. *Do not* attempt to lock the flywheel in position using the crankshaft pulley locking tool described in Section 3.

3 Slacken and remove the flywheel retaining bolts, and remove the flywheel from the end

16.12a ... then refit the flywheel, and tighten the bolts to the specified torque

of the crankshaft. Be careful not to drop it; it is heavy. If the flywheel locating dowel is a loose fit in the crankshaft end, remove it and store it with the flywheel for safe-keeping. Discard the flywheel bolts; new ones must be used on refitting.

Driveplate

4 Remove the transmission as described in Chapter 7B. Lock the driveplate as described in paragraph 2 of this Section. Mark the relationship between the torque converter plate and the driveplate, and slacken all the driveplate retaining bolts.

5 Remove the retaining bolts, along with the torque converter plate and the two shims (one fitted on each side of the torque converter plate). Note that the shims are of different thickness, the thicker one being on the outside of the torque converter plate. Discard the driveplate retaining bolts; new ones must be used on refitting.

6 Remove the driveplate from the end of the crankshaft. If the locating dowel is a loose fit in the crankshaft end, remove it and store it with the driveplate for safe-keeping.

Inspection

7 On models with manual transmission, examine the flywheel for scoring of the clutch face, and for wear or chipping of the ring gear teeth. If the clutch face is scored, the flywheel may be surface-ground, but renewal is preferable. Seek the advice of a Peugeot dealer or engine reconditioning specialist to see if machining is possible. If the ring gear is worn or damaged, the flywheel must be renewed, as it is not possible to renew the ring gear separately.

8 On models with automatic transmission, check the torque converter driveplate carefully for signs of distortion. Look for any hairline cracks around the bolt holes or radiating outwards from the centre, and inspect the ring gear teeth for signs of wear or chipping. If any sign of wear or damage is found, the driveplate must be renewed.

Refitting

Flywheel

9 Clean the mating surfaces of the flywheel and crankshaft. Remove any remaining locking compound from the threads of the

16.12b Torx bolts are fitted to the flywheel (DW12 engine with two section flywheel)

16.10 If the new flywheel bolt threads are not supplied with their threads precoated, apply a suitable thread-locking compound to them ...

crankshaft holes, using the correct size of tap, if available.

> **HAYNES HiNT** *If a suitable tap is not available, cut two slots along the threads of one of the old flywheel bolts, and use the bolt to remove the locking compound from the threads.*

10 If the new flywheel retaining bolts are not supplied with their threads already precoated, apply a suitable thread-locking compound to the threads of each bolt (see illustration).

11 Ensure that the locating dowel is in position. Offer up the flywheel, locating it on the dowel, and fit the new retaining bolts.

12 Lock the flywheel using the method employed on dismantling, and tighten the retaining bolts to the specified torque (see illustrations).

13 Refit the clutch as described in Chapter 6. Remove the flywheel locking tool, and refit the transmission as described in Chapter 7A.

Driveplate

14 Carry out the operations described above in paragraphs 9 and 10, substituting 'driveplate' for all references to the flywheel.

15 Locate the driveplate on its locating dowel.

16 Offer up the torque converter plate, with the thinner shim positioned behind the plate and the thicker shim on the outside, and align the marks made prior to removal.

17 Fit the new retaining bolts, then lock the driveplate using the method employed on dismantling. Tighten the retaining bolts to the specified torque wrench setting.

18 Remove the driveplate locking tool, and refit the transmission (see Chapter 7B).

17 Engine/transmission mountings – inspection and renewal

Inspection

1 If improved access is required, firmly apply the handbrake, then jack up the front of the

car and support it on axle stands (see *Jacking and vehicle support*).

2 Check the mounting rubbers to see if they are cracked, hardened or separated from the metal at any point; renew the mounting if any such damage or deterioration is evident.

3 Check that all the mountings' fasteners are securely tightened; use a torque wrench to check if possible.

4 Using a large screwdriver or a crowbar, check for wear in each mounting by carefully levering against it to check for free play. Where this is not possible, enlist the aid of an assistant to move the engine/transmission back-and-forth, or from side-to-side, while you watch the mounting. While some free play is to be expected even from new components, excessive wear should be obvious. If excessive free play is found, check first that the fasteners are correctly secured, then renew any worn components as described below.

Renewal

Right-hand mounting

5 Disconnect the battery negative lead (refer to *Disconnecting the battery* at the end of this manual).

6 Remove the engine management ECU and housing box from the right-hand side of the engine compartment with reference to Chapter 4B, Section 13, and position it to one side. There is no need to disconnect the wiring.

7 Release all the relevant hoses and wiring from their retaining clips near the mounting. Place the hoses/wiring clear of the mounting so that the removal procedure is not hindered.

8 Unscrew the mounting bolts and remove the torque reaction link from the right-hand mounting and body.

9 Place a jack beneath the right-hand end of the engine, with a block of wood on the jack head. Raise the jack until it is supporting the weight of the engine.

17.11 Removing the right-hand upper engine mounting bracket

10 Slacken and remove the three bolts securing the upper mounting bracket to the lower (engine) bracket.

11 Unscrew the nut securing the upper mounting bracket to the flexible engine mounting, and withdraw the bracket **(see illustration)**.

12 Unscrew the mounting rubber from the body, and remove it from the vehicle **(see illustration)**. A strap wrench or similar may be used to unscrew the mounting, or alternatively fabricate a tool from suitable metal tube with projections to engage in the cut-outs in the mounting.

13 If necessary, the lower mounting bracket can be unbolted and removed from the engine after removing the timing covers.

14 Check all components carefully for signs of wear or damage, and renew them where necessary.

15 On reassembly, screw the mounting rubber into the vehicle body, and tighten it securely. Where removed, refit the lower mounting bracket to the engine, apply a drop of locking compound to the retaining bolts and tighten them to the specified torque.

16 Refit the upper mounting bracket to the flexible mounting, then tighten the retaining nuts/bolts to the specified torque setting.

17 Refit and tighten the domed buffer nut,

then refit the torque reaction link and hoses removed.

18 Refit the ECU and housing box, then reconnect the battery.

Left-hand mounting

19 Remove the battery, battery tray, and mounting plate as described in Chapter 5A.

20 Place a jack beneath the transmission, with a block of wood on the jack head. Raise the jack until it is supporting the weight of the transmission.

21 Unscrew and remove the centre nut and washer from the left-hand mounting, then undo the nuts securing the mounting in position and remove it from the engine compartment **(see illustration)**.

22 If necessary, slide the spacer and small washer off the mounting stud, then unscrew the stud from the top of the transmission housing, and remove it along with its large washer. To improve access to the mounting stud, undo the retaining bolts and remove the mounting bracket from the body.

23 Check all components carefully for signs of wear or damage, and renew as necessary.

24 Clean the threads of the mounting stud, and apply a coat of thread-locking compound to its threads. Refit the stud and washer to the top of the transmission, and tighten it to the specified torque setting.

25 Slide the spacer (where fitted) onto the mounting stud, then refit the rubber mounting. Tighten both the mounting-to-body bolts and the mounting centre nut to their specified torque settings, and remove the jack from underneath the transmission.

26 Refit the battery mounting plate, battery tray and battery as described in Chapter 5A.

Rear mounting

27 If not already done, firmly apply the handbrake, then jack up the front of the car and support it securely on axle stands (see *Jacking and vehicle support*). Remove the engine undertray.

17.12 Right-hand engine mounting rubber

17.21 Removing the left-hand engine mounting

17.28 Removing the rear engine mounting connecting link

28 Unscrew and remove the bolt securing the rear mounting connecting link to the mounting on the rear of the cylinder block **(see illustration)**.

29 Remove the bolt securing the rear mounting connecting link to the bracket on the subframe/underbody. Withdraw the link.

30 To remove the mounting assembly it will first be necessary to remove the right-hand driveshaft as described in Chapter 8.

31 With the driveshaft removed, undo the retaining bolts and remove the mounting from the rear of the cylinder block.

32 Check carefully for signs of wear or damage on all components, and renew them where necessary.

33 On reassembly, fit the rear mounting assembly to the rear of the cylinder block, and tighten its retaining bolts to the specified torque. Refit the driveshaft as described in Chapter 8.

34 Refit the connecting link, and tighten both its bolts to their specified torque settings.

35 Refit the engine undertray and lower the vehicle to the ground.

Chapter 2 Part D:
Engine removal and overhaul procedures

Contents

Balance shaft housing (DW12 diesel engine) – removal, inspection and refitting 10
Crankshaft – inspection 15
Crankshaft – refitting and main bearing running clearance check .. 19
Crankshaft – removal 12
Cylinder block/crankcase – cleaning and inspection 13
Cylinder head – dismantling 7
Cylinder head – reassembly 9
Cylinder head and valves – cleaning and inspection 8
Engine – initial start-up after overhaul 21
Engine and automatic transmission – removal, separation and refitting 5

Engine and manual transmission – removal, separation and refitting 4
Engine overhaul – dismantling sequence 6
Engine overhaul – general information 2
Engine overhaul – reassembly sequence 17
Engine/transmission removal – methods and precautions 3
General information 1
Main and big-end bearings – inspection 16
Piston rings – refitting 18
Piston/connecting rod assembly – inspection 14
Piston/connecting rod assembly – removal 11
Pistons/connecting rods – refitting and big-end bearing running clearance check 20

Degrees of difficulty

Easy, suitable for novice with little experience	Fairly easy, suitable for beginner with some experience	Fairly difficult, suitable for competent DIY mechanic	Difficult, suitable for experienced DIY mechanic	Very difficult, suitable for expert DIY or professional

Specifications

Note: *At the time of writing, some specifications for certain engines were not available. Where the relevant specifications are not given here, refer to your Peugeot dealer for further information.*

Cylinder head

Maximum gasket face distortion:
    XU engine (LFY) .... 0.05 mm
    EW engines (6FZ, RFR and RFN) .... 0.05 mm
    DW engines (RHY, RHZ and 4HX) .... 0.03 mm
Cylinder head height:
    XU engine (LFY):
        Nominal .... 137.00 ± 0.05 mm
        Minimum (after grinding) .... 136.80 mm
    EW engines (6FZ, RFR and RFN):
        Nominal .... 137.00 ± 0.05 mm
        Minimum (after grinding) .... 136.70 ± 0.05 mm
    DW engines (RHY, RHZ and 4HX):
        Nominal .... 133.0 ± 0.05 mm
        Minimum (after grinding) .... 132.8 mm

Valves

	Inlet	Exhaust
Valve head diameter:		
XU engine	34.7 +0.0, –0.2 mm	29.7 +0.0, –0.2 mm
EW7 engine	29.8 ± 0.1 mm	27.2 ± 0.1 mm
EW10 engine	33.3 ± 0.1 mm	29.0 ± 0.1 mm
Diesel engines:		
2.0 litre engine	Not available	Not available
2.2 litre engine	29.9 ± 0.1 mm	25.0 ± 0.1 mm
Valve stem diameter:		
XU engine	6.98 +0.0, –0.015 mm	6.96 +0.0, –0.015 mm
EW engines	5.985 +0.0, –0.015 mm	5.975 +0.0, –0.015 mm
Diesel engines:		
2.0 litre engine	Not available	Not available
2.2 litre engine	5.968 ± 0.05 mm	5.968 ± 0.05 mm
Overall length:		
XU engine	104.38 +0.4, + 0.0	102.9 +0.4, +0.0
EW7 engine	104.17 ± 0.1 mm	104.10 ± 0.1 mm
EW10 engine	106.18 ± 0.3 mm	103.66 ± 0.1 mm
Diesel engines:		
2.0 litre engine	Not available	Not available
2.2 litre engine	102.55 ± 0.15 mm	102.48 ± 0.15 mm
Valve head recess below cylinder head surface (maximum):		
DW12 diesel engine	0.5 to 1.0 mm	0.9 to 1.4 mm

Balance shafts (DW12 diesel engine)

Endfloat	0.03 to 0.20 mm
Backlash clearance between shafts	0.01 to 0.7 mm
Backlash clearance between driver shaft and crankshaft gear	0.01 to 0.26 mm

Cylinder block

Cylinder bore diameter:	
XU engine:	
Category A	83.00 +0.010, +0.0
Category B	83.01 +0.010, +0.0
Category C	83.02 +0.010, +0.0
EW7 engine:	
Nominal	82.7 +0.018, +0.0 mm
Oversize	83.3 +0.018, +0.0 mm
EW10 engine:	
Nominal	85.0 +0.018, +0.0 mm
Oversize	85.6 +0.018, +0.0 mm
Diesel engines:	
2.0 litre engine:	
Standard	85.000 to 85.018 mm
Oversize A1	85.030 to 85.048 mm
Oversize R1	85.250 to 85.268 mm
Oversize R2	85.600 to 85.618 mm
2.2 litre engine:	
Standard	85.000 to 85.018 mm
Oversize R1	85.600 to 85.618 mm
Liner protrusion above block mating surface – XU7 aluminium-block engine only:	
Standard	0.03 to 0.10 mm
Maximum difference between any two liners	0.05 mm

Piston rings

End gaps:	
Petrol engines:	
Top compression ring:	
XU engine	Not available
EW engines	0.2 +0.25, +0.0 mm
Second compression ring:	
XU engine	Not available
EW engines	0.2 +0.25, +0.0 mm
Diesel engines:	
Top compression ring	0.20 to 0.35 mm
Second compression ring	0.80 to 1.00 mm
Oil control ring	0.25 to 0.50 mm

Pistons

Piston diameter:
  XU7 (LFY) engine:
    Category A:
      PDC type . . . . 82.970 ± 0.007 mm
      SMM type . . . . 82.912 ± 0.005 mm
      FM type . . . . 82.962 ± 0.005 mm
    Category B:
      PDC type . . . . 82.980 ± 0.007 mm
      SMM type . . . . 82.922 ± 0.005 mm
      FM type . . . . 82.972 ± 0.005 mm
    Category C:
      PDC type . . . . –
      SMM type . . . . 82.932 ± 0.005 mm
      FM type . . . . –
  EW7 engine:
    Nominal . . . . 82.657 mm
    Oversize . . . . 83.257 mm
  EW10 engine:
    Nominal . . . . 84.948 mm
    Oversize . . . . 85.548 mm
  DW10 engine:
    Standard . . . . 84.210 to 84.228 mm
    Maximum difference in weight between any two pistons . . . . 4.0 g
  DW12 engine:
    Standard . . . . 84.931 ± 0.009 mm
    1st oversize . . . . 85.531 ± 0.009 mm
Piston weight class:
  DW12 engine:
    P1 . . . . From 605 to 609
    P2 . . . . From 610 to 614
    P3 . . . . From 615 to 619
    P4 . . . . From 620 to 625

Note: *All 4 pistons must be of the same weight class*

Crankshaft

Endfloat . . . . 0.07 to 0.32 mm
Main bearing journal diameter:
  XU engine . . . . 60.0 +0, –0.019 mm
  EW engines:
    Nominal . . . . 60.0 +0, –0.025 mm
    Undersize . . . . 59.7 +0, –0.019 mm
  Diesel engines:
    Standard . . . . 60.0 +0, –0.025 mm
    Undersize . . . . 59.7 +0, –0.025 mm
Big-end bearing journal diameter:
  XU engine:
    Nominal . . . . 45.0 –0.025, –0.009 mm
    Undersize . . . . 44.7 –0.025, –0.009 mm
  EW engines:
    Nominal . . . . 60.0 +0, –0.025 mm
    Undersize . . . . 59.7 +0, –0.019 mm
  Diesel engines:
    Standard . . . . 50.0 +0, –0.016 mm
    Undersize . . . . 49.7 +0, –0.016 mm
Maximum bearing journal out-of-round (all models) . . . . 0.007 mm
Main bearing running clearance:
  XU engine . . . . 0.025 to 0.062 mm
  EW engines . . . . 0.030 to 0.054 mm
  Diesel engines* . . . . 0.025 to 0.050 mm
Big-end bearing running clearance – all models* . . . . 0.025 to 0.050 mm

* These are suggested figures, typical for this type of engine – no exact values are stated by Peugeot

Torque wrench settings

XU series (petrol) engine . . . . Refer to Chapter 2A Specifications
EW series (petrol) engine . . . . Refer to Chapter 2B Specifications
DW series (diesel) engine . . . . Refer to Chapter 2C Specifications

1 General information

Included in this Part of Chapter 2 are details of removing the engine/transmission from the car and general overhaul procedures for the cylinder head, cylinder block/crankcase and all other engine internal components.

The information given ranges from advice concerning preparation for an overhaul and the purchase of parts, to detailed step-by-step procedures covering removal, inspection, renovation and refitting of engine internal components.

After Section 6, all instructions are based on the assumption that the engine has been removed from the car. For information concerning in-car engine repair, as well as the removal and refitting of those external components necessary for full overhaul, refer to Part A, B or C of this Chapter (as applicable) and to Section 6. Ignore any preliminary dismantling operations described in Part A, B or C that are no longer relevant once the engine has been removed from the car.

Apart from torque wrench settings, which are given at the beginning of Part A, B or C (as applicable), all specifications relating to engine overhaul are at the beginning of this Part of Chapter 2.

2 Engine overhaul –
general information

It is not always easy to determine when, or if, an engine should be completely overhauled, as a number of factors must be considered.

High mileage is not necessarily an indication that an overhaul is needed, while low mileage does not preclude the need for an overhaul. Frequency of servicing is probably the most important consideration. An engine which has had regular and frequent oil and filter changes, as well as other required maintenance, should give many thousands of miles of reliable service. Conversely, a neglected engine may require an overhaul very early in its life.

Excessive oil consumption is an indication that piston rings, valve seals and/or valve guides are in need of attention. Make sure that oil leaks are not responsible before deciding that the rings and/or guides are worn. Perform a compression test, as described in Part A or B (petrol engines) or C (diesel engine) of this Chapter, to determine the likely cause of the problem.

Check the oil pressure with a gauge fitted in place of the oil pressure switch, and compare it with that specified. If it is extremely low, the main and big-end bearings, and/or the oil pump, are probably worn out.

Loss of power, rough running, knocking or metallic engine noises, excessive valve gear noise, and high fuel consumption may also point to the need for an overhaul, especially if they are all present at the same time. If a complete service does not cure the situation, major mechanical work is the only solution.

An engine overhaul involves restoring all internal parts to the specification of a new engine. During an overhaul, the cylinder liners (XU7 engine), the pistons and the piston rings are renewed. New main and big-end bearings are generally fitted; if necessary, the crankshaft may be renewed to restore the journals. The valves are also serviced as well, since they are usually in less-than-perfect condition at this point. While the engine is being overhauled, other components, such as the distributor, starter and alternator, can be overhauled as well. The end result should be an as-new engine that will give many trouble-free miles.

Note: Critical cooling system components such as the hoses, thermostat and coolant pump should be renewed when an engine is overhauled. The radiator should be checked carefully, to ensure that it is not clogged or leaking. Also, it is a good idea to renew the oil pump whenever the engine is overhauled.

Before beginning the engine overhaul, read through the entire procedure, to familiarise yourself with the scope and requirements of the job. Overhauling an engine is not difficult if you follow carefully all of the instructions, have the necessary tools and equipment, and pay close attention to all specifications. It can, however, be time-consuming. Plan on the car being off the road for a minimum of two weeks, especially if parts must be taken to an engineering works for repair or reconditioning. Check on the availability of parts and make sure that any necessary special tools and equipment are obtained in advance. Most work can be done with typical hand tools, although a number of precision measuring tools are required for inspecting parts to determine if they must be renewed. Often the engineering works will handle the inspection of parts and offer advice concerning reconditioning and renewal.

Always wait until the engine has been completely dismantled, and until all components (especially the cylinder block/crankcase and the crankshaft) have been inspected, before deciding what service and repair operations must be performed by an engineering works. The condition of these components will be the major factor to consider when determining whether to overhaul the original engine, or to buy a reconditioned unit. Do not, therefore, purchase parts or have overhaul work done on other components until they have been thoroughly inspected. As a general rule, time is the primary cost of an overhaul, so it does not pay to fit worn or sub-standard parts.

As a final note, to ensure maximum life and minimum trouble from a reconditioned engine, everything must be assembled with care, in a spotlessly-clean environment.

3 Engine/transmission removal –
methods and precautions

If you have decided that the engine must be removed for overhaul or major repair work, several preliminary steps should be taken.

Locating a suitable place to work is extremely important. Adequate work space, along with storage space for the car, will be needed. If a workshop or garage is not available, at the very least, a flat, level, clean work surface is required.

Cleaning the engine compartment and engine/transmission before beginning the removal procedure will help keep tools clean and organised.

An engine hoist or A-frame will also be necessary. Make sure the equipment is rated in excess of the combined weight of the engine and transmission. Safety is of primary importance, considering the potential hazards involved in lifting the engine/transmission out of the car.

If this is the first time you have removed an engine, an assistant should ideally be available. Advice and aid from someone more experienced would also be helpful. There are many instances when one person cannot simultaneously perform all of the operations required when removing the engine from the vehicle.

Plan the operation ahead of time. Before starting work, arrange for the hire of or obtain all of the tools and equipment you will need. Some of the equipment necessary to perform engine/transmission removal and installation safely and with relative ease (in addition to an engine hoist) is as follows: a heavy duty trolley jack, complete sets of spanners and sockets, wooden blocks, and plenty of rags and cleaning solvent for mopping-up spilled oil, coolant and fuel. If the hoist must be hired, make sure that you arrange for it in advance, and perform all of the operations possible without it beforehand. This will save you money and time.

Plan for the car to be out of use for quite a while. An engineering works will be required to perform some of the work which the do-it-yourselfer cannot accomplish without special equipment. These places often have a busy schedule, so it would be a good idea to consult them before removing the engine, in order to accurately estimate the amount of time required to rebuild or repair components that may need work.

During the engine removal procedure, it is advisable to make notes of the locations of all brackets, cable ties, earthing points, etc, as well as how the wiring harnesses, hoses and electrical connections are attached and routed around the engine and engine compartment. An effective way of doing this is to take a series of photographs of the various components before they are disconnected or removed. A simple inexpensive disposable camera is ideal for this and the resulting photographs will prove invaluable when the engine is refitted.

Always be extremely careful when removing and refitting the engine/transmission. Serious injury can result from careless actions. Plan ahead and take your time, and a job of this nature, although major, can be accomplished successfully.

Note 1: *All manual transmission petrol engines and the DW10 diesel engine are removed upwards from the car as a complete unit together with the transmission, then the transmission is separated from the engine on the bench. The DW12 diesel engine and all engines with automatic transmission are best removed by lowering them from the engine compartment after removing the subframe.*

Note 2: *Such is the complexity of the power unit arrangement on these vehicles, and the variations that may be encountered according to model and optional equipment fitted, that the following should be regarded as a guide to the work involved, rather than a step-by-step procedure. Where differences are encountered, or additional component disconnection or removal is necessary, make notes of the work involved as an aid to refitting.*

4	Engine and manual transmission – removal, separation and refitting

Removal

1 Disconnect the battery negative lead (refer to *Disconnecting the battery* at the end of this manual).

2 Apply the handbrake, then jack up the front of the vehicle and support it on axle stands (see *Jacking and vehicle support*). Remove both front roadwheels. Also remove the undertray from beneath the engine and transmission where fitted.

3 Remove the engine top cover. If necessary for use of the lifting hoist, disconnect the bonnet support struts as described in Chapter 11, Section 8, and tie or support the bonnet in the vertical position. Alternatively, remove the bonnet completely.

4 Drain the cooling system with reference to Chapter 1A or 1B.

5 Drain the transmission oil as described in Chapter 7A **(see illustration)**. Refit the drain and filler plugs, and tighten them to their specified torque settings.

6 If the engine is to be dismantled, drain the engine oil and remove the oil filter as described in Chapter 1A or 1B **(see illustrations)**. Clean and refit the drain plug, tightening it securely.

7 Refer to Chapter 11, Section 24, and remove the front wheelarch liners from both sides.

8 Refer to Chapter 8 and remove both front driveshafts **(see illustration)**.

9 Refer to Chapter 1A or 1B and remove the auxiliary drivebelt.

4.5 Manual transmission oil drain plug

4.6b Engine oil filter on the EW10 engine ...

4.8 Removing the driveshaft/hub nuts

10 On diesel engines with an intercooler, remove the air duct leading from the turbocharger to the intercooler.

11 Remove the exhaust system with reference to Chapter 4A or 4B.

12 From underneath the vehicle, slacken and remove the nuts and bolts securing the rear engine mounting connecting link to the mounting assembly and subframe, and remove the connecting link. Refer to Chapter 2A, 2B or 2C.

13 On models with air conditioning, refer to Chapter 3 and unbolt the compressor from the engine. On the DW12 diesel engine, it will be necessary to unbolt the auxiliary drivebelt idler for access to the upper compressor mounting bolt **(see illustration)**. **Do not** disconnect the refrigerant lines. Support or tie the compressor to one side.

14 Unclip the power steering fluid pipe from beneath the transmission. On models where

4.6a Unscrewing the sump drain plug (EW10 engine)

4.6c ... and on the DW12 engine (same on the DW10 engine)

the engine/transmission assembly is lowered from the engine compartment, carefully tie the pipe to the right-hand side of the engine compartment.

15 On diesel engines with an intercooler, remove the air duct leading from the intercooler to the air cleaner.

16 Refer to Chapter 4A or 4B and remove the air cleaner and its bracket, and all air inlet ducts.

17 Refer to Chapter 5A and remove the battery and battery tray.

18 Refer to Chapter 3 and remove the radiator. Although not essential, this will ensure the radiator is not damaged as the engine/transmission assembly is being removed. Alternatively, a piece of wood or card may be placed over the radiator as protection. If the radiator is left in position, remove the bottom hose from the thermostat housing and radiator.

4.13 Air conditioning compressor on the DW12 engine – auxiliary drivebelt idler has been removed for access to the upper bolt

4.29 Unbolting the power steering pump from its bracket

19 On diesel engines, remove the preheating control unit cover, then remove the preheating control unit housing.

20 Refer to Chapter 4A or 4B and remove the engine management ECU and housing.

21 Where applicable, disconnect the two engine/transmission wiring connectors at the left-hand front of the engine/transmission. If necessary, trace the wiring harness back from the engine to the main harness connectors at the fuse/relay box, and/or at the bulkhead connection behind the battery tray location. Release the locking rings by twisting them anti-clockwise and disconnect the connectors. Also trace the wiring connectors back to the transmission and disconnect all engine related wiring and earth leads in this area. Check that all the relevant connectors have been disconnected, and that the harness is released from all the clips or ties, so that it is free to be removed with the engine/transmission. On some models it may be necessary to disconnect all the relevant wiring from the engine, then unbolt the harness conduit and move it to one side.

22 Remove the battery support bracket.

23 Unbolt the accelerator control and bracket from the left-hand side of the engine compartment.

24 Disconnect the gear linkage cable end fittings from the levers on the top of the transmission then unclip the outer cables from their supports and tie them to one side.

25 On models with a clutch release cable, disconnect the cable from the transmission release lever and support it to one side. On models with a hydraulic clutch, remove the slave cylinder from the transmission with reference to Chapter 6, Section 4; this will necessitate disconnecting the hydraulic pipe first, as there is insufficient movement with the pipe in position.

26 On diesel models disconnect the brake vacuum pipe from the vacuum pump on the left-hand end of the cylinder head. Also disconnect the vacuum pipes from throttle bodies and swirl-control unit.

27 On diesel models, disconnect the wiring from the EGR valve.

28 At the bulkhead, disconnect the coolant hoses from the heater matrix.

29 Refer to Chapter 10 and unbolt the power steering pump from the engine, without disconnecting the hydraulic hoses – access to the front bolts is through the pulley **(see illustration)**. Tie it to one side. Note on models where the engine is lowered from the engine compartment, it will be necessary to pull the power steering fluid pipe from under the transmission to the right-hand side before lowering the engine. Take care not to damage the pipe at its connection to the steering gear. Alternatively, disconnect the fluid pipe either from the steering gear or pump.

30 Disconnect the fuel supply and return hoses with reference to the appropriate part of Chapter 4. Tape over or plug the holes in the fuel rail and the ends of the hoses, to prevent entry of dust and dirt.

31 On the DW12 diesel engine and all automatic transmission models, remove the front suspension subframe with reference to Chapter 10.

32 Using a hoist attached to the lifting eyes on the cylinder head, take the weight of the engine and transmission.

33 Refer to Chapter 2A, 2B or 2C and unbolt the right-hand engine mounting torque reaction link and the mounting itself.

34 Unscrew and remove the left-hand engine mounting centre nut and washer, then unbolt the rubber mounting from the body support bracket.

35 Remove the spacer, then unscrew the left-hand engine mounting centre stud from the transmission and remove its washer. On the ML5T transmission, unbolt the bracket together with the stud.

36 Make a final check that any components which would prevent the removal of the engine/transmission from the car have been removed or disconnected. Ensure that components such as the gearchange selector cables are secured so that they cannot be damaged on removal.

37 On models where the engine is lifted upwards from the engine compartment (see note in Section 3), raise the engine hoist and carefully lift the engine/transmission upwards, clear of the mountings, ensuring that nothing is trapped or damaged. Enlist the help of an assistant during this procedure, as it will be necessary to tilt and twist the assembly slightly to clear the body panels and adjacent components. Once the engine/transmission

assembly is high enough to clear the front crossmember, withdraw the unit forward and out of the engine compartment. Move the unit clear of the car and lower it to the ground.

38 On models where the engine is lowered from the engine compartment, carefully lower the assembly to the ground, making sure it clears the surrounding engine compartment components **(see illustration)**. On the DW12 engine, make sure that the power steering fluid pipe is tied to the right-hand side of the engine compartment, so that it will clear the engine.

Separation

39 With the engine/transmission assembly removed, support the assembly on suitable blocks of wood on a workbench (or failing that, on a clean area of the workshop floor).

40 Undo the retaining bolts, and remove the flywheel lower cover plate(s) from the transmission.

41 Slacken and remove the retaining bolts, and remove the starter motor from the transmission.

42 Undo the bolts and release the coolant heating housing from the transmission, noting the location of the earth leads and cable clips also secured by the housing retaining bolts.

43 Disconnect any remaining wiring connectors at the transmission, then move the main engine wiring harness to one side.

44 Ensure that both engine and transmission are adequately supported, then slacken and remove the remaining bolts securing the transmission housing to the engine. Note the correct fitted positions of each bolt (and the relevant brackets) as they are removed, to use as a reference on refitting.

45 Carefully withdraw the transmission from the engine, ensuring that the weight of the transmission is not allowed to hang on the input shaft while it is engaged with the clutch friction disc. On models with the 'pull-type' clutch, make sure that the release fork disengages fully from the release bearing.

46 If they are loose, remove the locating dowels from the engine or transmission, and keep them in a safe place.

Refitting

47 If the engine and transmission have not been separated, perform the operations described below from paragraph 58 onwards.

48 Apply a smear of high-melting-point grease (Peugeot recommend the use of Molykote BR2 plus – available from your Peugeot dealer) to the splines of the transmission input shaft. Do not apply too much, otherwise there is a possibility of the grease contaminating the clutch friction disc.

49 On models with the 'pull-type' clutch, fit the release bearing to the release fork with reference to Chapter 6, ensuring that the snap-ring is correctly in position in its groove.

50 Ensure that the locating dowels are correctly positioned in the engine or transmission.

4.38 Lowering the engine/transmission assembly to the ground (DW12 engine)

51 Carefully offer the transmission to the engine, until the locating dowels are engaged. Ensure that the weight of the transmission is not allowed to hang on the input shaft as it is engaged with the clutch friction disc.

52 Refit the transmission housing-to-engine bolts, ensuring that all the necessary brackets are correctly positioned, and tighten them securely.

53 On models with the 'pull-type' clutch, use the special tool described in Chapter 6 to pull the release fork in order to force the release bearing through the friction disc.

54 Locate the main engine wiring harness on the transmission and reconnect the relevant wiring connectors. On the DW12 engine in the project car, the wiring connectors are coloured as follows:

Fuel filter	Green
High-pressure fuel pump	White
Oil pressure switch	Grey
Oil level sensor	Green
Fuel rail	Red
Coolant temperature sensor	Green
Glow plugs	Grey
Air conditioning compressor	Grey

55 Refit the coolant heating housing to the transmission, ensuring that the earth leads and cable clips are correctly attached.

56 Refit the starter motor, and securely tighten its retaining bolts.

57 Refit the lower flywheel cover plate(s) to the transmission, and securely tighten the bolts.

58 Reconnect the hoist and lifting tackle to the engine lifting brackets. With the aid of an assistant, lift the assembly into the engine compartment, taking care not to damage surrounding components.

59 Refit the right-hand engine mounting and torque reaction link, but leave the link bolts finger-tight at this stage.

60 Working on the left-hand mounting, refit the left-hand engine mounting stud to the transmission together with its washer, then refit the spacer and coat it with grease. Refit the rubber mounting to the body and tighten the bolts, then refit the centre nut and washer and finger-tighten. On models with the ML5T transmission, refit the bracket to the transmission and tighten the bolts.

61 Position the engine and transmission on the mountings, and refit the mounting nuts/bolts hand-tight at this stage. Remove the hoist.

62 From underneath the vehicle, refit the rear mounting connecting link and finger-tighten the bolts.

63 Rock the engine to settle it on its mountings, then go around and tighten all the mounting nuts and bolts to their specified torque settings.

64 The remainder of the refitting procedure is a direct reversal of the removal sequence, with reference to the relevant chapters and noting the following points:

a) Ensure that the wiring loom is correctly routed and retained by all the relevant retaining clips; all connectors should be correctly and securely reconnected.

b) Prior to refitting the driveshafts to the transmission, renew the driveshaft oil seals as described in Chapter 7A.

c) Refer to Chapter 10 when refitting the power steering pump; the rear mounting bolt must be tightened last **(see illustration)**.

d) Ensure that all coolant hoses are correctly reconnected, and securely retained by their retaining clips.

e) Refill the engine and transmission with the correct quantity and type of lubricant, as described in Chapters 1A or 1B, and 7A.

f) Refill the cooling system as described in Chapter 1A or 1B.

g) Bleed the power steering system as described in Chapter 10.

h) Initialise the engine management ECU as follows. Start the engine and run to normal temperature. Carry out a road test during which the following procedure should be made. Engage third gear and stabilise the engine at 1000 rpm. Now accelerate fully to 3500 rpm.

---

5 Engine and automatic transmission – removal, separation and refitting

Removal

1 The procedure is essentially the same as described in Section 4, but carry out the following operations with reference to Chapter 7B.

a) Carefully prise the selector cable balljoint from the selector lever on the transmission multi-function switch. Extract the horseshoe-shaped clip securing the cable to the mounting bracket on the transmission.

b) Trace the wiring back from the multi-function switch to the wiring connector. Release the connector from the support bracket and disconnect it. Release the switch wiring from the support clip on the transmission.

c) Disconnect the wiring harness at the large connector adjacent to the transmission fluid cooler. Cover the wiring connector socket on the transmission to prevent water ingress when the fluid cooler hoses are disconnected.

d) Using hose clamps or similar, clamp both the fluid cooler coolant hoses to minimise coolant loss during subsequent operations.

e) Disconnect both coolant hoses from the fluid cooler being prepared for some coolant spillage. Wash off any spilt coolant immediately with cold water, and dry the surrounding area before proceeding further.

f) Unclip the wiring connector from the support bracket located just above the fluid cooler, then remove the support bracket.

4.64 The power steering pump rear bolt must be tightened last

g) Disconnect the earth cable from the stud on the transmission.

h) Remove the wiring harness bracket and the hose support bracket from the transmission.

i) Disconnect the wiring from the speedometer transducer (speedometer drive) and crankshaft (RPM) sensor, then remove the sensor from the bellhousing.

j) Remove the starter motor.

k) Label and disconnect any remaining wiring connectors and support brackets connected to the transmission.

Separation

2 With the engine/transmission assembly removed, support the assembly on suitable blocks of wood, on a workbench (or failing that, on a clean area of the workshop floor).

3 Locate the access hole at the lower rear of the cylinder block, then turn the crankshaft, by means of a socket on the crankshaft pulley bolt, until one of the torque converter retaining bolts is accessible through the access hole.

4 Undo the accessible torque converter bolt then turn the crankshaft as necessary and undo the remaining two bolts.

5 Slacken and remove the bolts securing the transmission housing to the engine. Note the correct fitted positions of each bolt and brackets, as they are removed, to use as a reference on refitting. Make a final check that all components have been disconnected, and are positioned clear of the transmission so that they will not hinder the removal procedure.

6 With the bolts removed, pull the transmission off the engine, to free it from its locating dowels. Once the transmission is free, and sufficient clearance exists, insert a bolt with a suitable washer through the crankshaft (RPM) sensor hole in the transmission bellhousing, to retain the torque converter on the transmission.

Preparation for reconnection

7 Prior to reconnection it is necessary to make a simple tool to align the torque converter with the driveplate as the transmission is refitted. To make the tool, obtain a bolt of the same size as the torque converter retaining bolts, but long enough to extend through the access hole in the cylinder block when the transmission is refitted.

7.2 Crankcase ventilation elbow on the DW12 diesel engine

8 Cut the head off the bolt and cut a slot (to enable it to be unscrewed) in the plain end. Check that the tool will slide easily through the torque converter retaining bolt hole in the driveplate.

9 Turn the engine crankshaft so that one of the torque converter retaining bolt holes in the driveplate, is aligned with the access hole in the cylinder block. Screw the alignment tool (finger-tight only) into one of the retaining bolt holes in the torque converter. Turn the torque converter so that the alignment tool is in approximately the correct position, relative to the cylinder block access hole. As the transmission is refitted, the alignment tool will pass through the retaining bolt hole in the driveplate and through the access hole. It can then be unscrewed with a screwdriver and the first torque converter retaining bolt fitted in its place.

10 Check that the torque converter support bush fitted to the centre of the crankshaft is in good condition, and in place.

11 Ensure that the engine/transmission locating dowels are correctly positioned prior to installation.

Reconnection

12 The transmission is reconnected by a reversal of the removal procedure, bearing in mind the following points:
a) Guide the transmission into position ensuring that the alignment tool passes through the driveplate and access hole.
b) Remove the bolt used to retain the torque converter in place, just before the transmission engages with the engine.
c) Once the transmission is bolted to the

7.3 Removing the camshaft chain guide

engine, remove the alignment tool and fit the first torque converter retaining bolt. Turn the crankshaft as necessary and fit the other two bolts.

Refitting

13 Refit the starter motor, and securely tighten its retaining bolts.

14 Refit the engine unit to the vehicle as described in the relevant refitting paragraphs of Section 4.

15 The remainder of the refitting procedure is a reversal of the removal sequence, noting the following points:
a) Ensure that the wiring loom is correctly routed, and retained by all the relevant retaining clips; all connectors should be correctly and securely reconnected.
b) Prior to refitting the driveshafts to the transmission, renew the driveshaft oil seals as described in Chapter 7B.
c) Ensure that all coolant hoses are correctly reconnected, and securely retained by their retaining clips.
d) Adjust the accelerator cable as described in the appropriate part of Chapter 4.
e) Refill the engine and transmission with correct quantity and type of lubricant, as described in Chapter 1A or 1B, and 7B.
f) Refill the cooling system (se Chapter 1A or 1B).
g) Initialise the engine management ECU as follows. Start the engine and run to normal temperature. Carry out a road test during which the following procedure should be made. Engage third gear and stabilise the engine at 1000 rpm. Now accelerate fully to 3500 rpm.

6 Engine overhaul – dismantling sequence

1 It is much easier to dismantle and work on the engine if it is mounted on a portable engine stand. These stands can often be hired from a tool hire shop. Before the engine is mounted on a stand, the flywheel/driveplate should be removed, so that the stand bolts can be tightened into the end of the cylinder block/crankcase.

2 If a stand is not available, it is possible to dismantle the engine with it blocked up on a sturdy workbench, or on the floor. Be extra-careful not to tip or drop the engine when working without a stand.

3 If you are going to obtain a reconditioned engine, all the external components must be removed first, to be transferred to the new engine (just as they will if you are doing a complete engine overhaul yourself). These components include the following:
a) Engine wiring harness and support brackets.
b) Alternator, power steering pump and air conditioning compressor mounting brackets (as applicable).
c) Coolant inlet and outlet housings.

d) Dipstick tube.
e) Fuel system components.
f) All electrical switches and sensors.
g) Inlet and exhaust manifolds and, where fitted, the turbocharger.
h) Oil filter and oil cooler.
i) Flywheel/driveplate.

Note: When removing the external components from the engine, pay close attention to details that may be helpful or important during refitting. Note the fitted position of gaskets, seals, spacers, pins, washers, bolts, and other small items.

4 If you are obtaining a 'short' engine (which consists of the engine cylinder block/crank-case, crankshaft, pistons and connecting rods all assembled), then the cylinder head, sump, oil pump, and timing belt will have to be removed also.

5 If you are planning a complete overhaul, the engine can be dismantled, and the internal components removed, in the order given below, referring to Part A, B or C of this Chapter unless otherwise stated.
a) Inlet and exhaust manifolds (Chapter 4A or 4B).
b) Timing belt, sprockets and tensioner.
c) Coolant pump (Chapter 3).
d) Cylinder head.
e) Flywheel/driveplate.
f) Sump.
g) Oil pump.
h) Balance shaft housing – DW12 diesel engine (Section 10 of this Chapter).
i) Pistons/connecting rods (Section 11 of this Chapter).
j) Crankshaft (Section 12 of this Chapter).

6 Before beginning the dismantling and overhaul procedures, make sure that you have all of the correct tools necessary. See *Tools and working facilities* for further information.

7 Cylinder head – dismantling

Note: New and reconditioned cylinder heads are available from the manufacturer, and from engine overhaul specialists. Be aware that some specialist tools are required for the dismantling and inspection procedures, and new components may not be readily available. It may therefore be more practical and economical for the home mechanic to purchase a reconditioned head, rather than dismantle, inspect and recondition the original head.

1 Remove the cylinder head as described in Part A, B or C of this Chapter (as applicable).

2 If not already done, remove the inlet and exhaust manifolds with reference to Chapter 4A or 4B. Remove any remaining brackets or housings as required **(see illustration)**.

3 Remove the camshaft(s), hydraulic tappets and rockers (as applicable) as described in Part A, B or C of this Chapter. On the 2.2 litre DW12 diesel engine, remove the camshaft drive chain guide from the cylinder head **(see illustration)**.

7.6a Use an Allen key to unscrew the grub screws securing the swirl-control butterflies on the shaft (DW12 engine)

7.6b Butterfly shaft retainer and stop (DW12 engine)

7.7a Compress the valve spring using a spring compressor . . .

7.7b . . . then extract the collets and release the spring compressor

7.7c Remove the spring retainer . . .

7.7d . . . followed by the valve spring . . .

4 If not already done on petrol models, remove the spark plugs as described in Chapter 1A.

5 If not already done on diesel models, remove the glow plugs as described in Chapter 5C.

6 On the 2.2 litre DW12 diesel engine, remove the swirl-control butterflies as follows. First, identify each butterfly for location and fitted position, to ensure correct refitting. Working on each butterfly in turn, unscrew the grub screws and slide the butterfly from the shaft. Mark the position of the stop, then remove it together with the retainer, and withdraw the shaft from the cylinder head **(see illustrations)**.

7 On all models, using a valve spring compressor, compress each valve spring in turn until the split collets can be removed. Release the compressor, and lift off the spring retainer, spring and, where fitted, the spring seat. Using a pair of pliers, carefully extract the valve stem oil seal from the top of the guide. On 16-valve engines, the valve stem oil seal also forms the spring seat and is deeply recessed in the cylinder head. It is also a tight fit on the valve guide making it difficult to remove with pliers or a conventional valve stem oil seal removal tool. It can be easily removed, however, using a self-locking nut of suitable diameter screwed onto the end of a bolt and locked with a second nut. Push the nut down onto the top of the seal; the locking portion of the nut will grip the seal allowing it to be withdrawn from the top of the valve guide. Access to the valves is limited, and it may be necessary to make up an adaptor out of metal

tube – cut out a 'window' so that the valve collets can be removed **(see illustrations)**.

8 If, when the valve spring compressor is screwed down, the spring retainer refuses to

7.7e . . . and the spring seat (not all models)

7.7g A metal tube adaptor for access to the valve collets

free and expose the split collets, gently tap the top of the tool, directly over the retainer, with a light hammer. This will free the retainer.

9 Withdraw the valve from the combustion

7.7f Remove the valve stem oil seal using a pair of pliers

7.7h Secure a self-locking nut of suitable diameter to a long bolt, then use this tool to remove the valve stem oil seal

chamber. Remove the valve stem oil seal from the top of the guide, then lift out the spring seat where fitted.

10 It is essential that each valve is stored together with its collets, retainer, spring, and spring seat. The valves should also be kept in their correct sequence, unless they are so badly worn that they are to be renewed. If they are going to be kept and used again, place each valve assembly in a labelled polythene bag or similar small container **(see illustration)**. Note that No 1 valve is nearest to the transmission (flywheel/driveplate) end of the engine.

8 Cylinder head and valves – cleaning and inspection

1 Thorough cleaning of the cylinder head and valve components, followed by a detailed inspection, will enable you to decide how much valve service work must be carried out during the engine overhaul. **Note:** *If the engine has been severely overheated, it is best to assume that the cylinder head is warped – check carefully for signs of this.*

Cleaning

2 Scrape away all traces of old gasket material from the cylinder head.

3 Scrape away the carbon from the combustion chambers and ports, then wash the cylinder head thoroughly with paraffin or a suitable solvent.

4 Scrape off any heavy carbon deposits that

7.10 Place each valve and its associated components in a labelled polythene bag

may have formed on the valves, then use a power-operated wire brush to remove deposits from the valve heads and stems.

Inspection

Note: *Be sure to perform all the following inspection procedures before concluding that the services of a machine shop or engine overhaul specialist are required. Make a list of all items that require attention.*

Cylinder head

5 Inspect the head very carefully for cracks, evidence of coolant leakage, and other damage. If cracks are found, a new cylinder head should be obtained. Use a straight-edge and feeler blade to check that the cylinder head gasket surface is not distorted **(see illustration)**. If it is, it may be possible to have it machined, provided that the cylinder head height is not significantly reduced.

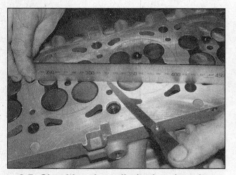

8.5 Checking the cylinder head gasket surface for distortion

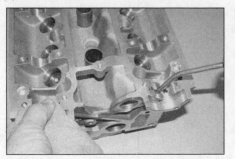

8.9a Apply compressed air to the oil feed bore of the inlet camshaft and seal the bore in the exhaust camshaft with a rag . . .

8.6 Checking the distance from the valve head to the cylinder head gasket surface

8.9b . . . the camshaft oil supply non-return valve will be ejected from the underside of the head

6 Examine the valve seats in each of the combustion chambers. If they are severely pitted, cracked, or burned, they will need to be renewed or recut by an engine overhaul specialist. If they are only slightly pitted, this can be removed by grinding-in the valve heads and seats with fine valve-grinding compound, as described below. Note on the DW12 diesel engine, however, that the valve heads must not be recessed below the surface of the cylinder head by more than the maximum amount given in the Specifications. After grinding-in the valves (described later), use a dial gauge to check the distance of recession for each valve in relation to the gasket surface and compare to that given in the Specifications. To do this, zero the dial gauge on the gasket surface, then move the probe onto each valve in turn. Alternatively, a straight-edge can be positioned on the gasket surface and the valve lifted until it contacts the straight-edge **(see illustration)**.

7 Check the valve guides for wear by inserting the relevant valve, and checking for side-to-side motion of the valve. A very small amount of movement is acceptable. If the movement seems excessive, remove the valve. Measure the valve stem diameter (see below), and renew the valve if it is worn. If the valve stem is not worn, the wear must be in the valve guide, and the guide must be renewed. The renewal of valve guides is best carried out by a Peugeot dealer or engine overhaul specialist, who will have the necessary tools available. Where no valve stem diameter is specified, seek the advice of a Peugeot dealer on the best course of action.

8 If renewing the valve guides, the valve seats should be recut or reground only *after* the guides have been fitted.

9 On the EW petrol engines, examine the camshaft oil supply non-return valve in the oil feed bore at the timing belt end of the cylinder head. Check that the valve is not loose in the cylinder head and that the ball is free to move within the valve body. If the valve is a loose fit in its bore, or if there is any doubt about its condition, it should be renewed. The non-return valve can be removed (assuming it is not loose), using compressed air, such as that generated by a tyre foot pump. Place the pump nozzle over the oil feed bore of the inlet camshaft No 4 bearing journal and seal the corresponding oil feed bore in the exhaust camshaft with a rag. Apply the compressed air and the valve will be forced out of its location in the underside of the cylinder head **(see illustrations)**. Fit the new non-return valve to its bore on the underside of the head ensuring it is fitted the correct way. Oil should be able to pass upwards through the valve to the camshafts, but the ball in the valve should prevent the oil from returning back to the cylinder block. Use a thin socket or similar to push the valve fully into position.

Valves

10 Examine the head of each valve for pitting, burning, cracks, and general wear.

Check the valve stem for scoring and wear ridges. Rotate the valve, and check for any obvious indication that it is bent. Look for pits or excessive wear on the tip of each valve stem. Renew any valve that shows any such signs of wear or damage.

11 If the valve appears satisfactory at this stage, measure the valve stem diameter at several points using a micrometer **(see illustration)**. Any significant difference in the readings obtained indicates wear of the valve stem. Should any of these conditions be apparent, the valve must be renewed.

12 If the valves are in satisfactory condition, they should be ground (lapped) into their respective seats, to ensure a smooth, gas-tight seal. If the seat is only lightly pitted, or if it has been recut, fine grinding compound *only* should be used to produce the required finish. Coarse valve-grinding compound should *not* be used, unless a seat is badly burned or deeply pitted. If this is the case, the cylinder head and valves should be inspected by an expert, to decide whether seat recutting, or even the renewal of the valve or seat insert (where possible) is required.

13 Valve grinding is carried out as follows. Place the cylinder head upside-down on a bench.

14 Smear a trace of (the appropriate grade of) valve-grinding compound on the seat face, and press a suction grinding tool onto the valve head **(see illustration)**. With a semi-rotary action, grind the valve head to its seat, lifting the valve occasionally to redistribute the grinding compound. A light spring placed under the valve head will greatly ease this operation.

15 If coarse grinding compound is being used, work only until a dull, matt even surface is produced on both the valve seat and the valve, then wipe off the used compound, and repeat the process with fine compound. When a smooth unbroken ring of light grey matt finish is produced on both the valve and seat, the grinding operation is complete. *Do not* grind-in the valves any further than absolutely necessary, or the seat will be prematurely sunk into the cylinder head.

16 When all the valves have been ground-in, carefully wash off *all* traces of grinding compound using paraffin or a suitable solvent, before reassembling the cylinder head.

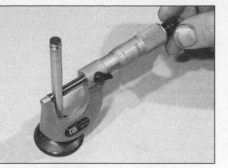
8.11 Measuring a valve stem diameter

Valve components

17 Examine the valve springs for signs of damage and discoloration. No minimum free length is specified by Peugeot, so the only way of judging valve spring wear is by comparison with a new component.

18 Stand each spring on a flat surface, and check it for squareness. If any of the springs are damaged, distorted or have lost their tension, obtain a complete new set of springs. It is normal to renew the valve springs as a matter of course if a major overhaul is being carried out.

19 Renew the valve stem oil seals regardless of their apparent condition.

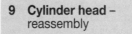

9 Cylinder head – reassembly

1 Working on the first valve assembly, refit the spring seat then dip the new valve stem oil seal in fresh engine oil. Locate the seal on the valve guide and press the seal firmly onto the guide using a suitable socket **(see illustrations)**.

2 Lubricate the stem of the first valve, and insert it in the guide **(see illustration)**.

3 Locate the valve spring on top of its seat, then refit the spring retainer. Note that on the EW7 engine, the larger diameter of the spring must face the cylinder head.

4 Compress the valve spring, and locate the split collets in the recess in the valve stem. Release the compressor, then repeat the procedure on the remaining valves. Ensure

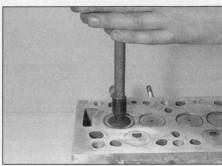
8.14 Grinding-in a valve

that each valve is inserted into its original location. If new valves are being fitted, insert them into the locations to which they have been ground.

> **HAYNES HiNT** *Use a little dab of grease to hold the collets in position on the valve stem while the spring compressor is released.*

5 With all the valves installed, support the cylinder head and, using a hammer and interposed block of wood, tap the end of each valve stem to settle the components.

6 On the 2.2 litre DW12 diesel engine, refit the swirl-control butterflies as follows. Lubricate the shaft with engine oil, then insert it into the cylinder head and refit the retainer and stop. Fit each butterfly in its correct location and tighten the grub screws securely. The stop must now be adjusted. First, loosen the locknut and position the stop eccentric so that the butterflies can be completely closed in their bores. At this stage, the butterflies will slightly 'bind' in their bores when pressure is applied. Now adjust the stop so that the butterflies do not 'bind' in their bores. Tighten the locknut with the stop in this position.

7 Refit the camshafts, hydraulic tappets and rocker arms (as applicable) as described in Part A, B or C of this Chapter.

8 Refit any remaining components using the reverse of the removal sequence and with new seals or gaskets as necessary.

9 The cylinder head can then be refitted as described in Part A, B or C of this Chapter.

9.1a Locate the valve stem oil seal on the valve guide . . .

9.1b . . . and press the seal firmly onto the guide using a suitable socket

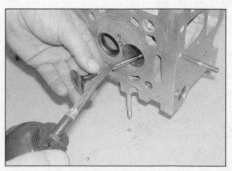
9.2 Lubricate the stem of the valve and insert it in the guide

10.1a Unscrew the oil pump mounting bolts . . .

10.1b . . . then tilt the pump from the crankcase and unhook the drive chain

10.2 TDC timing pin inserted through the crankcase hole into the flywheel

10.3 Marking the position of the balance shafts with a scriber prior to removing them

10.4 Bolts securing the balance shaft housing to the crankcase

10 Balance shaft housing (DW12 diesel engine) – removal, inspection and refitting

Note: *If a new housing is to be fitted, a Peugeot setting tool and adjustment shims will be required. Note that the balance shafts are timed accurately in relation to the crankshaft to ensure correct functioning, and therefore it is important to mark them accurately during the dismantling procedure.*

Removal

1 With the engine supported upside down on the workbench, remove the sump and oil pump as described in Chapter 2C **(see illustration)**.
2 Set the engine to TDC and lock the flywheel/driveplate with the timing pin **(see illustration)**.
3 Mark each balance shaft in relation to the housing to ensure correct refitting. Use a pin punch to mark the ends of each shaft in line with the cap housing joint face, or alternatively use a scriber and rule to mark the cap housing in line with the centres of the two vertical holes on the shafts **(see illustration)**.
4 Progressively unscrew the bolts securing the balance shaft housing to the crankcase. There are 8 bolts – do not unscrew the bolts securing the cap housing to the main housing at this stage **(see illustration)**.

5 Carefully lift the balance shaft housing from the crankcase, noting the location of adjustment shims for gear engagement. Remove the shims.

Inspection

6 Place the balance shaft housing on the bench with its lower side facing upwards (ie, the cap housing uppermost).
7 Position the balance shafts with the previously-made marks aligned with the marks on the housing. If a new balance shaft housing is being fitted, transfer the marks from the old balance shafts to the new ones, or, preferably, obtain the special Peugeot setting tool. If the Peugeot tool is obtained, position the balance shafts so that the blind holes at their timing ends are facing upwards (ie, towards the lower side of the housing) **(see illustration)**. The tool must now be used to lock the balance shafts in their TDC position. Engage the 5.0 mm pins of the tool in the blind holes, then fit the flange onto the housing and lightly tighten the tool bolt to lock it.
8 Position the special Peugeot gear engagement adjustment shims on the crankcase.
9 Lower the balance shafts and housing onto the shims and crankcase location dowels, and engage the crankshaft gear with the gears on the shafts. Check that the balance shafts are still aligned correctly, then remove the setting tool and timing pin.
10 Insert the bolts and finger-tighten them, then progressively tighten them in the order shown **(see illustration)**.
11 The endfloat of the balance shafts must now be checked. Attach a dial test gauge indicator (DTI) to the timing end of the engine, with the probe touching the end face of one of the balance shafts **(see illustration)**. Push the shaft fully in the direction of the flywheel/driveplate, then zero the DTI. Now move the shaft fully in the direction of the timing end of the engine, and record the endfloat. Carry out the procedure on the remaining balance shaft and record the endfloat. Check that the endfloat is as given in the Specifications.
12 The backlash clearance between the two balance shafts must now be checked. To do

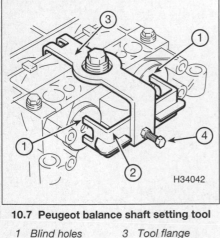

10.7 Peugeot balance shaft setting tool

1　*Blind holes*　　3　*Tool flange*
2　*Positioning gauge*　4　*Locking bolt*

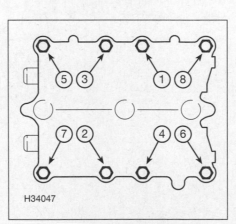

10.10 Balance shaft housing bolt tightening sequence

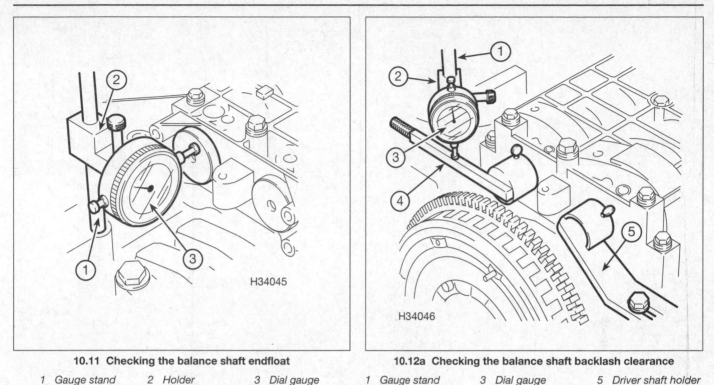

10.11 Checking the balance shaft endfloat

1 *Gauge stand*   2 *Holder*   3 *Dial gauge*

10.12a Checking the balance shaft backlash clearance

1 *Gauge stand*   3 *Dial gauge*   5 *Driver shaft holder*
2 *Holder*   4 *Driven shaft holder*

this, lock the driver shaft (front of the engine) using a suitable tool clamped to the flywheel/driveplate end of the shaft. The Peugeot tool consists of a sleeve which locates over the shaft, with a thumb screw to lock it onto the shaft, and an extension of the sleeve bolted to the crankcase. A further tool is clamped to the driven shaft, and the probe of a DTI positioned on the tool, 35.0 mm from the centre of the shaft. Move the driven shaft fully in one direction and zero the DTI, then move the shaft in the other direction and record the clearance. Check that the clearance is as given in the Specifications. A home-made version of the Peugeot tool can be made out of a Jubilee clip and a length of welding rod. Drill the clip to accept the rod, then tighten the clip onto the balance shaft **(see illustrations)**.

13 The backlash clearance between the driver balance shaft and the crankshaft gear must now be checked, and if necessary, a different shim selected for fitting between the housing and crankcase. First, clamp the special tool to the flywheel/driveplate end of the shaft, and arrange the DTI with its probe on the tool. Turn the shaft fully in one direction and zero the DTI, then turn it in the other direction and record the clearance. Turn the shaft by hand so that the crankshaft remains stationary. If the special tool is not available, a dial test gauge may be used through the window on the front of the balance shaft housing **(see illustrations)**.

14 Remove the tool from the balance shaft, and rotate the engine an eighth of a turn in its normal direction in order to obtain a quarter

rotation of the balance shafts. Repeat the backlash clearance check as described in paragraph 13 and record the result. Carry out 7 more checks and record each result; the engine will now have turned one complete turn.

10.12b Home-made tool for checking the backlash clearance between the two balance shafts

10.13a Gear on the crankshaft which is engaged with the rearmost balance shaft

10.12c Using the dial test gauge to check the backlash

10.13b Checking the backlash between the driver balance shaft and the crankshaft gear

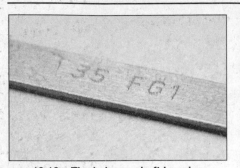

10.16a The balance shaft housing adjustment shims are marked to identify their thickness . . .

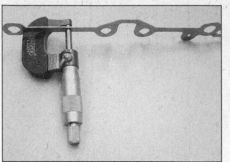

10.16b . . . however, the thickness can be checked with a micrometer

10.16c Locate the correct shims on the cylinder block

15 Calculate the average backlash clearance, then refer to the following list to select the correct shims to fit instead of the Peugeot adjustment shims.

Minimum clearance	Shim thickness	Shim marking
0.01≤ but <0.05	1.57	57
0.05	1.51	51
0.06	1.49	49
0.07	1.47	47
0.08	1.47	47
0.09	1.45	45
0.10	1.43	43
0.11	1.41	41
0.12	1.41	41
0.13	1.39	39
0.14	1.37	37
0.15	1.35	35
0.16	1.35	35
0.17	1.33	33
0.18	1.31	31
0.19	1.29	29
0.20	1.29	29
0.21	1.27	27
0.22	1.25	25
0.23	1.23	23
0.24	1.23	23
0.25	1.21	21
0.26	1.19	19
0.26<	1.19	19

16 Remove the tools, then unbolt the balance shaft housing from the crankcase and replace the adjustment shims with the shims chosen from the chart **(see illustrations)**.

Refitting

17 Refit the balance shaft housing as

previously described and progressively tighten the bolts in the order shown.
18 Repeat the clearance checking procedure again. The clearance should be between 0.01 and 0.07 mm.
19 Refit the sump as described in Chapter 2C.

11 Piston/connecting rod assembly – removal

1 Remove the cylinder head, sump and oil pump as described in Part A, B or C of this Chapter. On the DW12 diesel engine, also remove the balance shaft housing as described in Section 10.
2 If there is a pronounced wear ridge at the top of any bore, it may be necessary to remove it with a scraper or ridge reamer, to avoid piston damage during removal. Such a ridge indicates excessive wear of the cylinder bore.
3 Using quick-drying paint, mark each connecting rod and big-end bearing cap with its respective cylinder number on the flat machined surface provided; if the engine has been dismantled before, note carefully any identifying marks made previously **(see illustration)**. Note that No 1 cylinder is at the transmission (flywheel) end of the engine.
4 Turn the crankshaft to bring pistons 1 and 4 to BDC (bottom dead centre).
5 Unscrew the nuts or bolts, as applicable from No 1 piston big-end bearing cap. Take off the cap, and recover the bottom half bearing shell **(see illustration)**. If the bearing

shells are to be re-used, tape the cap and the shell together.
6 To prevent the possibility of damage to the crankshaft bearing journals on the XU engine, tape over the connecting rod stud threads **(see illustration)**.
7 Using a hammer handle, push the piston up through the bore, and remove it from the top of the cylinder block. Recover the bearing shell, and tape it to the connecting rod for safe-keeping.
8 Loosely refit the big-end cap to the connecting rod, and secure with the nuts/ bolts – this will help to keep the components in their correct order.
9 Remove No 4 piston assembly in the same way.
10 Turn the crankshaft through 180° to bring pistons 2 and 3 to BDC (bottom dead centre), and remove them in the same way.

12 Crankshaft – removal

1 Remove the crankshaft sprocket and the oil pump as described in Part A, B or C of this Chapter (as applicable). On the DW12 diesel engine, also remove the balance shaft housing as described in Section 10 of this Chapter.
2 Remove the pistons and connecting rods, as described in Section 11. If no work is to be done on the pistons and connecting rods, there is no need to remove the cylinder head, or to push the pistons out of the cylinder bores. The pistons should just be pushed far

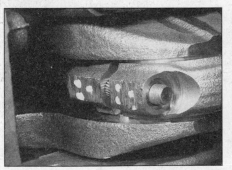

11.3 Connecting rod and big-end bearing cap identification marks (No 3 shown)

11.5 Removing a big-end bearing cap and shell

11.6 To protect the crankshaft journals, tape over the connecting rod stud threads

12.4 Removing the oil seal carrier from the right-hand end of the block

12.5a Remove the oil pump drive chain . . .

12.5b . . . then slide off the drive sprocket . . .

12.5c . . . and remove the Woodruff key from the crankshaft

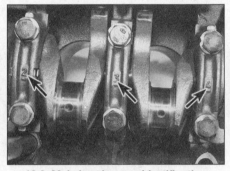

12.6 Main bearing cap identification markings (arrowed)

12.8 Removing No 2 main bearing cap. Note the thrustwasher (arrowed)

enough up the bores so that they are positioned clear of the crankshaft journals.

3 Check the crankshaft endfloat as described in Section 15, then proceed as follows.

XU and DW engines

4 Slacken and remove the retaining bolts, and remove the oil seal carrier from the timing belt end of the cylinder block, along with its gasket (where fitted) **(see illustration)**.

5 Remove the oil pump drive chain, and slide the drive sprocket and spacer (where fitted) off the end of the crankshaft. Remove the Woodruff key, and store it with the sprocket for safe-keeping **(see illustrations)**.

6 The main bearing caps should be numbered 1 to 5, starting from the transmission (flywheel/driveplate) end of the engine **(see illustration)**. If not, mark them accordingly using quick-drying paint. Also note the correct fitted depth of the crankshaft oil seal in the bearing cap.

7 On the XU petrol engine, undo the two bolts (one at the front of the block, and one at the rear) securing the centre main bearing cap to the block. Remove the bolts, along with their sealing washers.

8 On all engines, slacken and remove the main bearing cap retaining bolts/nuts, and lift off each bearing cap. Recover the lower

bearing shells, and tape them to their respective caps for safe-keeping. Also recover the lower thrustwasher halves from the side of No 2 main bearing cap **(see illustration)**. Remove the rubber sealing strips from the sides of No 1 main bearing cap, and discard them.

9 Lift out the crankshaft, and discard the oil seal **(see illustration)**.

10 Recover the upper bearing shells from the cylinder block, and tape them to their respective caps for safe-keeping **(see illustration)**. Remove the upper thrustwasher halves from the side of No 2 main bearing, and store them with the lower halves.

12.9 Lifting out the crankshaft

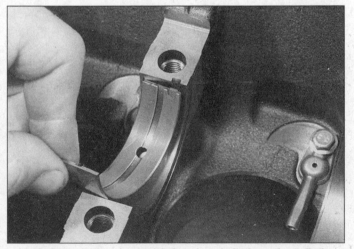

12.10 Remove the upper main bearing shells from the cylinder block/crankcase, and store them with their lower shells

12.13 Removing the crankshaft bearing cap housing

EW engines

11 Working around the inner periphery of the crankcase, unscrew the 16 small (M6) bolts securing the crankshaft bearing cap housing to the base of the cylinder block. Note the correct fitted depth of the left-hand crankshaft oil seal in the cylinder block/bearing cap housing.

12 Working in the reverse of the tightening sequence, evenly and progressively slacken the ten large (M11) bearing cap housing retaining bolts by a turn at a time. Once all the bolts are loose, remove them from the housing.

13 With all the retaining bolts removed, tap around the outer periphery of the bearing cap housing using a soft-faced mallet to break the seal between the housing and cylinder block. Once the seal is released and the housing is clear of the locating dowels, lift it up and off

the crankshaft and cylinder block **(see illustration)**. Recover the lower main bearing shells, and tape them to their respective locations in the housing. If the two locating dowels are a loose fit, remove them and store them with the housing for safe-keeping.

14 Lift out the crankshaft, and collect the left-hand oil seal.

15 Recover the upper main bearing shells, and store them along with the relevant lower bearing shell. Also recover the two thrustwashers (one fitted either side of No 2 main bearing) from the cylinder block.

13 Cylinder block/crankcase – cleaning and inspection

Cleaning

1 Remove all external components and electrical switches/sensors from the block. For complete cleaning, the core plugs should ideally be removed **(see illustrations)**. Drill a small hole in the plugs, then insert a self-tapping screw into the hole. Pull out the plugs by pulling on the screw with a pair of grips, or by using a slide hammer.

2 On aluminium block engines with wet liners, remove the liners, referring to paragraph 18.

3 Where applicable, undo the retaining bolts and remove the piston oil jet spray tubes from inside the cylinder block **(see illustration)**.

4 Scrape all traces of gasket from the cylinder block/crankcase, and from the main bearing

ladder (where fitted), taking care not to damage the gasket/sealing surfaces.

5 Remove all oil gallery plugs (where fitted). The plugs are usually very tight – they may have to be drilled out, and the holes retapped. Use new plugs when reassembling.

6 If any of the castings are extremely dirty, all should be steam-cleaned.

7 After the castings are returned, clean all oil holes and oil galleries one more time. Flush all internal passages with warm water until the water runs clear. Dry thoroughly, and apply a light film of oil to all mating surfaces, to prevent rusting. On cast-iron block engines, also oil the cylinder bores. If you have access to compressed air, use it to speed up the drying process, and to blow out all the oil holes and galleries.

⚠️ *Warning: Wear eye protection when using compressed air.*

8 If the castings are not very dirty, you can do an adequate cleaning job with hot (as hot as you can stand), soapy water and a stiff brush. Take plenty of time, and do a thorough job. Regardless of the cleaning method used, be sure to clean all oil holes and galleries very thoroughly, and to dry all components well. On cast-iron block engines, protect the cylinder bores as described above, to prevent rusting.

9 All threaded holes must be clean, to ensure accurate torque readings during reassembly. To clean the threads, run the correct-size tap into each of the holes to remove rust, corrosion, thread sealant or sludge, and to restore damaged threads **(see illustration)**. If possible, use compressed air to clear the holes of debris produced by this operation.

10 Apply suitable sealant to the new oil gallery plugs, and insert them into the holes in the block. Tighten them securely. Apply suitable sealant to the new core plugs, and insert them into the holes in the block. Tap them into place with a close-fitting tube or socket.

11 Where applicable, clean the threads of the piston oil jet retaining bolt, and apply a drop of thread-locking compound to the bolt threads. Refit the piston oil jet spray tube to the cylinder block, and tighten its retaining bolt to the specified torque setting.

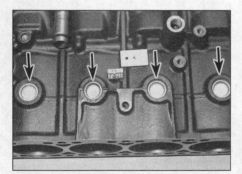

13.1a Cylinder block core plugs (arrowed)

13.1b Removing the air conditioning compressor mounting bracket

13.1c Removing the crankcase ventilation/oil separation box

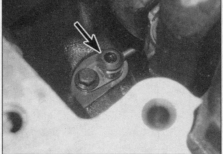

13.3 A piston oil jet spray tube in the cylinder block (DW12 engine)

13.9 Cleaning a cylinder block threaded hole using a suitable tap

12 If the engine is not going to be reassembled right away, cover it with a large plastic bag to keep it clean; protect all mating surfaces and the cylinder bores as described above, to prevent rusting.

Inspection

Cast-iron cylinder block

13 Visually check the castings for cracks and corrosion. Look for stripped threads in the threaded holes. If there has been any history of internal water leakage, it may be worthwhile having an engine overhaul specialist check the cylinder block/crankcase with special equipment. If defects are found, have them repaired if possible, or renew the assembly.

14 Check each cylinder bore for scuffing and scoring. Check for signs of a wear ridge at the top of the cylinder, indicating that the bore is excessively worn.

15 If the necessary measuring equipment is available, measure the bore diameter of each cylinder liner at the top (just under the wear ridge), centre, and bottom of the cylinder bore, parallel to the crankshaft axis.

16 Next, measure the bore diameter at the same three locations, at right-angles to the crankshaft axis. Compare the results with the figures given in the Specifications. If there is any doubt about the condition of the cylinder bores seek the advice of a Peugeot dealer or suitable engine reconditioning specialist.

17 At the time of writing, it was not clear whether oversize pistons were available for all models. Consult your Peugeot dealer for the latest information on piston availability. If oversize pistons are available, then it may be possible to have the cylinder bores rebored and oversize pistons fitted. If oversize pistons are not available, and the bores are worn, renewal of the block is the only option.

Aluminium cylinder block

18 Remove the liner clamps, then use a hard wood drift to tap out each liner from the inside of the cylinder block. When all the liners are released, tip the cylinder block/crankcase on its side and remove each liner from the top of the block. As each liner is removed, stick masking tape on its left-hand (transmission side) face, and write the cylinder number on the tape. No 1 cylinder is at the transmission (flywheel/driveplate) end of the engine. Remove the O-ring from the base of each liner, and discard it **(see illustrations)**.

19 Check each cylinder liner for scuffing and scoring. Check for a wear ridge at the top of the liner, indicating that the bore is badly worn.

20 If the necessary measuring equipment is available, measure the bore diameter of each cylinder liner at the top (just under the wear ridge), centre, and bottom of the cylinder bore, parallel to the crankshaft axis.

21 Next, measure the bore diameter at the same three locations, at right-angles to the crankshaft axis. Compare the results with the figures given in the Specifications.

13.18a On aluminium block engines, remove each liner . . .

22 Repeat the procedure for the remaining cylinder liners.

23 If the liner wear exceeds the permitted tolerances at any point, or if the cylinder liner walls are badly scored or scuffed, then renewal of the relevant liner assembly will be necessary. If there is any doubt about the condition of the cylinder bores, seek the advice of a Peugeot dealer or engine reconditioning specialist.

24 If renewal is necessary, new liners, complete with pistons and piston rings, can be purchased from a Peugeot dealer. Note that it is not possible to buy liners individually – they are supplied only as a matched assembly complete with piston and rings.

25 To allow for manufacturing tolerances, pistons and liners are separated into three size groups. The size group of each piston is indicated by a letter (A, B or C) stamped onto its crown, and the size group of each liner is indicated by a series of 1 to 3 notches on the upper lip of the liner; a single notch for group A, two notches for group B, and three notches for group C. Ensure that each piston and its respective liner are both of the same size group. It is permissible to have different size group piston and liner assemblies fitted to the same engine, but never fit a piston of one size group to a liner in a different group.

26 Prior to installing the liners, thoroughly clean the liner mating surfaces in the cylinder block, and use fine abrasive paper to polish away any burrs or sharp edges which might damage the liner O-rings. Clean the liners and wipe dry, then fit a new O-ring to the base of each liner. To aid installation, apply a smear of oil to each O-ring and to the base of the liner.

27 If the original liners are being refitted, use the marks made on removal to ensure that each is refitted the correct way round, and is inserted into its original bore. Insert each liner into the cylinder block, taking care not to damage the O-ring, and press it home as far as possible by hand. Using a hammer and a block of wood, tap each liner lightly but fully onto its locating shoulder. Wipe clean, then lightly oil, all exposed liner surfaces, to prevent rusting.

28 With all four liners correctly installed, use a dial gauge (or a straight-edge and feeler blade) to check that the protrusion of each

13.18b . . . and recover the bottom O-ring seal

liner above the upper surface of the cylinder block is within the limits given in the Specifications. The maximum difference between any two liners must not be exceeded.

29 If new liners are being fitted, it is permissible to interchange them to bring the difference in protrusion within limits. Remember to keep each piston with its respective liner.

30 If liner protrusion cannot be brought within limits, seek the advice of a Peugeot dealer or engine reconditioning specialist before proceeding with the engine rebuild.

14 Piston/connecting rod assembly – inspection

1 Before the inspection process can begin, the piston/connecting rod assemblies must be cleaned, and the original piston rings removed from the pistons.

2 Carefully expand the old rings over the top of the pistons. The use of two or three old feeler blades will be helpful in preventing the rings dropping into empty grooves **(see illustration)**. Be careful not to scratch the piston with the ends of the ring. The rings are brittle, and will snap if they are spread too far. They are also very sharp – protect your hands and fingers. Note that the third ring incorporates an expander. Always remove the rings from the top of the piston.

14.2 Removing a piston ring with the aid of a feeler blade

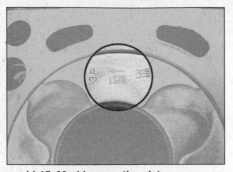

14.15 Markings on the piston crown (DW12 engine)

3 Scrape away all traces of carbon from the top of the piston. A hand-held wire brush (or a piece of fine emery cloth) can be used, once the majority of the deposits have been scraped away.

4 Remove the carbon from the ring grooves in the piston, using an old ring. Break the ring in half to do this. Be careful to remove only the carbon deposits – do not remove any metal, and do not nick or scratch the sides of the ring grooves.

5 Once the deposits have been removed, clean the piston/connecting rod assembly with paraffin or a suitable solvent, and dry thoroughly. Make sure that the oil return holes in the ring grooves are clear.

6 If the pistons and cylinder bores are not damaged or worn excessively, and if the cylinder block does not need to be rebored, the original pistons can be refitted. Normal piston wear shows up as even vertical wear on the piston thrust surfaces, and slight looseness of the top ring in its groove. New piston rings should always be used when the engine is reassembled.

7 Carefully inspect each piston for cracks around the skirt, around the gudgeon pin holes, and at the piston ring 'lands' (between the ring grooves).

8 Look for scoring and scuffing on the piston skirt, holes in the piston crown, and burned areas at the edge of the crown. If the skirt is scored or scuffed, the engine may have been suffering from overheating, and/or abnormal combustion which caused excessively high operating temperatures. The cooling and

lubrication systems should be checked thoroughly. Scorch marks on the sides of the pistons show that blow-by has occurred. A hole in the piston crown, or burned areas at the edge of the piston crown, indicates that abnormal combustion (pre-ignition, knocking, or detonation) has been occurring. If any of the above problems exist, the causes must be investigated and corrected, or the damage will occur again.

9 Corrosion of the piston, in the form of pitting, indicates that coolant has been leaking into the combustion chamber and/or the crankcase. Again, the cause must be corrected, or the problem may persist in the rebuilt engine.

10 On aluminium-block engines with wet liners, it is not possible to renew the pistons separately; pistons are only supplied with piston rings and a liner, as a part of a matched assembly. On iron-block engines, pistons can be purchased from a Peugeot dealer.

11 Examine each connecting rod carefully for signs of damage, such as cracks around the big-end and small-end bearings. Check that the rod is not bent or distorted. Damage is highly unlikely, unless the engine has been seized or badly overheated. Detailed checking of the connecting rod assembly can only be carried out by a Peugeot dealer or engine repair specialist with the necessary equipment.

12 The big-end cap bolts/nuts must be renewed as a complete set prior to refitting. This should be done after the big-end bearing running clearance check has been carried out. On the XU engine, the bolts can be simply tapped out of the connecting rods and new bolts fitted in the same way.

13 On petrol engines, the gudgeon pins are an interference fit in the connecting rod small-end bearing, therefore piston and/or connecting rod renewal should be entrusted to a Peugeot dealer or engine repair specialist, who will have the necessary tooling to remove and install the gudgeon pins.

14 On diesel engines, the gudgeon pins are of the floating type, secured in position by two circlips. On these engines, the pistons and connecting rods can be separated as described in the following paragraphs 15 to 21.

15 Before separating the piston and

connecting rod, check the position of the valve recesses or markings on the piston crown in relation to the connecting rod big-end bearing shell cut-outs and make a note of the orientation. On the DW12 diesel engine, the arrow on the piston crown points towards the timing end of the engine, and the big-end bearing location cut-outs are on the rear side of the engine **(see illustration)**.

16 Using a small flat-bladed screwdriver, prise out the circlips, and push out the gudgeon pin **(see illustrations)**. Hand pressure should be sufficient to remove the pin. Identify the piston and rod to ensure correct reassembly. Discard the circlips – new ones *must* be used on refitting.

17 Examine the gudgeon pin and connecting rod small-end bearing for signs of wear or damage. Wear can be cured by renewing both the pin and bush. Bush renewal, however, is a specialist job – press facilities are required, and the new bush must be reamed accurately.

18 The connecting rods themselves should not be in need of renewal, unless seizure or some other major mechanical failure has occurred. Check the alignment of the connecting rods visually, and if the rods are not straight, take them to an engine overhaul specialist for a more detailed check.

19 Examine all components, and obtain any new parts from your Peugeot dealer. If new pistons are purchased, they will be supplied complete with gudgeon pins and circlips. Circlips can also be purchased individually.

20 Position the piston in relation to the connecting rod big-end bearing shell cut-outs as noted during separation.

21 Apply a smear of clean engine oil to the gudgeon pin and slide it into the piston and through the connecting rod small-end. Check that the piston pivots freely on the rod, then secure the gudgeon pin in position with two new circlips. Ensure that each circlip is correctly located in its groove in the piston.

15 Crankshaft – inspection

Checking endfloat

1 If the crankshaft endfloat is to be checked, this must be done when the crankshaft is installed in the cylinder block/crankcase, but is free to move.

2 Check the endfloat using a dial gauge in contact with the end of the crankshaft. Push the crankshaft fully one way, and then zero the gauge. Push the crankshaft fully the other way, and check the endfloat. The result can be compared with the specified amount, and will give an indication as to whether new thrustwashers are required **(see illustration)**.

3 If a dial gauge is not available, feeler gauges can be used. First push the crankshaft fully towards the flywheel end of the engine,

14.16a Prise out the circlip . . .

14.16b . . . and withdraw the gudgeon pin

15.2 Checking crankshaft endfloat using a dial gauge

15.3 Checking crankshaft endfloat using feeler blades

15.10 Measuring a crankshaft big-end journal diameter

then use feeler gauges to measure the gap between the web of No 2 crankpin and the thrustwasher **(see illustration)**.

Inspection

4 Clean the crankshaft using paraffin or a suitable solvent, and dry it, preferably with compressed air if available. Be sure to clean the oil holes with a pipe cleaner or similar probe, to ensure that they are not obstructed.

 Warning: Wear eye protection when using compressed air.

5 Check the main and big-end bearing journals for uneven wear, scoring, pitting and cracking.

6 Big-end bearing wear is accompanied by distinct metallic knocking when the engine is running (particularly noticeable when the engine is pulling from low speed) and by some loss of oil pressure.

7 Main bearing wear is accompanied by severe engine vibration and rumble – getting progressively worse as engine speed increases – and again by loss of oil pressure.

8 Check the bearing journal for roughness by running a finger lightly over the bearing surface. Any roughness (which will be accompanied by obvious bearing wear) indicates that the crankshaft requires regrinding (where possible) or renewal.

9 If the crankshaft has been reground, check for burrs around the crankshaft oil holes (the holes are usually chamfered, so burrs should not be a problem unless regrinding has been carried out carelessly). Remove any burrs with a fine file or scraper, and thoroughly clean the oil holes as described previously.

10 Using a micrometer, measure the diameter of the main and big-end bearing journals, and compare the results with the Specifications **(see illustration)**. By measuring the diameter at a number of points around each journal's circumference, you will be able to determine whether or not the journal is out-of-round. Take the measurement at each end of the journal, near the webs, to determine if the journal is tapered. Compare the results obtained with those given in the Specifications.

11 Check the oil seal contact surfaces at each end of the crankshaft for wear and

damage. If the seal has worn a deep groove in the surface of the crankshaft, consult an engine overhaul specialist; repair may be possible, but otherwise a new crankshaft will be required.

12 Peugeot produce a set of undersize bearing shells for both the main and big-end bearings on most engines. Where the crankshaft journals have not already been reground, it may be possible to have the crankshaft reconditioned, and to fit undersize shells. If no undersize shells are available and the crankshaft has worn beyond the specified limits, the crankshaft will have to be renewed. Consult your Peugeot dealer or engine specialist for further information on parts availability.

16 Main and big-end bearings – inspection

1 Even though the main and big-end bearings should be renewed during the engine overhaul, the old bearings should be retained

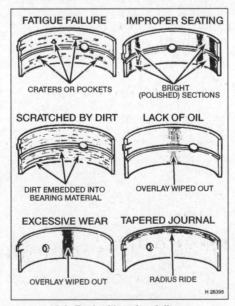

16.2 Typical bearing failures

FATIGUE FAILURE — CRATERS OR POCKETS

IMPROPER SEATING — BRIGHT (POLISHED) SECTIONS

SCRATCHED BY DIRT — DIRT EMBEDDED INTO BEARING MATERIAL

LACK OF OIL — OVERLAY WIPED OUT

EXCESSIVE WEAR — OVERLAY WIPED OUT

TAPERED JOURNAL — RADIUS RIDE

H 28395

for close examination, as they may reveal valuable information about the condition of the engine. The bearing shells are graded by thickness, the grade of each shell being indicated by the colour code marked on it.

2 Bearing failure can occur due to lack of lubrication, the presence of dirt or other foreign particles, overloading the engine, or corrosion **(see illustration)**. Regardless of the cause of bearing failure, the cause must be corrected (where applicable) before the engine is reassembled, to prevent it from happening again.

3 When examining the bearing shells, remove them from the cylinder block/crankcase, the main bearing ladder/caps (as appropriate), the connecting rods and the connecting rod big-end bearing caps. Lay them out on a clean surface in the same general position as their location in the engine. This will enable you to match any bearing problems with the corresponding crankshaft journal. *Do not touch any shell's bearing surface with your fingers while checking it, or the delicate surface may be scratched.*

4 Dirt and other foreign matter gets into the engine in a variety of ways. It may be left in the engine during assembly, or it may pass through filters or the crankcase ventilation system. It may get into the oil, and from there into the bearings. Metal chips from machining operations and normal engine wear are often present. Abrasives are sometimes left in engine components after reconditioning, especially when parts are not thoroughly cleaned using the proper cleaning methods. Whatever the source, these foreign objects often end up embedded in the soft bearing material, and are easily recognised. Large particles will not embed in the bearing, and will score or gouge the bearing and journal. The best prevention for this cause of bearing failure is to clean all parts thoroughly, and keep everything spotlessly-clean during engine assembly. Frequent and regular engine oil and filter changes are also recommended.

5 Lack of lubrication (or lubrication breakdown) has a number of interrelated causes. Excessive heat (which thins the oil), overloading (which squeezes the oil from the bearing face) and oil leakage (from excessive bearing clearances, worn oil pump or high

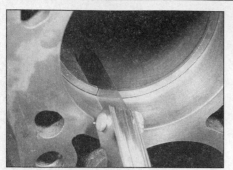

18.5 Measuring a piston ring end gap

engine speeds) all contribute to lubrication breakdown. Blocked oil passages, which usually are the result of misaligned oil holes in a bearing shell, will also oil-starve a bearing, and destroy it. When lack of lubrication is the cause of bearing failure, the bearing material is wiped or extruded from the steel backing of the bearing. Temperatures may increase to the point where the steel backing turns blue from overheating.

6 Driving habits can have a definite effect on bearing life. Full-throttle, low-speed operation (labouring the engine) puts very high loads on bearings, tending to squeeze out the oil film. These loads cause the bearings to flex, which produces fine cracks in the bearing face (fatigue failure). Eventually, the bearing material will loosen in pieces, and tear away from the steel backing.

7 Short-distance driving leads to corrosion of bearings, because insufficient engine heat is produced to drive off the condensed water and corrosive gases. These products collect in the engine oil, forming acid and sludge. As the oil is carried to the engine bearings, the acid attacks and corrodes the bearing material.

8 Incorrect bearing installation during engine assembly will lead to bearing failure as well. Tight-fitting bearings leave insufficient bearing running clearance, and will result in oil

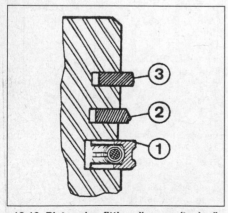

18.10 Piston ring fitting diagram (typical)

1 Oil control ring
2 Second compression ring
3 Top compression ring

starvation. Dirt or foreign particles trapped behind a bearing shell result in high spots on the bearing, which lead to failure.

9 *Do not* touch any shell's bearing surface with your fingers during reassembly; there is a risk of scratching the delicate surface, or of depositing particles of dirt on it.

10 As mentioned at the beginning of this Section, the bearing shells should be renewed as a matter of course during engine overhaul; to do otherwise is false economy. Refer to Sections 19 and 20 for details of bearing shell selection.

17 Engine overhaul – reassembly sequence

1 Before reassembly begins, ensure that all new parts have been obtained, and that all necessary tools are available. Read through the entire procedure to familiarise yourself with the work involved, and to ensure that all items necessary for reassembly of the engine are at hand. In addition to all normal tools and materials, thread-locking compound will be needed. A suitable tube of liquid sealant will also be required for the joint faces that are fitted without gaskets. It is recommended that Peugeot's own products are used, which are specially formulated for this purpose; the relevant product names are quoted in the text of each Section where they are required.

2 In order to save time and avoid problems, engine reassembly can be carried out in the following order:
a) *Crankshaft (Section 19).*
b) *Piston/connecting rod assemblies (Section 20).*
c) *Balance shaft housing – DW12 diesel engine (Section 10).*
d) *Oil pump (See Part A, B or C – as applicable).*
e) *Sump (See Part A, B or C – as applicable).*
f) *Flywheel (See Part A, B or C – as applicable).*
g) *Cylinder head (See Part A, B or C – as applicable).*
h) *Timing belt tensioner and sprockets, and timing belt (See Part A, B or C – as applicable).*
i) *Engine external components.*

3 At this stage, all engine components should be absolutely clean and dry, with all faults repaired. The components should be laid out (or in individual containers) on a completely clean work surface.

18 Piston rings – refitting

1 Before fitting new piston rings, the ring end gaps must be checked as follows.

2 Lay out the piston/connecting rod

assemblies and the new piston ring sets, so that the ring sets will be matched with the same piston and cylinder during the end gap measurement and subsequent engine reassembly.

3 Insert the top ring into the first cylinder, and push it down the bore using the top of the piston. This will ensure that the ring remains square with the cylinder walls. Position the ring near the bottom of the cylinder bore, at the lower limit of ring travel. Note that the top and second compression rings are different. The second ring is easily identified by the step on its lower surface, and by the fact that its outer face is tapered.

4 Measure the end gap using feeler gauges.

5 Repeat the procedure with the ring at the top of the cylinder bore, at the upper limit of its travel, and compare the measurements with the figures given in the Specifications **(see illustration)**. Where no figures are given, seek the advice of a Peugeot dealer or engine reconditioning specialist.

6 If the gap is too small (unlikely if genuine Peugeot parts are used), it must be enlarged, or the ring ends may contact each other during engine operation, causing serious damage. Ideally, new piston rings providing the correct end gap should be fitted. As a last resort, the end gap can be increased by filing the ring ends very carefully with a fine file. Mount the file in a vice equipped with soft jaws, slip the ring over the file with the ends contacting the file face, and slowly move the ring to remove material from the ends. Take care, as piston rings are sharp, and are easily broken.

7 With new piston rings, it is unlikely that the end gap will be too large. If the gaps are too large, check that you have the correct rings for your engine and for the particular cylinder bore size.

8 Repeat the checking procedure for each ring in the first cylinder, and then for the rings in the remaining cylinders. Remember to keep rings, pistons and cylinders matched up.

9 Once the ring end gaps have been checked and if necessary corrected, the rings can be fitted to the pistons.

10 Fit the piston rings using the same technique as for removal. Fit the bottom (oil control) ring first, and work up. When fitting the oil control ring, first insert the expander (where fitted), then fit the ring with its gap positioned 180° from the expander gap. Ensure that the second compression ring is fitted the correct way up, with its identification mark (either a dot of paint or the word TOP stamped on the ring surface) at the top, and the stepped surface at the bottom **(see illustration)**. Arrange the gaps of the top and second compression rings 120° either side of the oil control ring gap. Note: *Always follow any instructions supplied with the new piston ring sets – different manufacturers may specify different procedures. Do not mix up the top and second compression rings, as they have different cross-sections.*

19 Crankshaft –
refitting and main bearing running clearance check

New main bearing shells

1 To ensure that the main bearing running clearance is correct, the bearing shells are supplied in various thicknesses or grades. The grades are indicated by a colour-coding marked on the edge of each shell. The grade of the new bearing shells required (either standard size or undersize) is selected using the reference marks on the cylinder block and on the crankshaft. The cylinder block marks identify the diameter of the bearing bores in the block, and the crankshaft marks identify the diameter of the crankshaft journals.

2 Note that on the engines described in this Manual, the upper shells are all of the same size, and the running clearance is controlled by fitting a lower bearing shell of the required thickness.

3 Numerous grades of standard and oversize bearing shells are available, depending on the engine type, year of manufacture, and country of export. Using the cylinder block and crankshaft reference marks together with the crankshaft journal diameter, a Peugeot dealer or engine overhaul specialist will be able to supply the correct bearing shells to give the required bearing running clearance for each journal **(see illustration)**.

4 Whether the original shells or new shells are being fitted, it is recommended that the running clearance is checked as follows prior to crankshaft installation.

Running clearance check

5 The running clearance check can be carried out using the original bearing shells. However, it is preferable to use a new set, since the results obtained will be more conclusive.

6 Clean the backs of the bearing shells, and the bearing locations in both the cylinder block/crankcase and the main bearing caps.

7 Press the bearing shells into their locations, ensuring that the tab on each shell engages in the notch in the cylinder block/crankcase or bearing cap **(see illustrations)**. Take care not to touch any shell's bearing surface with your fingers. Note that the upper bearing shells all have a grooved bearing surface, whereas the lower shells have a plain bearing surface. If the original bearing shells are being used for the check, ensure that they are refitted in their original locations.

8 The clearance can be checked in either of two ways.

9 One method (which will be difficult to achieve without a range of internal micrometers or internal/external expanding calipers) is to refit the main bearing caps to the cylinder block/crankcase, with bearing shells in place. With the cap retaining bolts tightened to the specified torque, measure the internal diameter of each assembled pair of

bearing shells. If the diameter of each corresponding crankshaft journal is measured and then subtracted from the bearing internal diameter, the result will be the main bearing running clearance.

10 The second (and more accurate) method is to use a product known as Plastigauge. This consists of a fine thread of perfectly-round plastic, which is compressed between the bearing shell and the journal. When the shell is removed, the plastic is deformed, and can be measured with a special card gauge supplied with the kit. The running clearance is determined from this gauge. Plastigauge should be available from your Peugeot dealer; otherwise, enquiries at one of the larger specialist motor factors should produce the name of a stockist in your area. The procedure for using Plastigauge is as follows.

11 With the main bearing upper shells in place, carefully lay the crankshaft in position **(see illustration)**. Do not use any lubricant; the crankshaft journals and bearing shells must be perfectly clean and dry.

12 Cut several lengths of the appropriate-size Plastigauge (they should be slightly shorter than the width of the main bearings), and place one length on each crankshaft journal axis **(see illustration)**.

13 With the main bearing lower shells in position, refit the main bearing caps or bearing cap housing (as applicable) and tighten the bolts as described later in this Section. Take care not to disturb the Plastigauge, and *do not* rotate the crankshaft at any time during this operation.

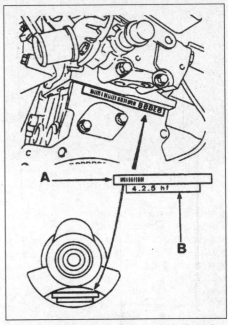

19.3 Cylinder block and crankshaft main bearing reference markings – XU series engine

A Bar code (for production use only)
B Reference marks

14 Remove the main bearing caps/housing, again taking great care not to disturb the Plastigauge or rotate the crankshaft.

15 Compare the width of the crushed Plastigauge on each journal to the scale

19.7a Fit the bearing shells, ensuring that the tab engages in the notch in the cylinder block/crankcase . . .

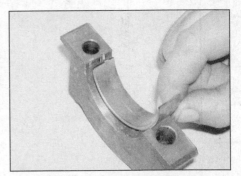

19.7b . . . and in the bearing cap

19.11 Lower the crankshaft into the cylinder block

19.12 Plastigauge in place on a crankshaft main bearing journal

19.15 Measure the width of the deformed Plastigauge using the scale on the card

19.21 Fit the upper thrustwashers to No 2 main bearing location with the oil way grooves facing outwards

19.23 Lower the crankshaft into position in the cylinder block/crankcase

printed on the Plastigauge envelope, to obtain the main bearing running clearance **(see illustration)**. Compare the clearance measured with that in the Specifications at the start of this Chapter.

16 If the clearance is significantly different from that expected, the bearing shells may be the wrong size (or excessively worn, if the original shells are being re-used). Before deciding that different-size shells are required, make sure that no dirt or oil was trapped between the bearing shells and the caps or block when the clearance was measured. If the Plastigauge was wider at one end than at the other, the crankshaft journal may be tapered.

17 If the clearance is not as specified, use the reading obtained, along with the shell thicknesses quoted above, to calculate the necessary grade of bearing shells required. When calculating the bearing clearance required, bear in mind that it is always better to have the running clearance towards the lower end of the specified range, to allow for wear in use.

18 Where necessary, obtain the required grades of bearing shell, and repeat the running clearance checking process described above.

19 On completion, carefully scrape away all traces of the Plastigauge material from the crankshaft and bearing shells. Use your fingernail, or a wooden or plastic scraper which is unlikely to score the bearing surfaces.

Final crankshaft refitting

XU and DW engines

20 Carefully lift the crankshaft out of the cylinder block once more.

21 Using a little grease, stick the upper thrustwashers to each side of the No 2 main bearing upper location. Ensure that the oil way grooves on each thrustwasher face outwards (away from the cylinder block) **(see illustration)**.

22 Place the bearing shells in their locations as described earlier. If new shells are being fitted, ensure that all traces of protective grease are cleaned off using paraffin. Wipe dry the shells and connecting rods with a lint-free cloth. Liberally lubricate each bearing shell in the cylinder block/crankcase and cap with clean engine oil.

23 Lower the crankshaft into position so that Nos 2 and 3 cylinder crankpins are at TDC; Nos 1 and 4 cylinder crankpins will be at BDC, ready for fitting No 1 piston **(see illustration)**. Check the crankshaft endfloat, referring to Section 15.

24 Lubricate the lower bearing shells in the main bearing caps with clean engine oil. Make sure that the locating lugs on the shells engage with the corresponding recesses in the caps.

25 Fit main bearing caps Nos 2 to 5 to their correct locations, ensuring that they are fitted the correct way round (the bearing shell tab recesses in the block and caps must be on the same side). Insert the bolts/nuts,

tightening them only loosely at this stage.

26 Apply a small amount of sealant to the No 1 main bearing cap mating face on the cylinder block, around the sealing strip holes **(see illustration)**.

27 Locate the tab of each sealing strip over the pins on the base of No 1 bearing cap, and press the strips into the bearing cap grooves. It is now necessary to obtain two thin metal strips, of 0.25 mm thickness or less, in order to prevent the strips moving when the cap is being fitted. Peugeot garages use the tool shown, which acts as a clamp. Metal strips (such as old feeler blades) can be used, provided all burrs which may damage the sealing strips are first removed **(see illustration)**.

28 Where applicable, oil both sides of the metal strips, and hold them on the sealing strips. Fit the No 1 main bearing cap, insert the bolts loosely, then carefully pull out the metal strips in a horizontal direction, using a pair of pliers **(see illustration)**.

29 Tighten all the main bearing cap bolts/nuts evenly to the specified torque. Using a sharp knife, trim off the ends of the No 1 bearing cap sealing strips, so that they protrude above the cylinder block/crankcase mating surface by approximately 1 mm **(see illustrations)**.

30 On the XU petrol engine, refit the centre main bearing side retaining bolts and sealing washers (one at the front of the block, and one at the rear) and tighten them both to the specified torque.

19.26 Apply sealant to the No 1 main bearing cap mating face on the cylinder block, around the sealing strip holes and in the corners

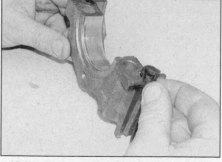

19.27 Fit the sealing strips to No 1 main bearing cap

19.28 Use two metal strips (arrowed) to hold the sealing strips in place as the bearing cap is fitted

19.29a Tighten all the main bearing cap bolts to the specified torque . . .

19.29b . . . and, where necessary, additionally through the specified angle

19.29c Trim off the ends of No 1 bearing cap sealing strips, so that they protrude by approximately 1.0 mm

19.34a Drive out the old oil seal . . .

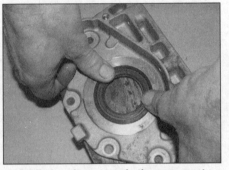

19.34b . . . then press in the new one to the previously noted depth

19.35a Apply the sealant . . .

31 Fit a new crankshaft left-hand oil seal as described in Part A or C of this Chapter (as applicable).

32 Refit the piston/connecting rod assemblies to the crankshaft as described in Section 20.

33 Refit the Woodruff key, then slide on the oil pump drive sprocket and spacer (where fitted), and locate the drive chain on the sprocket.

34 Ensure that the mating surfaces of the right-hand oil seal carrier and cylinder block are clean and dry. Note the correct fitted depth of the oil seal then, lever or drive out the old oil seal from the housing. If preferred, a new oil seal can be pressed into the housing at this stage (see illustrations).

35 Apply a smear of suitable sealant to the oil seal carrier mating surface. Ensure that the locating dowels are in position, then slide the carrier over the end of the crankshaft and into position on the cylinder block (see illustrations). Tighten the carrier retaining bolts to the specified torque.

36 If not already done, fit a new crankshaft right-hand oil seal as described in Part A or C of this Chapter.

37 Ensuring that the drive chain is correctly located on the sprocket, refit the oil pump and sump as described in Part A or C of this Chapter.

38 Where removed, refit the cylinder head as described in Part A or C, or this Part.

EW engines

39 Carefully lift the crankshaft out of the cylinder block once more.

40 Place the bearing shells in their locations as described earlier. If new shells are being fitted, ensure that all traces of protective grease are cleaned off using paraffin. Wipe dry the shells with a lint-free cloth.

41 Liberally lubricate each bearing shell in the cylinder block with clean engine oil then lower the crankshaft into position (see illustration).

42 Insert the thrustwashers to either side of No 2 main bearing upper location and push them around the bearing journal until their edges are horizontal (see illustration). Ensure that the oil way grooves on each thrustwasher face outwards (away from the bearing journal).

43 Thoroughly degrease the mating surfaces of the cylinder block and the crankshaft bearing cap housing. Apply a thin bead of RTV sealant to the bearing cap housing mating surface (see illustration). Peugeot

19.35b . . . then fit the oil seal carrier . . .

19.41 Lubricate the bearing shells and lower the crankshaft into the cylinder block

19.42 Insert the thrustwashers either side of No 2 main bearing upper location

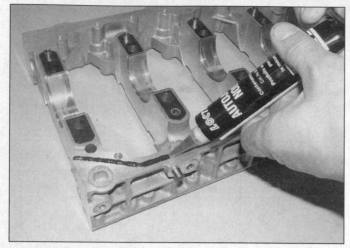

19.43 Apply a thin bead of RTV sealant to the bearing cap housing mating surface

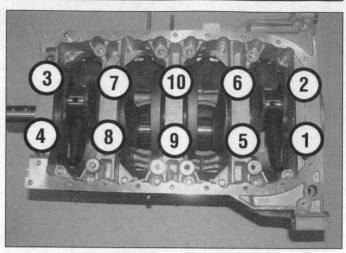

19.46 Crankshaft bearing cap housing retaining bolt tightening sequence

recommend the use of Loctite Autojoint Noir for this purpose.

44 Lubricate the lower bearing shells with clean engine oil, then refit the bearing cap housing, ensuring that the shells are not displaced, and that the locating dowels engage correctly.

45 Install the ten M11, and sixteen M6 crankshaft bearing cap housing retaining bolts, and screw them in until they are just making contact with the housing.

46 Working in the sequence shown, tighten all the M11 bolts to the Stage 1 torque setting given in the Specifications **(see illustration)**. Now tighten all the M6 bolts to the Stage 2 torque setting (finger-tight).

47 Fully slacken all the M11 bolts (Stage 3), then tighten them to the Stage 4 setting, working in the correct sequence.

48 Finally tighten all the M11 bolts, in the correct sequence, through the specified Stage 5 angle, using an angle tightening gauge.

49 The M6 bolts can now be tightened to the Stage 6 torque setting.

50 With the bearing cap housing in place, check that the crankshaft rotates freely.

51 Refit the piston/connecting rod assemblies to the crankshaft as described in Section 20.

52 Refit the oil pump and sump as described in Part B.

53 Fit a new crankshaft left-hand oil seal, then refit the flywheel as described in Part B.

54 Where removed, refit the cylinder head, crankshaft sprocket and timing belt also as described in Part B.

---

20 Pistons/connecting rods – refitting and big-end bearing running clearance check

New big-end bearing shells

1 There are two sizes of big-end bearing shell available; a standard size for use with the standard crankshaft, and an undersize for use once the crankshaft journals have been reground.

2 Consult your Peugeot dealer for the latest information on parts availability. To be safe, always quote the diameter of the crankshaft big-end crankpins when ordering bearing shells.

3 Prior to refitting the piston/connecting rod assemblies, it is recommended that the big-end bearing running clearance is checked as follows.

Running clearance check

4 Clean the backs of the bearing shells, and the bearing locations in both the connecting rod and bearing cap.

5 Press the bearing shells into their locations, ensuring that the tab on each shell engages in the notch in the connecting rod and cap. Take care not to touch any shell's bearing surface with your fingers **(see illustrations)**. If the original bearing shells are being used for the check, ensure they are refitted in their original locations. The clearance can be checked in either of two ways.

6 One method is to refit the big-end bearing cap to the connecting rod, ensuring they are fitted the correct way around, with the bearing shells in place. With the cap retaining nuts correctly tightened, use an internal micrometer or Vernier caliper to measure the internal diameter of each assembled pair of bearing shells. If the diameter of each corresponding crankshaft journal is measured and then subtracted from the bearing internal diameter, the result will be the big-end bearing running clearance.

7 The second, and more accurate method is to use Plastigauge (see Section 19).

8 Ensure that the bearing shells are correctly fitted. Place a strand of Plastigauge on each (cleaned) crankpin journal.

9 Refit the (clean) piston/connecting rod assemblies to the crankshaft, and refit the big-end bearing caps, using the marks made or noted on removal to ensure they are fitted the correct way around.

10 Tighten the bearing cap nuts as described later in this Section. Take care not to disturb the Plastigauge or rotate the connecting rod during the tightening sequence.

11 Dismantle the assemblies without rotating the connecting rods. Use the scale printed on the Plastigauge envelope to obtain the big-end bearing running clearance.

12 If the clearance is significantly different from that expected, the bearing shells may be

20.5a Fit the big-end bearing shells ensuring that the tab engages in the notch in the connecting rod . . .

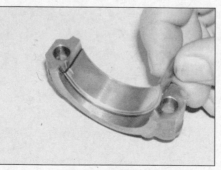

20.5b . . . and in the connecting rod cap

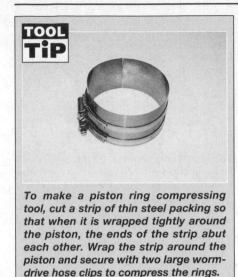

To make a piston ring compressing tool, cut a strip of thin steel packing so that when it is wrapped tightly around the piston, the ends of the strip abut each other. Wrap the strip around the piston and secure with two large worm-drive hose clips to compress the rings.

20.19a Insert the piston/connecting rod assembly into the top of the relevant cylinder

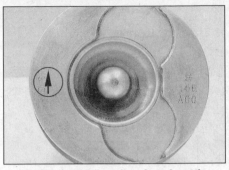

20.19b On 2.0 litre diesel engines the arrow on the piston crown must point towards the timing belt end of the engine

20.19c Tap the assembly into the cylinder bore until the piston crown is flush with the top of the block

the wrong size (or excessively worn, if the original shells are being re-used). Make sure that no dirt or oil was trapped between the bearing shells and the caps or block when the clearance was measured. If the Plastigauge was wider at one end than at the other, the crankshaft journal may be tapered.

13 Note that Peugeot do not specify a recommended big-end bearing running clearance. The figure given in the Specifications is a guide figure, which is typical for this type of engine. Before condemning the components concerned, refer to your Peugeot dealer or engine reconditioning specialist for further information on the specified running clearance. Their advice on the best course of action to be taken can then also be obtained.

14 On completion, carefully scrape away all traces of the Plastigauge material from the crankshaft and bearing shells. Use your fingernail, or some other object which is unlikely to score the bearing surfaces.

Piston/connecting rod refitting

15 Note that the following procedure assumes that the cylinder liners (where fitted) are in position in the cylinder block/crankcase, and that the crankshaft and main bearing caps are in place.

16 Ensure that the bearing shells are correctly fitted as described earlier. If new shells are being fitted, ensure that all traces of the protective grease are cleaned off using paraffin. Wipe dry the shells and connecting rods with a lint-free cloth.

17 Lubricate the cylinder bores, the pistons, and piston rings, then lay out each piston/connecting rod assembly in its respective position.

18 Start with assembly No 1. Make sure that the piston rings are still spaced as described in Section 18, then clamp them in position with a piston ring compressor. Due to the construction and small size of the oil control

piston ring on the EW engines, it is very easy to damage the ring when fitting the piston/connecting rod assembly if a conventional piston ring compressor is used. The lower part of the ring slips out of the ring compressor just before it enters the cylinder bore and can easily be bent or distorted if the fitting process continues. Peugeot specify the use of a tapered cone type piston ring compressor tool, but a suitable alternative can easily be fabricated **(see Tool Tip)**.

19 Insert the piston/connecting rod assembly into the top of cylinder/liner No 1. On petrol engines, ensure that the arrow on the piston crown is pointing towards the timing belt end of the engine and on diesel engines, ensure that the cloverleaf-shaped cut-out on the piston crown is towards the front (oil filter side) of the cylinder block. Using a block of wood or hammer handle against the piston crown, tap the assembly into the cylinder/liner until the piston crown is flush with the top of the cylinder/liner **(see illustrations)**.

20 Ensure that the bearing shell is still correctly installed. Liberally lubricate the crankpin and both bearing shells. Taking care not to mark the cylinder/liner bores, pull the piston/connecting rod assembly down the bore and onto the crankpin.

21 Refit the big-end bearing cap, tightening its retaining nuts finger-tight at first. Note that the faces with the identification marks must match (which means that the bearing shell locating tabs abut each other).

22 Tighten the bearing cap retaining nuts evenly and progressively in the Stages given in the appropriate Specifications **(see illustrations)**.

23 On all engines, once the bearing cap retaining nuts have been correctly tightened, rotate the crankshaft. Check that it turns freely; some stiffness is to be expected if new components have been fitted, but there should be no signs of binding or tight spots.

24 Refit the remaining three piston/connecting rod assemblies in the same way.

25 Refit the cylinder head and oil pump as described in Part A, B or C of this Chapter.

20.22a Tighten the bearing cap retaining nuts evenly and progressively to the torque setting . . .

20.22b . . . then angle-tighten them through the specified angle

21 Engine –
initial start-up after overhaul

1 With the engine refitted in the vehicle, double-check the engine oil and coolant levels. Make a final check that everything has been reconnected, and that there are no tools or rags left in the engine compartment.

Petrol engine models

2 Remove the spark plugs and disable the fuel system by disconnecting the wiring connectors from the fuel injectors, referring to Chapter 4A for further information.
3 Turn the engine on the starter until the oil pressure warning light goes out. Refit the spark plugs, and reconnect the wiring.

Diesel engine models

4 On the models covered in this Manual, the oil pressure warning light is linked to the STOP warning light, and is not illuminated when the ignition is initially switched on. Therefore it is not possible to check the oil pressure warning light when turning the engine on the starter motor.
5 Prime the fuel system (refer to Chapter 4B). Although the system is self-priming, it will help if the ignition is switched on and off several times before attempting to start the engine in order to purge air from the system.
6 Fully depress the accelerator pedal, turn the ignition key to position M, and wait for the preheating warning light to go out.

All models

7 Start the engine, noting that this may take a little longer than usual, due to the fuel system components having been disturbed.
8 While the engine is idling, check for fuel, water and oil leaks. Don't be alarmed if there are some odd smells and smoke from parts getting hot and burning off oil deposits.
9 Assuming all is well, keep the engine idling until hot water is felt circulating through the top hose, then switch off the engine.
10 After a few minutes, recheck the oil and coolant levels as described in *Weekly Checks*, and top-up as necessary.
11 Note that there is no need to retighten the cylinder head bolts once the engine has first run after reassembly.
12 If new pistons, rings or crankshaft bearings have been fitted, the engine must be treated as new, and run-in for the first 500 miles (800 km). *Do not* operate the engine at full-throttle, or allow it to labour at low engine speeds in any gear. It is recommended that the oil and filter be changed at the end of this period.

Please take your bo
to a self issue
machine to issue to
your account

Go to 'Account' if you
need to pay for your
reservation

Thank you

THOMAS
··

'9 1 / /145

Chapter 3
Cooling, heating and ventilation systems

Contents

Air conditioning compressor (auxiliary) drivebelt – checking and
  renewal ....See Chapter 1A or 1B
Air conditioning system – general information and precautions 10
Air conditioning system components – removal and refitting 11
Antifreeze mixture ....See Chapter 1A or 1B
Coolant level check ....See Weekly checks
Coolant pump – removal and refitting 7
Cooling system – draining ....See Chapter 1A or 1B
Cooling system – filling ....See Chapter 1A or 1B
Cooling system – flushing ....See Chapter 1A or 1B

Cooling system electrical switches and sensors – testing, removal
  and refitting 6
Cooling system hoses – disconnection and renewal 2
Electric cooling fan(s) – testing, removal and refitting 5
General information and precautions 1
Heater/ventilation components – removal and refitting 9
Heating and ventilation system – general information 8
Radiator – removal, inspection and refitting 3
Thermostat – removal, testing and refitting 4

Degrees of difficulty

Easy, suitable for novice with little experience	**Fairly easy,** suitable for beginner with some experience	**Fairly difficult,** suitable for competent DIY mechanic	**Difficult,** suitable for experienced DIY mechanic	**Very difficult,** suitable for expert DIY or professional

Specifications

General
Maximum system pressure .... 1.4 bar

Thermostat
Opening temperature:
  Petrol models .... 89°C
  Diesel models .... 83°C

Air conditioning system
Compressor:
  Petrol engines:
    Make .... SANDEN
    Model SD7V16
    Oil capacity .... 135 ± 15 cc
    Oil type SP10
  Diesel engines:
    Make .... DELPHI
    Model V5
    Oil capacity .... 265 ± 15 cc
    Oil type .... UCON 488

Torque wrench settings	Nm	lbf ft
Air conditioning pump to cylinder block:		
Bolts from crankshaft pulley side	42	31
Bolts from oil filter side	39	29
Coolant pump:		
XU petrol engines:		
Aluminium block:		
Smaller bolts	30	22
Larger bolts	65	48
Iron block	15	11
EW petrol engines	15	11
DW diesel engines	16	12
Coolant temperature sensor:		
EW petrol engines	18	13
Coolant cylinder block drain screw:		
EW petrol engines	25	18

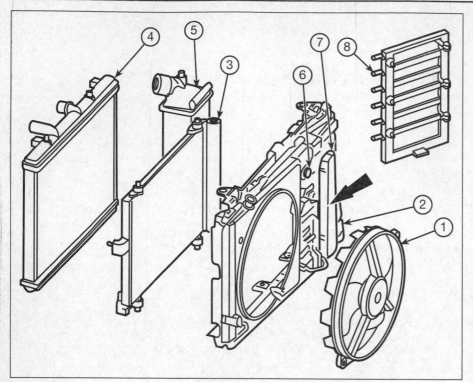

1.1a Radiator fan assembly

1 Fan	4 Radiator	6 Fan resistors
2 Fan cowling	5 Intercooler	7 Relay housing
3 Air conditioning condensor	(Turbo models)	8 Anti-recirculation grille

1 General information and precautions

General information

The cooling system is of pressurised type, comprising a coolant pump driven by the timing belt, an aluminium crossflow radiator, electric cooling fan, a thermostat, heater matrix, and all associated hoses and switches.

The system functions as follows. Cold coolant in the bottom of the radiator passes through the bottom hose to the coolant pump, where it is pumped around the cylinder block and head passages, and through the oil cooler(s) (where fitted). After cooling the cylinder bores, combustion surfaces and valve seats, the coolant reaches the underside of the thermostat, which is initially closed. The coolant passes through the heater, and is returned via the cylinder block to the coolant pump.

When the engine is cold, the coolant circulates only through the cylinder block, cylinder head, and heater. When the coolant reaches a predetermined temperature, the thermostat opens, and the coolant passes through the top hose to the radiator. As the coolant circulates through the radiator, it is cooled by the inrush of air when the car is in forward motion. The airflow is supplemented by the action of the electric cooling fan which

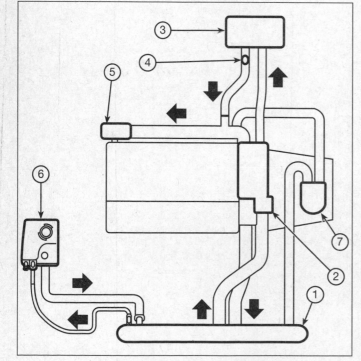

1.1b Cooling circuit for petrol engines

1 Radiator	5 Coolant pump	
2 Coolant inlet manifold	6 Expansion bottle	
3 Heater matrix	7 Oil cooler (automatic	
4 Bleed screw	gearbox only)	

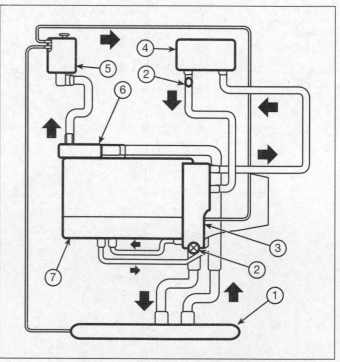

1.1c Cooling circuit for diesel engines

1 Radiator	5 Expansion bottle	
2 Bleed screw	6 Coolant outlet	
3 Coolant inlet manifold	manifold	
4 Heater matrix	7 Coolant pump	

is controlled by the ECU and has three operating speeds. Upon reaching the bottom of the radiator, the coolant has now cooled, and the cycle is repeated.

When the engine is at normal operating temperature, the coolant expands, and some of it is displaced into the expansion tank. Coolant collects in the tank, and is returned to the radiator when the system cools.

On models with automatic transmission, a proportion of the coolant is recirculated from the bottom of the radiator through the transmission fluid cooler mounted on the transmission. On models fitted with an engine oil cooler, the coolant is also passed through the oil cooler.

The electric cooling fan in front of the radiator is controlled by a temperature sensor in the thermostat housing, which gives information to the ECU. **Note:** *On XU engines, the temperature sensor gives information to the air conditioning/coolant temperature unit before the ECU. The temperature unit is situated behind the left-hand front headlight unit.* At a predetermined coolant temperature, the engine management control unit (ECU) actuates the fan.

The fan cowling has an anti-recirculation grille, this has six flaps that open when the car is travelling forwards, when the fan starts to operate the flaps close. This is to improve cooling, and allow extra passages to the radiator when the fan is not operating. When the fan operates it draws the air through the fan aperture in the cowling, thus closing the flaps and allowing all the air drawn in to cool down the radiator **(see illustrations)**.

Precautions

⚠️ *Warning: Do not attempt to remove the expansion tank filler cap, or to disturb any part of the cooling system, while the engine is hot, as there is a high risk of scalding. If the expansion tank filler cap must be removed before the engine and radiator have fully cooled (even though* this is not recommended), the pressure in the cooling system must first be relieved. Cover the cap with a thick layer of cloth to avoid scalding, and slowly unscrew the filler cap until a hissing sound is heard. When the hissing has stopped, indicating that the pressure has reduced, slowly unscrew the filler cap until it can be removed; if more hissing sounds are heard, wait until they have stopped before unscrewing the cap completely. At all times, keep well away from the filler cap opening, and protect your hands.*

⚠️ *Warning: Do not allow antifreeze to come into contact with your skin, or with the painted surfaces of the vehicle. Rinse off spills immediately, with plenty of water. Never leave antifreeze lying around in an open container, or in a puddle in the driveway or on the garage floor. Children and pets are attracted by its sweet smell, but antifreeze can be fatal if ingested.*

⚠️ *Warning: If the engine is hot, the electric cooling fan may start rotating even if the engine is not running. Be careful to keep your hands, hair, and any loose clothing well clear when working in the engine compartment.*

⚠️ *Warning: Refer to Section 10 for precautions to be observed when working on models equipped with air conditioning.*

2 Cooling system hoses – disconnection and renewal

Note: *Refer to the warnings given in Section 1 of this Chapter before proceeding. Hoses should only be disconnected once the engine has cooled sufficiently to avoid scalding.*

1 If the checks described in Chapter 1A or 1B reveal a faulty hose, it must be renewed as follows.

2 First drain the cooling system (Chapter 1A or 1B). If the coolant is not due for renewal, it may be re-used, providing it is collected in a clean container.

3 To disconnect a hose, proceed as follows, according to the type of hose connection.

Standard hose connections

4 On conventional connections, the clips used to secure the hoses in position may be standard worm drive clips, spring clips or disposable crimped types. The crimped type of clip is not designed to be re-used, and a worm drive or spring clip type used on reassembly.

5 To disconnect a hose, use a screwdriver to slacken or release the worm drive clips, or squeeze the tags together with a pair of pliers on the spring type **(see illustrations)**. Move the clips along the hose, clear of the relevant inlet/outlet then carefully work the hose free. The hoses can be removed with relative ease when new – on an older car, they may have stuck.

6 If a hose proves to be difficult to remove, try to release it by rotating its ends before attempting to free it. Gently prise the end of the hose with a blunt instrument (such as a flat-bladed screwdriver), but do not apply too much force, and take care not to damage the pipe stubs or hoses. Note in particular that the radiator inlet stub is fragile; do not use excessive force when attempting to remove the hose. If all else fails, cut the hose with a sharp knife, then slit it so that it can be peeled off in two pieces. Although this may prove expensive if the hose is otherwise undamaged, it is preferable to buying a new radiator. Check first, however, that a new hose is readily available.

> **HAYNES HiNT** *If the hose is stiff, use a little soapy water as a lubricant, or soften the hose by soaking it in hot water. Do not use oil or grease, which may attack the rubber.*

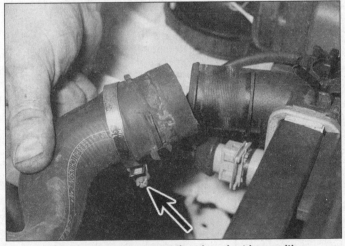

2.5a Disconnect a conventional coolant hose with a screwdriver . . .

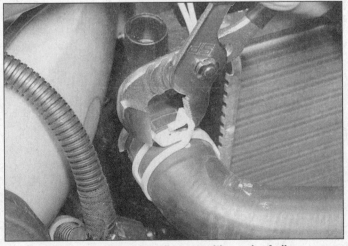

2.5b . . . or the spring clip type with a pair of pliers

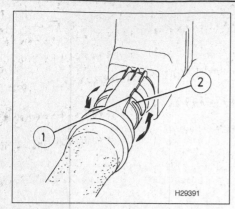

2.12 To release a bayonet-type hose, turn the locking ring (2) until it contacts the stop (1) . . .

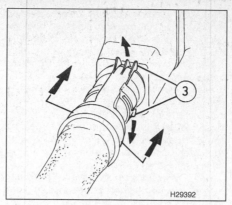

2.13 . . . then press the connector away from the hose to ensure that the retaining lugs (3) are free

7 When fitting a hose, first slide the clips onto the hose, then work the hose into position. If crimped-type clips were originally fitted, use standard worm drive clips when refitting the hose.

8 Work the hose into position, checking that it is correctly routed, then slide each clip back along the hose until it passes over the flared end of the relevant inlet/outlet, before tightening the clip securely.

9 Refill the cooling system (see Chapter 1A or 1B).

10 Check thoroughly for leaks as soon as possible after disturbing any part of the cooling system.

Bayonet-type connections

Note: *A new sealing ring should be used when reconnecting the hose.*

11 On certain models, some hoses may be secured in position using a plastic bayonet-type connection. To disconnect this type of connector, proceed as follows.

12 Turn the locking ring (2) anti-clockwise until it contacts the stop (1) **(see illustration)**.

13 Press the connector away from the hose, to ensure that the two retaining lugs (3) are free **(see illustration)**.

14 Pull the hose and its connector from the radiator.

15 Recover the sealing ring from the connector, and discard it; a new one must be used on refitting.

16 On refitting, wipe the connector and the stub on the radiator thoroughly with a clean, lint-free cloth.

17 Fit a new sealing ring to the male half of the connector, ensuring that it is correctly seated **(see illustration)**.

18 Turn the locking ring clockwise until it clicks.

19 Offer the hose to the union making sure the cut-out is correctly positioned to align with the locating lug **(see illustration)**.

20 Push the connector fully into position until both the retaining lugs click into position. Make sure that the sealing ring is not trapped.

21 Pull the connector rearwards (away from the stub) to adjust the position of the retaining lugs if necessary.

22 Refill the cooling system (see Chapter 1A or 1B).

23 Check thoroughly for leaks as soon as possible after disturbing any part of the cooling system.

Click-fit connections

Note: *A new sealing ring should be used when reconnecting the hose.*

24 On certain models, some cooling system hoses are secured in position with click-fit connectors where the hose union is retained by a large circlip.

25 To disconnect this type of hose, using a small flat-bladed screwdriver, carefully prise the circlip out of position. The hose connection can then be slid out of position and the sealing ring removed **(see illustrations)**. Once the hose is disconnected, refit the circlip to the female end of the connection.

26 On refitting, ensure that the circlip is correctly located in its groove in the female end of the connection, and fit the new sealing ring to the hose union. Push the hose connection into position, taking care not trap the sealing ring, until it clicks into position.

27 Ensure that the hose is securely retained by the circlip then refill the cooling system as described in Chapter 1A or 1B.

28 Check thoroughly for leaks as soon as possible after disturbing any part of the cooling system.

2.17 Prior to refitting, fit a new sealing ring (arrowed) to the hose union

2.19 When the hose is reconnected ensure its cut-out (arrowed) is correctly positioned

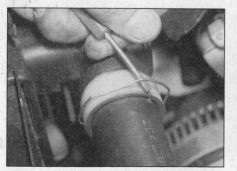

2.25a To disconnect a click-fit connector, lever out the circlip . . .

2.25b . . . then ease the hose union out of position and remove the sealing ring (arrowed)

3 Radiator –
removal, inspection and refitting

Note: *New sealing rings must be used when reconnecting bayonet-type/click-fit radiator hoses – see Section 2. If leakage is the reason for removing the radiator, bear in mind that minor leaks can often be cured using a radiator sealant with the radiator in situ.*

Removal

1 Disconnect the battery negative lead.

2 Drain the cooling system (see Chapter 1A or 1B).

3 Where necessary, disconnect the wiring connector from the cooling fan switch which is screwed into the radiator.

4 Disconnect the coolant hoses from the radiator with reference to Section 2.

5 Remove the radiator grille as described in Chapter 11.

6 Undo the four retaining bolts (two each side) and remove the front crossmember from across the top of the radiator (**see illustration**). The bonnet release cable can be left attached to the lock, and the cross-member moved to one side of the engine bay

7 Working at the top of the radiator, undo the two retaining bolts and release the top radiator mounting brackets (**see illustration**).

8 On diesel models, it will be necessary to free the intercooler from the side of the radiator as it is removed. Where applicable, undo the retaining bolts and remove the heat exchanger from the radiator (**see illustrations**).

9 On all models, disengage the air conditioning condenser and the electric fan cowling from the radiator.

10 Lift the radiator out of position, taking care not to damage the radiator fins on surrounding components. Take care not to lose the radiator lower mounting rubbers.

Inspection

11 If the radiator has been removed due to suspected blockage, reverse-flush it as described in Chapter 1A or 1B. Clean dirt and debris from the radiator fins, using an air line (in which case, wear eye protection) or a soft brush. Be careful, as the fins are sharp, and easily damaged.

12 If necessary, a radiator specialist can perform a 'flow test' on the radiator, to establish whether an internal blockage exists.

13 A leaking radiator must be referred to a specialist for permanent repair. Do not attempt to weld or solder a leaking radiator, as damage to the plastic components may result.

14 If the radiator is to be sent for repair or renewed, remove all hoses and the cooling fan switch (where fitted).

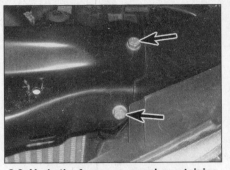

3.6 Undo the four crossmember retaining bolts (two on left-hand side arrowed)

3.8a Undo the two upper mounting bolts (arrowed) . . .

15 Inspect the condition of the radiator mounting rubbers, and renew them if necessary.

Refitting

16 Refitting is a reversal of removal, bearing in mind the following points:

a) Ensure that the lower lugs on the radiator are correctly engaged with the mounting rubbers in the body panel. On diesel models, also ensure that the intercooler is correctly engaged with the radiator.

b) Reconnect the hoses with reference to Section 2, using new sealing rings where applicable.

c) On completion, refill the cooling system as described in Chapter 1A or 1B.

3.7 Undo the two retaining bolts (arrowed) from the radiator top mountings

3.8b . . . and the lower mounting bolt (arrowed) to release the heat exchanger from the radiator

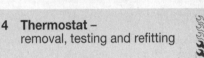

4 Thermostat –
removal, testing and refitting

Note: *A new thermostat sealing ring/gasket will be required on refitting.*

Removal

1 Disconnect the battery negative lead.

2 Drain the cooling system as described in Chapter 1A or 1B. On all models, the thermostat housing is mounted on the left-hand end of the cylinder head (**see illustrations**).

3 Where necessary, release any relevant wiring and hoses from the retaining clips, and position clear of the thermostat housing to improve access.

4.2a On petrol (EW engines) models, the thermostat housing (arrowed) is at the front . . .

4.2b . . . on diesel models it is on the top of the coolant housing on the left-hand side of the cylinder head (arrowed) . . .

4.2c . . . and on petrol (XU engines) it is on the side of the cylinder head (arrowed)

5.6 Undo the four fan shroud retaining bolts (arrowed)

5.7 Undo the three retaining bolts (arrowed) to remove the fan motor from its mounting bracket

4 Disconnect the coolant hose(s) from the thermostat housing (see Section 2).

5 Unscrew the retaining nuts/bolts (as applicable) and carefully withdraw the thermostat housing cover to expose the thermostat.

6 Lift the thermostat from the housing, and recover the sealing ring.

Testing

7 A rough test of the thermostat may be made by suspending it with a piece of string in a container full of water. Heat the water to bring it to the boil – the thermostat must open by the time the water boils. If not, renew it.

8 If a thermometer is available, the precise opening temperature of the thermostat may be determined; compare with the figures given in the Specifications. The opening temperature is also marked on the thermostat.

9 A thermostat which fails to close as the water cools must also be renewed.

Refitting

10 Refitting is a reversal of removal, bearing in mind the following points:
a) *Always fit a new sealing ring and ensure that the thermostat is fitted the correct way round, with the spring(s) facing into the housing.*
b) *On models where the coolant hose is secured to the housing with a click-fit connector, renew the connector sealing ring (see Section 2).*
c) *On completion, refill the cooling system as described in Chapter 1A or 1B.*

5 Electric cooling fan(s) – testing, removal and refitting

Testing

1 Current supply to the cooling fan(s) is via the ignition switch and a fuse (Chapter 12), and are controlled by the Bitron sensor – see Section 6.

2 If a fan does not appear to work, run the engine until normal operating temperature is reached, then allow it to idle. The fan should cut in within a few minutes (before the temperature gauge needle enters the red

section, or before the coolant temperature warning light comes on).

3 If the fan fails to operate, check that battery voltage is available at the feed wire to the switch; if not, then there is a fault in the feed wire (possibly due to a fault in the fan motor, or a blown fuse).

4 If the switch and the wiring are in good condition, the fault must lie in the motor itself. The motor can be checked by disconnecting it from the wiring loom and connecting a 12 volt supply directly to it.

Removal

5 Remove the radiator grille as described in Chapter 11.

6 Slacken and remove the four retaining bolts **(see illustration)**, then remove the outer fan shroud from the radiator cowling.

7 Undo the three retaining bolts to release the fan motor from the mounting bracket **(see illustration)**, then manoeuvre it out from between the shroud and bumper (the wiring connector will disconnect automatically).

8 If necessary, slide off retaining clip/undo the retaining screw (as applicable) and remove the fan from the motor spindle.

9 If the motor is faulty, the complete unit must be renewed, as no spares were available at the time of writing.

Refitting

10 Refitting is a reversal of removal, noting the following points.
a) *Prior to refitting, inspect the fan shroud mountings, renewing them if they show signs of wear or damage.*

6.7a Remove the retaining clip . . .

b) *Ensure that any wiring is correctly routed and secured in position with all the relevant clips and ties so that it is no danger of contacting the fan.*
c) *Refit the radiator grille as described in Chapter 11.*

6 Cooling system electrical switches and sensors – testing, removal and refitting

Coolant temperature sensor

Testing

1 The coolant temperature sensor is screwed into the alloy thermostat/coolant housing. On models with a plastic thermostat/coolant housing it is held in place by a retaining clip. The thermostat/coolant housing is bolted onto the left-hand end of the cylinder head. The sensor can be identified by its green wiring connector.

2 The sensor is a thermistor (see paragraph 18). The fuel injection/engine management electronic control unit (ECU) supplies the sensor with a set voltage and then, by measuring the current flowing in the sensor circuit, it determines the engine's temperature. This information is then used, in conjunction with other inputs, to control the injector opening time (pulse width). On some models, the idle speed and/or ignition timing settings are also temperature-dependent.

3 If the sensor circuit should fail to provide adequate information, the ECU's back-up facility will override the sensor signal. In this event, the ECU assumes a predetermined setting which will allow the fuel injection/engine management system to run, albeit at reduced efficiency. When this occurs, the warning light on the instrument panel will come on, and the advice of a Peugeot dealer should be sought. The sensor itself can only be tested using special Peugeot diagnostic equipment. *Do not* attempt to test the circuit using any other equipment, as there is a high risk of damaging the ECU.

Removal

4 The sensor is located in the coolant housing on the left-hand side of the cylinder head. The engine and radiator should be cold before removing the sensor.

5 Disconnect the battery negative lead. On some models, access to the sensor is very poor, and certain components may need to be removed before the sensor can be reached.

6 Partially drain the cooling system to just below the level of the sensor (as described in Chapter 1A or 1B). Alternatively, have ready a suitable bung to plug the switch aperture when the sensor is removed.

7 On models with a plastic thermostat/coolant housing, disconnect the wiring plug from the sensor, then release the retaining clip and remove the sensor **(see illustrations)**. Recover the sealing ring on removal. If the system has not been drained, plug the switch aperture to prevent further coolant loss.

8 On models with an alloy thermostat/coolant housing, disconnect the wiring plug from the sensor, then carefully unscrew the sensor. Where fitted recover the sealing ring. If the system has not been drained, plug the switch aperture to prevent further coolant loss.

Refitting

9 Refitting is a reversal of removal, noting the following points:
   a) Use a new sealing ring on refitting.
   b) Make sure the sensor retaining clip is correctly located.
   c) Refill (or top-up) the cooling system as described in Chapter 1A or 1B.

10 On completion, start the engine and run it until it reaches normal operating temperature. Continue to run the engine, and check that the cooling fan cuts in and out correctly.

Fan sensor – XU engine

11 The cooling fans are controlled by the air conditioning/coolant temperature unit which is located behind the left-hand front headlight unit. The coolant temperature sensor is located in the thermostat housing, which is bolted onto the left-hand end of the cylinder head (see illustration).

12 The sensor forms part of the air conditioning/coolant control system (see Section 10). Testing of the sensor should be entrusted to a Peugeot dealer.

Removal

13 Carry out the procedures as described in paragraphs 4 to 6.

14 Disconnect the wiring plug from the sensor, then carefully unscrew the sensor from the thermostat housing, where fitted recover the sealing ring. If the system has not been drained, plug the switch aperture to prevent further coolant loss.

Refitting

15 Refitting is a reversal of removal, noting the following points:
   a) Where applicable, use a new sealing ring on refitting.
   b) Make sure the sensor retaining clip is correctly located.
   c) Refill (or top-up) the cooling system as described in Chapter 1A or 1B.

16 On completion, start the engine and run it until it reaches normal operating temperature. Continue to run the engine, and check that the cooling fan cuts in and out correctly.

Temperature gauge/warning light sender – XU engine

Testing

17 The coolant temperature gauge/warning light sender is screwed into the left-hand end of the cylinder head. The sender can be identified by its blue wiring connector (see illustration 6.11).

18 The temperature gauge (where fitted) is fed with a stabilised voltage from the instrument panel feed (via the ignition switch and a fuse). The gauge earth is controlled by

6.7b . . . and withdraw the temperature sensor (renew the sealing ring on refitting)

the sender. The sender contains a thermistor – an electronic component whose electrical resistance decreases at a predetermined rate as its temperature rises. When the coolant is cold, the sender resistance is high, current flow through the gauge is reduced, and the gauge needle points towards the blue (cold) end of the scale. As the coolant temperature rises and the sender resistance falls, current flow increases, and the gauge needle moves towards the upper end of the scale. If the sender is faulty, it must be renewed.

19 On models with a temperature warning light, the light is fed with a voltage from the instrument panel. The light earth is controlled by the sender. The sender is effectively a switch, which operates at a predetermined temperature to earth the light and complete the circuit. If the light is fitted in addition to a gauge, the senders for the gauge and light are incorporated in a single unit, with two wires, one each for the light and gauge earths.

20 If the gauge develops a fault, first check the other instruments; if they do not work at all, check the instrument panel electrical feed. If the readings are erratic, there may be a fault in the voltage stabiliser, which will necessitate renewal of the stabiliser (the stabiliser is integral with the instrument panel printed circuit board – see Chapter 12). If the fault lies in the temperature gauge alone, check it as follows.

21 If the gauge needle remains at the 'cold' end of the scale when the engine is hot, disconnect the sender wiring plug, and earth the relevant wire to the cylinder head. If the needle then deflects when the ignition is switched on, the sender unit is proved faulty, and should be renewed. If the needle still does not move, remove the instrument panel (Chapter 12) and check the continuity of the wire between the sender unit and the gauge, and the feed to the gauge unit. If continuity is shown, and the fault still exists, then the gauge is faulty, and the gauge unit should be renewed.

22 If the gauge needle remains at the 'hot' end of the scale when the engine is cold, disconnect the sender wire. If the needle then returns to the 'cold' end of the scale when the ignition is switched on, the sender unit is proved faulty, and should be renewed. If the

6.11 On XU engine models, the switches/senders are screwed into the thermostat housing (arrowed)

needle still does not move, check the remainder of the circuit as described previously.

23 The same basic principles apply to testing the warning light. The light should illuminate when the relevant sender wire is earthed.

Removal and refitting

24 The procedure is similar to that described previously in this Section for the electric cooling fan thermostatic sensor. On some models, access to the switch is very poor, and other components may need to be removed before the sender unit can be reached.

---

7 Coolant pump – removal and refitting

Removal

1 The coolant pump is located in a housing at the timing belt end of the engine and is driven by the timing belt.

2 Drain the cooling system as described in Chapter 1A or 1B.

3 Remove the timing belt as described in the relevant part of Chapter 2.

4 Slacken and remove the retaining bolts (see illustration) and withdraw the pump assembly from the engine, along with its gasket/sealing ring. Discard the gasket/sealing ring, a new one must be used on refitting.

7.4 Undo the retaining bolts (arrowed) to remove the coolant pump – 2.2 litre diesel engine

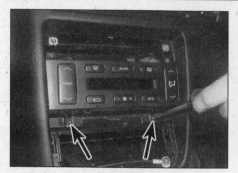

9.3 Undo the retaining screws (arrowed) . . .

Refitting

5 Ensure that the pump and cylinder block/housing mating faces are clean and dry.
6 Offer up the new gasket/sealing ring and fit the pump assembly, tighten its retaining bolts securely.
7 Refit the timing belt as described in the relevant Part of Chapter 2.
8 Refill the cooling system as described in Chapter 1A or 1B.

8 Heating and ventilation system – general information

The heating/ventilation system consists of a fully adjustable blower motor (housed behind the facia), face level vents in the centre and at each end of the facia, and air ducts to the front footwells.

The control unit is located in the facia, and the controls operate flap valves to deflect and mix the air flowing through the various parts of the heating/ventilation system. The flap valves are contained in the air distribution housing, which acts as a central distribution unit, passing air to the various ducts and vents.

Cold air enters the system through the grille at the rear of the engine compartment. If required, the airflow is boosted by the blower, and then flows through the various ducts, according to the settings of the controls. Stale air is expelled through ducts at the rear of the vehicle. If warm air is required, the cold air is

9.14a Undo the retaining screw (shown with the facia removed for clarity) . . .

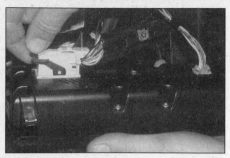

9.5 . . . then manoeuvre the control unit out of position, and disconnect its wiring connectors (fully automatic unit shown)

passed over the heater matrix, which is heated by the engine coolant.

A recirculation lever/switch enables the outside air supply to be closed off, while the air inside the vehicle is recirculated. This can be useful to prevent unpleasant odours entering from outside the vehicle, but should only be used briefly, as the recirculated air inside the vehicle will soon become stale.

9 Heater/ventilation components – removal and refitting

Note: *On models with fully automatic air conditioning system, there are no heater/ventilation control cables fitted.*

Control unit

Removal

1 Disconnect the battery negative lead.
2 Remove the radio/cassette unit and the facia centre switch panel unit as described in Chapter 12.
3 Remove the control unit retaining screws and carefully withdraw the control unit from the facia **(see illustration)**.
4 Working at the rear of the control unit, release the securing clips, and disconnect the control cables (where applicable) from the unit. Note the locations of the cables to ensure correct refitting.
5 Disconnect the wiring connector(s) from the rear of the control unit and withdraw the unit from the facia **(see illustration)**.

9.14b . . . then disconnect the coolant pipes from the heater matrix and recover the sealing rings (arrowed)

Refitting

6 Refitting is a reversal of removal, but ensure that the control cables (where fitted) are securely reconnected to their original locations. Check the operation of the controls prior to refitting the radio/cassette and display units.

Control cables

Removal

7 Disconnect the cables from the heater/ventilation control unit, as described previously in this Section during the control unit removal procedure.
8 Working through the facia aperture or under the facia (it may be necessary to remove certain facia panels for access – refer to Chapter 11 – depending on which cable is to be removed), release the clips and disconnect the relevant cable from the heater assembly. Note the routing of the cable to ensure correct refitting.

Refitting

9 Refitting is a reversal of removal, ensuring that the cables are correctly routed, and securely reconnected. Check the cable operation before refitting the trim panels.

Heater matrix

Note: *New heater matrix union sealing rings must be used on refitting. If leakage is the reason for removing the matrix, bear in mind that minor leaks can often be cured using a radiator sealant with the matrix in situ.*

Removal

10 Drain the cooling system as described in Chapter 1A or 1B. Alternately, clamp the heater matrix hoses as close as possible to the engine compartment bulkhead.
11 On left-hand drive models, remove the steering column as described in Chapter 10. Undo the retaining bolts and remove the facia mounting support bracket to gain access to the heater matrix.
12 On right-hand drive models remove the glovebox as described in Chapter 11, Section 28. Remove the retaining clips and lower the undercover away from the passenger side of the facia.
13 Position a container beneath the unions on the side of the heater matrix, and place absorbent rags around the container as a precaution.
14 Slacken and remove the retaining bolt, and ease the coolant pipes away from the matrix, allowing the coolant to drain into the container. Remove the sealing rings from the pipe ends and discard them; new ones must be used on refitting **(see illustrations)**.
15 Slacken and remove the heater matrix screws, and slide the matrix out of position **(see illustrations)**. **Note:** *On some models, the end of the facia mounting bracket may prevent removal of the matrix. If so, trim the end of the bracket off to gain the necessary clearance. As the matrix is being removed, try to keep the pipe unions uppermost to*

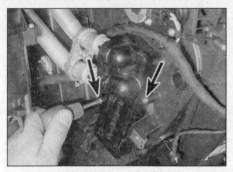

9.15a Undo the retaining screws (arrowed) . . .

9.15b . . . then carefully slide the heater matrix out from its housing

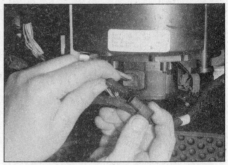

9.19 Disconnect the wiring connectors, then undo the retaining screws . . .

minimise coolant spillage. Mop up any spilt coolant immediately with a damp cloth to prevent staining.

Refitting

16 Refitting is a reversal of removal, bearing in mind the following points:
  a) *Fit new sealing rings to the pipe unions.*
  b) *Slide the matrix into position and engage the pipes fully with the matrix union. Refit the retaining bolts and union bolt, and tighten them securely. Remove the hose clamps (where fitted).*
  c) *Refill/top-up the cooling system as described in Chapter 1A or 1B.*

Heater blower motor

Removal

17 The blower motor assembly is located on the passenger side of the facia, in the base of the blower motor housing.

18 Disconnect the battery negative lead. Remove the retaining clips, and unclip the undercover from the bottom of the passenger side of the facia. If necessary, to further improve access remove the glovebox as described in Chapter 11, Section 28.
19 Disconnect the wiring connector(s) from the motor and release the wiring harness from its retaining clips (see illustration).
20 Slacken and remove the motor retaining screws, and lower the motor assembly away from the housing (see illustration).

Refitting

21 Refitting is a reversal of removal.

Blower motor control module

Removal

22 Remove the blower motor as described in paragraphs earlier in this Section.
23 Release the wiring harness grommet from

the base of the motor assembly. Disconnect the connector from the module/motor and remove the harness (see illustration).
24 Depress the motor retaining clips and separate the motor from its mounting plate (see illustrations).
25 Slacken and remove the retaining screws and remove the control module from the mounting plate (see illustration).

Refitting

26 Refitting is the reverse of removal, ensuring that the motor is clipped securely into position on the mounting plate. Also make sure that the wiring is correctly routed and retained by all the necessary clips.

10 Air conditioning system – general information and precautions

General information

1 An air conditioning system is available on all models. It enables the temperature of incoming air to be lowered, and also dehumidifies the air, which makes for rapid demisting and increased comfort.
2 The cooling side of the system works in the same way as a domestic refrigerator. Refrigerant gas is drawn into a belt-driven compressor, and passes into a condenser mounted on the front of the radiator, where it loses heat and becomes liquid. The liquid passes through an expansion valve to an evaporator, where it changes from liquid

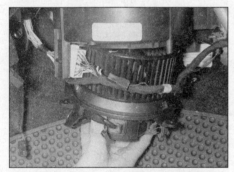

9.20 . . . and lower the blower motor out of position (facia removed for clarity)

9.23 Disconnect the wiring connector . . .

9.24a . . . then release the retaining clips (arrowed) . . .

9.24b . . . and separate the blower motor and mounting plate

9.25 Undo the screws (arrowed) and remove the blower motor control module

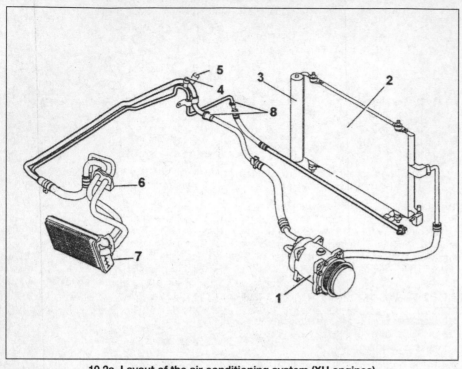

10.2a Layout of the air conditioning system (XU engines)

1 *Compressor*	4 *High pressure valve*	7 *Evaporator*
2 *Condenser*	5 *Low pressure valve*	8 *'Click-on' connections*
3 *Dehydrator reservoir*	6 *Pressure relief valve*	

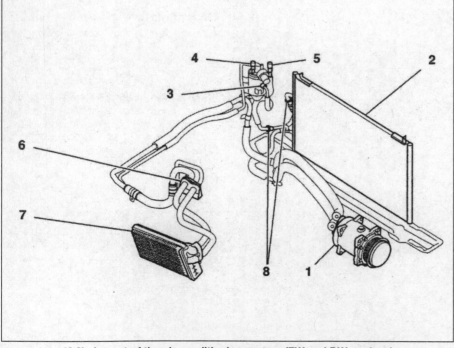

10.2b Layout of the air conditioning system (EW and DW engines)

1 *Compressor*	4 *High pressure valve*	7 *Evaporator*
2 *Condenser*	5 *Low pressure valve*	8 *'Click-on' connections*
3 *Dehydrator reservoir*	6 *Pressure relief valve*	

under high pressure to gas under low pressure. This change is accompanied by a drop in temperature, which cools the evaporator. The refrigerant returns to the compressor, and the cycle begins again **(see illustrations)**.

3 Air blown through the evaporator passes to the air distribution unit, where it is mixed with hot air blown through the heater matrix to achieve the desired temperature.

4 The heating side of the system works the same way as on models without air conditioning (see Section 8).

5 The operation of the system is controlled electronically by the ECU, which controls the electric cooling fan(s), the compressor and the facia-mounted warning light. Any problems with the system should be referred to a Peugeot dealer.

Precautions

6 When an air conditioning system is fitted, it is necessary to observe special precautions whenever dealing with any part of the system, or its associated components. If for any reason the system must be disconnected, entrust this task to your Peugeot dealer or a refrigeration engineer.

⚠️ *Warning: The refrigeration circuit contains a liquid refrigerant (Freon), and it is therefore dangerous to disconnect any part of the system without specialised knowledge and equipment.*

7 The refrigerant is potentially dangerous, and it should therefore only be handled by qualified persons, such as your Peugeot dealer. If it is splashed onto the skin, it can cause frostbite. It is not itself poisonous, but in the presence of a naked flame (including a cigarette) it forms a poisonous gas. Uncontrolled discharging of the refrigerant is dangerous, and potentially damaging to the environment.

8 Do not operate the air conditioning system if it is known to be short of refrigerant, as this may damage the compressor.

11 Air conditioning system components – removal and refitting

⚠️ *Warning: Do not attempt to open the refrigerant circuit. Refer to the precautions in Section 10.*

1 The only operation which can be carried out easily without discharging the refrigerant is the renewal of the compressor drivebelt. This is described in Chapter 1A or 1B. The temperature sensor may be renewed using the information in Section 6. All other operations must be referred to a Peugeot dealer or an air conditioning specialist.

2 If necessary, the compressor can be unbolted and moved aside, without disconnecting its flexible hoses, after removing the drivebelt.

Chapter 4 Part A:
Fuel and exhaust system – petrol models

Contents

Accelerator cable – removal, refitting and adjustment 3
Accelerator pedal – removal and refitting 4
Air cleaner assembly and intake ducts – removal and refitting 2
Air cleaner filter element renewal . . . . .See Chapter 1A
Bosch Motronic and Sagem Lucas system components – removal and
   refitting 13
Exhaust manifold – removal and refitting 16
Exhaust system – general information, removal and refitting 17
Fuel filter – renewal . . . . .See Chapter 1A
Fuel gauge sender unit – removal and refitting 9

Fuel injection system – depressurisation 7
Fuel injection system – testing 11
Fuel injection systems – general information 6
Fuel pump – removal and refitting 8
Fuel tank – removal and refitting 10
General information and precautions 1
Inlet manifold – removal and refitting 15
Magneti Marelli system components – removal and refitting 14
Throttle housing – removal and refitting 12
Unleaded petrol – general information and usage 5

Degrees of difficulty

Easy, suitable for novice with little experience	**Fairly easy,** suitable for beginner with some experience	**Fairly difficult,** suitable for competent DIY mechanic	**Difficult,** suitable for experienced DIY mechanic	**Very difficult,** suitable for expert DIY or professional

Specifications

System type
1.8 litre XU7JP4 models . . . . Bosch Motronic MP5.1.1, MP7.3 or Sagem SL96
1.8 litre EW7J4 models . . . . Sagem S2000 MPI
2.0 litre EW10J4 models . . . . Magneti Marelli 4.8P

Fuel system data
Fuel pump type . . . . Electric, immersed in tank
Specified idle speed:
   1.8 litre engine . . . . 700 ± 50 rpm (not adjustable – controlled by ECU)
   2.0 litre engine . . . . 850 ± 50 rpm (not adjustable – controlled by ECU)
Idle mixture CO content . . . . Less than 0.4 % (not adjustable- controlled by ECU)

Recommended fuel
Minimum octane rating . . . . 95 RON unleaded (UK unleaded premium)

Torque wrench settings

	Nm	lbf ft
Exhaust manifold nuts	35	26
Inlet manifold nuts	20	15

2.1 Slacken the clip (arrowed) and disconnect the intake duct from the throttle housing

1 General information and precautions

The fuel supply system consists of a fuel tank (which is mounted under the rear of the car, with an electric fuel pump immersed in it), a fuel filter, fuel feed and return lines. The fuel pump supplies fuel to the fuel rail, which acts as a reservoir for the four fuel injectors which inject fuel into the inlet tracts. The fuel filter incorporated in the feed line from the pump to the fuel rail ensures that the fuel supplied to the injectors is clean.

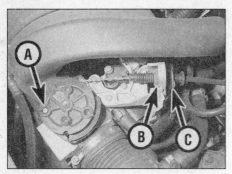

3.1a Accelerator cable connections – 1.8 litre XU7 engine

A Inner cable attachment at throttle housing cam
B Mounting bracket rubber grommet
C Flat washer and spring clip

3.1b Releasing the inner cable from the throttle housing cam – 1.8 litre EW7 engine

Refer to Section 6 for further information on the operation of each fuel injection system. Throughout this Section, it is also occasionally necessary to identify vehicles by their engine codes rather than by engine capacity alone. Refer to the relevant Part of Chapter 2 for further information on engine code identification.

> ⚠️ **Warning: Many of the procedures in this Chapter require the removal of fuel lines and connections, which may result in some fuel spillage. Before carrying out any operation on the fuel system, refer to the precautions given in 'Safety first!' at the beginning of this manual, and follow them implicitly. Petrol is a highly dangerous and volatile liquid, and the precautions necessary when handling it cannot be overstressed.**

Note: Residual pressure will remain in the fuel lines long after the vehicle was last used. When disconnecting any fuel line, first depressurise the fuel system (see Section 7).

2 Air cleaner assembly and intake ducts – removal and refitting

Removal

1 Slacken the retaining clips and disconnect the intake duct from the throttle housing and air cleaner housing lid **(see illustration)**.
2 Undo the screws securing the lid to the air cleaner housing body. Lift off the lid and take out the filter element.
3 Lift the housing body upward to disengage it from the lower locating lugs. On some models, as the housing is lifted up, it will be necessary to disengage a small plastic retaining tag at the front securing the housing to the cold air intake duct underneath.
4 To remove the cold air intake duct, undo the air cleaner housing mounting bracket bolts and withdraw the bracket. Release the cold air intake from the bracket as it is removed.
5 Release the other end of the cold air intake from its body attachments and manipulate the duct from the car.

3.4 Accelerator cable end fitting (A) and outer cable plastic retainer (B)

Refitting

6 Refitting is a reversal of the removal procedure, ensuring that all hoses are properly reconnected, and that all ducts are correctly seated and securely held by their retaining clips.

3 Accelerator cable – removal, refitting and adjustment

Removal

1 Working in the engine compartment, free the accelerator inner cable from the cam on the throttle housing, then pull the outer cable out from its mounting bracket rubber grommet. Slide the flat washer off the end of the cable, and remove the spring clip **(see illustrations)**.
2 Working back along the length of the cable, free it from any retaining clips or ties, noting its correct routing.
3 Working from inside the vehicle, rotate the fastener through 90° and lower the fusebox cover. Disconnect the wiring connector from the key pad then slacken and remove the retaining screws and remove the driver's side lower panel from the facia.
4 Release the retaining clip, and detach the inner cable from the top of the accelerator pedal **(see illustration)**.
5 Release the outer cable from its retainer on the pedal mounting bracket, then tie a length of string to the end of the cable.
6 Return to the engine compartment, release the cable grommet from the bulkhead and withdraw the cable. When the end of the cable appears, untie the string and leave it in position – it can then be used to draw the cable back into position on refitting.

Refitting

7 Tie the string to the end of the cable, then use the string to draw the cable into position through the bulkhead. Once the cable end is visible, untie the string, then clip the outer cable into its pedal bracket retainer, and clip the inner cable into position in the pedal end.
8 Check that the cable is securely retained, then refit the lower panel to the facia.
9 Within the engine compartment, ensure the outer cable is correctly seated in the bulkhead grommet, then work along the cable, securing it in position with the retaining clips and ties, and ensuring the cable is correctly routed.
10 Slide the flat washer onto the cable end, and refit the spring clip.
11 Pass the outer cable through the mounting bracket grommet on the throttle housing, and reconnect the inner cable to the throttle cam. Adjust the cable as described below.

Adjustment

12 Remove the spring clip from the accelerator outer cable **(see illustration)**.

3.12 Accelerator cable adjustment ferrule and spring clip – 2.0 litre EW10 engine

Ensuring that the throttle cam is fully against its stop, gently pull the cable out of its grommet until all free play is removed from the inner cable.

13 With the cable held in this position, refit the spring clip to the last exposed outer cable groove in front of the rubber grommet and washer. When the clip is refitted and the outer cable is released, there should be only a small amount of free play in the inner cable.

14 Have an assistant depress the accelerator pedal, and check that the throttle cam opens fully and returns smoothly to its stop.

4 Accelerator pedal – removal and refitting

Removal

1 Disconnect the accelerator cable from the pedal as described in Section 3.

2 According to type either remove the screws from the pedal pivot bush, or unscrew the nut (or remove the spring clip) from the end of the pedal pivot shaft. Where a pivot shaft and nut arrangement is used, unscrew the nut whilst retaining the pivot shaft with an open-ended spanner on the flats provided.

3 Remove the pedal, or pull the pedal and pivot shaft assembly from the support bracket according to type.

Refitting

4 Refitting is a reversal of the removal procedure, applying a little multi-purpose grease to the pedal pivot point. On completion, adjust the accelerator cable as described in Section 3.

5 Unleaded petrol – general information and usage

Note: *The information given in this Chapter is correct at the time of writing. If updated information is thought to be required, check with a Peugeot dealer. If travelling abroad, consult one of the motoring organisations (or a similar authority) for advice on the fuel available.*

1 All Peugeot 406 petrol engines are designed to run on unleaded fuel with a minimum octane rating of 95 (RON). All engines have a catalytic converter, and so must be run on unleaded fuel **only**. Under no circumstances should leaded fuel, or lead replacement petrol (LRP) be used, as this will damage the converter.

2 The manufacturer's do state, however, that for improved vehicle performance (and possibly increased fuel economy), 98 (RON) unleaded petrol may be used, where this is available.

6 Fuel injection systems – general information

Note: *The fuel injection ECU is of the 'self-learning' type, meaning that as it operates, it also monitors and stores the settings which give optimum engine performance under all operating conditions. When the battery is disconnected, these settings are lost and the ECU reverts to the base settings programmed into its memory at the factory. On restarting, this may lead to the engine running/idling roughly for a short while, until the ECU has relearned the optimum settings. This process is best accomplished by taking the vehicle on a road test (for approximately 15 minutes), covering all engine speeds and loads, concentrating mainly in the 2500 to 3500 rpm region.*

On all engines, the fuel injection and ignition functions are combined into a single engine management system. The systems fitted are manufactured by Bosch, Sagem Lucas and Magneti Marelli, and are very similar to each other in most respects, the only significant differences being within the system ECUs **(see illustrations overleaf)**. Each system incorporates a closed-loop catalytic converter and an evaporative emission control system, and complies with the latest emission control standards. Refer to Chapter 5B for information on the ignition side of each system; the fuel side of the system operates as follows.

The fuel pump supplies fuel from the tank to the fuel rail, via a renewable cartridge filter mounted underneath the rear of the vehicle. The pump itself is mounted inside the fuel tank, the pump motor is permanently immersed in fuel, to keep it cool. The fuel rail is mounted directly above the fuel injectors and acts as a fuel reservoir.

Fuel rail supply pressure is controlled by the pressure regulator, mounted at the end of the fuel rail or, on later Bosch systems, in front of the fuel tank. The regulator contains a spring-loaded valve, which lifts to allow excess fuel to return to the tank when the optimum operating pressure of the fuel system is exceeded (eg, during low speed, light load cruising). The regulator also contains a diaphragm which is supplied with vacuum from the inlet manifold. This allows the regulator to reduce the fuel supply pressure during light load, high manifold depression conditions (eg, during idling or deceleration) to prevent excess fuel being 'sucked' through the open injectors.

The fuel injectors are electromagnetic valves, which spray atomised fuel into the inlet manifold tracts under the control of the engine management system ECU. There are four injectors, one per cylinder, mounted in the inlet manifold close to the cylinder head. Each injector is mounted at an angle that allows it to spray fuel directly onto the back of the inlet valve(s). The ECU controls the volume of fuel injected by varying the length of time for which each injector is held open.

The fuel injection systems are typically of the simultaneous injection type, whereby all four injectors open at the same time and fuel is injected into each cylinder's inlet tract twice per engine cycle; once during the power stroke and once during the induction stroke. On later Bosch systems, however, sequential fuel injection is used whereby each injector operates individually in cylinder sequence.

The electrical control system consists of the ECU, along with the following sensors:

a) *Throttle potentiometer – informs the ECU of the throttle valve position, and the rate of throttle opening/closing.*

b) *Coolant temperature sensor – informs the ECU of engine temperature.*

c) *Inlet air temperature sensor – informs the ECU of the temperature of the air passing through the throttle housing.*

d) *Lambda sensor – informs the ECU of the oxygen content of the exhaust gases (explained in greater detail in Part C of this Chapter).*

e) *Manifold pressure sensor – informs the ECU of the load on the engine (expressed in terms of inlet manifold vacuum).*

f) *Crankshaft sensor – informs the ECU of engine speed and crankshaft angular position.*

g) *Vehicle speed sensor – informs the ECU of the vehicle speed.*

h) *Knock sensor – informs the ECU of pre-ignition (detonation) within the cylinders. Not all systems utilise this sensor.*

i) *Camshaft sensor – informs the ECU of which cylinder is on the firing stroke on later systems with sequential injection.*

Signals from each of the sensors are compared by the ECU and, based on this information, the ECU selects the response appropriate to those values, and controls the fuel injectors (varying the pulse width – the length of time the injectors are held open – to provide a richer or weaker air/fuel mixture, as appropriate). The air/fuel mixture is constantly varied by the ECU, to provide the best settings for cranking, starting (with either a hot or cold engine) and engine warm-up, idle, cruising and acceleration.

The ECU also has full control over the engine idle speed, typically via a stepper

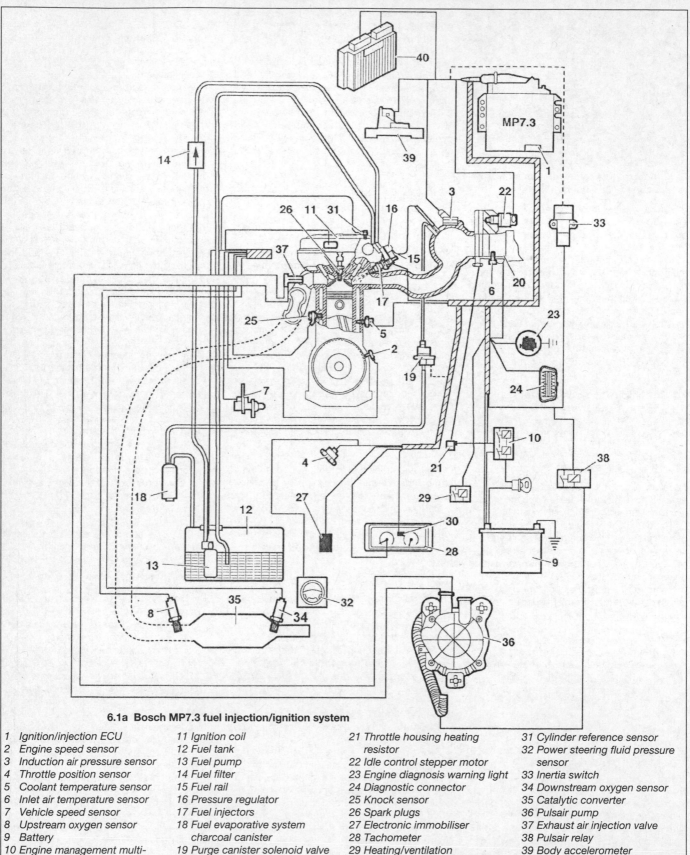

6.1a Bosch MP7.3 fuel injection/ignition system

1 Ignition/injection ECU
2 Engine speed sensor
3 Induction air pressure sensor
4 Throttle position sensor
5 Coolant temperature sensor
6 Inlet air temperature sensor
7 Vehicle speed sensor
8 Upstream oxygen sensor
9 Battery
10 Engine management multi-
   function double relay

11 Ignition coil
12 Fuel tank
13 Fuel pump
14 Fuel filter
15 Fuel rail
16 Pressure regulator
17 Fuel injectors
18 Fuel evaporative system
   charcoal canister
19 Purge canister solenoid valve
20 Throttle housing

21 Throttle housing heating
   resistor
22 Idle control stepper motor
23 Engine diagnosis warning light
24 Diagnostic connector
25 Knock sensor
26 Spark plugs
27 Electronic immobiliser
28 Tachometer
29 Heating/ventilation
30 Fuel consumption data

31 Cylinder reference sensor
32 Power steering fluid pressure
   sensor
33 Inertia switch
34 Downstream oxygen sensor
35 Catalytic converter
36 Pulsair pump
37 Exhaust air injection valve
38 Pulsair relay
39 Body accelerometer
40 Automatic transmission ECU

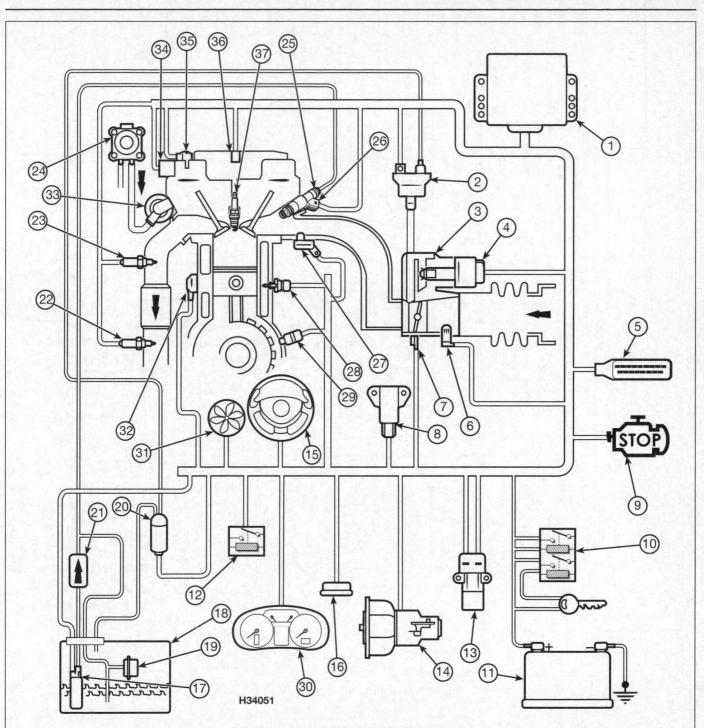

6.1b Sagem 2000 fuel injection/ignition system

1 Ignition/injection ECU
2 Purge canister solenoid valve
3 Throttle housing
4 Idle control stepper motor
5 Diagnostic connector
6 Inlet air temperature sensor
7 Throttle housing heating resistor
8 Throttle position sensor
9 Engine diagnosis warning light

10 Engine management multi-function double relay
11 Battery
12 Air conditioning relay
13 Inertia switch
14 Vehicle speed sensor
15 Power steering fluid pressure sensor
16 Electronic immobiliser
17 Fuel pump
18 Fuel tank

19 Fuel pressure regulator
20 Fuel evaporative system charcoal canister
21 Fuel filter
22 Upstream oxygen sensor
23 Downstream oxygen sensor
24 Pulsair pump
25 Fuel rail
26 Fuel injectors
27 Induction air pressure sensor

28 Coolant temperature sensor
29 Crankshaft position sensor
30 Instrument panel
31 Electric cooling fans
32 Knock sensor
33 Secondary air valve
34 Camshaft position sensor
35 EGR valve
36 Ignition coil module
37 Spark plugs

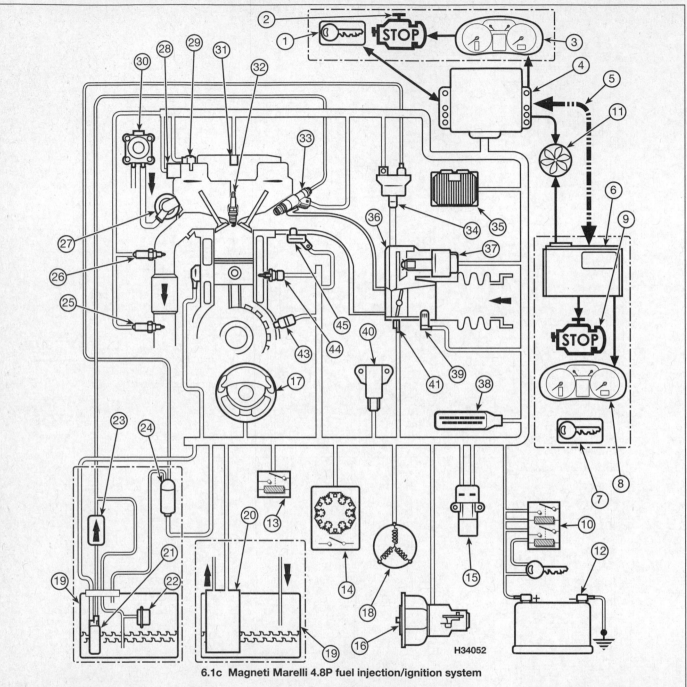

6.1c Magneti Marelli 4.8P fuel injection/ignition system

1 Decoder – non-multiplexed	11 Fans	22 Fuel pressure regulator	33 Fuel injectors and supply rail
2 Engine management warning light – non-multiplexed	12 Battery	23 Fuel filter	34 Purge valve
	13 Air conditioning relay	24 Charcoal canister	35 Automatic transmission ECU
3 Rev counter and instrument panel – non-multiplexed	14 Air conditioning pressure switch	25 Lambda (oxygen) sensor (downstream)	36 Throttle body
4 ECU	15 Inertia switch (where fitted)	26 Lambda (oxygen) sensor (upstream)	37 Idle control stepper motor
5 Multiplex network	16 Vehicle speed transmitter (where fitted)	27 Air inlet valve	38 Diagnostic socket
6 Control box – multiplexed	17 Power steering fluid pressure switch	28 Exhaust gas recirculation (EGR) valve	39 Inlet air temperature sensor
7 Immobiliser – multiplexed	18 Alternator	29 Camshaft position sensor	40 Throttle position potentiometer
8 Instrument panel – multiplexed	19 Fuel tank	30 Secondary air pump	41 Throttle body heating element
9 Engine management warning light – non-multiplexed	20 Fuel pump	31 Ignition coil module	42 Knock sensor
10 Double relay or built-in systems interface	21 Fuel pump	32 Spark plugs	43 Engine speed sensor
			44 Coolant temperature sensor
			45 Inlet air pressure sensor

motor fitted to the throttle housing. The stepper motor pushrod controls the amount of air passing through a bypass drilling at the side of the throttle. When the throttle valve is closed (accelerator pedal released), the ECU uses the motor to alter the position of the pushrod, controlling the amount of air bypassing the throttle valve and so controlling the idle speed. The ECU also carries out 'fine tuning' of the idle speed by varying the ignition timing to increase or reduce the torque of the engine as it is idling. This helps to stabilise the idle speed when electrical or mechanical loads (such as headlights, air conditioning, etc) are switched on and off.

On certain Bosch systems, ECU control of the engine idle speed is by means of an auxiliary air valve which bypasses the throttle valve. When the throttle valve is closed, the ECU controls the opening of the air valve, which in turn regulates the amount of air entering the manifold, and so controls the idle speed.

The throttle housing on most engines is fitted with an electric heating element. The heater is supplied with current by the ECU, warming the throttle housing on cold-starts to help prevent icing of the throttle valve.

The exhaust and evaporative loss emission control systems are described in more detail in Chapter 4C.

If there is any abnormality in any of the readings obtained from the coolant temperature sensor, the inlet air temperature sensor or the lambda sensor, the ECU enters its 'back-up' mode. If this happens, the erroneous sensor signal is overridden, and the ECU assumes a pre-programmed 'back-up' value, which will allow the engine to continue running, albeit at reduced efficiency. If the ECU enters this mode, the warning lamp on the instrument panel will be illuminated, and the relevant fault code will be stored in the ECU memory.

If the warning light illuminates, the vehicle should be taken to a Peugeot dealer at the earliest opportunity. Once there, a complete test of the engine management system can be carried out, using a special electronic diagnostic test unit, which is plugged into the system's diagnostic connector.

7.2 Pressure release valve on the fuel rail

7 Fuel injection system – depressurisation

Note: *Refer to the warning note in Section 1 before proceeding.*

> **⚠ Warning: The following procedure will merely relieve the pressure in the fuel system – remember that fuel will still be present in the system components and take precautions accordingly before disconnecting any of them.**

1 The fuel system referred to in this Section is defined as the tank-mounted fuel pump, the fuel filter, the fuel injectors, the fuel rail and the pressure regulator, and the metal pipes and flexible hoses of the fuel lines between these components. All these contain fuel which will be under pressure while the engine is running, and/or while the ignition is switched on. The pressure will remain for some time after the ignition has been switched off, and must be relieved in a controlled fashion when any of these components are disturbed for servicing work.

2 Peugeot technicians connect a special tube to the Schrader valve on the fuel rail in order to depressurize the fuel system **(see illustration)**. The tube incorporates a union nut which is screwed onto the valve, and an inner cable which is used to depress the valve core. If this tube is not available, cover the valve and surrounding area with cloth rag, and depress the valve with a screwdriver through

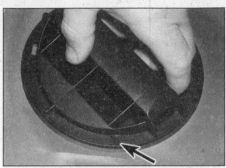

8.3 Note the position of the arrow when removing the plastic access cover

the rag. Make sure that enough rag is used to soak up the fuel. Access to the valve is gained by first removing the engine top cover.

3 With the pressure released, refit the cap to the valve.

4 Note that pressure may increase again in the fuel system due to an increase in ambient temperature, so any work required on the system should be started immediately after releasing the pressure.

8 Fuel pump – removal and refitting

Note: *Refer to the warning note in Section 1 before proceeding.*

Removal

1 Disconnect the battery negative lead (refer to *Disconnecting the battery* at the end of this manual). This is important, since any stray electrical discharge in the vicinity of the open fuel tank would be extremely dangerous.

2 For access to the fuel pump, remove the rear seat as described in Chapter 11.

3 Remove the plastic access cover from the floor to expose the fuel pump. Note the position of the arrow on the cover to assist refitting **(see illustration)**.

4 Disconnect the wiring connector from the top of the fuel pump **(see illustration)**.

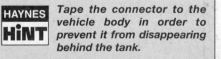

HAYNES HiNT *Tape the connector to the vehicle body in order to prevent it from disappearing behind the tank.*

5 Mark the fuel supply hose (and, where applicable, the return hose) for identification purposes, then disconnect from the top of the pump. Note that quick-release unions are fitted. The supply hose is indicated by an arrow on the top of the pump **(see illustration)**.

6 Noting the alignment arrows on the tank, pump and locking ring **(see illustration)**, unscrew the locking ring and remove it from the tank. Although Peugeot recommend the use of tool 1601 to unscrew the locking ring,

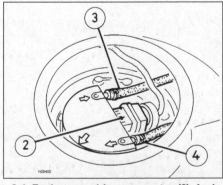

8.4 Fuel pump wiring connector (2), fuel feed hose (3) and return hose (4)

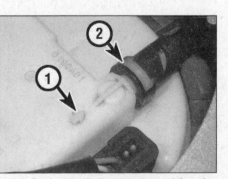

8.5 Fuel outlet indication arrow (1) and outlet hose (2)

this can be accomplished by using a screwdriver on the raised studs of the locking ring. Carefully tap the screwdriver to turn the ring anti-clockwise and release it. Alternatively, a home-made tool may be fabricated out of metal rod, bent to locate on the studs.

7 Lift the fuel pump assembly out of the fuel tank, taking great care not to damage the float arm, or to spill fuel inside the car. Recover the seal from the assembly and discard it; a new one must be obtained for the refitting procedure.

8 Note that the fuel pump is only available as a complete assembly – no components are available separately.

Refitting

9 Wipe clean the contact surfaces of the pump/gauge and tank, then locate a new seal on the tank. Manoeuvre the assembly into the fuel tank, ensuring that the alignment arrows are positioned correctly. Refit the locking ring and securely tighten it using the same method as for removal. The alignment arrow on the locking ring must be positioned pointing to the arrow on the tank.

10 Reconnect the supply and return hoses to the top of the fuel pump, then reconnect the wiring.

11 Refit the plastic access cover with its notch facing forwards, then refit the rear seat with reference to Chapter 11.

12 Reconnect the battery negative lead.

9 Fuel gauge sender unit – removal and refitting

The fuel gauge sender unit is incorporated in the fuel pump – refer to Section 8.

10 Fuel tank – removal and refitting

Note: *Refer to the warning note in Section 1 before proceeding.*

Removal

1 Before removing the fuel tank, all fuel must

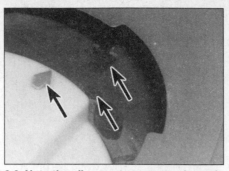

8.6 Note the alignment arrows on the tank, pump and locking ring

be drained from the tank. Since a fuel tank drain plug is not provided, it is preferable to carry out the removal operation when the tank is nearly empty. If there is any fuel remaining in the fuel tank, it can be removed by disconnecting the fuel supply hose and connecting a suitable hose leading to a container outside the vehicle.

2 Remove the fuel pump/gauge assembly as described in Section 8. Remove the fuel pump relay located in the engine compartment fuse/relay box, and connect a bridging wire between the terminals.

3 Chock the front wheels then jack up the rear of the vehicle and support on axle stands (see *Jacking and vehicle support*).

4 Remove the exhaust system from the catalytic converter rearward (see Section 17).

5 Unbolt and remove the exhaust heat shield from the underbody.

6 Disconnect the fuel filler pipe, breather pipe and vapour collection pipe at their tank attachments **(see illustration)**. Where the crimped-type Peugeot hose clips are fitted, cut the clips and discard them; use standard worm drive hose clips on refitting.

7 Disconnect the fuel supply and return pipes at their fuel tank connections **(see illustration)**.

8 Unclip the handbrake cable and move it aside as far as possible.

9 Place a trolley jack with an interposed block of wood beneath the tank, then raise the jack until it is supporting the weight of the tank. Position the jack so as to allow room to remove the fuel tank cradle.

10 Unscrew the fuel tank cradle mounting bolts and remove the cradle **(see illustration)**.

11 Lower the fuel tank and remove it from under the car.

12 If the tank is contaminated with sediment or water, remove the fuel pump and swill the tank out with clean fuel. The tank is injection-moulded from a synthetic material – if seriously damaged, it should be renewed. However, in certain cases, it may be possible to have small leaks or minor damage repaired. Seek the advice of a specialist before attempting to repair the fuel tank.

Refitting

13 Refitting is the reverse of the removal procedure, noting the following points:

a) When lifting the tank back into position, take care to ensure none of the hoses get trapped between the tank and body.

b) Ensure that all pipes and hoses are correctly routed, and securely held in position with their retaining clips.

c) On completion, refill the tank with a small amount of fuel, and check for signs of leakage prior to taking the vehicle out on the road.

11 Fuel injection system – testing

Testing

1 If a fault appears in the fuel injection/engine management system, first ensure that all the system wiring connectors are securely connected and free of corrosion. Ensure that the fault is not due to poor maintenance; ie, check that the air cleaner filter element is clean, the spark plugs are in good condition and correctly gapped, the cylinder compression pressures are correct, and that the engine breather hoses are clear and undamaged, referring to the relevant Parts of Chapters 1, 2 and 5 for further information.

2 If these checks fail to reveal the cause of the problem, the vehicle should be taken to a Peugeot dealer or suitably-equipped garage for testing. A diagnostic socket is located adjacent to the passenger compartment fusebox in which a fault code reader or other suitable test equipment can be connected. By

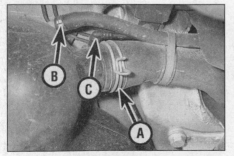

10.6 Fuel filler pipe (A), breather pipe (B) and vapour collection pipe (C) attachments at the fuel tank

10.7 Fuel supply and return pipe connections at the fuel tank

10.10 Fuel tank cradle mounting bolt

using the code reader or test equipment, the engine management ECU (and the various other vehicle system ECUs) can be interrogated, and any stored fault codes can be retrieved. This will allow the fault to be quickly and simply traced, alleviating the need to test all the system components individually, which is a time-consuming operation that carries a risk of damaging the ECU.

Adjustment

3 Experienced home mechanics with a considerable amount of skill and equipment (including a tachometer and an accurately calibrated exhaust gas analyser) may be able to *check* the exhaust CO level and the idle speed. However, if these are found to be outside the specified tolerance, the car must be taken to a suitably-equipped garage for further testing. Neither the mixture adjustment (exhaust gas CO level) nor the idle speed are adjustable, and should either be incorrect, a fault may be present in the engine management system.

12 Throttle housing –
removal and refitting

Removal

1 Disconnect the battery negative lead (refer to *Disconnecting the battery* at the end of this manual).
2 Remove the air cleaner-to-throttle housing duct as described in Section 2.

13.2 Fuel pressure regulator vacuum pipe (Bosch system)

13.3b . . . and on the EW7 engine

3 Disconnect the accelerator inner cable from the throttle cam then withdraw the outer cable from the mounting bracket along with its flat washer and spring clip. Where applicable, also disconnect the arm from the diaphragm canister **(see illustration)**.
4 Depress the retaining clips, and disconnect the wiring connectors from the throttle potentiometer, the electric heating element, the inlet air temperature sensor and idle speed control stepper motor (as applicable).
5 Release the retaining clips (where fitted), and disconnect all the relevant vacuum and breather hoses from the throttle housing. Make identification marks on the hoses, to ensure that they are connected correctly on refitting.
6 Where necessary, undo the bolts or screws and release the accelerator cable bracket and housing support bracket.
7 Slacken and remove the retaining screws, and remove the throttle housing from the inlet manifold. Remove the O-ring from the manifold, and discard it – a new one must be used on refitting.

Refitting

8 Refitting is a reversal of the removal procedure, noting the following points:
  a) Fit a new O-ring to the manifold, then refit the throttle housing and securely tighten its retaining nuts or screws (as applicable).
  b) Ensure that all hoses are correctly reconnected and, where necessary, are securely held in position by the retaining clips.

13.3a Disconnecting the fuel feed and return hoses from the fuel rail and fuel pressure regulator on the XU7 engine . . .

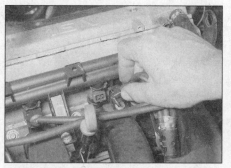

13.5a Disconnect the wiring connectors from the fuel injectors on the XU7 engine . . .

12.3 Accelerator inner cable (1) and diaphragm canister arm (2)

  c) Ensure that all wiring is correctly routed, and that the connectors are securely reconnected.
  d) On completion, adjust the accelerator cable as described in Section 3.

13 Bosch Motronic and Sagem Lucas system components –
removal and refitting

Fuel rail and injectors

Note: *Refer to the warning note in Section 1 before proceeding. If a faulty injector is suspected, before condemning the injector, it is worth trying the effect of one of the proprietary injector-cleaning treatments which are available from car accessory shops.*

1 Disconnect the battery negative lead (refer to *Disconnecting the battery* at the end of this manual).
2 Disconnect the vacuum pipe from the fuel pressure regulator **(see illustration)**.
3 Bearing in mind the information given in Section 7, depress the catch on the fuel feed hose quick-release fitting, and disconnect the fuel feed (and return hoses, where applicable) from the fuel rail **(see illustrations)**. Suitably seal or plug the hose and the fuel rail union(s) after disconnection.
4 Open the retaining clips and release the wiring and hoses running along the front of the fuel rail.
5 Depress the retaining tangs and disconnect the wiring connectors from the four injectors **(see illustrations)**.

13.5b . . . and on the EW7 engine

13.6a Slacken and remove the fuel rail retaining bolts . . .

13.6b . . . then carefully ease the fuel rail and injector assembly from the inlet manifold on the XU7 engine

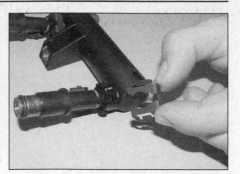

13.7a Slide out the retaining clip . . .

13.7b . . . and remove the injector from the fuel rail

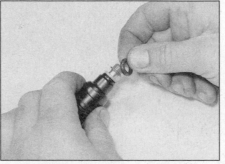

13.8 Fit new O-rings to the injectors before refitting – 1.8 litre XU7 engines

13.11 Disconnect the vacuum pipe from the regulator – 1.8 litre XU7 engines

6 Slacken and remove the fuel rail retaining bolts then carefully ease the fuel rail and injector assembly out from the inlet manifold and remove it from the engine **(see illustrations)**. Remove the O-rings from the end of each injector and discard them; they must be renewed whenever they are disturbed.

7 Slide out the retaining clip(s) and remove the relevant injector(s) from the fuel rail **(see illustrations)**. Remove the upper O-ring from each disturbed injector and discard; all disturbed O-rings must be renewed.

8 Refitting is a reversal of the removal procedure, noting the following points.

a) Fit new O-rings to all disturbed injector unions **(see illustration)**.

b) Apply a smear of engine oil to the O-rings to aid installation then ease the injectors and fuel rail into position ensuring that none of the O-rings are displaced.

c) On completion start the engine and check for fuel leaks.

Fuel pressure regulator

Note 1: Refer to the warning note in Section 1 before proceeding.

Note 2: On the S2000 MPI system, the pressure regulator is located in the fuel tank.

9 Disconnect the battery negative lead (refer to Disconnecting the battery at the end of this manual).

10 Bearing in mind the information given in Section 7, slacken the retaining clips and disconnect the fuel feed and return hoses from the fuel rail and pressure regulator.

11 Disconnect the vacuum pipe from the regulator **(see illustration)**.

12 Place some rags under the regulator, to catch any spilt fuel. Remove the retaining clip and ease the regulator out from the fuel rail **(see illustrations)**.

13 Refitting is a reversal of the removal procedure. Examine the regulator seal for signs of damage or deterioration and renew if necessary.

Throttle potentiometer

14 Depress the retaining clip and disconnect the wiring connector from the throttle potentiometer located beneath the throttle housing **(see illustrations)**.

15 Slacken and remove the two retaining screws then disengage the potentiometer from the throttle valve spindle and remove it from the vehicle.

16 Refitting is a reverse of the removal procedure ensuring that the potentiometer is correctly engaged with the throttle valve spindle.

Electronic Control Unit

17 The ECU is located in a plastic box which is mounted on the right-hand front wheelarch.

13.12a Remove the retaining clip . . .

13.12b . . . and ease the regulator from the fuel rail. Check the sealing ring condition (arrowed) before refitting – XU7 engines

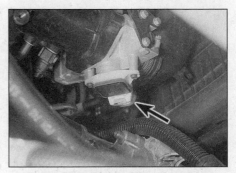

13.14a Throttle potentiometer wiring connector on the XU7 engine . . .

13.14b . . . and on the EW7 engine

13.18 Lift the lid for access to the ECU module

13.19 Wiring connector on the top of the Electronic Control Unit (ECU)

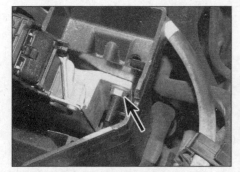

13.20 The ECU mounting bolts

13.23 Idle speed control stepper motor

13.27 Disconnecting the wiring from the manifold absolute pressure sensor

18 Ensure that the ignition is switched off then lift off the ECU module box lid **(see illustration)**. On automatic transmission models there will be two ECUs in the box; the fuel injection/ignition ECU is the unit nearest to the engine.

19 Release the wiring connector by lifting the locking lever on top of the connector upwards. Lift the connector at the rear, disengage the tag at the front and carefully withdraw the connector from the ECU pins **(see illustration)**.

20 Unscrew the mounting bolts, then lift the ECU upwards and remove it from its location **(see illustration)**.

21 Refitting is a reversal of removal. Note that if a new ECU has been fitted, the vehicle should be taken on an extensive road test. Initially, engine performance may be less than acceptable, but should improve as the ECU control circuitry adapts to the engine parameters.

Idle speed stepper motor

22 The idle speed control stepper motor is located on the side of the throttle housing assembly.

23 Release the retaining clip, and disconnect the wiring connector from the motor **(see illustration)**.

24 Slacken and remove the two retaining screws, and withdraw the motor from the throttle housing.

25 Refitting is a reversal of the removal procedure.

Manifold absolute pressure sensor

26 The MAP sensor is situated on the underside of the inlet manifold.

27 Disconnect the wiring connector from the sensor **(see illustration)**.

28 Undo the securing screw, then pull the sensor out of the manifold.

29 Refitting is the reverse of the removal procedure.

Coolant temperature sensor

30 Refer to Chapter 3, Section 6.

Inlet air temperature sensor

31 The inlet air temperature sensor is located on the underside or front of the throttle housing **(see illustration)**.

32 Loosen the retaining clip, and release the air inlet duct from the throttle housing. The inlet air temperature sensor is visible in the top of the housing.

33 Trace the wiring back from the sensor to

its wiring connector on the throttle housing, and unplug the connector.

34 The sensor itself can be pressed out of the throttle housing. Note that it is sealed in place, to prevent air leaks; a suitable sealant will be required for refitting.

35 Refitting is the reverse of removal.

Camshaft position sensor

36 The camshaft position sensor is located at the left-hand end of the exhaust camshaft cylinder head cover.

37 Undo the six screws and lift off the engine cover.

38 Disconnect the crankcase breather hose at the quick-fit connector on the rear cylinder head cover.

39 Disconnect the wiring connector at the camshaft position sensor, then undo the bolt and remove the sensor from the cylinder head cover **(see illustrations)**.

13.31 Inlet air temperature sensor

13.39a Disconnect the wiring . . .

13.39b . . . and remove the camshaft position sensor

40 Refitting is the reverse of removal but fit a new sealing O-ring to the sensor body.

Crankshaft (RPM) sensor

41 The crankshaft sensor is situated on the front face of the transmission clutch housing.

14.2 Removing the engine top cover – 2.0 litre EW engine

14.3 Removing the throttle body-to-air cleaner air duct – 2.0 litre EW engine

14.5b . . . and remove the inlet elbow from the throttle body – 2.0 litre EW engine

42 Trace the wiring back from the sensor to the wiring connector and disconnect it from the main harness.
43 Undo the retaining bolt and withdraw the sensor from the transmission.
44 Refitting is the reverse of the removal procedure.

Vehicle speed sensor

45 The vehicle speed sensor is an integral part of the transmission speedometer drive assembly. Refer to the relevant Part of Chapter 7 for removal and refitting details.

Knock sensor

46 Refer to Chapter 5B, Section 5.

Fuel injection relay unit

47 The relay unit is located in the ECU module box which is mounted on the right-hand front wheelarch.
48 Ensure that the ignition is switched off then lift off the ECU module box lid.
49 Disconnect the wiring connector and remove the relay unit from the mounting plate.
50 Refitting is the reverse of removal.

---

14 Magneti Marelli system components – removal and refitting

Fuel rail and injectors

Note: *Refer to the warning note in Section 1 before proceeding. If a faulty injector is suspected, before condemning the injector, it*

14.4 Disconnect the wiring from the inlet air temperature sensor . . .

14.8 Disconnecting the wiring from the injectors – 2.0 litre EW engine

is worth trying the effect of one of the proprietary injector-cleaning treatments.
1 Disconnect the battery negative lead (refer to *Disconnecting the battery* at the end of this manual).
2 Unbolt and remove the engine top cover **(see illustration)**.
3 Disconnect the air duct from between the air cleaner and throttle body elbow **(see illustration)**.
4 Disconnect the wiring from the inlet air temperature sensor **(see illustration)**.
5 Loosen the clamp and remove the inlet elbow from the throttle body **(see illustrations)**.
6 Disconnect the accelerator cable from the throttle body with reference to Section 3.
7 Unbolt the wiring tray from the top of the inlet manifold, and position to one side.
8 Depress the retaining clip(s), and disconnect the wiring connector(s) from the injector(s) **(see illustration)**.
9 Unscrew the mounting bolts and carefully ease the fuel rail complete with injectors from the inlet manifold **(see illustration)**. Remove the O-rings from the end of each injector, and discard them; these must be renewed whenever they are disturbed.
10 Slide out the retaining clip(s) and remove the relevant injector(s) from the fuel rail. Remove the upper O-ring from each disturbed injector and discard; all disturbed O-rings must be renewed.
11 Refitting is a reversal of the removal procedure, noting the following points.
a) Fit new O-rings to all disturbed injector unions.

14.5a . . . then loosen the clamp . . .

14.9 Fuel rail mounting bolt

14.13 Throttle potentiometer on the throttle body

14.18 Idle speed control stepper motor

14.22 Inlet air pressure sensor

b) *Apply a smear of engine oil to the O-rings to aid installation then ease the injectors and fuel rail into position ensuring that none of the O-rings are displaced.*

c) *On completion start the engine and check for fuel leaks.*

Fuel pressure regulator

12 The fuel pressure regulator is located in the fuel tank, and is removed together with the fuel pump and gauge sender.

Throttle potentiometer

13 The throttle potentiometer is fitted to the right-hand side of the throttle housing (see illustration).

14 Release the retaining clip, and disconnect the potentiometer wiring connector.

15 Slacken and remove the two retaining screws, and remove the potentiometer from the throttle housing.

16 Refitting is the reverse of removal, ensuring that the potentiometer is correctly engaged with the throttle valve spindle.

Electronic Control Unit

17 Refer to Section 13.

Idle speed stepper motor

18 The idle speed control stepper motor is located on the front of the throttle housing assembly (see illustration).

19 Release the retaining clip, and disconnect the wiring connector from the motor.

20 Slacken and remove the two retaining screws, and withdraw the motor from the throttle housing.

21 Refitting is a reversal of the removal procedure.

Inlet air pressure sensor

22 The inlet air pressure sensor is located on the inlet manifold, below the throttle housing (see illustration).

23 Disconnect the wiring from the sensor.

24 Undo the screw and withdraw the sensor from the inlet manifold.

25 Refitting is the reverse of the removal procedure.

Coolant temperature sensor

26 Refer to Chapter 3, Section 6.

14.27 Inlet air temperature sensor

Inlet air temperature sensor

27 The inlet air temperature sensor is located on the front of the throttle housing (see illustration) and cannot be removed separately.

Throttle housing heater

28 The throttle housing heating element is integral with the throttle housing and cannot be removed separately (see illustration).

Crankshaft (RPM) sensor

29 Refer to Section 13.

Camshaft position sensor

30 Refer to Section 13.

Vehicle speed sensor

31 Refer to Section 13.

Knock sensor

32 Refer to Chapter 5B, Section 5.

15.3a Disconnecting the inlet manifold breather hoses from the cylinder head cover – XU7 engine

14.28 Throttle housing heating element wiring

Fuel injection relay unit

33 Refer to Section 13.

15 Inlet manifold – removal and refitting

Removal

1 Disconnect the battery negative lead (refer to *Disconnecting the battery* at the end of this manual).

2 Remove the throttle housing as described in Section 12 and the fuel rail and injectors as described in Section 13 or 14.

3 Disconnect the braking system vacuum servo unit hose, and all the relevant vacuum/breather hoses, from the manifold (see illustrations). Where necessary, make

15.3b Brake vacuum servo hose connection to the inlet manifold – EW10 engine

15.3c Disconnect the left-hand breather hose . . .

15.3d . . . and right-hand breather hose from their connections at the rear of the throttle housing – EW7 engine

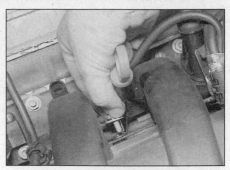
15.4a Slacken and remove the bolt securing the dipstick tube to the rear of the manifold – XU7 engine

15.4b Throttle diaphragm canister on the inlet manifold

15.4c Disconnecting the EGR pipe from the cylinder head – EW7 engine

15.5a Withdraw the inlet manifold . . .

identification marks on the hoses, to ensure that they are correctly reconnected on refitting.

4 Where applicable, slacken and remove the bolt securing the dipstick tube to the side of the manifold, and also remove throttle diaphragm canister where fitted, and disconnect the EGR pipe **(see illustrations)**.

5 Undo the nuts and bolts securing the manifold to the cylinder head, and remove the manifold from the engine compartment **(see illustrations)**. Note the location of the engine top cover support bracket.

6 Recover the manifold gasket/seals, and discard them – new ones must be used on refitting **(see illustrations)**.

Refitting

7 Refitting is a reverse of the relevant removal procedure, noting the following points:

a) Ensure that the manifold and cylinder head mating surfaces are clean and dry, then locate the new gasket/seals on the manifold. Refit the manifold and tighten its retaining nuts and bolts to the specified torque setting.

b) Ensure that all relevant hoses are reconnected to their original positions and are securely held (where necessary) by the retaining clips.

c) Adjust the accelerator cable as described in Section 3.

16 Exhaust manifold – removal and refitting

Removal

1 Remove the top cover from the engine.

2 Disconnect the hot-air inlet hose from the manifold shroud and remove it from the vehicle.

3 Slacken and remove the three retaining screws, and remove the shroud from the top of the exhaust manifold.

4 Apply the handbrake, then jack up the front of the vehicle and support it on axle stands (see *Jacking and vehicle support*).

15.5b . . . and disconnect the manifold pressure sensor wiring connector – 1.8 litre XU7 engine

15.6a Recover the seals from the recesses in the manifold on the 1.8 litre XU7 engine . . .

15.6b . . . and on the 1.8 litre EW7 engine

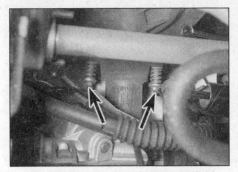

17.6a Exhaust front pipe-to-manifold retaining nuts and springs – 1.8 litre XU7 engine

17.6b Clamp bolt and front pipe flexible exhaust section – 2.0 litre EW10 engine

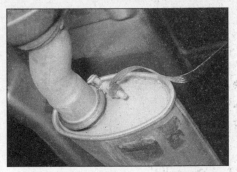

17.8 Earth strap attachment at the exhaust intermediate pipe clamp

5 Where necessary, disconnect the wiring from the lambda (oxygen) sensor. Alternatively, support the exhaust front pipe, to avoid any strain being placed on the sensor wiring.

6 Undo the nuts securing the exhaust front pipe to the manifold and recover the springs. Note on some models a clamp ring is fitted. Where applicable, remove the bolt securing the front pipe to its mounting bracket. Disconnect the front pipe from the manifold, and recover the gasket.

7 Undo the retaining nuts securing the exhaust manifold to the cylinder head. Manoeuvre the manifold out of the engine compartment, and discard the manifold gaskets.

Refitting

8 Refitting is the reverse of the removal procedure, noting the following points:
  a) Examine all the exhaust manifold studs for signs of damage and corrosion; remove all traces of corrosion, and repair or renew any damaged studs.
  b) Ensure that the manifold and cylinder head sealing faces are clean and flat, and fit the new manifold gasket(s). Tighten the manifold retaining nuts to the specified torque setting.
  c) Reconnect the front pipe to the manifold, using the information given in Section 17.

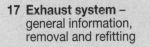

17 Exhaust system –
general information, removal and refitting

General information

1 A multi-section exhaust system is fitted. The exhaust sections are joined by clamping rings or flanges, with a flexible section incorporated in the front pipe to cater for engine movement.

2 A catalytic converter is located on the front section of the exhaust. The system is suspended throughout its entire length by rubber mountings.

Removal

3 Each exhaust section can be removed individually, or the system can be removed complete, then separated after removal.

4 To remove part of the system, first jack up the front or rear of the car and support it on axle stands. Alternatively, position the car over an inspection pit or on car ramps.

Front pipe/catalytic converter

5 Trace the wiring back from the downstream lambda sensor to the wiring connector and disconnect the connector.

6 Where applicable, undo the nuts and bolts securing the front pipe flange joint to the manifold, and recover the springs. Separate the joint and recover the sealing ring. On the EW10 engine, unscrew the clamp bolt and release the ring, then separate the flexible exhaust pipe section from the exhaust manifold **(see illustrations)**.

7 Loosen the clamp bolt securing the front pipe flange joint to the intermediate pipe/rear pipe and separate the joint. Withdraw the front pipe from underneath the vehicle, and recover the sealing ring.

Intermediate pipe and silencer

8 Slacken the clamping ring bolts and disengage the clamps from the front and rear flange joints. Note that there may be an earth strap attached to one of the clamp bolts **(see illustration)**.

9 Unhook the intermediate pipe and silencer from its mounting rubber and remove it from underneath the vehicle.

Tailpipe and silencer

10 Slacken the clamping ring bolt and disengage the clamp from the flange joint.

11 Unhook the tailpipe and silencer from its mounting rubbers and remove it from the car.

Complete system

12 Disconnect the lambda sensor wiring connectors from the main wiring harness.

13 Undo the nut and remove the through bolt, then spread the clamping ring securing the front pipe flange joint to the exhaust manifold.

14 Free the system from all its mounting rubbers and lower it from under the vehicle.

Heat shield(s)

15 The heat shields are secured to the underbody by various nuts and bolts. Each shield can be removed once the relevant exhaust section has been removed. If a shield is being removed to gain access to a component located behind it, it may prove sufficient in some cases to remove the retaining nuts and/or bolts, and simply lower the shield, without disturbing the exhaust system.

Refitting

16 Each section is refitted by reversing the removal sequence, noting the following:
  a) Ensure that all traces of corrosion have been removed from the flanges.
  b) Inspect the rubber mountings for damage or deterioration, and renew as necessary.
  c) Prior to assembling the spring-loaded joint, a smear of high-temperature grease should be applied to the joint mating surfaces.
  d) Prior to tightening the exhaust system fasteners, ensure that all rubber mountings are correctly located, and that there is adequate clearance between the exhaust system and vehicle underbody.
  e) Ensure that the lambda sensor wiring is reconnected correctly and secured to the underbody by the relevant retaining clips.

Notes

Chapter 4 Part B:
Fuel and exhaust systems – diesel models

Contents

Accelerator cable – removal, refitting and adjustment 5
Accelerator pedal – removal and refitting 6
Accumulator rail – removal and refitting 11
Air cleaner assembly and inlet ducts – removal and refitting 4
Air cleaner filter element renewal . . . . See Chapter 1B
Electronic control system components – testing, removal and
   refitting 13
Exhaust manifold – removal and refitting 15
Exhaust system – general information and component renewal 19
Fuel filter renewal . . . . See Chapter 1B
Fuel filter water draining . . . . See Chapter 1B
Fuel gauge sender unit – removal and refitting 8

Fuel injectors – removal and refitting 12
Fuel lift pump – removal and refitting 7
Fuel system – priming and bleeding 3
Fuel tank – removal and refitting 9
General information and system operation 1
High-pressure diesel injection system – special information 2
High-pressure fuel pump – removal and refitting 10
Inlet manifold – removal and refitting 14
Intercooler – removal and refitting 18
Turbocharger – description and precautions 16
Turbocharger – removal, inspection and refitting 17

Degrees of difficulty

Easy, suitable for novice with little experience	**Fairly easy,** suitable for beginner with some experience	**Fairly difficult,** suitable for competent DIY mechanic	**Difficult,** suitable for experienced DIY mechanic	**Very difficult,** suitable for expert DIY or professional

Specifications

General
System type . . . . HDi (High-pressure Diesel injection) with full electronic control, direct injection and turbocharger
Designation . . . . Bosch EDC 15C2
Firing order . . . . 1-3-4-2 (No 1 at flywheel end)
Fuel system operating pressure . . . . 200 to 1350 bars (according to engine speed)

High-pressure fuel pump
Type . . . . Bosch CP 1
Direction of rotation . . . . Clockwise, viewed from sprocket end

Injectors
Type . . . . Electromagnetic

Turbocharger
Type:
   DW10 engine . . . . Garrett GT15 or KKK K03
   DW12 engine . . . . Allied Signal GT 1549P
Boost pressure (approximate) . . . . 1 bar at 3000 rpm

Torque wrench settings

	Nm	lbf ft
Accumulator rail mounting bolts	23	17
Accumulator rail-to-fuel injector fuel pipe unions	25	18
Clamping ring nuts	20	15
Exhaust manifold nuts	20	15
Exhaust system fasteners:		
Catalytic converter-to-manifold nuts	10	7
Fuel injector clamp nuts:		
DW10 engine	30	22
DW12 engine:		
Stage 1	4	3
Stage 2	Angle-tighten a further 45°	
Fuel injector clamp stud	7	5
Fuel pressure sensor to accumulator rail	45	33
Fuel pump-to-accumulator rail fuel pipe unions	20	15
High-pressure fuel pipe union nuts*:		
High-pressure fuel pump front mounting bolts and nut	20	15
High-pressure fuel pump rear mounting bolt and nut	22	16
High-pressure fuel pump sprocket nut	50	37

* These torque settings are using Peugeot crow's-foot adaptors – see Section 2

1 General information and system operation

The fuel system consists of a rear-mounted fuel tank and fuel lift pump, a fuel filter with integral water separator, on some models a fuel cooler mounted under the car, and an electronically-controlled High-pressure Diesel injection (HDi) system, together with a turbocharger (see illustrations).

The exhaust system is conventional, but to meet the latest emission levels an unregulated catalytic converter and an exhaust gas recirculation system are fitted to all models.

The HDi system (generally known as a 'common rail' system) derives its name from the fact that a common rail (referred to as an accumulator rail), or fuel reservoir, is used to supply fuel to all the fuel injectors. Instead of an in-line or distributor type injection pump, which distributes the fuel directly to each injector, a high-pressure pump is used, which generates a very high fuel pressure (1350 bars at high engine speed) in the accumulator rail. The accumulator rail stores fuel, and maintains a constant fuel pressure, with the aid of a pressure control valve. Each injector is supplied with high-pressure fuel from the accumulator rail, and the injectors are individually controlled via signals from the system electronic control unit (ECU). The injectors are electromagnetically-operated.

In addition to the various sensors used on models with a conventional fuel injection pump, common rail systems also have a fuel pressure sensor. The fuel pressure sensor allows the ECU to maintain the required fuel pressure, via the pressure control valve.

System operation

For the purposes of describing the operation of a common rail injection system, the components can be divided into three sub-systems; the low-pressure fuel system, the high-pressure fuel system and the electronic control system.

Low-pressure fuel system

The low-pressure fuel system consists of the following components:
a) Fuel tank.
b) Fuel lift pump.
c) Fuel cooler (not all models).
d) Fuel filter/water trap.
e) Low-pressure fuel lines.

The low-pressure system (fuel supply system) is responsible for supplying clean fuel to the high-pressure fuel system.

High-pressure fuel system

The high-pressure fuel system consists of the following components:
a) High-pressure fuel pump with pressure control valve.

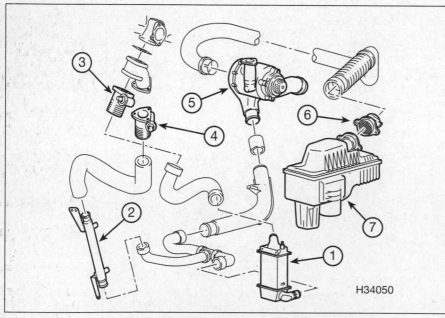

1.1a Fuel inlet system on the 2.2 litre DW12 engine

1 Intercooler (air-to-air heat exchanger)
2 Water-to-air heat exchanger
3 Cold air inlet
4 Hot air inlet
5 Turbocharger
6 Airflow sensor
7 Air filter

1.1b Fuel cooler mounted under the vehicle

b) *High-pressure fuel accumulator rail.*
c) *Fuel injectors.*
d) *High-pressure fuel lines.*

After passing through the fuel filter, the fuel reaches the high-pressure pump, which forces it into the accumulator rail. As diesel fuel has a certain elasticity, the pressure in the accumulator rail remains constant, even though fuel leaves the rail each time one of the injectors operates. Additionally, a pressure control valve mounted on the high-pressure pump ensures that the fuel pressure is maintained within preset limits.

The pressure control valve is operated by the ECU. When the valve is opened, fuel is returned from the high-pressure pump to the tank, via the fuel return lines, and the pressure in the accumulator rail falls. To enable the ECU to trigger the pressure control valve correctly, the pressure in the accumulator rail is measured by a fuel pressure sensor.

The electromagnetically-controlled fuel injectors are operated individually, via signals from the ECU, and each injector injects fuel directly into the relevant combustion chamber. The fact that high fuel pressure is always available allows very precise and highly flexible injection in comparison to a conventional injection pump: for example combustion during the main injection process can be improved considerably by the pre-injection of a very small quantity of fuel.

Electronic control system

The electronic control system consists of the following components:

a) *Electronic control unit (ECU).*
b) *Crankshaft speed/position sensor.*
c) *Camshaft position sensor.*
d) *Accelerator pedal position sensor.*
e) *Coolant temperature sensor.*
f) *Fuel temperature sensor.*
g) *Air mass meter.*
h) *Fuel pressure sensor.*
i) *Fuel injectors.*
j) *Fuel pressure control valve.*
k) *Preheating control unit.*
l) *EGR solenoid valve.*

The information from the various sensors is passed to the ECU, which evaluates the signals. The ECU contains electronic 'maps' which enable it to calculate the optimum quantity of fuel to inject, the appropriate start of injection, and even pre- and post-injection fuel quantities, for each individual engine cylinder under any given condition of engine operation.

Additionally, the ECU carries out monitoring and self-diagnostic functions. Any faults in the system are stored in the ECU memory, which enables quick and accurate fault diagnosis using appropriate diagnostic equipment (such as a suitable fault code reader).

System Components

Fuel lift pump

The fuel lift pump and integral fuel gauge sender unit is electrically-operated, and is mounted in the fuel tank.

High-pressure pump

The high-pressure pump is mounted on the engine in the position normally occupied by the conventional distributor fuel injection pump. The pump is driven at half engine speed by the timing belt, and is lubricated by the fuel which it pumps.

The fuel lift pump forces the fuel into the high-pressure pump chamber, via a safety valve.

The high-pressure pump consists of three radially-mounted pistons and cylinders. The pistons are operated by an eccentric cam mounted on the pump drive spindle. As a piston moves down, fuel enters the cylinder through an inlet valve. When the piston reaches bottom dead centre (BDC), the inlet valve closes, and as the piston moves back up the cylinder, the fuel is compressed. When the pressure in the cylinder reaches the pressure in the accumulator rail, an outlet valve opens, and fuel is forced into the accumulator rail. When the piston reaches top dead centre (TDC), the outlet valve closes, due to the pressure drop, and the pumping cycle is repeated. The use of multiple cylinders provides a steady flow of fuel, minimising pulses and pressure fluctuations.

As the pump needs to be able to supply sufficient fuel under full-load conditions, it will supply excess fuel during idle and part-load conditions. This excess fuel is returned from the high-pressure circuit to the low-pressure circuit (to the tank) via the pressure control valve.

The pump incorporates a facility to effectively switch off one of the cylinders to improve efficiency and reduce fuel consumption when maximum pumping capacity is not required. When this facility is operated, a solenoid-operated needle holds the inlet valve in the relevant cylinder open during the delivery stroke, preventing the fuel from being compressed.

Accumulator rail

As its name suggests, the accumulator rail acts as an accumulator, storing fuel and preventing pressure fluctuations. Fuel enters the rail from the high-pressure pump, and each injector has its own connection to the rail. The fuel pressure sensor is mounted in the rail, and the rail also has a connection to the fuel pressure control valve on the pump.

Pressure control valve

The pressure control valve is operated by the ECU, and controls the system pressure. The valve is integral with the high-pressure pump and cannot be separated.

If the fuel pressure is excessive, the valve opens, and fuel flows back to the tank. If the pressure is too low, the valve closes, enabling the high-pressure pump to increase the pressure.

The valve is an electromagnetically-operated ball valve. The ball is forced against its seat, against the fuel pressure, by a powerful spring, and also by the force provided by the electromagnet. The force generated by the electromagnet is directly proportional to the current applied to it by the ECU. The desired pressure can therefore be set by varying the current applied to the electromagnet. Any pressure fluctuations are damped by the spring.

Fuel pressure sensor

The fuel pressure sensor is mounted in the accumulator rail, and provides very precise information on the fuel pressure to the ECU.

Fuel injector

The injectors are mounted on the engine in a similar manner to conventional diesel fuel injectors. The injectors are electro-magnetically-operated via signals from the ECU, and fuel is injected at the pressure existing in the accumulator rail. The injectors are high-precision instruments and are manufactured to very high tolerances.

Fuel flows into the injector from the accumulator rail, via an inlet valve and an inlet throttle, and an electromagnet causes the injector nozzle to lift from its seat, allowing injection. Excess fuel is returned from the injectors to the tank via a return line. The injector operates on a hydraulic servo principle: the forces resulting inside the injector due to the fuel pressure effectively amplify the effects of the electromagnet, which does not provide sufficient force to open the injector nozzle directly. The injector functions as follows. Five separate forces are essential to the operation of the injector.

a) *A nozzle spring forces the nozzle needle against the nozzle seat at the bottom of the injector, preventing fuel from entering the combustion chamber.*
b) *In the valve at the top of the injector, the valve spring forces the valve ball against the opening to the valve control chamber. The fuel in the chamber is unable to escape through the fuel return.*
c) *When triggered, the electromagnet exerts a force which overcomes the valve spring force, and moves the valve ball away from its seat. This is the triggering force for the start of injection. When the valve ball moves off its seat, fuel enters the valve control chamber.*
d) *The pressure of the fuel in the valve control chamber exerts a force on the valve control plunger, which is added to the nozzle spring force.*
e) *A slight chamfer towards the lower end of the nozzle needle causes the fuel in the control chamber to exert a force on the nozzle needle.*

When these forces are in equilibrium, the injector is in its rest (idle) state, but when a voltage is applied to the electromagnet, the forces work to lift the nozzle needle, injecting fuel into the combustion chamber. There are four phases of injector operation as follows:

a) *Rest (idle) state – all forces are in equilibrium. The nozzle needle closes off the nozzle opening, and the valve spring forces the valve ball against its seat.*

1.26 The control vacuum servos on the bulkhead

b) *Opening – the electromagnet is triggered which opens the nozzle and triggers the injection process. The force from the electromagnet allows the valve ball to leave its seat. The fuel from the valve control chamber flows back to the tank via the fuel return line. When the valve opens, the pressure in the valve control chamber drops, and the force on the valve plunger is reduced. However, due to the effect of the input throttle, the pressure on the nozzle needle remains unchanged. The resulting force in the valve control chamber is sufficient to lift the nozzle from its seat, and the injection process begins.*

c) *Injection – within a few milliseconds, the triggering current in the electromagnet is reduced to a lower holding current. The nozzle is now fully open, and fuel is injected into the combustion chamber at the pressure present in the accumulator rail.*

d) *Closing – the electromagnet is switched off, at which point the valve spring forces the valve ball firmly against its seat, and in the valve control chamber, the pressure is the same as that at the nozzle needle. The force at the valve plunger increases, and the nozzle needle closes the nozzle opening. The forces are now in equilibrium once more, and the injector is once more in the idle state, awaiting the next injection sequence.*

ECU and sensors

The ECU and sensors are described earlier in this Section – see *Electronic control system*.

2.4 Typical plastic plug and cap set for sealing disconnected fuel pipes and components

Air inlet sensor and turbocharger

An airflow sensor is fitted downstream of the air filter to monitor the quantity of air supplied to the turbocharger. On models with the 2.2 litre diesel engine (DW12), air from the high-pressure side of the turbocharger is channelled either through the intercooler and cold air throttle body, or through the coolant heat exchanger and hot air throttle body. The throttle bodies are controlled by the engine management ECU via vacuum servos located on the bulkhead **(see illustration)**.

2 High-pressure diesel injection system – special information

Warnings and precautions

1 It is essential to observe strict precautions when working on the fuel system components, particularly the high-pressure side of the system. Before carrying out any operations on the fuel system, refer to the precautions given in *Safety first!* at the beginning of this manual, and to the following additional information.

Do not carry out any repair work on the high-pressure fuel system unless you are competent to do so, have all the necessary tools and equipment required, and are aware of the safety implications involved.

Before starting any repair work on the fuel system, wait at least 30 seconds after switching off the engine to allow the fuel circuit pressure to reduce.

Never work on the high-pressure fuel system with the engine running.

Keep well clear of any possible source of fuel leakage, particularly when starting the engine after carrying out repair work. A leak in the system could cause an extremely high-pressure jet of fuel to escape, which could result in severe personal injury.

Never place your hands or any part of your body near to a leak in the high-pressure fuel system.

Do not use steam cleaning equipment or compressed air to clean the engine or any of the fuel system components.

Procedures and information

2 Strict cleanliness must be observed at all times when working on any part of the fuel system. This applies to the working area in general, the person doing the work, and the components being worked on.

3 Before working on the fuel system components, they must be thoroughly cleaned with a suitable degreasing fluid. Specific cleaning products may be obtained from Peugeot dealers. Alternatively, a suitable brake cleaning fluid may be used. Cleanliness is particularly important when working on the fuel system connections at the following components:

a) *Fuel filter.*
b) *High-pressure fuel pump.*
c) *Accumulator rail.*
d) *Fuel injectors.*
e) *High-pressure fuel pipes.*

4 After disconnecting any fuel pipes or components, the open union or orifice must be immediately sealed to prevent the entry of dirt or foreign material. Plastic plugs and caps in various sizes are available in packs from motor factors and accessory outlets, and are particularly suitable for this application **(see illustration)**. Fingers cut from disposable rubber gloves should be used to protect components such as fuel pipes, fuel injectors and wiring connectors, and can be secured in place using elastic bands. Suitable gloves of this type are available at no cost from most petrol station forecourts.

5 Whenever any of the high-pressure fuel pipes are disconnected or removed, new pipes must be obtained for refitting.

6 On the completion of any repair on the high-pressure fuel system, Peugeot recommend the use of a leak-detecting compound. This is a powder which is applied to the fuel pipe unions and connections and turns white when dry. Any leak in the system will cause the product to darken indicating the source of the leak.

7 The torque wrench settings given in the Specifications must be strictly observed when tightening component mountings and connections. This is particularly important when tightening the high-pressure fuel pipe unions. To enable a torque wrench to be used on the fuel pipe unions, two Peugeot crow-foot adaptors are required. Suitable alternatives are available from motor factors and accessory outlets **(see illustration)**.

3 Fuel system – priming and bleeding

1 The fuel system is entirely self-bleeding because the fuel lift pump supplies fuel to the high-pressure pump whenever the ignition is switched on.

2 In the case of running out of fuel, or after

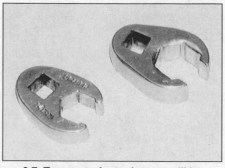

2.7 Two crow-foot adaptors will be necessary for tightening the fuel pipe unions

4.2 Undo the four plastic nuts and lift off the engine cover

4.3 Disconnect the flexible air inlet duct from the air mass meter and turbocharger rigid inlet duct

4.4 Disconnect the wiring plug from the accelerator pedal position sensor

4.5 Rotate the pedal position sensor quadrant, and release the accelerator inner cable

4.7 Disconnect the wiring connector from the air mass meter

4.8 Undo the nuts securing the base of the air cleaner housing to the front and rear support brackets

disconnecting any part of the fuel supply system, ensure that there is fuel in the tank, then start the engine in the normal way.

4 Air cleaner assembly and inlet ducts – removal and refitting

Removal

Air cleaner and front inlet ducts

1 Disconnect the battery negative terminal (refer to *Disconnecting the battery* in the Reference Section of this manual).
2 Undo the four plastic nuts and lift off the engine cover **(see illustration)**.
3 Slacken the retaining clips and disconnect the flexible air inlet duct from the air mass meter and turbocharger rigid inlet duct **(see**

illustration**). Plug or cover the turbocharger rigid inlet duct, using clean rag to prevent any dirt or foreign material from entering.
4 Disconnect the wiring plug from the accelerator pedal position sensor, adjacent to the air cleaner housing **(see illustration)**.
5 Rotate the accelerator pedal position sensor quadrant, and release the inner cable from the quadrant **(see illustration)**.
6 Withdraw the outer cable from the grommet in the pedal position sensor body, and recover the flat washer from the end of the cable.
7 Disconnect the wiring connector from the air mass meter on the side of the air cleaner lid **(see illustration)**.
8 Undo the nuts securing the base of the air cleaner housing to the front and rear support brackets **(see illustration)**.
9 Undo the bolt securing the wiring harness retaining clip to the air cleaner bracket.
10 Lift the air cleaner housing upwards at the

rear, disengage the two front locating lugs and remove the assembly from the engine compartment **(see illustration)**.
11 To remove the air cleaner air inlet duct, undo the bolt securing the front of the inlet duct to the front body panel **(see illustration)**. Detach and remove the duct from the flexible tube.
12 Undo the two bolts securing the flexible tube to the air cleaner support bracket and remove the tube from the engine compartment **(see illustration)**.

Turbocharger inlet and outlet ducts

13 The rigid ducts at the rear of the engine, connecting the turbocharger to the flexible air inlet duct and to the inlet manifold are inaccessible with the engine in the car. To gain access it will be necessary to remove the front suspension subframe as described in Chapter 10.

4.10 Lift the air cleaner housing upwards at the rear and disengage the two front locating lugs

4.11 Undo the bolt securing the front of the air inlet duct to the front body panel

4.12 Undo the two bolts and remove the flexible tube from the engine compartment

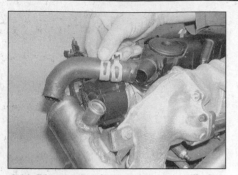

4.14 Disconnect the crankcase ventilation hose at the top of the turbocharger rigid inlet duct

4.15 Undo the bolt (arrowed) securing the rigid inlet duct to the inlet manifold elbow

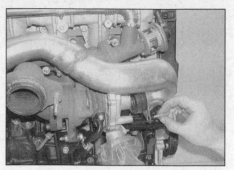

4.16 Undo the bolt securing the rigid inlet duct to the turbocharger and remove the duct

4.17 Slacken the clip and release the plastic duct connecting hose from the inlet manifold elbow

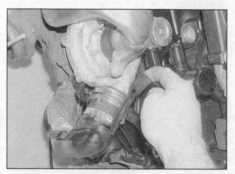

4.18 Slacken the connecting hose clip, release the attachment strap and withdraw the plastic duct from the engine

14 Once access has been gained, begin removal of the turbocharger rigid inlet duct by disconnecting the crankcase ventilation hose at the top of the duct **(see illustration)**.

15 Undo the bolt securing the duct to the inlet manifold elbow **(see illustration)**.

16 At the lower end, undo the bolt securing the duct to the turbocharger **(see illustration)**. Lift off the duct and recover the seal from the lower end.

17 To remove the turbocharger-to-inlet manifold rigid plastic duct, slacken the retaining clip and release the connecting hose from the inlet manifold elbow **(see illustration)**.

18 Slacken the clip securing the connecting hose at the lower end of the duct to the turbocharger. Release the attachment strap from the lug on the turbocharger and

withdraw the duct from the engine **(see illustration)**.

Refitting

19 Refitting is a reverse of the removal procedure. Examine the condition of the seals and retaining clips and renew if necessary.

20 Where applicable, refit the front suspension subframe as described in Chapter 10.

21 Reconnect and adjust the accelerator cable as described in Section 5.

---

5 Accelerator cable – removal, refitting and adjustment

Removal

1 Undo the four plastic nuts and lift off the engine cover.

2 Rotate the accelerator pedal position sensor quadrant, and release the inner cable from the quadrant.

3 Withdraw the outer cable from the grommet in the pedal position sensor body, recover the flat washer from the end of the cable and remove the spring clip.

4 Release the cable from the remaining clips and brackets in the engine compartment, noting its routing.

5 Working in the passenger compartment, reach up under the facia, depress the ends of the cable end fitting, and detach the inner cable from the top of the accelerator pedal.

6 Release the outer cable grommet from the pedal mounting bracket, then tie a length of string to the end of the cable.

7 Return to the engine compartment, release the cable grommet from the bulkhead and withdraw the cable. When the end of the cable appears, untie the string and leave it in position – it can then be used to draw the cable back into position on refitting.

Refitting

8 Refitting is a reversal of removal, but ensure that the cable is routed as noted before removal and, on completion, adjust the cable as follows.

Adjustment

9 Remove the spring clip from the accelerator outer cable. Ensuring that the pedal position sensor quadrant is against its stop, gently pull the cable out of its grommet until all free play is removed from the inner cable.

10 With the cable held in this position, refit the spring clip to the last exposed outer cable groove in front of the rubber grommet and washer. When the clip is refitted and the outer cable is released, there should be only a small amount of free play in the inner cable.

11 Have an assistant depress the accelerator pedal, and check that the pedal position sensor quadrant opens fully and returns smoothly to its stop.

12 Refit the engine cover on completion.

---

6 Accelerator pedal – removal and refitting

Refer to Chapter 4A.

---

7 Fuel lift pump – removal and refitting

The diesel fuel lift pump is located in the same position as the conventional fuel pump on petrol models, and the removal and refitting procedures are virtually identical **(see illustration)**. Refer to Chapter 4A.

7.1 Fuel pump/level gauge wiring and fuel supply and return pipes on the fuel tank – DW12 engine

10.2 Undo the bolt (arrowed) to release the plastic wiring harness guide

10.4 Disconnect the fuel supply and return hose quick-release fittings at the connections above the fuel pump

10.6 Using the home-made tools to remove the fuel pump sprocket

8 Fuel gauge sender unit – removal and refitting

The fuel gauge sender unit is integral with the fuel lift pump. Refer to Section 7.

9 Fuel tank – removal and refitting

Refer to Chapter 4A.

10 High-pressure fuel pump – removal and refitting

 Warning: Refer to the information contained in Section 2 before proceeding.

Note: *A new fuel pump-to-accumulator rail high-pressure fuel pipe will be required for refitting.*

Removal

1 Disconnect the battery negative lead and remove the timing belt as described in Chapter 2C. After removal of the timing belt,

temporarily refit the right-hand engine mounting but do not fully tighten the bolts.
2 Undo the bolts securing the plastic wiring harness guide to the front of the engine **(see illustration)**. It will be necessary to lift up the wiring harness as far as possible for access to the rear of the fuel pump. If necessary, disconnect the relevant wiring connectors to enable the harness and guide assembly to be moved further for additional access.
3 Place a suitable container beneath the fuel filter, then loosen the drain plug and drain the fuel. Retighten the plug.
4 Clean the feed and supply lines to the fuel filter, then unclip the fuel filter from its bracket and disconnect the quick-release feed and supply lines **(see illustration)**. Tape over or plug the openings in the filter and lines, to prevent entry of dust and dirt. **Note:** *The fuel lines must be renewed every time they are removed, as it is possible for minute metal particles to enter them as a result of tightening the union nuts. If these particles enter the fuel injectors, fuel at high-pressure can enter the combustion chambers unrestricted.*
5 Unbolt and remove the fuel filter support bracket.
6 Hold the pump pulley/sprocket stationary, and loosen the centre nut securing it to the pump shaft. The manufacturers recommend using a pin inserted through the pulley and

into the cylinder head, however, a home-made forked tool engaged with the pulley holes can be used instead **(see illustration and Tool Tip 1)**.
7 The fuel pump sprocket is a taper fit on the pump shaft and it will be necessary to make up a tool to release it from the taper **(see Tool Tip 2)**. Partially unscrew the sprocket retaining nut, fit the home-made tool, and secure it to the sprocket with two 7.0 mm bolts. Prevent the sprocket from rotating as before, and unscrew the sprocket retaining nut. The nut will bear against the tool as it is undone, forcing the sprocket off the shaft taper. Once the taper is released, remove the tool, unscrew the nut fully, and remove the sprocket from the pump shaft.
8 Thoroughly clean the high-pressure fuel pipe unions on the fuel pump and accumulator rail. Using an open-ended spanner, unscrew the union nuts securing the high-pressure fuel pipe to the fuel pump and accumulator rail. Counterhold the unions on the pump and accumulator rail with a second spanner, while unscrewing the union nuts. Withdraw the high-pressure fuel pipe and plug or cover the open unions to prevent dirt entry **(see illustration)**. Note that a new high-pressure fuel pipe will be required for refitting.
9 On the DW10 engine, unscrew the nut and bolt securing the fuel pump rear mounting to the mounting bracket. On the DW12 engine, unscrew the two bolts securing the mounting plate to the rear of the fuel pump, then loosen only the single bolt securing the plate to the bracket and tilt the plate outwards **(see illustrations)**.

Tool Tip 1: *A sprocket holding tool can be made from two lengths of steel strip bolted together to form a forked end. Bend the ends of the strip through 90° to form the fork 'prongs'.*

Tool Tip 2: *Make a sprocket releasing tool from a short strip of steel. Drill two holes in the strip to correspond with the two 7.0 mm holes in the sprocket. Drill a third hole just large enough to accept the flats of the sprocket retaining nut.*

10.8 Unscrew the unions and remove the high pressure fuel pipe

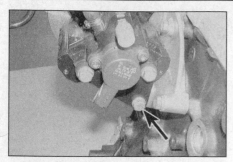

10.9a Undo the nut and bolt (arrowed) securing the fuel pump rear mounting to the mounting bracket – DW10

10.9b Move the rear mounting plate to one side – DW12 engine

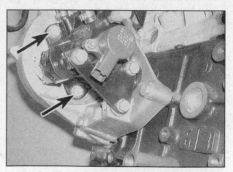

10.12a Fuel pump front mounting bolts (arrowed) . . .

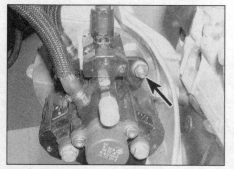

10.12b . . . and mounting nut (arrowed) – DW10 engine

10.12c High-pressure fuel pump removed from the engine – DW12 engine

10.19 Tighten the fuel pipe union nuts using a torque wrench and crow-foot adaptor

10 Disconnect the wiring connector at the pressure control valve on the rear of the fuel pump (orange wire), and at the piston de-activator switch on the top of the pump.

11 Disconnect the low pressure hoses from the fuel pump, then tape over the openings. Move the hoses to one side.

12 Unscrew the nut and two bolts securing the front of the fuel pump to the mounting bracket **(see illustrations)**. Withdraw the pump and lift it off the engine.

Caution: The high-pressure fuel pump is manufactured to extremely close tolerances and must not be dismantled in any way. Do not unscrew the fuel pipe male union on the rear of the pump, or attempt to remove the pressure control valve, piston de-activator switch, or the seal on the pump shaft. No parts for the pump are available separately and if the unit is in any way suspect, it must be renewed.

Refitting

13 Locate the pump on the mounting bracket, and refit the front retaining nut and the two bolts. Refit the nut and bolt securing the fuel pump rear mounting to the mounting bracket, then tighten all the mountings to the specified torque.

14 Refit the low pressure hoses and tighten the clips.

15 Reconnect the wiring to the pressure control valve and piston de-activator switch.

16 Refit the mounting bracket to the rear of the fuel pump and tighten the bolts.

17 Remove the blanking plugs from the fuel

pipe unions on the pump and accumulator rail. Locate a new high-pressure fuel pipe over the unions and screw on the union nuts finger tight at this stage.

18 Refit the pump sprocket and retaining nut and tighten the nut to the specified torque. Prevent the sprocket rotating as the nut is tightened using the sprocket holding tool.

19 Using a torque wrench and crow-foot adaptor, tighten the fuel pipe union nuts to the specified torque. Counterhold the unions on the pump and accumulator rail with an open-ended spanner, while tightening the union nuts **(see illustration)**.

20 Reposition and secure the plastic wiring harness guide to the front of the engine, and reconnect any additional wiring disconnected for access.

21 Refit the filter mounting bracket to the engine and securely tighten the retaining bolts. Locate the fuel filter back in position in the mounting bracket.

22 Remove the blanking plugs and reconnect the supply and return hose quick-release fittings at the fuel filter, and at the connections above the fuel pump. Secure the hoses with their respective retaining clips.

23 Refit the timing belt as described in Chapter 2C.

24 With everything reassembled and reconnected, and observing the precautions listed in Section 2, start the engine and allow it to idle. Check for leaks at the high-pressure fuel pipe unions with the engine idling. If satisfactory, increase the engine speed to 4000 rpm and check again for leaks.

25 Take the car for a short road test and check for leaks once again on return. If any leaks are detected, obtain and fit another new high-pressure fuel pipe. **Do not** attempt to cure even the slightest leak by further tightening of the pipe unions. During the road test, initialise the engine management ECU as follows. Engage third gear and stabilise the engine at 1000 rpm, then accelerate fully up to 3500 rpm.

11 Accumulator rail – removal and refitting

⚠️ *Warning: Refer to the information contained in Section 2 before proceeding.*

Note: *A complete new set of high-pressure fuel pipes will be required for refitting.*

Removal

1 Disconnect the battery negative terminal (refer to *Disconnecting the battery* in the Reference Section of this manual).

2 Undo the four plastic nuts and lift off the engine cover.

3 Disconnect the wiring connectors at the fuel injectors and at the piston de-activator switch on the top of the fuel pump **(see illustrations)**.

4 Release the retaining clip and disconnect the crankcase ventilation hose from the cylinder head cover. Position it to one side.

5 Undo the two nuts securing the plastic wiring harness guide to the cylinder head. Lift

11.3a Disconnect the wiring connectors at the fuel injectors . . .

11.3b . . . and at the piston de-activator switch on top of the fuel pump

11.5 Undo the two nuts and lift off the plastic wiring harness guide

11.9a Using two spanners, unscrew the fuel pipe unions at the accumulator rail . . .

11.9b . . . and at each injector

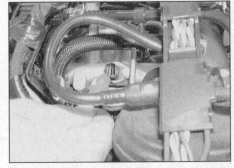

11.10 Disconnect the wiring connector at the fuel temperature sensor

the guide off the two mounting studs and move it clear of the accumulator rail **(see illustration)**. Disconnect any additional wiring connectors as necessary to enable the harness and guide assembly to be moved further for increased access.

6 At the connections above the fuel pump, disconnect the fuel supply and return hose quick-release fittings using a small screwdriver to release the locking clip. Suitably plug or cover the open unions to prevent dirt entry.

7 Similarly disconnect the supply and return hose quick-release fittings at the fuel filter and plug or cover the open unions. Release the fuel hoses from the relevant retaining clips.

8 Thoroughly clean all the high-pressure fuel pipe unions on the accumulator rail, fuel pump and injectors. Using an open-ended spanner, unscrew the union nuts securing the high-pressure fuel pipe to the fuel pump and

accumulator rail. Counterhold the unions on the pump and accumulator rail with a second spanner, while unscrewing the union nuts. Withdraw the high-pressure fuel pipe and plug or cover the open unions to prevent dirt entry.

9 Again using two spanners, hold the unions and unscrew the union nuts securing the high-pressure fuel pipes to the fuel injectors and accumulator rail **(see illustrations)**. Withdraw the high-pressure fuel pipes and plug or cover the open unions to prevent dirt entry.

10 Disconnect the wiring connectors at the fuel temperature sensor and fuel pressure sensor on the accumulator rail **(see illustration)**.

11 Undo the three bolts securing the accumulator rail to the cylinder head and withdraw the rail from its location **(see illustrations)**.

Caution: Do not attempt to remove the four high-pressure fuel pipe male unions from

the accumulator rail. These parts are not available separately and if disturbed are likely to result in fuel leakage on reassembly.

12 Obtain a complete new set of high-pressure fuel pipes for refitting.

Refitting

13 Locate the accumulator rail in position, refit the three securing bolts and tighten to the specified torque.

14 Reconnect the fuel temperature sensor and fuel pressure sensor wiring connectors.

15 Working on one fuel injector at a time, remove the blanking plugs from the fuel pipe unions on the accumulator rail and the relevant injector. Locate a new high-pressure fuel pipe over the unions and screw on the union nuts finger tight at this stage.

16 When all four fuel pipes are in place, hold the unions with a spanner and tighten the

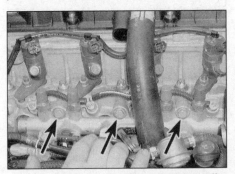

11.11a Undo the three accumulator rail retaining bolts (arrowed) . . .

11.11b . . . and withdraw the accumulator rail from the engine – DW10 engine

11.11c Removing the accumulator rail – DW12 engine

11.16 Using a torque wrench and crow-foot adaptor, tighten the fuel pipe union nuts

union nuts to the specified torque using a torque wrench and crow-foot adaptor **(see illustration)**.

17 Similarly, fit a new high-pressure fuel pipe to the fuel pump and accumulator rail, and tighten the union nuts to the specified torque.

18 Remove the blanking plugs and reconnect the supply and return hose quick-release fittings at the fuel filter, and at the connections above the fuel pump. Secure the hoses with their respective retaining clips.

19 Reconnect the crankcase ventilation hose to the cylinder head cover.

20 Reposition the plastic wiring harness guide over the two mounting studs and secure with the retaining nuts.

21 Reconnect the fuel injector and pump piston de-activator switch wiring connectors, and reconnect any additional wiring disconnected for access.

22 Check that everything has been

reconnected and secured with the relevant retaining clips then reconnect the battery negative terminal.

23 Refit the engine cover on completion.

24 Observing the precautions listed in Section 2, start the engine and allow it to idle. Check for leaks at the high-pressure fuel pipe unions with the engine idling. If satisfactory, increase the engine speed to 4000 rpm and check again for leaks. Take the car for a short road test and check for leaks once again on return. If any leaks are detected, obtain and fit additional new high-pressure fuel pipes as required. **Do not** attempt to cure even the slightest leak by further tightening of the pipe unions. During the road test, initialise the engine management ECU as follows. Engage third gear and stabilise the engine at 1000 rpm, then accelerate fully up to 3500 rpm.

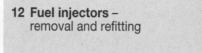

12 Fuel injectors – removal and refitting

⚠️ **Warning: Refer to the information contained in Section 2 before proceeding.**

Note: *The following procedure describes the removal and refitting of the injectors as a complete set, however each injector may be removed individually if required. New copper washers, upper seals, injector clamp retaining nuts and a high-pressure fuel pipe will be required for each disturbed injector when refitting.*

Removal

1 Disconnect the battery negative lead (refer to *Disconnecting the battery* at the end of this manual).

2 Undo the four plastic nuts and lift off the engine top cover.

3 Disconnect the wiring connectors at the fuel injectors. If necessary, unclip the wiring conduit and move it to one side **(see illustration)**.

4 Release the retaining clip and disconnect the crankcase ventilation hose from the cylinder head cover. Position it to one side.

5 Undo the two nuts securing the plastic wiring harness guide to the cylinder head **(see illustration)**. Lift the guide off the two mounting studs and move it clear of the accumulator rail. Disconnect any additional wiring connectors as necessary to enable the harness and guide assembly to be moved to one side.

6 At the connections above the fuel pump, disconnect the fuel supply and return hose quick-release fittings using a small screwdriver to release the locking clip. Suitably plug or cover the open unions to prevent dirt entry, then release the fuel hoses from the relevant retaining clips.

7 Thoroughly clean all the high-pressure fuel pipe unions on the fuel injectors and accumulator rail. Using two open-ended spanners, unscrew the union nuts securing the high-pressure fuel pipes to the fuel injectors and accumulator rail **(see illustrations)**. Withdraw the high-pressure fuel pipes and plug or cover the open unions on the injectors and accumulator rail to prevent dirt entry. Note that a new high-pressure fuel pipe will be required for each removed injector when refitting.

8 Extract the retaining circlip and disconnect the leak-off pipe from each fuel injector **(see illustration)**.

9 Unscrew the nut(s) and remove the washer(s) securing each injector clamp to its cylinder head stud(s) **(see illustrations)**. Note that new clamp nuts will be required for refitting.

10 Withdraw the injectors, together with their clamps, from the cylinder head or inlet manifold, as applicable. Slide the clamp off the injector once it is clear of the mounting

12.3 Disconnect the wiring . . .

12.5 . . . and move the harness conduit to one side – DW12 engine

12.7a Unscrew the union nuts using two spanners . . .

12.7b . . . and remove the two pairs of high-pressure fuel pipes

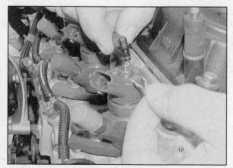

12.8 Extract the circlip and disconnect the injector leak-off pipes – DW10 engine

12.9a Unscrew the injector clamp retaining nut . . .

12.9b . . . and remove the washer – DW10 engine

12.9c Using a key to unscrew the injector clamp nuts – DW12 engine

stud. If the injectors are a tight fit in the cylinder head and cannot be released, two screwdrivers may be used to carefully lever them out **(see illustrations)**. Alternatively, unscrew one mounting stud using a stud extractor and slide off the injector clamp. Using an open-ended spanner engaged with the clamp locating slot on the injector body, free the injector by twisting it and at the same time lifting it upwards.

11 Recover the injector clamp locating dowel from the cylinder head **(see illustration)**.

12 Remove the copper washer and the upper seal from each injector, or from the cylinder head if they remained in place during injector removal. New copper washers and upper seals will be required for refitting.

13 Examine each injector visually for any signs of obvious damage or deterioration. If any defects are apparent, renew the injector(s).

Caution: The injectors are manufactured to extremely close tolerances and must not be dismantled in any way. Do not unscrew the fuel pipe union on the side of the injector, or separate any parts of the injector body. Do not attempt to clean carbon deposits from the injector nozzle or carry out any form of ultrasonic or pressure testing.

14 If the injectors are in a satisfactory condition, plug the fuel pipe union (if not already done) and suitably cover the electrical element and the injector nozzle.

15 Prior to refitting, obtain new copper washers, upper seals, injector clamp retaining nuts and high-pressure fuel pipes for each removed injector.

Refitting

16 Locate a new upper seal on the body of each injector, and place a new copper washer on the injector nozzle **(see illustrations)**.

17 Refit the injector clamp locating dowels to the cylinder head.

18 Place the injector clamp in the slot on each injector body and refit the injectors to the cylinder head. Guide the clamp over the mounting stud and onto the locating dowel as each injector is inserted.

19 Fit the washer and a new injector clamp retaining nut to each mounting stud. Tighten the nuts finger tight only at this stage.

20 Working on one fuel injector at a time, remove the blanking plugs from the fuel pipe unions on the accumulator rail and the relevant injector. Locate a new high-pressure fuel pipe over the unions and screw on the union nuts. Take care not to cross-thread the nuts or strain the fuel pipes as they are fitted. Once the union nut threads have started, tighten the nuts moderately tight only at this stage.

21 When all the fuel pipes are in place,

12.10a Withdraw the injectors, together with their clamps, from the cylinder head – DW10 engine

12.10b Using two screwdrivers . . .

12.10c . . . to remove the injectors – DW12 engine

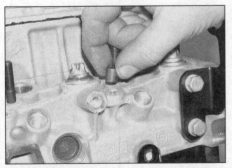

12.11 Recover the injector clamp locating dowel from the cylinder head – DW10 engine

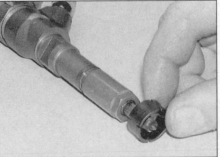

12.16a Locate a new upper seal on the body of each injector . . .

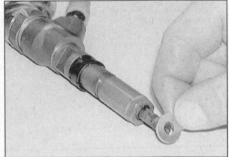

12.16b . . . and place a new copper washer on the injector nozzle – DW10 engine

12.21 Angle-tightening the injector clamp nuts – DW12 engine

12.22 Tightening the fuel pipe union nuts – DW12 engine

tighten the injector clamp retaining nuts to the specified torque (and angle where applicable) **(see illustration)**.

22 Using an open-ended spanner, hold each fuel pipe union in turn and tighten the union nut to the specified torque using a torque wrench and crow-foot adaptor **(see illustration)**. Tighten all the disturbed union nuts in the same way.

23 Connect the leak-off pipes to each fuel injector and secure with the retaining circlips.

24 Remove the blanking plugs and reconnect the supply and return hose quick-release fittings at the connections above the fuel pump. Secure the hoses with their respective retaining clips.

25 Reposition the plastic wiring harness guide over the two mounting studs and secure with the retaining nuts.

26 Reconnect the fuel injector wiring connectors, and reconnect any additional

wiring disconnected for access.

27 Check that everything has been reconnected and secured with the relevant retaining clips then reconnect the battery negative terminal.

28 Observing the precautions listed in Section 2, start the engine and allow it to idle. Check for leaks at the high-pressure fuel pipe unions with the engine idling. If satisfactory, increase the engine speed to 4000 rpm and check again for leaks. Take the car for a short road test and check for leaks once again on return. If any leaks are detected, obtain and fit additional new high-pressure fuel pipes as required. **Do not** attempt to cure even the slightest leak by further tightening of the pipe unions. During the road test, initialise the engine management ECU as follows. Engage third gear and stabilise the engine at 1000 rpm, then accelerate fully up to 3500 rpm.

29 Refit the engine cover on completion.

13.6a Lift the locking lever upwards . . .

13.6b . . . and disconnect the wiring connector

13.7 Lift the ECU upwards and remove it from the module box

13.8a Undo the internal and external retaining bolts . . .

13 Electronic control system components – testing, removal and refitting

Testing

1 If a fault is suspected in the electronic control side of the system, first ensure that all the wiring connectors are securely connected and free of corrosion. Ensure that the suspected problem is not of a mechanical nature, or due to poor maintenance; ie, check that the air cleaner filter element is clean, the engine breather hoses are clear and undamaged, and that the cylinder compression pressures are correct, referring to Chapters 1B and 2C for further information.

2 If these checks fail to reveal the cause of the problem, the vehicle should be taken to a Peugeot dealer or suitably-equipped garage for testing. A diagnostic socket is located adjacent to the passenger compartment fusebox in which a fault code reader or other suitable test equipment can be connected. By using the code reader or test equipment, the engine management ECU (and the various other vehicle system ECUs) can be interrogated, and any stored fault codes can be retrieved. This will allow the fault to be quickly and simply traced, alleviating the need to test all the system components individually, which is a time-consuming operation that carries a risk of damaging the ECU.

Removal and refitting

3 Before carrying out any of the following procedures, disconnect the battery negative terminal (refer to *Disconnecting the battery* in the Reference Section of this manual). Reconnect the battery on completion of refitting.

Electronic control unit (ECU)

Note: *If a new ECU is to be fitted, this work must be entrusted to a Peugeot dealer. It is necessary to initialise the new ECU after installation, which requires the use of dedicated Peugeot diagnostic equipment.*

4 The ECU is located in a plastic box which is mounted on the right-hand front wheelarch.

5 Lift off the ECU module box lid.

6 Release the wiring connector by lifting the locking lever on top of the connector upwards. Lift the connector at the rear, disengage the tag at the front and carefully withdraw the connector from the ECU pins **(see illustrations)**

7 Lift the ECU upwards and remove it from its location **(see illustration)**.

8 To remove the ECU module box, undo the internal and external retaining bolts and remove the module box **(see illustrations)**.

9 Refitting is a reversal of removal.

Crankshaft speed/position sensor

10 The crankshaft speed/position sensor is located at the top of the transmission bellhousing, directly above the engine flywheel.

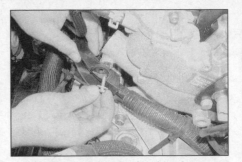

13.11 Release the plastic wiring harness guide for access to the crankshaft speed/position sensor

13.13 Slacken the bolt securing the sensor to the bellhousing

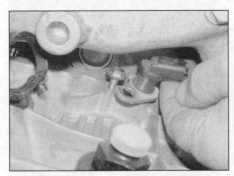

13.14 Turn the sensor body to clear the bolt and withdraw it from the bellhousing

13.18 Disconnect the wiring . . .

13.19 . . . and remove the camshaft position sensor

To gain access, remove the air cleaner assembly as described in Section 4, then remove the battery and battery tray as described in Chapter 5A.

11 Undo the retaining nuts and bolts and release the plastic wiring harness guide from its mountings (see illustration).

12 Working below the thermostat housing, disconnect the wiring connector from the crankshaft speed/position sensor.

13 Slacken the bolt securing the sensor to the bellhousing (see illustration). It is not necessary to remove the bolt completely as the sensor mounting flange is slotted.

14 Turn the sensor body to clear the mounting bolt, then withdraw the sensor from the bellhousing (see illustration).

15 Refitting is reverse of the removal procedure ensuring the sensor retaining bolt is securely tightened.

Camshaft position sensor

16 The camshaft position sensor is mounted on the right-hand end of the cylinder head cover, directly behind the camshaft sprocket.

17 Remove the timing belt upper and intermediate covers as described in Chapter 2C.

18 Disconnect the sensor wiring connector (see illustration).

19 Undo the retaining bolt and lift the sensor off the cylinder head cover (see illustration).

20 To refit and adjust the sensor position, locate the sensor on the cylinder head cover and loosely refit the retaining bolt.

21 The air gap between the tip of the sensor and the target plate at the rear of the camshaft sprocket hub must be set to 1.2 mm,

using feeler blades. Clearance for the feeler blades is limited with the timing belt and camshaft sprocket in place, but it is just possible if the feeler blades are bent through 90° so they can be inserted through the holes in the sprocket, to rest against the inner face of the target plate.

22 With the feeler blades placed against the target plate, move the sensor toward the sprocket until it just contacts the feeler blades. Hold the sensor in this position and tighten the retaining bolt (see illustration).

23 With the gap correctly adjusted, reconnect the sensor wiring connector, then refit the timing belt upper and intermediate covers as described in Chapter 2C.

Accelerator pedal position sensor

24 The accelerator pedal position sensor is located on the left-hand side of the engine

compartment, adjacent to the air cleaner housing.

25 Remove the air cleaner assembly as described in Section 4.

26 Undo the two nuts and bolts and remove the sensor assembly from the mounting bracket on the side of the air cleaner housing (see illustration).

27 Refitting is reverse of the removal procedure.

Coolant temperature sensor

28 Refer to Chapter 3, Section 6.

Fuel temperature sensor

⚠️ *Warning: Refer to the information contained in Section 2 before proceeding.*

Note: *Do not remove the sensor from the accumulator rail unless there is a valid reason*

13.22 Insert feeler blades bent through 90° through the sprocket to measure the camshaft position sensor air gap

13.26 Removing the accelerator pedal position sensor

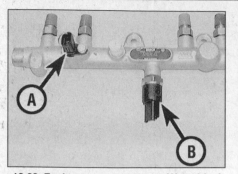

13.29 Fuel temperature sensor (A) and fuel pressure sensor (B) locations on the accumulator rail (shown removed for clarity)

to do so. At the time of writing there was no information as to the availability of the sensor seal as a separate item. Consult a Peugeot parts stockist for the latest information before proceeding.

29 The fuel temperature sensor is located towards the right-hand end of the accumulator rail **(see illustration)**.

30 Undo the four plastic nuts and lift off the engine cover.

31 Disconnect the fuel temperature sensor wiring connector.

32 Thoroughly clean the area around the sensor and its location on the accumulator rail.

33 Suitably protect the components below the sensor and have plenty of clean rags handy. Be prepared for considerable fuel spillage.

34 Undo the retaining bolt and withdraw the sensor from the accumulator rail. Plug the opening in the accumulator rail as soon as the sensor is withdrawn.

35 Prior to refitting, if the original sensor is to be refitted, renew the sensor seal, where applicable (see the note at the start of this sub-Section).

36 Locate the sensor in the accumulator rail and refit the retaining bolt, tightened securely.

37 Refit the sensor wiring connector.

38 Observing the precautions listed in Section 2, start the engine and allow it to idle. Check for leaks at the fuel temperature sensor with the engine idling. If satisfactory, increase the engine speed to 4000 rpm and check again for leaks. Take the car for a short road test and check for leaks once again on return.

13.67 Removing the throttle bodies from the inlet manifold

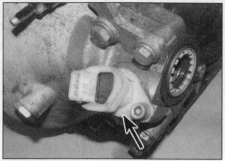

13.63 The vehicle speed sensor (speedometer transducer) is located on the final drive casing

If any leaks are detected, obtain and fit a new sensor.

39 Refit the engine cover on completion.

Air mass meter

40 The air mass meter is attached to the lid of the air cleaner housing.

41 Undo the four plastic nuts and lift off the engine cover.

42 Slacken the retaining clips and disconnect the flexible air inlet duct from the air mass meter and turbocharger rigid inlet duct. Suitably plug or cover the turbocharger rigid inlet duct, using clean rag to prevent any dirt or foreign material from entering.

43 Disconnect the wiring connector from the air mass meter.

44 Undo the screws securing the lid to the air cleaner housing and lift off the lid, complete with air mass meter.

45 Undo the two screws and withdraw the air mass meter from the air cleaner lid.

46 Refitting is reverse of the removal procedure.

Fuel pressure sensor

 Warning: Refer to the information contained in Section 2 before proceeding.

Note: *Peugeot special tool (-).4220 TH (27 mm forked adaptor) or suitable equivalent will be required for this operation.*

47 The fuel pressure sensor is located centrally on the underside of the accumulator rail.

48 Undo the four plastic nuts and lift off the engine cover.

49 Release the retaining clip and disconnect the crankcase ventilation hose from the cylinder head cover.

50 Disconnect the fuel supply and return hose quick-release fittings at the fuel filter, using a small screwdriver to release the locking clip. Suitably plug or cover the open unions to prevent dirt entry. Release the fuel hoses from the relevant retaining clips.

51 Disconnect the fuel pressure sensor wiring connector.

52 Thoroughly clean the area around the sensor and its location on the accumulator rail.

53 Suitably protect the components below the

sensor and have plenty of clean rags handy. Be prepared for considerable fuel spillage.

54 Using the Peugeot special tool (or suitable alternative 27 mm forked adaptor) and a socket bar, unscrew the fuel pressure sensor from the base of the accumulator rail.

55 Obtain and fit a new sealing ring to the sensor prior to refitting.

56 Locate the sensor in the accumulator rail and tighten it to the specified torque using the special tool (or alternative) and a torque wrench.

57 Refit the sensor wiring connector.

58 Observing the precautions listed in Section 2, start the engine and allow it to idle. Check for leaks at the fuel pressure sensor with the engine idling. If satisfactory, increase the engine speed to 4000 rpm and check again for leaks. Take the car for a short road test and check for leaks once again on return. If any leaks are detected, obtain and fit another new sensor sealing ring.

59 Refit the engine cover on completion.

Fuel pressure control valve

60 The fuel pressure control valve is integral with the high-pressure fuel pump and cannot be separated.

Preheating system control unit

61 Refer to Chapter 5C.

EGR solenoid valve

62 Refer to Chapter 4C, Section 2.

Vehicle speed sensor

63 The vehicle speed sensor is located on the final drive casing on the rear of the transmission **(see illustration)**. To remove it, unscrew the retaining screw and withdraw it from the transmission casing.

64 Refitting is a reversal of removal.

Throttle bodies (DW12 engine)

65 Remove the air cleaner and inlet air ducts with reference to Section 4.

66 Disconnect the vacuum hoses from the servos, and disconnect the air inlet ducts from the throttle bodies.

67 Unbolt the throttle body assembly from the inlet manifold, and withdraw from the engine compartment **(see illustration)**. Recover the gaskets.

68 If necessary, unbolt the throttle bodies from the elbow.

69 Refitting is a reversal of removal, but fit new gaskets.

14 Inlet manifold – removal and refitting

DW10 engine

Note: *Renew the manifold gasket when refitting.*

Removal

1 The inlet manifold is located on the rear of the cylinder head together with the exhaust

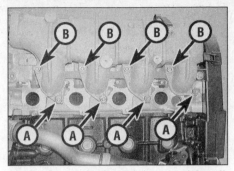

14.2 Inlet manifold retaining nuts (A) and bolts (B)

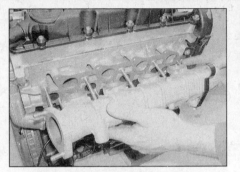

14.3a Lift the manifold off the cylinder head studs . . .

14.3b . . . and recover the gasket

manifold. First, remove the exhaust manifold as described in Section 15.

2 Undo the four bolts and four nuts securing the inlet manifolds flanges to the cylinder head **(see illustration)** and recover the washers. If preferred, the lower mounting nuts may be loosened and not removed, as the lower inlet manifold holes are slotted to allow the manifold to be lifted upwards once the upper bolts have been removed.

3 Lift the manifold off the cylinder head studs and recover the gasket **(see illustrations)**.

Refitting

4 Refitting is reverse of the removal procedure, bearing in mind the following points.
 a) *Ensure that the manifold and cylinder head mating faces are clean, with all traces of old gasket removed.*
 b) *Use a new gasket when refitting the manifold.*

 c) *Ensure that all fixings and attachments are securely tightened.*
 d) *Refit the exhaust manifold as described in Section 15.*

DW12 engine

Removal and refitting

5 The inlet manifold is located on the top of the cylinder head, and incorporates the camshaft bearing housing. Refer to Chapter 2C, and follow the procedure for removing and refitting the camshafts.

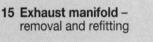

15 Exhaust manifold – removal and refitting

Removal

1 The exhaust manifold is located on the rear

of the cylinder head and access is very limited. On the DW10 engine, the inlet manifold is also located on the rear of the cylinder head, however on the DW12 engine access is easier since the inlet manifold is located on the front of the engine. First, apply the handbrake, then jack up the front of the vehicle and support it on axle stands (see *Jacking and vehicle support*).

2 Disconnect the battery negative terminal (refer to *Disconnecting the battery* in the Reference Section of this manual).

3 Remove the catalytic converter with reference to Section 19.

4 Remove the turbocharger inlet and outlet ducts as described in Section 4.

5 Unscrew the union nut securing the turbocharger oil feed pipe to the cylinder block, then withdraw the pipe from its location **(see illustration)**.

6 Remove the filter from the end of the oil feed pipe, and examine it for contamination **(see illustration)**. Clean or renew if necessary.

7 Undo the two bolts securing the oil return pipe flange to the turbocharger. Separate the flange and recover the gasket **(see illustrations)**.

8 Remove the exhaust gas recirculation (EGR) valve and connecting pipe from the exhaust manifold as described in Chapter 4C.

9 Undo the exhaust manifold retaining nuts and recover the spacers from the studs **(see illustrations)**.

10 Undo the nut and bolt securing the base of the turbocharger to the support bracket on the cylinder block.

15.5 Unscrew the turbocharger oil feed pipe union nut

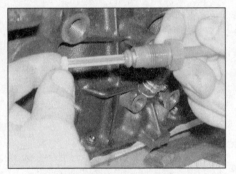

15.6 Withdraw the oil feed pipe and remove the filter

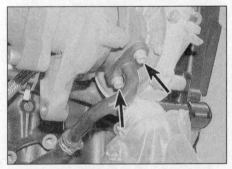

15.7a Undo the oil return pipe flange securing bolts . . .

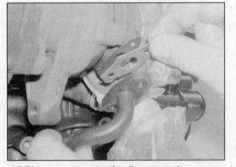

15.7b . . . separate the flange and recover the gasket

15.9a Undo the exhaust manifold retaining nuts . . .

15.9b . . . and recover the spacers from the studs – DW10 engine

15.9c Exhaust manifold – DW12 engine

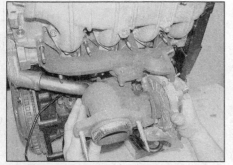

15.11a Withdraw the turbocharger and exhaust manifold off the mounting studs . . .

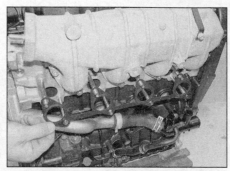

15.11b . . . and recover the gasket

11 Withdraw the turbocharger and exhaust manifold off the mounting studs and remove the assembly from the engine. Recover the manifold gasket **(see illustrations)**.

Refitting

12 Refitting is a reverse of the removal procedure, bearing in mind the following points:

a) Ensure that the manifold and cylinder head mating faces are clean, with all traces of old gasket removed.
b) Use new gaskets when refitting the manifold to the cylinder head and the oil return pipe flange to the turbocharger.
c) Tighten the exhaust manifold retaining nuts to the specified torque.
d) Refit the EGR valve and connecting pipe as described in Chapter 4C, Section 2.
e) Refit the turbocharger rear inlet and outlet ducts as described in Section 4.
f) Refit the catalytic converter as described in Section 19.

16 Turbocharger –
description and precautions

Description

1 A turbocharger is fitted to increase engine efficiency by raising the pressure in the inlet manifold above atmospheric pressure. Instead of the air simply being sucked into the cylinders, it is forced in.
2 Energy for the operation of the turbocharger comes from the exhaust gas. The gas flows through a specially-shaped housing (the turbine housing) and, in so doing, spins the turbine wheel. The turbine wheel is attached to a shaft, at the end of which is another vaned wheel known as the compressor wheel. The compressor wheel spins in its own housing, and compresses the inlet air on the way to the inlet manifold.
3 Boost pressure (the pressure in the inlet manifold) is limited by a wastegate, which diverts the exhaust gas away from the turbine wheel in response to a pressure-sensitive actuator. On 2.2 litre engines, the turbocharger is controlled by the ECU, however on the 2.0 litre engine, it is controlled by a conventional wastegate.
4 The turbo shaft is pressure-lubricated by an oil feed pipe from the main oil gallery. The shaft 'floats' on a cushion of oil. A drain pipe returns the oil to the sump.

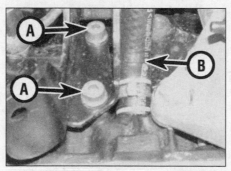

17.10 Turbocharger lower mounting bracket bolts (A) and oil drain pipe (B)

Precautions

5 The turbocharger operates at extremely high speeds and temperatures. Certain precautions must be observed, to avoid premature failure of the turbo, or injury to the operator.
6 Do not operate the turbo with any of its parts exposed, or with any of its hoses removed. Foreign objects falling onto the rotating vanes could cause excessive damage, and (if ejected) personal injury.
7 Do not race the engine immediately after start-up, especially if it is cold. Give the oil a few seconds to circulate.
8 Always allow the engine to return to idle speed before switching it off – do not blip the throttle and switch off, as this will leave the turbo spinning without lubrication.
9 Allow the engine to idle for several minutes before switching off after a high-speed run.
10 Observe the recommended intervals for oil and filter changing, and use a reputable oil of the specified quality. Neglect of oil changing, or use of inferior oil, can cause carbon formation on the turbo shaft, leading to subsequent failure.

17 Turbocharger –
removal, inspection and refitting

Removal

1 Apply the handbrake, then jack up the front of the vehicle and support it on axle stands (see *Jacking and vehicle support*). Remove the engine compartment undertray where fitted.
2 Remove the exhaust system as described in Section 19. **Note:** *This is necessary to prevent damage to the exhaust flexible joint, when the engine mountings are disconnected.*
3 On models with an intercooler, loosen the clips and remove the intercooler air hose from beneath the engine.
4 Unbolt and remove the torque reaction link from between the cylinder block and subframe.
5 From under the engine, unscrew the turbocharger air inlet pipe mounting bolt, then disconnect and remove the pipe.
6 On models without an intercooler, unclip the power steering pipes and tie them to one side. Also disconnect the transmission control cables (see Chapter 7A) for access to the turbocharger.
7 Remove the engine top cover, and the air cleaner assembly (see Section 4).
8 Unbolt the EGR solenoid valve assembly and move it to one side.
9 Unscrew the bolt securing the turbocharger inlet air duct to the left-hand rear of the cylinder head, then remove both air ducts. Access to the lower duct is best from under the car. Tape over the turbocharger openings to prevent dirt entry.
10 Unbolt the turbocharger upper and lower mounting brackets **(see illustration)**.

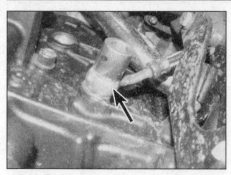

17.11 Turbocharger oil supply pipe banjo on the rear of the cylinder block

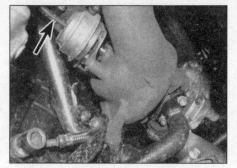

17.12 Turbocharger vacuum control pipe

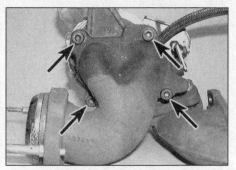

17.14a Exhaust outlet elbow-to-turbocharger retaining bolts

17.14b Turbocharger-to-exhaust manifold retaining nuts

11 Unscrew the union nuts and disconnect the oil supply and return pipes from the turbocharger and engine cylinder block **(see illustration)**. Tape over the openings.

12 On models with an intercooler, disconnect the vacuum control pipe **(see illustration)**.

13 On models without an intercooler, unscrew the three retaining nuts and withdraw the turbocharger from the exhaust manifold studs.

14 On DW10 engines with an intercooler, first loosen only the three nuts securing the turbocharger to the exhaust manifold, then unscrew the nuts securing the exhaust manifold to the cylinder head, and recover the spacers. Withdraw the turbocharger together with the exhaust manifold from the cylinder head, then fully unscrew the nuts and separate the turbocharger from the manifold **(see illustrations)**. Recover the gasket from the cylinder head.

15 On DW12 engines, improved access can be gained by removing the front suspension subframe (see Chapter 10). Unscrew the three nuts (2 from below and 1 from above) securing the turbocharger to the exhaust manifold, then unscrew the bolt securing the turbocharger to the bracket and lower the unit from under the engine.

Inspection

16 With the turbocharger removed, inspect the housing for cracks or other visible damage.

17 Spin the turbine or the compressor wheel, to verify that the shaft is intact and to feel for excessive shake or roughness. Some play is normal, since in use, the shaft is 'floating' on a film of oil. Check that the wheel vanes are undamaged.

18 If oil contamination of the exhaust or induction passages is apparent, it is likely that turbo shaft oil seals have failed.

19 No DIY repair of the turbo is possible and none of the internal or external parts are available separately. If the turbocharger is suspect in any way a complete new unit must be obtained.

Refitting

20 Refitting is a reverse of the removal procedure, bearing in mind the following points:

a) *Renew the turbocharger retaining nuts and gaskets.*

b) *If a new turbocharger is being fitted, change the engine oil and filter. Also renew the filter in the oil feed pipe.*

c) *Prime the turbocharger by injecting clean engine oil through the oil feed pipe union before reconnecting the union.*

18 Intercooler – removal and refitting

Removal

1 The intercooler is located at the front of the engine compartment, on the left-hand side of the radiator. First apply the handbrake, then jack up the front of the vehicle and support it on axle stands (see *Jacking and vehicle support*).

2 Remove the engine top cover(s).

3 Remove the air filter assembly as described in Section 4.

4 Remove the battery as described in Chapter 5A.

5 Loosen the clip and disconnect the outlet air duct from the intercooler.

6 Working under the car, loosen the clip and disconnect the inlet air duct from the intercooler.

7 Unbolt the upper mounting plate from the engine compartment front crossmember.

8 Lift the intercooler from its lower mountings and remove from the vehicle.

Refitting

9 Refitting is a reversal of removal.

19 Exhaust system – general information and component renewal

General information

1 According to model, the exhaust system consists of either two, three or four sections. Three section systems consist of a catalytic converter, an intermediate pipe, and a tailpipe. The four section system fitted to the DW12 diesel engine, consists of a particulate filter with flexible coupling, catalytic converter, intermediate pipe, and tailpipe. On two

section systems, the catalytic converter and intermediate pipe are combined to form a single section.

2 The exhaust joints are of either the spring-loaded ball type (to allow for movement in the exhaust system) or clamp-ring type.

3 The system is suspended throughout its entire length by rubber mountings.

Removal

4 Each exhaust section can be removed individually, or alternatively, the complete system can be removed as a unit. Even if only one part of the system needs attention, it is often easier to remove the whole system and separate the sections on the bench.

5 To remove the system or part of the system, first jack up the front or rear of the car, and support it on axle stands (see *Jacking and vehicle support*). Alternatively, position the car over an inspection pit, or on car ramps.

Catalytic converter

6 Unscrew the catalytic converter rear clamp ring bolt, and disengage the rear of the converter from the intermediate section. On the DW12 engine, also disconnect the wiring from the lambda/temperature sensors **(see illustrations)**. If the converter is being renewed, unscrew and remove the sensor(s).

7 Except on the DW12 engine, unscrew the front clamp ring bolt, and disengage the converter from the turbocharger. Remove the catalytic converter from underneath the vehicle. On the DW12 engine, unscrew the front clamp ring bolt and

19.6a Catalytic converter rear clamp

19.6b Lambda sensor on the DW12 exhaust

19.7a Removing the front clamp ring

19.7b Particulate filter mounted on the front of the catalytic converter – DW12 engine

19.11 Tailpipe mounting rubber

19.13 Disconnecting the front pipe from the turbocharger – DW12 engine

disengage the particulate filter from the flexible coupling, then remove the catalytic converter and unbolt the particulate filter on the bench **(see illustrations)**.

Intermediate pipe

8 Slacken the clamping ring bolts, and disengage both clamps from the flange joints.
9 Release the pipe from its mounting rubber and remove it from underneath the vehicle.

Tailpipe

10 Slacken the tailpipe clamping ring bolts, and disengage the clamp from the flange joint.
11 Unhook the tailpipe from its mounting rubbers, and remove it from the vehicle **(see illustration)**.

Particulate filter (DW12 engine)

12 The procedure is identical to that for the removal of the catalytic converter.

Complete system

13 Unscrew the front clamp ring bolt and release the catalytic converter or front pipe from the turbocharger **(see illustration)**. Free the system from its mounting rubbers and remove it from underneath the vehicle.

Heat shield(s)

14 The heat shields are secured to the underside of the body by various nuts and bolts. Each shield can be removed once the relevant exhaust section has been removed. If a shield is being removed to gain access to a component located behind it, it may prove sufficient in some cases to remove the retaining nuts and/or bolts, and simply lower the shield, without disturbing the exhaust system.

Refitting

15 Each section is refitted by reversing the removal sequence, noting the following points:

a) *Ensure that all traces of corrosion have been removed from the flanges, and renew all necessary gaskets.*
b) *Inspect the rubber mountings for signs of damage or deterioration, and renew as necessary.*
c) *On joints secured together by a clamping ring, apply a smear of exhaust system jointing paste to the flange joint, to ensure a gas-tight seal. Tighten the clamping ring nuts evenly and progressively, so that the clearance between the clamp halves remains equal on either side.*
d) *Prior to tightening the exhaust system fasteners, ensure that all rubber mountings are correctly located, and that there is adequate clearance between the exhaust system and vehicle underbody.*

Chapter 4 Part C:
Emission control systems

Contents

Catalytic converter – general information and precautions 3
Emission control systems – testing and component renewal 2

General information 1

Degrees of difficulty

Easy, suitable for novice with little experience	Fairly easy, suitable for beginner with some experience	Fairly difficult, suitable for competent DIY mechanic	Difficult, suitable for experienced DIY mechanic	Very difficult, suitable for expert DIY or professional

---

1 General information

All petrol engines use unleaded petrol and also have various other features built into the fuel system to help minimise harmful emissions. In addition, all engines are equipped with the crankcase emission control system described below. All engines are also equipped with a catalytic converter and an evaporative emission control system. 1.8 litre engines equipped to emission standard L4 also utilise a secondary air injection system to quickly bring the catalytic converter up to normal working temperature.

All diesel engines are also designed to meet the strict emission requirements and are equipped with a crankcase emission control system and a catalytic converter. To further reduce exhaust emissions, all diesel engines are also fitted with an exhaust gas recirculation (EGR) system. Additionally, 2.2 litre diesel models are equipped with a particulate emission filter which uses porous silicon carbide substrate to trap particulates of carbon as the exhaust gases pass through.

The emission control systems function as follows.

Petrol engines

Crankcase emission control

To reduce the emission of unburned hydrocarbons from the crankcase into the atmosphere, the engine is sealed and the blow-by gases and oil vapour are drawn from inside the crankcase, through a wire mesh oil separator, into the inlet tract to be burned by the engine during normal combustion.

Under all conditions the gases are forced out of the crankcase by the (relatively) higher crankcase pressure; if the engine is worn, the raised crankcase pressure (due to increased blow-by) will cause some of the flow to return under all manifold conditions.

Exhaust emission control

To minimise the amount of pollutants which escape into the atmosphere, a catalytic converter is fitted in the exhaust system. On all models where a catalytic converter is fitted, the system is of the closed-loop type, in which a lambda (oxygen) sensor in the exhaust system provides the fuel-injection/ignition system ECU with constant feedback, enabling the ECU to adjust the mixture to provide the best possible conditions for the converter to operate.

The lambda sensor has a heating element built-in that is controlled by the ECU through the lambda sensor relay to quickly bring the sensor's tip to an efficient operating temperature. The sensor's tip is sensitive to oxygen and sends the ECU a varying voltage depending on the amount of oxygen in the exhaust gases; if the inlet air/fuel mixture is too rich, the exhaust gases are low in oxygen so the sensor sends a low-voltage signal, the voltage rising as the mixture weakens and the amount of oxygen rises in the exhaust gases. Peak conversion efficiency of all major pollutants occurs if the inlet air/fuel mixture is maintained at the chemically-correct ratio for the complete combustion of petrol of 14.7 parts (by weight) of air to 1 part of fuel (the 'stoichiometric' ratio). The sensor output voltage alters in a large step at this point, the ECU using the signal change as a reference point and correcting the inlet air/fuel mixture accordingly by altering the fuel injector pulse width.

Evaporative emission control

To minimise the escape into the atmosphere of unburned hydrocarbons, an evaporative emission control system is fitted to models equipped with a catalytic converter. The fuel tank filler cap is sealed and a charcoal canister is mounted behind the radiator on the left-hand side of the engine compartment to collect the petrol vapours generated in the tank when the car is parked. It stores them until they can be cleared from the canister (under the control of the fuel-injection/ignition system ECU) via the purge valve into the inlet tract to be burned by the engine during normal combustion.

To ensure that the engine runs correctly when it is cold and/or idling and to protect the catalytic converter from the effects of an over-rich mixture, the purge control valve is not opened by the ECU until the engine has warmed-up, and the engine is under load; the valve solenoid is then modulated on and off to allow the stored vapour to pass into the inlet tract.

Secondary air injection

1.8 litre engines equipped to emission standard L4 are also equipped with a secondary air injection system. This system is designed to reduce exhaust emissions in the period between first starting the engine, and until the catalytic converter reaches operating (functioning) temperature. Introduction of air into the exhaust system during the initial start-up period, creates an 'afterburner' effect which quickly increases the temperature in the exhaust system front pipe, thus bringing the catalytic converter up to normal operating temperatures very quickly.

The system consists of an air pump, mounted at the front left-hand side of the car, an air injection valve, mounted on a bracket at the front of the cylinder head, a connecting pipe linking the valve to the exhaust manifold, and interconnecting air hoses.

The system operates for between 10 and 45 seconds after engine start-up, dependant on coolant temperature.

Diesel models

Crankcase emission control

Refer to the description for petrol engines.

Exhaust emission control

To minimise the level of exhaust pollutants released into the atmosphere, a catalytic converter is fitted in the exhaust system of all models.

The catalytic converter consists of a canister containing a fine mesh impregnated with a catalyst material, over which the hot exhaust gases pass. The catalyst speeds up the oxidation of harmful carbon monoxide, unburnt hydrocarbons and soot, effectively reducing the quantity of harmful products released into the atmosphere via the exhaust gases.

Exhaust gas recirculation system

This system is designed to recirculate small quantities of exhaust gas into the inlet tract, and therefore into the combustion process. This process reduces the level of oxides of nitrogen present in the final exhaust gas which is released into the atmosphere.

The volume of exhaust gas recirculated is controlled by the system electronic control unit.

A vacuum-operated valve is fitted to the exhaust manifold, to regulate the quantity of exhaust gas recirculated. The valve is operated by the vacuum supplied by the solenoid valve.

Particulate filter system

The particulate emission filter is located upstream of the catalytic converter in the exhaust system, and its purpose it to trap particulates of carbon (soot) as the exhaust gases pass through, in order to comply with latest emission regulations.

The filter can be automatically regenerated (cleaned) by a Peugeot dealership using a special diagnostic tool in conjunction with the system's ECU on-board the vehicle. The engine's high pressure injection system is utilized to inject fuel into the exhaust gases during the post-injection period; this causes the filter temperature to increase sufficient to oxidize the particulates, leaving an ash residue. The regeneration period is automatically controlled by the on-board ECU. Subsequently, every 48 000 miles (80 000 km), the filter must be removed from the exhaust system, and the ash residue flushed away with water.

To assist the combustion of the trapped carbon (soot) during the regeneration process, a fuel additive (cerium-based Eolys) is automatically mixed with the diesel fuel in the fuel tank. The additive is stored in a 5 litre container attached to the bottom of the fuel tank, and the ECU regulates the amount of additive to send to the fuel tank by means of an additive injector located on the top of the fuel tank.

| 2 | Emission control systems – testing and component renewal | ⚒ |

Petrol models

Crankcase emission control

1 The components of this system require no attention other than to check that the hose(s) are clear and undamaged at regular intervals.

Evaporative emission control

2 If the system is thought to be faulty, disconnect the hoses from the charcoal canister and purge control valve and check that they are clear by blowing through them. If the purge control valve or charcoal canister are thought to be faulty, they must be renewed.

Charcoal canister renewal

3 The charcoal canister is located under the wheelarch on the right-hand side. To gain access, jack up the front of the car and support it on axle stands. Remove the roadwheel and the wheelarch liner (where necessary).

4 Identify the location of the two hoses then disconnect them from the top of the canister. Where the crimped-type hose clips are fitted, cut the clips and discard them, replace them with standard worm drive hose clips on refitting. Where the hoses are equipped with quick-release fittings depress the centre collar of the fitting with a small flat-bladed screwdriver then detach the hose from the canister.

5 Unscrew the mounting nuts and remove the canister from its mounting bracket. If necessary unbolt and remove the mounting bracket.

6 Refitting is a reverse of the removal procedure ensuring that the hoses are correctly reconnected.

Purge valve renewal

7 The purge valve is located in the right-hand side of the engine compartment near the front suspension strut tower.

8 To renew the purge valve, disconnect the battery negative terminal then depress the retaining clip and disconnect the wiring connector from the valve.

9 Disconnect the hoses from either end of the valve then release the valve from its retaining clip and remove it from the engine compartment, noting which way around it is fitted.

10 Refitting is a reversal of the removal procedure ensuring that the valve is fitted the correct way around and the hoses are securely connected.

Exhaust emission control

11 The performance of the catalytic converter can be checked only by measuring the exhaust gases using a good-quality, carefully-calibrated exhaust gas analyser.

12 If the CO level at the tailpipe is too high, the vehicle should be taken to a Peugeot dealer so that the complete fuel injection and ignition systems, including the lambda sensor, can be thoroughly checked using the special diagnostic equipment. Once these have been checked and are known to be free from faults, the fault must be in the catalytic converter, which must be renewed as described in Part A of this Chapter.

Catalytic converter renewal

13 Refer to Part A of this Chapter.

Lambda sensor renewal

Note: *The lambda sensor is delicate and will not work if it is dropped or knocked, if its power supply is disrupted, or if any cleaning materials are used on it.*

14 Trace the wiring back from the lambda sensor, which is screwed into the top of the exhaust front pipe, to the top of the transmission. Disconnect both wiring connectors and free the wiring from any relevant retaining clips or ties.

15 Unscrew the sensor from the exhaust system front pipe and remove it along with its sealing washer.

16 Refitting is a reverse of the removal procedure using a new sealing washer. Prior

to installing the sensor apply a smear of high temperature grease to the sensor threads. Ensure that the sensor is securely tightened and that the wiring is correctly routed and in no danger of contacting either the exhaust system or engine.

Testing secondary air injection

17 The components of this system require no attention other than to check that the hose(s) are clear and undamaged at regular intervals.
18 Accurate testing of the system operation entails the use of diagnostic test equipment and should be entrusted to a Peugeot dealer.

Air pump renewal

19 The air pump is located at the front left-hand side of the engine compartment.
20 Disconnect the battery negative terminal (refer to *Disconnecting the battery* in the Reference Section of this manual).
21 Slacken and remove the three nuts and withdraw the pump from the mounting bracket.
22 Disconnect the air hoses and wiring connector and remove the pump.
23 Refitting is a reverse of the removal procedure, ensuring that the hoses are correctly reconnected.

Air injection valve renewal

24 Disconnect the battery negative terminal (refer to *Disconnecting the battery* in the Reference Section of this manual).
25 Slacken and remove the retaining screws, and remove the shroud from the top of the exhaust manifold.
26 Undo the two bolts securing the connecting pipe flange to the exhaust manifold.
27 Undo the two bolts securing the valve mounting bracket to the cylinder head.
28 Withdraw the valve and connecting pipe, disconnect the air hose and remove the air injection valve and connecting pipe as an assembly.
29 If necessary, the air pipe can be removed from the valve and the valve removed from the mounting bracket after undoing the two retaining nuts. Collect the flange gasket after removal.
30 Refitting is a reverse of the removal procedure, but use a new gasket between the valve and mounting bracket.

Diesel models

Crankcase emission control

31 The components of this system require no attention other than to check that the hose(s) are clear and undamaged at regular intervals.

Exhaust emission control

32 The performance of the catalytic converter can be checked only by measuring the exhaust gases using a good-quality, carefully-calibrated exhaust gas analyser.
33 If the catalytic converter is thought to be faulty, before assuming the catalytic converter is faulty, it is worth checking the problem is

2.36 On 2.0 litre diesel engines, undo the bolts securing the EGR pipe support clips to the inlet manifold . . .

not due to a faulty injector(s). Refer to your Peugeot dealer for further information.

Catalytic converter renewal

34 Refer to Part B of this Chapter.

Exhaust gas recirculation system

35 Testing of the system should ideally be entrusted to a Peugeot dealer since a vacuum pump and vacuum gauge are required.

EGR valve renewal (DW10)

36 Undo the bolts securing the EGR pipe support clips to the inlet manifold **(see illustration)**.
37 Disconnect the vacuum hose, then undo the two nuts securing the EGR valve to the exhaust manifold **(see illustration)**.
38 Undo the two bolts securing the EGR pipe to the inlet manifold elbow. Withdraw the EGR valve and pipe assembly from the manifold and recover the gasket at the EGR pipe-to-inlet manifold flange **(see illustrations)**.
39 To separate the EGR pipe from the valve, remove the clip securing the upper flexible portion of the pipe to the valve. If the original crimped clip is still in place, cut it off; new clips are supplied by Peugeot parts stockists with a screw clamp fixing. If a screw clamp type clip is fitted, undo the screw and manipulate the clip off the pipe.
40 To remove the EGR solenoid valve, disconnect the two vacuum hoses and the wiring connector. Undo the mounting bracket bolts and remove the valve from the engine compartment.

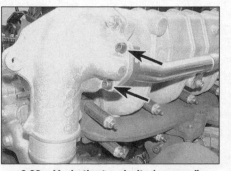
2.38a Undo the two bolts (arrowed) securing the EGR pipe to the inlet manifold elbow . . .

2.37 . . . then undo the nuts securing the EGR valve to the exhaust manifold

41 Refitting is a reversal of removal.

EGR valve and heat exchanger renewal (DW12)

42 Drain the cooling system with reference to Chapter 1B. Alternatively, fit hose clamps to the hoses connected to the EGR heat exchanger.
43 Remove the engine top cover, then remove the air filter assembly and inlet ducts.
44 Loosen the clips and disconnect the coolant hoses from the EGR heat exchanger.
45 Disconnect the vacuum hose from the EGR valve.
46 Unscrew the bolts securing the EGR valve to the exhaust manifold.
47 Unscrew the nut securing the heat exchanger to the exhaust manifold.
48 Unscrew the bolts securing the flexible pipe to the inlet manifold.
49 Unscrew the remaining mounting bolts and withdraw the assembly of the EGR valve together with the heat exchanger and pipe from the engine.
50 With the assembly on the bench, loosen the clips and separate the heat exchanger from the EGR valve.
51 Refitting is a reversal of removal, but renew the gaskets.

Fuel additive system (DW12)

52 It is possible to check the fuel additive pump delivery pressure, however, this should be made by a Peugeot dealer.

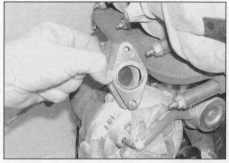
2.38b . . . then withdraw the valve and pipe assembly and recover the gasket at the EGR pipe flange

2.55 Additive reservoir heat shield retaining bolt

2.56 Injector pipes and wiring plug on the rear of the additive reservoir

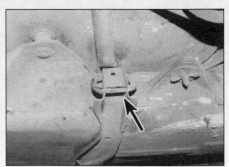

2.59 Additive reservoir retaining bracket

Fuel additive reservoir renewal

Note: *Ideally, the additive reservoir should be empty before removing it, otherwise take precautions against spillage.*

⚠ **Warning: Wear protective gloves and eye protection when handling the reservoir.**

53 To remove the fuel additive reservoir, chock the front wheels then jack up the rear of the vehicle and support on axle stands (see *Jacking and vehicle support*).
54 Disconnect the battery negative lead (refer to *Disconnecting the battery* at the end of this manual).
55 Remove the heat shield from beneath the additive reservoir **(see illustration)**.
56 Note the location of the two additive injector pipes on the rear of the reservoir, then disconnect them **(see illustration)**. Tape over or plug the openings.
57 Disconnect the tank top-up pipe, and tape over or plug the openings.
58 Disconnect the wiring from the level sensor on the rear of the reservoir.
59 Unbolt the bracket from under the reservoir **(see illustration)**.
60 Have a suitable container available to catch spilled additive. Unscrew the single outer mounting bolt, then tilt the reservoir to

release it from the inner fixings. Withdraw the reservoir from under the vehicle, and pour any remaining additive into the container.
61 Refitting is a reversal of removal.
62 Have the reservoir refilled by a Peugeot dealer.

---

3 Catalytic converter –
general information
and precautions

1 The catalytic converter is a reliable and simple device which needs no maintenance in itself, but there are some facts of which an owner should be aware if the converter is to function properly for its full service life.

Petrol models

a) *DO NOT use leaded petrol in a car equipped with a catalytic converter – the lead will coat the precious metals, and will eventually destroy the converter.*
b) *Always keep the ignition and fuel systems well-maintained to the service schedule.*
c) *If the engine develops a misfire, do not drive the car at all (or at least as little as possible) until the fault is cured.*
d) *DO NOT push- or tow-start the car – this will soak the catalytic converter in*

unburned fuel, causing it to overheat when the engine does start.
e) *DO NOT switch off the ignition at high engine speeds.*
f) *DO NOT use fuel or engine oil additives – these may contain substances harmful to the catalytic converter.*
g) *DO NOT continue to use the car if the engine burns oil to the extent of leaving a visible trail of blue smoke.*
h) *Remember that the catalytic converter operates at very high temperatures. DO NOT, therefore, park the car in dry undergrowth, over long grass or piles of dead leaves after a long run.*
i) *Remember that the catalytic converter is FRAGILE – do not strike it with tools.*
j) *In some cases a sulphurous smell (like that of rotten eggs) may be noticed from the exhaust. This is common to many catalytic converter-equipped cars and once the car has covered a few thousand miles the problem should disappear.*
k) *If the converter is no longer effective it must be renewed.*

Diesel models

2 Refer to parts f, g, h and i of the *petrol models* information given above.

Chapter 5 Part A:
Starting and charging systems

Contents

Alternator – removal and refitting 7
Alternator – testing and overhaul 8
Alternator drivebelt – removal, refitting and tensioning 6
Battery – removal and refitting 4
Battery – testing and charging 3
Charging system – testing 5
Electrical fault finding – general information 2

General information and precautions 1
Ignition switch – removal and refitting 12
Oil level sensor – removal and refitting 14
Oil pressure warning light switch – removal and refitting 13
Starter motor – removal and refitting 10
Starter motor – testing and overhaul 11
Starting system – testing 9

Degrees of difficulty

Easy, suitable for novice with little experience	**Fairly easy,** suitable for beginner with some experience	**Fairly difficult,** suitable for competent DIY mechanic	**Difficult,** suitable for experienced DIY mechanic	**Very difficult,** suitable for expert DIY or professional

Specifications

System type .... 12 volt, negative earth

Battery

Type .... Low maintenance or 'maintenance-free' sealed for life
Charge condition:
  Poor .... 12.5 volts
  Normal .... 12.6 volts
  Good .... 12.7 volts

Alternator

Type .... Valeo or Mitsubishi (depending on model)

Starter motor

Type .... Valeo or Bosch (depending on model)

Torque wrench settings	**Nm**	**lbf ft**
Battery mounting plate retaining bolts	45	33
Starter motor	35	26

---

1 General information and precautions

General information

The engine electrical system consists mainly of the charging and starting systems. Because of their engine-related functions, these components are covered separately from the body electrical devices such as the lights, instruments, etc (which are covered in Chapter 12). On petrol engine models refer to Part B for information on the ignition system, and on diesel models refer to Part C for information on the preheating system.

The electrical system is of the 12 volt negative earth type.

The battery is of the low maintenance or 'maintenance-free' (sealed for life) type and is charged by the alternator, which is belt-driven from the crankshaft pulley.

The starter motor is of the pre-engaged type incorporating an integral solenoid. On starting, the solenoid moves the drive pinion into engagement with the flywheel ring gear before the starter motor is energised. Once the engine has started, a one-way clutch prevents the motor armature being driven by the engine until the pinion disengages from the flywheel.

Precautions

Further details of the various systems are given in the relevant Sections of this Chapter. While some repair procedures are given, the usual course of action is to renew the component concerned. The owner whose interest extends beyond mere component renewal should obtain a copy of the *Automotive Electrical & Electronic Systems Manual*, available from the publishers of this manual.

It is necessary to take extra care when working on the electrical system to avoid damage to semi-conductor devices (diodes and transistors), and to avoid the risk of personal injury. In addition to the precautions given in *Safety first!* at the beginning of this manual, observe the following when working on the system:

Always remove rings, watches, etc, before working on the electrical system. Even with the battery disconnected, capacitive discharge could occur if a component's live terminal is earthed through a metal object. This could cause a shock or nasty burn.

Do not reverse the battery connections. Components such as the alternator, electronic control units, or any other components having semi-conductor circuitry could be irreparably damaged.

If the engine is being started using jump leads and a slave battery, connect the batteries positive-to-positive and negative-to-negative (see 'Jump starting'). This also applies when connecting a battery charger.

Never disconnect the battery terminals, the alternator, any electrical wiring or any test instruments when the engine is running.

Do not allow the engine to turn the alternator when the alternator is not connected.

Never 'test' for alternator output by 'flashing' the output lead to earth.

Never use an ohmmeter of the type incorporating a hand-cranked generator for circuit or continuity testing.

Always ensure that the battery negative lead is disconnected when working on the electrical system.

Before using electric-arc welding equipment on the car, disconnect the battery, alternator and components such as the fuel injection/ignition electronic control unit to protect them from the risk of damage.

Several systems fitted to the vehicle require battery power to be available at all times, either to ensure their continued operation (such as the clock) or to maintain control unit memories of security codes which would be wiped if the battery were to be disconnected. To ensure that there are no unforeseen consequences of this action, refer to 'Disconnecting the battery' in the Reference Section of this manual for further information.

2 Electrical fault finding –
general information

Refer to Chapter 12.

3 Battery –
testing and charging

Testing

Standard and low maintenance battery

1 If the vehicle covers a small annual mileage, it is worthwhile checking the specific gravity of the electrolyte every three months to determine the state of charge of the battery. Use a hydrometer to make the check and compare the results with the following table. Note that the specific gravity readings assume an electrolyte temperature of 15°C (60°F); for every 10°C (18°F) below 15°C (60°F) subtract 0.007. For every 10°C (18°F) above 15°C (60°F) add 0.007.

	Above 25°C	Below 25°C
Fully-charged	1.210 to 1.230	1.270 to 1.290
70% charged	1.170 to 1.190	1.230 to 1.250
Discharged	1.050 to 1.070	1.110 to 1.130

2 If the battery condition is suspect, first check the specific gravity of electrolyte in each cell. A variation of 0.040 or more between any cells indicates loss of electrolyte or deterioration of the internal plates.

3 If the specific gravity variation is 0.040 or more, the battery should be renewed. If the cell variation is satisfactory but the battery is discharged, it should be charged as described later in this Section.

Maintenance-free battery

4 In cases where a 'sealed for life' maintenance-free battery is fitted, topping-up and testing of the electrolyte in each cell is not possible. The condition of the battery can therefore only be tested using a battery condition indicator or a voltmeter.

5 Certain models may be fitted with a 'Delco' type maintenance-free battery, with a built-in charge condition indicator. The indicator is located in the top of the battery casing, and indicates the condition of the battery from its colour. If the indicator shows green, then the battery is in a good state of charge. If the indicator shows black, then the battery requires charging, as described later in this Section. If the indicator shows blue, then the electrolyte level in the battery is too low to allow further use, and the battery should be renewed.
Caution: Do not attempt to charge, load or jump start a battery when the indicator shows clear/yellow.

6 If testing the battery using a voltmeter, connect the voltmeter across the battery and compare the result with those given in the Specifications under 'charge condition'. The test is only accurate if the battery has not been subjected to any kind of charge for the previous six hours. If this is not the case, switch on the headlights for 30 seconds, then wait four to five minutes before testing the battery after switching off the headlights. All other electrical circuits must be switched off, so check that the doors, boot and/or tailgate are fully shut when making the test.

7 If the voltage reading is less than 12.2 volts, then the battery is discharged, whilst a reading of 12.2 to 12.4 volts indicates a partially discharged condition.

8 If the battery is to be charged, remove it from the vehicle (Section 4) and charge it as described later in this Section.

Charging

Standard and low maintenance battery

Note: *The following is intended as a guide only. Always refer to the manufacturer's recommendations (often printed on a label attached to the battery) before charging a battery.*

9 Charge the battery at a rate of 3.5 to 4 amps and continue to charge the battery at this rate until no further rise in specific gravity is noted over a four hour period.

10 Alternatively, a trickle charger charging at the rate of 1.5 amps can safely be used overnight.

11 Specially rapid 'boost' charges which are claimed to restore the power of the battery in 1 to 2 hours are not recommended, as they can cause serious damage to the battery plates through overheating.

12 While charging the battery, note that the temperature of the electrolyte should never exceed 37.8°C (100°F).

Maintenance-free battery

Note: *The following is intended as a guide only. Always refer to the manufacturer's recommendations (often printed on a label attached to the battery) before charging a battery.*

13 This battery type takes considerably longer to fully recharge than the standard type, the time taken being dependent on the extent of discharge, but it can take anything up to three days.

14 A constant voltage type charger is required to be set, when connected, to 13.9 to 14.9 volts with a charger current below 25 amps. Using this method, the battery should be usable within three hours, giving a voltage reading of 12.5 volts, but this is for a partially discharged battery and, as mentioned, full charging can take considerably longer.

15 If the battery is to be charged from a fully discharged state (condition reading less than 12.2 volts), have it recharged by your Peugeot dealer or local automotive electrician, as the charge rate is higher and constant supervision during charging is necessary.

4 Battery –
removal and refitting

Note: *The radio/cassette/CD player/auto-changer unit fitted as standard equipment by Peugeot is equipped with an anti-theft system, to deter thieves. If the power source is disconnected, the radio/cassette will automatically recode itself as long as it is still fitted to the correct vehicle. If the unit is removed it will not operate in another vehicle.*

Removal

1 The battery is located on the front left-hand side of the engine compartment.

2 Lift off the battery cover then slacken the battery negative (earth) terminal connector (coloured green). Lift the terminal connector off the battery post.

3 Disconnect the positive terminal connector (coloured red) in the same way.

4 Unscrew the two bolts and remove the battery retaining clamp.

5 Lift the battery out of the engine compartment.

6 To remove the battery box, remove the air cleaner assembly as described in the relevant Part of Chapter 4.

7 On models equipped with air conditioning, undo the screw securing the dehydrator retaining strap to the front of the battery box **(see illustration)**.

8 Undo the internal bolts securing the battery box and metal base to the mounting bracket, and the single outer bolt securing the box to the air cleaner mounting bracket **(see illustrations)**.

9 Carefully move aside all cables and hoses, then lift the battery box out of the engine compartment **(see illustration)**.

Refitting

10 Refitting is a reversal of removal, but smear petroleum jelly on the terminals after reconnecting the leads, and always reconnect the positive lead first, and the negative lead last.

11 With the battery reconnected, switch on the ignition and wait ten seconds before starting the engine. This will allow the vehicle electronic systems and control units to stabilise.

4.7 Undo the screw (arrowed) securing the air conditioning dehydrator retaining strap to the front of the battery box

4.8b . . . and the single outer bolt securing the box to the air cleaner mounting bracket

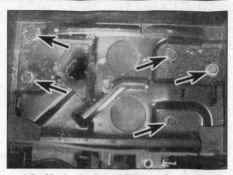

4.8a Undo the internal bolts (arrowed) securing the battery box and metal base to the mounting bracket . . .

4.9 Lift the battery box out of the engine compartment

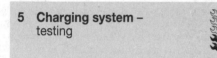

5 Charging system – testing

Note: *Refer to the warnings given in 'Safety first!' and in Section 1 of this Chapter before starting work.*

1 If the ignition warning light fails to illuminate when the ignition is switched on, first check the alternator wiring connections for security. If satisfactory, check that the warning light bulb has not blown, and that the bulbholder is secure in its location in the instrument panel. If the light still fails to illuminate, check the continuity of the warning light feed wire from the alternator to the bulbholder. If all is satisfactory, the alternator is at fault and should be renewed or taken to an auto-electrician for testing and repair.

2 If the ignition warning light illuminates when the engine is running, stop the engine and check that the drivebelt is correctly fitted and tensioned (see Chapter 1A or 1B) and that the alternator connections are secure. If all is so far satisfactory, have the alternator checked by an auto-electrician for testing and repair.

3 If the alternator output is suspect even though the warning light functions correctly, the regulated voltage may be checked as follows.

4 Connect a voltmeter across the battery terminals and start the engine.

5 Increase the engine speed until the voltmeter reading remains steady; the reading should be approximately 12 to 13 volts, and no more than 14 volts.

6 Switch on as many electrical accessories (eg, the headlights, heated rear window and heater blower) as possible, and check that the alternator maintains the regulated voltage at around 13 to 14 volts.

7 If the regulated voltage is not as stated, the fault may be due to worn brushes, weak brush springs, a faulty voltage regulator, a faulty diode, a severed phase winding or worn or damaged slip rings. The alternator should be renewed or taken to an auto-electrician for testing and repair.

6 Alternator drivebelt – removal, refitting and tensioning

Refer to the procedure given for the auxiliary drivebelt in Chapter 1A or 1B.

7.3 Alternator wiring connections

7 Alternator – removal and refitting

Removal

1 Disconnect the battery negative lead (refer to *Disconnecting the battery* at the end of this manual).

2 Remove the auxiliary drivebelt as described in Chapter 1A or 1B.

3 Remove the rubber covers (where fitted) from the alternator terminals, then unscrew the retaining nuts and disconnect the wiring from the rear of the alternator **(see illustration)**.

4 Where applicable on diesel models, unbolt the power steering pump and move it to one side without disconnecting any hydraulic pipes or hoses (see Chapter 10).

5 Unscrew the nut(s) and/or bolt(s) securing the alternator to the upper mounting bracket.

6 Unscrew the lower nut(s) and/or mounting bolt(s), or undo the nut securing the adjuster bolt bracket to the alternator (as applicable). Note that, where a long through-bolt is used to secure the alternator in position, the bolt does not need to be fully removed; the alternator can be disengaged from the bolt once it has been slackened sufficiently. On some models, it may be necessary to remove the drivebelt idler/tensioner pulley to gain access to the alternator mounting nuts and bolts (depending on specification). On diesel models, the lower front mounting bolt also

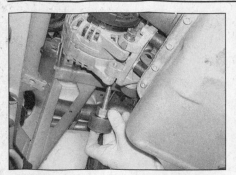

7.6 On diesel models, the lower mounting bolt also carries the auxiliary drivebelt pulley

7.7 Removing the alternator from its bracket

7.8 On diesel engines, the upper bolt acts as a centraliser

carries the auxiliary drivebelt idler pulley which can be left in position on the bolt as it is removed **(see illustration)**.

7 Manoeuvre the alternator away from its mounting brackets and out from the engine compartment **(see illustration)**.

Refitting

8 Refitting is a reversal of removal, tensioning the auxiliary drivebelt as described in Chapter 1A or 1B, and ensuring that the alternator mountings are securely tightened. Note that on diesel models, the upper bolt acts as a centraliser and should be tightened first **(see illustration)**.

8 Alternator – testing and overhaul

If the alternator is thought to be suspect, it should be removed from the vehicle and taken to an auto-electrician for testing. Most auto-electricians will be able to supply and fit brushes at a reasonable cost. However, check on the cost of repairs before proceeding as it may prove more economical to obtain a new or exchange alternator.

9 Starting system – testing

Note: *Refer to the precautions given in 'Safety first!' and in Section 1 of this Chapter before starting work.*

1 If the starter motor fails to operate when the ignition key is turned to the appropriate position, the following possible causes may be to blame.

a) *The coded anti-start system is engaged.*
b) *The battery is faulty.*
c) *The electrical connections between the switch, solenoid, battery and starter motor are somewhere failing to pass the necessary current from the battery through the starter to earth.*
d) *The solenoid is faulty.*
e) *The starter motor is mechanically or electrically defective.*

2 To check the battery, switch on the headlights. If they dim after a few seconds, this indicates that the battery is discharged – recharge (see Section 3) or renew the battery. If the headlights glow brightly, operate the ignition switch and observe the lights. If they dim, then this indicates that current is reaching the starter motor, therefore the fault must lie in the starter motor. If the lights continue to glow brightly (and no clicking sound can be heard from the starter motor solenoid), this indicates that there is a fault in the circuit or solenoid – see following paragraphs. If the starter motor turns slowly when operated, but the battery is in good condition, then this indicates that either the starter motor is faulty, or there is considerable resistance somewhere in the circuit.

3 If a fault in the circuit is suspected, disconnect the battery leads (including the earth connection to the body), the starter/solenoid wiring and the engine/transmission earth strap. Thoroughly clean the connections, and reconnect the leads and wiring, then use a voltmeter or test lamp to check that full battery voltage is available at the battery positive lead connection to the solenoid, and that the earth is sound. Smear petroleum jelly around the battery terminals to prevent corrosion – corroded connections are amongst the most frequent causes of electrical system faults.

4 If the battery and all connections are in good condition, check the circuit by disconnecting the wire from the solenoid blade terminal. Connect a voltmeter or test

10.3 Remove the two retaining nuts (arrowed) and disconnect the wiring from the starter motor solenoid

lamp between the wire end and a good earth (such as the battery negative terminal), and check that the wire is live when the ignition switch is turned to the 'start' position. If it is, then the circuit is sound – if not the circuit wiring can be checked as described in Chapter 12.

5 The solenoid contacts can be checked by connecting a voltmeter or test lamp between the battery positive feed connection on the starter side of the solenoid, and earth. When the ignition switch is turned to the 'start' position, there should be a reading or lighted bulb, as applicable. If there is no reading or lighted bulb, the solenoid is faulty and should be renewed.

6 If the circuit and solenoid are proved sound, the fault must lie in the starter motor. In this event, it may be possible to have the starter motor overhauled by a specialist, but check on the cost of spares before proceeding, as it may prove more economical to obtain a new or exchange motor.

10 Starter motor – removal and refitting

Removal

1 Disconnect the battery negative lead (refer to *Disconnecting the battery* at the end of this manual).

2 So that access to the motor can be gained both from above and below, apply the handbrake then jack up the front of the vehicle and support it on axle stands (see *Jacking and vehicle support*). Where applicable, to improve access to the motor, remove the air cleaner and ducting as necessary as described in the relevant Part of Chapter 4.

3 Slacken and remove the two retaining nuts and disconnect the wiring from the starter motor solenoid. Recover the washers under the nuts **(see illustration)**.

4 Undo the three mounting bolts (two at the rear of the motor, and one which comes through from the top of the transmission housing), supporting the motor as the bolts are withdrawn. Recover the washers from

10.4 Note the main engine earth strap connection on one of the starter motor mounting bolts

10.5 Removing the starter motor – DW12 engine

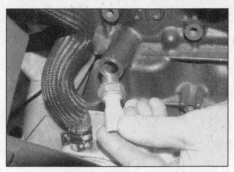

13.4 Removing the oil pressure switch from the block

14.2 Removing the oil level sensor from the cylinder block – XU engine

under the bolt heads and note the locations of any wiring or hose brackets secured by the bolts **(see illustration)**.

5 Manoeuvre the starter motor out from underneath the engine and recover the locating dowel(s) from the motor/transmission (as applicable) **(see illustration)**.

Refitting

6 Refitting is a reversal of removal, ensuring that the locating dowel(s) are correctly positioned. Also make sure that any wiring or hose brackets are in place under the bolt heads as noted prior to removal.

11 Starter motor – testing and overhaul

If the starter motor is thought to be suspect, it should be removed from the vehicle and taken to an auto-electrician for testing. Most auto-electricians will be able to supply and fit brushes at a reasonable cost. However, check on the cost of repairs before proceeding as it may prove more economical to obtain a new or exchange motor.

12 Ignition switch – removal and refitting

The ignition switch is integral with the steering column lock, and can be removed as described in Chapter 10.

13 Oil pressure warning light switch – removal and refitting

Removal

1 The switch is located at the front of the cylinder block, above the oil filter mounting. Note that on some models access to the switch may be improved if the vehicle is jacked up and supported on axle stands so that the switch can be reached from underneath (see *Jacking and vehicle support*).

2 Disconnect the battery negative lead (refer to *Disconnecting the battery* at the end of this manual).

3 Remove the protective sleeve from the wiring plug (where applicable), then disconnect the wiring from the switch.

4 Unscrew the switch from the cylinder block, and recover the sealing washer **(see illustration)**. Be prepared for oil spillage, and if the switch is to be left removed from the engine for any length of time, plug the hole in the cylinder block.

Refitting

5 Examine the sealing washer for signs of damage or deterioration and if necessary renew.

6 Refit the switch, complete with washer, and tighten it securely. Reconnect the wiring connector.

7 Lower the vehicle to the ground then check and, if necessary, top-up the engine oil as described in *Weekly Checks*.

14 Oil level sensor – removal and refitting

1 The sensor is located on the front side of the cylinder block, just to the right of the oil filter.

2 The removal and refitting procedure is as described for the oil pressure switch in Section 13. Access is most easily obtained from underneath the vehicle **(see illustration)**.

Notes

Notes

Chapter 5 Part B:
Ignition system (petrol models)

Contents

Ignition coil module – removal, testing and refitting 3
Ignition system – general information 1
Ignition system – testing 2
Ignition timing – checking and adjustment 4
Knock sensor – removal and refitting 5
Spark plug renewal and ignition system check . . . . . . .See Chapter 1A

Degrees of difficulty

Easy, suitable for novice with little experience	**Fairly easy,** suitable for beginner with some experience	**Fairly difficult,** suitable for competent DIY mechanic	**Difficult,** suitable for experienced DIY mechanic	**Very difficult,** suitable for expert DIY or professional

Specifications

System type . . . . Static (distributorless) ignition system controlled by engine management ECU

Firing order . . . . 1-3-4-2 (number 1 cylinder at transmission end)

Spark plugs . . . . See Chapter 1A Specifications

Ignition timing . . . . Controlled by engine management ECU

Torque wrench settings	**Nm**	**lbf ft**
Ignition coil block (XU7 engine)	10	7
Knock sensor securing bolt	20	15

---

1 Ignition system – general information

On all models, the ignition system is integrated with the fuel injection system to form a combined engine management system under the control of one ECU (see Chapter 4A for further information).

The ignition side of the system is of the static (distributorless) type and consists of ignition coils located in a module fitted over the centre of the cylinder head. The coils are integral with the spark plug caps and are pushed directly onto the spark plugs, one for each plug. This removes the need for any HT leads connecting the coils to the plugs.

Under the control of the ECU, the ignition coils operate on the 'wasted spark' principle, ie, each spark plug sparks twice for every cycle of the engine, once on the compression stroke and once on the exhaust stroke. The spark voltage is greatest in the cylinder which is under compression; in the cylinder on its exhaust stroke the compression is low, and this produces a very weak spark which has no effect on the exhaust gases.

The ECU uses its inputs from the various sensors to calculate the required ignition advance setting and coil charging time, depending on engine temperature, load and speed. At idle speeds, the ECU varies the ignition timing to alter the torque characteristic of the engine, enabling the idle speed to be controlled. This system operates in conjunction with the idle speed stepper motor – see Chapter 4A for additional details.

A knock sensor is also incorporated into the ignition system. Mounted onto the cylinder block, the sensor detects the high-frequency vibrations caused when the engine starts to pre-ignite, or 'pink'. Under these conditions, the knock sensor sends an electrical signal to the ECU which in turn retards the ignition advance setting in small steps until the 'pinking' ceases.

2 Ignition system – testing

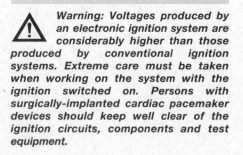

Warning: Voltages produced by an electronic ignition system are considerably higher than those produced by conventional ignition systems. Extreme care must be taken when working on the system with the ignition switched on. Persons with surgically-implanted cardiac pacemaker devices should keep well clear of the ignition circuits, components and test equipment.

1 If a fault appears in the engine management (fuel injection/ignition) system first ensure that the fault is not due to a poor electrical connection or poor maintenance; ie, check that the air cleaner filter element is clean, the spark plugs are in good condition and correctly gapped, that the engine breather hoses are clear and undamaged, referring to Chapter 1A for further information. Also check that the accelerator cable is correctly adjusted as described in Chapter 4A. If the engine is running very roughly, check the compression pressures as described in Chapter 2A or 2B.

2 If these checks fail to reveal the cause of the problem, the car should be taken to a Peugeot dealer for testing. A wiring block connector is incorporated in the engine management circuit into which a special electronic diagnostic tester can be plugged. The tester will locate the fault quickly and simply, alleviating the need to test all the system components individually which is a time consuming operation that carries a high risk of damaging the ECU.

3 The only ignition system checks which can be carried out by the home mechanic are those described in Chapter 1A relating to the spark plugs. If necessary, the system wiring and wiring connectors can be checked as described in Chapter 12 ensuring that the ECU wiring connector(s) have first been disconnected.

3 Ignition coil module – removal, testing and refitting

Removal

1 Disconnect the battery negative lead (refer to *Disconnecting the battery* at the end of this manual).
2 Unplug the wiring connector from the end of the ignition coil module **(see illustration)**.
3 Unscrew the retaining bolts then carefully lift the ignition module from the spark plugs and withdraw it from the top of the cylinder head.

Testing

4 The circuitry arrangement of the ignition coils and the coil unit on these engines is such that testing in isolation from the remainder of the engine management system is unlikely to prove effective in diagnosing a particular fault. Should there be any reason to suspect a faulty individual coil, the engine management system should be tested by a Peugeot dealer using diagnostic test equipment (see Section 2).

Refitting

5 Refitting is a reversal of the removal procedure ensuring that the wiring connector is securely reconnected.

4 Ignition timing – checking and adjustment

1 There are no timing marks on the flywheel or crankshaft pulley. The timing is constantly being monitored and adjusted by the engine management ECU, and nominal values cannot be given. Therefore, it is not possible for the home mechanic to check the ignition timing.
2 The only way in which the ignition timing can be checked is using special electronic test equipment, connected to the engine management system diagnostic connector.

5 Knock sensor – removal and refitting

Removal

1 The knock sensor is screwed into the front face of the cylinder block.
2 To gain access to the sensor, apply the handbrake, then jack up the front of the vehicle and support it on axle stands (see *Jacking and vehicle support*). Remove the splash guard from under the engine.
3 Trace the wiring back from the sensor to its wiring connector, and disconnect it from the main loom.

3.2 Disconnect the wiring connector from the ignition coil unit – EW7 engine

4 Undo the bolt securing the sensor to the cylinder block, and remove it from under the vehicle.

Refitting

5 Refitting is a reversal of the removal procedure. Ensure that the sensor and its seating on the cylinder block are completely clean and tighten the sensor securing bolt to the specified torque wrench setting. It is essential that these measures are scrupulously observed as if the sensor is not correctly secured to a clean mating surface it may not be able to detect the impulses caused by pre-ignition. If this were to happen the correction of ignition timing would not take place, with the consequent risk of severe engine damage.

Chapter 5 Part C:
Preheating system (diesel models)

Contents

Glow plugs – removal, inspection and refitting 2
Pre-post heating system – description and testing 1
Pre-post heating system control unit – removal and refitting 3

Degrees of difficulty

Easy, suitable for novice with little experience		**Fairly easy,** suitable for beginner with some experience		**Fairly difficult,** suitable for competent DIY mechanic		**Difficult,** suitable for experienced DIY mechanic		**Very difficult,** suitable for expert DIY or professional	

Specifications

Preheating system

Preheating period at ambient temperature of:

–30°C	20 seconds
–10°C	5 seconds
0°C	0.5 seconds
18°C	0 seconds

Post-heating system

Post-heating period at ambient temperature of:

–30°C	3 minutes
–10°C	3 minutes
0°C	1 minute
18°C	30 seconds
40°C	0 seconds

Glow plugs

Resistance (typical)	Less than 1 ohm
Type:	
DW10 engine	Bosch 0 250 202 032
DW12 engine	Not specified

Torque wrench setting	Nm	lbf ft
Glow plugs	22	16

1 Pre-post heating system – description and testing

Description

1 To assist cold starting, diesel engines are fitted with a preheating system, which consists of four of glow plugs (one per cylinder), a glow plug control unit (in the engine management ECU on later models), a facia-mounted warning lamp, a coolant temperature sensor mounted on the cylinder head, an ambient air temperature sensor, and the associated electrical wiring.

2 The glow plugs are miniature electric heating elements, encapsulated in a metal case with a probe at one end and electrical connection at the other. Each combustion chamber has one glow plug threaded into it, with the tip of the glow plug probe positioned directly in line with incoming spray of fuel from the injectors. When the glow plug is energised, It heats up rapidly, causing the fuel passing over the glow plug probe to be heated to its optimum combustion temperature, ready for combustion. In addition, some of the fuel passing over the glow plugs is ignited and this helps to trigger the combustion process.

3 The preheating system begins to operate as soon as the ignition key is switched to the second position, but only if the engine coolant temperature is below 20°C and the engine is turned at more than 70 rpm for 0.2 seconds. A facia-mounted warning lamp informs the driver that preheating is taking place. The lamp extinguishes when sufficient preheating has taken place to allow the engine to be started, but power will still be supplied to the glow plugs for a further period until the engine is started. If no attempt is made to start the engine, the power supply to the glow plugs is switched off after 10 seconds, to prevent battery drain and glow plug burn-out.

4 With the electronically-controlled diesel injection systems fitted to models in this manual, the glow plug control unit is controlled by the injection system ECU, which determines the necessary preheating time based on inputs from the various system sensors. The system monitors the temperature of the air in the engine bay by an air temperature sensor, then alters the preheating time (the length for which the glow plugs are supplied with current) to suit the conditions.

5 Post-heating takes place after the ignition key has been released from the 'Start' position, but only if the engine coolant temperature is below 20°C, the injected fuel flow is less than a certain rate, and the engine speed is less than 2000 rpm. The glow plugs continue to operate for a maximum of 60 seconds, helping to improve fuel combustion whilst the engine is warming-up, resulting in quieter, smoother running and reduced exhaust emissions.

2.2 Removing the shunt from the glow plugs

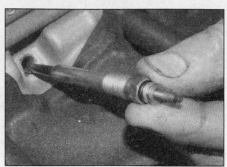

2.4 Removing a glow plug – DW12 engine

Testing

6 If the system malfunctions, testing is ultimately by substitution of known good units, but some preliminary checks may be made as follows.

7 Connect a voltmeter or 12 volt test lamp between the glow plug supply cable and earth (engine or vehicle metal). Make sure that the live connection is kept clear of the engine and bodywork.

8 Have an assistant switch on the ignition, and check that voltage is applied to the glow plugs. Note the time for which the warning light is lit, and the total time for which voltage is applied before the system cuts out. Switch off the ignition.

9 Compare the results with the information given in the Specifications. Warning light time will increase with lower temperatures and decrease with higher temperatures.

10 If there is no supply at all, the control unit or associated wiring is at fault.

11 To gain access to the glow plugs for further testing, refer to Chapter 4B, where necessary, and remove the following components, according to model:

DW10 2.0 litre engine – Release the four plastic fasteners and remove the engine cover from the top of the engine. It may also be necessary to move the wiring harness tray to one side after undoing the two retaining nuts, for access to No 4 glow plug.

DW12 2.2 litre engine – Remove the engine top cover, then remove the air filter and ducts, and the EGR valve and gasket together with the EGR heat exchanger.

12 Disconnect the main supply cable and the interconnecting wire or strap from the top of the glow plugs. Be careful not to drop the nuts and washers.

13 Use a continuity tester, or a 12 volt test lamp connected to the battery positive terminal, to check for continuity between each glow plug terminal and earth. The resistance of a glow plug in good condition is very low

(less than 1 ohm), so if the test lamp does not light or the continuity tester shows a high resistance, the glow plug is certainly defective.

14 If an ammeter is available, the current draw of each glow plug can be checked. After an initial surge of 15 to 20 amps, each plug should draw 12 amps. Any plug which draws much more or less than this is probably defective.

15 As a final check, the glow plugs can be removed and inspected as described in the following Section. On completion, refit any components removed for access.

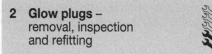

2   Glow plugs –
removal, inspection and refitting

Caution: If the preheating system has just been energised, or if the engine has been running, the glow plugs will be very hot.

Removal

1 Disconnect the battery negative terminal (refer to *Disconnecting the battery* in the Reference Section of this manual). To gain access to the glow plugs, remove the components described in Section 1, according to model.

2 Unscrew the nuts from the glow plug terminals, and recover the washers. Note that an interconnecting wire/shunt is fitted between the four plugs **(see illustration)**.

3 Where applicable, carefully move any obstructing pipes or wires to one side to enable access to the relevant glow plug(s).

4 Unscrew the glow plug(s) and remove from the cylinder head **(see illustration)**.

Inspection

5 Inspect each glow plug for physical damage. Burnt or eroded glow plug tips can be caused by a bad injector spray pattern. Have the injectors checked if this sort of damage is found.

6 If the glow plugs are in good physical condition, check them electrically using a 12 volt test lamp or continuity tester as described in the previous Section.

7 The glow plugs can be energised by applying 12 volts to them to verify that they heat up evenly and in the required time. Observe the following precautions.

a) Support the glow plug by clamping it carefully in a vice or self-locking pliers. Remember it will become red-hot.

b) Make sure that the power supply or test lead incorporates a fuse or overload trip to protect against damage from a short-circuit.

c) After testing, allow the glow plug to cool for several minutes before attempting to handle it.

8 A glow plug in good condition will start to glow red at the tip after drawing current for 5 seconds or so. Any plug which takes much longer to start glowing, or which starts glowing in the middle instead of at the tip, is defective.

Refitting

9 Refit by reversing the removal operations. Apply a smear of copper-based anti-seize compound to the plug threads and tighten the glow plugs to the specified torque. Do not overtighten, as this can damage the glow plug element.

10 Refit any components removed for access.

3   Pre-post heating
system control unit –
removal and refitting

Note: *The pre-post heating system control unit is not fitted to later models, as its function is controlled by the engine management ECU.*

Removal

1 The unit is located on the left-hand side of the engine compartment where it is mounted on a bracket just in front of the fuse/relay box.

2 Disconnect the battery negative terminal (refer to *Disconnecting the battery* in the Reference Section of this manual).

3 Unscrew the retaining nut securing the unit to the mounting bracket.

4 Unscrew the two retaining nuts and free the main feed and supply wires from the base of the unit, then disconnect the wiring connector. Remove the unit from the engine compartment.

Refitting

5 Refitting is a reversal of removal, ensuring that the wiring connectors are correctly connected.

Chapter 6
Clutch

Contents

Clutch assembly – removal, inspection and refitting 6
Clutch cable – removal and refitting 2
Clutch hydraulic system – bleeding 5
Clutch hydraulic system components – removal and refitting 4
Clutch operation check . . . . See Chapter 1A or 1B
Clutch pedal – removal and refitting 3
Clutch release mechanism – removal, inspection and refitting 7
General information 1

Degrees of difficulty

Easy, suitable for novice with little experience	Fairly easy, suitable for beginner with some experience	Fairly difficult, suitable for competent DIY mechanic	Difficult, suitable for experienced DIY mechanic	Very difficult, suitable for expert DIY or professional

Specifications

Type . . . . Single dry plate with diaphragm spring, cable or hydraulic operation

Friction disc diameter

1.8 litre petrol engine:
XU7JP4 . . . . 200 mm
EW7J4 . . . . 228 mm
2.0 litre petrol engine . . . . 228.6 mm
2.0 litre diesel engine . . . . 225 mm
2.2 litre diesel engine . . . . 242 mm

Torque wrench settings	**Nm**	**lbf ft**
Clutch slave cylinder	20	15
Pressure plate retaining bolts	20	15

1 General information

The clutch consists of a friction disc, a pressure plate assembly, a release bearing and the release mechanism, all of these components being contained in the transmission bellhousing, sandwiched between the engine and the transmission. The release mechanism is mechanical, and is operated by cable on early models with the XU7 engine, or hydraulically on other models by means of a master and slave cylinder together with interconnecting hydraulic pipework **(see illustrations)**.

The friction disc is fitted between the engine flywheel and the clutch pressure plate, and is free to slide along the transmission input shaft splines.

The pressure plate assembly is bolted to the engine flywheel. When the engine is running, drive is transmitted from the crankshaft, through the flywheel, to the friction disc (these components being clamped securely together by the pressure plate assembly) and from the friction disc to the transmission input shaft.

The disc is held in position between the flywheel and the pressure plate by the pressure of the diaphragm spring. Friction lining material is riveted to the disc which, on all petrol engines and the non-intercooled DW10TD engine, has a spring-cushioned hub

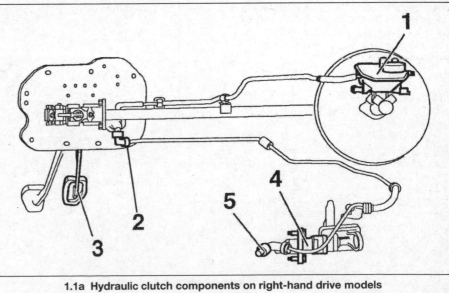

1.1a Hydraulic clutch components on right-hand drive models

1 Brake fluid reservoir
2 Clutch master cylinder
3 Clutch pedal
4 Slave cylinder
5 Bleed screw

to absorb transmission shocks and help ensure a smooth take-up of the drive. There is no spring-cushioned hub on the DW10ATED and DW12TED diesel engines, however, the flywheel is designed in two sections with an internal cushion to take up transmission shocks.

Two different types of clutch release mechanism are used. The first is a conventional 'push-type' mechanism, where an independent clutch release bearing, fitted concentrically around the transmission input shaft, is pushed onto the pressure plate assembly; this type is fitted to all petrol engines and the 2.0 litre DW10TD (non-intercooled) diesel engine. The second is a 'pull-type' mechanism, where the clutch release bearing is an integral part of the pressure plate assembly, and is lifted away from the friction disc; this type is fitted to the 2.0 litre DW10ATED (intercooled) diesel engine and the DW12TED diesel engine.

On models with the conventional 'push-type' mechanism, the clutch release mechanism consists of a release fork and bearing which are in permanent contact with the fingers of the diaphragm spring. Depressing the clutch pedal actuates the release arm by means of the cable or hydraulic master and slave cylinders, and the release bearing is pushed against the diaphragm fingers, so moving the centre of the diaphragm spring inwards. As the centre of the spring is pushed in, the outside of the spring pivots out, so moving the pressure plate backwards and disengaging its grip on the friction disc.

On models with the 'pull-type' mechanism, the clutch release mechanism consists of a release fork which pivots on a spindle inside the gearbox bellhousing. Depressing the clutch pedal rotates the release fork on its spindle, and lifts the release bearing, which is attached to the pressure plate springs, away

from the friction disc, and releases the clamping force exerted at the pressure plate periphery.

Adjustment of the clutch to compensate for wear of the friction disc linings is automatically taken up by the self-adjusting cable or hydraulic clutch components.

Some early models may be fitted with a sealed hydraulic system, where the master cylinder, fluid reservoir, and slave cylinder are of monobloc construction.

2 Clutch cable – removal and refitting

Removal

1 Disconnect the battery negative lead (refer to *Disconnecting the battery* at the end of this manual).
2 Open up the engine immobiliser key pad, then rotate the fastener through 90° and lower the fusebox cover. Disconnect the wiring connector from the key pad then slacken and remove the retaining screws and remove the driver's side lower panel from the facia.
3 Remove the air cleaner housing and intake duct components as described in the relevant Part of Chapter 4.
4 Working in the engine compartment, release the inner cable and outer cable fittings from the clutch release lever and mounting bracket and free the cable from the transmission housing.
5 Working inside the vehicle, release the inner cable from the pedal. On some models it may be necessary to depress a plastic clip located just beneath the top of the pedal to release the cable.
6 Return to the engine compartment, then release the cable guide from the bulkhead and withdraw the cable forwards, releasing it from

any relevant retaining clips and guides. Note its correct routing, and remove it from the vehicle.
7 Examine the cable, looking for worn end fittings or a damaged outer casing, and for signs of fraying of the inner wire. Renew the cable if it shows signs of excessive wear or any damage.

Refitting

8 Apply a thin smear of multi-purpose grease to the cable end fittings, then pass the cable through the engine compartment bulkhead.
9 Hold the clutch pedal in its raised position by wedging a suitable tool beneath it.
10 Guide the end of the cable into the pedal end (or plastic clip) making sure that it is fully engaged.
11 In the engine compartment refit the cable to the transmission housing and release lever. Resecure the cable with any relevant retaining clips and guides.
12 Depress and release the clutch pedal several times to operate the self-adjusting mechanism and check that the clutch pedal operates correctly.
13 Refit the lower panel to the facia then refit the air cleaner components and reconnect the battery.

3 Clutch pedal – removal and refitting

Removal

1 Disconnect the battery negative lead (refer to *Disconnecting the battery* at the end of this manual).
2 Open up the engine immobiliser key pad, then rotate the fastener through 90° and lower the fusebox cover. Disconnect the wiring connector from the key pad then slacken and remove the retaining screws and remove the driver's side lower panel from the facia.
3 On models with a cable-operated clutch, release the inner cable from the pedal. On some models it may be necessary to depress a plastic clip located just beneath the top of the pedal to release the cable. Carefully release the pedal-assist spring assembly from the pedal.
4 On models with a hydraulically-operated clutch, release the master cylinder pushrod balljoint from the pedal and allow the pedal to rise until it reaches its stop.
5 Slacken and remove the pivot bolt and nut, and remove the clutch pedal from the vehicle. Slide the spacer out from the pedal pivot. Examine all components for signs of wear or damage, renewing them as necessary.

Refitting

6 Apply a smear of multi-purpose grease to the spacer, and insert it into the pedal pivot bore.
7 Manoeuvre the pedal into position, and

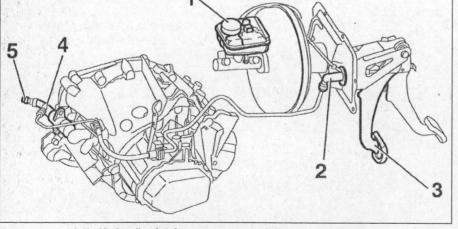

1.1b Hydraulic clutch components on left-hand drive models

| 1 Brake fluid reservoir | 3 Clutch pedal | 5 Bleed screw |
| 2 Clutch master cylinder | 4 Slave cylinder | |

insert the pivot bolt. Refit the nut to the pivot bolt and tighten it securely.

8 Reconnect the clutch cable or master cylinder pushrod to the pedal. On cable-operated versions, refit the pedal assist spring assembly.

9 Depress and release the clutch pedal several times and check for correct operation.

10 Refit the lower panel to the facia and reconnect the battery.

4 Clutch hydraulic system components – removal and refitting

Note: *Early models may have a sealed monobloc system, where the complete hydraulic system is removed as a complete assembly. This system is described at the end of this Section.*

Clutch master cylinder

Removal

1 Remove the air cleaner housing and intake duct components as described in the relevant Part of Chapter 4.

2 Open up the engine immobiliser key pad, then rotate the fastener through 90° and lower the fusebox cover. Disconnect the wiring connector from the key pad then slacken and remove the retaining screws and remove the driver's side lower panel from the facia.

3 Working on the clutch pedal, release the clutch master cylinder pushrod from the pedal and allow the pedal to rise until it reaches its stop. The pushrod is retained on the pedal by a clevis pin and spring clip.

4 Working in the engine compartment, syphon out the hydraulic fluid from the brake fluid reservoir. Disconnect the clutch hydraulic supply hose from the reservoir then tape over or plug the hose and aperture.

5 On right-hand drive models, apply the handbrake, then jack up the front of the vehicle and support it on axle stands (see

4.6 Hydraulic pipe leading from the clutch master cylinder to the slave cylinder

Jacking and vehicle support); access to the master cylinder is gained from under the car. On left-hand drive models, remove the brake master cylinder and the brake vacuum servo unit with reference to Chapter 9.

6 Unclip the slave cylinder hydraulic line from the bottom of the clutch master cylinder **(see illustration)**.

7 Turn the clutch master cylinder 90° clockwise to release it from the bulkhead attachment. If necessary, make up a tool from metal tube to engage the master cylinder, so that it can be turned easily.

Refitting

8 Locate the master cylinder in position, aligning the white mark on the cylinder with the corresponding white mark on the bulkhead. Push and turn the cylinder 90° anticlockwise to secure.

9 Refit the slave cylinder hydraulic line to the bottom of the clutch master cylinder.

10 On right-hand drive models, lower the car to the ground. On left-hand drive models, refit the brake vacuum servo unit and the master cylinder with reference to Chapter 9.

11 Reconnect the clutch hydraulic supply hose to the brake fluid reservoir.

12 Working inside the car, lubricate the master cylinder pushrod balljoint, then lift the clutch pedal and connect the pushrod. Refit the clevis pin and secure with the spring clip.

13 Top-up the hydraulic brake fluid in the reservoir, then bleed the clutch hydraulic system as described in Section 5 and the brake hydraulic system as described in Chapter 9.

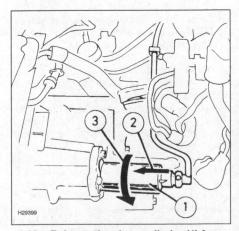

4.19a Release the slave cylinder (1) from the transmission by pushing it in (2) and turning it 90° anti-clockwise (3)

4.18 Unclipping the hydraulic pipe from the clutch slave cylinder

14 Refit the lower facia panel.

15 Refit the air cleaner housing.

Clutch slave cylinder

Removal

16 Remove the air cleaner housing and intake duct components as described in the relevant Part of Chapter 4.

17 Syphon out the hydraulic fluid from the brake fluid reservoir until the fluid level is below the clutch master cylinder supply hose.

18 Unclip the hydraulic pipe from the clutch slave cylinder and move it to one side **(see illustration)**.

19 Where fitted, remove the clip from over the slave cylinder. Release the slave cylinder from the transmission by pushing it in by hand and at the same time turning it 90° anticlockwise **(see illustrations)**. Withdraw the cylinder from the engine compartment.

Refitting

Note: *On a new assembly, the slave cylinder pushrod is retained in the cylinder by a plastic collar which will automatically break off when the clutch pedal is depressed for the first time. Do not attempt to release this collar manually prior to fitting or the pushrod may be ejected.*

20 Lubricate the end of the slave cylinder pushrod with molybdenum disulphide grease then locate the slave cylinder in the transmission. Push it in by hand and at the same time turn it 90° clockwise to secure.

21 Reconnect the hydraulic pipe to the slave cylinder.

22 Top-up the hydraulic brake fluid in the

4.19b Remove the cover . . .

4.19c . . . then twist and remove the clutch slave cylinder

6.2 Marking the relationship of the pressure plate assembly to the flywheel

reservoir, then bleed the clutch hydraulic system as described in Section 5.

23 Refit the air cleaner housing with reference to the relevant Part of Chapter 4.

Sealed system (early models)

Note: *Access to the master cylinder is extremely limited and Peugeot recommend the use of a special slotted socket (tool 0216J) for this purpose. A suitable alternative can be fabricated from a box spanner with a slot cut in the side to accommodate the hydraulic hose.*

Removal

24 Disconnect the battery negative terminal.

25 Remove the air cleaner housing and intake duct components as described in the relevant Part of Chapter 4.

26 Release the master cylinder pushrod balljoint from the pedal and allow the pedal to rise until it reaches its stop.

27 Working in the engine compartment, unclip the master cylinder fluid reservoir from the bulkhead.

28 Engage the Peugeot special tool, or the home-made alternative over the master cylinder and turn the cylinder 90° clockwise to release it from the bulkhead attachment.

29 Release the slave cylinder from the transmission by pushing it in by hand and at the same time turning it 90° anti-clockwise.

30 Release the hydraulic pipework from the retaining clips and attachments in the engine compartment and remove the complete assembly from the vehicle.

6.4 Removing the pressure plate assembly (pull-type) and friction disc from the flywheel

Refitting

Note: *On a new assembly, the slave cylinder pushrod is retained in the cylinder by a plastic collar which will automatically break off when the clutch pedal is depressed for the first time. Do not attempt to release this collar manually prior to fitting or the pushrod may be ejected.*

31 Push the clutch pedal to the floor by hand and retain it in this position.

32 Locate the master cylinder in position, aligning the white mark on the cylinder with the corresponding white mark on the bulkhead. Using the tool, push and turn the cylinder 90° anti-clockwise to secure.

33 Clip the master cylinder fluid reservoir into place on the bulkhead. Ensure that the fluid hoses are correctly routed and not chafing.

34 Lubricate the end of the slave cylinder pushrod with molybdenum disulphide grease then locate the slave cylinder in the transmission. Push it in by hand and at the same time turn it 90° clockwise to secure.

35 Reconnect the hydraulic pipework to the retaining clips and attachments in the engine compartment

36 Lubricate the master cylinder pushrod balljoint, then lift the clutch pedal and connect the pushrod.

37 With the assembly installed, slowly depress the clutch pedal to the floor, then slowly lift it again by hand. Wait for ten seconds and repeat this procedure. Depress the pedal again, release it and check that it rises correctly after being released.

38 Refit the lower panel to the facia then refit the air cleaner components and reconnect the battery.

5 Clutch hydraulic system – bleeding

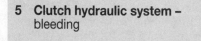

Note: *The manufacturers do not recommend the use of an automatic bleeding kit, as there is the risk of foaming in the hydraulic circuit. This Section does not apply to early (sealed) systems.*

1 Bleeding of the clutch hydraulic system is carried out in the same manner as bleeding the brake hydraulic system (see Chapter 9). First top up the brake fluid reservoir.

2 Remove the air cleaner housing and intake duct components as described in the relevant Part of Chapter 4.

3 Connect a bleed tube to the bleed screw on the clutch slave cylinder, and place the free end of the tube in a suitable jar with sufficient hydraulic fluid to cover the end of the tube.

4 Loosen the bleed screw, then have an assistant depress and release the clutch pedal fully 7 times. On the last stroke, have the assistant hold the pedal depressed. Tighten the bleed screw and have the pedal released.

5 Top-up the hydraulic fluid, then repeat the procedure described in paragraph 4.

6 Top-up the fluid again, then operate the clutch pedal 40 times at the rate of 1 forward and backward movement per second.

7 With the handbrake applied, start the engine and engage a gear. Check that the start of friction of the clutch pedal occurs at a distance of at least 35 mm from the floor. If it occurs at less than 35 mm from the floor, air must still be present in the hydraulic system and it will be necessary to bleed the system again. An alternative method of checking the operation of the clutch pedal is to place a 35 mm thick spacer beneath the pedal on the floor, and check that all gears can be engaged normally when the pedal is depressed onto the spacer.

8 On completion, refit the air cleaner housing.

6 Clutch assembly – removal, inspection and refitting

⚠ **Warning: Dust created by clutch wear and deposited on the clutch components may contain asbestos, which is a health hazard. DO NOT blow it out with compressed air, or inhale any of it. DO NOT use petrol or petroleum-based solvents to clean off the dust. Brake system cleaner or methylated spirit should be used to flush the dust into a suitable receptacle. After the clutch components are wiped clean with rags, dispose of the contaminated rags and cleaner in a sealed, marked container.**

Note: *Although some friction materials may no longer contain asbestos, it is safest to assume that they do, and to take precautions accordingly.*

Removal

1 Unless the complete engine/transmission is to be removed from the car and separated for major overhaul (see Chapter 2D), the clutch can be reached by removing the transmission as described in Chapter 7A.

2 Before disturbing the clutch, mark the relationship of the pressure plate assembly to the flywheel, using a marker pen or similar **(see illustration)**.

3 Working in a diagonal sequence, slacken the pressure plate bolts by half a turn at a time, until spring pressure is released and the bolts can be unscrewed by hand.

4 Prise the pressure plate assembly off its locating dowels, and collect the friction disc, noting which way round the friction disc is fitted **(see illustration)**.

5 On models with the 'pull-type' release mechanism (DW10ATED and DW12TED diesel engines), first press down the pressure plate on the bench, then use a screwdriver to prise out the circlip and remove the release bearing from the pressure plate diaphragm spring **(see illustrations)**. Take care not to deform the circlip, and after removing the bearing, refit the circlip in its groove.

6.5a Press down on the pressure plate . . .

6.5b . . . then prise out the circlip . . .

6.5c . . . and remove the release bearing from the pressure plate diaphragm

Inspection

Note: *Due to the amount of work necessary to remove and refit clutch components, it is usually considered good practice to renew the clutch friction disc, pressure plate assembly and release bearing as a matched set, even if only one of these is actually worn enough to require renewal. It is also worth considering the renewal of the clutch components on a preventative basis if the engine and/or transmission have been removed for some other reason.*

6 When cleaning clutch components, read first the warning at the beginning of this Section; remove dust using a clean, dry cloth, and working in a well-ventilated atmosphere.

7 Check the friction disc facings for signs of wear, damage or oil contamination. If the friction material is cracked, burnt, scored or damaged, or if it is contaminated with oil or grease (shown by shiny black patches), the friction disc must be renewed.

8 If the friction material is still serviceable, check that the centre boss splines are unworn, that the torsion springs (where fitted) are in good condition and securely fastened, and that all the rivets are tight. If any wear or damage is found, the friction disc must be renewed.

9 If the friction material is fouled with oil, this must be due to an oil leak from the crankshaft left-hand oil seal, from the sump-to-cylinder block joint, or from the transmission input shaft. Renew the seal or repair the joint, as appropriate, as described in the relevant Part of Chapter 2 or 7, before installing the new friction disc.

10 Check the pressure plate assembly for obvious signs of wear or damage; shake it to check for loose rivets or worn or damaged fulcrum rings, and check that the drive straps securing the pressure plate to the cover do not show signs (such as a deep yellow or blue discoloration) of overheating. If the diaphragm spring is worn or damaged, or if its pressure is in any way suspect, the pressure plate assembly should be renewed.

11 Examine the machined bearing surfaces of the pressure plate and flywheel; they should be clean, completely flat, and free from scratches or scoring. If either is discoloured from excessive heat, or shows signs of cracks, it should be renewed – although minor damage of this nature can sometimes be polished away using emery paper.

12 Check that the release bearing contact surface rotates smoothly and easily, with no sign of noise or roughness. Also check that the surface itself is smooth and unworn, with no signs of cracks, pitting or scoring. If there is any doubt about its condition, the bearing must be renewed. On clutches with a 'pull-type' release mechanism, check that the retaining circlip is in good condition, and renew it if necessary.

Refitting

13 On reassembly, ensure that the bearing surfaces of the flywheel and pressure plate are completely clean, smooth, and free from oil or grease. Use solvent to remove any protective grease from new components.

14 Fit the friction disc so its spring hub faces away from the flywheel; there may also be a marking to show which way round the plate is to be refitted **(see illustration)**. On most models, the thickness of the spring hub makes it impossible to fit it with the hub against the flywheel.

15 Refit the pressure plate assembly, aligning the marks made on dismantling (if the original pressure plate is re-used), and locating the pressure plate on its locating dowels. Fit the pressure plate bolts, but tighten them only finger-tight, so that the friction disc can still be moved.

16 The friction disc must now be centralised, so that when the transmission is refitted, its input shaft will pass through the splines at the centre of the friction disc.

17 Centralisation can be achieved by passing a screwdriver or other long bar through the friction disc and into the hole in the crankshaft; the friction disc can then be moved around until it is centred on the crankshaft hole. Alternatively, a clutch-aligning tool can be used to eliminate the guesswork; these can be obtained from most accessory shops **(see illustration)**. A home-made alignment tool can be fabricated from a length of metal rod or wooden dowel which fits closely inside the crankshaft hole, and has insulating tape wound around it to match the diameter of the friction disc splined hole.

18 When the friction disc is centralised, tighten the pressure plate bolts evenly and in a diagonal sequence to the specified torque setting.

19 Refit the transmission as described in Chapter 7A. On models with the 'pull-type' release mechanism, use the tool described in Chapter 7A, Section 9, to engage the release bearing with the pressure plate diaphragm spring before refitting the slave cylinder.

7 Clutch release mechanism – removal, inspection and refitting

Note: *Refer to the warning concerning the dangers of asbestos dust at the beginning of Section 6.*

Removal

1 Unless the complete engine/transmission is to be removed from the car and separated for major overhaul (see Chapter 2D), the clutch release mechanism can be reached by

6.14 Ensure the friction disc is fitted the correct way round then install the pressure plate

6.17 Using a clutch-aligning tool to centralise the friction disc

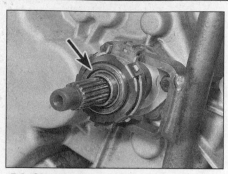

7.2 Clutch release bearing (arrowed) and release fork and shaft

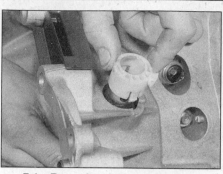

7.4a Removing the upper bush . . .

7.4b . . . release fork shaft . . .

7.4c . . . and lower bush

7.5a Using a lever to remove the release fork shaft

7.5b Remove the release fork shaft . . .

removing the transmission only, as described in Chapter 7A.

Push-type release mechanism

2 Unhook the release bearing from the fork, and slide it off the input shaft (see illustration).
3 Drive out the roll pin, and remove the release lever from the top of the release fork shaft. Discard the roll pin – a new one must be used on refitting.
4 Depress the retaining tabs, then slide the upper bush off the end of the release fork shaft. Disengage the shaft from its lower bush, and manoeuvre it out from the transmission. Depress the retaining tabs, and remove the lower pivot bush from the transmission housing (see illustrations).

Pull-type release mechanism

5 Access to the inner end of the release fork shaft is not possible, and the shaft must be pulled or levered out from the outside of the

bellhousing. A slide hammer may be attached to the groove in the end of the shaft, or alternatively a lever may be used taking care not to damage the transmission casing (see illustrations).
6 With the shaft removed, withdraw the release fork from the bellhousing, noting which way round it is fitted (see illustration).

Inspection

7 Check the release mechanism, renewing any component which is worn or damaged. Carefully check all bearing surfaces and points of contact.
8 When checking the release bearing itself, note that it is often considered worthwhile to renew it as a matter of course. Check that the contact surface rotates smoothly and easily, with no sign of noise or roughness, and that the surface itself is smooth and unworn, with no signs of cracks, pitting or scoring. If there

is any doubt about its condition, the bearing must be renewed.

Refitting

Push-type release mechanism

9 Apply a smear of molybdenum disulphide grease to the shaft pivot bushes and the contact surfaces of the release fork.
10 Locate the lower pivot bush in the transmission, ensuring that it is securely retained by its locating tangs, and refit the release fork. Slide the upper bush down the shaft, and clip it into position in the transmission housing.
11 Refit the release lever to the shaft. Align the lever with the shaft hole, and secure it in position by tapping a new roll pin fully into position. Slide the release bearing onto the input shaft, and engage it with the release fork.

Pull-type release mechanism

12 Apply a smear of molybdenum disulphide grease to the shaft and contact surfaces of the release fork.
13 Insert the shaft through the transmission casing then locate the release fork inside the bellhousing and insert the shaft through it into the inner location hole. Make sure that the slave cylinder contact point is facing the correct direction.
14 Using a soft-metal drift, drive the shaft fully into the casing, taking care not to damage the inner blind hole (see illustration).

All models

15 Refit the transmission as described in Chapter 7A.

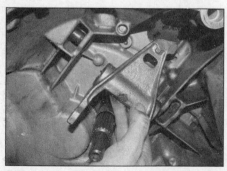

7.6 . . . and withdraw the release fork from the bellhousing

7.14 Driving the release shaft into the casing

Chapter 7 Part A:
Manual transmission

Contents

Gearchange cables (BE4/5 and ML5T transmissions) – removal and refitting ... 4
Gearchange linkage (BE3/5 transmission) – removal and refitting .. 3
General information ... 1
Manual transmission – draining and refilling ... 2
Manual transmission (BE3/5 and BE4/5) – removal and refitting ... 8
Manual transmission (ML5T) – removal and refitting ... 9
Manual transmission oil level check ... See Chapter 1A or 1B
Manual transmission overhaul – general information ... 10
Oil seals – renewal ... 5
Reversing light switch – testing, removal and refitting ... 6
Speedometer drive – removal and refitting ... 7

Degrees of difficulty

Easy, suitable for novice with little experience

Fairly easy, suitable for beginner with some experience

Fairly difficult, suitable for competent DIY mechanic

Difficult, suitable for experienced DIY mechanic

Very difficult, suitable for expert DIY or professional

Specifications

General

Type ... Manual, five forward speeds and reverse. Synchromesh on all forward speeds

Designation:
XU petrol engine ... BE3/5
EW petrol engines ... BE4/5
DW10TD diesel engine ... BE4/5
DW10ATED and DW12TED4 diesel engines ... ML5T

Lubrication

Recommended oil ... See *Lubricants and fluids*
Capacity ... 1.9 litres (1.8 litres after draining)

Torque wrench settings

	Nm	lbf ft
BE3 and BE4 transmissions		
Clutch release bearing guide sleeve bolts	12	9
Differential extension	15	11
Engine movement limiter to driveshaft intermediate bearing housing	45	33
Engine movement limiter to subframe	85	63
Engine-to-transmission fixing bolts	55	41
Gearbox control plate	15	11
Gearchange cable bracket (BE4)	20	15
Gearchange linkage bellcrank pivot bolt (BE3)	28	21
Gearchange selector rod to lever pivot bolt (BE3)	15	11
Left-hand engine/transmission mounting:		
Centre nut	65	48
Mounting stud bracket to transmission	60	44
Mounting stud to transmission	50	37
Rubber mounting-to-bracket bolts	30	22
Oil drain plug	30	22
Oil filler/level plug	20	15
Reversing light switch	25	18
Right-hand driveshaft intermediate bearing retaining bolt nuts	10	7
Roadwheel bolts	90	66

Torque wrench settings (continued)

	Nm	lbf ft
ML5T transmission		
Clutch release bearing guide sleeve bolts	12	9
Engine movement limiter to driveshaft intermediate bearing housing ..	50	37
Engine movement limiter to subframe	85	63
Engine-to-transmission fixing bolts	60	44
Gearchange lever housing bolts	7	5
Left-hand engine/transmission mounting:		
Centre nut	65	48
Mounting bracket to transmission	30	22
Mounting to bracket	30	22
Oil drain plug	30	22
Oil filler/level plug	20	15
Reversing light switch	25	18
Right-hand driveshaft intermediate bearing retaining bolt nuts	10	7
Roadwheel bolts	90	66

1 General information

The transmission is contained in a cast-aluminium alloy casing bolted to the engine's left-hand end, and consists of the gearbox and final drive differential. Three transmission types are fitted according to model, the types being BE3/5, BE4/5 and ML5T. All transmission types have 5 forward gears and 1 reverse gear, and are similar in operation.

Drive is transmitted from the crankshaft through the clutch to the input shaft, which has a splined extension to accept the clutch friction disc, and which rotates in sealed ball-bearings. From the input shaft, drive is transmitted to the output shaft, which rotates in a roller bearing at its right-hand end, and a sealed ball-bearing at its left-hand end. From the output shaft, the drive is transmitted to the differential crown wheel, which rotates with the differential case and planetary gears, thus driving the sun gears and driveshafts. The rotation of the planetary gears on their shaft allows the inner roadwheel to rotate at a slower speed than the outer roadwheel when the car is cornering.

The input and output shafts are arranged side-by-side, parallel to the crankshaft and driveshafts, so that their gear pinion teeth are in constant mesh. In the neutral position, the relevant input shaft and output shaft gear pinions rotate freely, so that drive cannot be transmitted to the output shaft and crown wheel.

Gear selection is by a floor-mounted lever actuating a selector rod mechanism on BE3/5 transmission, or a selector cable mechanism on the BE4/5 and ML5T units. The selector rod/cables cause the appropriate selector fork to move its respective synchro sleeve along the shaft, to lock the gear pinion to the synchro-hub. Since the synchro-hubs are splined to the input and output shafts, this locks the pinion to the shaft, so that drive can be transmitted. To ensure that gearchanging can be made quickly and quietly, a synchromesh system is fitted to all forward gears, consisting of baulk rings and spring-loaded fingers, together with the gear pinions and synchro-hubs. The synchromesh cones are formed on the mating faces of the baulk rings and gear pinions.

2 Manual transmission – draining and refilling

Note: *A suitable square section wrench may be required to undo the transmission filler/level and drain plugs on some models. These wrenches can be obtained from most motor factors or your Peugeot dealer.*

1 This operation is much quicker and more efficient if the car is first taken on a journey of sufficient length to warm the engine/transmission up to operating temperature.

2 Park the car on level ground, switch off the ignition and apply the handbrake firmly. To ensure that the car remains level when refilling, jack up the front and rear of the car and support it securely on axle stands.

3 On models equipped with the BE3 and BE4 transmissions, remove the left-hand front roadwheel then release the screws and clips and remove the wheelarch liner from under the wing for access to the filler/level plug. On all models, remove the splash guard from under the engine.

4 Wipe clean the area around the filler/level plug. On the BE3 and BE4 transmissions, the filler/level plug is the largest bolt among those securing the end cover to the transmission; on the ML5T transmission, the filler/level plug is located on the rear face of the differential housing. A hexagon key will be required to unscrew the plug. Remove the filler/level plug from the transmission and recover the sealing washer **(see illustration)**.

5 Position a suitable container under the drain plug (situated on the final drive casing at the rear of the transmission) and unscrew the plug **(see illustrations)**.

6 Allow the oil to drain completely into the container **(see illustration)**. If the oil is hot, take precautions against scalding. Clean both the filler/level and the drain plugs, being especially careful to wipe any metallic particles off the magnetic inserts. Discard the original sealing washers; they should be renewed whenever they are disturbed.

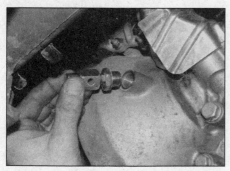

2.4 Removing the filler/level plug on the ML5T transmission

2.5a Unscrewing the drain plug situated on the final drive casing on the BE3 transmission

2.5b Drain plug on the ML5T transmission

7 When the oil has finished draining, clean the drain plug threads and those of the transmission casing, fit a new sealing washer and refit the drain plug, tightening it to the specified torque wrench setting.

8 Refilling the transmission is an extremely awkward operation. Above all, allow plenty of time for the oil level to settle properly before checking it. Note that the car must be level when checking the oil level.

9 Refill the transmission with the exact amount of the specified type of oil **(see illustration)** then check the oil level as described in the relevant Part of Chapter 1; if the correct amount was poured into the transmission and a large amount flows out on checking the level, refit the filler/level plug and take the car on a short journey so that the new oil is distributed fully around the transmission components, then check the level again on your return.

10 When the level is correct, fit a new sealing washer to the filler/level plug. Tighten the plug to the specified torque wrench setting. Wash off any spilt oil. Where necessary, refit the wheelarch liner and splash guard, and secure with the retaining screws and clips. Refit the roadwheel where removed then lower the car to the ground.

2.6 Draining the transmission oil

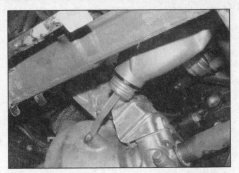

2.9 Refilling the transmission with oil (view from under the vehicle)

the transmission **(see illustration)**. Disengage the selector rod from the bellcrank pivot, and remove it from underneath the vehicle.

6 Carefully prise the plastic cap off the bolt securing the gearchange linkage bellcrank to the subframe.

7 Slacken and remove the bellcrank pivot bolt and washer, then manoeuvre the bellcrank and link rod out from under the vehicle, and recover the spacer and pivot bushes from the centre of the bellcrank.

8 Inspect all the linkage components for signs of wear or damage, paying particular attention to the pivot bushes and link rod balljoints, and renew worn components as necessary. If necessary, the gearchange lever can be removed and inspected as follows.

9 Slacken and remove the selector lever retaining nuts and lift off the retaining plate then lower the lever out from underneath the vehicle.

10 Peel back the lower gaiter from the base of the gearchange lever, then disengage the lever mounting plate, and slide the upper gaiter up the lever to gain access to the gearchange lever pivot ball. Examine the lever components for signs of wear or damage, paying particular attention to the rubber gaiters, and renew components as necessary. The lever can be separated from its baseplate after the retaining ring has been unclipped.

3 Gearchange linkage (BE3/5 transmission) – removal and refitting

Removal

1 Remove the centre console (Chapter 11).

2 Chock the rear wheels, then jack up the front of the vehicle and support it on axle stands.

3 Refer to Chapter 4A and remove the air inlet ducts, exhaust system and heat shields, as necessary for access to the gearchange linkage.

4 Slacken and remove the nut, and withdraw the pivot bolt securing the selector rod to the base of the gearchange lever.

5 Using a flat-bladed screwdriver, carefully lever the three link rods off their balljoints on

Refitting

11 Refitting is a reversal of the removal procedure, noting the following points:

a) *Apply a smear of molybdenum disulphide grease to the gearchange lever pivot ball, the link rod balljoints and the bellcrank ball and pivot bushes.*

b) *Ensure that the gearchange lever rubber gaiters are correctly seated before refitting the lever assembly to the vehicle.*

c) *Ensure that the link rods are securely pressed onto their balljoints.*

d) *Refit the heat shields and exhaust components (Chapter 4A) and the centre console (Chapter 11).*

4 Gearchange cables (BE4/5 and ML5T transmissions) – removal and refitting

Removal

1 Remove the air cleaner assembly and air inlet ducts as described in the relevant Part of Chapter 4.

2 Remove the centre console (see Chapter 11).

3 Working in the engine compartment, carefully prise the two gearchange cable balljoints from the selector levers on the transmission **(see illustration)**.

3.5 Disconnect the three gearchange linkage link rods (arrowed) from their transmission balljoints

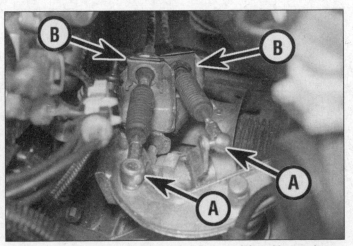

4.3 Gearchange cable balljoint attachments (A) and horseshoe-shaped clips (B) securing the cables to the mounting bracket

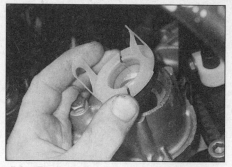

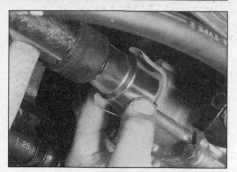

5.8 Use a large flat-bladed screwdriver to prise the driveshaft oil seals out of position

5.9a Fit the new seal to the transmission, noting the plastic seal protector . . .

5.9b . . . and tap it into position using a tubular drift

4 Extract the two horseshoe-shaped clips securing the cables to the mounting bracket on the transmission.

5 Apply the handbrake, then jack up the front of the vehicle and support it on axle stands (see *Jacking and vehicle support*).

6 Refer to the relevant Part of Chapter 4 and remove the exhaust system and heat shields, as necessary for access to the cables and gearchange lever housing.

7 From inside the car, remove the sound-proofing shim then unscrew the bolts securing the lever housing to the floor. Release any clips or ties securing the gearchange cables, then remove the lever housing and gearchange cables as an assembly from under the car.

Refitting

8 Refitting is a reversal of the removal procedure, noting the following points:
a) *Ensure that the sound-proofing shim is correctly positioned when refitting the lever housing.*
b) *Ensure that the cables are fitted to the correct selector levers on the transmission – the 13.0 mm diameter balljoint connects to the upper lever and the 10.0 mm diameter balljoint connects to the side lever.*
c) *Refit the heat shields, exhaust components and air cleaner assembly, and the centre console.*

5 Oil seals – renewal

Driveshaft oil seals

Note: *A new suspension lower balljoint nut will be required on refitting.*
1 Apply the handbrake, then jack up the front of the vehicle and support it on axle stands (see *Jacking and vehicle support*). Remove the appropriate front roadwheel, and remove the splash guard from under the engine.
2 Drain the transmission oil as described in Section 2.
3 On models with ABS, remove the wheel sensor as described in Chapter 9, Section 24.
4 Slacken and remove the nut securing the front suspension lower balljoint to the swivel

hub, and free the balljoint from the lower arm (see Chapter 10). Discard the nut and remove the protector plate (if loose).

Right-hand seal

5 Loosen the two intermediate bearing retaining bolt nuts, then rotate the bolts through 90° so that their offset heads are clear of the bearing outer race.
6 Carefully pull the swivel hub assembly outwards, and pull on the inner end of the driveshaft to free the intermediate bearing from its mounting bracket.
7 Once the driveshaft end is free from the transmission, slide the dust seal off the inner end of the shaft, noting which way around it is fitted, and support the inner end of the driveshaft to avoid damaging the constant velocity joints or gaiters.
8 Carefully prise the oil seal out of the transmission, using a large flat-bladed screwdriver **(see illustration)**.
9 Remove all traces of dirt from the area around the oil seal aperture, then fill the space between the lips of the new oil seal with grease. Fit the new seal into its aperture, and drive it squarely into position using a suitable tubular drift (such as a socket) which bears only on the hard outer edge of the seal, until it abuts its locating shoulder. If the seal was supplied with a plastic protector sleeve, leave this in position until the driveshaft has been refitted **(see illustrations)**.
10 Thoroughly clean the driveshaft splines, then apply a thin film of grease to the oil seal lips and to the driveshaft inner end splines.

5.19 The left-hand oil seal is beneath the differential bearing stop plate on the ML5T transmission

11 Slide the dust seal into position on the end of the shaft, ensuring that its flat surface is facing the transmission.
12 Carefully locate the inner driveshaft splines with those of the differential sun gear, taking care not to damage the oil seal, then align the intermediate bearing with its mounting bracket, and push the driveshaft fully into position. If necessary, use a soft-faced mallet to tap the outer race of the bearing into position in the mounting bracket.
13 Ensure that the intermediate bearing is correctly seated, then rotate its retaining bolts back through 90° so that their offset heads are resting against the bearing outer race, and tighten the retaining nuts to the specified torque. Remove the plastic seal protector (where supplied), and slide the dust seal tight up against the oil seal.
14 Refit the protector plate (where removed) to the lower balljoint, then align the balljoint with the lower arm. Fit the new balljoint nut and tighten it to the specified torque setting (see Chapter 10).
15 Where necessary, refit the ABS wheel sensor as described in Chapter 9, Section 24.
16 Refit the roadwheel and the engine splash guard, then lower the vehicle to the ground and tighten the roadwheel bolts to the specified torque.
17 Refill the transmission with the specified type and amount of oil, and check the level using the information given in the relevant Part of Chapter 1.

Left-hand seal

18 Pull the swivel hub assembly outwards and withdraw the driveshaft inner constant velocity joint from the transmission, taking care not to damage the driveshaft oil seal. Support the driveshaft, to avoid damaging the constant velocity joints or gaiters.
19 On BE3 and BE4 transmissions, renew the oil seal as described in paragraphs 8 to 10. On ML5T transmissions, unbolt the differential bearing stop plate **(see illustration)**, and prise or drift the oil seal out of the stop plate. Also remove the sealing O-ring. Thoroughly clean the stop plate, then fill the space between the lips of the new oil seal with grease. Fit the new seal into its aperture, and drive it squarely into position using a suitable tubular drift (such as a socket) which bears only on the hard outer

5.23a Clutch release bearing guide sleeve retaining bolts (arrowed) on the BE3 transmission . . .

5.23b . . . and on the ML5T transmission (arrowed)

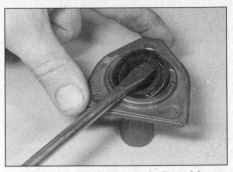

5.24 Removing the input shaft seal from the guide sleeve

edge of the seal, until it is fully seated. Locate a new O-ring in position then refit the stop plate to the transmission.

20 Carefully locate the inner constant velocity joint splines with those of the differential sun gear, taking care not to damage the oil seal, and push the driveshaft fully into position. Where fitted, remove the plastic protector from the oil seal.

21 Carry out the operations described above in paragraphs 14 to 17.

Input shaft oil seal

22 Remove the transmission as described in Section 8 or 9 as applicable.

23 Undo the bolts securing the clutch release bearing guide sleeve in position, and slide the guide off the input shaft, along with its O-ring or gasket **(see illustrations)**. Recover any shims or thrust washers which have stuck to the rear of the guide sleeve, and refit them to the input shaft.

24 Carefully lever the oil seal out of the guide using a suitable flat-bladed screwdriver **(see illustration)**.

25 Before fitting a new seal, check the input shaft's seal rubbing surface for signs of burrs, scratches or other damage, which may have caused the seal to fail in the first place. It may be possible to polish away minor faults of this sort using fine abrasive paper; however, more serious defects will require the renewal of the input shaft. Ensure the input shaft is clean and greased, to protect the seal lips on refitting.

26 Dip the new seal in clean oil, and fit it to the guide sleeve.

27 Fit a new O-ring or gasket (as applicable) to the rear of the guide sleeve, then carefully slide the sleeve into position over the input shaft **(see illustration)**. Refit the retaining bolts and tighten them to the specified torque.

28 Take the opportunity to inspect the clutch components if not already done (Chapter 6). Finally, refit the transmission (Section 8 or 9).

Selector shaft oil seal

BE3 and BE4 transmissions

29 Park the car on level ground and chock the rear wheels. Apply the handbrake and jack up the front of the vehicle and support it on axle stands (see *Jacking and vehicle support*). Remove the left-hand front roadwheel, then release the screws and clips and remove the wheelarch liner from under the wing.

30 Using a large flat-bladed screwdriver, lever the gearchange balljoint off the transmission selector shaft.

31 Carefully prise the selector shaft seal out of the housing, and slide it off the end of the shaft **(see illustrations)**.

32 Before fitting a new seal, check the selector shaft's seal rubbing surface for signs of burrs, scratches or other damage, which may have caused the seal to fail in the first place. It may be possible to polish away minor faults of this sort using fine abrasive paper; however, more serious defects will require the renewal of the selector shaft.

33 Apply a smear of grease to the new seal's outer edge and sealing lip, then carefully slide the seal along the selector rod. Press the seal fully into position in the transmission housing.

34 Reconnect the gearchange to the selector shaft, ensuring that its balljoint is pressed firmly onto the shaft.

35 Refit the wheelarch liner and secure it in position with its retaining screws and clips. Refit the roadwheel then lower the car to the ground.

6 Reversing light switch – testing, removal and refitting

Testing

1 The reversing light circuit is controlled by a plunger-type switch that is screwed into the top of the transmission casing. If a fault develops in the circuit, first ensure that the circuit fuse has not blown.

2 To test the switch, remove the air cleaner components as required for access (see the relevant Part of Chapter 4) then disconnect the wiring connector, and use a multimeter (set to the resistance function) or a battery-and-bulb test circuit to check that there is continuity between the switch terminals only when reverse gear is selected. If this is not the case, and there are no obvious breaks or other damage to the wires, the switch is faulty, and must be renewed.

5.27 Fit a new O-ring/gasket (as applicable) to the guide sleeve

5.31a On the BE3 transmission, use a screwdriver to prise the selector shaft seal out of position . . .

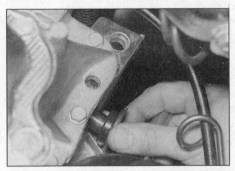

5.31b . . . then slide the seal off the shaft

Removal

3 Remove the air cleaner components as described in the relevant Part of Chapter 4.

4 Disconnect the wiring connector, then unscrew it from the transmission casing along with its sealing washer (**see illustrations**).

Refitting

5 Fit a new sealing washer to the switch, then screw it back into position in the top of the transmission housing and tighten it to the specified torque setting. Reconnect the wiring connector, and test the operation of the circuit. Refit any components removed for access.

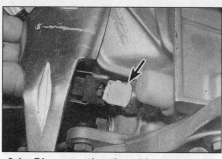

6.4a Disconnecting the wiring connector from the reversing light switch on the BE3 transmission . . .

6.4b . . . and on the ML5T transmission

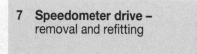

7 Speedometer drive – removal and refitting

Note: The following description is for BE3 and BE4 gearboxes. On the ML5T transmission, major dismantling is necessary which must be entrusted to a dealer.

Removal

1 Chock the rear wheels, then jack up the front of the car and support it on axle stands. Remove the splash guard from under the engine. The speedometer drive is situated on the rear of the transmission housing, next to the inner end of the right-hand driveshaft. All models covered by this Manual are fitted with a transducer unit (**see illustration**).

2 Disconnect the wiring from the transducer.

3 Slacken and remove the retaining bolt, along with the heat shield (where fitted), and withdraw the speedometer drive and driven pinion assembly from the transmission housing, along with its O-ring (**see illustrations**).

4 If necessary, the pinion can be slid out of the housing, and the oil seal can be removed from the top of the housing. Examine the pinion for signs of damage, and renew if necessary. Renew the housing O-ring as a matter of course.

5 If the driven pinion is worn or damaged, also examine the drive pinion in the transmission housing for similar signs. The drive pinion can be renewed as described below.

6 To remove the drive pinion, first disengage the right-hand driveshaft from the transmission, as described in paragraphs 1 to 7 of Section 5. Undo the three retaining bolts, and remove the speedometer drive housing from

the transmission, along with its O-ring. Remove the drive pinion from the differential gear, and recover any adjustment shims from the gear (**see illustrations**).

Refitting

7 Refit the adjustment shims to the differential gear, then locate the speedometer drive on the gear, ensuring it is correctly engaged in the gear slots (**see illustration**). Fit a new O-ring to the rear of the speedometer drive housing, then refit the housing to the transmission and securely tighten its retaining bolts. Inspect the driveshaft oil seal for signs of wear, and renew if necessary. Refit the driveshaft to the transmission, using the information given in Section 5.

8 Apply a smear of grease to the lips of the seal and to the driven pinion shaft, and slide the pinion into position in the speedometer drive.

7.1 Speedometer transducer unit as fitted to the ML5T transmission

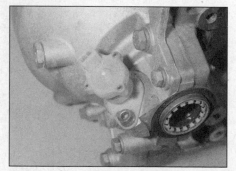

7.3a Slacken and remove the retaining bolt . . .

7.3b . . . then withdraw the speedometer drive from the transmission (transmission removed for clarity)

7.6a Undo the three retaining bolts . . .

7.6b . . . and remove the housing, O-ring and drive pinion from the transmission (transmission removed for clarity)

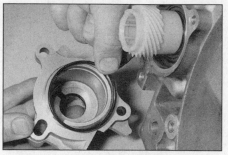

7.7 Ensure the drive pinion dogs are correctly engaged with the gear slots (arrowed)

9 Fit a new O-ring to the speedometer drive and refit it to the transmission, ensuring that the drive and driven pinions are correctly engaged.

10 Refit the retaining bolt and the heat shield (where fitted), and tighten the bolt.

11 Reconnect the wiring to the transducer.

12 Refit the splash guard under the engine then lower the vehicle to the ground.

8 Manual transmission (BE3/5 and BE4/5) – removal and refitting

Removal

1 Disconnect the battery negative lead (refer to *Disconnecting the battery* at the end of this manual).

2 Apply the handbrake, then jack up the front of the vehicle and support it on axle stands (see *Jacking and vehicle support*). Remove both front roadwheels, then release the screws and clips and remove the wheelarch liner from under the left-hand wing. Remove the splash guard from under the engine.

3 Drain the transmission oil as described in Section 2, then refit the drain and filler plugs, and tighten them to their specified torque settings.

4 Remove the air cleaner assembly and intake ducting (see Chapter 4A or 4B, as applicable).

5 Remove both driveshafts as described in Chapter 8.

6 From under the car, undo the bolts securing the engine movement limiter/link to the right-hand driveshaft intermediate bearing housing, and subframe. Manipulate the movement limiter from its location **(see illustration)**.

7 Disconnect the wiring from the transmission including the reversing light switch, speedometer transducer, engine speed sensor and earth wiring.

8 Unbolt and remove the clutch slave cylinder and support to one side without disconnecting the hydraulic line.

9 Remove the cable guide, bracket and the RPM/TDC sensor.

10 Undo the starter motor mounting bolts and move the starter clear without disconnecting the wiring.

11 On the BE3 transmission, using a flat-bladed screwdriver, carefully lever the three gearchange mechanism link rods off their respective balljoints on the transmission. On the BE4 transmission, lever the two gearchange cable sockets from their balljoints and unbolt the retaining brackets. Position the rods/cables clear of the transmission.

12 Remove the exhaust system with reference to the relevant Part of Chapter 4. This is necessary to avoid damage to the flexible section of the exhaust.

13 Unscrew the retaining bolt, along with the heat shield (where fitted), and withdraw the speedometer drive and driven pinion

8.6 Engine movement limiter attachments to the intermediate bearing housing and subframe

assembly from the transmission housing, along with its O-ring. Undo the three retaining bolts, and remove the speedometer drive housing from the transmission, along with its O-ring. Remove the drive pinion from the differential gear, and recover any adjustment shims from the gear.

14 Unscrew the nut and remove the gearbox cover plate.

15 Attach a hoist or support bar to the engine left-hand lifting eye and just take the engine weight.

16 Place a jack and block of wood beneath the transmission, and raise the jack to take the weight of the transmission.

17 Slacken and remove the centre nut and washer from the left-hand engine/transmission mounting **(see illustration)**. Undo the two bolts and remove the rubber mounting from the mounting bracket and transmission mounting stud. If the mounting stud is screwed into a separate bracket bolted to the transmission, undo the bolts and remove the transmission bracket. If the mounting stud is screwed directly into the transmission, slide off the spacer and unscrew the stud. If it is tight, use a universal stud extractor to unscrew it.

18 Unscrew the retaining bolts and remove the flywheel lower cover plate (where fitted) from the transmission.

19 Unscrew and remove the transmission mounting bolt located on the rear of the cylinder block.

20 With the jack positioned beneath the transmission taking the weight, slacken and

8.17 Engine/transmission left-hand mounting details

remove the remaining bolts securing the transmission housing to the engine. Note the correct fitted positions of each bolt, and the necessary brackets, as they are removed, to use as a reference on refitting. Make a final check that all components have been disconnected, and are positioned clear of the transmission so that they will not hinder the removal procedure.

21 With the bolts removed, lower the engine and move the trolley jack and transmission to the left, to free it from its locating dowels. Once the transmission is free, lower the jack and manoeuvre the unit out from under the car. Remove the locating dowels from the transmission or engine if they are loose, and keep them in a safe place.

Refitting

22 The transmission is refitted by a reversal of the removal procedure, bearing in mind the following points:

a) *Check the clutch release bearing and fork with reference to Chapter 6.*

b) *Renew the driveshaft oil seals, as described in Section 5, prior to refitting the transmission.*

c) *Ensure that the locating dowels are correctly positioned prior to installation.*

d) *Apply thread-locking fluid to the left-hand engine/transmission mounting stud and mounting bolt threads, prior to refitting. Tighten the stud/bolts to the specified torque.*

e) *Tighten all nuts and bolts to the specified torque (where given).*

f) *Refit the driveshafts as described in Chapter 8.*

g) *On completion, refill the transmission with the specified type and quantity of lubricant, as described in the relevant Part of Chapter 1.*

9 Manual transmission (ML5T) – removal and refitting

Note: *Peugeot special tool 0216K will be required for the refitting procedure, although details of a suitable home-made alternative are given. Read through the entire procedure before starting and make sure that either the Peugeot tool or the alternative described, are available before proceeding.*

Removal

1 Disconnect the battery negative lead (refer to *Disconnecting the battery* at the end of this manual).

2 Apply the handbrake, then jack up the front of the vehicle and support it on axle stands (see *Jacking and vehicle support*). Remove both front roadwheels, then release the screws and clips and remove the wheelarch liner from under the left-hand wing **(see illustration)**. Remove the splash guard from under the engine.

9.2 Removing the left-hand front wheelarch liner

9.5 Removing the intercooler air duct

9.6 Removing the exhaust clamp from the manifold

9.7a Unbolt the power steering pipe bracket bolts under the transmission (arrowed) . . .

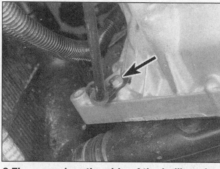

9.7b . . . and on the side of the bellhousing (arrowed)

9.8a Removing the rear cover plate . . .

9.8b . . . and front cover plate from the bellhousing

9.12 Disconnecting the gearchange cable balljoints from the selector levers

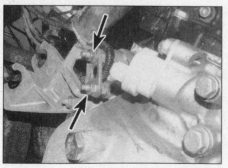

9.13 Gearchange cable support bracket mounting nuts

9.14a Disconnect the engine earth cable . . .

3 Drain the transmission oil as described in Section 2, then refit the drain and filler plugs, and tighten them to their specified torque settings.

4 Remove the air cleaner assembly and intake ducting as described in Chapter 4B.

5 Loosen the clips and remove the intercooler air duct from under the engine (see illustration).

6 Unbolt the clamp and disconnect the exhaust downpipe from the exhaust manifold (see illustration). Alternatively, remove the complete exhaust system with reference to Chapter 4B. If the exhaust system is left in position, make sure that the flexible section is not damaged during the removal procedure.

7 Unbolt the power steering hydraulic fluid pipe from under the transmission (see illustrations).

8 Unscrew the retaining bolts and remove the flywheel lower cover plates from the transmission (see illustrations).

9 Remove the engine top cover.

10 Remove the turbocharger air intake pipe from its location between the engine sump and transmission bellhousing.

11 Unbolt the accelerator pedal sensor and bracket with reference to Chapter 4B, Section 13, and move it to one side.

12 Carefully prise the two gearchange cable balljoints from the selector levers on the transmission (see illustration).

13 Extract the two horseshoe-shaped clips securing the cables to the mounting bracket on the transmission, then tie the cables to one side. Unscrew the nuts and remove the cable support bracket from the transmission (see illustration).

14 Disconnect the wiring from the transmission including the reversing light switch, speedometer transducer and earth wiring. Note that the speedometer transducer is protected by a cover clipped into position. Unbolt and remove the TDC sensor from the top of the transmission bellhousing. Release the wiring harness from the bracket (see illustrations).

9.14b . . . and reversing light switch lead . . .

9.14c . . . then remove the cover . . .

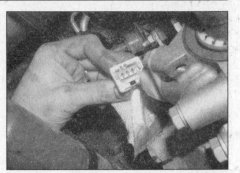

9.14d . . . disconnect the wiring from the speedometer transducer . . .

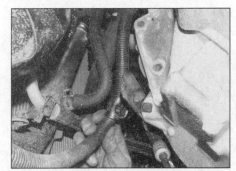

9.14e . . . and release the wiring harness from the bracket

9.16 Releasing the slave cylinder hydraulic pipe from the support over the transmission

9.17a Withdraw the clutch slave cylinder from the transmission . . .

15 Remove the filler cap from the brake hydraulic fluid reservoir, and draw out sufficient fluid to lower the fluid level below the clutch master cylinder supply outlet. Alternatively, fit a hose clamp to the clutch hydraulic fluid supply hose.

16 Position a suitable container beneath the clutch slave cylinder to accept spilt fluid, then release the clip and disconnect the hydraulic pipe. Also release the pipe from the support over the transmission **(see illustration)**.

17 Release the clutch slave cylinder from the transmission by pushing it in by hand and at the same time turning it 90° anti-clockwise. Withdraw the slave cylinder, together with its pushrod from the transmission. With the slave cylinder removed, retain the pushrod in place using a cable tie and suitable slotted tube or a similar arrangement **(see illustrations)**. **Do not** depress the clutch pedal with the slave cylinder removed or the push rod will be ejected. It is advisable to place a block of wood under the clutch pedal to prevent it being accidentally depressed.

18 Undo the starter motor mounting bolts and move the starter clear without disconnecting the wiring. Note that one of the bolts secures an earth wire **(see illustration)**.

19 Undo the bolts securing the engine movement limiter to the right-hand driveshaft intermediate bearing housing, and subframe. Manipulate the movement limiter from its location **(see illustration)**.

20 Remove the front suspension subframe as described in Chapter 10, and noting the location of spacers **(see illustrations)**. If the

exhaust system is still in position, support the front end on a block of wood or axle stand.

21 Remove both driveshafts as described in Chapter 8 **(see illustrations)**.

22 Attach a hoist or support bar to the engine

9.17b . . . and retain the pushrod using a cable tie and suitable slotted tube arrangement

9.19 Removing the movement limiter bolts

left-hand lifting eye and just take the engine weight **(see illustration)**.

23 Unscrew the retaining bolts and remove the flywheel lower cover plate (where fitted) from the transmission.

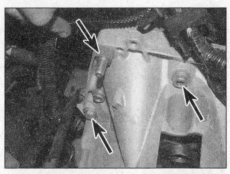

9.18 The starter motor retaining bolts

9.20a Remove the mounting bolts . . .

9.20b . . . and lower the front suspension subframe from the underbody

9.21a Unscrew the driveshaft nut . . .

9.21b . . . then detach the steering track rod end . . .

9.21c . . . anti-roll bar link . . .

9.21d . . . separate the lower balljoint . . .

9.21e . . . and remove the left-hand driveshaft

24 Place a jack and block of wood beneath the transmission, and raise the jack to take the weight of the transmission. Move the transmission slightly towards the radiator.

25 Slacken and remove the centre nut and washer from the left-hand engine/transmission mounting. Undo the bolts and remove the rubber mounting from the mounting bracket and transmission mounting stud. Undo the bolts and remove the transmission support bracket. On diesel models, access to the left-hand mounting is improved by unbolting the accelerator cable sensor bracket and moving it to one side (see **illustrations**).

9.21f To remove the right-hand driveshaft, remove the intermediate shaft bearing nuts and bolts . . .

9.21g . . . and withdraw the driveshaft from the transmission

9.22 Using a support bar across the engine compartment

9.25a Remove the accelerator cable sensor and bracket for access to the left-hand engine mounting

9.25b Undo the left-hand mounting centre nut then undo the bolts . . .

9.25c . . . and remove the mounting . . .

9.25d . . . followed by the sleeve . . .

9.25e . . . and the mounting bracket

9.25f Removing the mounting bracket –
DW12 engine

9.27 Removing the transmission from the
engine

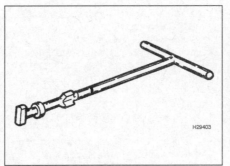

9.29 Peugeot tool for securing the release
bearing to the clutch pressure plate

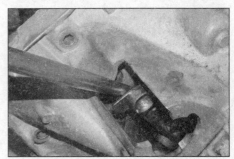

9.30 Using a screwdriver to lever the
release fork and engage the release
bearing with the pressure plate

26 With the jack positioned beneath the transmission taking the weight, slacken and remove the bolts securing the transmission housing to the engine. Note the correct fitted positions of each bolt, and the necessary brackets, as they are removed, to use as a reference on refitting. Make a final check that all components have been disconnected, and are positioned clear of the transmission so that they will not hinder the removal procedure.

27 With the bolts removed, lower the engine and move the trolley jack and transmission to the left, to free it from its locating dowels (see illustration). Once the transmission is free, lower the jack and manoeuvre the unit out from under the car. Remove the locating dowels from the transmission or engine if they are loose, and keep them in a safe place.

Preparation for refitting

28 The design of the clutch release bearing and clutch release fork is unusual on this type of transmission in that it is necessary to remove the 'pull-type' release bearing from the clutch pressure plate, and reposition it on the transmission, before the transmission is re-attached to the engine. With the transmission refitted, the release bearing is then secured back on the pressure plate by means of a special tool. If the following procedure is not followed exactly, it will be impossible to operate the clutch on completion.

29 The Peugeot special tool (0216K) for securing the release bearing in place, consists

of a T-shaped rod with a rectangular end (see illustration). The rod is inserted through the slave cylinder aperture in the transmission bellhousing so that the rectangular end engages through the slot in the clutch release fork. When the tool is turned through 90° the rectangular end locks in the release fork slot. Pulling the tool sharply rearwards pivots the release fork and forces the release bearing hard against the pressure plate, causing a snap-ring on the bearing to lock into the pressure plate.

30 Before proceeding, either obtain the Peugeot special tool, or fabricate an

alternative on the same pattern that will operate as described above. Note, however, on later models, a cut-out (with plastic cover) is provided in the clutch bellhousing, and it is possible to lever the release fork with a screwdriver (see illustration).

31 Begin by removing the clutch assembly as described in Chapter 6.

32 Using a screwdriver, carefully remove the release bearing retaining snap-ring from the inside of the pressure plate diaphragm spring (see illustration). The snap-ring may not be immediately visible, in which case it will be necessary to press down on the pressure plate to push out the inner end of the release bearing. Take care not to deform the snap-ring as it is removed.

33 Remove the release bearing from the pressure plate, then refit the snap-ring back into the groove in the release bearing boss (see illustration).

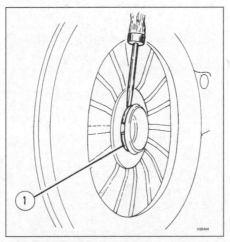

9.32 Remove the release bearing retaining
snap-ring (1) from the inside of the
pressure plate diaphragm spring . . .

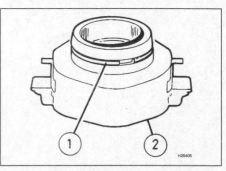

9.33 . . . then refit the snap-ring (1) back
into the release bearing (2)

9.35a Lightly lubricate the input shaft splines with high melting point grease . . .

9.35b . . . and engage the release bearing with the fork

9.38 Refitting the transmission to the engine

34 Refit the clutch assembly (see Chapter 6).

35 Lightly lubricate the transmission input shaft splines and guide tube with high-melting point grease, and slide the release bearing onto the guide tube on the transmission input shaft, while at the same time engaging the release fork between the contact lugs on the release bearing **(see illustrations)**. Check that the release fork and bearing operate smoothly and that the fork ends are correctly engaged between the bearing lugs.

36 Using the Peugeot tool or the home-made alternative, check that the tool will enter the release fork slot, and lock when turned through 90° enabling the fork to be pulled away from the bellhousing end of the transmission by means of the tool. If all is satisfactory, remove the tool.

37 Renew the driveshaft oil seals as described in Section 5 before refitting the transmission. The transmission can now be refitted.

Refitting

38 The transmission is refitted by a reversal of the removal procedure **(see illustration)**, bearing in mind the following points:

a) *Ensure the release bearing is in position on the transmission as previously described.*

b) *Ensure that the locating dowels are correctly positioned prior to installation.*

c) *Once the transmission is bolted to the engine, engage the Peugeot tool, or the home-made alternative as described previously, and pull on the tool so that the release bearing snap-ring engages with the clutch pressure plate. Check for*

correct engagement by attempting to push the release fork back towards the engine with a screwdriver; there should be slight play but no appreciable travel.

d) *Refit the front suspension subframe as described in Chapter 10.*

e) *Tighten all nuts and bolts to the specified torque (where given).*

f) *When refitting the clutch slave cylinder, remove the tie used to retain the pushrod, and lubricate the pushrod end with molybdenum disulphide grease. Locate the slave cylinder in the transmission, push it in by hand, and at the same time turn it 90° clockwise to secure. With the cylinder installed, slowly depress the clutch pedal to the floor, then slowly lift it again by hand. Wait for ten seconds and repeat this procedure. Depress the pedal again, release it and check that it rises correctly after being released.*

g) *Ensure that the gearchange cables are fitted to the correct selector levers on the transmission – the 13.0 mm diameter balljoint connects to the upper lever and the 10.0 mm diameter balljoint connects to the side lever.*

h) *On completion, refill the transmission with the specified type and quantity of lubricant, as described in Chapter 1B.*

10 Manual transmission overhaul – general information

Overhauling a manual transmission is a

difficult and involved job for the DIY home mechanic. In addition to dismantling and reassembling many small parts, clearances must be precisely measured and, if necessary, changed by selecting shims and spacers. Internal transmission components are also often difficult to obtain, and in many instances, extremely expensive. Because of this, if the transmission develops a fault or becomes noisy, the best course of action is to have the unit overhauled by a specialist repairer, or to obtain an exchange reconditioned unit.

Nevertheless, it is not impossible for the more experienced mechanic to overhaul the transmission, provided the special tools are available, and the job is done in a deliberate step-by-step manner, so nothing is overlooked.

The tools necessary for an overhaul include internal and external circlip pliers, bearing pullers, a slide hammer, a set of pin punches, a dial test indicator, and possibly a hydraulic press. In addition, a large, sturdy workbench and a vice will be required.

During dismantling of the transmission, make careful notes of how each component is fitted, to make reassembly easier and more accurate.

Before dismantling the transmission, it will help if you have some idea what area is malfunctioning. Certain problems can be closely related to specific areas in the transmission, which can make component examination and replacement easier. Refer to the *Fault finding* Section at the rear of this manual for more information.

Chapter 7 Part B:
Automatic transmission

Contents

Automatic transmission – removal and refitting	10
Automatic transmission fluid – draining and refilling	2
Automatic transmission fluid level check	See Chapter 1A
Automatic transmission overhaul – general information	11
Electronic control unit (ECU) – removal and refitting	8
Electronic system components (AL4) – removal and refitting	9
Fluid cooler – removal and refitting	6
General information	1
Multi-function switch (4HP20) – removal and refitting	7
Oil seals – renewal	4
Selector cable – removal and refitting	3
Speedometer drive – removal and refitting	5

Degrees of difficulty

Easy, suitable for novice with little experience	**Fairly easy,** suitable for beginner with some experience	**Fairly difficult,** suitable for competent DIY mechanic	**Difficult,** suitable for experienced DIY mechanic	**Very difficult,** suitable for expert DIY or professional

Specifications

General
Type	Automatic, four forward speeds and reverse
Codes	4HP20 and AL4

Lubrication
Recommended fluid	Refer to *Lubricants and fluids*
Capacity (approximate):	
4HP20:	
Drain and refill	3.0 litres
Total capacity (including torque converter)	8.0 litres
AL4:	
Drain and refill	4.5 litres
Total capacity (including torque converter)	6.0 litres

Torque wrench settings

	Nm	lbf ft
4HP20 transmission		
Engine movement limiter to driveshaft intermediate bearing housing	50	37
Engine movement limiter to subframe	85	63
Engine-to-transmission securing bolts	60	44
Fluid cooler mounting bolts	40	30
Left-hand engine/transmission mounting:		
Centre nut	65	48
Mounting stud	50	37
Multi-function switch retaining bolts	10	7
Selector lever to multi-function switch shaft	21	15
Torque converter-to-driveplate bolts	30	22
AL4 transmission		
Engine/transmission left-hand mounting:		
Mounting stud to transmission	50	37
Rubber mounting centre nut	65	48
Rubber mounting-to-body bolts	27	20
Engine-to-transmission securing bolts	52	38
Fluid cooler centre bolt	50	37
Input speed sensor	10	7
Oil drain plug	33	24
Oil filler and level plugs	24	18
Output speed sensor	10	7
Selector lever position switch bolts	15	11
Torque converter-to-driveplate bolts:		
Stage 1	10	7
Stage 2	30	22
Transmission selector shaft lever clamp bolt and nut	15	11

1 General information

4HP20 transmission

Certain models are fitted with the 4HP20 computer-controlled four-speed fully-automatic transmission, consisting of a torque converter, an epicyclic geartrain, and hydraulically-operated clutches and brakes.

The unit is controlled by an electronic control unit (ECU) which receives signal inputs from various sensors relating to transmission operating conditions. Information on engine parameters are also sent to the ECU from the engine management system. From this data, the ECU can establish the optimum gear shifting speeds according to the driving mode selected.

Drive is taken from the engine to the transmission by a torque converter. The torque converter provides a fluid coupling between the engine and transmission, and acts as an automatic clutch, also providing a degree of torque multiplication when accelerating.

The epicyclic geartrain provides either of the four forward or one reverse gear ratios, according to which of its component parts are held stationary or allowed to turn. The components of the geartrain are held or released by brakes and clutches which are activated by a hydraulic control unit. A fluid pump within the transmission provides the necessary hydraulic pressure to operate the brakes and clutches.

Driver control of the transmission is by a seven-position selector lever. The transmission has a 'drive' position, and a 'hold' facility on the first three gear ratios. The 'drive' position D provides automatic changing throughout the range of all four gear ratios, and is the one to select for normal driving. An automatic kickdown facility shifts the transmission down a gear if the accelerator pedal is fully depressed. This is useful when extra acceleration is required. Kickdown, like the other transmission functions, is controlled by the ECU. The 'hold' facility is very similar, but limits the number of gear ratios available – ie, when the selector lever is in the 3 position, only the first three ratios can be selected; in the 2 position, only the first two can be selected, and so on. The lower ratio 'hold' is useful for providing engine braking when travelling down steep gradients, or for preventing unwanted selection of top gear on twisty roads. Additionally, three driving programs, controlled by a switch to the left of the selector lever, provides additional driver control of the transmission according to road conditions. In Normal mode the transmission adopts conventional automatic operation. In Sport mode, priority is given to engine performance and gearchanges occur at higher engine rpm. In Snow mode, the vehicle starts in the second gear ratio when D is selected. In positions 1, 2 and 3, the gears are selected manually and the kickdown facility is inhibited.

AL4 transmission

The AL4 transmission, available on cars with EW7 (6FZ) and EW10 (RFN) petrol engines as well as the HDi 110 diesel engine model, incorporates electronic control; the automatic gearchanges are electronically-controlled, rather than hydraulically. The advantage of electronic management is to provide a faster gearchange response. A kickdown facility is also provided, to enable a faster acceleration response when required.

The torque converter incorporates an automatic lock-up feature which eliminates any possibility of converter slip in the top two gears; this aids performance and economy. In addition to the normal alternative of manual change, the three-position mode switch on the centre console (adjacent to the selector lever) provides Normal, Sport or Snow settings, as required. In Sport mode, upshifts are delayed longer, to make full use of engine power. In Snow mode, either 2nd or 3rd gear is used to pull away from rest, maximising traction in slippery conditions.

Another feature of this transmission is the Park Lock, which is partly a safety, and partly a security, feature. Moving the lever out of the P position requires the ignition to be on, and the brake pedal must also be depressed.

The gear selector cable has an automatic adjuster mechanism, meaning that cable adjustment should not be required. The AL4 transmission is also regarded as being 'lubricated for life', with routine fluid changes not featuring in the manufacturer's maintenance schedule.

In the event of a problem developing with the transmission, the transmission ECU may select one of two emergency back-up modes, to enable the car to continue being driven. When operating in this back-up mode, shifting out of N or R will become more jerky, or the transmission will only select 3rd gear (no gearchanges). If a fault is suspected, your Peugeot dealer will be able to download fault codes from the transmission ECU memory, to speed-up diagnosis.

All transmission types

Due to the complexity of the automatic transmission, any repair or overhaul work must be left to a Peugeot dealer with the necessary special equipment for fault diagnosis and repair. The contents of the following Sections are therefore confined to supplying general information, and any service information and instructions that can be used by the owner.

2 Automatic transmission fluid – draining and refilling

Note: *Transmission fluid renewal on the AL4 transmission is not a service requirement and the following operations will normally only be necessary to allow transmission repair work to be carried out.*

1 Take the vehicle on a short run, to warm the transmission up to normal operating temperature.

2 Park the vehicle on level ground, switch off the ignition and apply the handbrake firmly. For improved access, apply the handbrake, then jack up the front of the vehicle and support it on axle stands (see *Jacking and vehicle support*). Remove the engine undertray if fitted. Note that the vehicle must be lowered to the ground and be level, to ensure accuracy when refilling and checking the fluid level.

3 Remove the dipstick (where applicable), then position a suitable container under the transmission drain plug. The drain plug is located in the centre of the transmission casing.

4 Unscrew the drain plug and allow the fluid to drain completely into the container. Note that on the AL4 transmission, the inner oil level plug is screwed into the outer drain plug, and both must be removed to drain the fluid **(see illustration)**. Also note that only approximately 3.0 litres will drain out as it is not possible to completely drain the torque converter. If the fluid is hot, take precautions against scalding. Clean the drain plug, being especially careful to wipe any metallic particles off the magnetic insert. Discard the original sealing washer which should be renewed whenever it is disturbed.

5 When the fluid has finished draining, clean the drain plug threads and those of the transmission casing, fit a new sealing washer to the drain plug and refit it to the transmission, tightening securely. On the AL4 transmission, only fit the drain plug and do not fit the centre level plug. If the vehicle was raised for the draining operation, lower it to the ground.

6 Refilling the transmission with fluid is made through the dipstick tube on the 4HP20 transmission, or through the fluid filler plug on the AL4 transmission **(see illustration)**.

4HP20 transmission

7 Add the specified type of fluid a little at a time, and use a funnel with a fine mesh gauze, to avoid spillage and to ensure that no foreign matter enters the transmission. Allow plenty of time for the fluid level to settle properly before checking. Note that the vehicle must be parked on flat level ground when checking the fluid level.

8 After adding approximately 3.0 litres, check the level on the dipstick and top-up if necessary. Refit the dipstick, then start the engine and allow it to idle for a few minutes. Switch the engine off and recheck the level, topping-up if necessary. Take the vehicle on a short run to fully distribute the new fluid around the transmission, then recheck the fluid level with reference to the relevant Part of Chapter 1.

AL4 transmission

9 Position a container beneath the level plug, then add the specified type of fluid through

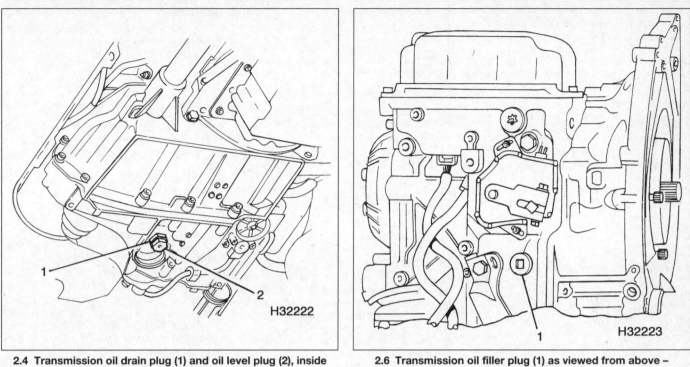

2.4 Transmission oil drain plug (1) and oil level plug (2), inside drain plug – AL4 transmission

H32222

2.6 Transmission oil filler plug (1) as viewed from above – AL4 transmission

H32223

the filler plug aperture until it starts to flow from the level plug. Note that the vehicle must be parked on flat level ground when checking the fluid level.

10 Refit and tighten the filler and level plugs, then start the engine and allow it to idle for a few minutes. Switch the engine off and recheck the level, topping-up if necessary. Take the vehicle on a short run to fully distribute the new fluid around the transmission, then recheck the fluid level with reference to the relevant Part of Chapter 1.

3 Selector cable – removal and refitting

Removal

4HP20 transmission

1 Remove the air cleaner assembly as described in the relevant Part of Chapter 4.
2 Move the gear selector lever to the P position.
3 Working in the engine compartment, carefully prise the selector cable balljoint from the selector lever on the transmission multi-function switch.
4 Extract the horseshoe-shaped clip securing the cable to the mounting bracket on the transmission.
5 Remove the centre console (Chapter 11).
6 Chock the rear wheels, then jack up the front of the car and support it on axle stands.
7 Refer to the relevant Part of Chapter 4 and remove the exhaust system and heat shields,

as necessary for access to the cable and gear selector lever housing.
8 Work back along the selector cable, releasing it from any relevant retaining clips, and noting its correct routing.
9 From inside the car, remove the selector lever control grid illumination bulbholder, the control grid and the sound-proofing gaiter. Unscrew the nuts securing the selector lever housing to the floor. Release any remaining clips or ties, then remove the selector lever housing and cable as an assembly from under the car.

AL4 transmission

10 Release the Park Lock by switching on the ignition and pressing the brake pedal. Position the selector lever in the 2nd gear position, then switch off the ignition.
11 Remove the air cleaner assembly and air inlet ducting as described in the relevant Part of Chapter 4.
12 Remove the battery, battery tray and mounting plate as described in Chapter 5A.
13 Using a suitable forked tool (a fork type balljoint splitter could be used, or failing that, a large flat-bladed screwdriver), carefully prise the selector cable balljoint off the selector lever **(see illustration)**.
14 Extract the retaining C-clip and release the outer cable and cable grommet from the transmission bracket.
15 Firmly apply the handbrake, then jack up the front of the car and support it securely on axle stands (see *Jacking and vehicle support*).
16 Detach and lower the exhaust system in the area below the passenger compartment selector lever, and remove the heat shield in

order to release the selector cable retaining clamp.
17 Remove the centre console as described in Chapter 11.
18 Undo the two screws and withdraw the Park Lock solenoid valve from the front of the selector lever upper housing.
19 Pull the selector lever knob upwards off the lever, without twisting it.
20 Undo the two nuts securing the selector lever upper housing to the lower housing and

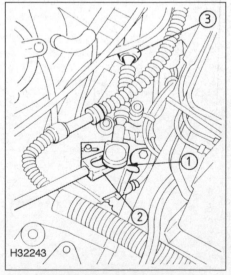

H32243

3.13 Prise off the selector cable balljoint (1) using a forked tool (2), then remove the cable from the bracket (3) – AL4 transmission

lift off the upper housing. On later models, there may be two additional upper housing retaining screws which are accessible through the selector lever gate.

21 Undo the remaining nuts and bolts securing the selector lever lower housing to the floor, then withdraw the lower housing and cable from the car.

Refitting

22 Refitting is the reverse of removal, ensuring that the selector lever is in the P position and the cable is correctly routed and retained with any relevant clips and ties. If a new cable is being fitted, remove the automatic adjuster locking key from the cable end fitting by turning it anti-clockwise and lifting off **(see illustration)**.

4 Oil seals – renewal

Driveshaft oil seals

1 Refer to Chapter 7A.

Selector shaft oil seal

AL4 transmission

2 Remove the selector lever position switch as described in Section 9 for access to the oil seal.

3 Punch or drill two small holes opposite each other in the seal. Screw a self-tapping screw into each, and pull on the screws with pliers to extract the seal.

4 Clean the seal housing, and polish off any burrs or raised edges, which may have caused the seal to fail in the first place. Small imperfections can be removed using emery paper, but larger defects will require the renewal of the selector shaft.

5 Lubricate the lips of the new seal with clean engine oil, and carefully ease the seal into position over the end of the shaft, taking great care not to damage its sealing lip. Tap the seal into position until it is flush with the transmission casing, using a suitable tubular drift (such as a socket) which bears only on the hard outer edge of the seal. Note that the seal lips should face inwards.

6 Refit the selector lever position switch as described in Section 9.

5 Speedometer drive – removal and refitting

Removal

1 Chock the rear wheels, then jack up the front of the car and support it on axle stands. Remove the splash guard from under the engine. The speedometer drive is situated on the rear of the transmission housing, next to the inner end of the right-hand driveshaft.

2 Disconnect the wiring connector from the speedometer drive housing.

3 Slacken and remove the retaining bolt, along with the heat shield, and withdraw the speedometer drive and driven pinion assembly from the transmission housing, along with its O-ring. As the drive is withdrawn, hold the pinion assembly in place as there is a possibility that it can be dislodged and fall into the transmission casing.

4 If necessary, the pinion can be slid out of the housing, and the oil seal can be removed from the top of the housing. Renew the housing O-ring as a matter of course.

Refitting

5 Fit a new O-ring to the speedometer drive and refit it to the transmission, ensuring the drive and driven pinions are correctly engaged.

6 Refit the retaining bolt and the heat shield and tighten the bolt. Reconnect the wiring.

7 Refit the undertray under the engine then lower the vehicle to the ground.

6 Fluid cooler – removal and refitting

Removal

1 The fluid cooler is mounted on the top (4HP20) or rear (AL4) of the transmission housing.

2 To gain access to the fluid cooler on the 4HP20 type transmission, remove the air cleaner assembly and intake ducts as described in the relevant Part of Chapter 4, then unbolt and remove the wiring support bracket. On the AL4 type transmission, apply the handbrake, jack up the front of the vehicle and support it on axle stands (see *Jacking and vehicle support*).

3 Using hose clamps or similar, clamp both of the fluid cooler coolant hoses to minimise coolant loss during subsequent operations.

4 Disconnect both coolant hoses from the fluid cooler being prepared for some coolant spillage. Wash off any spilt coolant immediately with cold water, and dry the surrounding area before proceeding further.

5 Slacken and remove the fluid cooler mounting bolt(s), and remove the cooler from the transmission. Remove the mounting bolt seal(s), and the two seals fitted to the base of the cooler, and discard them; new ones must be used on refitting **(see illustrations)**.

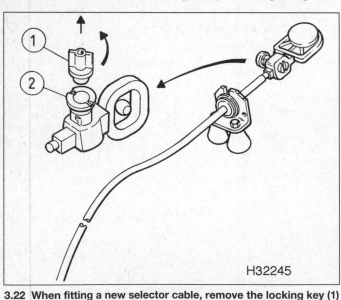

H32245

3.22 When fitting a new selector cable, remove the locking key (1) from the cable adjuster boss (2) – AL4 transmission

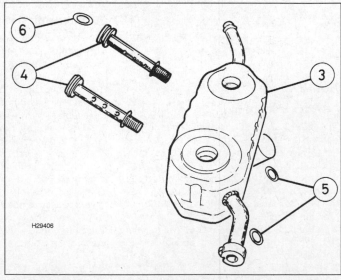

H29406

6.5a Transmission fluid cooler details – 4HP20 transmission

3 *Fluid cooler*   5 *Fluid cooler lower seals*
4 *Mounting bolts*   6 *Mounting bolt seals*

Refitting

6 Lubricate the new seals with clean automatic transmission fluid, then fit the two new seals to the base of the fluid cooler, and a new seal to the mounting bolt(s).

7 Locate the fluid cooler on the transmission housing, then refit the mounting bolt(s), and tighten to the specified torque setting.

8 Reconnect the coolant hoses to the fluid cooler and remove the hose clamps.

9 Refit the intake duct/air cleaner or support bracket components.

10 On completion, top-up the cooling system and check the automatic transmission fluid level as described in the relevant Part of Chapter 1.

7 Multi-function switch (4HP20) – removal and refitting

Removal

1 To improve access to the switch, remove the air cleaner assembly and intake ducts as necessary, as described in the relevant Part of Chapter 4.

2 Place the gear selector in the N position.

3 If the original switch is to be refitted, mark the position of the selector lever in relation to the switch body. Ensure that the lever is in this position (N) when refitting the switch. If a new switch is to be fitted, it will be supplied already in the N position.

4 Carefully prise the gear selector cable balljoint from the selector lever on the multi-function switch.

5 Trace the wiring back from the switch to the wiring connector. Release the connector from the support bracket and disconnect it.

6 Release the switch wiring from the support clip on the transmission.

7 Hold the selector lever on the switch and unscrew the lever retaining nut. Remove the selector lever from the switch shaft.

8 Unscrew the switch, and remove it from the transmission housing.

Refitting

9 Refit the switch to the transmission ensuring that it is seated correctly and secure it with the retaining bolts tightened to the specified torque.

10 Ensure that the switch is in the N position then locate the selector lever on the switch shaft. Hold the lever to prevent internal damage to the switch, and fit and tighten the retaining nut to the specified torque.

11 Ensure that the gear selector lever is still in the N position then reconnect the selector cable balljoint to the selector lever.

12 Reconnect the switch wiring, locate the connector in the support bracket and secure the harness with the retaining clip.

13 Reconnect the switch wiring, then refit the support tray and securely tighten its retaining bolts.

14 Refit the air cleaner and intake ducts as described in the relevant Part of Chapter 4.

8 Electronic control unit (ECU) – removal and refitting

Note: *The automatic transmission ECU, together with the engine management ECU, is located in the ECU module box, situated at the front right-hand side of the engine compartment, adjacent to the cooling system expansion tank.*

Removal

1 Ensure that the ignition is switched off then lift off the ECU module box lid. The automatic transmission ECU is the unit nearest to the side of the car.

2 Release the wiring connector by lifting the locking lever on top of the connector upwards. Lift the connector at the rear, disengage the tag at the front and carefully withdraw the connector from the ECU pins.

3 Lift the ECU upwards and remove it from its location.

Refitting

4 Refitting is a reversal of removal. Note that if a new ECU has been fitted, the vehicle should be taken on an extensive road test, on a route which will allow numerous gearchanges and full use of the transmission mode settings. Initially, transmission response and gearchange quality may be less than acceptable, but should improve as the ECU control circuitry adapts to the transmission parameters.

9 Electronic system components (AL4) – removal and refitting

Note: *Renewal of the transmission oil temperature sensor involves removing the hydraulic block, therefore this work should be carried out by a Peugeot dealer.*

Input speed sensor

1 The input speed sensor is located on the left-hand end of the transmission, in front of the driveshaft.

2 Remove the battery, battery tray and mounting plate as described in Chapter 5A, then remove the air cleaner and air inlet ducts as described in the relevant Part of Chapter 4. If necessary for improved access, apply the handbrake, jack up the front of the vehicle and support it on axle stands (see *Jacking and vehicle support*), then remove the left-hand front roadwheel and wheelarch liner.

3 Remove the two securing screws from the modular connector located at the rear of the transmission, and disconnect the wiring as it is removed.

4 Extract the yellow three-way wiring connector from the modular connector.

5 Detach the wiring harness from the transmission as necessary for access to the sensor. Unscrew and remove the sensor retaining bolt, then withdraw the sensor from the transmission. Recover the sensor O-ring seal, and discard it.

6 Refitting is a reversal of removal. Use a new O-ring seal when refitting the sensor, and tighten its retaining bolt to the specified torque. Ensure that all wiring connections are securely remade.

Output speed sensor

7 The output speed sensor is fitted to the rear

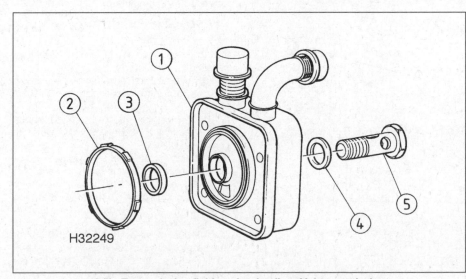

6.5b Transmission fluid cooler details – AL4 transmission

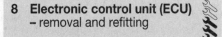

1 Fluid cooler	*3 Small square-section seal*
2 Large square-section seal (to transmission)	*4 Centre bolt seal*
	5 Centre bolt

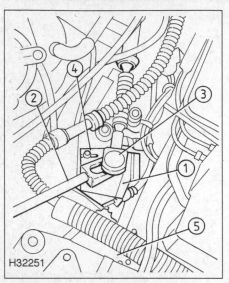

9.15 Selector lever position switch details – AL4 transmission

1 Selector lever position switch
2 Forked tool
3 Selector cable balljoint
4 Transmission selector lever clamp bolt and nut
5 Wiring harness support bracket

of the transmission, just below the selector cable bracket.

8 Disconnect the battery negative terminal (refer to *Disconnecting the battery* in the Reference Section of this manual). For improved access, apply the handbrake, jack up the front of the vehicle and support it on axle stands (see *Jacking and vehicle support*), then remove the left-hand front roadwheel and wheelarch liner.

9 Disconnect the speed sensor wiring plug located behind the modular connector.

10 Unscrew and remove the sensor retaining bolt, then withdraw the sensor from the transmission. Recover the sensor O-ring seal, and discard it.

11 Refitting is a reversal of removal. Use a new O-ring seal when refitting the sensor, and tighten its retaining bolt to the specified torque. Ensure that the wiring connection is securely remade.

Selector lever position switch

12 The selector lever position switch is situated on top of the transmission, attached to the selector cable.

13 Remove the battery, battery tray and mounting plate as described in Chapter 5A, then remove the air inlet duct as described in the relevant Part of Chapter 4.

14 From inside the car, move the selector lever to the N position.

15 Using a suitable forked tool (a fork type balljoint splitter could be used, or failing that, a large flat-bladed screwdriver), carefully prise the selector cable balljoint off the transmission selector lever **(see illustration)**. Take care not to bend the transmission selector lever during this operation.

16 Mark the position of the transmission selector lever in relation to the splined shaft of the switch, for use when refitting. Unscrew and remove the clamp bolt and nut from the selector lever, and remove the lever from the shaft splines.

17 Detach the wiring harness and its support bracket from in front of the switch.

18 If the original switch is to be refitted, mark the position of the two switch retaining bolts in the slotted holes of the switch. If the switch is refitted in exactly the same position, there should be no need to check the switch resistance on refitting.

19 Unscrew the switch retaining bolts, disconnect the switch wiring, and remove the switch from the engine compartment.

20 With the switch removed, check the condition of the selector shaft oil seal. If signs of leakage are evident, renew the seal as described in Section 8.

21 Refitting is a reversal of removal, but the switch position must be set to ensure correct operation.

22 If the original switch is being refitted, the switch bolts can be aligned in the switch slots as marked on removal.

23 If a new switch is being fitted, or the marks have been lost, connect an ohmmeter between the two pins provided on the front of the switch (do not use a test light, or any multimeter which supplies more than 100 mA, or the switch will be damaged). Fit the switch retaining bolts loosely at this stage.

24 Refit the transmission selector lever to the splined shaft of the switch and tighten the clamp bolt and nut to the specified torque.

25 Ensure that the transmission selector lever is in the neutral N position.

26 Turn the switch body until the resistance measured on the ohmmeter falls to zero **(see illustration)**.

27 When the switch position is correct, tighten the retaining bolts to the specified torque.

28 Refit all remaining components removed for access, and check for satisfactory operation on completion.

Park Lock solenoid

29 The Park Lock solenoid is located on the front of the gear selector lever housing in the passenger compartment.

30 To gain access to the solenoid, remove the centre console as described in Chapter 11.

31 Unscrew the two retaining bolts, disconnect the wiring plug, and remove the solenoid.

32 Refitting is a reversal of removal.

33 In the event of a fault in the system, such that the selector lever cannot be moved out of P with the ignition on and the brake pedal depressed, the system can be disabled manually, as follows.

34 Carefully prise out the trim panel around the selector lever, and remove it.

35 Using a suitable flat-bladed screwdriver, carefully ease the central plunger away from the switch body to release the locking mechanism. Move the selector lever to the N position and it should now be possible to start the engine and drive the car.

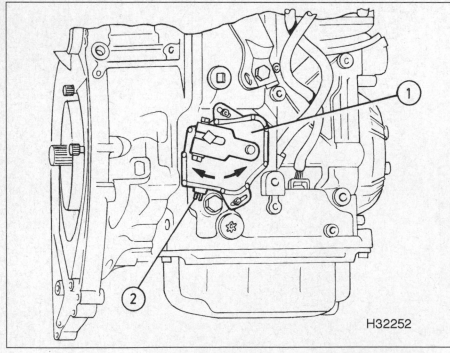

9.26 Turn switch (1) until resistance measured at terminals (2) falls to zero – AL4 transmission

Oil pressure sensor

Note: *It is not necessary to drain the transmission before carrying out this work.*

36 Apply the handbrake, then jack up the front of the vehicle and support it on axle stands (see *Jacking and vehicle support*). Remove the left-hand front roadwheel and wheelarch.

37 Remove the battery, battery tray and mounting plate as described in Chapter 5A, then remove the air cleaner and air inlet ducts as described in the relevant Part of Chapter 4.

38 Undo the screws and disconnect the wiring connector.

39 Extract the green wire from the wiring connector.

40 Disconnect the wiring from the oil pressure sensor.

41 Undo the mounting screws and withdraw the oil pressure sensor from the transmission. Remove the O-ring and discard it; a new one must be fitted on reassembly.

42 Refitting is a reversal of removal, but fit a new O-ring.

10 Automatic transmission – removal and refitting

Removal

4HP20 transmission

1 Remove the battery and battery box as described in Chapter 5A.

2 Remove the air cleaner assembly and intake ducting as described in the relevant Part of Chapter 4.

3 Chock the rear wheels, then jack up the front of the vehicle, and securely support it on axle stands. Remove both front roadwheels, then release the screws and clips and remove the wheelarch liner from under the left-hand wing. Remove the splash guard from under the engine.

4 Drain the transmission fluid as described in Section 2, then refit the drain plug, and tighten securely.

5 Release the cable ties or clips and move aside the brake pad wear warning light harness and/or the ABS wiring harness.

6 Carefully prise the selector cable balljoint from the selector lever on the transmission multi-function switch. Extract the horseshoe-shaped clip securing the cable to the mounting bracket on the transmission.

7 Trace the wiring back from the multi-function switch to the wiring connector. Release the connector from the support bracket and disconnect it. Release the switch wiring from the support clip on the transmission.

8 Disconnect the wiring harness at the large connector adjacent to the transmission fluid cooler. Cover the wiring connector socket on the transmission to prevent water ingress when the fluid cooler hoses are disconnected.

9 Using hose clamps or similar, clamp both the fluid cooler coolant hoses to minimise coolant loss during subsequent operations.

10 Disconnect both coolant hoses from the fluid cooler being prepared for some coolant spillage. Wash off any spilt coolant immediately with cold water, and dry the surrounding area before proceeding further.

11 Unclip the wiring connector from the support bracket located just above the fluid cooler, then remove the support bracket.

12 Disconnect the earth cable from the stud on the transmission.

13 Remove the wiring harness bracket and the hose support bracket from the transmission.

14 Disconnect the wiring from the speedometer transducer (speedometer drive) and RPM sensor, then remove the RPM sensor from the bellhousing.

15 Undo the starter motor mounting bolts and move the starter clear without disconnecting the wiring.

16 Label and disconnect any remaining wiring connectors and support brackets connected to the transmission.

17 Remove both driveshafts as described in Chapter 8.

18 From under the car, undo the bolts securing the engine movement limiter to the right-hand driveshaft intermediate bearing housing, and subframe. Manipulate the movement limiter from its location **(see illustration)**.

19 Undo the bolts securing the power steering pipes to the transmission.

20 Remove the front suspension subframe as described in Chapter 10.

21 Attach a hoist or support bar to the engine left-hand lifting eye and just take the engine weight.

22 Attach a second hoist to the transmission lifting eye located next to the fluid cooler.

23 Locate the access hole at the lower rear of the cylinder block, then turn the crankshaft, by means of a socket on the crankshaft pulley bolt, until one of the torque converter retaining bolts is accessible through the access hole.

24 Undo the accessible torque converter bolt then turn the crankshaft as necessary and undo the remaining two bolts.

25 With the transmission securely supported on the hoist, slacken and remove the centre nut and washer from the left-hand engine/transmission mounting stud, then unscrew the stud from the transmission **(see illustration)**.

26 Slacken and remove the bolts securing the transmission housing to the engine. Note the correct fitted positions of each bolt, and the necessary brackets, as they are removed, to use as a reference on refitting. Make a final check that all components have been disconnected, and are positioned clear of the transmission so that they will not hinder the removal procedure.

27 With the bolts removed, pull the transmission to the left, to free it from its

10.18 Engine movement limiter attachments to the intermediate bearing housing and subframe

locating dowels. Once the transmission is free, and sufficient clearance exists, insert a bolt with a suitable washer, through the RPM sensor hole in the transmission bellhousing, to retain the torque converter on the transmission.

28 Lower the engine and transmission hoists and manoeuvre the transmission out from under the car. Remove the locating dowels from the transmission or engine if they are loose, and keep them in a safe place.

29 With the transmission removed make sure that the bolt used initially is capable of retaining the torque converter in place.

AL4 transmission

Note: *If a new transmission unit is being fitted, it will be necessary for the transmission ECU to be initialised and matched electronically to the engine management ECU on completion – the initialisation must be referred to a Peugeot dealer.*

30 Chock the rear wheels, apply the handbrake, and place the selector lever in the N (neutral) position. Jack up the front of the vehicle, and securely support it on axle stands (see *Jacking and vehicle support*). Remove both front roadwheels, and the engine undertray.

31 Remove the battery, battery tray and mounting plate as described in Chapter 5A, then remove the air cleaner and air inlet duct(s) as described in the relevant Part of Chapter 4.

32 Disconnect the transmission ECU wiring connector and the support bracket.

10.25 Engine/transmission left-hand mounting details

33 Disconnect the output speed sensor wiring plug located behind the modular connector. Also, disconnect the engine TDC/speed sensor wiring plug.

34 Drain the transmission fluid as described in Section 2, then refit the drain plug, and tighten securely.

35 Using a suitable forked tool (a fork type balljoint splitter could be used, or failing that, a large flat-bladed screwdriver), carefully prise the selector cable balljoint off the selector lever.

36 Extract the retaining C-clip and release the selector outer cable and cable grommet from the transmission bracket.

37 Using a hose clamp or similar, clamp both the fluid cooler coolant hoses to minimise coolant loss during subsequent operations.

38 Slacken the retaining clips, and disconnect both coolant hoses from the fluid cooler – be prepared for some coolant spillage. Wash off any spilt coolant immediately with cold water, and dry the surrounding area before proceeding further.

39 Remove the driveshafts as described in Chapter 8.

40 Unbolt the earth wire(s) from the transmission.

41 Remove the front suspension subframe as described in Chapter 10, and noting the location of spacers. If the exhaust system is still in position, support the front end on a block of wood or axle stand.

42 Remove the fluid heat exchanger.

43 Remove the starter motor as described in Chapter 5A.

44 Undo the retaining bolts and remove the lower driveplate cover plate from the transmission, to gain access to the torque converter retaining nuts. Slacken and remove the visible nut then, using a socket and extension bar to rotate the crankshaft pulley, undo the remaining nuts securing the torque converter to the driveplate as they become accessible. There are three nuts in total.

45 To ensure that the torque converter does not fall out as the transmission is removed, secure it in position using a length of metal strip bolted to one of the starter motor bolt holes.

46 Attach a hoist or support bar to the engine left-hand lifting eye and just take the engine weight.

47 Place a jack and block of wood beneath the transmission, and raise the jack to take the weight of the transmission. Move the transmission slightly towards the radiator.

48 Slacken and remove the centre nut and washer from the left-hand engine/transmission mounting. Undo the bolts and remove the rubber mounting from the mounting bracket and transmission mounting stud. Undo the bolts and remove the transmission support bracket. On diesel models, access to the left-hand mounting is improved by unbolting the accelerator cable sensor bracket and moving it to one side

49 With the jack positioned beneath the transmission taking the weight, slacken and remove the bolts securing the transmission housing to the engine. Note the correct fitted positions of each bolt as it is removed, to use as a reference on refitting. Make a final check that all necessary components have been disconnected, and positioned clear of the transmission so that they will not hinder the removal procedure.

50 With the bolts removed, move the trolley jack and transmission to the left, to free it from its locating dowels.

51 Once the transmission is free, lower the jack and manoeuvre the unit out from under the car. If they are loose, remove the locating dowels from the transmission or engine, and keep them in a safe place.

Refitting

52 Both transmission types are refitted using a reversal of the removal procedure, bearing in mind the following points:

a) *Ensure that the bush fitted to the centre of the crankshaft is in good condition, and apply a little Molykote G1 grease to the torque converter centring pin. Do not apply too much, otherwise there is a possibility of the grease contaminating the torque converter.*

b) *On the AL4 transmission, turn the torque converter so that one of the mounting studs is positioned opposite the right-hand driveshaft output shaft (approximately the 9 o'clock position). Turn the engine crankshaft so that the corresponding mounting hole in the driveplate is in the same position. The torque converter mounting studs and the corresponding holes in the driveplate should then be in alignment when the transmission is fitted.*

c) *Ensure that the engine/transmission locating dowels are correctly positioned prior to installation.*

d) *Once the transmission and engine are correctly joined, refit the securing bolts, tightening them to the specified torque setting, then remove the metal strip used to retain the torque converter.*

e) *Tighten all nuts and bolts to the specified torque (where given).*

f) *Renew the driveshaft oil seals with reference to Chapter 7A.*

g) *Refit the driveshafts to the transmission as described in Chapter 8.*

h) *On the 4HP20 transmission, adjust the selector cable and kickdown cable.*

i) *On completion, top-up the cooling system, then refill the transmission with the specified type and quantity of fluid as described in Section 2.*

11 Automatic transmission overhaul – general information

In the event of a fault occurring with the transmission, it is first necessary to determine whether it is of an electrical, mechanical or hydraulic nature, and to do this, special test equipment is required. It is therefore essential to have the work carried out by a Peugeot dealer if a transmission fault is suspected.

Do not remove the transmission from the car for possible repair before professional fault diagnosis has been carried out, since most tests require the transmission to be in the vehicle.

Chapter 8
Driveshafts

Contents

Driveshaft overhaul – general information 4
Driveshaft rubber gaiter and constant velocity (CV) joint
  check . . . . .See Chapter 1A or 1B
Driveshaft rubber gaiters – renewal 3
Driveshafts – removal and refitting 2
General information 1
Right-hand driveshaft intermediate bearing – renewal 5

Degrees of difficulty

Easy, suitable for novice with little experience	Fairly easy, suitable for beginner with some experience	Fairly difficult, suitable for competent DIY mechanic	Difficult, suitable for experienced DIY mechanic	Very difficult, suitable for expert DIY or professional

Specifications

Lubrication (overhaul only – see text)

Lubricant type/specification . . . . Use only special grease supplied in sachets with gaiter kits – joints are otherwise pre-packed with grease and sealed

Torque wrench settings	Nm	lbf ft
Driveshaft retaining nut	325	240
Lower suspension arm balljoint retaining nuts	45	33
Right-hand driveshaft intermediate bearing retaining bolt nuts	10	7
Road wheel bolts	90	66

1 General information

Drive is transmitted from the differential to the front wheels by means of two solid-steel driveshafts of unequal length.

Both driveshafts are splined at their outer ends, to accept the wheel hubs, and are threaded so that each hub can be fastened by a large nut. The inner end of each driveshaft is splined, to accept the differential sun gear.

Constant velocity (CV) joints are fitted to each end of the driveshafts, to ensure that the smooth and efficient transmission of power at all suspension and steering angles. The outer constant velocity joints are of the ball-and-cage type, and the inner constant velocity joints are of the tripod type.

On the right-hand side, due to the length of the driveshaft, the inner constant velocity joint is situated approximately halfway along the shaft's length, and an intermediate support bearing is mounted in the engine/transmission rear mounting bracket. The inner end of the driveshaft passes through the bearing (which prevents any lateral movement of the driveshaft inner end) and the inner constant velocity joint outer member.

2 Driveshafts – removal and refitting

Removal

Note: *A new suspension lower balljoint nut will be required on refitting.*

1 Remove the wheel trim/hub cap (as applicable) then withdraw the R-clip and remove the locking cap from the driveshaft retaining nut. Slacken the driveshaft nut with the vehicle resting on its wheels. Also slacken the wheel bolts.

2 Chock the rear wheels of the car, firmly apply the handbrake, then jack up the front of the car and support it on axle stands. Remove the appropriate front roadwheel.

3 On manual transmission models drain the transmission oil as described in Chapter 7A, and on automatic transmission models drain the fluid as described in Chapter 7B.

4 On models equipped with ABS, remove the wheel sensor as described in Chapter 9, Section 24.

5 Slacken and remove the driveshaft retaining nut. If the nut was not slackened with the wheels on the ground (see paragraph 1), withdraw the R-clip and remove the locking cap. Refit at least two roadwheel bolts to the front hub, tightening them securely, then have an assistant firmly depress the brake pedal to prevent the front hub from rotating, whilst you slacken and remove the driveshaft retaining nut. Alternatively, a tool can be fabricated from two lengths of steel strip (one long, one short) and a nut and bolt; the nut and bolt forming the pivot of a forked tool **(see Tool tip)**.

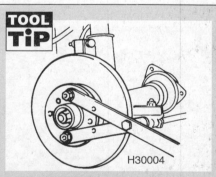

Using a fabricated tool to hold the front hub stationary whilst the driveshaft retaining nut is slackened.

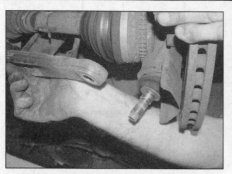

2.6 Release the balljoint from the lower suspension arm . . .

2.7 . . . then withdraw the outer joint from the hub assembly

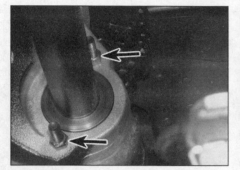

2.9a On the right-hand driveshaft, slacken the two intermediate bearing retaining bolt nuts (arrowed) . . .

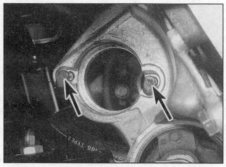

2.9b . . . then turn the bolts through 90° to disengage their offset heads (arrowed) from the bearing (driveshaft removed for clarity)

6 Slacken and remove the nut securing the front suspension lower balljoint to the swivel hub, and free the balljoint from the lower arm (see illustration). Discard the nut and remove the protector plate (if loose).

Left-hand driveshaft

7 Carefully pull the swivel hub assembly outwards, and withdraw the driveshaft outer constant velocity joint from the hub assembly (see illustration). If necessary, the shaft can be tapped out of the hub using a soft-faced mallet.
8 Support the driveshaft, then withdraw the inner constant velocity joint from the transmission, taking care not to damage the driveshaft oil seal. Remove the driveshaft from the vehicle. **Note:** *Do not allow the vehicle to rest on its wheels with one or both driveshafts removed, as damage to the wheel bearing(s)*

may result. If moving the vehicle is unavoidable, temporarily insert the outer end of the driveshaft(s) in the hub(s) and tighten the driveshaft nut(s). Support the inner end(s) of the driveshaft(s) to avoid damage.

Right-hand driveshaft

9 Loosen the two intermediate bearing retaining bolt nuts, then rotate the bolts through 90°, so that their offset heads are clear of the bearing outer race (see illustrations).
10 Carefully pull the swivel hub assembly outwards, and withdraw the driveshaft outer constant velocity joint from the hub assembly. If necessary, the shaft can be tapped out of the hub using a soft-faced mallet.
11 Support the outer end of the driveshaft, then pull on the inner end of the shaft to free the intermediate bearing from its mounting bracket.

2.18a Tighten the driveshaft nut to the specified torque, then refit the locking cap . . .

2.18b . . . and secure it in position with the R-clip

12 Once the driveshaft end is free from the transmission, slide the dust seal (where fitted) off the inner end of the shaft, noting which way around it is fitted, and remove the driveshaft from the vehicle. **Note:** *Do not allow the vehicle to rest on its wheels with one or both driveshafts removed, as damage to the wheel bearing(s) may result. If moving the vehicle is unavoidable, temporarily insert the outer end of the driveshaft(s) in the hub(s) and tighten the driveshaft nut(s). Support the inner end(s) of the driveshaft(s) to avoid damage.*

Refitting

13 Before installing the driveshaft, examine the driveshaft oil seal in the transmission for signs of damage or deterioration and, if necessary, renew it as described in Chapter 7A. It is highly recommended that the seal is renewed, regardless of its apparent condition.
14 Thoroughly clean the driveshaft splines, and the apertures in the transmission and hub assembly. Apply a thin film of grease to the oil seal lips, and to the driveshaft splines and shoulders. Check that all gaiter clips are securely fastened.

Left-hand driveshaft

15 Offer up the driveshaft, and locate the joint splines with those of the differential sun gear, taking great care not to damage the oil seal. Push the joint fully into position.
16 Locate the outer constant velocity joint splines with those of the swivel hub, and slide the joint back into position in the hub.
17 Refit the protector plate (where removed) to the lower balljoint, then align the balljoint with the lower arm. Fit the new balljoint nut and tighten it to the specified torque setting.
18 Lubricate the inner face and threads of the driveshaft nut with clean engine oil, and refit it to the end of the driveshaft. Use the method employed on removal to prevent the hub from rotating (see paragraph 5), and tighten the driveshaft retaining nut to the specified torque. Check that the hub rotates freely then engage the locking cap with the driveshaft nut, so that one of its cut-outs is aligned with the driveshaft hole, and secure the cap in position with the R-clip (see illustrations). Alternatively, lightly tighten the nut at this stage, and tighten it to the specified torque once the car is resting on its wheels again.
19 Where necessary, refit the ABS wheel sensor as described in Chapter 9.
20 Refit the roadwheel, then lower the vehicle to the ground and tighten the roadwheel bolts to the specified torque. If not already done, tighten the driveshaft retaining nut to the specified torque then refit the locking cap, aligning its cut-outs with the driveshaft hole, and secure it in position with the R-clip.
21 Refill the transmission with the specified type and amount of fluid/oil, and check the level using the information given in the relevant Part of Chapter 1.

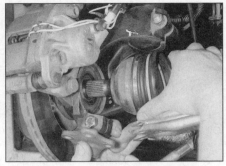

2.24 Locate the dust seal (where fitted) on the inner end of the right-hand driveshaft, ensuring it is fitted the right way around

2.26 Pull out the swivel hub assembly and locate the outer constant velocity joint splines with those of the swivel hub

2.27 Secure the intermediate bearing in position then (if necessary) slide the dust seal up tight against the driveshaft oil seal

Right-hand driveshaft

22 Check that the intermediate bearing rotates smoothly, without any sign of roughness or undue free play between its inner and outer races. If necessary, renew the bearing as described in Section 5. Examine the dust seal for signs of damage or deterioration, and renew if necessary.

23 Apply a smear of grease to the outer race of the intermediate bearing, and to the inner lip of the dust seal (where fitted).

24 Pass the inner end of the shaft through the bearing mounting bracket then, where necessary, carefully slide the dust seal into position on the driveshaft, ensuring that its flat surface is facing the transmission **(see illustration)**.

25 Carefully locate the inner driveshaft splines with those of the differential sun gear, taking care not to damage the oil seal. Align the intermediate bearing with its mounting bracket, and push the driveshaft fully into position. If necessary, use a soft-faced mallet to tap the outer race of the bearing into position in the mounting bracket.

26 Locate the outer constant velocity joint splines with those of the swivel hub, and slide the joint back into position in the hub **(see illustration)**.

27 Ensure that the intermediate bearing is correctly seated, then rotate its retaining bolts back through 90°, so that their offset heads are resting against the bearing outer race. Tighten the retaining nuts to the specified

torque. Where necessary, ensure that the dust seal is tight against the driveshaft oil seal **(see illustration)**.

28 Carry out the operations described above in paragraphs 17 to 21.

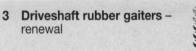

3 Driveshaft rubber gaiters – renewal

Outer joint

1 Remove the driveshaft from the vehicle as described in Section 2.

2 Secure the driveshaft in a vice equipped with soft jaws, and release the two outer gaiter retaining clips. If necessary, the gaiter retaining clips can be cut to release them.

3 Slide the rubber gaiter down the shaft, to expose the outer constant velocity joint. Scoop out the excess grease.

4 Using a hammer and suitable soft metal drift, sharply strike the inner member of the outer joint to drive it off the end of the shaft. The joint is retained on the driveshaft by a circlip, and striking the joint in this manner forces the circlip into its groove, so allowing the joint to slide off.

5 Once the joint assembly has been removed, remove the circlip from the groove in the driveshaft splines, and discard it. A new circlip must be fitted on reassembly.

6 Withdraw the rubber gaiter from the

driveshaft. Where necessary, slide off the gaiter inner end plastic bush.

7 With the constant velocity joint removed from the driveshaft, thoroughly clean the joint using paraffin, or a suitable solvent, and dry it thoroughly. Carry out a visual inspection of the joint.

8 Move the inner splined driving member from side-to-side, to expose each ball in turn at the top of its track. Examine the balls for cracks, flat spots, or signs of surface pitting.

9 Inspect the ball tracks on the inner and outer members. If the tracks have widened, the balls will no longer be a tight fit. At the same time, check the ball cage windows for wear or cracking between the windows.

10 If on inspection, any of the constant velocity joint components are found to be worn or damaged, it will be necessary to renew the complete joint assembly (where available), or even the complete driveshaft (where no joint components are available separately). Refer to your Peugeot dealer for further information on parts availability. If the joint is in satisfactory condition, obtain a repair kit consisting of a new gaiter, circlip, retaining clips, and the correct type and quantity of grease.

11 To install the new gaiter, perform the operations shown **(see illustrations)**. Be sure to stay in order, and follow the captions carefully. Note that the hard plastic rings and plastic bushes are not fitted to all gaiters, and the gaiter retaining clips supplied with the repair kit may be different to those shown in

3.11a Fit the hard plastic rings to the outer CV joint gaiter . . .

3.11b . . . then slide on the new plastic bush (arrowed – where fitted), and seat it in its recess in the shaft. Slide the gaiter onto the shaft . . .

3.11c . . . and seat the gaiter inner end on top of the plastic bush/shaft (as applicable)

3.11d Fit the new circlip to its groove in the driveshaft splines . . .

3.11e . . . then locate the joint outer member on the splines, and slide it into position over the circlip. Ensure that the joint is securely retained by the circlip

3.11f Pack the joint with the grease supplied, working it into the ball tracks while twisting the joint, then locate the gaiter outer lip in its groove on the outer member

3.11g Fit the outer gaiter retaining clip and, using a hook fabricated out of welding rod and a pair of pliers, pull the clip tightly to remove all slack

3.11h Bend the clip end back over the buckle, then cut off the excess clip

3.11i Fold the clip end underneath the buckle . . .

12 Check that the constant velocity joint moves freely in all directions, then refit the driveshaft to the vehicle as described in Section 2.

Inner joint

13 Remove the driveshaft from the vehicle as described in Section 2.
14 Remove the outer constant velocity joint as described above in paragraphs 1 to 5.
15 Tape over the splines on the driveshaft, and carefully remove the outer constant velocity joint rubber gaiter, and (where fitted) the gaiter inner end plastic bush. It is recommended that the outer joint gaiter is also renewed, regardless of its apparent condition.
16 Release the retaining clips, then slide the inner gaiter off the shaft and (where fitted) remove its plastic bush. As the gaiter is released, the joint outer member will also be freed from the end of the shaft **(see illustrations)**.

3.11j . . . then fold the buckle firmly down onto the clip to secure the clip in position

the sequence. To secure this other type of clip in position, lock the ends of the clip together, then remove any slack in the clip by carefully

3.11k Carefully lift the gaiter inner end to equalise air pressure in the gaiter, then secure the inner gaiter retaining clip in position using the same method

compressing the raised section of the clip using a pair of side-cutters.

3.16a Release the inner gaiter retaining clips, and remove the joint outer member

3.16b Slide the gaiter off the end of the driveshaft . . .

3.16c . . . and remove the plastic bush

17 Thoroughly clean the joint using paraffin, or a suitable solvent, and dry it thoroughly. Check the tripod joint bearings and joint outer member for signs of wear, pitting or scuffing on their bearing surfaces. Check that the bearing rollers rotate smoothly and easily around the tripod joint, with no traces of roughness.

18 If on inspection, the tripod joint or outer member reveal signs of wear or damage, it will be necessary to renew the complete driveshaft assembly, since the joint is not available separately. If the joint is in satisfactory condition, obtain a repair kit consisting of a new gaiter, retaining clips, and the correct type and quantity of grease. Although not strictly necessary, it is also recommended that the outer constant velocity joint gaiter is renewed, regardless of its apparent condition.

19 On reassembly, pack the inner joint with the grease supplied in the gaiter kit. Work the grease well into the bearing tracks and rollers, while twisting the joint.

20 Clean the shaft, using emery cloth to remove any rust or sharp edges which may damage the gaiter, then slide the plastic bush (where fitted) and inner joint gaiter along the driveshaft. Locate the plastic bush in its recess on the shaft, and seat the inner end of the gaiter on top of the bush; where no bush is fitted, seat the inner end of the driveshaft in the recess on the shaft.

21 Fit the outer member over the end of the shaft, and locate the gaiter in the groove on the joint outer member. Push the outer member onto the joint, so that its spring-loaded plunger is compressed, then lift the outer edge of the gaiter to equalise air pressure in the gaiter. Fit both the inner and outer retaining clips, securing them in position using the information given in paragraph 11. Ensure that the gaiter retaining clips are securely tightened, then check that the joint moves freely in all directions.

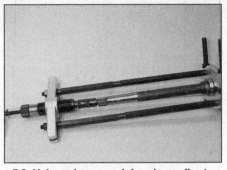

5.3 Using a long-reach bearing puller to remove the intermediate bearing from the right-hand driveshaft

22 Refit the outer constant velocity joint components using the information given in paragraph 11.

4 Driveshaft overhaul – general information

1 If any of the checks described in Chapter 1A or 1B reveal wear in any driveshaft joint, first remove the roadwheel trim or centre cap (as appropriate).

2 If the R-clip is still in position, the driveshaft nut should be correctly tightened; if in doubt, remove the R-clip and locking cap, and use a torque wrench to check that the nut is securely fastened. Once tightened, refit the locking cap and R-clip, then refit the centre cap or trim. Repeat this check on the remaining driveshaft nut.

3 Road test the vehicle, and listen for a metallic clicking from the front as the vehicle is driven slowly in a circle on full-lock. If a clicking noise is heard, this indicates wear in the outer constant velocity joint. This means that the joint must be renewed; reconditioning is not possible.

4 If vibration, consistent with road speed, is felt through the car when accelerating, there is a possibility of wear in the inner constant velocity joints.

5 To check the joints for wear, remove the driveshafts, then dismantle them as described in Section 3; if any wear or free play is found, the affected joint must be renewed. In the case of the inner joints (and on some models, the outer joints), this means that the complete driveshaft assembly must be renewed, as the joints are not available separately. Refer to your Peugeot dealer for latest information on the availability of driveshaft components.

5 Right-hand driveshaft intermediate bearing – renewal

Note: *A suitable bearing puller will be required, to draw the bearing and collar off the driveshaft end.*

1 Remove the right-hand driveshaft as described in Section 2 of this Chapter.

2 Check that the bearing outer race rotates smoothly and easily, without any signs of roughness or undue free play between the inner and outer races. If necessary, renew the bearing as follows.

3 Using a long-reach universal bearing puller, carefully draw the collar and intermediate bearing off the driveshaft inner end **(see illustration)**. Apply a smear of grease to the inner race of the new bearing, then fit the bearing over the end of the driveshaft. Using a hammer and suitable piece of tubing which bears only on the bearing inner race, tap the new bearing into position on the driveshaft, until it abuts the constant velocity joint outer member. Once the bearing is correctly positioned, tap the bearing collar onto the shaft until it contacts the bearing inner race.

4 Check that the bearing rotates freely, then refit the driveshaft as described in Section 2.

Notes

Chapter 9
Braking system

Contents

Anti-lock Braking System (ABS) – general information 23
Anti-lock Braking System (ABS) components – removal and
  refitting 24
Brake pedal – removal and refitting 14
Front brake caliper – removal, overhaul and refitting 10
Front brake disc – inspection, removal and refitting 7
Front brake pad wear check . . . . .See Chapter 1A or 1B
Front brake pads – renewal 4
General information 1
Handbrake – adjustment 17
Handbrake cables – removal and refitting 19
Handbrake lever – removal and refitting 18
Handbrake shoes (rear disc brake models) – removal and refitting . 20
Hydraulic fluid level check . . . . .See Weekly checks
Hydraulic fluid renewal .See Chapter 1A or 1B
Hydraulic pipes and hoses – renewal 3
Hydraulic system – bleeding 2
Master cylinder – removal, overhaul and refitting 13
Rear brake caliper – removal, overhaul and refitting 11
Rear brake disc – inspection, removal and refitting 8
Rear brake drum – removal, inspection and refitting 9
Rear brake pad wear check . . . . .See Chapter 1A or 1B
Rear brake pads – renewal 5
Rear brake pressure-regulating valve – testing, removal and
  refitting 21
Rear brake shoe wear check . . . . .See Chapter 1A or 1B
Rear brake shoes – renewal 6
Rear wheel cylinder – removal and refitting 12
Stop-light switch – removal, refitting and adjustment 22
Vacuum pump (diesel engine models) – removal and refitting 25
Vacuum pump (diesel engine models) – testing 26
Vacuum servo unit – testing, removal and refitting 15
Vacuum servo unit check valve – removal, testing and refitting 16

Degrees of difficulty

Easy, suitable for novice with little experience	Fairly easy, suitable for beginner with some experience	Fairly difficult, suitable for competent DIY mechanic	Difficult, suitable for experienced DIY mechanic	Very difficult, suitable for expert DIY or professional

Specifications

Front brakes

Type	Disc, with single-piston sliding caliper
Disc diameter:	
1.6 and 1.8 litre petrol models	260 mm
All other models	283 mm
Disc thickness:	
1.6 and 1.8 litre petrol models:	
New	24.0 mm
Minimum	22.0 mm
All other models:	
New	26.0 mm
Minimum	24.0 mm
Maximum disc run-out	0.05 mm
Brake pad friction material thickness:	
New	13.0 mm
Minimum	2.0 mm

Rear drum brakes

Drum internal diameter	
New	228.6 mm
Maximum diameter after machining	230.0 mm
Brake shoe friction material thickness:	
New	4.8 mm
Minimum	1.5 mm
Maximum drum run-out	0.07 mm

Rear disc brakes

Disc diameter	290 mm
Disc thickness:	
New	10.0 mm
Minimum thickness	8.0 mm
Maximum disc run-out	0.05 mm
Brake pad friction material thickness:	
New	11.0 mm
Minimum	2.0 mm

Torque wrench settings

	Nm	lbf ft
ABS system components:		
Electronic control unit (ECU) bolts	5	4
Regulator unit nuts	20	15
Wheel sensor retaining bolts*	10	7
Brake pedal pivot shaft nut	40	30
Crossover linkage housing nuts and bolts (right-hand drive models)	25	18
Disc retaining screws	10	7
Front brake caliper:		
Guide pin bolts*	30	22
Mounting bracket bolts*	120	89
Handbrake lever nuts	20	15
Hydraulic hose/pipe union nuts	15	11
Master cylinder retaining nuts	20	15
Pressure regulating valve bolts*	20	15
Rear brake caliper:		
Guide pin bolt*	30	22
Mounting bolt*	50	37
Rear wheel cylinder bolts	10	7
Roadwheel bolts	90	66
Vacuum servo unit mounting nuts	20	15

Use thread-locking compound.

1 General information

The braking system is of the servo-assisted, dual-circuit hydraulic type. The arrangement of the hydraulic system is such that each circuit operates one front and one rear brake from a tandem master cylinder. Under normal circumstances, both circuits operate in unison. However, in the event of hydraulic failure in one circuit, full braking force will still be available at two wheels.

Most models have disc brakes all round as standard; although some earlier models where fitted with front disc brakes and rear drum brakes. ABS is fitted as standard (refer to Section 23 for further information on ABS operation).

The front disc brakes are actuated by single-piston sliding type calipers, which ensure that equal pressure is applied to each disc pad.

On models with rear drum brakes, the rear brakes incorporate leading and trailing shoes, which are actuated by twin-piston wheel cylinders. A self-adjust mechanism is incorporated, to automatically compensate for brake shoe wear. As the brake shoe linings wear, the footbrake operation automatically operates the adjuster mechanism, which effectively lengthens the shoe strut and repositions the brake shoes, to reduce the lining-to-drum clearance.

On models with rear disc brakes, the brakes are actuated by single-piston sliding calipers.

On some models, a pressure-regulating valve arrangement is situated in the hydraulic circuit to the rear brakes; this can be a separate valve arrangement fitted to the rear suspension lower arm or, on some models with rear drum brakes, the valves are incorporated into the rear wheel cylinders. The valves control the hydraulic pressure applied to the rear brakes to help to prevent rear wheel lock-up during emergency braking (see Section 21).

On all models, the handbrake provides an independent mechanical means of rear brake application. On models with rear disc brakes, the handbrake is in the form of a separate drum brake arrangement fitted in the centre of the brake disc; on models with drum brakes, the handbrake applies the rear brake shoes.

On diesel engines, there is insufficient vacuum in the inlet manifold to operate the braking system servo effectively at all times. To overcome this problem, a vacuum pump is fitted to the engine, to provide sufficient vacuum to operate the servo unit. The vacuum pump is mounted on the end of the cylinder head, and is driven directly off the end of the camshaft.

Note: *When servicing any of the system, work carefully and methodically; also observe scrupulous cleanliness when overhauling any of the hydraulic system. Always renew components (in axle sets, where applicable) if in doubt about their condition, and use only genuine Peugeot replacement parts, or at least those of known good quality. Note the warnings given in 'Safety first!' and at relevant points in this Chapter concerning the dangers of asbestos dust and hydraulic fluid.*

2 Hydraulic system – bleeding

Warning: Hydraulic fluid is poisonous; wash off immediately and thoroughly in the case of skin contact, and seek immediate medical advice if any fluid is swallowed or gets into the eyes. Certain types of hydraulic fluid are inflammable, and may ignite when allowed into contact with hot components; when servicing any hydraulic system, it is safest to assume that the fluid is inflammable, and to take precautions against the risk of fire as though it is petrol that is being handled. Hydraulic fluid is also an effective paint stripper, and will attack plastics; if any is spilt, it should be washed off immediately, using copious quantities of fresh water. Finally, it is hygroscopic (it absorbs moisture from the air) – old fluid may be contaminated and unfit for further use. When topping-up or renewing the fluid, always use the recommended type, and ensure that it comes from a freshly-opened sealed container.

Note: *If difficulty is experienced in bleeding the braking circuit on models with ABS, this maybe due to air being trapped in the ABS regulator unit. If this is the case then the vehicle should be taken to a Peugeot dealer so that the system can be bled using special electronic test equipment.*

Note: *A hydraulic clutch shares its fluid reservoir with the braking system, and may also need to be bled (see Chapter 6).*

General

1 The correct operation of any hydraulic system is only possible after removing all air from the components and circuit; this is achieved by bleeding the system.

2 During the bleeding procedure, add only clean, unused hydraulic fluid of the recommended type; never re-use fluid that has already been bled from the system. Ensure that sufficient fluid is available before starting work.

3 If there is any possibility of incorrect fluid being already in the system, the brake components and circuit must be flushed completely with uncontaminated, correct fluid, and new seals should be fitted to the various components.

4 If hydraulic fluid has been lost from the system, or air has entered because of a leak, ensure that the fault is cured before proceeding further.

5 Park the vehicle on level ground, switch off the engine and select first or reverse gear, then chock the wheels and release the handbrake.

6 Check that all pipes and hoses are secure, unions tight and bleed screws closed. Clean any dirt from around the bleed screws.

7 Unscrew the master cylinder reservoir cap, and top the master cylinder reservoir up to the MAX level line; refit the cap loosely, and remember to maintain the fluid level at least above the MIN/DANGER level line throughout the procedure, or there is a risk of further air entering the system.

8 There are a number of one-man, do-it-yourself brake bleeding kits currently available from motor accessory shops. It is recommended that one of these kits is used whenever possible, as they greatly simplify the bleeding operation, and also reduce the risk of expelled air and fluid being drawn back into the system. If such a kit is not available, the basic (two-man) method must be used, which is described in detail below.

9 If a kit is to be used, prepare the vehicle as described previously, and follow the kit manufacturer's instructions, as the procedure may vary slightly according to the type being used; generally, they are as outlined below in the relevant sub-section.

10 Whichever method is used, the same sequence must be followed (paragraphs 11 and 12) to ensure that the removal of all air from the system.

Bleeding

Sequence

11 If the system has been only partially disconnected, and suitable precautions were taken to minimise fluid loss, it should be necessary only to bleed that of the system (ie, the primary or secondary circuit).

12 If the complete system is to be bled, then it should be done working in the following sequence:

   a) *Right-hand front brake.*
   b) *Left-hand front brake.*
   c) *Right-hand rear brake.*
   d) *Left-hand rear brake.*

Basic (two-man) method

13 Collect a clean glass jar, a suitable length of plastic or rubber tubing which is a tight fit over the bleed screw, and a ring spanner to fit the screw. The help of an assistant will also be required.

14 Remove the dust cap from the first screw in the sequence. Fit the spanner and tube to the screw, place the other end of the tube in the jar, and pour in sufficient fluid to cover the end of the tube.

15 Ensure that the master cylinder reservoir fluid level is maintained at least above the MIN/DANGER level line throughout the procedure.

16 Have the assistant fully depress the brake pedal several times to build-up pressure, then maintain it on the final downstroke.

17 While pedal pressure is maintained, unscrew the bleed screw (approximately one turn) and allow the compressed fluid and air to flow into the jar. The assistant should maintain pedal pressure, following it down to the floor if necessary, and should not release it until instructed to do so. When the flow stops, tighten the bleed screw again, have the assistant release the pedal slowly, and recheck the reservoir fluid level.

18 Repeat the steps given in paragraphs 16 and 17 until the fluid emerging from the bleed screw is free from air bubbles. If the master cylinder has been drained and refilled, and air is being bled from the first screw in the sequence, allow approximately five seconds between cycles for the master cylinder passages to refill.

19 When no more air bubbles appear, tighten the bleed screw securely, remove the tube and spanner, and refit the dust cap. Do not overtighten the bleed screw.

20 Repeat the procedure on the remaining screws in the sequence, until all air is removed from the system and the brake pedal feels firm again.

Using a one-way valve kit

21 As their name implies, these kits consist of a length of tubing with a one-way valve fitted, to prevent expelled air and fluid being drawn back into the system; some kits include a translucent container, which can be positioned so that the air bubbles can be more easily seen flowing from the end of the tube.

22 The kit is connected to the bleed screw, which is then opened **(see illustration)**. The user returns to the driver's seat, depresses the brake pedal with a smooth, steady stroke, and slowly releases it; this is repeated until the expelled fluid is clear of air bubbles.

23 Note that these kits simplify work so much that it is easy to forget the master cylinder reservoir fluid level; ensure that this is maintained at least above the MIN/DANGER level line at all times.

Using a pressure-bleeding kit

24 These kits are usually operated by the reservoir of pressurised air contained in the spare tyre. However, note that it will probably be necessary to reduce the pressure to a lower level than normal; refer to the instructions supplied with the kit.

25 By connecting a pressurised, fluid-filled container to the master cylinder reservoir, bleeding can be carried out simply by opening each screw in turn (in the specified sequence), and allowing the fluid to flow out until no more air bubbles can be seen in the expelled fluid.

26 This method has the advantage that the large reservoir of fluid provides an additional safeguard against air being drawn into the system during bleeding.

27 Pressure-bleeding is particularly effective when bleeding 'difficult' systems, or when bleeding the complete system at the time of routine fluid renewal.

All methods

28 When bleeding is complete, and firm pedal feel is restored, wash off any spilt fluid, tighten the bleed screws securely, and refit their dust caps.

29 Check the hydraulic fluid level in the master cylinder reservoir, and top-up if necessary (see *Weekly checks*).

30 Discard any hydraulic fluid that has been bled from the system; it will not be fit for re-use.

31 Check the feel of the brake pedal. If it feels at all spongy, air must still be present in the system, and further bleeding is required. Failure to bleed satisfactorily after a reasonable repetition of the bleeding procedure may be due to worn master cylinder seals.

2.22 Bleeding a rear brake caliper

3.3 Using a brake pipe spanner to slacken a union nut

3 Hydraulic pipes and hoses – renewal

Caution: On models equipped with ABS, disconnect the battery before disconnecting any braking system hydraulic union and do not reconnect the battery until after the hydraulic system has been bled. Failure to do this could lead to air entering the regulator unit requiring the unit to be bled using special Peugeot test equipment (see Section 2).

Note: *Before starting work, refer to the note at the beginning of Section 2 concerning the dangers of hydraulic fluid.*

1 If any pipe or hose is to be renewed, minimise fluid loss by first removing the master cylinder reservoir cap, then tightening it down onto a piece of polythene to obtain an airtight seal. Alternatively, flexible hoses can be sealed, if required, using a proprietary brake hose clamp; metal brake pipe unions can be plugged (if care is taken not to allow dirt into the system) or capped immediately they are disconnected. Place a wad of rag under any union that is to be disconnected, to catch any spilt fluid.

2 If a flexible hose is to be disconnected, unscrew the brake pipe union nut before removing the spring clip which secures the hose to its mounting bracket.

3 To unscrew the union nuts, it is preferable to obtain a brake pipe spanner of the correct size; these are available from most large motor accessory shops **(see illustration)**. Failing this, a close-fitting open-ended spanner will be required, though if the nuts are tight or corroded, their flats may be rounded-off if the spanner slips. In such a case, a self-locking wrench is often the only way to unscrew a stubborn union, but it follows that the pipe and the damaged nuts must be renewed on reassembly. Always clean a union and surrounding area before disconnecting it. If disconnecting a component with more than one union, make a careful note of the connections before disturbing any of them.

4 If a brake pipe is to be renewed, it can be obtained, cut to length and with the union nuts and end flares in place, from Peugeot dealers. All that is then necessary is to bend it to shape, following the line of the original, before fitting it to the car. Alternatively, most motor accessory shops can make up brake pipes from kits, but this requires very careful measurement of the original, to ensure that the replacement is of the correct length. The safest answer is usually to take the original to the shop as a pattern.

5 On refitting, do not overtighten the union nuts. It is not necessary to exercise brute force to obtain a sound joint.

6 Ensure that the pipes and hoses are correctly routed, with no kinks, and that they are secured in the clips or brackets provided. After fitting, remove the polythene from the reservoir, and bleed the hydraulic system as described in Section 2. Wash off any spilt fluid, and check carefully for fluid leaks.

4 Front brake pads – renewal

Warning: Renew both sets of front brake pads at the same time – never renew the pads on only one wheel, as uneven braking may result. Note that the dust created by wear of the pads may contain asbestos, which is a health hazard. Never blow it out with compressed air, and don't inhale any of it. An approved filtering mask should be worn when working on the brakes. DO NOT use petrol or petroleum-based solvents to clean brake parts; use brake cleaner or methylated spirit only.

Note: *New guide pin bolts must be used on refitting.*

1 Apply the handbrake, then jack up the front of the vehicle and support it on axle stands. Remove the front roadwheels.

2 Trace the brake pad wear sensor wiring back from the pads, and disconnect it from the wiring connector. Note the routing of the wiring, and free it from any relevant retaining clips **(see illustration)**.

3 Push the piston into its bore by pulling the caliper outwards.

4 Slacken and remove the caliper lower guide pin bolt, using a slim open-ended spanner to prevent the guide pin itself from rotating **(see illustration)**. Discard the guide pin bolt – a new one must be used on refitting.

5 With the lower guide pin bolt removed, pivot the caliper away from the brake pads and mounting bracket, and tie it to the suspension strut using a suitable piece of wire **(see illustration)**.

6 Withdraw the two brake pads from the caliper mounting bracket; the shims (where fitted) should be bonded to the pad, but may have come unstuck in use **(see illustration)**.

7 First measure the thickness of each brake pad's friction material **(see illustration)**. If either pad is worn at any point to the specified minimum thickness or less, all four pads must be renewed. Also, the pads should be renewed if any are fouled with oil or grease;

4.2 Disconnect the pad wear sensor wiring connectors and release the wiring from its retaining clips

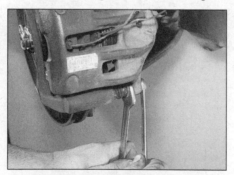

4.4 Slacken and remove the caliper lower guide pin bolt . . .

4.5 . . . then pivot the caliper upwards and away from the brake pads and tie it to the suspension strut . . .

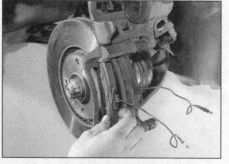

4.6 . . . the brake pads can then be removed from the mounting bracket

there is no satisfactory way of degreasing friction material, once contaminated. If any of the brake pads are worn unevenly, or are fouled with oil or grease, trace and rectify the cause before reassembly.

8 If the brake pads are still serviceable, carefully clean them using a clean, fine wire brush or similar, paying particular attention to the sides and back of the metal backing. Clean out the grooves in the friction material, and pick out any large embedded particles of dirt or debris. Carefully clean the pad locations in the caliper mounting bracket.

9 Prior to fitting the pads, check that the guide pins are free to slide easily in the caliper mounting bracket, and check that the rubber guide pin gaiters are undamaged **(see illustration)**. Brush the dust and dirt from the caliper and piston, but **do not** inhale it, as it is a health hazard. Inspect the dust seal around the piston for damage, and the piston for evidence of fluid leaks, corrosion or damage. If attention to any of these components is necessary, refer to Section 10.

10 If new brake pads are to be fitted, the caliper piston must be pushed back into the cylinder to make room for them. Either use a G-clamp or similar tool, or use suitable pieces of wood as levers. Provided that the master cylinder reservoir has not been overfilled with hydraulic fluid, there should be no spillage, but keep a careful watch on the fluid level while retracting the piston. If the fluid level rises above the MAX level line at any time, the surplus should be syphoned off or ejected via a plastic tube connected to the bleed screw (see Section 2). **Note:** *Do not syphon the fluid by mouth, as it is poisonous; use a syringe or an old poultry baster.*

11 Ensuring that the friction material of each pad is against the brake disc, fit the pads to the caliper mounting bracket. If the shims (where fitted) have become detached, ensure that they are correctly positioned on each pads backing plate.

12 Pivot the caliper down into position over the pads, passing the pad warning sensor wiring through the caliper aperture. If the threads of the new guide pin bolt are not already pre-coated with locking compound, apply a suitable thread-locking compound to them (Peugeot recommend Loctite Frenetanch – available from your Peugeot dealer). Press the caliper into position, then install the guide pin bolt, tightening it to the specified torque setting while retaining the guide pin with an open-ended spanner **(see illustrations)**.

13 Reconnect the brake pad wear sensor wiring connectors, ensuring that the wiring is correctly routed through the loop of the caliper bleed screw cap.

14 Depress the brake pedal repeatedly, until the pads are pressed into firm contact with the brake disc, and normal (non-assisted) pedal pressure is restored.

15 Repeat the above procedure on the remaining front brake caliper.

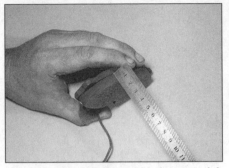

4.7 Measuring brake pad friction material thickness

4.12a Pivot the caliper back into position, passing the pad wear sensor wiring through the aperture . . .

16 Refit the roadwheels, then lower the vehicle to the ground and tighten the roadwheel bolts to the specified torque.

17 Check the hydraulic fluid level as described in *Weekly checks*.

Caution: New pads will not give full braking efficiency until they have bedded-in. Be prepared for this, and avoid hard braking as far as possible for the first hundred miles or so after pad renewal.

---

5 Rear brake pads – renewal

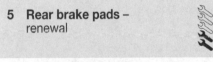

⚠ *Warning: Renew both sets of rear brake pads at the same time – never renew the pads on only one*

5.2a Remove the spring clips (arrowed) . . .

4.9 Examine the guide pin gaiters for signs of damage and renew if necessary

4.12b . . . then fit the new guide pin bolt and tighten it to the specified torque

wheel, as uneven braking may result. Note that the dust created by wear of the pads may contain asbestos, which is a health hazard. Never blow it out with compressed air, and don't inhale any of it. An approved filtering mask should be worn when working on the brakes. DO NOT use petrol or petroleum-based solvents to clean brake parts; use brake cleaner or methylated spirit only.

1 Chock the front wheels, then jack up the rear of the vehicle and support it on axle stands. Remove the rear wheels.

2 Extract the small spring clip from the each pad retaining pin then slide the retaining pins out from the caliper, noting the correct fitted location of the pad anti-rattle spring **(see illustrations)**. Remove the anti-rattle spring.

5.2b . . . then withdraw the retaining pins and recover the anti-rattle spring, noting which way around it is fitted

5.3 Removing the rear brake pads from the caliper

5.9 Ensure the upper retaining pin passes through the centre of the anti-rattle spring and the spring ends are located behind the lower pin

3 Using pliers if necessary, withdraw both the inner and outer pads from the caliper; the inner pad has an anti-squeal shim which should have the rubber surface side facing towards the pad **(see illustration)**.

4 First measure the thickness of the friction material of each brake pad. If either pad is worn at any point to the specified minimum thickness or less, all four pads must be renewed. Also, the pads should be renewed if any are fouled with oil or grease; there is no satisfactory way of degreasing friction material, once contaminated. If any of the brake pads are worn unevenly, or fouled with oil or grease, trace and rectify the cause before reassembly. Examine the retaining pins for signs of wear and renew if necessary. New brake pads and retaining pin kits are available from Peugeot dealers.

5 If the brake pads are still serviceable, carefully clean them using a clean, fine wire brush or similar, paying particular attention to the sides and back of the metal backing. Clean out the grooves in the friction material, and pick out any large embedded particles of dirt or debris. Carefully clean the pad locations in the caliper body/mounting bracket.

6 Prior to fitting the pads, check that the guide sleeves are free to slide easily in the caliper body, and check that the rubber guide sleeve gaiters are undamaged. Brush the dust and dirt from the caliper and piston, but **do not** inhale it, as it is a health hazard. Inspect the dust seal around the piston for damage, and the piston for evidence of fluid leaks, corrosion or damage. If attention to any of these components is necessary, refer to Section 11.

7 If new brake pads are to be fitted, the caliper piston must be pushed back into the cylinder to make room for them. Either use a G-clamp or similar tool, or use suitable pieces of wood as levers. Provided that the master cylinder reservoir has not been overfilled with hydraulic fluid, there should be no spillage, but keep a careful watch on the fluid level while retracting the piston. If the fluid level rises above the MAX level line at any time, the surplus should be syphoned off or ejected via

a plastic tube connected to the bleed screw (see Section 2). **Note:** *Do not syphon the fluid by mouth, as it is poisonous; use a syringe or an old poultry baster.*

8 Slide the brake pads into position in the caliper, ensuring each pad's friction material is facing the brake disc. If the shims (where fitted) have become detached, ensure that they are correctly positioned on each pad's backing plate

9 Fit the anti-rattle spring to the top of the pads, making sure it is fitted the correct way up. Slide the first pad retaining pin into position, ensuring it passes through the holes in both pad backing plates and the centre of the anti-rattle spring. Slide the second pad retaining pin into position, ensuring that the anti-rattle spring ends are correctly located behind the pin **(see illustration)**. Ensure that the anti-rattle spring and pads are correctly engaged with the retaining pins, then secure the pins in position with the spring clips.

10 Depress the brake pedal repeatedly until the pads are pressed into firm contact with the brake disc, and normal (non-assisted) pedal pressure is restored. Check that the inner pad lug is correctly engaged with one of the caliper piston slots.

11 Repeat the above procedure on the remaining rear brake caliper.

12 Refit the roadwheels, then lower the vehicle to the ground and tighten the road-wheel bolts to the specified torque setting.

13 Check the hydraulic fluid level as described in *Weekly checks*.

6.6 Removing a shoe retainer spring cup

6 Rear brake shoes – renewal

⚠ *Warning: Brake shoes must be renewed on both rear wheels at the same time – never renew the shoes on only one wheel, as uneven braking may result. Also, the dust created by wear of the shoes may contain asbestos, which is a health hazard. Never blow it out with compressed air, and don't inhale any of it. An approved filtering mask should be worn when working on the brakes. DO NOT use petrol or petroleum-based solvents to clean brake parts; use brake cleaner or methylated spirit only.*

1 Remove the brake drum as described in Section 9.

2 Working carefully, and taking the necessary precautions, remove all traces of brake dust from the brake drum, backplate and shoes.

3 Measure the thickness of the friction material of each brake shoe at several points; if either shoe is worn at any point to the specified minimum thickness or less, all four shoes must be renewed as a set. The shoes should also be renewed if any are fouled with oil or grease; there is no satisfactory way of degreasing friction material, once contaminated.

4 If any of the brake shoes are worn unevenly, or fouled with oil or grease, trace and rectify the cause before reassembly.

5 If all the components are in good condition, refit the brake drum as described in Section 9. To renew the brake shoes, proceed as follows.

6 Note the correct fitted location of all components then, using a pair of pliers, remove the shoe retainer spring cups by depressing and turning them through 90°. With the cups removed, lift off the springs and withdraw the retainer pins **(see illustration)**.

7 Ease the shoes out one at a time from the lower pivot point, to release the tension of the return spring, then disconnect the lower return spring from both shoes.

8 Ease the upper end of both shoes out from their wheel cylinder locations, taking care not to damage the wheel cylinder seals, and disconnect the handbrake cable from the trailing shoe. The brake shoe and adjuster strut assembly can then be manoeuvred out of position and away from the backplate. Do not depress the brake pedal until the brakes are reassembled; wrap a strong elastic band around the wheel cylinder pistons to retain them.

9 With the shoe and adjuster strut assembly on a bench, make a note of the correct fitted positions of the springs and adjuster strut, to use as a guide on reassembly **(see illustration)**. Release the handbrake lever stop-peg (if not already done), then carefully detach the adjuster strut bolt retaining spring from the leading shoe. Disconnect the upper return spring, then detach the leading shoe and return spring from the trailing shoe and strut assembly. Unhook the spring securing the adjuster strut to the trailing shoe, and separate the two.

10 Depending on the type of brake shoes being installed, it may be necessary to remove the handbrake lever from the original trailing shoe, and install it on the new shoe. Secure the lever in position with a new retaining clip. All return springs should be renewed, regardless of their apparent condition; spring kits are available from Peugeot dealers.

11 Withdraw the adjuster bolt from the strut, and carefully examine the assembly for signs of wear or damage. Pay particular attention to the threads of the adjuster bolt and the knurled adjuster wheel, and renew if necessary. Note that left-hand and right-hand struts are not interchangeable – they are marked G (gauche/left) and D (droit/right) respectively. Also note that the strut adjuster bolts are not interchangeable; the left-hand strut bolt has a left-handed thread (unscrews **clockwise**), and the right-hand bolt a right-handed thread.

12 Ensure that the components on the end of the strut are correctly positioned, then apply a little high-melting-point grease to the threads of the adjuster bolt. Screw the adjuster wheel onto the bolt until only a small gap exists between the wheel and the head of the bolt, then install the bolt in the strut.

13 Fit the adjuster strut retaining spring to the trailing shoe, ensuring that the shorter hook of the spring is engaged with the shoe. Attach the adjuster strut to the spring end, then ease the strut into position in its slot in the trailing shoe.

14 Engage the upper return spring with the trailing shoe, then hook the leading shoe onto the other end of the spring, and lever the leading shoe down until the adjuster bolt head is correctly located in its groove. Once the bolt is correctly located, hook its retaining spring into the slot on the leading shoe.

15 Peel back the rubber protective caps, and check the wheel cylinder for fluid leaks or other damage; check that both cylinder pistons are free to move easily. Refer to Section 12, if necessary, for information on wheel cylinder renewal.

16 Prior to installation, clean the backplate, and apply a thin smear of high-temperature brake grease or anti-seize compound to all those surfaces of the backplate which bear on the shoes, particularly the wheel cylinder pistons and lower pivot point **(see illustration)**. Do not allow the lubricant to foul the friction material.

17 Ensure that the handbrake lever stop-peg is correctly located against the edge of the

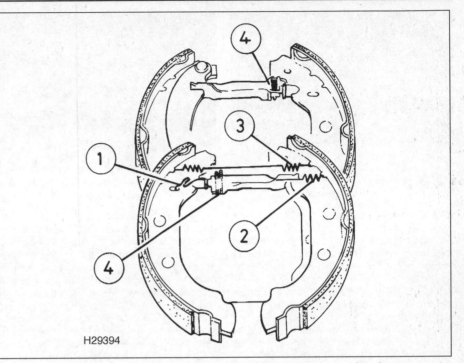

6.9 Correct fitted locations of the brake shoe adjuster strut and associated components

1 *Adjuster strut bolt retaining spring*
2 *Adjuster strut spring*
3 *Upper return spring*
4 *Adjuster strut assembly*

trailing shoe, and remove the elastic band fitted to the wheel cylinder.

18 Manoeuvre the shoe and strut assembly into position on the vehicle, and locate the upper end of both shoes with the wheel cylinder pistons. Attach the handbrake cable to the trailing shoe lever. Fit the lower return spring to both shoes, and ease the shoes into position on the lower pivot point.

19 Tap the shoes to centralise them with the backplate, then refit the shoe retainer pins and springs, and secure them in position with the spring cups.

20 Using a screwdriver, turn the strut adjuster wheel to expand the shoes until the brake drum just slides over the shoes.

21 Refit the brake drum as described in Section 9.

22 Repeat the above procedure on the remaining rear brake.

6.16 Apply a little high-melting point grease to the shoe contact points on the backplate

23 Once both sets of rear shoes have been renewed, adjust the lining-to-drum clearance by repeatedly depressing the brake pedal. Whilst depressing the pedal, have an assistant listen to the rear drums, to check that the adjuster strut is functioning correctly; if so, a clicking sound will be emitted by the strut as the pedal is depressed.

24 Check and, if necessary, adjust the handbrake as described in Section 17.

25 On completion, check the hydraulic fluid level as described in *Weekly checks*.

Caution: New shoes will not give full braking efficiency until they have bedded-in. Be prepared for this, and avoid hard braking as far as possible for the first hundred miles or so after shoe renewal.

7 Front brake disc – inspection, removal and refitting

Note: *Before starting work, refer to the note at the beginning of Section 4 concerning the dangers of asbestos dust.*

Inspection

Note: *If either disc requires renewal, BOTH should be renewed at the same time, to ensure even and consistent braking. New brake pads should also be fitted.*

1 Apply the handbrake, then jack up the front of the car and support it on axle stands. Remove the appropriate front roadwheel.

2 Slowly rotate the brake disc so that the full

7.3 Measuring brake disc thickness using a micrometer

7.4 Using a dial gauge to check brake disc run-out

area of both sides can be checked; remove the brake pads if better access is required to the inboard surface. Light scoring is normal in the area swept by the brake pads, but if heavy scoring or cracks are found, the disc must be renewed.

3 It is normal to find a lip of rust and brake dust around the disc's perimeter; this can be scraped off if required. If, however, a lip has formed due to excessive wear of the brake pad swept area, then the disc's thickness must be measured using a micrometer. Take measurements at several places around the disc, at the inside and outside of the pad swept area; if the disc has worn at any point to the specified minimum thickness or less, the disc must be renewed **(see illustration)**.

4 If the disc is thought to be warped, it can be checked for run-out. Either use a dial gauge mounted on any convenient fixed point, while the disc is slowly rotated, or use feeler blades

to measure (at several points all around the disc) the clearance between the disc and a fixed point, such as the caliper mounting bracket **(see illustration)**. If the measurements obtained are at the specified maximum or beyond, the disc is excessively warped, and must be renewed; however, it is worth checking first that the hub bearing is in good condition (Chapter 1A or 1B). Also try the effect of removing the disc and turning it through 180º, to reposition it on the hub; if the run-out is still excessive, the disc must be renewed.

5 Check the disc for cracks, especially around the wheel bolt holes, and any other wear or damage, and renew if necessary.

Removal

6 Slacken and remove the two bolts securing the brake caliper mounting bracket to the swivel hub. Slide the caliper assembly off the disc and tie the assembly to the front coil

spring, using a piece of wire or string, to avoid placing any strain on the hydraulic brake hose.

7 Use chalk or paint to mark the relationship of the disc to the hub, then remove the screws securing the brake disc to the hub, and remove the disc. If it is tight, lightly tap its rear face with a hide or plastic mallet.

Refitting

8 Refitting is the reverse of the removal procedure, noting the following points:
   a) Ensure that the mating surfaces of the disc and hub are clean and flat.
   b) Align (if applicable) the marks made on removal, and tighten the disc retaining screws to the specified torque setting.
   c) If a new disc has been fitted, use a suitable solvent to wipe any preservative coating from the disc, before refitting the caliper.
   d) Prior to installation, clean the threads of the caliper bracket mounting bolts and coat them with thread-locking compound (Peugeot recommend Loctite Frenetanch – available from your Peugeot dealer). Slide the caliper into position, making sure the pads pass either side of the disc, and tighten the caliper bracket bolts to the specified torque setting.
   e) Refit the roadwheel then lower the vehicle to the ground and tighten the wheel bolts to the specified torque. Apply the footbrake several times to force the pads back into contact with the disc before driving the vehicle.

8 Rear brake disc – inspection, removal and refitting

Note: Before starting work, refer to the note at the beginning of Section 5 concerning the dangers of asbestos dust.

Inspection

Note: If either disc requires renewal, BOTH should be renewed at the same time, to ensure even and consistent braking. New brake pads should also be fitted.

1 Firmly chock the front wheels, then jack up the rear of the car and support it on axle stands. Remove the relevant rear roadwheel.
2 Inspect the disc as described in Section 7.

Removal

3 Slide out the retaining clip and release the brake pipe from its clip on the front of the hub assembly **(see illustration)**.
4 Slacken and remove the caliper mounting bolt then remove the protective cap from the guide bush and slacken and remove the guide pin bolt. Slide the caliper assembly off the disc and tie the assembly to the coil spring, using a piece of wire or string, to avoid placing any strain on the hydraulic brake pipe **(see illustrations)**.

8.3 Slide out the retaining clip (arrowed) and free the brake pipe from the hub assembly

8.4a Slacken and remove the mounting bolt . . .

8.4b . . . then remove the cap from the guide bush . . .

8.4c . . . and unscrew the guide pin bolt

8.4d Slide the caliper assembly off the disc and tie it to the rear suspension to avoid straining the brake pipe

8.5a Undo the retaining screws (arrowed) . . .

8.5b . . . and remove the rear brake disc from the vehicle

5 Use chalk or paint to mark the relationship of the disc to the hub, then remove the screws securing the brake disc to the hub. Ensure that the handbrake is fully released then remove the disc from the vehicle, if necessary gently tap the disc to free it from the hub. If the disc is still tight on the handbrake shoes even with the brake fully released, back off the adjuster as described in Section 17 **(see illustrations)**.

Refitting

6 Refitting is the reverse of the removal procedure, noting the following points:
  a) *Ensure that the mating surfaces of the disc and hub are clean and flat.*
  b) *Align (if applicable) the marks made on removal, and tighten the disc retaining screws to the specified torque.*
  c) *If a new disc has been fitted, use a suitable solvent to wipe any preservative coating from the disc, before refitting the caliper.*
  d) *Clean the threads of the caliper mounting and guide pin bolts and coat them with thread-locking compound. Slide the caliper into position, making sure the pads pass either side of the disc, then refit the bolts tightening them to the specified torque settings (see illustrations). Refit the cap to the guide bush.*
  e) *Prior to refitting the roadwheel, adjust the handbrake shoes (refer to Section 17).*
  f) *Refit the roadwheel, then lower the vehicle to the ground and tighten the roadwheel bolts to the specified torque. Depress the brake pedal several times to force the pads back into contact with the disc.*

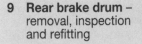 **9 Rear brake drum –**
removal, inspection
and refitting

Note: *Before starting work, refer to the note at the beginning of Section 6 concerning the dangers of asbestos dust.*

Removal

1 Chock the front wheels, then jack up the

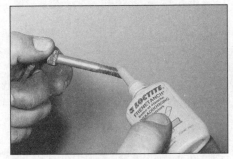

8.6a Apply locking compound to the threads of the caliper mounting and guide pin bolts . . .

rear of the vehicle and support it on axle stands. Remove the appropriate rear wheel.
2 Slacken and remove the screws securing the brake drum to the hub.
3 Ensure that the handbrake is fully released and remove the brake drum from the vehicle. It may be difficult to remove the drum due to the drum being corroded onto the hub, or the brake shoes binding on the inner circumference of the drum. If the drum is tight, tap the periphery of the drum using a hide or plastic mallet. If the brake shoes are binding, first check that the handbrake is fully released, then proceed as follows.
4 Referring to Section 17, fully slacken the handbrake cable adjuster to obtain maximum freeplay in the cable. Remove the access plug from the rear of the brake backplate (the plug is usually coloured blue) then, using a screwdriver or punch, push the handbrake lever outwards until the stop-peg slips behind the brake shoe web **(see illustration)**. This will retract the brake shoes fully and so allow the brake drum to be withdrawn easily. Once the drum is removed, refit the access plug to the backplate.

Inspection

Note: *If either drum requires renewal, BOTH should be renewed at the same time, to ensure even and consistent braking. New brake shoes should also be fitted.*
5 Working carefully, remove all traces of brake dust from the drum, but *avoid inhaling the dust, as it is a health hazard.*
6 Clean the outside of the drum, and check it for obvious signs of wear or damage, such as

8.6b . . . and tighten them to the specified torque settings

cracks around the roadwheel bolt holes; renew the drum if necessary.
7 Examine carefully the inside of the drum. Light scoring of the friction surface is normal, but if heavy scoring is found, the drum must be renewed. It is usual to find a lip on the drum's inboard edge which consists of a mixture of rust and brake dust; this should be scraped away, to leave a smooth surface which can be polished with fine (120- to 150-grade) emery paper. If, however, the lip is due to the friction surface being recessed by excessive wear, then the drum must be renewed.
8 If the drum is thought to be excessively

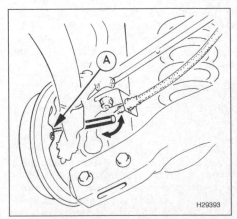

9.4 To fully release the handbrake lever, remove the access plug and use a screwdriver or punch (A) to push the lever outwards

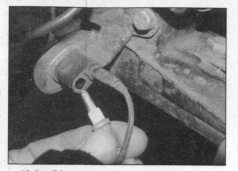

10.3a Disconnect the pad wear sensor wiring . . .

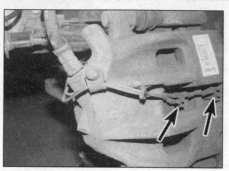

10.3b . . . and free it from its retaining clips (arrowed)

worn, or oval, its internal diameter must be measured at several points using an internal micrometer. Take measurements in pairs, the second at right-angles to the first, and compare the two, to check for signs of ovality. Provided that it does not enlarge the drum to beyond the specified maximum diameter, it may be possible to have the drum refinished by skimming or grinding; if this is not possible, the drums on both sides must be renewed. Note that if the drum is to be skimmed, BOTH drums must be refinished, to maintain a consistent internal diameter on both sides.

Refitting

9 If a new brake drum is to be installed, use a suitable solvent to remove any preservative coating that may have been applied to its interior. Note that it may also be necessary to shorten the adjuster strut length, by rotating the strut wheel, to allow the drum to pass over the brake shoes.

10 Ensure that the handbrake lever stop-peg is correctly repositioned against the edge of the brake shoe web and that the mating surfaces of the drum and hub are clean and dry.

11 Manoeuvre the drum into position and tighten its retaining screws.

12 Depress the footbrake several times to operate the self-adjusting mechanism.

13 Repeat the above procedure on the remaining rear brake assembly (where necessary), then check and, if necessary, adjust the handbrake cable (see Section 17).

14 On completion, refit the roadwheel(s), then lower the car to the ground and tighten the wheel bolts to the specified torque.

---

10 Front brake caliper –
removal, overhaul and refitting

Caution: On models equipped with ABS, disconnect the battery before disconnecting any braking system hydraulic union and do not reconnect the battery until after the hydraulic system has been bled. Failure to do this could lead to air entering the regulator unit requiring the unit to be bled using special Peugeot test equipment (see Section 2).

Note: *Before starting work, refer to the note at the beginning of Section 2 concerning the dangers of hydraulic fluid, and to the warning at the beginning of Section 4 concerning the dangers of asbestos dust.*

Note: *New guide pin bolts will be required on refitting.*

Removal

1 Apply the handbrake, then jack up the front of the vehicle and support it on axle stands. Remove the appropriate roadwheel.

2 Minimise fluid loss by first removing the master cylinder reservoir cap, and then tightening it down onto a piece of polythene, to obtain an airtight seal. Alternatively, use a brake hose clamp, a G-clamp or a similar tool to clamp the flexible hose.

3 Clean the area around the caliper hose union, then loosen the union. Disconnect the pad wear warning sensor wiring connector, and free it from any relevant retaining clips **(see illustrations)**.

4 Slacken and remove the upper and lower caliper guide pin bolts, using a slim open-ended spanner to prevent the guide pin itself from rotating. Discard the bolts, new ones must be used on refitting. Lift the caliper away from the brake disc, then unscrew the caliper from the end of the brake hose. Note that the brake pads need not be disturbed, and can be left in position in the caliper mounting bracket.

Overhaul

5 With the caliper on the bench, wipe away all traces of dust and dirt, but *avoid inhaling the dust, as it is a health hazard.*

6 Withdraw the partially ejected piston from the caliper body, and remove the dust seal.

HAYNES HiNT *If the piston cannot be withdrawn by hand, it can be pushed out by applying compressed air to the brake hose union hole. Only low pressure should be required, such as is generated by a foot pump. As the piston is expelled, take great care not to trap your fingers between the piston and caliper.*

---

7 Using a small screwdriver, extract the

piston hydraulic seal, taking great care not to damage the caliper bore.

8 Thoroughly clean all components, using only methylated spirit, isopropyl alcohol or clean hydraulic fluid as a cleaning medium. Never use mineral-based solvents such as petrol or paraffin, as they will attack the hydraulic system's rubber components. Dry the components immediately, using compressed air or a clean, lint-free cloth. Use compressed air to blow clear the fluid passages.

9 Check all components, and renew any that are worn or damaged. Check particularly the cylinder bore and piston; these should be renewed (note that this means the renewal of the complete body assembly) if they are scratched, worn or corroded in any way. Similarly check the condition of the guide pins and their gaiters; both pins should be undamaged and (when cleaned) a reasonably tight sliding fit in the caliper bracket. If there is any doubt about the condition of any component, renew it.

10 If the assembly is fit for further use, obtain the appropriate repair kit; the components are available from Peugeot dealers in various combinations. All rubber seals should be renewed as a matter of course; these should never be re-used.

11 On reassembly, ensure that all components are clean and dry.

12 Soak the piston and the new piston (fluid) seal in clean hydraulic fluid. Smear clean fluid on the cylinder bore surface.

13 Fit the new piston (fluid) seal, using only your fingers (no tools) to manipulate it into the cylinder bore groove.

14 Fit the new dust seal to the rear of the piston and seat the outer lip of the seal in the caliper body groove. Carefully ease the piston squarely into the cylinder bore using a twisting motion. Press the piston fully into position, and seat the inner lip of the dust seal in the piston groove.

15 If the guide pins are being renewed, lubricate the pin shafts with the special grease supplied in the repair kit, and fit the gaiters to the pin grooves. Insert the pins into the caliper bracket and seat the gaiters correctly in the bracket grooves.

Refitting

16 Screw the caliper body fully onto the flexible hose union.

17 Ensure that the brake pads are still correctly fitted in the caliper mounting bracket and refit the caliper, passing the pad warning sensor wiring through the caliper aperture.

18 If the threads of the new guide pin bolts are not already precoated with locking compound, apply a suitable locking compound to them (Peugeot recommend Loctite Frenetanch – available from your Peugeot dealer). Fit the new lower guide pin bolt, then press the caliper into position and fit the new upper guide pin bolt. Tighten both guide pin bolts to the specified torque while retaining the guide pin with an open-ended spanner.

19 Reconnect the brake pad wear sensor wiring connectors, ensuring that the wiring is correctly routed through the loop of the caliper bleed screw cap.

20 Tighten the brake hose union nut to the specified torque, then remove the brake hose clamp or polythene (where fitted).

21 Bleed the hydraulic system as described in Section 2. Note that, providing the precautions described were taken to minimise brake fluid loss, it should only be necessary to bleed the relevant front brake.

22 Refit the roadwheel, then lower the vehicle to the ground and tighten the roadwheel bolts to the specified torque.

11 Rear brake caliper – removal, overhaul and refitting

Caution: On models equipped with ABS, disconnect the battery before disconnecting any braking system hydraulic union and do not reconnect the battery until after the hydraulic system has been bled. Failure to do this could lead to air entering the regulator unit requiring the unit to be bled using special Peugeot test equipment (see Section 2).

Note: *Before starting work, refer to the note at the beginning of Section 2 concerning the dangers of hydraulic fluid, and to the warning at the beginning of Section 5 concerning the dangers of asbestos dust.*

Removal

1 Chock the front wheels, then jack up the rear of the vehicle and support on axle stands. Remove the relevant rear wheel.

2 Remove the brake pads as described in Section 5.

3 Minimise fluid loss by first removing the master cylinder reservoir cap, and then tightening it down onto a piece of polythene, to obtain an airtight seal. Alternatively, use a brake hose clamp, a G-clamp or a similar tool to clamp the flexible hose at the nearest convenient point to the brake caliper.

4 Wipe away all traces of dirt around the brake hose union on the caliper. Unscrew the union nut and disconnect the brake pipe from the caliper. Plug the pipe and caliper unions to minimise fluid loss and prevent dirt entry.

5 Slacken and remove the caliper mounting bolt then remove the protective cap from the guide bush and slacken and remove the guide pin bolt. Remove the caliper from the vehicle.

Overhaul

6 The caliper can be overhauled as described in Section 10. The only notable difference between the front and rear caliper is in the guide pin/bush arrangement. If either the guide bush or spacer show signs of wear or damage they must be renewed; both components are available in repair kits from Peugeot dealers.

11.8a Apply locking compound to the guide pin and mounting bolt threads . . .

Refitting

7 Clean the threads of the caliper mounting and guide pin bolts and coat them with thread-locking compound (Peugeot recommend Loctite Frenetanch – available from your Peugeot dealer).

8 Refit the caliper and insert the mounting and guide pin bolts, tightening them to the specified torque settings **(see illustrations)**. Refit the protective cap to the guide bush.

9 Reconnect the brake pipe to the caliper, and tighten the brake hose union nut to the specified torque. Remove the brake hose clamp or polythene (where fitted).

10 Refit the brake pads as described in Section 5.

11 Bleed the hydraulic system as described in Section 2. Note that, providing the precautions described were taken to minimise brake fluid loss, it should only be necessary to bleed the relevant front brake.

12 Refit the roadwheel, then lower the vehicle to the ground and tighten the roadwheel bolts to the specified torque.

12 Rear wheel cylinder – removal and refitting

Caution: On models equipped with ABS, disconnect the battery before disconnecting any braking system hydraulic union and do not reconnect the battery until after the hydraulic system has been bled. Failure to do this could lead to air

12.2 To minimise fluid loss, clamp the brake hose at the nearest convenient point to the wheel cylinder

11.8b . . . and tighten them to the specified torque

entering the regulator unit requiring the unit to be bled using special Peugeot test equipment (see Section 2).

Note: *Before starting work, refer to the note at the beginning of Section 2 concerning the dangers of hydraulic fluid, and to the warning at the beginning of Section 6 concerning the dangers of asbestos dust.*

Removal

1 Remove the brake drum as described in Section 9.

2 Minimise fluid loss by first removing the master cylinder reservoir cap, and then tightening it down onto a piece of polythene, to obtain an airtight seal. Alternatively, use a brake hose clamp, a G-clamp or a similar tool to clamp the flexible hose at the nearest convenient point to the wheel cylinder **(see illustration)**.

3 Using pliers, carefully unhook the upper brake shoe return spring, and remove it from both brake shoes. Pull the upper ends of the shoes away from the wheel cylinder to disengage them from the pistons.

4 Wipe away all traces of dirt around the brake pipe union at the rear of the wheel cylinder, and unscrew the union nut **(see illustration)**. Carefully ease the pipe out of the wheel cylinder, and plug or tape over its end to prevent dirt entry. Wipe off any spilt fluid immediately.

5 Unscrew the two wheel cylinder retaining bolts from the rear of the backplate, and remove the cylinder, taking great care not to allow surplus hydraulic fluid to contaminate the brake shoe linings.

12.4 Using a brake pipe spanner to unscrew the wheel cylinder union nut

6 Note that it is not possible to overhaul the cylinder, since no components are available separately. If faulty, the complete wheel cylinder assembly must be renewed.

Refitting

7 Ensure that the backplate and wheel cylinder mating surfaces are clean, then spread the brake shoes and manoeuvre the wheel cylinder into position.

8 Engage the brake pipe, and screw in the union nut two or three turns to ensure that the thread has started.

9 Insert the two wheel cylinder retaining bolts, tightening them to the specified torque, then tighten the brake pipe union nut to the specified torque.

10 Remove the clamp from the flexible brake hose, or the polythene from the master cylinder reservoir (as applicable).

11 Ensure that the brake shoes are correctly located in the cylinder pistons, then carefully refit the brake shoe upper return spring, using a screwdriver to stretch the spring into position.

12 Refit the brake drum as described in Section 9.

13 Bleed the brake hydraulic system as described in Section 2. Providing suitable precautions were taken to minimise loss of fluid, it should only be necessary to bleed the relevant rear brake.

13 Master cylinder –
removal, overhaul and refitting

Caution: On models equipped with ABS, disconnect the battery before disconnecting any braking system hydraulic union and do not reconnect the battery until after the hydraulic system has been bled. Failure to do this could lead to air entering the regulator unit requiring the unit to be bled using special Peugeot test equipment (see Section 2).

Note: *Before starting work, refer to the warning at the beginning of Section 2 concerning the dangers of hydraulic fluid.*

Removal

1 To provide improved access on some models it will be necessary to remove the air cleaner housing duct (see the relevant Part of Chapter 4).

2 Remove the master cylinder reservoir cap and filter, and syphon the hydraulic fluid from the reservoir. **Note:** *Do not syphon the fluid by mouth, as it is poisonous; use a syringe or an old antifreeze tester.* Alternatively, open any convenient bleed screw in the system, and gently pump the brake pedal to expel the fluid through a plastic tube connected to the screw (see Section 2). Disconnect the wiring connector from the brake fluid level sender unit.

3 Remove the retaining clip then slide out the

14.3 Release the retaining clip (arrowed) and withdraw the clevis pin

fluid reservoir retaining pin. Lift the reservoir upwards and away from the master cylinder body, and recover the mounting seals from the cylinder ports. If the mounting seals show signs of wear or deterioration, they must be renewed.

4 Wipe clean the area around the brake pipe unions on the side of the master cylinder, and place absorbent rags beneath the pipe unions to catch any surplus fluid. Make a note of the correct fitted positions of the unions, then unscrew the union nuts and carefully withdraw the pipes. Plug or tape over the pipe ends and master cylinder orifices, to minimise the loss of brake fluid, and to prevent the entry of dirt into the system. Wash off any spilt fluid immediately with cold water.

5 Slacken and remove the two nuts securing the master cylinder to the vacuum servo unit, then withdraw the unit from the engine compartment. If the sealing ring fitted to the rear of the master cylinder shows signs of damage or deterioration, it must be renewed.

Overhaul

6 The master cylinder can be overhauled after obtaining the relevant repair kit from a Peugeot dealer. Ensure that the correct repair kit is obtained for the master cylinder being worked on. Note the locations of all components to ensure correct refitting, and lubricate the new seals using clean brake fluid. Follow the assembly instructions supplied with the repair kit.

Refitting

7 Prior to refitting, measure the distance from

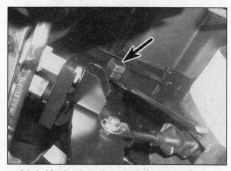

14.4 Undo the pivot bolt (arrowed) and remove the brake pedal

the end of the vacuum servo unit pushrod to the servo master cylinder mating surface. This should be 22.3 ± 0.1 mm; if not seek the advice of a Peugeot dealer before refitting the master cylinder.

8 Remove all traces of dirt from the master cylinder and servo unit mating surfaces and ensure that the sealing ring is correctly fitted to the rear of the master cylinder.

9 Fit the master cylinder to the servo unit, ensuring that the servo unit pushrod enters the master cylinder bore centrally. Refit the master cylinder mounting nuts, and tighten them to the specified torque.

10 Wipe clean the brake pipe unions and refit them to the master cylinder ports, tightening them to the specified torque.

11 Press the mounting seals fully into the master cylinder ports then carefully ease the fluid reservoir into position. Slide the reservoir retaining pin into position and secure it in position, making sure the retaining clip is correctly located in the pin groove.

12 Refit any components removed to improve access then refill the master cylinder reservoir with new fluid. Bleed the complete hydraulic system as described in Section 2. **Note:** *A hydraulic clutch shares its fluid reservoir with the braking system, and may also need to be bled (see Chapter 6).*

14 Brake pedal –
removal and refitting

Removal

1 Disconnect the battery negative terminal.

2 Rotate the fastener through 90° and lower the fusebox cover, then slacken and remove the retaining screws and remove the driver's side lower panel from the facia.

3 Slide off the retaining clip and withdraw the clevis pin securing the pedal crossover linkage/servo unit pushrod to the pedal **(see illustration)**.

4 Slacken and remove the pivot bolt and nut **(see illustration)**, and remove the brake pedal from the vehicle. Slide the spacer out from the pedal pivot. Examine all components for signs of wear or damage, renewing them as necessary.

Refitting

5 Apply a smear of multi-purpose grease to the spacer, and insert it into the pedal pivot bore.

6 Manoeuvre the pedal into position, making sure it is correctly engaged with the pushrod, and insert the pivot bolt. Refit the nut to the pivot bolt and tighten it to the specified torque.

7 Align the pedal with the pushrod and insert the clevis pin, securing it in position with the retaining clip(s).

8 Refit the lower panel to the facia and reconnect the battery.

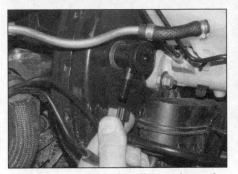

15.5 Press the securing clip to release the vacuum pipe

15.6 Rubber cover (arrowed) over the pedal crossover linkage

15.8 Slacken and remove the four securing nuts (one nut arrowed) behind the servo unit

15 Vacuum servo unit – testing, removal and refitting

Testing

1 To test the operation of the servo unit, depress the footbrake several times to exhaust the vacuum, then start the engine whilst keeping the pedal firmly depressed. As the engine starts, there should be a noticeable 'give' in the brake pedal as the vacuum builds-up. Allow the engine to run for at least two minutes, then switch it off. If the brake pedal is now depressed it should feel normal, but further applications should result in the pedal feeling firmer, with the pedal stroke decreasing with each application.

2 If the servo does not operate as described, first inspect the servo unit check valve as described in Section 16. On diesel engine models, also check the operation of the vacuum pump as described in Section 26.

3 If the servo unit still fails to operate satisfactorily, the fault lies within the unit itself. Repairs to the unit are not possible – if faulty, the servo unit must be renewed.

Removal

4 Remove the master cylinder as described in Section 13.

5 Slacken or release the retaining clip (depending on type of securing clip), then disconnect the vacuum pipe from the servo unit check valve (see illustration). Proceed as described under the relevant sub-heading.

Right-hand drive models

Note: Access to the servo unit and crossover linkage is exceptionally poor (especially on diesel models) but can be improved by removing the cylinder head (where possible) or the engine!

6 Undo the six retaining nuts and remove the rubber cover from the right-hand end of the pedal crossover linkage housing (see illustration).

7 Slacken and remove the pivot bolt and nut securing the crossover linkage rod to the pedal end pivot, then unscrew the two bolts securing the linkage housing to the pedal end bracket.

8 Unclip the cover (where fitted) from the servo end of the crossover linkage housing then slacken and remove the four nuts securing the housing to the bulkhead (see illustration).

9 Ease the housing away from the bulkhead, then slacken and remove the servo unit retaining nuts. Remove the retaining clip, then slide out the clevis pin securing the servo unit to the linkage pivot.

10 Manoeuvre the servo unit out of position, along with its gasket which is fitted between the servo and housing. Renew the gasket if it shows signs of damage.

Left-hand drive models

11 Disconnect the servo unit pushrod from the brake pedal as described in paragraphs 2 and 3 of Section 14.

12 Slacken and remove the nuts securing the servo unit to the bulkhead, and manoeuvre the unit out of position. Recover the seal which is fitted between the servo and bulkhead.

Refitting

Right-hand drive models

13 Refitting is the reverse of removal, noting the following points.

a) Prior to refitting, measure the distance from the end of the vacuum servo unit pushrod to the servo master cylinder mating surface. This should be 22.3 ± 0.1 mm; if not seek the advice of a Peugeot dealer before refitting the master cylinder.

b) Lubricate all crossover linkage pivot points with multi-purpose grease.

c) Tighten the servo unit and mounting bracket nuts and bolts to their specified torque settings.

d) Refit the master cylinder as described in Section 13 and bleed the complete hydraulic system as described in Section 2.

Left-hand drive models

14 Prior to refitting, measure the distance from the end of the vacuum servo unit pushrod to the servo master cylinder mating surface. This should be 22.3 ± 0.1 mm; if not seek the advice of a Peugeot dealer before refitting the master cylinder.

15 Ensure that the gasket is correctly fitted to the rear of the servo unit, then manoeuvre the unit into position.

16 Make sure the pushrod is correctly engaged with the pedal, then refit the servo unit mounting nuts and tighten them to the specified torque.

17 Align the pedal with the pushrod and insert the clevis pin, securing it in position with the retaining clip(s). Refit the lower panel to the facia.

18 Connect the vacuum hose to the check valve and securely tighten its retaining clip.

19 Refit the master cylinder as described in Section 13, and bleed the complete hydraulic system as described in Section 2.

16 Vacuum servo unit check valve – removal, testing and refitting

Removal

1 Slacken or release the retaining clip (depending on type of securing clip), then disconnect the vacuum hose from the servo unit check valve (see illustration).

2 Withdraw the valve from its rubber sealing grommet, using a pulling and twisting motion (see illustration). Remove the grommet from the servo.

Testing

3 Examine the check valve for signs of damage, and renew if necessary. The valve may be tested by blowing through it in both

16.1 Press the securing clip to release the vacuum pipe . . .

16.2 . . . and pull the check valve to release it from the rubber grommet in the servo unit

directions. Air should flow through the valve in one direction only – when blown through from the servo unit end of the valve. Renew the valve if this is not the case.

4 Examine the rubber sealing grommet and flexible vacuum hose for signs of damage or deterioration, and renew as necessary.

Refitting

5 Fit the sealing grommet into position in the servo unit.

6 Carefully ease the check valve into position, taking great care not to displace or damage the grommet. Reconnect the vacuum hose to the valve and, where necessary, securely tighten its retaining clip.

7 On completion, start the engine and check for air leaks from the check valve-to-servo unit connection.

17 Handbrake – adjustment

Rear drum brake models

1 To check the handbrake adjustment, fully release the handbrake then apply the footbrake firmly several times to establish correct shoe-to-drum clearance, then apply and release the handbrake several times to ensure that the self-adjust mechanism is fully adjusted. Applying normal moderate pressure, pull the handbrake lever to the fully-applied position, counting the number of clicks emitted from the handbrake ratchet mechanism. If adjustment is correct, there should be between 10 and 11 clicks before the handbrake is fully applied. If this is not the case, adjust as follows.

2 Chock the front wheels, then jack up the rear of the vehicle and support it on axle stands.

3 To gain access to the handbrake adjuster, unscrew the retaining nuts/bolts and remove the exhaust system rear heat shield.

4 With the handbrake lever fully released, slacken the locknut and rotate the adjuster on the left-hand side of the relay mechanism. Screw the adjuster in or out (as applicable) until there is approximately 0.5 to 1.0 mm of freeplay between the front cable and the right-hand rear cable **(see illustrations)**. Once the adjuster is correctly positioned, securely tighten the locknut.

5 Check the handbrake adjustment by applying the handbrake fully, counting the clicks emitted from the handbrake ratchet and, if necessary, re-adjust.

6 Refit the heat shield then lower the vehicle to the ground.

Rear disc brake models

7 To check the handbrake adjustment, applying normal moderate pressure, pull the handbrake lever to the fully-applied position, counting the number of clicks emitted from the handbrake ratchet mechanism. If adjustment is correct, there should be between 6 and 7 clicks before the handbrake is fully applied. If this is not the case, adjust as follows noting that it should only be necessary to adjust the cable if the handbrake shoes have not been disturbed.

Adjusting the handbrake shoes

8 Chock the front wheels, then jack up the rear of the vehicle and support it on axle stands. Remove both rear roadwheels.

9 Working on the first disc, using a pair of pointed-nose pliers, remove the adjuster access plug from the front of the brake disc **(see illustration)**.

10 Rotate the disc and position the access hole directly opposite the brake caliper so that access can be gained to the handbrake shoe adjuster knurled ring.

11 Make sure the handbrake is fully released, then insert a screwdriver in through the access hole and fully expand the handbrake shoes by rotating the adjuster knurled ring **(see illustrations)**. When the disc can no longer be turned, back the knurled ring off by 5 or 6 teeth (catches) so that the wheel is free to rotate easily.

12 Refit the access plug to the brake disc. Ensure that the plug is positioned correctly so that its slot is at right-angles to the centre line from the hub to the plug hole.

13 Repeat paragraphs 9 to 12 on the opposite disc.

14 Refit the roadwheels then adjust the cable as follows.

Adjusting the handbrake cable

15 The handbrake cable is adjusted as described in paragraphs 2 to 6.

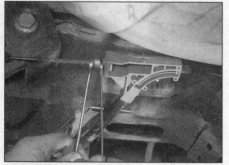

17.4a Slacken the locknut and rotate the adjuster nut . . .

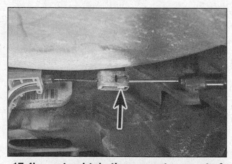

17.4b . . . to obtain the correct amount of freeplay (arrowed) between the right-hand cable and front cable end fittings

17.9 On models with rear disc brakes, remove the access plug from brake disc

17.11a Using a flat-bladed screwdriver inserted through the access hole . . .

17.11b . . . rotate the adjuster knurled ring (shown with disc removed) to correctly set the handbrake shoe-to-drum clearance

18 Handbrake lever –
removal and refitting

Removal

1 Chock the front wheels then jack up the rear of the vehicle and support it on axle stands.
2 Referring to Section 17, release the handbrake lever and back off the adjuster to obtain maximum freeplay in the cable.
3 Remove the centre console as described in Chapter 11.
4 Peel back the gaiter (where necessary) and disconnect the wiring connector from the handbrake warning light switch.
5 Detach the handbrake cable from the lever then slacken and remove the lever retaining nuts, and remove the lever from the vehicle.

Refitting

6 Refitting is a reversal of removal. Tighten the lever retaining nuts to the specified torque, and adjust the handbrake (see Section 17).

19 Handbrake cables –
removal and refitting

Removal

1 The handbrake cable consists of three sections, a front section which incorporates the adjuster mechanism and right- and left-hand rear sections which connect the rear brakes to the adjuster mechanism on the front cable. Each section can be removed individually.
2 Firmly chock the front wheels, then jack up the rear of the vehicle and support it on axle stands.
3 Referring to Section 17, remove the heat shield and slacken the adjuster to obtain maximum freeplay in the cable. Proceed as described under the relevant sub-heading.

Front cable

4 Remove the centre console (Chapter 11).
5 Fully release the handbrake then detach the cable from the handbrake lever, and release the cable from its retaining clips and ties.
6 From underneath the vehicle, detach the right-hand rear cable from the front cable adjuster, then unscrew the adjuster and detach the left-hand rear cable.
7 Free the front cable from its retaining clips and ties, and withdraw the cable from underneath the vehicle.

Rear cable – drum brake models

8 Remove the relevant rear brake drum as described in Section 9.
9 Detach the end of the inner cable from the brake shoe lever, and tap the outer cable out of the rear of the backplate.
10 Work back along the length of the cable, freeing it from any relevant retaining clips and ties. Free the cable from the adjuster

19.12a Tap the handbrake outer cable out from the backplate . . .

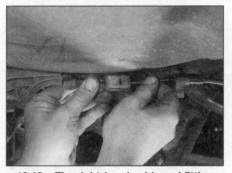

19.12c The right-hand cable end fitting simply unhooks from the front cable . . .

mechanism (the right-hand cable is clipped in position and the left-hand cable screwed in) and remove it from underneath the vehicle.

Rear cable – disc brake models

11 Remove the relevant set of handbrake shoes as described in Section 20, and detach the expander mechanism from the end of the cable.
12 Tap the outer cable out of the backplate then work back along the length of the cable, freeing it from any relevant retaining clips and ties. Free the cable from the adjuster mechanism (the right-hand cable is clipped in position and the left-hand cable screwed in) and remove it from underneath the vehicle **(see illustrations)**.

Refitting

13 Refitting is a reversal of the removal

20.2 Rotate the handbrake upper shoe retaining spring through 90° and remove it from the vehicle

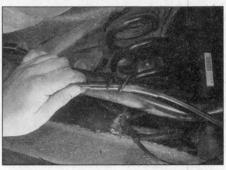

19.12b . . . and free the cable from its retaining clips

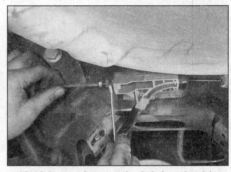

19.12d . . . whereas the left-hand cable needs to be unscrewed

procedure, adjusting the handbrake as described in Section 17.

20 Handbrake shoes (rear disc brake models) –
removal and refitting

Removal

1 Remove the brake disc as described in Section 8, and make a note of the correct fitted position of all components.
2 Using an Allen key, compress the upper shoe retaining spring, then rotate it through 90° and remove it from the backplate **(see illustration)**.
3 Carefully unhook and remove the handbrake shoe upper return spring then free the adjuster, noting which way around it is fitted, and remove it from between the shoes **(see illustrations)**.

20.3a Unhook the upper return spring . . .

20.3b . . . and remove the adjuster from between the handbrake shoes

20.4 Disengage the upper shoe from the expander then remove the shoe and lower return spring

20.5a Remove the retaining spring and lower shoe . . .

20.5b . . . and detach the expander mechanism from the end of the cable, noting its fitted arrangement and taking care not to lose the pivot pin (arrowed)

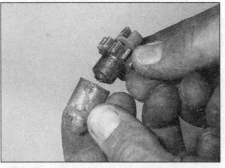

20.7 Examine the adjuster mechanism for signs of wear or damage

10 Ensure that the expander legs are correctly positioned against the back plate stops, then fit the lower handbrake shoe. Ensure that the shoe is correctly engaged with the expander and secure it in position retaining spring **(see illustration)**.

11 Offer up the upper shoe and lower return spring. Hook the spring into position on both shoes, then manoeuvre the upper shoe into position on the backplate. Ensure that the upper shoe is correctly engaged with the expander, then secure it in position with the retaining spring.

12 Fully retract the adjuster assembly and manoeuvre it into position between the shoes. Using pliers, hook the upper return spring onto the lower shoe, then stretch it into position in the upper shoe.

13 Check all components are correctly fitted, and centralise the handbrake shoes.

14 Refit the brake disc (see Section 8). Prior to refitting the roadwheel, adjust the handbrake shoes and cable (see Section 17).

4 Free the upper shoe from the expander mechanism, then carefully unhook the lower return spring and remove both components **(see illustration)**.

5 Remove the lower shoe retaining spring (see paragraph 2) and remove the handbrake shoe, taking great care not to drop the expander. Note the correct fitted orientation of the expander assembly, then detach it from the end of the handbrake cable **(see illustrations)**.

6 Inspect the handbrake shoes for signs of wear or contamination, and renew if necessary. It is recommended that the return springs are renewed as a matter of course. Peugeot do not state any wear limit for the shoe friction material thickness, but anything less than 1 mm is not ideal.

7 Whilst the shoes are removed, clean and inspect the condition of the shoe adjuster and expander mechanisms, renew them if they show signs of wear or damage **(see illustration)**. If all is well, apply a fresh coat of high-temperature grease to the threads of the adjuster and sliding surfaces of the expander mechanism. Do allow the grease to contact the shoe friction material.

Refitting

8 Prior to installation, clean the backplate, and apply a thin smear of high-temperature brake grease or anti-seize compound to all those surfaces of the backplate which bear on the shoes. Do not allow the lubricant to foul the friction material.

9 Ensure that the expander mechanism is correctly assembled, then engage it with the end of the handbrake cable **(see illustration)**.

21 Rear brake pressure-regulating valve – testing, removal and refitting

Caution: On models equipped with ABS, disconnect the battery before disconnecting any braking system hydraulic union, and do not reconnect the battery until after the hydraulic system has been bled. Failure to do this could lead to air entering the regulator unit, requiring the unit to be bled using special Peugeot test equipment (see Section 2).

Note: On models where the pressure regulator is an integral part of the wheel cylinder, renew the wheel cylinder as described in Section 12.

Testing

1 On models with a load-sensitive pressure regulating valve, it will be fitted into the hydraulic circuit to the rear brakes.

2 The valve is mounted onto the underside of the rear of the vehicle, and is attached to the rear suspension anti-roll bar by a spring. The valve measures the load on the rear axle, via the movement of the anti-roll bar, and

20.9 Ensure the expander mechanism is correctly engaged with the cable . . .

20.10 . . . then fit the lower handbrake shoe and secure it in position with the retaining spring

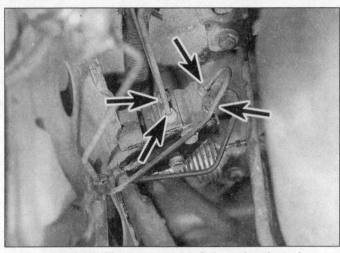

21.6 Load-sensitive pressure regulating valve pipe unions (arrowed)

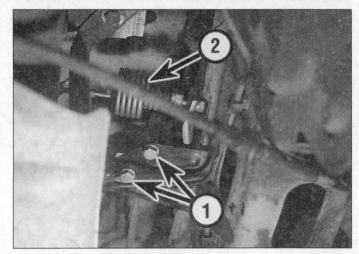

21.8 Undo the retaining bolts (1) then detach the spring (2) and remove the valve from underneath the vehicle

regulates the hydraulic pressure being applied to the rear brakes to help prevent rear wheels locking-up under hard braking.

3 Specialist equipment is required to check the performance of the valve, so if the valve is thought to be faulty, the car should be taken to a suitably-equipped Peugeot dealer for testing. Repairs are not possible and, if faulty, the valve must be renewed, adjustment is possible, but again specialist equipment is needed to carry out this procedure.

Removal

Note: *Before starting work, refer to the warning at the beginning of Section 2 concerning the dangers of hydraulic fluid.*

4 Firmly chock the front wheels, then jack up the rear of the vehicle and support it on axle stands.

5 Minimise fluid loss by first removing the master cylinder reservoir cap, and then tightening it down onto a piece of polythene, to obtain an airtight seal.

6 Wipe clean the area around the brake pipe unions on the valve, and place absorbent rags beneath the pipe unions to catch any surplus fluid **(see illustration)**. To avoid confusion on refitting, make alignment marks between the pipes and valve assembly.

7 Slacken the union nuts and disconnect the brake pipes from the valve. Plug or tape over the pipe ends and valve orifices, to minimise the loss of brake fluid, and to prevent the entry of dirt into the system. Wash off any spilt fluid immediately with cold water.

8 Slacken and remove the valve retaining bolts, then unhook the valve spring from its bracket and remove the valve assembly from underneath the vehicle **(see illustration)**.

Refitting

9 Prior to refitting, thoroughly clean the valve retaining bolt threads and apply a few drops of thread-locking compound (Peugeot recommend Loctite Frenetanch – available from your Peugeot dealer) to each one.

10 Manoeuvre the valve assembly into position, and hook the spring into the bracket on the anti-roll bar. Align the valve with its mounting bracket, and refit the retaining bolts, tightening them to the specified torque setting.

11 Refit the brake pipes to their specific unions on the valve, and tighten the union nuts to the specified torque setting.

12 Remove the polythene from the master cylinder reservoir, and bleed the complete hydraulic system as described in Section 2. If a new valve assembly has been fitted, it is recommended that the vehicle is taken to a Peugeot dealer so that the valve operation can be checked and, if necessary, adjusted using their special test equipment.

22 Stop-light switch – removal, refitting and adjustment

Note: *On some models it will be necessary to remove the steering column to gain access to the switch.*

1 The stop-light switch is located on the pedal bracket behind the facia. On models with automatic transmission or cruise control there are two switches fitted to the bracket – the stop-light switch is the left-hand of the two.

22.2 Stop-light switch (arrowed) viewed with the steering column removed

Removal

2 Open up the engine immobiliser key pad, then rotate the fastener through 90° and lower the fusebox cover. Disconnect the wiring connector from the key pad, then slacken and remove the retaining screws and remove the driver's side lower panel from the facia. Access to the switch is very poor, and can only be improved by removing the steering column (see Chapter 10) **(see illustration)**.

3 Disconnect the wiring, then unscrew the switch and remove it from the bracket.

Refitting and adjustment

4 Screw the switch back into position in the mounting bracket, until the gap between the end of the main body of the switch and the lug on the brake pedal is around 2 to 3 mm.

5 Once the stop-light switch is correctly positioned, reconnect the wiring connector, and check the operation of the stop-lights. The stop-lights should illuminate after the brake pedal has travelled about 5 mm. Adjust the switch as necessary, then refit the steering column (where removed) lower facia panel.

23 Anti-lock braking system (ABS) – general information

ABS is fitted to all models as standard, the system comprises a hydraulic regulator unit and the four roadwheel sensors. The regulator unit contains the electronic control unit (ECU), the eight hydraulic solenoid valves (two for each brake – one inlet and one outlet) and the electrically-driven return pump. The purpose of the system is to prevent the wheel(s) locking during heavy braking. This is achieved by automatic release of the brake on the relevant wheel, followed by re-application of the brake. In the case of the rear wheels both brakes are applied at the same time.

The solenoid valves are controlled by the ECU, which itself receives signals from the

24.2 Pull out the securing clip to release the wiring block connector from the ABS unit

four wheel sensors (front sensors are fitted to the hubs, and the rear sensors are fitted to the caliper mounting brackets), which monitor the speed of rotation of each wheel. By comparing these signals, the ECU can determine the speed at which the vehicle is travelling. It can then use this speed to determine when a wheel is decelerating at an abnormal rate, compared to the speed of the vehicle, and therefore predicts when a wheel is about to lock. During normal operation, the system functions in the same way as a non-ABS braking system.

If the ECU senses that a wheel is about to lock, it closes the relevant outlet solenoid valves in the hydraulic unit, which then isolates the relevant brake(s) on the wheel(s) which is/are about to lock from the master cylinder, effectively sealing-in the hydraulic pressure.

If the speed of rotation of the wheel continues to decrease at an abnormal rate, the ECU opens the inlet solenoid valves on the relevant brake(s), and operates the electrically-driven return pump which pumps the hydraulic fluid back into the master cylinder, releasing the brake. Once the speed of rotation of the wheel returns to an acceptable rate, the pump stops; the solenoid valves switch again, allowing the hydraulic master cylinder pressure to return to the caliper, which then re-applies the brake. This cycle can be carried out many times a second.

The action of the solenoid valves and return pump creates pulses in the hydraulic circuit. When the ABS system is functioning, these pulses can be felt through the brake pedal.

The operation of the ABS system is entirely dependent on electrical signals. To prevent the system responding to any inaccurate signals, a built-in safety circuit monitors all signals received by the ECU. If an inaccurate signal or low battery voltage is detected, the ABS system is automatically shut-down, and the warning light on the instrument panel is illuminated, to inform the driver that the ABS system is not operational. Normal braking should still be available, however.

If a fault does develop in the ABS system, the vehicle must be taken to a Peugeot dealer for fault diagnosis and repair.

24 Anti-lock braking system (ABS) components – removal and refitting

Regulator assembly

Caution: Disconnect the battery before disconnecting the regulator hydraulic unions, and do not reconnect the battery until after the hydraulic system has been bled. Also ensure that the unit is stored upright (in the same position as it is fitted to the vehicle) and is not tipped onto its side or upside down. Failure to do this could lead to air entering the regulator unit, requiring the unit to be bled using special Peugeot test equipment on refitting (see Section 2).

Note: *Before starting work, refer to the warning at the beginning of Section 2 concerning the dangers of hydraulic fluid.*

Removal

1 Disconnect the battery negative lead.
2 Release the retaining clip and disconnect the main wiring connector from the regulator assembly **(see illustration)**. Where applicable, unscrew the retaining nut and disconnect the earth lead from the regulator.
3 Mark the locations of the hydraulic fluid pipes to ensure correct refitting, then unscrew the union nuts, and disconnect the pipes from the regulator assembly **(see illustration)**. Be prepared for fluid spillage, and plug the open ends of the pipes and the regulator, to prevent dirt ingress and further fluid loss.
4 Slacken and remove the regulator mounting nuts and remove the assembly from the engine compartment. If necessary, the mounting bracket can then be unbolted and removed from the vehicle. Renew the regulator mountings if they show signs of wear or damage.

Refitting

5 Manoeuvre the regulator into position and locate it in the mounting bracket. Refit the mounting nuts and tighten them to the specified torque setting.
6 Reconnect the hydraulic pipes to the correct unions on the regulator and tighten the union nuts to the specified torque.
7 Reconnect the wiring connector to the regulator and connect the earth lead, tightening its retaining nut securely.
8 Bleed the complete hydraulic system as described in Section 2. Once the system is correctly bled, reconnect the battery.

Electronic control unit (ECU)

Note: *Check with your local Peugeot dealer before attempting to remove the ECU. The ECU may be part of the regulator assembly depending on the type of brake system being worked on.*

Removal

9 Where the ECU can be removed from the regulator unit, use the following procedures. To gain access to the ECU, remove the battery and battery tray (see Chapter 5A).
10 Release the retaining clip and disconnect the wiring connector from the ECU.
11 Slacken and remove the retaining bolts/screws, and carefully ease the ECU squarely away from the regulator.

Refitting

12 Align the ECU with the regulator connectors, and ease the unit into position.

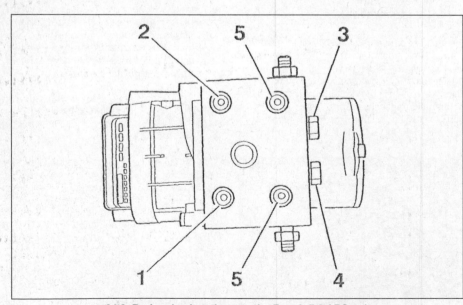

24.3 Brake pipe locations on the Bosch 5.3 ABS unit

1	Front left-hand wheel	3	Rear left-hand wheel	5	Master cylinder
2	Front right-hand wheel	4	Rear right-hand wheel		

24.17a Slacken and remove the retaining bolt . . .

24.17b . . . and withdraw the front wheel sensor from the hub

Refit the retaining bolts and tighten them to the specified torque setting.

13 Reconnect the wiring connector and refit the battery.

Front wheel sensor

Removal

14 Disconnect the battery negative lead.

15 Apply the handbrake, then jack up the front of the vehicle and support securely on axle stands. To improve access, remove the roadwheel.

16 Trace the wiring back from the sensor, releasing it from all the relevant clips and ties whilst noting its correct routing, and disconnect the wiring connector.

17 Slacken and remove the retaining bolt and withdraw the sensor from the swivel hub **(see illustrations)**.

Refitting

18 Ensure that the mating faces of the sensor and the swivel hub are clean, and apply a little grease to the swivel hub bore before refitting.

19 Make sure the sensor tip is clean and ease it into position in the swivel hub.

20 Clean the threads of the sensor bolt and apply a few drops of thread-locking compound (Peugeot recommend Loctite Frenetanch – available from your Peugeot

dealer). Refit the retaining bolt and tighten it to the specified torque.

21 Work along the sensor wiring, making sure it is correctly routed, securing it in position with all the relevant clips and ties. Reconnect the wiring connector.

22 Lower the vehicle and (where necessary) tighten the wheel bolts to the specified torque.

Rear wheel sensor

Removal

23 Chock the front wheels, then jack up the rear of the vehicle and support it on axle stands. To improve access, remove the appropriate roadwheel.

24 Trace the wiring back from the sensor, releasing it from all the relevant clips and ties whilst noting its correct routing, and disconnect the wiring connector **(see illustrations)**.

25 Slacken and remove the retaining bolt and withdraw the sensor **(see illustration)**.

Refitting

26 Ensure that the mating faces of the sensor and the hub are clean, and apply a little grease to the hub bore before refitting.

27 Make sure the sensor tip is clean and ease it into position in the swivel hub.

28 Clean the threads of the sensor bolt and apply a few drops of thread-locking compound (Peugeot recommend Loctite Frenetanch – available from your Peugeot dealer). Refit the retaining bolt and tighten it to the specified torque.

29 Work along the sensor wiring, making sure it is correctly routed, securing it in position with all the relevant clips and ties. Reconnect the wiring connector, then lower the vehicle and (where necessary) tighten the wheel bolts to the specified torque.

25 Vacuum pump (diesel engine models) – removal and refitting

Removal

1 If necessary, to improve access to the vacuum pump, remove the air cleaner duct (see Chapter 4B).

2 Release the retaining clip and disconnect the vacuum hose from the pump.

3 Slacken and remove the retaining bolts/nut (as applicable) securing the pump to the left-hand end of the cylinder head, then remove the pump **(see illustration)**. Discard the sealing rings – new ones must be used on refitting.

24.24a Free the rear wheel sensor wiring from its retaining clips . . .

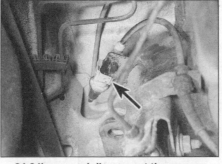

24.24b . . . and disconnect the sensor wiring connector (arrowed) . . .

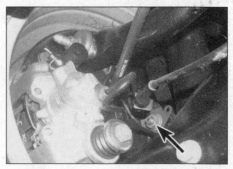

24.25 . . . then remove the retaining nut (arrowed) and remove the sensor

25.3 Undo the retaining bolts and remove the vacuum pump –
2.2 litre engine

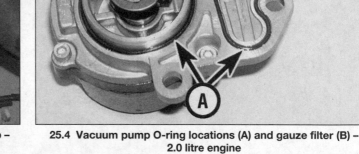

25.4 Vacuum pump O-ring locations (A) and gauze filter (B) –
2.0 litre engine

Refitting

4 Fit new sealing ring(s) to the pump recess(es), then align the drive dog with the slot in the end of the camshaft, and refit the pump to the cylinder head, ensuring that the sealing ring(s) remain correctly seated **(see illustration)**.

5 Refit the pump mounting bolts/nut (as applicable) and tighten them securely.

6 Reconnect the vacuum hose to the pump, tightening its retaining clip securely, and (where necessary) refit the air cleaner duct.

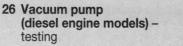

26 Vacuum pump (diesel engine models) – testing

1 The operation of the braking system vacuum pump can be checked using a vacuum gauge.

2 Disconnect the vacuum pipe from the pump, and connect the gauge to the pump union using a suitable length of hose.

3 Start the engine and allow it to idle, then measure the vacuum created by the pump. As a guide, after one minute, a minimum of approximately 500 mm Hg should be recorded. If the vacuum registered is significantly less than this, it is likely that the pump is faulty. However, seek the advice of a Peugeot dealer before condemning the pump.

4 Overhaul of the vacuum pump is not possible, since no components are available separately for it. If faulty, the complete pump assembly must be renewed.

Chapter 10
Suspension and steering

Contents

Front hub bearings – renewal 3
Front suspension anti-roll bar – removal and refitting 8
Front suspension anti-roll bar connecting link – removal and
    refitting 9
Front suspension lower arm – removal, overhaul and refitting 6
Front suspension lower balljoint – removal and refitting 7
Front suspension strut – overhaul 5
Front suspension strut – removal and refitting 4
Front suspension subframe – removal and refitting 10
Front swivel hub assembly – removal and refitting 2
General information 1
Ignition switch/lock cylinder – removal and refitting 25
Power steering fluid level check .... See *Weekly checks*
Power steering pump – removal and refitting 29
Power steering pump drivebelt check, adjustment and
    renewal .... See Chapter 1A or 1B
Power steering system – bleeding 28
Rear hub assembly – removal and refitting 11
Rear hub bearings – renewal 12
Rear suspension anti-roll bar – removal and refitting 20

Rear suspension anti-roll bar connecting link – removal and refitting . 21
Rear suspension coil spring – removal and refitting 14
Rear suspension trailing arm – removal, overhaul and refitting 18
Rear suspension lower arm – removal, overhaul and refitting 16
Rear suspension shock absorber – removal, testing and refitting .. 13
Rear suspension stub axle – removal, overhaul and refitting 15
Rear suspension track arm – removal and refitting 19
Rear suspension upper arm – removal and refitting 17
Steering and suspension check .... See Chapter 1A or 1B
Steering column – removal, inspection and refitting 23
Steering column intermediate shaft – removal, inspection and
    refitting 24
Steering gear assembly – removal, overhaul and refitting 26
Steering gear rubber gaiters – renewal 27
Steering wheel – removal and refitting 22
Track rod – removal and refitting 31
Track rod balljoint – removal and refitting 30
Wheel alignment and steering angles – general information, checking
    and adjustment 32
Wheel and tyre maintenance .... See Chapter 1A or 1B

Degrees of difficulty

Easy, suitable for novice with little experience	**Fairly easy,** suitable for beginner with some experience	**Fairly difficult,** suitable for competent DIY mechanic	**Difficult,** suitable for experienced DIY mechanic	**Very difficult,** suitable for expert DIY or professional

Specifications

Wheel alignment and steering angles
Front wheel:
  Toe setting .... 0 ± 0.5 mm
  Camber .... 0° ± 30'
  Castor .... 3° 30' ± 30'
  King pin inclination .... 11° 30' ± 30'
Rear wheel:
  Toe setting .... 1.5 ± 0.5 mm toe-in
  Camber .... 1° 50' ± 30'

Roadwheels
Type .... Pressed-steel or aluminium alloy (depending on model)
Size .... 5J x 14, 6J x 15 or 6.5J x 15 (depending on model)
Tyre pressures .... See end of *Weekly checks* on page 0•18

Torque wrench settings	Nm	lbf ft
Front suspension		
Anti-roll bar:		
Connecting link nuts	65	48
Mounting clamp bolts	65	48
Driveshaft retaining nut	325	240
Lower arm:		
Front pivot bolt	130	96
Rear mounting bracket bolts	60	44
Lower balljoint:		
Balljoint to swivel hub	250	185
Retaining nut	45	33
Subframe mounting bolts	120	89
Suspension strut:		
Upper mounting bolts	40	30
Upper mounting plate nut	65	48
Swivel hub clamp bolt	55	41
Rear suspension		
Anti-roll bar:		
Connecting link nuts	40	30
Mounting clamp bolts	40	30
Hub nut	275	203
Lower arm:		
Inner pivot bolt	75	55
Outer pivot bolt	95	70
Shock absorber:		
Lower mounting bolt	75	55
Upper mounting nut	35	26
Subframe mounting bolts	65	48
Track arm:		
Balljoint nut	65	48
Inner pivot bolt nut	40	30
Trailing arm:		
Front pivot bolt	95	70
Mounting bracket to body bolts	100	74
Rear pivot bolt	75	55
Upper arm:		
Inner pivot bolt	95	70
Outer pivot bolt	75	55
Steering		
Column-to-intermediate shaft clamp bolt	22	16
Intermediate shaft-to-steering gear clamp bolt	25	18
Steering column mounting bolts	20	15
Steering gear mounting bolts	80	59
Steering wheel bolt	35	26
Track rod:		
Balljoint-to-swivel hub nut	35	26
Balljoint locknut	60	44
Inner balljoint to steering rack	50	37
Roadwheels		
Wheel bolts	90	66

1 General information

The independent front suspension is of the MacPherson strut type, incorporating coil springs and integral telescopic shock absorbers. The MacPherson struts are located by transverse lower suspension arms, which utilise rubber inner mounting bushes, and incorporate a balljoint at the outer ends. The front swivel hubs, which carry the wheel bearings, brake calipers and the hub/disc assemblies, are bolted to the MacPherson struts, and connected to the lower arms via the balljoints. A front anti-roll bar is fitted to all models. The anti-roll bar is rubber-mounted onto the subframe, and is connected directly to the front suspension struts.

The independent rear suspension is of multi-link type. The stub axles are linked to the subframe by upper and lower arms and a track arm, and are attached to the vehicle underbody by trailing arms. The anti-roll bar is mounted onto the subframe and is attached to the swivel hubs by connecting links.

The steering column has a universal joint fitted to its lower end, which is connected to an intermediate shaft having a second universal joint at its lower end. The lower universal joint is clamped to the steering gear pinion by means of a clamp bolt.

The steering gear is mounted onto the front subframe, and is connected by two track rods, with balljoints at their outer ends, to the steering arms projecting rearwards from the swivel hubs. The track rod ends are threaded, to facilitate adjustment. The hydraulic steering system is powered by a belt-driven pump, which is driven off the crankshaft pulley.

There are two different types of power steering fitted to the models covered in this manual; the steering can be either variable or invariable (depending on model). The hydraulic pump on the variable system alters the hydraulic pressure supplied to the steering gear to suit all conditions, ie, supplies high pressure when the vehicle is being driven slowly/parked and lower pressure when the vehicle is being driven at speed. On the invariable system the pump supplies the fluid at constant pressure, regardless of the vehicle speed.

2 Front swivel hub assembly – removal and refitting

Note: *A new track rod balljoint nut, lower balljoint nut, and swivel hub clamp bolt and nut will be required on refitting.*

Removal

1 Remove the wheel trim/hub cap (as applicable) then withdraw the R-clip and remove the locking cap from the driveshaft retaining nut. Slacken the driveshaft nut with the vehicle resting on its wheels **(see illustrations)**. Also slacken the wheel bolts.
2 Chock the rear wheels of the car, firmly apply the handbrake, then jack up the front of the car and support it on axle stands. Remove the appropriate front roadwheel.
3 On models equipped with ABS, unbolt the wheel sensor and position it clear of the hub assembly (see Chapter 9, Section 24). Note that there is no need to disconnect the wiring.
4 Slacken and remove the driveshaft retaining nut. If the nut was not slackened with the wheels on the ground (see paragraph 1), withdraw the R-clip and remove the locking cap. Refit at least two roadwheel bolts to the front hub, tightening them securely, then have an assistant firmly depress the brake pedal to prevent the front hub from rotating, whilst you slacken and remove the driveshaft retaining nut. Alternatively, a tool can be fabricated to hold the hub stationary (see Chapter 8, Section 2).
5 Slacken and remove the nut securing the steering gear track rod to the swivel hub then free the balljoint from the hub and recover the protector plate. If the balljoint is tight, use a universal balljoint separator to free it. Discard the nut, a new one should be used on refitting.
6 If the hub bearings are to be disturbed, remove the brake disc as described in Chapter 9. If not, unscrew the two bolts securing the brake caliper/mounting bracket assembly to the swivel hub, and slide the caliper assembly off the disc. Using a piece of wire or string, tie the caliper to the front suspension coil spring, to avoid placing any strain on the hydraulic brake hose.
7 Where necessary, slacken and remove the

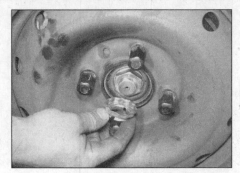

2.1a Withdraw the R-clip . . .

bolts securing the bracket to the top of the swivel hub **(see illustration)**.
8 Slacken and remove the lower balljoint nut and free the balljoint shank from the lower arm, if necessary, using a universal balljoint separator. Discard the nut and lift off the protector plate (if loose).
9 Undo the nut and withdraw the swivel hub-to-suspension strut clamp bolt, noting that the bolt fits from the rear of the vehicle. Discard the nut and clamp bolt, they should be renewed whenever they are disturbed.
10 Free the swivel hub assembly from the end of the strut, then release it from the outer constant velocity joint splines, and remove it from the vehicle. If the swivel hub is a tight fit on the strut, use a large flat-bladed screwdriver to carefully open up the clamp a little.

Refitting

11 Ensure that the driveshaft outer constant velocity joint and hub splines are clean, then slide the hub fully onto the driveshaft splines.
12 Slide the hub assembly fully onto the suspension strut, aligning the split in the hub clamp with the lug on the back of the strut. Also ensure that the raised rim on the strut is in contact with the top surface of the swivel hub. Insert the new clamp bolt from the rear side of the strut then fit the new nut and tighten it to the specified torque.
13 Refit the protector plate (where removed) to the lower balljoint. Align the balljoint with the lower arm and fit the new retaining nut, tightening it to the specified torque.
14 Refit the protector plate and engage the track rod balljoint in the swivel hub, then fit the new retaining nut and tighten it to the specified torque.
15 Where necessary, refit the brake disc to the hub, referring to Chapter 9 for further information. Thoroughly clean the threads of the caliper bracket mounting bolts and coat them with thread locking compound (Peugeot recommend Loctite Frenetanch – available from your Peugeot dealer). Slide the caliper into position, making sure the pads pass either side of the disc, and tighten the caliper bracket bolts to the specified torque setting (see Chapter 9).
16 On models with ABS, refit the wheel sensor as described in Chapter 9.
17 Where applicable, refit the wiring retaining

2.1b . . . then remove the locking cap and slacken the driveshaft nut

bracket to the top of the swivel hub, and tighten its retaining bolt securely.
18 Lubricate the inner face and threads of the driveshaft retaining nut with clean engine oil, and refit it to the end of the driveshaft. Use the method employed on removal to prevent the hub from rotating (see paragraph 4), and tighten the driveshaft retaining nut to the specified torque. Check that the hub rotates freely then engage the locking cap with the driveshaft nut, so that one of its cut-outs is aligned with the driveshaft hole, and secure the cap in position with the R-clip. Alternatively, lightly tighten the nut at this stage and tighten it to the specified torque once the vehicle is resting on its wheels again.
19 Refit the roadwheel, then lower the vehicle to the ground and tighten the roadwheel bolts to the specified torque. If not already having done so, tighten the driveshaft retaining nut to the specified torque then refit the locking cap, aligning its cut-outs with the driveshaft hole, and secure it in position with the R-clip.

3 Front hub bearings – renewal

Note: *The bearing is a sealed, pre-adjusted and prelubricated, double-row roller type, and is intended to last the car's entire service life without maintenance or attention. Never overtighten the driveshaft nut beyond the specified torque wrench setting in an attempt to 'adjust' the bearing.*

2.7 Undo the bolts (arrowed) and free the mounting bracket from the swivel hub

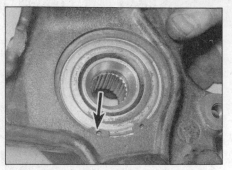

3.3 Front wheel bearing retaining clip (arrowed)

Note: *A press will be required to dismantle and rebuild the assembly; if such a tool is not available, a large bench vice and spacers (such as large sockets) will serve as an adequate substitute. The bearing's inner races are an interference fit on the hub; if the inner race remains on the hub when it is pressed out of the hub carrier, a knife-edged bearing puller will be required to remove it. A new bearing retaining circlip must be used on refitting.*

1 Remove the swivel hub assembly as described in Section 2.

2 Support the swivel hub securely on blocks or in a vice. Using a tubular spacer which bears only on the inner end of the hub flange, press the hub flange out of the bearing. If the bearing's outboard inner race remains on the hub, remove it using a bearing puller (see note above).

3 Extract the bearing retaining circlip from the inner end of the swivel hub assembly **(see illustration)**.

4 Where necessary, refit the inner race back in position over the ball cage, and securely support the inner face of the swivel hub. Using a tubular spacer which bears only on the inner race, press the complete bearing assembly out of the swivel hub.

5 Thoroughly clean the hub and swivel hub, removing all traces of dirt and grease, and polish away any burrs or raised edges which might hinder reassembly. Check both for cracks or any other signs of wear or damage, and renew them if necessary. Renew the circlip, regardless of its apparent condition.

6 On reassembly, apply a light film of oil (Peugeot recommend Molykote 321R – available from your Peugeot dealer) to the bearing outer race and hub flange shaft, to aid installation of the bearing.

7 Securely support the swivel hub, and locate the bearing in the hub. Press the bearing fully into position, ensuring that it enters the hub squarely, using a tubular spacer which bears only on the bearing outer race.

8 Once the bearing is correctly seated, secure the bearing in position with the new circlip, ensuring that it is correctly located in the groove in the swivel hub.

9 Securely support the outer face of the hub flange, and locate the swivel hub bearing inner race over the end of the hub flange. Press the bearing onto the hub, using a tubular spacer which bears only on the inner race of the hub bearing, until it seats against

the hub shoulder. Check that the hub flange rotates freely, and wipe off any excess oil or grease.

10 Refit the swivel hub assembly as described in Section 2.

4 Front suspension strut – removal and refitting

Note: *At the time of writing, no information on the active suspension system was available. If your car has active suspension, consult your Peugeot dealer for details of any relevant changes to the following procedure before attempting to remove/refit the strut assembly.*
Note: *A new swivel hub clamp bolt and nut, a lower balljoint nut and a anti-roll bar connecting link nut will be required on refitting.*

Removal

1 Chock the rear wheels, apply the handbrake, then jack up the front of the car and support on axle stands. Remove the appropriate roadwheel.

2 Unclip the wiring and/or hoses from the strut/body then undo the retaining bolts and free the mounting bracket from the swivel hub **(see illustrations)**.

3 Slacken and remove the lower balljoint nut and free the balljoint shank from the lower arm, if necessary, using a universal balljoint separator. Discard the nut and lift off the protector plate (if loose).

4 Unscrew the nut securing the anti-roll bar connecting link to the strut, and position the link clear of the strut; if necessary, retain the balljoint shank with an Allen key to prevent rotation whilst the nut is slackened **(see illustration)**. Discard the nut, a new one should be used on refitting.

5 Undo the nut and withdraw the swivel hub-to-suspension strut clamp bolt, noting that the bolt fits from the rear of the strut; discard the nut and bolt, new ones will be needed on refitting **(see illustrations)**. To prevent the swivel hub assembly dropping whilst the strut is removed support the lower arm or alternately tie the hub to the subframe with a piece of wire.

4.2a Unclip the wiring . . .

4.2b . . . then with the retaining bolts removed, free the mounting bracket from the hub

4.4 Undo the retaining nut and free the anti-roll bar connecting link from the strut

4.5a Slacken and remove the securing nut . . .

4.5b . . . then withdraw the clamp bolt securing the swivel hub to the strut

4.7a Undo the upper mounting bolts (arrowed) . . .

4.7b . . . and remove the front suspension strut from underneath the wheelarch

4.8 Make sure the locating pin (arrowed) is correctly positioned when refitting the strut

6 Release the strut from the swivel hub. If the swivel hub is a tight fit on the strut, carefully open up the clamp a little using a large flat-bladed screwdriver or similar tool. Take care not to strain the brake hose and the wiring attached to the brake caliper and the swivel hub.

7 Working in the engine compartment, remove the plastic cover (where fitted) then slacken and remove the suspension strut upper mounting bolts and withdraw the strut from under the wheelarch **(see illustrations)**. Temporarily locate the hub assembly balljoint in the lower arm to help support it whilst the strut is removed.

Refitting

8 Manoeuvre the strut assembly into position, ensuring that the top mounting plate locating pin is correctly located in the corresponding hole in the inner wing **(see illustration)**. Engage the lower end of the strut with the hub

assembly aligning the split in the hub clamp with the lug on the back of the strut.

9 Refit the strut upper mounting bolts and tighten them to the specified torque setting.

10 Ensure that the raised rim on the strut is in contact with the top surface of the swivel hub then insert the new clamp bolt from the rear side of the strut. Fit the new nut to the clamp bolt and tighten it to the specified torque.

11 Refit the protector plate (where removed) to the lower balljoint. Align the balljoint with the lower arm and fit the new retaining nut, tightening it to the specified torque.

12 Reconnect the anti-roll bar connecting link to the strut. Fit a new nut to the connecting link, and tighten it to the specified torque.

13 Where applicable, clip any wiring/hoses into position on the strut.

14 Refit the roadwheel, then lower the vehicle to the ground and tighten the roadwheel bolts to the specified torque.

5 Front suspension strut – overhaul

> **Warning: Before attempting to dismantle the front suspension strut, a suitable tool to hold the coil spring in compression must be obtained. Adjustable coil spring compressors are readily-available, and are recommended for this operation. Any attempt to dismantle the strut without such a tool is likely to result in damage or personal injury.**

Note: *A new mounting plate nut will be required.*

1 With the strut removed from the car (as described in Section 4), clean away all external dirt, then mount it upright in a vice. Fit the spring compressor and compress the coil spring until tension is relieved from the spring seats **(see illustration)**.

2 Slacken and remove the upper mounting plate nut whilst retaining the shock absorber piston with a suitable Allen key **(see illustration)**.

3 Remove the nut and washer then lift off the mounting plate followed by the spacer and upper spring seat **(see illustrations)**.

4 Lift off the coil spring and remove the washer, dust gaiter and rubber bump stop from the shock absorber piston **(see illustrations)**. Slide off the lower spring seat.

5 Examine the shock absorber for signs of fluid leakage. Check the piston for signs of pitting along its entire length, and check the

5.1 Using spring compressors, compress the spring sufficiently to relieve pressure from the spring seats

5.2 Slacken and remove the upper mounting plate nut . . .

5.3a . . . then lift off the upper mounting plate . . .

5.3b . . . the spacer and the upper spring seat (arrowed)

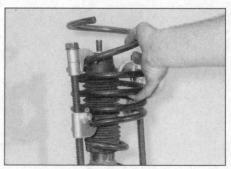

5.4a Lift off the coil spring . . .

5.4b . . . then slide off the washer, dust gaiter . . .

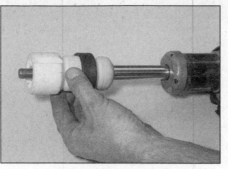

5.4c . . . rubber bump stop . . .

5.4d . . . and lower spring seat

5.7 On refitting ensure the dust gaiter is correctly located on the strut body

5.8 Ensure the upper spring seat stop (arrowed) is correctly located against the spring end

shock body for signs of damage. While holding it in an upright position, test the operation of the shock absorber by moving the piston through a full stroke, and then through short strokes of 50 to 100 mm. In both cases, the resistance felt should be smooth and continuous. If the resistance is jerky, or uneven, or if there is any visible sign of wear or damage to the shock absorber, renewal is necessary.

6 Inspect all other components for signs of damage or deterioration, and renew any that are suspect.

7 Fit the lower spring seat to the shock absorber then slide the rubber bump stop onto the piston. Fit the dust gaiter and washer making sure the lower end of gaiter is correctly positioned over the shock absorber end **(see illustration)**.

8 Refit the coil spring, making sure its lower end is correctly seated against the spring seat stop. Fit the upper spring seat, aligning its

stop with the spring end, then fit the spacer and mounting plate **(see illustration)**.

9 Refit the washer and screw on the new nut. Retain the shock absorber piston and tighten the mounting plate nut to the specified torque.

---

6 Front suspension lower arm – removal, overhaul and refitting

Note: *A new lower balljoint nut will be required on refitting.*

Removal

1 Chock the rear wheels, firmly apply the handbrake, then jack up the front of the vehicle and support on axle stands. Remove the appropriate front roadwheel.

2 Slacken and remove the nut, then free the lower balljoint shank from the lower arm, if necessary, using a universal balljoint separator. Discard the nut and lift off the protector plate (if loose).

3 Slacken and remove the lower arm front pivot bolt and nut **(see illustration)**.

4 Unscrew the two bolts securing the lower arm rear mounting bush to the subframe **(see illustration)**.

5 Manoeuvre the lower arm assembly out from underneath the vehicle.

Overhaul

6 Thoroughly clean the lower arm and the area around the arm mountings, removing all traces of dirt and underseal if necessary, then check carefully for cracks, distortion or any

other signs of wear or damage, paying particular attention to the pivot bushes, and renew components as necessary.

7 Renewal of the front pivot bush and rear mounting bracket will required the use of a hydraulic press, a bearing puller and several spacers and should therefore be entrusted to a Peugeot dealer with access to the necessary equipment.

Refitting

8 Manoeuvre the lower arm assembly into position, and refit the front pivot bolt and nut, tightening it finger-tight only.

9 Refit the rear mounting bracket bolts and tighten them to the specified torque.

10 Refit the protector plate (where removed) to the lower balljoint, then locate the balljoint shank in the lower arm. Fit the new retaining nut and tighten it to the specified torque.

11 Refit the roadwheel, then lower the vehicle and tighten the roadwheel bolts to the specified torque. Rock the car to settle the disturbed components in position, then tighten the lower arm front pivot bolt to the specified torque.

12 Check and, if necessary, adjust the front wheel alignment as described in Section 32.

---

7 Front suspension lower balljoint – removal and refitting

Note: *A special peg socket (Peugeot number 0615J) is required to remove and refit the balljoint. If access to this tool is not available,*

6.3 Front suspension lower arm front pivot bolt (arrowed)

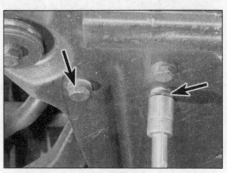

6.4 Front suspension lower arm rear mounting bush bolts (arrowed)

then balljoint renewal should be entrusted to a Peugeot dealer.

Removal

1 Remove the swivel hub assembly as described in Section 2.

2 Remove the protector plate from the balljoint and mount the assembly securely in a vice **(see illustration)**.

3 Using a hammer and pointed-nose chisel, tap up the staking securing the balljoint in position.

4 Fit the special tool to the balljoint, engaging the tool with the cut-outs in the balljoint, and secure it in position by screwing on the old balljoint nut **(see illustration)**. Unscrew the balljoint and remove it from the swivel hub.

Refitting

5 Screw the balljoint into the swivel hub assembly. Fit the special tool, taking care not to damage the balljoint gaiter, and tighten the balljoint to the specified torque. Secure the balljoint in position by firmly staking it into one of the swivel hub notches using a hammer and punch.

6 Fit the new protector plate to the balljoint and secure it in position by staking it into the one of the balljoint notches.

7 Refit the swivel hub (see Section 2).

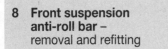

8 Front suspension anti-roll bar – removal and refitting

Note: *New connecting link nuts will be required on refitting.*

Removal

1 Chock the rear wheels, firmly apply the handbrake, then jack up the front of the vehicle and support on axle stands. Remove both front roadwheels.

2 Slacken and remove the nuts securing the left- and right-hand connecting links to the anti-roll bar, and position the links clear of the bar; if necessary, retain the balljoint shank with an Allen key to prevent rotation whilst the nut is slackened **(see illustration)**. Discard the nuts new ones should be used on refitting.

3 Slacken the two anti-roll bar mounting clamp retaining bolts and nuts, and remove both clamps from the top of the subframe **(see illustration)**.

4 Manoeuvre the anti-roll bar out from underneath the vehicle, and remove the mounting bushes from the bar.

5 Carefully examine the anti-roll bar components for signs of wear, damage or deterioration, paying particular attention to the mounting bushes. Renew worn components as necessary.

Refitting

6 Fit the rubber mounting bushes to the anti-roll bar. Position each bush so that its flat surface is at the bottom and its internal flats

7.2 Tapping off the lower balljoint protector plate

are correctly engaged with the flats on the anti-roll bar; the bush split should be facing towards the rear.

7 Offer up the anti-roll bar, and manoeuvre it into position on the subframe. Refit the mounting clamps, ensuring that their ends are correctly located in the hooks on the subframe, and refit the retaining bolts and nuts. Engage the connecting links with the ends of the bar then tighten the mounting clamp retaining bolts to the specified torque.

8 Fit the new retaining nuts to the connecting links and tighten them to the specified torque setting.

9 Refit the roadwheels then lower the vehicle to the ground and tighten the wheel bolts to the specified torque.

9 Front suspension anti-roll bar connecting link – removal and refitting

Note: *New connecting link nuts will be required on refitting.*

Removal

1 Chock the rear wheels, firmly apply the handbrake, then jack up the front of the vehicle and support on axle stands. Remove the relevant roadwheel.

2 Slacken and remove the nuts securing the connecting link to the anti-roll bar and suspension strut and remove the link from the vehicle; if necessary, retain the balljoint shanks with an Allen key to prevent rotation whilst each nut is slackened **(see illustration 4.4)**.

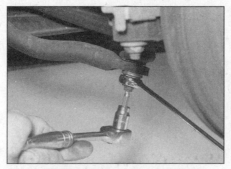

8.2 Unscrew the nut and detach the connecting rods from the anti-roll bar ends

7.4 Engage the special tool with the cut-outs (arrowed) in the balljoint

Discard the nuts, new ones should be used on refitting.

3 Inspect the link for signs of wear or damage and renew if necessary.

Refitting

4 Refitting is the reverse of removal, using new nuts and tightening them to the specified torque setting.

10 Front suspension subframe – removal and refitting

Note: *New connecting link nuts and lower balljoint nuts will be required on refitting.*

Removal

1 Chock the rear wheels, firmly apply the handbrake, then jack up the front of the vehicle and support it on axle stands. Remove both front roadwheels.

2 Remove the anti-roll bar connecting links as described in Section 9.

3 Slacken and remove the engine/transmission rear lower mounting bolt and nut, then undo the nut and bolt securing the mounting bracket to the subframe and remove the bracket **(see illustration)**.

4 Slacken and remove the left-hand lower balljoint nut and free the balljoint shank from the lower arm, if necessary, using a universal balljoint separator. Discard the nut and lift off the protector plate (if loose). Repeat the procedure on the right-hand side.

5 Slacken and remove the steering gear

8.3 Slacken and remove the retaining bolt and nut, and remove the anti-roll bar mounting clamp (arrowed)

10.3 Remove the mounting retaining bolt (A) and the bracket retaining bolt (B)

11.2 Tap the cap out from the centre of the hub and discard it

mounting bolts and washers then recover the washers from the top of the steering gear and the spacers which are fitted between the steering gear and subframe. Free the power steering pipes/hoses from their brackets on the subframe so the subframe can be removed, leaving the steering gear in position.

6 Referring to Chapter 7A, on XU7 engine models, slacken and remove the bolt securing the gearchange linkage bellcrank to the subframe. Withdraw the spacer from the bellcrank and store it with the pivot bolt for safe-keeping.

7 Make a final check that all control cables/hoses that are attached to the subframe have been released and positioned clear so that they will not hinder the removal procedure.

8 Place a jack and a suitable block of wood under the subframe to support the subframe as it is lowered.

9 Slacken and remove the subframe mounting bolts then carefully lower the subframe assembly out of position and remove it from underneath the vehicle, taking great care to ensure that the subframe assembly does not catch the power steering pipes as it is lowered out of position.

Refitting

10 Refitting is a reversal of the removal procedure, noting the following points:

a) Use new connecting link and lower balljoint nuts.
b) Tighten all nuts and bolts to the specified torque settings (where given).
c) On completion check and, if necessary, adjust the front wheel alignment as described in Section 32.

11 Rear hub assembly – removal and refitting

Note: *Do not remove the hub assembly unless it is absolutely necessary. A puller will be required to draw the hub assembly off the stub axle, and the hub bearing will almost certainly be damaged by the removal procedure, necessitating renewal of the hub assembly. A new hub nut and centre cap must be used on refitting.*

Removal

1 Remove the rear brake drum/disc (as applicable) as described in Chapter 9.

2 Prise out the cap from the centre of the hub and discard; a new cap should be used on refitting **(see illustration)**.

3 Using a hammer and punch, tap up the staking securing the hub retaining nut to the groove in the stub axle **(see illustration)**.

4 Using a socket and long bar, unscrew the

rear hub nut and discard it; a new hub nut should be used on refitting.

5 Using a puller, draw the hub assembly off the stub axle, along with the outer bearing race **(see illustration)**. If necessary, with the hub removed, use the puller to draw the inner bearing race off the stub axle.

6 Check the hub bearing for signs of roughness. It is recommended that the hub bearings should be renewed as a matter of course, as it is likely to have been damaged during removal. This means that the complete hub assembly must be renewed, since it is not possible to obtain the bearing separately.

7 With the hub removed, examine the stub axle shaft for signs of wear or damage, and if necessary renew it (see Section 15).

Refitting

8 Ensure that the bearing is packed with grease and lubricate the stub axle shaft with clean engine oil.

9 Fit the new bearing assembly, tapping it fully onto the stub axle using a hammer and a tubular drift which bears only on the flat inside edge of the bearing inner race.

10 Fit the new hub nut and tighten it to the specified torque. Stake the nut firmly into the groove on the stub axle to secure it in position, then tap the new hub cap into place in the centre of the hub **(see illustrations)**.

11.3 Using a hammer and punch, tap out the hub nut staking

11.5 Using a puller to remove the rear hub assembly from the stub axle

11.10a Fit the new hub nut . . .

11.10b . . . and tighten it to the specified torque

11.10c Stake the hub nut firmly into the stub axle groove . . .

11.10d . . . and securely fit a new cap to the centre of the hub assembly

11 Refit the rear brake disc/drum as described in Chapter 9.

12 Rear hub bearings – renewal

The hub bearing is an integral part of the hub assembly and is not available separately. If the bearing is worn, renew the complete hub assembly as described in Section 11.

13 Rear suspension shock absorber – removal, testing and refitting

Note: *At the time of writing, no information on the active suspension system was available. If your car has active suspension, consult your Peugeot dealer for details of any relevant changes to the following procedure before attempting to remove/refit the shock absorber.*

Note: *A new shock absorber upper mounting nut and lower mounting bolt nut will be required on refitting.*

Removal

1 On Saloon models, from inside the vehicle luggage compartment, slacken and remove the retaining screws and remove the rear trim panel. Release the retaining clips (pull out the centre pins then prise out the complete clip) and peel back the trim panel to gain access to the strut upper mounting, it may also prove

necessary to undo the retaining screw and remove the tie-down hook **(see illustration)**. On some models, if work is being carried out on the left-hand side it will also be necessary to unscrew the fastener and remove the storage compartment to gain the necessary clearance required.

2 On Estate models, open up the tailgate and peel the sealing strip away from the base and relevant side of the body. Undo the retaining screws and remove the rear trim plate then unclip and remove the side storage compartment cover. Remove the retaining clips (pull out the centre pins then remove the complete clip) securing the side of the carpet to the floor then release the retaining clips and remove the plastic storage compartment. Peel back the side trim panel to reveal the strut upper mounting **(see illustration)**.

3 Chock the front wheels, then jack up the rear of the vehicle and support it on axle stands. Remove the relevant rear roadwheel.

4 Using a trolley jack, raise the lower arm until the rear suspension coil spring is slightly compressed.

5 From inside the luggage compartment, slacken and remove the upper mounting nut; discard the nut, a new one should be used on refitting, and lift off the upper mounting rubber, noting which way around it is fitted.

6 From underneath the vehicle, slacken and remove the lower mounting bolt and nut then manoeuvre the shock absorber out of position complete with its mounting rubber and bump stop/dust cover **(see illustration)**. Slide off the mounting, noting which way around it is fitted, and lift off the bump stop/dust cover.

Testing

7 Examine the shock absorber for signs of fluid leakage or damage. Test the operation of the shock absorber, while holding it in an upright position, by moving the piston through a full stroke and then through short strokes of 50 to 100 mm. In both cases, the resistance felt should be smooth and continuous. If the resistance is jerky, or uneven, or if there is any visible sign of wear or damage, renewal is necessary. Also check the rubber mountings for damage and deterioration. Renew worn components as necessary. Inspect the shank of the mounting bolt for signs of wear or damage, and renew as necessary. The self-locking nuts should be renewed as a matter of course.

Refitting

8 Prior to refitting the shock absorber, mount it upright in the vice, and operate it fully through several strokes in order to prime it. Apply a smear of multi-purpose grease to the lower mounting bolt and contact face of the new nut (Peugeot recommend Molykote G Rapide Plus – available from your Peugeot dealer).

9 Fit the bump stop/dust cover to the shock absorber piston followed by the mounting rubber.

10 Fully extend the piston and manoeuvre the assembly into position. Have an assistant refit the upper mounting cup and rubber to the inside of the vehicle and screw the new upper mounting nut on a few turns.

11 Align the shock absorber lower mounting

13.1 On Saloon models, peel back the luggage compartment side trim panel to gain access to the shock absorber upper mounting (arrowed)

13.2 On Estate models, release the side trim panel to gain access to the shock absorber upper mounting (arrowed)

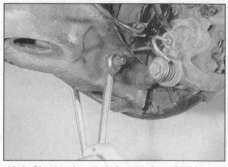

13.6 Slackening the shock absorber lower mounting bolt

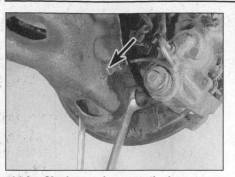

14.3a Slacken and remove the lower arm outer pivot bolt and nut (shock absorber bolt arrowed) . . .

14.3b . . . and loosen the inner pivot bolt

with the lower arm and refit the mounting bolt. Fit the new nut, tightening it lightly only at this stage.

12 Tighten the upper mounting nut to the specified torque and refit the trim panel(s) in the luggage compartment.

13 Refit the rear roadwheel then lower the vehicle to the ground and tighten the wheel bolts to the specified torque. Rock the vehicle to settle the shock absorber in position then tighten the shock absorber lower mounting to the specified torque setting.

14 Rear suspension coil spring – removal and refitting

Note: *A new shock absorber lower mounting bolt nut and lower arm pivot bolt nuts will be required on refitting.*

Removal

1 Chock the front wheels, then jack up the rear of the vehicle and support it on axle stands. Remove the relevant rear roadwheel.
2 Position a trolley jack underneath the outer end of the lower arm and raise the arm until the rear suspension coil spring is slightly compressed.
3 Slacken and remove the lower arm outer pivot bolt and nut then unscrew the nut from the inner pivot bolt **(see illustrations)**.
4 Unscrew the shock absorber lower mounting bolt nut and withdraw the bolt. Discard the nut; a new should be used on refitting.
5 Unclip the brake hose and wiring (as applicable) from any relevant clips on the lower arm, so that the arm is free to be lowered.
6 Slowly lower the jack until all spring pressure is released, then remove the coil spring along with its upper and lower spring seats.
7 Inspect the coil spring and its seats for signs of wear or damage and renew if necessary.

Refitting

8 Fit the lower spring seat in position on the lower arm, and seat the upper seat on top of the coil spring. Lubricate the shanks of the shock absorber and lower arm bolts and the contact faces of the new nuts with multi-purpose grease (Peugeot recommend Molykote G Rapide Plus – available from your Peugeot dealer).

9 Manoeuvre the spring into position and carefully raise the lower arm with the jack, ensuring that the coil spring ends are correctly aligned with both seats.
10 Align the lower arm with the swivel hub and insert the outer pivot bolt. Fit the new nuts to the inner and outer pivot bolts tightening them by hand only at this stage.
11 Align the shock absorber with the lower arm and refit its mounting bolt. Fit the new nut to bolt, tightening it lightly only at this stage.
12 Remove the jack from underneath the lower arm and secure the brake hose and wiring (as applicable) in position with all the relevant clips and ties.
13 Refit the rear roadwheel then lower the vehicle to the ground and tighten the wheel bolts to the specified torque. Rock the vehicle to settle the lower arm in position then tighten the shock absorber lower mounting and the lower arm pivot bolts to their specified torque settings.

15 Rear suspension stub axle – removal, overhaul and refitting

Note: *On refitting new trailing arm, lower arm and upper arm pivot bolt nuts will be required on refitting as will a track arm balljoint nut and an anti-roll bar connecting link nut. It is almost certain that a new hub assembly will also be required on refitting.*

Removal

1 Chock the front wheels then jack up the rear of the vehicle and support it on axle stands. Remove the relevant roadwheel.
2 On models equipped with ABS, unbolt the wheel sensor and position it clear of the stub axle (see Chapter 9, Section 24). Note that there is no need to disconnect the wiring.
3 Remove the hub assembly as described in Section 11. Proceed as described under the relevant sub-heading.

Models with rear drum brakes

4 Minimise fluid loss by first removing the master cylinder reservoir cap, and then tightening it down onto a piece of polythene, to obtain an airtight seal. Alternatively, use a brake hose clamp, a G-clamp or a similar tool to clamp the flexible hose at the nearest convenient point to the wheel cylinder.
5 Wipe away all traces of dirt around the brake hose union on the wheel cylinder then unscrew the union nut and disconnect the brake pipe. Plug the pipe and wheel cylinder unions to minimise fluid loss and prevent dirt entry.
6 Unclip the handbrake cable then slacken and remove the four bolts securing the brake backplate assembly in position then carefully ease the assembly off the stub axle. Position the plate clear of the stub axle so that it does not hinder removal.
7 Position a hydraulic jack underneath the outer end of the lower arm and raise the jack until the coil spring is slightly compressed.
8 Unscrew the retaining nut and free the anti-roll bar connecting link from the stub axle.
9 Unscrew the retaining nut and free the track arm balljoint from the stub axle.
10 Slacken and remove the upper and lower arm outer pivot bolts and nuts.
11 Unscrew the nut and withdraw the bolt securing the trailing arm to the stub axle and remove the stub axle from the vehicle.
12 Inspect the stub axle for signs of wear or damage paying particular attention to the pivot bush. If the stub axle shaft is worn or damaged then the assembly must be renewed. The pivot bush is available separately, however renewal is best entrusted to a Peugeot dealer since a hydraulic press and spacers will be required.

Models with rear disc brakes

13 Remove the stub axle as described in paragraphs 6 to 12.

Refitting

14 Obtain all the new nuts required (see Note) and lubricate the shanks of the pivot bolts and contact faces of the new nuts with multi-purpose grease (Peugeot recommend Molykote G Rapide Plus – available from your Peugeot dealer).
15 Offer up the stub axle and insert the upper and lower arm pivot bolts and the trailing arm bolt. Fit the new nuts to the bolts, tightening them lightly only at this stage.
16 Locate the anti-roll bar connecting link and track arm balljoints correctly in position then fit the new nuts and tighten them to their specified torque settings.
17 Locate the backplate assembly on the stub axle and tighten its retaining bolts securely.
18 Fit the new hub assembly as described in Section 11.
19 On models with rear drum brakes, working as described in Chapter 9, reconnect the pipe to the wheel cylinder and tighten its union nut to the specified torque. Remove the clamp/polythene (as applicable) and bleed the

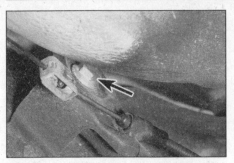

17.1 Removal of the rear suspension right-hand upper arm may require removal of the subframe – see text

hydraulic system noting that if the precautions described have been taken it should only be necessary to bleed the relevant rear brake.

20 On models with ABS, refit the wheel sensor to the stub axle (see Chapter 9).

21 Refit the rear roadwheel then lower the vehicle to the ground and tighten the wheel bolts to the specified torque. Rock the vehicle to settle the stub axle in position then tighten the upper and lower arm pivot bolts and the trailing arm pivot bolt to their specified torque settings.

22 Check and, if necessary, adjust the rear wheel alignment as described in Section 32.

16 Rear suspension lower arm – removal, overhaul and refitting

Note: *A new shock absorber lower mounting bolt nut and lower arm pivot bolt nuts will be required on refitting.*

Removal

1 Remove the coil spring as described in Section 14.

2 Withdraw the inner pivot bolt and remove the lower arm from the vehicle.

Overhaul

3 Thoroughly clean the lower arm and the area around the arm mountings, removing all traces of dirt and underseal if necessary, then check carefully for cracks, distortion or any other signs of wear or damage, paying particular attention to the pivot bushes (the outer bush is pressed into the stub axle), and renew components as necessary.

4 Renewal of the inner pivot bush will required the use of a hydraulic press and several spacers and should therefore be entrusted to a Peugeot dealer with access to the necessary equipment. If renewal of outer pivot bush is necessary, it will be necessary to remove the stub axle (see Section 15).

Refitting

5 Lubricate the shanks of the pivot bolts and the contact faces of the new nuts with multi-purpose grease (Peugeot recommend Molykote G Rapide Plus – available from your Peugeot dealer).

17.5a Slacken and remove the inner pivot bolt and nut . . .

6 Offer up the lower arm and insert the inner pivot bolt.

7 Refit the coil spring with reference to Section 14. On completion check and, if necessary, adjust the rear wheel alignment as described in Section 32.

17 Rear suspension upper arm – removal and refitting

Right-hand arm

1 To gain the necessary clearance required to withdraw the inner pivot bolt, it is necessary to drop the complete rear suspension and subframe assembly out of position **(see illustration)**. This task should be entrusted to a Peugeot dealer. On refitting they will fit the bolt the opposite way around so that it can be removed in future, should the need arise.

2 A way around this is to cut the head off the original pivot bolt (making sure a new bolt is available) so that it can be withdrawn in the opposite direction. This avoids the need to remove the rear suspension and subframe assembly, so saving a lot of time and effort. Using this method, the arm can be removed and refitted as described below.

Left-hand arm

Note: *New pivot bolt nuts will be required on refitting.*

Removal

3 Chock the front wheels then jack up the rear of the vehicle and support it on axle stands. Remove the relevant roadwheel.

4 Position a hydraulic jack underneath the outer end of the lower arm and raise the jack until the coil spring is slightly compressed.

5 Slacken and remove the nuts then withdraw the inner and outer pivot bolts and remove the arm from underneath the vehicle, freeing it from the handbrake cable **(see illustrations)**.

6 Thoroughly clean the arm and the area around the arm mountings, removing all traces of dirt and underseal if necessary, then check carefully for cracks, distortion or any other signs of wear or damage, paying particular attention to the pivot bushes. If there is any sign of wear or damage the arm must be renewed.

17.5b . . . and the outer pivot bolt and nut, and remove the upper arm from the rear suspension

Refitting

7 Lubricate the shanks of the pivot bolts and the contact faces of the nuts with multi-purpose grease (Peugeot recommend Molykote G Rapide Plus – available from your Peugeot dealer).

8 Offer up the arm and insert the pivot bolts. Fit the new nuts to the bolts tighten them lightly only at this stage.

9 Refit the rear roadwheel then lower the vehicle to the ground and tighten the wheel bolts to the specified torque. Rock the vehicle to settle the stub axle in position then tighten the upper arm pivot bolts to the specified torque setting.

10 On completion check and, if necessary, adjust the rear wheel alignment as described in Section 32.

18 Rear suspension trailing arm – removal, overhaul and refitting

Note: *New trailing arm pivot bolt nuts will be required on refitting.*

Removal

1 Chock the front wheels then jack up the rear of the vehicle and support it on axle stands. Remove the relevant roadwheel.

2 Position a hydraulic jack underneath the outer end of the lower arm and raise the jack until the coil spring is slightly compressed.

3 Unscrew the nut and remove the washer then withdraw the pivot bolt and washer securing the trailing arm to the stub axle **(see illustration)**.

18.3 Slacken and remove the pivot bolt and nut (arrowed) securing the leading arm to the stub axle . . .

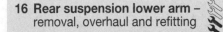

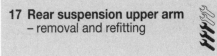

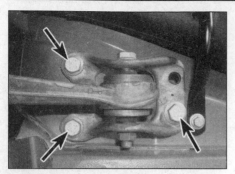

18.4 . . . then undo the three mounting bracket-to-body bolts (arrowed), and remove the trailing arm assembly

4 Unscrew the three bolts securing the trailing arm mounting bracket to the vehicle body and remove the arm assembly **(see illustration)**. Note: *Do not slacken the trailing arm pivot bush bolt unless renewal of the bush/mounting bracket is necessary.*

Overhaul

5 Slacken and remove the nut and pivot bolt and separate the front mounting bracket and trailing arm.
6 Thoroughly clean the trailing arm and the area around the arm mountings, removing all traces of dirt and underseal if necessary, then check carefully for cracks, distortion or any other signs of wear or damage paying particular attention to the mounting bushes. If either bush requires renewal, it is recommended that the task is entrusted to a Peugeot dealer or suitably-equipped garage with access to a hydraulic press and spacers which will be needed to press the bushes out of position and install the new ones. If the front bush requires renewal, it may prove easier/more cost effective to renew the complete mounting bracket assembly. Inspect the pivot bolts for signs of wear or damage and renew as necessary.

Refitting

7 Lubricate the shanks of the bolts and the contact faces of the new nuts with multi-purpose grease (Peugeot recommend Molykote G Rapide Plus – available from your Peugeot dealer).

8 If the trailing arm and bracket were separated, refit the pivot bolt and screw on the new nut, tightening it by hand only at this stage.
9 Manoeuvre the arm assembly into position and refit the mounting bracket retaining bolts.
10 Insert the pivot bolt and washer securing the arm to the stub axle then fit the washer and new nut, tightening it lightly only at this stage.
11 Tighten the mounting bracket to body bolts to the specified torque then refit the roadwheel and lower the vehicle to the ground. Tighten the wheel bolts to the specified torque then rock the vehicle to settle the stub axle in position. Tighten the trailing arm front and (where slackened) rear pivot bolt to their specified torque settings.
12 On completion check and, if necessary, adjust the rear wheel alignment (Section 32).

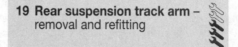

19 Rear suspension track arm – removal and refitting

Note: *A new track arm pivot bolt nut and balljoint nut will be required on refitting.*

Removal

1 Chock the front wheels then jack up the rear of the vehicle and support it on axle stands. Remove the relevant roadwheel.
2 Position a hydraulic jack underneath the outer end of the lower arm and raise the jack until the coil spring is slightly compressed.
3 Prior to disturbing the track arm, make alignment marks between the inner pivot bolt special washer and subframe. These marks can then be used on refitting to set the rear wheel alignment.
4 Slacken and remove the nut securing the track arm balljoint to the stub axle and free the balljoint shank; if necessary, prevent the balljoint shank from rotating by retaining it with an Allen key whilst the nut is slackened **(see illustration)**.
5 Unscrew the nut from the inner pivot bolt and remove the special washer **(see illustration)**. Withdraw the pivot bolt and remove the track arm from the vehicle.

6 Thoroughly clean the arm and the area around the arm mountings, removing all traces of dirt and underseal if necessary, then check carefully for cracks, distortion or any other signs of wear or damage, paying particular attention to the balljoint. If there is any sign of wear or damage the complete arm must be renewed.

Refitting

7 Clean the threads of the pivot bolt and balljoint and lubricate the contact faces of the new nuts with multi-purpose grease (Peugeot recommend Molykote G Rapide Plus – available from your Peugeot dealer).
8 Manoeuvre the track arm into position and insert the pivot bolt. Slide the special washer onto the rear of the bolt, making sure it is correctly engaged with the bolts and is positioned against the lug on the subframe, and fit the new nut tightening it lightly only. Align the marks made prior to removal and tighten the bolt to the specified torque setting.
9 Locate the balljoint shank in the stub axle and fit the new nut, tightening it to the specified torque setting.
10 Refit the rear roadwheel then lower the vehicle to the ground and tighten the wheel bolts to the specified torque.
11 On completion check and, if necessary, adjust the rear wheel alignment as described in Section 32.

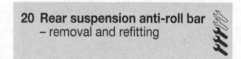

20 Rear suspension anti-roll bar – removal and refitting

Note: *New connecting link nuts will be required on refitting.*

Removal

1 Chock the front wheels then jack up the rear of the vehicle and support it on axle stands. Remove both rear roadwheels.
2 Unscrew the retaining nuts and free the connecting links from either end of the anti-roll bar **(see illustration)**.
3 Prior to removal make alignment marks between the mounting bushes and the anti-roll.

19.4 Unscrew the nut (arrowed) and free the track arm balljoint from the stub axle . . .

19.5 . . . then remove the inner pivot bolt arrangement (arrowed) and remove the arm

20.2 Unscrew the nut (arrowed), and free the connecting link from the anti-roll bar end – right-hand side

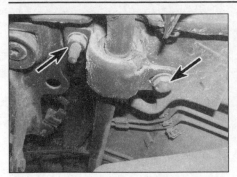

20.4 Unscrew the nuts/bolts (arrowed) and remove the anti-roll bar mounting clamps

4 Slacken and remove the retaining nuts/bolt (as applicable) and remove the anti-roll bar mounting clamps **(see illustration)**.
5 Manoeuvre the anti-roll bar out from underneath the vehicle, and remove the mounting bushes from the bar.
6 Carefully examine the anti-roll bar components for signs of wear, damage or deterioration, paying particular attention to the mounting bushes. Renew worn components as necessary.

Refitting

7 Fit the rubber mounting bushes to the anti-roll bar. Align the bushes with the marks made prior to removal and position them so that their flat surfaces are at the top and the bush splits are facing towards the front.
8 Offer up the anti-roll bar, and manoeuvre it into position. Refit the mounting clamps and refit the retaining bolt and nuts. Engage the connecting links with the ends of the bar then tighten the mounting clamp retaining bolts to the specified torque.
9 Fit the new retaining nuts to the connecting links and tighten them to the specified torque setting.
10 Refit the roadwheels then lower the vehicle to the ground and tighten the wheel bolts to the specified torque.

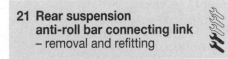

21 Rear suspension anti-roll bar connecting link – removal and refitting

Note: *New connecting link nuts will be required on refitting.*

Removal

1 Chock the front wheels then jack up the rear of the vehicle and support on axle stands. Remove the relevant roadwheel.
2 Slacken and remove the nuts securing the connecting link to the anti-roll bar and stub axle and remove the link from the vehicle; if necessary, retaining the balljoint shank with an Allen key to prevent rotation as the nut is slackened. Discard the nuts, new ones should be used on refitting.
3 Inspect the link for signs of wear or damage and renew if necessary.

22.3 Remove the steering wheel retaining bolt . . .

Refitting

4 Refitting is the reverse of removal. Use new nuts and tighten them to the specified torque setting.

22 Steering wheel – removal and refitting

Note: *All models are equipped with a driver's airbag which has the word AIRBAG stamped on the steering wheel pad.*

⚠ **Warning: Refer to the precautions given in Chapter 12 before proceeding.**

Removal

1 Remove the air bag unit as described in Chapter 12, Section 26.
2 Position the front wheels in the straight-ahead position and engage the steering lock.
3 Slacken and remove the steering wheel retaining bolt then mark the steering wheel and steering column shaft in relation to each other **(see illustration)**.
4 Release the airbag unit wiring connector from its retaining clips and lift the steering wheel off the column splines, taking care not to damage the wiring **(see illustration)**.

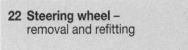

HAYNES HiNT *If the wheel is tight, tap it up near the centre, using the palm of your hand, or twist it from side-to-side, whilst carefully pulling it upwards to release it from the shaft splines.*

23.5a Undo the retaining screw (arrowed) from under the right-hand side of the facia panel . . .

22.4 . . . and disconnect/release the wiring connectors from the steering wheel

Refitting

5 Prior to refitting the steering wheel, ensure that the front wheels are still in the straight-ahead position and check that the airbag contact unit is correctly centralised (see Chapter 12, Section 26). On completion, refit the airbag unit as described in Chapter 12.
6 Refitting is a reversal of removal, noting the following points:
a) *Prior to refitting, ensure that the indicator switch stem is in its central position. Failure to do this could lead to the steering wheel lug breaking the switch tab as the steering wheel is refitted.*
b) *On refitting, align the marks made on removal, taking great care not to damage the airbag unit wiring, then tighten the retaining bolt to the specified torque.*

23 Steering column – removal, inspection and refitting

Note: *On models equipped with a driver's airbag, refer to the precautions given in Chapter 12 before proceeding.*
Note: *A special TORX socket will be required to remove/refit the column mounting bolts. A new clamp bolt nut will also be needed on refitting.*

Removal

1 Disconnect the battery negative terminal.
2 Remove the steering wheel as described in Section 22.
3 On early models, remove the contact unit from the top of the steering column as described in Chapter 12, Section 26.
4 On all models, remove the combination switches from the top of the steering column as described in Chapter 12, Section 4.
5 Undo the lower retaining screw from the right-hand side of the facia panel, then rotate the three fastener through 90° and lower the fusebox cover. Slacken and remove the left-hand side retaining screw, and remove the driver's side lower panel from the facia **(see illustrations)**.
6 Trace the wiring back from the ignition switch and disconnect it at the wiring connectors **(see illustrations)**.

23.5b . . . and the left-hand side retaining screw (arrowed)

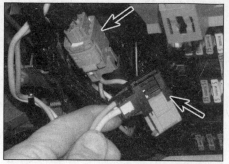

23.6a Disconnect the two wiring block connectors (arrowed) . . .

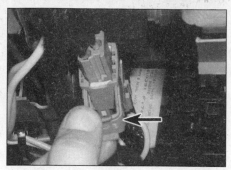

23.6b . . . to disconnect the connectors, first pull out the locking clip (arrowed)

23.7 Where applicable, undo the retaining bolt (arrowed) and free the wiring bracket from the steering column

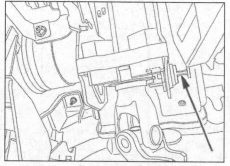

23.8 Lock the column in position by pressing in the locking button (arrowed) on the column base

23.9 Make alignment marks between the column joint and intermediate shaft, then remove the clamp bolt (arrowed)

7 Where applicable, undo the retaining bolt and free the wiring retaining bracket from the column **(see illustration)**. Release the wiring from its retaining clips and position it clear so that it does hinder column removal.

8 Lock the steering column in position by pressing in the locking button (approx 1 mm) on the base of the column shaft. This is important as it prevents any lateral movement in the steering column while it is off the vehicle **(see illustration)**.

9 Using paint or a suitable marker pen, make alignment marks between the column universal joint and the intermediate shaft then slacken and remove the clamp bolt **(see illustration)**.

10 Slacken and remove the mounting bolts from the top of the column **(see illustration)**. Slide the column assembly upwards, to release its rear retaining clip and free it from

the intermediate shaft, and remove it from the vehicle.

Inspection

11 Before refitting the steering column, examine the column and mountings for signs of damage and deformation, and renew as necessary. Check the steering shaft for signs of free play in the column bushes, and check the universal joints for signs of damage or roughness in the joint bearings. If any damage or wear is found on the steering column universal joint or shaft bushes, the column must be renewed as an assembly.

Refitting

12 Prior to refitting release the clamp bolt nut retainer tang and remove the old nut **(see illustration)**. Fit the new nut into the retainer, making sure it is fitted the correct way around,

and securely refit the retainer to the column.
13 Align the marks made prior to removal and engage the column universal joint with the intermediate shaft.
14 Slide the column assembly into position making sure its mounting bracket is correctly engaged with the bracket. Refit the column mounting bolts and tighten them to the specified torque setting.
15 Refit the universal joint clamp bolt and tighten it to the specified torque setting.
16 Unlock the column by pulling **out** the locking button by approx 1 mm **(see illustration 23.8)**.
17 The remainder of refitting is a direct reversal of the removal procedure, noting the following.
  a) Ensure that all wiring is correctly routed and retained by all the necessary clips and ties.
  b) Refit the steering wheel as described in Section 22.

23.10 Slacken and remove the two upper mounting bolts (arrowed)

23.12 Prior to refitting, remove the nut retainer (arrowed) and renew the clamp bolt nut

24 Steering column intermediate shaft – removal, inspection and refitting

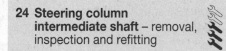

Note: New clamp bolt nuts will be required on refitting.

Removal

1 Remove the steering column as described in Section 23.
2 Firmly apply the handbrake then jack up the front of the vehicle and support it on axle stands.
3 Make alignment marks between the inter-

mediate shaft joint and the steering gear pinion then slacken and remove the clamp bolt and nut. Discard the nut, a new one should be used on refitting.

4 Slacken and remove the three nuts securing the intermediate shaft gaiter to the bulkhead.

5 From inside the car, slide the gaiter off the intermediate shaft then detach the shaft from the steering gear and remove it from the car.

Inspection

6 Inspect the intermediate shaft assembly for signs of wear or damage, paying particular attention to the universal joint. If the shaft or joint show any sign of wear then the complete shaft assembly must be renewed. Renew the rubber gaiter if it shows signs of damage or deterioration.

Refitting

7 Align the marks made prior to removal and engage the intermediate shaft with the steering gear pinion splines.

8 Slide the rubber gaiter along the intermediate shaft and into position in the bulkhead.

9 From underneath the vehicle, fit the intermediate shaft clamp bolt and the new retaining nut and tighten it to the specified torque setting.

10 Refit the gaiter retaining nuts and tighten them securely.

11 Refit the steering column as described in Section 23.

25 Ignition switch/lock cylinder – removal and refitting

Ignition switch

Removal

1 Disconnect the battery negative terminal.

2 Lift the steering column adjustment lever up, then turn the three fasteners through 90° and lower the fusebox cover.

3 Undo the retaining screws securing the steering column lower shroud in position then unclip both the upper and lower shrouds from the column (see illustration).

4 Carefully pull the transponder immobiliser unit, to release it from the ignition switch

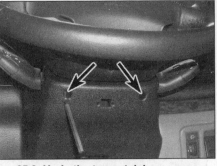
25.3 Undo the two retaining screws (arrowed) and unclip the lower shroud

25.7a Remove the securing screw (arrowed) . . .

housing (see illustration). The transponder can then be put to one side, with its wiring still connected. Take care not to damage the transponder assembly.

5 Trace the wiring back from the ignition switch, and disconnect its wiring connectors from the main wiring harness.

6 Insert the key into the steering lock and turn it to the first position.

7 Remove the cylinder lock retaining screw, then use a small screwdriver to release the locating peg and slide the lock cylinder out from the steering column housing (see illustrations).

8 Manoeuvre the ignition switch complete with the wiring block connectors out through the steering lock housing (see illustration).

Refitting

9 Slide the ignition switch wiring block connectors back through the steering lock housing.

25.4 Carefully unclip the transponder unit from around the ignition switch

25.7b . . . then press down the locating peg to release the ignition lock

10 Insert the key (if not already done) and turn the lock cylinder to the first position. Slide the lock cylinder back into the steering column housing, aligning it up with the locating peg and retaining screw holes in the housing. Refit the retaining screw.

11 Reconnect the wiring block connectors to the main harness ensuring it is correctly routed and retained by all the necessary clips.

12 The remainder of refitting is the reverse of removal.

Lock cylinder

Removal

13 Remove the ignition switch as described in paragraphs 1 to 8.

14 Slide out the locking pegs and unclip the wiring block retaining bracket (see illustrations).

15 Disengage the wiring block from the

25.8 Manoeuvre the ignition switch and wiring out from the steering column

25.14a Slide the locking pegs out of position (noting the correct fitted position) . . .

25.14b . . . and unclip the retaining bracket

25.15a Remove the wiring block from the ignition switch . . .

25.15b . . . then withdraw the lock cylinder from the switch housing

25.17 Make sure the locking pegs are located correctly

ignition switch, then the lock cylinder can be withdrawn from the ignition switch housing **(see illustrations)**.

Refitting

16 Slide the lock cylinder back into the ignition switch housing, and refit the wiring block connector.

17 Refit the wiring block retaining bracket and slide the locking pegs back into position **(see illustration)**.

18 Refit the ignition switch assembly as described earlier.

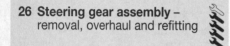

26 Steering gear assembly – removal, overhaul and refitting

Note: *New track rod balljoint nuts and an intermediate shaft clamp bolt nut will be required on refitting.*

Removal

1 Firmly apply the handbrake then jack up the front of the vehicle and support it on axle stands. Remove both front roadwheels.

2 Release the cable ties and unclip the heat shield from the top of the steering gear. Where necessary, depress the retaining clip and disconnect the wiring connector from the steering gear pinion housing.

3 Slacken and remove the nuts securing the steering gear track rod balljoints to the swivel hubs. Release the balljoint tapered shanks using a universal balljoint separator and

recover the protector plates. Discard the nuts, new ones will be needed on refitting.

4 Using paint or a suitable marker pen, make alignment marks between the intermediate shaft joint and the steering gear pinion, then slacken and remove the clamp bolt and nut. Discard the nut, a new one should be used on refitting **(see illustration)**.

5 Using brake hose clamps, clamp both the supply and return hoses near the power steering fluid reservoir. This will minimise fluid loss during subsequent operations.

6 Mark the unions to ensure that they are correctly positioned on reassembly, then unscrew the feed and return pipe union nuts/bolts (as applicable) from the steering gear assembly; be prepared for fluid spillage, and position a suitable container beneath the pipes whilst unscrewing the union nuts. Disconnect both pipes, and plug the pipe ends and steering gear orifices, to prevent fluid leakage and to keep dirt out of the hydraulic system **(see illustration)**.

7 Free the power steering pipes from any retaining clips, and position them clear of the steering gear.

8 Slacken the steering gear mounting bolts, and recover the nuts and washers from the top of the steering gear **(see illustration)**. Withdraw the mounting bolts, and recover the spacers which are fitted between the steering gear and the subframe.

9 Free the steering gear pinion from the intermediate shaft joint and manoeuvre it out towards the driver's side of the vehicle.

Overhaul

10 Examine the steering gear assembly for signs of wear or damage, and check that the rack moves freely throughout the full length of its travel, with no signs of roughness or excessive free play between the steering gear pinion and rack. Inspect all the steering gear fluid unions for signs of leakage, and check that all union nuts are securely tightened. On models with invariable pressure power steering, also examine the steering gear hydraulic ram for signs of fluid leakage or damage, and if necessary renew it.

11 It is possible to overhaul the steering gear assembly housing components, but this task should be entrusted to a Peugeot dealer. The only components which can be renewed easily by the home mechanic are the steering gear gaiters, the track rod balljoints and the track rods which are covered elsewhere in this Chapter.

Refitting

12 Manoeuvre the steering gear into position and engage it with the intermediate shaft, aligning the marks made prior to removal.

13 Slide the spacers into position between the subframe and steering gear and fit the washers and nuts to the top of the steering gear. Insert the mounting bolts and tighten them to the specified torque.

14 Reconnect the fluid pipes to the steering gear and securely tighten their union nuts/bolts. Secure the pipes in position with all the necessary clips and ties and remove the clamps from the hoses.

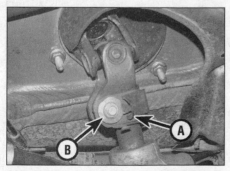

26.4 Release the retaining clip (A) and undo the steering gear pinion clamp bolt (B)

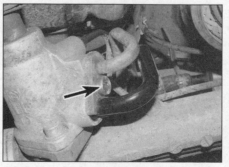

26.6 Slacken the retaining bolt (arrowed) and remove the fluid pipes

26.8 Slacken and remove the steering gear-to-subframe bolts (arrowed)

15 Fit the intermediate shaft clamp bolt and the new nut, tightening it to the specified torque.
16 Ensure that the protector plates are in position then locate the track rod balljoints in the swivel hubs. Fit the new retaining nuts and tighten them to the specified torque.
17 Reconnect the wiring connector (where fitted) then refit the heat shield to the steering gear and secure it in position with new cable ties. Refit the roadwheels then lower the vehicle to the ground and tighten the roadwheel bolts to the specified torque.
18 Top-up the fluid reservoir and bleed the hydraulic system as described in Section 28.
19 On completion check and, if necessary, adjust the front wheel alignment as described in Section 32.

27 Steering gear rubber gaiters – renewal

Variable pressure steering

1 Remove the track rod balljoint as described in Section 30.
2 Mark the correct fitted position of the gaiter on the track rod, then release the retaining clips and slide the gaiter off the steering gear housing and track rod end **(see illustration)**.
3 Thoroughly clean the track rod and the steering gear housing, using fine abrasive paper to polish off any corrosion, burrs or sharp edges, which might damage the new gaiter's sealing lips on installation. Scrape off all the grease from the old gaiter, and apply it to the track rod inner balljoint. (This assumes that grease has not been lost or contaminated as a result of damage to the old gaiter. Use fresh grease if in doubt.)
4 Carefully slide the new gaiter onto the track rod end, and locate it on the steering gear housing. Align the outer edge of the gaiter with the mark made on the track rod prior to removal, then secure it in position with new retaining clips (where fitted).

5 Refit the track rod balljoint as described in Section 30.

Invariable pressure steering

6 On these models, it is only possible to renew the gaiter nearest the drive pinion, ie, the right-hand gaiter on right-hand-drive models, and the left-hand gaiter on left-hand-drive models. This can be renewed as described above in paragraphs 1 to 5.
7 The task of renewing the opposite gaiter should be entrusted to a Peugeot dealer. This is necessary since it is not possible to pass the gaiter over the steering rack stud to which the hydraulic ram is fixed. Therefore, the steering gear must be dismantled and the rack removed from the housing to allow the gaiter to be renewed.
8 The only task on this end of the assembly which can be carried out by the home mechanic is the renewal of the track rod inner balljoint dust cover. The dust cover can be renewed once the track rod balljoint has been removed as described in Section 30. On refitting, ensure that the dust cover is correctly located on the track rod and steering rack, then refit the balljoint.

28 Power steering system – bleeding

1 This procedure will only be necessary when any of the hydraulic system has been disconnected.
2 Referring to *Weekly checks*, remove the fluid reservoir filler cap, and top-up with the specified fluid to the upper level mark.
3 With the engine stopped, slowly move the steering from lock-to-lock several times to purge out the trapped air, then top-up the level in the fluid reservoir. Repeat this procedure until the fluid level in the reservoir does not drop any further.
4 Start the engine, then slowly move the steering from lock-to-lock several times to purge out any remaining air in the system. Repeat this procedure until bubbles cease to appear in the fluid reservoir.
5 If, when turning the steering, an abnormal noise is heard from the fluid lines, it indicates that there is still air in the system. Check this by turning the wheels to the straight-ahead position and switching off the engine. If the fluid level in the reservoir rises, then air is present in the system, and further bleeding is necessary.
6 Once all traces of air have been removed from the power steering hydraulic system, turn the engine off and allow the system to cool. Once cool, check that fluid level is up to the upper mark on the power steering fluid reservoir, topping-up if necessary.

29 Power steering pump – removal and refitting

Removal

1 Release the drivebelt tension as described in the relevant Part of Chapter 1, and unhook the drivebelt from the pump pulley. The power steering pump is mounted directly above, or directly below the alternator, depending on engine type and specification level. If the pump is mounted below the alternator, access is most easily obtained from underneath the car.
2 Using brake hose clamps, clamp both the supply and return hoses near the power steering fluid reservoir. This will minimise fluid loss during subsequent operations.
3 Undo the retaining nut, and free the fluid hose retaining clip from the rear of the pump (where fitted).
4 Slacken the retaining clip, and disconnect the fluid supply hose from the pump then slacken the union nut, and disconnect the feed pipe **(see illustration)**. Be prepared for

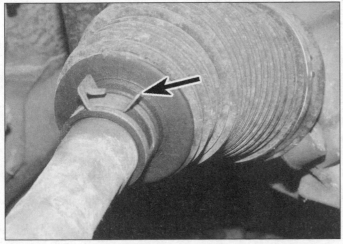
27.2 Use a pair of pliers to remove the outer retaining clip (arrowed)

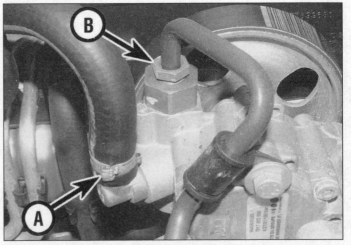
29.4 Release the retaining clip (A) from the supply hose, and undo the union nut (B) to disconnect the feed pipe – 2.2 litre diesel

30.4a Slacken and remove the track rod balljoint retaining nut . . .

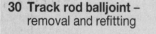

30.4b . . . then release the balljoint shank using a universal balljoint separator

some fluid spillage as the pipe and hose are disconnected, and plug the hose/pipe end and pump unions, to minimise fluid loss and prevent the entry of dirt into the system.
5 Slacken and remove the pump mounting bolts and withdraw the pump from its bracket.
6 If the power steering pump is faulty it must be renewed. The pump is a sealed unit and cannot be overhauled.

Refitting

7 Manoeuvre the pump into position, then refit its mounting bolts and tighten them securely.
8 Reconnect the feed pipe to the pump and securely tighten the union nut. Refit the supply pipe to the pump, and securely tighten its retaining clip. Remove the brake hose clamps used to minimise fluid loss.
9 Where applicable, refit the fluid hose retaining clip to the rear of the pump, and securely tighten its retaining nut.
10 Refit the drivebelt to the pump pulley, and tension it as described in the relevant Part of Chapter 1.
11 On completion, bleed the hydraulic system as described in Section 28.

30 Track rod balljoint – removal and refitting

Note: *A new balljoint retaining nut will be required on refitting.*

Removal

1 Apply the handbrake, then jack up the front of the vehicle and support it on axle stands. Remove the appropriate front roadwheel.
2 If the balljoint is to be re-used, use a straight-edge and a scriber, or similar, to mark its relationship to the track rod.
3 Hold the track rod, and unscrew the balljoint locknut by a quarter of a turn. Do not move the locknut from this position, as it will serve as a handy reference mark on refitting.
4 Slacken and remove the nut securing the track rod balljoint to the swivel hub; discard the nut a new one will be needed on refitting. Release the balljoint tapered shank using a universal balljoint separator and recover the protector plate (if loose) **(see illustrations)**.

5 Counting the **exact** number of turns necessary to do so, unscrew the balljoint from the track rod end.
6 Count the number of exposed threads between the end of the balljoint and the locknut, and record this figure. If a new balljoint is to be fitted, unscrew the locknut from the old balljoint.
7 Carefully clean the balljoint and the threads. Renew the balljoint if its movement is sloppy or too stiff, if excessively worn, or if damaged in any way; carefully check the stud taper and threads. If the balljoint gaiter is damaged, the complete balljoint assembly must be renewed; it is not possible to obtain the gaiter separately.

Refitting

8 If a new balljoint is to be fitted, screw the locknut onto its threads, and position it so that the same number of exposed threads are visible, as was noted prior to removal.
9 Screw the balljoint into the track rod by the number of turns noted on removal. This should bring the balljoint locknut to within a quarter of a turn from the track rod, with the alignment marks that were made on removal (if applicable) lined up.
10 Ensure that the protector plate is in position then locate the balljoint shank in the swivel hub. Fit a new retaining nut and tighten it to the specified torque.
11 Refit the roadwheel, then lower the vehicle to the ground and tighten the roadwheel bolts to the specified torque.
12 Check and, if necessary, adjust the front wheel alignment as described in Section 32, then securely tighten the balljoint locknut.

31 Track rod – removal and refitting

Note: *A special wrench (Peugeot number 0707) will be required to remove/refit the track rod inner balljoint from the end of the steering rack. The special wrench engages with the balljoint housing allowing the track rod to be easily slackened/tightened without the risk of damage. Note that without access to the special tool, track rod removal will be difficult, especially without causing damage.*

Note: *A new balljoint retaining nut will be required on refitting.*

Removal

1 Remove the track rod balljoint as described in Section 30.
2 Either release the retaining clips and slide the steering gear gaiter off the end of the track rod, or release the track rod balljoint dust cover from rack, and slide it off the track rod (as applicable). Refer to Section 27 for further information.
3 Using the special wrench (see note at the start of the Section), unscrew the track rod inner balljoint from the steering rack end. Take great care not to place excess strain on the rack as the joint is unscrewed, if necessary, prevent the steering rack from turning by holding it carefully with a pair of grips. Take great care not to mark the surfaces of the rack and balljoint.
4 Remove the track rod assembly. Examine the track rod inner balljoint for signs of slackness or tight spots, and check that the track rod itself is straight and free from damage. If necessary, renew the track rod; it is also recommended that the steering gear gaiter/dust cover is renewed.

Refitting

5 Screw the balljoint into the steering rack, and tighten it to the specified torque. If necessary, retain the steering rack with a pair of grips, again taking great care not to damage or mark the track rod balljoint or steering rack.
6 Where a gaiter was removed, carefully slide on the new gaiter, and locate it on the steering gear housing. Turn the steering fully from lock-to-lock, to check that the gaiter is correctly positioned on the track rod, then secure it in position with new retaining clips (where fitted).
7 Where a dust cover was removed, carefully slide on the new cover, and locate it in its grooves on the steering rack collar and track rod.
8 Refit the track rod balljoint as described in Section 30.

32 Wheel alignment and steering angles – information, checking and adjustment

Definitions

1 A car's steering and suspension geometry is defined in four basic settings – all angles are expressed in degrees (toe settings are also expressed as a measurement); the steering axis is defined as an imaginary line drawn through the axis of the suspension strut, extended where necessary to contact the ground.
2 Camber is the angle between each roadwheel and a vertical line drawn through its centre and tyre contact patch, when viewed from the front or rear of the car.

Positive camber is when the roadwheels are tilted outwards from the vertical at the top; negative camber is when they are tilted inwards. The camber angle is not adjustable

3 **Castor** is the angle between the steering axis and a vertical line drawn through each roadwheel's centre and tyre contact patch, when viewed from the side of the car. Positive castor is when the steering axis is tilted so that it contacts the ground ahead of the vertical; negative castor is when it contacts the ground behind the vertical. The castor angle is not adjustable.

4 **Toe** is the difference, viewed from above, between lines drawn through the roadwheel centres and the car's centre-line. 'Toe-in' is when the roadwheels point inwards, towards each other at the front, while 'toe-out' is when they splay outwards from each other at the front.

5 The front wheel toe setting is adjusted by screwing the track rod in or out of its balljoints, to alter the effective length of the track rod assembly.

6 Rear wheel toe setting is also adjustable. The toe setting is adjusted by slackening and rotating the track arm inner pivot bolt.

Checking and adjustment

7 Due to the special measuring equipment necessary to check the wheel alignment and steering angles, and the skill required to use it properly, the checking and adjustment of these settings is best left to a Peugeot dealer or similar expert. Note that most tyre-fitting shops now possess sophisticated checking equipment. The following is provided as a guide, should the owner decide to carry out a DIY check.

Front wheel toe setting

8 The front wheel toe setting is checked by measuring the distance between the front and rear inside edges of the roadwheel rims. Proprietary toe measurement gauges are available from motor accessory shops. Adjustment is made by screwing the balljoints in or out of their track rods, to alter the effective length of the track rod assemblies.

9 For **accurate** checking, the vehicle **must** be at the kerb weight, ie, unladen and with a full tank of fuel.

10 Before starting work, check first that the tyre sizes and types are as specified, then check the tyre pressures and tread wear, the roadwheel run-out, the condition of the hub

bearings, the steering wheel free play, and the condition of the front suspension components (see *Weekly checks* and the relevant Part of Chapter 1). Correct any faults found.

11 Park the vehicle on level ground, check that the front roadwheels are in the straight-ahead position, then rock the rear and front ends to settle the suspension. Release the handbrake, and roll the vehicle backwards 1 metre, then forwards again, to relieve any stresses in the steering and suspension components.

12 Measure the distance between the front edges of the wheel rims and the rear edges of the rims. Subtract one measurement from the other, and check that the result is within the specified range.

13 If adjustment is necessary, apply the handbrake, then jack up the front of the vehicle and support it securely on axle stands. Turn the steering wheel onto full-left lock, and record the number of exposed threads on the right-hand track rod end. Now turn the steering onto full-right lock, and record the number of threads on the left-hand side. If there are the same number of threads visible on both sides, then subsequent adjustment should be made equally on both sides. If there are more threads visible on one side than the other, it will be necessary to compensate for this during adjustment. **Note:** *It is most important that after adjustment, the same number of threads are visible on each track rod end.*

14 First clean the track rod threads; if they are corroded, apply penetrating fluid before starting adjustment. Release the rubber gaiter outboard clips (where necessary), and peel back the gaiters; apply a smear of grease to the inside of the gaiters, so that both are free, and will not be twisted or strained as their respective track rods are rotated.

15 Use a straight-edge and a scriber or similar to mark the relationship of each track rod to its balljoint then, holding each track rod in turn, unscrew its locknut fully.

16 Alter the length of the track rods, bearing in mind the note made in paragraph 13. **Note:** *One complete rotation of the track rod equals approximately 2 mm of adjustment.* Screw them onto or off the balljoints, rotating the track rod using an open-ended spanner fitted to the flats provided on the track rod. Shortening the track rods (screwing them into their balljoints) will reduce toe-in/increase toe-out.

32.20 Rear wheel toe setting is adjusted by slackening and rotating the track arm inner pivot bolt (arrowed)

17 When the setting is correct, hold the track rods and tighten the balljoint locknuts to the specified torque setting. Check that the balljoints are seated correctly in their sockets, and count the exposed threads to check the length of both track rods. If they are not the same, then the adjustment has not been made equally, and problems will be encountered with tyre scrubbing in turns; also, the steering wheel spokes will no longer be horizontal when the wheels are in the straight-ahead position.

18 If the track rod lengths are the same, lower the vehicle to the ground and recheck the toe setting; re-adjust if necessary. When the setting is correct, tighten the track rod balljoint locknuts to the specified torque. Ensure that the rubber gaiters are seated correctly, and are not twisted or strained, and secure them in position with new retaining clips (where necessary).

Rear wheel toe setting

19 The procedure for checking the rear toe setting is same as described for the front in paragraphs 8 to 12.

20 To adjust the setting, chock the front wheels then jack up the rear of the vehicle and support it on axle stands. Slacken the track arm inner pivot bolt nut and rotate the pivot bolt until the toe setting is correctly set **(see illustration)**. Hold the pivot bolt stationary and tighten the pivot bolt nut to the specified torque.

21 Check that the toe setting has been correctly adjusted by lowering the vehicle to the ground and rechecking the toe setting; re-adjust if necessary.

Notes

Chapter 11
Bodywork and fittings

Contents

Body exterior fittings – removal and refitting 24
Bonnet – removal, refitting and adjustment 8
Bonnet lock – removal and refitting 10
Bonnet release cable – removal and refitting 9
Boot lid – removal and refitting 15
Boot lid lock components – removal and refitting 16
Bumpers – removal and refitting 6
Central locking components – removal and refitting 19
Centre console – removal and refitting 29
Door – removal, refitting and adjustment 11
Door handle and lock components – removal and refitting 13
Door inner trim panel – removal and refitting 12
Door window glass and regulator – removal and refitting 14
Electric window components – general information 20
Exterior mirrors and associated components – removal and refitting 21

Facia panel assembly – removal and refitting 30
Front seat belt tensioning mechanism – general information 26
General information 1
Interior trim – removal and refitting 28
Maintenance – bodywork and underframe 2
Maintenance – upholstery and carpets 3
Major body damage – repair 5
Minor body damage – repair 4
Radiator grille – removal and refitting 7
Seat belt components – removal and refitting 27
Seats – removal and refitting 25
Sunroof – general information 23
Tailgate – removal and refitting 17
Tailgate lock components – removal and refitting 18
Windscreen and rear screen glass – general information 22

Degrees of difficulty

Easy, suitable for novice with little experience	**Fairly easy,** suitable for beginner with some experience	**Fairly difficult,** suitable for competent DIY mechanic	**Difficult,** suitable for experienced DIY mechanic	**Very difficult,** suitable for expert DIY or professional

Specifications

Torque wrench settings	Nm	lbf ft
Front seat belt reel	35	26
Front seat belt stalk/pretensioner bolt	35	26
Front seat belt to seat	25	18
Front seat belt-to-B-pillar upper mounting bolt	35	26
Rear seat belt mountings to floor	35	26
Rear seat belt reel	35	26

1 General information

The bodyshell is made of pressed-steel sections. Most components are welded together, but some use is made of structural adhesives.

The bonnet, door, and some other vulnerable panels are made of zinc-coated metal, and are further protected by being coated with an anti-chip primer before being sprayed.

Extensive use is made of plastic materials, mainly in the interior, but also in exterior components. The front and rear bumpers and front grille are injection-moulded from a synthetic material that is very strong and yet light. Plastic components such as wheelarch liners are fitted to the underside of the vehicle, to improve the body's resistance to corrosion.

2 Maintenance – bodywork and underframe

The general condition of a vehicle's bodywork is the one thing that significantly affects its value. Maintenance is easy, but needs to be regular. Neglect, particularly after minor damage, can lead quickly to further deterioration and costly repair bills. It is important also to keep watch on those parts of the vehicle not immediately visible, for instance the underside, inside all the wheelarches, and the lower part of the engine compartment.

The basic maintenance routine for the bodywork is washing – preferably with a lot of water, from a hose. This will remove all the loose solids which may have stuck to the vehicle. It is important to flush these off in such a way as to prevent grit from scratching the finish. The wheelarches and underframe need washing in the same way, to remove any accumulated mud, which will retain moisture and tend to encourage rust. Paradoxically enough, the best time to clean the underframe and wheelarches is in wet weather, when the mud is thoroughly wet and soft. In very wet weather, the underframe is usually cleaned of large accumulations automatically, and this is a good time for inspection.

Periodically, except on vehicles with a wax-based underbody protective coating, it is a good idea to have the whole of the underframe of the vehicle steam-cleaned, engine compartment included, so that a thorough inspection can be carried out to see what minor repairs and renovations are necessary. Steam-cleaning is available at many garages, and is necessary for the removal of the accumulation of oily grime, which sometimes is allowed to become thick in certain areas. If steam-cleaning facilities are not available, there are some excellent grease solvents available which can be brush-applied; the dirt can then be simply hosed off. Note that these methods should not be used on vehicles with wax-based underbody protective coating, or the coating will be removed. Such vehicles should be inspected annually, preferably just prior to Winter, when the underbody should be washed down, and any damage to the wax coating repaired. Ideally, a completely fresh coat should be applied. It would also be worth considering the use of such wax-based protection for injection into door panels, sills, box sections, etc, as an additional safeguard against rust damage, where such protection is not provided by the vehicle manufacturer.

After washing paintwork, wipe off with a chamois leather to give an unspotted clear finish. A coat of clear protective wax polish will give added protection against chemical pollutants in the air. If the paintwork sheen has dulled or oxidised, use a cleaner/polisher combination to restore the brilliance of the shine. This requires a little effort, but such dulling is usually caused because regular washing has been neglected. Care needs to be taken with metallic paintwork, as special non-abrasive cleaner/polisher is required to avoid damage to the finish. Always check that the door and ventilator opening drain holes and pipes are completely clear, so that water can be drained out. Brightwork should be treated in the same way as paintwork. Windscreens and windows can be kept clear of the smeary film which often appears, by the use of proprietary glass cleaner. Never use any form of wax or other body or chromium polish on glass.

3 Maintenance –
upholstery and carpets

Mats and carpets should be brushed or vacuum-cleaned regularly, to keep them free of grit. If they are badly stained, remove them from the vehicle for scrubbing or sponging, and make quite sure they are dry before refitting. Seats and interior trim panels can be kept clean by wiping with a damp cloth. If they do become stained (which can be more apparent on light-coloured upholstery), use a little liquid detergent and a soft nail brush to scour the grime out of the grain of the material. Do not forget to keep the headlining clean in the same way as the upholstery. When using liquid cleaners inside the vehicle, do not over-wet the surfaces being cleaned. Excessive damp could get into the seams and padded interior, causing stains, offensive odours or even rot.

HAYNES HINT
If the inside of the vehicle gets wet accidentally, it is worthwhile taking some trouble to dry it out properly, particularly where carpets are involved. Do not leave oil or electric heaters inside the vehicle for this purpose.

4 Minor body damage –
repair

Repairs of minor scratches in bodywork

If the scratch is very superficial, and does not penetrate to the metal of the bodywork, repair is very simple. Lightly rub the area of the scratch with a paintwork renovator, or a very fine cutting paste, to remove loose paint from the scratch, and to clear the surrounding bodywork of wax polish. Rinse the area with clean water.

Apply touch-up paint to the scratch using a fine paint brush; continue to apply fine layers of paint until the surface of the paint in the scratch is level with the surrounding paintwork. Allow the new paint at least two weeks to harden, then blend it into the surrounding paintwork by rubbing the scratch area with a paintwork renovator or a very fine cutting paste. Finally, apply wax polish.

Where the scratch has penetrated right through to the metal of the bodywork, causing the metal to rust, a different repair technique is required. Remove any loose rust from the bottom of the scratch with a penknife, then apply rust-inhibiting paint to prevent the formation of rust in the future. Using a rubber or nylon applicator, fill the scratch with bodystopper paste. If required, this paste can be mixed with cellulose thinners to provide a very thin paste which is ideal for filling narrow scratches. Before the stopper-paste in the scratch hardens, wrap a piece of smooth cotton rag around the top of a finger. Dip the finger in cellulose thinners, and quickly sweep it across the surface of the stopper-paste in the scratch; this will ensure that the surface of the stopper-paste is slightly hollowed. The scratch can now be painted over as described earlier in this Section.

Repairs of dents in bodywork

When deep denting of the vehicle's bodywork has taken place, the first task is to pull the dent out, until the affected bodywork almost attains its original shape. There is little point in trying to restore the original shape completely, as the metal in the damaged area will have stretched on impact, and cannot be reshaped fully to its original contour. It is better to bring the level of the dent up to a point which is about 3 mm below the level of the surrounding bodywork. In cases where the dent is very shallow anyway, it is not worth trying to pull it out at all. If the underside of the dent is accessible, it can be hammered out gently from behind, using a mallet with a wooden or plastic head. Whilst doing this, hold a suitable block of wood firmly against the outside of the panel, to absorb the impact from the hammer blows and thus prevent a large area of the bodywork from being 'belled-out'.

Should the dent be in a section of the bodywork which has a double skin, or some other factor making it inaccessible from behind, a different technique is called for. Drill several small holes through the metal inside the area – particularly in the deeper section. Then screw long self-tapping screws into the holes, just sufficiently for them to gain a good purchase in the metal. Now the dent can be pulled out by pulling on the protruding heads of the screws with a pair of pliers.

The next stage of the repair is the removal of the paint from the damaged area, and from an inch or so of the surrounding 'sound' bodywork. This is accomplished most easily by using a wire brush or abrasive pad on a power drill, although it can be done just as effectively by hand, using sheets of abrasive paper. To complete the preparation for filling, score the surface of the bare metal with a screwdriver or the tang of a file, or alternatively, drill small holes in the affected area. This will provide a really good 'key' for the filler paste.

To complete the repair, see the Section on filling and respraying.

Repairs of rust holes or gashes in bodywork

Remove all paint from the affected area, and from an inch or so of the surrounding 'sound' bodywork, using an abrasive pad or a wire brush on a power drill. If these are not available, a few sheets of abrasive paper will do the job most effectively. With the paint removed, you will be able to judge the severity of the corrosion, and therefore decide whether to renew the whole panel (if this is possible) or to repair the affected area. New body panels are not as expensive as most people think, and it is often quicker and more satisfactory to fit a new panel than to attempt to repair large areas of corrosion.

Remove all fittings from the affected area, except those which will act as a guide to the original shape of the damaged bodywork (eg headlight shells etc). Then, using tin snips or a hacksaw blade, remove all loose metal and any other metal badly affected by corrosion. Hammer the edges of the hole inwards, in order to create a slight depression for the filler paste.

Wire-brush the affected area to remove the powdery rust from the surface of the remaining metal. Paint the affected area with rust-inhibiting paint, if the back of the rusted area is accessible, treat this also.

Before filling can take place, it will be necessary to block the hole in some way. This can be achieved by the use of aluminium or plastic mesh, or aluminium tape.

Aluminium or plastic mesh, or glass-fibre matting, is probably the best material to use for a large hole. Cut a piece to the approximate size and shape of the hole to be filled, then position it in the hole so that its edges are below the level of the surrounding bodywork. It can be retained in position by several blobs of filler paste around its periphery.

Aluminium tape should be used for small or very narrow holes. Pull a piece off the roll, trim it to the approximate size and shape required, then pull off the backing paper (if used) and stick the tape over the hole; it can be overlapped if the thickness of one piece is insufficient. Burnish down the edges of the tape with the handle of a screwdriver or similar, to ensure that the tape is securely attached to the metal underneath.

Bodywork repairs – filling and respraying

Before using this Section, see the Sections on dent, deep scratch, rust holes and gash repairs.

Many types of bodyfiller are available, but generally speaking, those proprietary kits which contain a tin of filler paste and a tube of resin hardener are best for this type of repair. A wide, flexible plastic or nylon applicator will be found invaluable for imparting a smooth and well-contoured finish to the surface of the filler.

Mix up a little filler on a clean piece of card or board – measure the hardener carefully (follow the maker's instructions on the pack), otherwise the filler will set too rapidly or too slowly. Using the applicator, apply the filler paste to the prepared area; draw the applicator across the surface of the filler to achieve the correct contour and to level the surface. As soon as a contour that approximates to the correct one is achieved, stop working the paste – if you carry on too long, the paste will become sticky and begin to 'pick-up' on the applicator. Continue to add thin layers of filler paste at 20-minute intervals, until the level of the filler is just proud of the surrounding bodywork.

Once the filler has hardened, the excess can be removed using a metal plane or file. From then on, progressively-finer grades of abrasive paper should be used, starting with a 40-grade production paper, and finishing with a 400-grade wet-and-dry paper. Always wrap the abrasive paper around a flat rubber, cork, or wooden block – otherwise the surface of the filler will not be completely flat. During the smoothing of the filler surface, the wet-and-dry paper should be periodically rinsed in water. This will ensure that a very smooth finish is imparted to the filler at the final stage.

At this stage, the dent should be surrounded by a ring of bare metal, which in turn should be encircled by the finely 'feathered' edge of the good paintwork. Rinse the repair area with clean water, until all of the dust produced by the rubbing-down operation has gone.

Spray the whole area with a light coat of primer – this will show up any imperfections in the surface of the filler. Repair these imperfections with fresh filler paste or bodystopper, and once more smooth the surface with abrasive paper. Repeat this spray-and-repair procedure until you are satisfied that the surface of the filler, and the feathered edge of the paintwork, are perfect. Clean the repair area with clean water, and allow to dry fully.

HAYNES HiNT

If bodystopper is used, it can be mixed with cellulose thinners to form a really thin paste which is ideal for filling small holes.

The repair area is now ready for final spraying. Paint spraying must be carried out in a warm, dry, windless and dust-free atmosphere. This condition can be created artificially if you have access to a large indoor working area, but if you are forced to work in the open, you will have to pick your day very carefully. If you are working indoors, dousing the floor in the work area with water will help to settle the dust which would otherwise be in the atmosphere. If the repair area is confined to one body panel, mask off the surrounding panels; this will help to minimise the effects of a slight mis-match in paint colours. Bodywork fittings (eg chrome strips, door handles etc) will also need to be masked off. Use genuine masking tape, and several thicknesses of newspaper, for the masking operations.

Before commencing to spray, agitate the aerosol can thoroughly, then spray a test area (an old tin, or similar) until the technique is mastered. Cover the repair area with a thick coat of primer; the thickness should be built up using several thin layers of paint, rather than one thick one. Using 400-grade wet-and-dry paper, rub down the surface of the primer until it is really smooth. While doing this, the work area should be thoroughly doused with water, and the wet-and-dry paper periodically rinsed in water. Allow to dry before spraying on more paint.

Spray on the top coat, again building up the thickness by using several thin layers of paint. Start spraying at one edge of the repair area, and then, using a side-to-side motion, work until the whole repair area and about 2 inches of the surrounding original paintwork is covered. Remove all masking material 10 to 15 minutes after spraying on the final coat of paint.

Allow the new paint at least two weeks to harden, then, using a paintwork renovator, or a very fine cutting paste, blend the edges of the paint into the existing paintwork. Finally, apply wax polish.

Plastic components

With the use of more and more plastic body components by the vehicle manufacturers (eg bumpers. spoilers, and in some cases major body panels), rectification of more serious damage to such items has become a matter of either entrusting repair work to a specialist in this field, or renewing complete components. Repair of such damage by the DIY owner is not really feasible, owing to the cost of the equipment and materials required for effecting such repairs. The basic technique involves making a groove along the line of the crack in the plastic, using a rotary burr in a power drill. The damaged part is then welded back together, using a hot-air gun to heat up and fuse a plastic filler rod into the groove. Any excess plastic is then removed, and the area rubbed down to a smooth finish. It is important that a filler rod of the correct plastic is used, as body components can be made of a variety of different types (eg polycarbonate, ABS, polypropylene).

Damage of a less serious nature (abrasions, minor cracks etc) can be repaired by the DIY owner using a two-part epoxy filler repair material. Once mixed in equal proportions, this is used in similar fashion to the bodywork filler used on metal panels. The filler is usually cured in twenty to thirty minutes, ready for sanding and painting.

If the owner is renewing a complete component himself, or if he has repaired it with epoxy filler, he will be left with the problem of finding a suitable paint for finishing which is compatible with the type of plastic used. At one time, the use of a universal paint was not possible, owing to the complex range of plastics encountered in body component applications. Standard paints, generally speaking, will not bond to plastic or rubber satisfactorily. However, it is now possible to obtain a plastic body parts finishing kit which consists of a pre-primer treatment, a primer and coloured top coat. Full instructions are normally supplied with a kit, but basically, the method of use is to first apply the pre-primer to the component concerned, and allow it to dry for up to 30 minutes. Then the primer is applied, and left to dry for about an hour before finally applying the special-coloured top coat. The result is a correctly-coloured component, where the paint will flex with the plastic or rubber, a property that standard paint does not normally possess.

5 Major body damage – repair

Where serious damage has occurred, or large areas need renewal due to neglect, it means that complete new panels will need welding-in, and this is best left to professionals. If the damage is due to impact, it will also be necessary to check completely the alignment of the bodyshell, and this can only be carried out accurately by a Peugeot dealer using special jigs. If the body is left misaligned, it is primarily dangerous, as the car will not handle properly, and secondly, uneven stresses will be imposed on the steering, suspension and possibly transmission, causing abnormal wear, or complete failure, particularly to such items as the tyres.

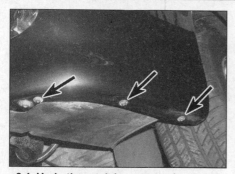

6.4 Undo the retaining screws (arrowed) and remove the lower splash shield

6.5a Release the wheelarch liners . . .

6.5b . . . and remove the bumper end retaining bolts

6 Bumpers – removal and refitting

Front bumper

Removal

1 Remove the radiator grille as described in Section 7 of this Chapter.
2 Remove the headlights as described in Chapter 12, Section 7.
3 For easier access, firmly apply the handbrake then jack up the front of the vehicle and support it on axle stands.
4 Undo the retaining screws securing the left- and right-hand front lower wheelarch liners/splash shields to the bumper **(see illustration)**.

5 Release each liner from the from the bumper then slacken and remove the retaining bolt securing the left- and right-hand ends of the bumper to the body **(see illustrations)**.
6 Undo the retaining bolt, holding the lower centre of the bumper to the crossmember **(see illustration)**.
7 On models with front foglights, depress the retaining clips and disconnect the wiring connectors from the foglights.
8 Release the left- and right-hand retaining clips (situated by the headlight apertures) by rotating them through 90° **(see illustration)**
9 With the aid of an assistant, unclip the outer ends of the bumper cover assembly from the front wing panels and manoeuvre it forwards and away from the vehicle **(see illustrations)**.
10 Undo the two mounting bolts from the

bumper crossmember and remove it from the vehicle **(see illustration)**. Inspect the bumper mountings for signs of damage and renew if necessary.

Refitting

11 Refitting is a reverse of the removal procedure, ensuring that the bumper mounting bolts are securely tightened.

Rear bumper

Removal

12 Open the tailgate/boot lid and lift up or remove the luggage compartment carpet, then carefully peel back the boot sealing strip **(see illustration)**.
13 Release the retaining clips (or screws) from the rear trim panel, then remove the rear

6.6 Remove the lower retaining bolt

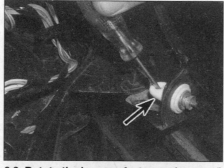

6.8 Rotate the bumper fasteners (arrowed) through 90° . . .

6.9a . . . unclip the ends of the bumper . . .

6.9b . . . and remove the front bumper cover from the vehicle

6.10a Undo the mounting bolts . . .

6.10b . . . and remove the front bumper crossmember

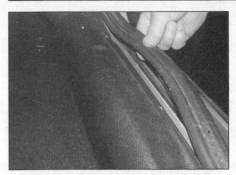

6.12 Carefully peel off the boot seal

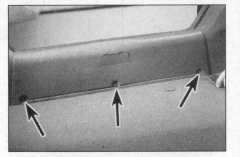

6.13a On Saloon models, release the securing clips, or undo the screws (arrowed) . . .

6.13b . . . and remove the rear trim panel from the luggage compartment

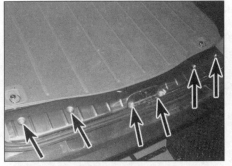

6.13c On Estate models, undo the trim plate retaining screws (arrowed)

6.14 Undo the screw and remove the tie-down hook

6.15 Prise out the fasteners and peel back the side trim panel to gain access to the bumper retaining nuts

trim panel unclipping it from the rear crossmember **(see illustrations)**.
14 Where applicable, undo the retaining screws and remove the tie-down hooks from

the left- and right-hand corners of the luggage compartment **(see illustration)**.
15 On Saloon models, release the retaining clips (pull out the centre pins then prise out

the complete clip) and peel back the side trim panels to gain access to the bumper mountings **(see illustration)**.
16 On Estate models, it will be necessary to unscrew the fastener and remove the storage compartments from each side to allow the trim panel to be freed.
17 Where applicable, remove the CD player from the rear side storage compartment **(see illustrations)**.
18 Undo the retaining nuts and remove the vent assembly from the right-hand rear corner of the luggage compartment **(see illustration)**.
19 From outside the vehicle, slacken and remove the retaining screws securing the rear of each wheelarch liner to the bumper. Free the liners from the bumper then slacken and remove the retaining nuts and rubbers securing the left- and right-hand ends of the bumper to the body **(see illustrations)**.

6.17a On Saloon models, the CD unit is under the side trim cover . . .

6.17b . . . and on the Estate models, unbolt the CD unit from inside the storage compartment

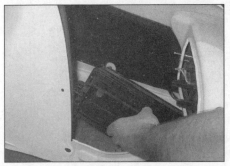

6.18 Undo the retaining nuts and remove the vent assembly from the right-hand side

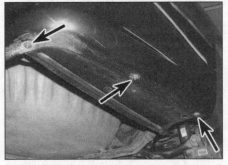

6.19a Undo the retaining screws (arrowed) and free the wheelarch liner . . .

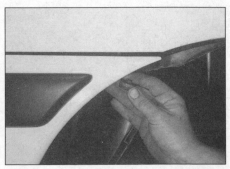

6.19b . . . then slacken and remove the bumper retaining nut and mounting rubber

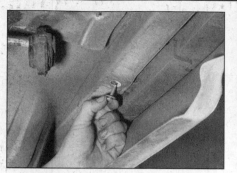

6.20 Slacken and remove the lower retaining bolts . . .

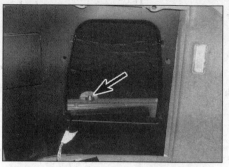

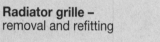

6.21 . . . then undo the upper mounting nuts (arrowed) – Estate model

6.22 Disconnect the number plate light wiring connector from the left-hand rear light cluster and free the wiring

20 Slacken and remove the lower bolts securing the rear of the bumper to the vehicle underbody **(see illustration)**.

21 Returning to the luggage compartment, slacken and remove the remaining bumper upper retaining nuts and mounting rubbers **(see illustration)**.

22 On Saloon models, trace the number plate light wiring back to the left-hand rear light cluster assembly and disconnect the wiring connector **(see illustration)**.

23 With the aid of an assistant, carefully release the bumper ends and remove the bumper from the vehicle, freeing the number plate light wiring grommet (Saloon models) from the body.

Refitting

24 Refitting is a reverse of the removal procedure. If any of the upper retaining nut studs were unscrewed from the mounting

plates on removal, prior to refitting, remove the nuts and rubbers from the stud, then refit the studs and plates to the bumper and tighten securely.

---

7 Radiator grille – removal and refitting

Removal

1 Open the bonnet, then use a small screwdriver to release the centre pins from the three mounting clips. The three clips can then be removed from the upper part of the radiator grille **(see illustrations)**.

2 Use a screwdriver to release the three lower retaining clips, then slide the radiator grille forward to remove it from the front bumper **(see illustrations)**.

Refitting

3 Refitting is a reverse of the removal procedure, ensuring the clips are located securely.

---

8 Bonnet – removal, refitting and adjustment

Removal

1 Open the bonnet to the vertical position and place a wad of rag underneath each corner of the bonnet to protect against possible damage should the bonnet slip.

2 Disconnect the washer hose from the right-hand side of the bonnet and release it from its retaining clip **(see illustration)**.

3 Using a pencil or felt tip pen, mark the outline of each retaining nut relative to the bonnet, to use as a guide on refitting.

4 With the aid of an assistant, support the bonnet then (where necessary) carefully lift the retaining clips and detach the support struts from the bonnet **(see illustration)**.

5 Slacken and remove the left- and right-hand hinge to bonnet nuts and carefully remove the bonnet from the vehicle **(see illustration)**.

6 Inspect the bonnet hinges for signs of wear and free play at the pivots, and if necessary renew; the hinges are bolted to the body.

Refitting and adjustment

7 With the aid of an assistant, engage the

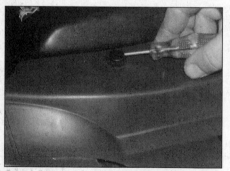

7.1a Use a small screwdriver to release the centre pins . . .

7.1b . . . and remove the retaining clips

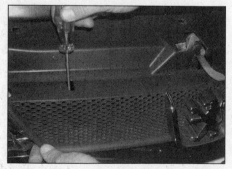

7.2a Use a screwdriver to release the outer . . .

7.2b . . . and centre grille retaining clips

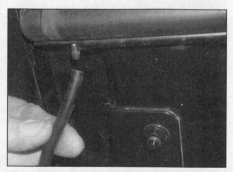

8.2 Disconnect the washer hose from the right-hand side of the bonnet

bonnet with the hinges. Refit the retaining nuts and tighten them by hand only. Align the nuts with the marks made on removal, then tighten them securely. Where necessary, clip the support struts securely onto the bonnet.

8 Close the bonnet, and check for alignment with the adjacent panels. If necessary, slacken the hinge bolts and re-align the bonnet to suit; the height of the bonnet is altered by moving the rubber stops on the bonnet crossmember. If necessary, further adjustment can be gained by slackening the hinge retaining bolts and repositioning the hinge slightly. Once the bonnet is correctly aligned, securely tighten the hinge nuts/bolts (as applicable). Once the bonnet is correctly aligned, check that the bonnet fastens and releases satisfactorily.

9 Bonnet release cable – removal and refitting

Removal

1 Open up the bonnet and remove the grille panel as described in Section 7, Section

2 If required (to improve access) remove the driver's side headlight as described in Chapter 12, Section 7.

3 Undo the retaining screw and release the cable retaining clamp from the headlight aperture and detach the cable from the lock assembly **(see illustration).**

4 Tie a piece of string to the end of the release cable and free the cable from all the necessary retaining clips and ties.

5 From inside the vehicle, undo the retaining bolt and withdraw the bonnet release handle from underneath the facia **(see illustration),** withdrawing the cable into the passenger compartment. When the end of the string appears from the bulkhead, untie it and leave it in position; the string can then be used on refitting to draw the cable back into position.

Refitting

6 Refitting is the reverse of removal, ensuring that the cable is correctly routed, and secured to all the relevant retaining clips. Prior to closing the bonnet, operate the release handle and have an assistant check that the lock hook moves easily and smoothly to its stop. The cable is adjusted by slackening the retaining clamp screw **(see illustration 9.3)** and repositioning the outer cable as necessary.

10 Bonnet lock – removal and refitting

Removal

1 Open the bonnet and remove the grille panel as described in Section 7.

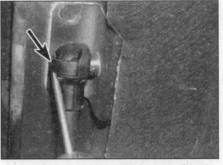

8.4 Lift the retaining clip (arrowed) and detach the support struts from the bonnet

9.3 Undo the retaining screw (arrowed) and detach the bonnet release cable from its clamp

2 Using a suitable marker pen, draw around the outline of each lock retaining bolt then slacken and remove the both bolts. Remove the lock from the vehicle, freeing it from the release cable **(see illustration).**

Refitting

3 Connect the release cable to the lock, and seat the lock on the crossmember.

4 Refit the retaining bolts, aligning them with the marks made prior to removal, and tighten them securely.

5 Check the lock operation then lubricate the lock with multi-purpose grease. If adjustment is necessary, slacken the release cable clamp retaining screw and reposition the cable **(see illustration).**

6 Once the lock is operating correctly, then clip the grille panel back into position and secure it with the fasteners.

10.2 Undo the retaining bolts (arrowed), then detach the lock from the release cable

8.5 Undo the bonnet hinge retaining nuts (arrowed) – right-hand side

9.5 Undo the retaining bolt from the bonnet release handle

11 Door – removal, refitting and adjustment

Removal

1 Disconnect the battery negative terminal.

2 Open up the front door to gain access to the door wiring connector (for rear doors access to wiring is easier via the front door). Rotate the connector locking ring anti-clockwise until it is possible to disconnect the wiring connector **(see illustration).**

3 Undo the retaining bolts securing the check link to the pillar and remove the rubber cover **(see illustrations).**

4 With the aid of an assistant, support the door then unscrew the hinge pins and remove the door from the vehicle **(see illustration).**

10.5 Adjust the release cable by slackening the clamp screw and repositioning the outer cable

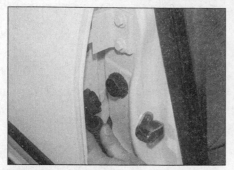

11.2 Unscrew the locking ring to detach the wiring connector from the pillar – rear door

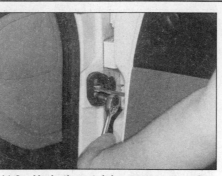

11.3a Undo the retaining screws securing the check link to the door pillar . . .

11.3b . . . and remove the rubber cover

11.4 Unscrew the hinge retaining bolts (arrowed) and remove the door

11.8 Secure the wiring connector by rotating the locking ring until the index marks are aligned (arrowed)

11.10 To reposition the door striker, slacken the two retaining screws (arrowed)

5 Examine the hinges for signs of wear or damage. If renewal is necessary, mark the position of the hinge(s) then undo the retaining bolts and remove them from the door. Fit the new hinge(s), align with the marks made before removal, and securely tighten the retaining bolts.

Refitting

6 Manoeuvre the door into position and refit the hinge pins (renew hinge pins if necessary).
7 Refit the rubber cover onto the check link, then align the link with the pillar and securely tighten its retaining bolts.
8 Reconnect the wiring connector and secure it in position by rotating the locking ring until the index marks align **(see illustration)**.
9 Check the door alignment and, if

necessary, adjust. If the paintwork around the hinges has been damaged, paint the affected area with a suitable touch-in brush to prevent corrosion.

Adjustment

10 Close the door and check the door alignment with surrounding body panels. If necessary, slight adjustment of the door position can be made by slackening the hinge retaining bolts and repositioning the hinge/door as necessary. Once the door is correctly positioned, tighten the hinge bolts securely. After adjustment, make sure that the door lock engages correctly with the striker on the body pillar. If necessary loosen the striker retaining screws, then reposition the striker and tighten the screws **(see illustration)**.

12 Door inner trim panel –
removal and refitting

Note: *Door trim panel design varies according to the equipment level of the vehicle, and therefore some trim panel fastener locations on your vehicle might be different to those shown in the accompanying illustrations.*

Removal

1 Disconnect the battery negative terminal and proceed as described under the relevant sub-heading.

Front door

2 Carefully unclip the exterior mirror inner trim panel from the front of the door **(see illustration)**. On models with manually-adjusted mirrors, remove the rubber gaiter from the adjustment handle prior to unclipping the trim panel.
3 Working as described in Chapter 12, Section 4, remove the switch(es) from the door armrest and also remove the loudspeaker from the door.
4 Carefully prise the door opening handle surround from the door interior trim panel **(see illustration)**.
5 Prise out the trim retaining screw cover from the lower rear corner of the trim panel, then slacken and remove the retaining screw **(see illustrations)**.

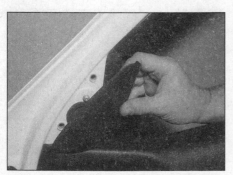

12.2 Removing the mirror inner trim panel from the door

12.4 Removing the inner handle surround

12.5a Prise out the lower trim retaining screw cover . . .

12.5b . . . then slacken and remove the trim panel retaining screw

12.6a Prise out the upper trim retaining screw cover . . .

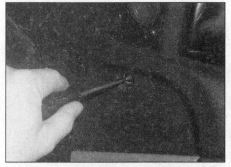

12.6b . . . then slacken and remove the trim panel retaining screw

12.7 Where fitted, unclip the door open warning light

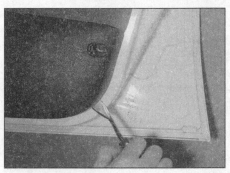

12.8a Unclip the trim panel . . .

6 Prise out the trim retaining screw cover from the upper front corner of the trim panel, then slacken and remove the retaining screw **(see illustrations)**.
7 Where fitted, unclip the door open warning

light from the lower part of the door trim under the armrest **(see illustration)**.
8 Make a final check that all the retaining screws have been removed, then carefully unclip the base of the trim panel from the door

and manoeuvre it upwards and out of position **(see illustrations)**. As the panel is removed, free the wiring harness noting its correct routing.

Rear door

9 On models with manually-operated windows, pull the window regulator handle off its spindle and remove the spacer.
10 On models with electrically-operated windows, remove the switch(es) from the door armrest, as described in Chapter 12, Section 4.
11 Where fitted, unclip the door open warning light from the lower part of the door trim under the armrest **(see illustration)**.
12 Undo the retaining screw from under the top end of the grab handle **(see illustration)**.
13 Prise out the trim retaining screw cover from the below the door grab handle, then slacken and remove the retaining screw **(see illustrations)**.

12.8b . . . and move it upwards and away from the door

12.11 Where fitted, unclip the door open warning light

12.12 Undo the retaining screw at the top end of the grab handle

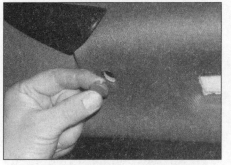

12.13a Prise out the trim retaining screw cover . . .

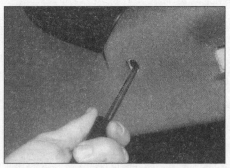

12.13b . . . then slacken and remove the trim panel retaining screw

12.14 Unclip the inner handle surround

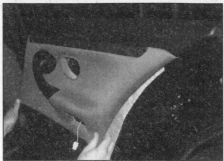

12.15 Unclip the trim panel and move it upwards and away from the door

16 Refitting of the trim panel is the reverse of removal. Prior to clipping the panel in position, ensure all the wiring (where necessary) is correctly routed and passed through the relevant apertures. On completion check the operation of all switches.

13 Door handle and lock components – removal and refitting

14 Carefully prise the door opening handle surround from the door interior trim panel **(see illustration)**.
15 Make a final check that all the retaining screws have been removed, then carefully

unclip the base of the trim panel from the door and manoeuvre it upwards and out of position **(see illustration)**. As the panel is removed, free the wiring harness noting its correct routing.

Removal

1 Remove the inner trim panel as described in Section 12.
2 To gain access to the handle and lock components, it is necessary to peel/cut the foam insulation panel away from the door **(see illustrations). Note:** *This is likely to result in the panel being damaged, necessitating its renewal. If the panel needs to be renewed, it will be necessary to drill out the rivets (see paragraph 4) and remove the armrest/trim panel brackets; new pop rivets will be required on refitting to secure the brackets in position.*

Door lock inner handle

Note: *A pop rivet gun and suitable rivets will be required on refitting.*
3 Peel/cut the insulation panel sufficiently away from the door to gain access to the handle (see paragraph 2).
4 Carefully drill the heads off the rivets securing the handle to the door, whilst taking great care not to damage the handle itself. Recover the remains of the rivets from inside the door.
5 Free the handle from the door, then disconnect the link rods and remove the handle assembly **(see illustration)**.

Front door lock cylinder

6 Peel/cut the insulation panel sufficiently away from the door to gain access to the lock assembly (see paragraph 2).
7 Slacken and remove the lower retaining nut and the upper retaining screws, and manoeuvre the lock protective cover out from inside the door assembly **(see illustrations)**.
8 To improve access to the lock cylinder, release the retaining clip and disconnect the

13.2a Carefully peel the insulation panel away from the door . . .

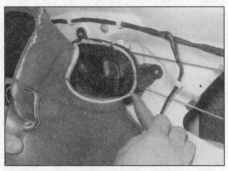

13.2b . . . and inner handle to gain access to the lock components

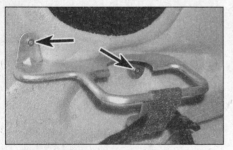

13.2c If the insulation panel is to be removed completely, drill out the rivets (arrowed) and remove the trim panel mounting brackets

13.5 Drill out the rivets then detach the inner handle from the link rods and remove it from the door

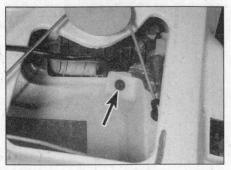

13.7a Undo the upper retaining screws (arrowed) . . .

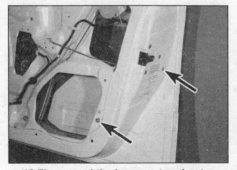

13.7b . . . and the lower nut and outer screw (arrowed) . . .

13.7c . . . and manoeuvre the lock protective cover from the front door

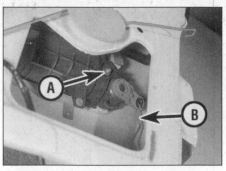

13.9a Undo the retaining nut (A) then detach the link rod (B) . . .

13.9b . . . and remove the lock cylinder mounting plate from the door

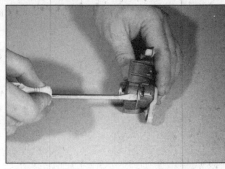

13.10a Slide out the retaining clip . . .

wiring connector from the lock assembly.

9 Slacken and remove the rear retaining nut from the exterior handle, then manoeuvre the lock cylinder mounting plate assembly out of position, disconnecting it from the link rod **(see illustrations)**.

10 To remove the lock cylinder, prise out the retaining clip then separate the lock cylinder, housing and mounting plate. Insert the key into the lock cylinder and withdraw it from the housing **(see illustrations)**.

Front door exterior handle

11 Remove the lock cylinder assembly as described in paragraphs 6 to 9.

12 Undo the front retaining nut then detach the link rod from the handle and manoeuvre the handle out from the door, along with its rubber seal **(see illustrations)**.

Front door lock assembly

13 Peel/cut the insulation panel sufficiently away from the door to gain access to the lock and handle components (see paragraph 2).

14 Slacken and remove the lower retaining nut and the upper retaining screws, and manoeuvre the lock protective cover out from inside the door assembly (see paragraph 7).

15 Remove the inner handle as described in paragraphs 4 and 5.

16 Release the retaining clip and disconnect the wiring connector from the lock assembly **(see illustration)**.

17 Slacken and remove the retaining screws, then unhook the link rods from the lock assembly and manoeuvre it out from the door **(see illustrations)**. Do not attempt to

dismantle the lock assembly, if it is faulty the complete unit must be renewed.

Rear door lock assembly

18 Peel/cut the insulation panel sufficiently

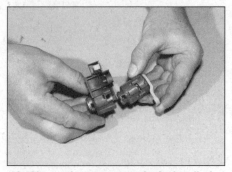

13.10b . . . then separate the lock cylinder housing and mounting plate

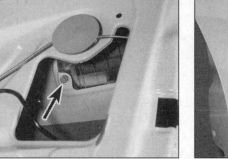

13.12a Undo the retaining nut (arrowed) . . .

away from the door to gain access to the lock and handle components (see paragraph 2).

19 Remove the inner handle as described in paragraphs 4 and 5.

20 Unhook the link rod connecting the lock

13.10c Insert the key and withdraw the lock cylinder from its housing

13.12b . . . and remove the handle and seal from the door

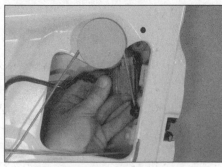

13.16 Lift the clip and disconnect the wiring connector from the lock assembly

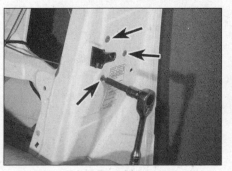

13.17a Undo the retaining screws (arrowed) . . .

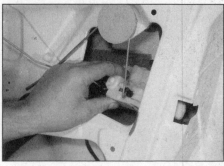

13.17b . . . and manoeuvre the lock assembly out of position

13.20a Detach the link rod (arrowed) . . .

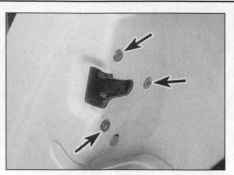

13.20b . . . then undo the lock retaining screws (arrowed)

13.21a Detach the link rods from the lock . . .

13.21b . . . and manoeuvre the lock out from the door

13.25a Remove the access plug from the rear of the door, then slacken and remove the handle rear retaining nut . . .

13.25b . . . then unscrew the front retaining nut . . .

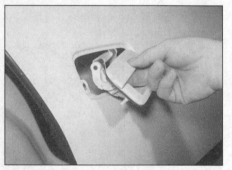

13.25c . . . and remove the handle and seal from the rear door

to the handle, then slacken and remove the lock retaining screws (**see illustrations**).

21 Manoeuvre the lock assembly out of position and remove it from the door. Note that it may be necessary to unhook the inner

handle link rods from the lock assembly, noting their correct fitted locations, in order to gain the clearance required (**see illustrations**).

Rear door exterior handle

22 Peel/cut the insulation panel sufficiently away from the door to gain access to the lock and handle components (see paragraph 2).

23 Release the retaining clip and disconnect the wiring connector from the lock.

24 Unhook the link rod from the door handle.

25 Remove the access plug from the rear of the door, then undo the retaining nuts and remove the handle and seal from the outside of the door (**see illustrations**).

Refitting

26 Refitting is the reverse of removal, ensuring that all link rods are clipped securely in position. Prior to sticking the insulation panel to the door, reconnect the battery and

check the operation of the lock and handles. If all is well, stick the insulation securely in position then refit the trim panel (Section 12).

14 Door window glass and regulator – removal and refitting

Note: *A pop rivet gun and suitable rivets will be required on refitting. The door foam insulation panel is almost certainly going to be damaged on removal, necessitating its renewal.*

Removal

1 Fully lower the window glass then remove the inner trim panel (see Section 12).

2 Noting each brackets correct fitted location, carefully drill off the head of the pop rivets and remove the armrest/trim panel mounting brackets from the door. New pop rivets will be required on refitting.

3 Carefully peel/cut the foam insulation panel away from the door to gain access to the window/regulator. If the panel is damaged on removal it should be renewed. Proceed as described under the relevant sub-heading.

Front door window

4 Remove the inner sealing strip away from the door, noting which way around it is fitted (**see illustration**).

5 Carefully peel the main sealing strip out from the door frame and remove it from the vehicle (**see illustration**).

6 Using a long, flat-bladed screwdriver, depress and release the retaining clip, and

14.4 To remove the front door glass, remove the inner sealing strip from the top of the door . . .

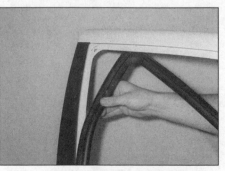

14.5 . . . then ease the main sealing strip out from the door frame

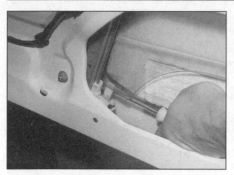

14.6 Carefully use a screwdriver to release the regulator guide clip . . .

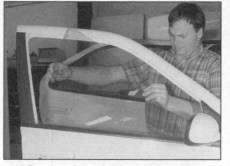

14.7 . . . and carefully work the window glass out through the top of the door

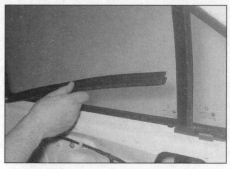

14.8 To remove the rear door glass, remove the inner sealing strip . . .

free the window glass from the regulator guide clip **(see illustration)**.

7 Carefully manoeuvre the glass upwards and out from the top of the door **(see illustration)**.

Rear door window

8 Carefully ease the window inner seal out of position, noting which way around it is fitted, and remove it from the door frame **(see illustration)**.

9 Free the window section of the outer sealing strip from the door, and position it clear of the glass **(see illustration)**.

10 Carefully peel the main sealing strip out from the door frame and remove it from the vehicle **(see illustration)**.

11 Slacken and remove the two retaining screws, then manoeuvre the window rear guide rail out of position and remove it from the door **(see illustrations)**.

12 Depress the retaining clip and free the window glass from the regulator guide. The

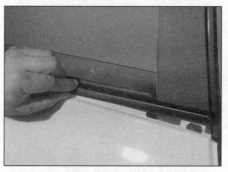

14.9 . . . then free the outer sealing strip . . .

window glass can then be removed from the top of the door **(see illustrations)**.

Window regulator

13 Depress the retaining clip (on the front

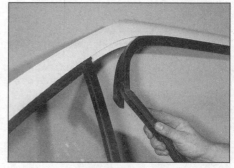

14.10 . . . and the main sealing strip from the door

door it will be necessary to use a screwdriver to reach the clip) and free the window glass from the regulator guide. Slide the window glass fully up and hold it in position by taping it to the door frame **(see illustration)**.

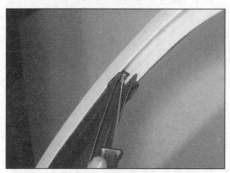

14.11a Undo the upper retaining screw . . .

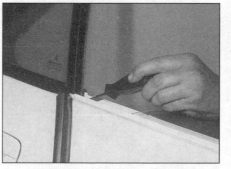

14.11b . . . and the lower retaining screws . . .

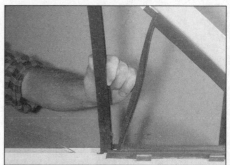

14.11c . . . and manoeuvre the window guide rail out of position

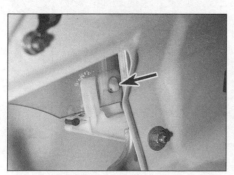

14.12a Release the regulator guide clip (arrowed) . . .

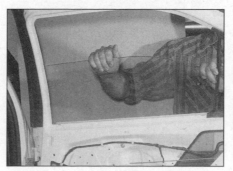

14.12b . . . and manoeuvre the glass out of the top of the door

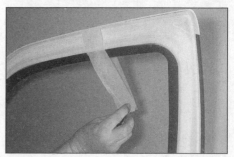

14.13 Release the glass from the regulator then slide up and tape it securely to the door frame

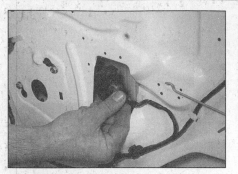

14.14 On models with electric windows, lift the retaining clip and detach the wiring connector from the window motor

14 On models with electric windows, lift the retaining clip and disconnect the wiring connector from the regulator motor **(see illustration)**.

15 On all models, undo the five retaining nuts securing the regulator assembly to the door, then carefully manoeuvre the assembly out through the door lower aperture **(see illustrations)**.

Rear door fixed window

16 Carry out the operations described in paragraphs 8 to 11, noting that it is not necessary to remove the main sealing strip completely, it only needs to be freed from window guide.

17 The fixed window can then be eased out position complete with the outer sealing strip.

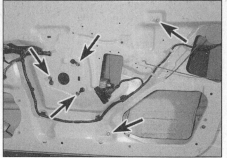

14.15a Undo the retaining nuts (arrowed) . . .

Refitting

18 Refitting is the reverse of the relevant removal procedure, noting the following:

a) Ensure that all sealing strips are correctly located in the door frame.

b) On refitting the window glass, take care to ensure it engages correctly with its guides and the regulator slide, and is clipped securely in position.

c) Check the operation of the window prior to sticking the insulation panel in position. On models with electric windows, the windows will not function correctly until they have been reprogrammed (see Section 20).

d) Fit the insulation panel securely to the door, and secure the armrest/trim panel brackets in position with new pop rivets. Refit the inner trim panel as described in Section 12.

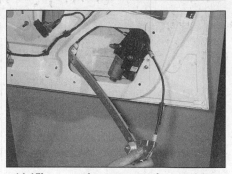

14.15b . . . and manoeuvre the regulator assembly out from the door

15 Boot lid – removal and refitting

Removal

Boot lid

1 Open up the boot lid and disconnect the battery negative terminal.

2 Remove the fasteners securing the inner trim panel to the boot lid, then unclip the panel and remove it from the vehicle; the fasteners are removed by pulling out their centre pins before prising out the complete clip **(see illustrations)**.

3 Prise out the retaining clip and release the wiring cover from the left-hand boot lid hinge to gain access to the wiring harness **(see illustrations)**.

4 Disconnect the wiring connectors from the boot lid electrical components, noting their correct fitted locations, and tie a piece of string to the end of the wiring. Noting the correct routing of the wiring harness, withdraw the wiring. When the end of the wiring appears, untie the string and leave it in position in the boot lid; it can then be used on refitting to draw the wiring into position.

5 Draw around the outline of each hinge with a suitable marker pen, then slacken and remove the hinge retaining bolts and remove the boot lid from the vehicle **(see illustration)**.

6 To remove the boot lid hinge, it will first be necessary to remove the parcel shelf (see rear seat belt removal – Section 27). The hinge

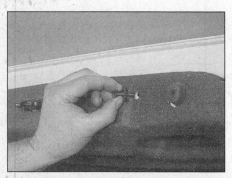

15.2a Withdraw the centre pin and remove the retaining fasteners . . .

15.2b . . . and lift the inner trim panel away from the boot lid

15.3a Remove the retaining clip . . .

15.3b . . . and detach the wiring cover from the boot lid hinge

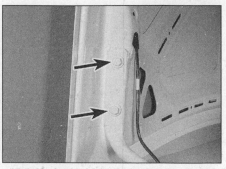

15.5 Undo the hinge bolts (arrowed) and remove the boot lid

pivot bolt can then be unscrewed and the hinge removed **(see illustration)**.

Support strut

7 To remove a support strut, using a small flat-bladed screwdriver, carefully lift the retaining clips and unhook the strut from its balljoints. **Note:** *Access to the strut front mounting can be improved by removing the rear seat back side cushion (models with a folding rear seat) or the complete seat back (models with a fixed rear seat – Section 25). The mounting can then be reached from the front* **(see illustration)**.

Refitting

Boot lid

8 Refitting is the reverse of removal, aligning the hinges with the marks made before removal.

9 On completion, close the boot lid and check its alignment with the surrounding

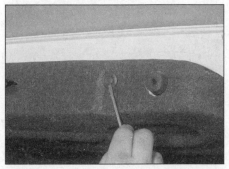

16.2 Remove the fasteners and detach the inner trim panel from the boot lid

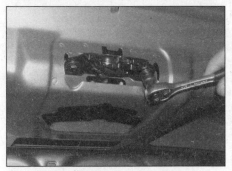

16.3a Undo the retaining bolts . . .

16.4b . . . and remove the trim cover and seal from the boot lid

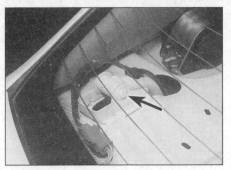

15.6 With the parcel shelf removed, the hinge pivot bolt (arrowed) can be removed

panels. If necessary, slight adjustment can be made by slackening the retaining bolts and repositioning the boot lid on its hinges. If the paintwork around the hinges has been damaged, paint the affected area with a suitable touch-in brush to prevent corrosion.

Support strut

10 Refitting is the reverse of removal, ensuring that the strut is securely clipped in position.

16 Boot lid lock components – removal and refitting

Removal

1 Open up the boot lid then disconnect the battery negative terminal.

2 Remove the retaining clips (pull out the

16.3b . . . then unhook the link rod and remove the lock from the boot lid

16.5 Detach any link rods and wiring connectors

15.7 Access to the support strut front mounting is best obtained from the front

centre pins then prise out the complete clip) and remove the inner trim panel from the boot lid **(see illustration)**. Proceed as described under the relevant sub-heading.

Lock mechanism

3 Slacken and remove the retaining bolts, then unhook the link rod and remove the lock from the boot lid **(see illustrations)**.

Lock cylinder housing

4 Slacken and remove the retaining screws securing the lock cylinder housing in position, then remove the trim cover and seal from the outside of the boot lid **(see illustrations)**.

5 Detach the link rods and wiring connector(s) as required, then remove the lock cylinder housing from the boot lid **(see illustration)**.

6 To disengage the lock cylinder assembly, slide out the retaining clip then separate the lock button and main housing, noting the correct fitted locations **(see illustration)**.

16.4a Undo the lock cylinder housing screws (arrowed)

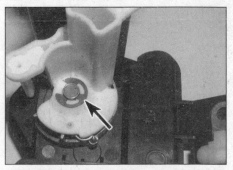

16.6 Slide out the retaining clip (arrowed) and remove the lock cylinder

17.2a Peel away the tailgate sealing strip . . .

17.2b . . . then unclip the upper trim panel(s) to gain access to the tailgate wiring

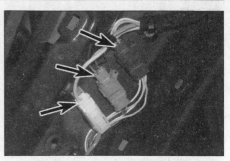

17.3a Working on the left-hand side, disconnect the wiring connectors (arrowed) . . .

17.3b . . . then free the grommet and withdraw the harness from the rear

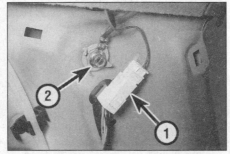

17.4a Working on the right-hand side, disconnect the wiring connector (1) then undo the earth lead bolt (2) . . .

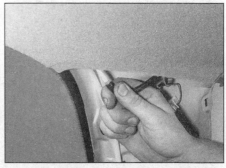

17.4b . . . and disconnect the tailgate washer jet hose from its union

Refitting

7 Refitting is the reverse of removal. Prior to refitting the trim panel, check the operation of the lock assembly and (where necessary) the central locking actuator.

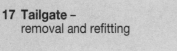

17 Tailgate –
removal and refitting

Removal

Tailgate

1 Disconnect the battery negative terminal.
2 Peel the tailgate sealing strip away from the left- and right-hand rear pillar upper trim panels, then carefully unclip both panels from the vehicle (see illustrations).
3 Disconnect the tailgate wiring connectors,

which are clipped to the left-hand rear pillar, then release the grommet and withdraw the wiring harness from the body (see illustrations).
4 Disconnect the wiring connector and undo the bolt securing the earth lead to the right-hand rear pillar. Work back along the washer hose and disconnect it, then free the grommet and withdraw the wiring and hose from the body (see illustrations).
5 Using a pencil or felt tip pen, mark the outline of each hinge on the tailgate, to use as a guide on refitting.
6 Have an assistant support the tailgate, then carefully lift the retaining clips and detach the support struts.
7 Slacken and remove the bolts securing the hinges to the tailgate and remove the tailgate from the vehicle (see illustration).
8 Inspect the hinges for signs of wear or damage. If renewal is necessary, draw around

the outline of the hinge then unclip the upper trim panel from the roof (see illustration). Carefully peel back the headlining then undo the retaining nuts and remove the hinges from the vehicle. Fit the new hinges, aligning them with the marks made prior to removal and securely tighten the retaining nuts. Clip the headlining back in position and refit the upper trim panel.

Support strut

9 Have an assistant support the tailgate then, using a small flat-bladed screwdriver, carefully lift the retaining clips and unhook the strut from its balljoints (see illustration).

Refitting

Tailgate

10 Refitting is the reverse of removal, aligning the hinges with the marks made before removal. Prior to refitting the trim

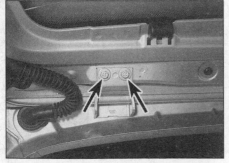

17.7 Undo the hinge bolts (arrowed) and remove the tailgate from the vehicle

17.8 To gain access to the hinge retaining nuts, unclip the upper trim panel and peel back the headlining

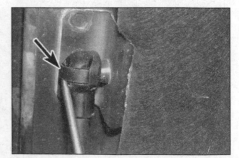

17.9 To remove a support strut, carefully lift the retaining clip (arrowed) using a small, flat-bladed screwdriver

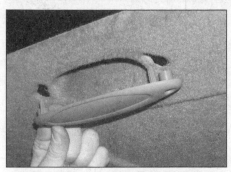

18.2a Undo the screws and remove the inner handle from the tailgate

18.2b Prise out the surround from the lock inner button . . .

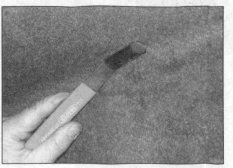

18.2c . . . then remove the retaining clips and remove the inner trim panel

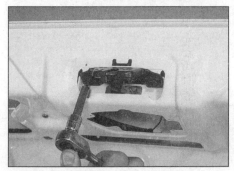

18.3a Undo the retaining bolts . . .

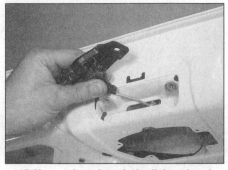

18.3b . . . then detach the link rod and remove the tailgate lock

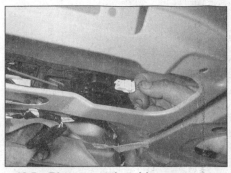

18.5a Disconnect the wiring connector from the central locking motor . . .

panels and sealing strip, connect the battery and check the operation of all the tailgate electrical components. On completion, ensure that the tailgate is correctly aligned with all its surrounding body components; adjustments can be made by slacken the hinge bolts and repositioning the tailgate.

Support strut

11 Refitting is the reverse of removal, making sure the strut is clipped securely in position.

18 Tailgate lock components – removal and refitting

Removal

1 Disconnect the battery negative terminal.

2 Open up the tailgate then undo the retaining screws and remove the inner handle. On 7-seat models, unclip the surround from the lock inner button, then prise out the trim clips and remove the trim panel from the tailgate **(see illustrations)**. Proceed as described under the relevant sub-heading.

Lock assembly

3 Undo the retaining screws then free the lock from the link rod and remove it from the tailgate **(see illustrations)**.

Lock cylinder housing

4 Release the clip and detach the link rod from the assembly.
5 Disconnect the wiring connector from the central locking motor then undo the retaining bolts and remove the assembly from the tailgate **(see illustrations)**. In order to gain the

necessary clearance required, it will probably be necessary to unclip the number plate lights.

Lock inner button (7-seat models)

6 Remove the lock assembly (refer to paragraph 3). Note how the link rod is engaged with the button, then detach the rod from the lock cylinder housing and remove it from the tailgate **(see illustration)**.
7 Slide out the retaining clip and remove the button assembly from the tailgate **(see illustration)**.

Refitting

8 Refitting is the reverse of removal. Check the operation of the lock assembly components prior to refitting the trim panel to the tailgate.

18.5b . . . then undo the retaining bolts and remove the lock cylinder housing

18.6 Note how the link rod engages with the inner button then unclip it from the lock and cylinder, and remove it

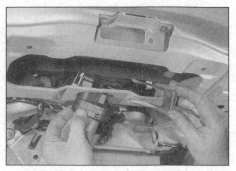

18.7 Slide out the retaining clip and remove the button from the tailgate

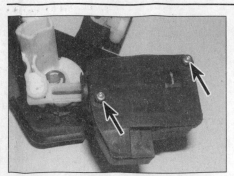

19.3a Undo the retaining screws (arrowed) . . .

19.5a Undo the retaining screws (arrowed) . . .

19 Central locking components – removal and refitting

Removal

Door lock motor

1 Each door lock motor is integral with the lock assembly, and cannot be renewed separately. If the motor is faulty, the complete lock assembly must be renewed (refer to Section 13).

Boot lid lock motor

2 Remove the lock cylinder housing as described in Section 16.
3 Undo the retaining screws and remove the motor from the lock assembly, disengaging it from the lock actuating arm **(see illustrations)**.

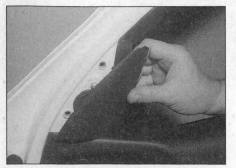

21.1 Unclip the inner trim panel . . .

19.3b . . . then disconnect the actuating arm and remove the central locking motor from the lock assembly

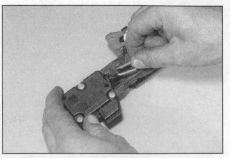

19.5b . . . then unhook the link rod and remove the central locking motor from the bracket

Tailgate lock motor

4 Remove the lock cylinder housing as described in Section 18.
5 Slacken and remove the retaining screws, then detach the motor from its link rod and remove it from the assembly **(see illustrations)**.

Electronic control units (ECU)

6 The door locking electronic control unit is an integral part of the vehicle system interface, which is located behind the passenger compartment fusebox on the right-hand side of the facia.
7 To gain access to the system interface, rotate the three fastener through 90° and lower the fusebox cover. The interface unit will then be found behind and below the fusebox.
8 If there is a fault in the vehicle system interface unit, then it should be checked by your local Peugeot dealer

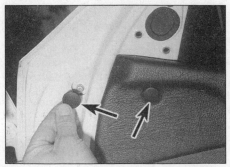

21.2a . . . then remove the trim covers (arrowed) . . .

Refitting

9 Refitting is the reverse of removal.

20 Electric window components – removal and refitting

Note: *If the battery is disconnected with a window open, the window will need to be reprogrammed once the battery is reconnected. To do this, turn on the ignition switch and fully lower the window to its stop. Hold the switch until the relay clicks then, within two seconds, fully raise the window (it will rise in short steps). Once the window is fully closed, keep the switch depressed for a few seconds; this will initialise the ECU so that it learns the fully closed position. Release the switch and check that the window operates normally. Repeat the procedure as necessary.*

Window switches

1 Refer to Chapter 12, Section 4.

Window winder motors

2 At the time of writing, it was unclear whether the window winder motors were available separately or whether the complete regulator assembly would have to be renewed. Refer to your Peugeot dealer for the latest information. Regulator removal and refitting is described in Section 14.

21 Exterior mirrors and associated components – removal and refitting

Mirror assembly

1 Carefully unclip the mirror inner trim panel from the door **(see illustration)**.
2 Prise out the trim covers to reveal the mirror lower retaining screws, then undo the retaining screws and remove the mirror from the door, disconnect the wiring connector as it becomes accessible **(see illustrations)**. Recover the rubber seal which is fitted between the door and mirror; if the seal is damaged it must be renewed.
3 Refitting is the reverse of removal.

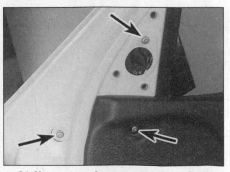

21.2b . . . to gain access to the mirror retaining screws (arrowed)

Mirror glass

Note: *The mirror glass is clipped into position. Removal of the glass is likely to result in breakage if carried out carelessly. It is advisable to wear gloves when carrying out this procedure.*

4 Tilt the mirror glass fully upwards, and insert a wide plastic or wooden wedge between the mirror glass and mirror housing. Release the lower retaining clip and carefully prise the glass from the motor/adjuster **(see illustration)**. Take great care when removing the glass; do not use excessive force, as the glass is easily broken.

5 Remove the glass from the mirror, where necessary, disconnect the wiring connectors from the mirror heating element **(see illustration)**.

6 On refitting, reconnect the wiring to the glass and clip the glass onto the motor/adjuster, taking great care not to break it. Ensure that the glass is clipped securely into position and adjust as necessary.

Mirror switch

7 Refer to Chapter 12, Section 4.

Mirror motor

8 Remove the mirror glass as described above.

9 Undo the retaining screws and remove the motor, disconnecting its wiring connector as it becomes accessible **(see illustration)**.

10 On refitting reconnect the wiring connector and securely tighten the motor screws. Check the operation of the motor then refit the glass as described above.

22 Windscreen and rear screen glass – general information

These areas of glass are secured by the tight fit of the weatherstrip in the body aperture, and are bonded in position with a special adhesive. Renewal of such fixed glass is a difficult, messy and time-consuming task, which is beyond the scope

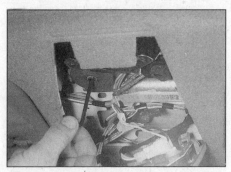
23.2 Using an Allen key to manually move the electric sunroof

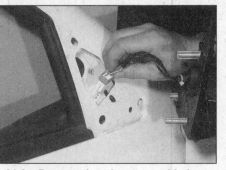
21.2c Remove the mirror assembly from the door and disconnect the wiring

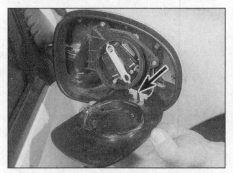
21.5 . . . then carefully unclip the glass from the mirror and (where necessary) disconnect its wiring connectors

of the home mechanic. It is difficult, unless one has plenty of practice, to obtain a secure, waterproof fit. Furthermore, the task carries a high risk of breakage; this applies especially to the laminated glass windscreen. In view of this, owners are strongly advised to have this sort of work carried out by one of the many specialist windscreen fitters.

23 Sunroof – general information

1 Due to the complexity of the sunroof mechanism, considerable expertise is needed to repair, renew or adjust the sunroof components successfully. Removal of the roof first requires the headlining to be removed, which is a complex and tedious operation in itself, and not a task to be undertaken lightly. Therefore, any problems with the sunroof should be referred to a Peugeot dealer.

2 On models with an electric sunroof, if the sunroof motor fails to operate, first check the relevant fuse. If the fault cannot be traced and rectified, the sunroof can be opened and closed manually using an Allen key to turn the motor spindle. To gain access to the motor, remove the overhead console from the roof (see Chapter 12, Section 4). Using the Allen key, rotate the motor spindle and move the sunroof to the required position **(see illustration)**.

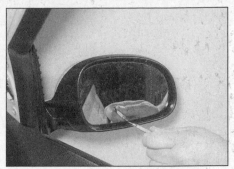
21.4 Release the retaining clip . . .

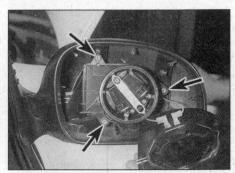
21.9 Mirror motor is retained by three screws (arrowed)

24 Body exterior fittings – removal and refitting

Wheelarch liners and body under-panels

1 The various plastic covers fitted to the underside of the vehicle are secured in position by a mixture of screws, nuts and retaining clips, and removal will be fairly obvious on inspection. Work methodically around the panel, removing its retaining screws and releasing its retaining clips until the panel is free and can be removed from the underside of the vehicle. Most clips used on the vehicle are simply prised out of position. Other clips can be released by unscrewing/prising out the centre pins and then removing the clip **(see illustration)**.

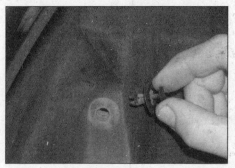
24.1 Prise out the centre pin to release the retaining clip

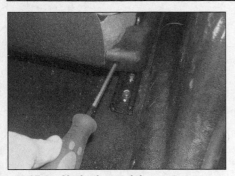

25.1a Undo the retaining screw . . .

25.1b . . . and unclip the outer trim panel from the front seat

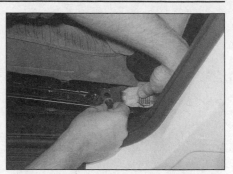

25.2 Undo the lower mounting bolt and detach the seat belt from the seat

25.3 Slide the seat fully forwards and undo the rear mounting bolts . . .

25.4 . . . then slide it fully backwards and undo the front mounting bolts

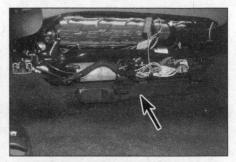

25.5 Unclip the seat wiring cover (arrowed) from the seat frame and disconnect the wiring connectors

2 On refitting, renew any retaining clips that may have been broken on removal, and ensure that the panel is securely retained by all the relevant clips and screws.

Body trim strips and badges

3 The various body trim strips and badges are held in position with a special adhesive tape. Removal requires the trim/badge to be heated, to soften the adhesive, and then cut away from the surface. Due to the high risk of damage to the vehicle's paintwork during this operation, it is recommended that this task should be entrusted to a Peugeot dealer.

25 Seats – removal and refitting

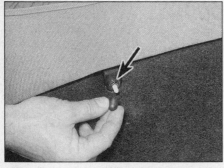

25.6 Remove the rubber cover then undo the seat cushion retaining nut (arrowed)

Removal

Front seat

⚠ **Warning: On models equipped with front seat belt tensioners, refer to Section 26 in this Chapter.**

On models equipped with side airbags, refer to Chapter 12, Section 25 (Airbag systems) before proceeding.

1 Slacken and remove the screw from the rear of the seat outer trim panel, then unclip the trim panel in an upwards direction **(see illustrations)**.

2 Slacken and remove the mounting bolt, and free the seat belt from the seat base **(see illustration)**.

3 Slide the seat fully forwards, then slacken and remove the bolts and washers securing the rear of the seat rails in position **(see illustration)**.

4 Slide the seat fully backwards, then slacken and remove the seat rail front mounting bolts **(see illustration)**.

5 Unclip the cover and disconnect the wiring connectors (for the seat belt tensioner and where applicable seat motors), from under the front of the seat **(see illustration)**. Carefully manoeuvre the seat out of position.

Folding rear seat

6 Remove the rubber covers from the seat cushion mounting studs then unscrew the seat retaining nuts **(see illustration)**. Slide the seat cushion forwards slightly and lift it to release it from the rear retaining pegs. Remove the cushion from the vehicle, freeing it from the seat belt buckles.

7 To remove the seat side cushions, slacken and remove the retaining bolt from the base of the cushion, then slide the cushion upwards and out of the vehicle **(see illustrations)**.

8 To remove the rear seat back assembly on models with a split rear seat, it is first

25.7a Undo the retaining bolt . . .

25.7b . . . then unclip the rear seat side section from the vehicle

25.8a On models with a split rear seat, remove the fasteners (arrowed) . . .

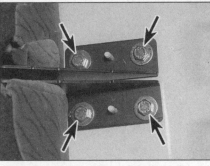

25.8b . . . and peel back the carpet to gain access to the centre bolts (arrowed)

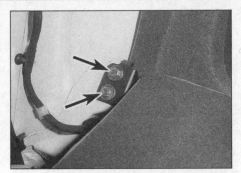

25.9a Rear seat back side mounting bolts – Saloon model

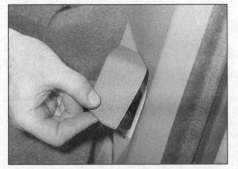

25.9b On Estate models, unclip the access cover to reveal the seat side bolts

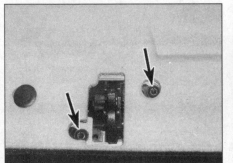

25.10 Undo the two seat catch retaining bolts (arrowed)

25.11 Undo the two retaining screws (arrowed) unclip the cable and remove the seat catch assembly

necessary to remove the retaining clips (prise out the centre pins then remove the complete clips) securing the front of the luggage compartment carpet to the floor; the carpet can then be folded back to gain access to the seat centre mounting bolts **(see illustrations)**. On Estate models, it will be necessary to unbolt the centre seat belt lower mounting from the body.

9 Slacken and remove all the mounting bolts and remove the seat assembly from the vehicle; on Estate models, it will be necessary to unclip the access covers from the side trim panels to gain access to the mounting bolts **(see illustrations)**.

Folding seat cable and catch

10 Fold the rear seat cushion forward, and undo the two seat catch retaining bolts **(see illustration)**.

11 From inside the luggage compartment, undo the two retaining screws from the seat release lever **(see illustration)**. Unclip the cable from under the rear parcel shelf and remove the seat catch assembly from the vehicle.

Fixed rear seat

12 Remove the seat cushion as described in paragraph 6.

13 Slacken and remove the seat back retaining bolts then lift the back upwards and out of position.

Refitting

14 Refitting is the reverse of removal, ensuring all bolts are securely tightened.

26 Front seat belt tensioning mechanism – general information

All models covered in this manual are fitted with a front seat belt pretensioning system. The system is designed to instantaneously take up any slack in the seat belt in the case of a sudden frontal impact, therefore reducing the possibility of injury to the front seat occupants. Each front seat is fitted with the system, the tensioner being attached directly to the seat belt stalk **(see illustration)**.

The seat belt tensioner is operated by the airbag control unit (see Chapter 12). The tensioner is electrically triggered by a frontal impact above a predetermined force. Lesser impacts, including impacts from behind, will not trigger the system.

When the system is triggered, the fuel inside the tensioner cylinder ignites. This forces the tensioner piston forwards which then removes all slack from the seat belt by retracting the seat belt stalk. The strength of the explosion in the tensioner cylinder is calibrated to retract the seat belt sufficiently to securely retain the occupant of the seat without forcing them into the seat. Once the tensioner has been triggered, the seat belt will be permanently locked and the assembly must be renewed.

To prevent the risk of injury if the system is triggered inadvertently when working on the vehicle, if any work is to be carried out on the seat, disconnect the battery and disable the tensioner. To do this, remove the centre console, and disconnect the wiring connector from the seat belt tensioning/airbag control unit (see Chapter 12).

Also note the following warnings carefully before contemplating any work on the front seat belts.

⚠️ *Warning: Before carrying out any operations on the seatbelt tensioning system, disconnect the battery negative terminal and wait at least two minutes. Remove the centre console (see Section 29) then release the retaining clip and disconnect the main wiring connector from the seat belt tensioning control unit (Chapter 12). When operations are complete, reconnect the control unit and refit the centre console.*

⚠️ *Warning: If the tensioner mechanism is dropped, it must be renewed, even it has suffered no apparent damage.*

26.1 Front seat belt stalk pretensioner

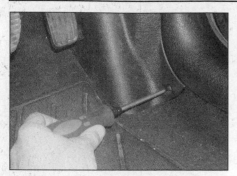

27.5a Undo the retaining screw(s) . . .

27.5b . . . and retaining clip(s), then remove the side panel from the footwell

27.6a Peel back the sealing strip and undo the retaining screw (arrowed) . . .

 Warning: Do not allow any solvents to come into contact with the tensioner mechanism.

Warning: Do not subject the seat to any form of shock, as this could accidentally trigger to the seat belt tensioner.

Warning: Do not subject the tensioner assembly to temperatures above 100°C.

27 Seat belt components – removal and refitting

Removal

Front seat belt

1 Disconnect the battery negative terminal.

2 Remove the relevant front seat as described in Section 25.

3 Prise out the retaining clips and remove the undercover from beneath the facia.

4 If the work is being carried out on the driver's side, slacken the retaining bolt(s) and free the bonnet release lever from the side of the footwell.

5 Remove the footwell side panel retaining screws/nut and clips (as applicable), and carefully unclip the panel from the vehicle **(see illustrations)**.

6 Slacken and remove the retaining screw, then peel away the sealing strip and unclip the front door sill trim panel and remove it from the vehicle **(see illustrations)**.

7 Peel away the front and rear sealing strips from the door centre pillar **(see illustration)**.

8 Unclip the centre pillar trim panel (starting at the top and working down) and free it from the seat belt **(see illustration)**.

9 Undo the front retaining screws, then carefully unclip the front of the rear door sill trim panel sufficiently to reveal the seat belt inertia reel **(see illustration)**. It is not necessary to remove the trim panel completely (this would require the rear seat to be removed).

10 Slacken and remove the two retaining screws, and remove the seat belt guide from the door pillar **(see illustration)**.

11 Unscrew the upper mounting nut and detach the seat belt from its height adjuster **(see illustration)**.

12 Slacken and remove the inertia reel mounting bolt and remove the seat belt assembly from the vehicle **(see illustration)**.

13 If necessary, the height adjustment mechanism can be removed once its retaining bolt has been undone.

Rear seat belt – Saloon

14 Remove the rear seat cushion and side

27.6b . . . then unclip the trim panel from the sill

27.7 Peel the front and rear sealing strips away from the pillar . . .

27.8 . . . then unclip the trim panel and remove it from the vehicle

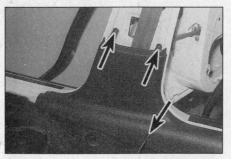

27.9 Undo the retaining screws (arrowed), and unclip the front of the rear door sill trim panel to gain access to the inertia reel

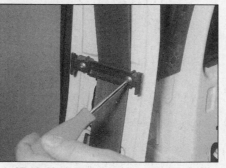

27.10 Undo the retaining screws and remove the seat belt guide from the pillar

27.11 Undo the upper mounting nut . . .

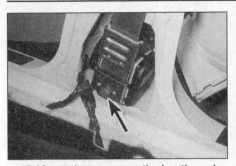

27.12 ... then unscrew the inertia reel mounting bolt (arrowed) and remove the front seat belt assembly from the vehicle

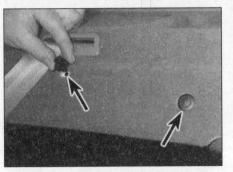

27.16 Remove the retaining clips securing the front of the parcel shelf in position

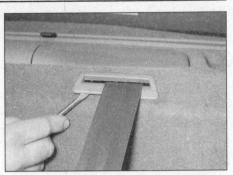

27.17a Carefully prise out the seat belt trim covers ...

27.17b ... and detach them from the seat belts

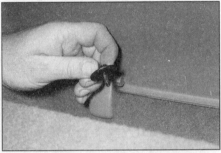

27.19 On models with a storage compartment, remove the parcel shelf bolt from the centre of the compartment

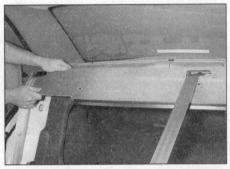

27.20 Unclip the front of the parcel shelf and remove it from the vehicle

cushions (models with a folding rear seat) or the complete seat back (models with a fixed rear seat) as described in Section 25.

15 Slacken and remove the lower mounting bolt securing the seat belt to the floor.

16 Pull out the centre pins and remove the retaining clips securing the front of the parcel shelf to the body **(see illustration)**.

17 Carefully unclip the seat belt trim covers from the front of the parcel shelf, then disengage them from the seat belts **(see illustrations)**.

18 Remove the rear loudspeakers as described in Chapter 12.

19 Where necessary, open up the storage compartment in the centre of the shelf and slacken and remove the shelf retaining bolt **(see illustration)**.

20 Release the front edge of the parcel shelf from the body, and slide the assembly forwards and out of position **(see illustration)**.

21 Slacken and remove the inertia reel retaining bolt, and remove the seat belt assembly from the vehicle **(see illustration)**.

Rear seat belt – Estate

Note: *The rear seat centre belt is built into the seat back. At the time of writing, it was unclear whether it is possible to separate the belt from the seat assembly. Refer to your Peugeot dealer for further information.*

22 Open up the tailgate and peel the sealing strip away from the relevant side of the vehicle. Carefully unclip the upper trim panel from the rear pillar **(see illustration)**, and

remove the luggage compartment side storage compartment cover. Release the luggage compartment cover assembly and remove it from the car.

23 Undo the retaining screws and remove

27.21 Rear seat belt inertia reel retaining bolt (arrowed)

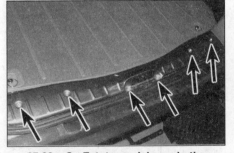

27.23a On Estate models, undo the retaining screws (arrowed) and remove the rear trim panel ...

the rear trim panel from the luggage compartment, then unclip the lower side trim panel **(see illustrations)**. Release the retaining clips and remove the storage compartment.

27.22 Unclip the upper trim panel from the rear pillar

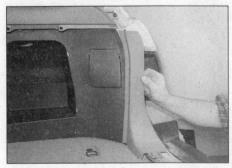

27.23b ... then unclip the lower side trim panel from the luggage compartment

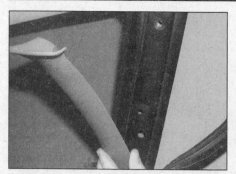

27.25 Unclip the upper trim cover from the pillar

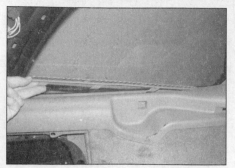

27.26 Unclip the rear side window ventilation grille

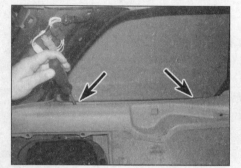

27.27a Undo the two upper retaining screws (arrowed) . . .

27.27b . . . and the rear retaining screw (arrowed) . . .

24 Unclip the trim cover then slacken and remove the seat belt lower mounting bolt.

25 Peel the rear door sealing strip away from the front edge of the upper trim panel, then carefully unclip the upper trim panel and remove it from the vehicle (see illustration).

26 Using a flat-bladed screwdriver, prise out the ventilation grille from the rear window lower trim panel (see illustration).

27 Slacken and remove the retaining screws, then unclip the trim panel and free it from the seat belts (see illustrations).

27.28 Rear seat belt inertia reel retaining bolts (arrowed) – Estate models

27.30a Undo the retaining screw . . .

27.30b . . . and unclip the trim panel from the front seat belt stalk

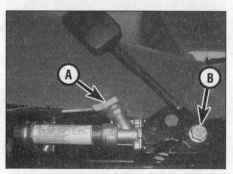

27.31 Disconnect the wiring connector (A) and undo the securing bolt (B)

28 Slacken and remove the retaining bolt and remove the relevant inertia reel seat belt from the vehicle (see illustration).

Front belt stalk and tensioner

29 Remove the front seat as described in Section 25.

30 Slacken and remove the screw from the seat belt stalk trim panel, then unclip the trim panel (see illustrations).

31 Disconnect the wiring plug and release the cable tie, then unbolt and remove the tensioner (see illustration).

Refitting

32 Refitting is the reverse of removal, making sure the inertia reel is correctly engaged with the body, and that all mounting bolts are securely tightened to the specified torque. Also ensure that all trim panels removed are correctly clipped into position and retained by all the relevant clips and screws.

28 Interior trim – removal and refitting

Interior trim panels

1 The interior trim panels are secured using either screws or various types of trim fasteners, usually studs or clips.

2 Check that there are no other panels overlapping the one to be removed; usually there is a sequence that has to be followed that will become obvious on close inspection.

3 Remove all obvious fasteners, such as screws. If the panel will not come free, it is held by hidden clips or fasteners. These are usually situated around the edge of the panel, and can be prised up to release them; note, however that they can break quite easily, so replacements should be available. The best way of releasing such clips without the correct type of tool, is to use a large flat-bladed screwdriver. Note in many cases that the adjacent sealing strip must be prised back to release a panel.

4 When removing a panel, **never** use excessive force or the panel may be damaged; always check carefully that all fasteners have been removed or released before attempting to withdraw a panel.

5 Refitting is the reverse of the removal procedure; secure the fasteners by pressing them firmly into place and ensure that all disturbed components are correctly secured to prevent rattles.

Glovebox

6 Open up the glovebox, then slide out the two hinge pins and remove the glovebox lid (see illustration).

7 Refitting is the reverse of removal.

Carpets

8 The passenger compartment floor carpet is in one piece, and is secured at its edges by screws

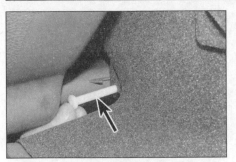

28.6 Slide out the hinge pins (outer pin arrowed) and remove the glovebox lid from the facia

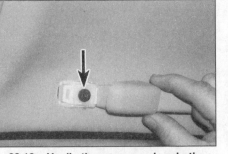

28.10a Unclip the covers and undo the retaining screws (arrowed) to remove the grab handles

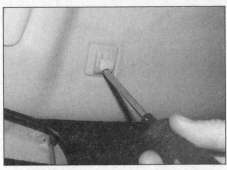

28.10b Undo the retaining screw to release the sun visor retaining clip

or clips, usually the same fasteners used to secure the various adjoining trim panels.

9 Carpet removal and refitting is reasonably straightforward but very time-consuming, because all adjoining trim panels must be removed first, as must components such as the seats, the centre console and seat belt lower anchorages.

Headlining

10 The headlining is clipped to the roof, and can be withdrawn only once all fittings such as the grab handles, sun visors, interior lights, sunroof (if fitted), windscreen and rear quarter windows and related trim panels have been removed and the door, tailgate and sunroof aperture sealing strips have been prised clear **(see illustrations)**.

11 Note that headlining removal requires considerable skill and experience if it is to be carried out without damage, and is therefore best entrusted to an expert.

28.10c Undo the retaining screw to remove the sun visor . . .

the ashtray/surround and remove it from the centre console, disconnecting the ashtray illumination bulb as it becomes accessible **(see illustrations)**.

4 Working inside the ashtray aperture,

28.10d . . . and disconnect the wiring connectors (arrowed) from behind the roof console, to withdraw the sun visor wiring

slacken and remove the retaining screws securing the left- and right-hand side panels to the centre console. Unclip the front of each panel and remove both panels from the console **(see illustrations)**.

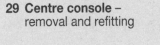
29 Centre console – removal and refitting

Removal

1 Slide the front seats fully forwards, then slacken and remove the rear retaining screws from the left- and right-hand sides of the centre console **(see illustration)**.

2 Slide the front seats fully backwards and disconnect the battery negative terminal.

3 Open up the ashtray then carefully unclip

29.1 Slide the seat forwards and remove the rear bolts (arrowed) from the centre console

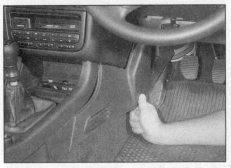

29.3a Unclip the ashtray assembly and remove it from the console . . .

29.3b . . . disconnecting the bulbholder as the ashtray is removed

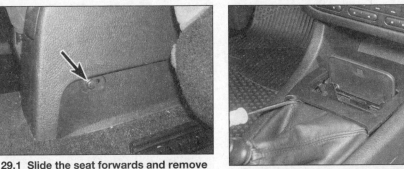

29.4a Undo the retaining screws in the ashtray aperture . . .

29.4b . . . and unclip the side panels from the front of the console

29.5 On manual transmission models, unclip the gearchange lever gaiter

29.7a Carefully prise the handbrake lever trim cover . . .

29.7b . . . and the switch panel out from the console

29.8 Press the button in, to release the armrest from the seat back

29.9 Undo the front mounting nuts (arrowed) . . .

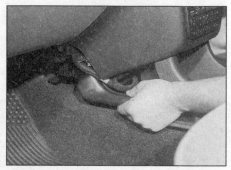

29.10 . . . and unclip the heater ducts from the housing

5 On manual transmission models, unclip the gearchange lever gaiter from the console **(see illustration)**.

6 On automatic transmission models, pull the knob off the top of the gear selector lever.

7 Carefully unclip the handbrake lever trim cover and the airbag on/off switch trim panel from the top of the console, disconnecting the wiring connector as the switch is removed **(see illustrations)**.

8 Where necessary, unclip the front seat armrest(s) to gain the necessary clearance required to remove the console **(see illustration)**.

9 Slacken and remove the two mounting nuts securing the front of the console to the floor **(see illustration)**.

10 Free the heater ducts (situated at the front of the console) from the base of the housing, then lift up the rear of the console **(see illustration)**. Reach in and push the console

switch panel (where fitted) out of position, disconnect the wiring connectors and remove the panel from the vehicle.

11 Disconnect the wiring connectors from the cigarette lighter, then lift up the console and remove it from the vehicle **(see illustrations)**.

Refitting

12 Refitting is the reverse of removal, making sure the heater ducts are correctly engaged with the housing. Ensure that all wiring is correctly routed and all fasteners are securely tightened. On completion, check the operation of all switches.

30 Facia panel assembly – removal and refitting

HAYNES HiNT *Attach an identification label to each wiring connector as it is disconnected. The labels can then be used on refitting to help ensure that all wiring is correctly routed through the relevant facia apertures.*

Removal

1 Remove the centre console as described in Section 29.

2 Working as described in Chapter 12, remove the following components.

　a) Instrument panel. The instrument panel

wiring can be clipped into the holder on the bulkhead to hold it in position whilst the facia is removed.

　b) Driver's side and centre facia switch panels. On the driver's side, disconnect the wiring connector from the lights-on warning buzzer and free the wiring harness from its retaining clips so that it does not hinder facia removal.

　c) Radio/cassette unit.

　d) Clock.

　e) Facia loudspeakers.

　f) Driver's airbag and contact unit. Also, where necessary, disconnect the passenger airbag wiring connectors from the control unit so the airbag is free to be removed with the facia.

　g) Windscreen wiper motor.

3 Remove the steering column (Chapter 10).

4 Referring to Chapter 3, undo the heater control panel retaining screws and free the

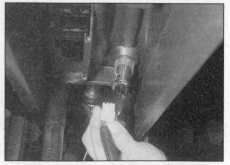

29.11a Lift the rear of the console and disconnect the cigarette lighter wiring . . .

29.11b . . . then manoeuvre the console out of position

30.5a Undo the retaining nuts . . .

30.5b . . . and free the wiring connector mounting plate from the facia

30.6a Slacken and remove the upper (arrowed) . . .

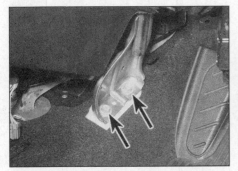

30.6b . . . and lower mounting bolts (arrowed) . . .

30.6c . . . and remove the facia support strut

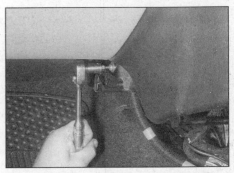

30.7 Undo the retaining screws securing the facia to the heater housing

panel from the facia. On models equipped with a fully-automatic air conditioning system, disconnect the wiring connectors and remove the panel from the vehicle. On all other models the panel can be left connected.

5 Undo the retaining nuts and free the facia wiring connector mounting plate from its bracket (see illustrations).
6 Slacken and remove the upper and lower mounting bolts and remove the facia

mounting bracket support strut from the side of the driver's footwell (see illustrations).
7 Slacken and remove the two heater housing-to-facia screws (see illustration).
8 Slide out the hinge pins and remove the glovebox lid (see illustration 28.6). Carefully prise the illumination light and switch out from the facia, and disconnect them from the wiring connectors (see illustrations). Prise out the retaining clips and remove the undercover from the passenger side of the facia.
9 On models with a fully-automatic air conditioning system, carefully prise the sunshine sensor out from the centre of the top of the facia. Free the sensor from its mounting plate so that it is free to pass through the facia aperture (see illustrations).
10 Carefully prise out the side cover from the passenger end of the facia (see illustration).

30.8a Prise out the glovebox illumination light . . .

30.8b . . . and the light switch, then remove them from the facia

30.9a On models with automatic air conditioning, carefully prise the sunshine sensor out from the top of the facia . . .

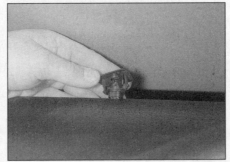

30.9b . . . and unclip the sensor mounting plate

30.10 Removing the side cover from the passenger end of the facia

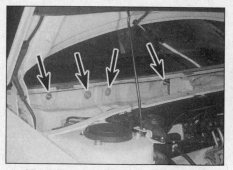

30.11 Facia retaining nuts and bolts (arrowed)

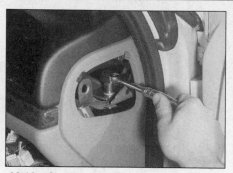

30.12a Slacken and remove the end bolts then release the retaining clips . . .

30.12b . . . and remove the facia from the vehicle

11 From within the engine compartment, slacken and remove the three nuts and two bolts securing the facia mounting bracket to the bulkhead **(see illustration)**.

12 From inside the vehicle, slacken and remove the facia mounting bolts from the left- and right-hand end of the mounting bracket. With the aid of an assistant, release the end clips then carefully manoeuvre the facia assembly away from the bulkhead and out from the vehicle, detaching the heater vents from the heater housing **(see illustrations)**.

Refitting

13 Refitting is a reversal of the removal procedure, ensuring that the heater vents engage correctly with the housing. Prior to refitting the facia mounting nuts and bolts, ensure that all the necessary wiring connectors are fed through the relevant facia apertures. Ensure that the facia bracket is clipped securely in position, then refit the mounting nuts and bolts; tighten them all by hand at first before going around and tightening them securely. On completion, reconnect the battery and check that all the electrical components and switches function correctly.

Chapter 12
Body electrical system

Contents

Airbag system – general information and precautions 25
Airbag system components – removal and refitting 26
Anti-theft alarm and engine immobiliser system – general
   information 23
Battery – removal and refitting . . . . See Chapter 5A
Battery check and maintenance . . . . .See *Weekly checks*
Bulbs (exterior lights) – renewal 5
Bulbs (interior lights) – renewal 6
Cigarette lighter – removal and refitting 12
Clock – general information 13
Cruise control system components – removal and refitting 22
Electric front seat components – removal and refitting 24
Electrical fault finding – general information 2
Exterior light units – removal and refitting 7
Fuses and relays – general information 3
General information and precautions 1

Headlight beam alignment – general information 8
Horn(s) – removal and refitting 14
Instrument panel – removal and refitting 9
Instrument panel components – general information 10
Loudspeakers – removal and refitting 20
Multi-function display – removal and refitting 11
Radio aerial – removal and refitting 21
Radio/cassette player – removal and refitting 19
Rear screen/tailgate wiper motor – removal and refitting 17
Stop-light switch – removal and refitting . . . . .See Chapter 9
Switches – removal and refitting 4
Washer system components – removal and refitting 18
Windscreen wiper blade check and renewal . . . . . .See *Weekly checks*
Windscreen wiper motor and linkage – removal and refitting 16
Wiper arm – removal and refitting 15

Degrees of difficulty

Easy, suitable for novice with little experience	**Fairly easy,** suitable for beginner with some experience	**Fairly difficult,** suitable for competent DIY mechanic	**Difficult,** suitable for experienced DIY mechanic	**Very difficult,** suitable for expert DIY or professional

Specifications

System type	12 volt negative earth

Bulbs	**Wattage**

Exterior lights

Headlight	55 (H7 type)
Front foglight	55 (H1 type)
Front sidelight	5
Direction indicator	21
Direction indicator side repeater	5
Stop/tail	21/5
High-level stop-light	5
Reversing light	21
Rear foglight	21
Number plate light	5

Interior lights

Front courtesy lights	5
Rear courtesy lights	5
Luggage compartment light	5

Torque wrench setting	**Nm**	**lbf ft**
Airbag control unit nuts	8	6

1 General information and precautions

⚠️ **Warning: Before carrying out any work on the electrical system, read through the precautions given in 'Safety First!' at the beginning of this manual and Chapter 5A.**

The electrical system is of the 12 volt negative earth type. Power for the lights and all electrical accessories is supplied by a lead/acid type battery which is charged by the alternator.

This Chapter covers repair and service procedures for the various electrical components not associated with engine. Information on the battery, alternator and starter motor can be found in Chapter 5A.

It should be noted that prior to working on any component in the electrical system, the battery negative terminal should first be disconnected, to prevent the possibility of electrical short circuits and/or fires.

2 Electrical fault finding – general information

Note: *Refer to the precautions given in 'Safety first!' and in Section 1 of this Chapter before starting work. The following tests relate to testing of the main electrical circuits, and should not be used to test delicate electronic circuits (such as anti-lock braking systems), particularly where an electronic control unit (ECU) is used.*

General

1 A typical electrical circuit consists of an electrical component, any switches, relays, motors, fuses, fusible links or circuit breakers related to that component, and the wiring and connectors which link the component to both the battery and the chassis. To help to pinpoint a problem in an electrical circuit, wiring diagrams are included at the end of this Chapter.

2 Before attempting to diagnose an electrical fault, first study the appropriate wiring diagram to obtain a complete understanding of the components included in the particular circuit concerned. The possible sources of a fault can be narrowed down by noting if other components related to the circuit are operating properly. If several components or circuits fail at one time, the problem is likely to be related to a shared fuse or earth connection.

3 Electrical problems usually stem from simple causes, such as loose or corroded connections, a faulty earth connection, a blown fuse, a melted fusible link, or a faulty relay (refer to Section 3 for details of testing relays). Visually inspect the condition of all fuses, wires and connections in a problem circuit before testing the components. Use the wiring diagrams to determine which terminal connections will need to be checked in order to pinpoint the trouble spot.

4 The basic tools required for electrical fault-finding include a circuit tester or voltmeter (a 12 volt bulb with a set of test leads can also be used for certain tests); a self-powered test light (sometimes known as a continuity tester); an ohmmeter (to measure resistance); a battery and set of test leads; and a jumper wire, preferably with a circuit breaker or fuse incorporated, which can be used to bypass suspect wires or electrical components. Before attempting to locate a problem with test instruments, use the wiring diagram to determine where to make the connections.

5 To find the source of an intermittent wiring fault (usually due to a poor or dirty connection, or damaged wiring insulation), a 'wiggle' test can be performed on the wiring. This involves wiggling the wiring by hand to see if the fault occurs as the wiring is moved. It should be possible to narrow down the source of the fault to a particular section of wiring. This method of testing can be used in conjunction with any of the tests described in the following sub-Sections.

6 Apart from problems due to poor connections, two basic types of fault can occur in an electrical circuit – open circuit, or short circuit.

7 Open circuit faults are caused by a break somewhere in the circuit, which prevents current from flowing. An open circuit fault will prevent a component from working, but will not cause the relevant circuit fuse to blow.

8 Short circuit faults are caused by a 'short' somewhere in the circuit, which allows the current flowing in the circuit to 'escape' along an alternative route, usually to earth. Short circuit faults are normally caused by a breakdown in wiring insulation, which allows a feed wire to touch either another wire, or an earthed component such as the bodyshell. A short circuit fault will normally cause the relevant circuit fuse to blow.

Finding an open circuit

9 To check for an open circuit, connect one lead of a circuit tester or voltmeter to either the negative battery terminal or a known good earth.

10 Connect the other lead to a connector in the circuit being tested, preferably nearest to the battery or fuse.

11 Switch on the circuit, bearing in mind that some circuits are live only when the ignition switch is moved to a particular position.

12 If voltage is present (indicated either by the tester bulb lighting or a voltmeter reading, as applicable), this means that the section of the circuit between the relevant connector and the battery is problem-free.

13 Continue to check the remainder of the circuit in the same fashion.

14 When a point is reached at which no voltage is present, the problem must lie between that point and the previous test point with voltage. Most problems can be traced to a broken, corroded or loose connection.

Finding a short circuit

15 To check for a short circuit, first disconnect the load(s) from the circuit (loads are the components which draw current from a circuit, such as bulbs, motors, heating elements, etc).

16 Remove the relevant fuse from the circuit, and connect a circuit tester or voltmeter to the fuse connections.

17 Switch on the circuit, bearing in mind that some circuits are live only when the ignition switch is moved to a particular position.

18 If voltage is present (indicated either by the tester bulb lighting or a voltmeter reading, as applicable), this means that there is a short circuit.

19 If no voltage is present, but the fuse still blows with the load(s) connected, this indicates an internal fault in the load(s).

Finding an earth fault

20 The battery negative terminal is connected to 'earth' – the metal of the engine/transmission and the car body – and most systems are wired so that they only receive a positive feed, the current returning through the metal of the car body. This means that the component mounting and the body form of that circuit. Loose or corroded mountings can therefore cause a range of electrical faults, ranging from total failure of a circuit, to a puzzling partial fault. In particular, lights may shine dimly (especially when another circuit sharing the same earth point is in operation), motors (eg, wiper motors or the radiator cooling fan motor) may run slowly, and the operation of one circuit may have an apparently unrelated effect on another. Note that on many vehicles, earth straps are used between certain components, such as the engine/transmission and the body, usually where there is no metal-to-metal contact between components due to flexible rubber mountings, etc.

21 To check whether a component is properly earthed, disconnect the battery and connect one lead of an ohmmeter to a known good earth point. Connect the other lead to the wire or earth connection being tested. The resistance reading should be zero; if not, check the connection as follows.

22 If an earth connection is thought to be faulty, dismantle the connection and clean back to bare metal both the bodyshell and the wire terminal or the component earth connection mating surface. Be careful to remove all traces of dirt and corrosion, then use a knife to trim away any paint, so that a clean metal-to-metal joint is made. On reassembly, tighten the joint fasteners securely; if a wire terminal is being refitted, use serrated washers between the terminal and the bodyshell to ensure a clean and secure connection. When the connection is remade, prevent the onset of corrosion in the future by applying a coat of petroleum jelly or silicone-based grease or by spraying on (at regular intervals) a proprietary ignition sealer or a water-dispersant lubricant.

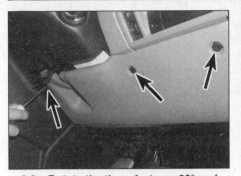

3.2a Rotate the three fastener 90° and lower the fusebox cover . . .

3.2b . . . to gain access to the main fusebox

3.2c Unclip the lid to gain access to the engine compartment fuses

3 Fuses and relays – general information

Fuses

1 The majority of fuses are located in the fusebox situated behind the driver's side lower facia panel. Additional fuses (including the larger, higher-rated fuses) are located in the fuse/relay box on the left-hand side of the engine compartment.

2 To gain access to the main fusebox, lift the steering column adjustment lever up, then turn the three fasteners through 90° and lower the fusebox cover. To gain access to the fuses in the engine compartment, simply unclip the cover from the fuse/relay box; some of the higher-rated fuses are located in a separate box mounted in front of the main box (see illustrations).

3 See wiring diagrams at the end of this Chapter to find a list of the circuits each fuse protects.

4 To remove a fuse, first switch off the circuit concerned (or the ignition), then pull the fuse out of its terminals. The wire within the fuse should be visible; if the fuse is blown it will be broken or melted.

5 Always renew a fuse with one of an identical rating; never use a fuse with a different rating from the original, nor substitute anything else. Never renew a fuse more than once without tracing the source of the trouble. The fuse rating is stamped on top of the fuse; note that the fuses are also colour-coded for easy recognition.

6 If a new fuse blows immediately, find the cause before renewing it again; a short to earth as a result of faulty insulation is most likely. Where a fuse protects more than one circuit, try to isolate the defect by switching on each circuit in turn (if possible) until the fuse blows again. Always carry a supply of spare fuses of each relevant rating on the vehicle, a spare of each rating should be clipped into the base of the fusebox.

Relays

7 The majority of relays are either located in the fuse/relay box in the engine compartment

or behind the driver's side lower facia panel; the exceptions are as follows.

a) *The sunroof relay – located behind the overhead console.*

b) *Rear screen/tailgate wiper relay – fitted to the wiper motor bracket.*

c) *Cooling fan relay(s) – located in the fan shroud or at the side of the radiator.*

8 If a circuit or system controlled by a relay develops a fault and the relay is suspect, operate the system; if the relay is functioning it should be possible to hear it click as it is energised. If this is the case, the fault lies with the components or wiring of the system. If the relay is not being energised, then either the relay is not receiving a main supply or a switching voltage or the relay itself is faulty. Testing is by the substitution of a known good unit, but be careful; while some relays are identical in appearance and in operation, others look similar but perform different functions.

9 To renew a relay, first ensure that the ignition switch is off. The relay can then simply be pulled out from the socket and the new relay pressed in.

4 Switches – removal and refitting

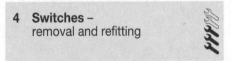

Note: *Disconnect the battery negative lead before removing any switch, and reconnect the lead after refitting the switch.*

4.3 Undo the retaining screws (arrowed) and remove the radio switch from the steering column lower shroud

Ignition switch/steering lock

1 Refer to Chapter 10.

Steering column switches

2 Undo the retaining screws securing the steering column lower shroud in position then unclip both the upper and lower shrouds from the column.

3 On early models, disconnect the cruise control and/or radio control switch wiring connectors. Remove the lower shroud and position the upper shroud clear of the switches. Undo the retaining screws and remove the relevant switch assembly from the lower shroud (see illustration).

4 On later models, to remove an individual cruise control and/or radio control switch, release the retaining clip and slide the switch out of its mounting bracket (see illustration).

5 To remove the complete switch assembly and mounting bracket it will first be necessary to remove the steering wheel (see Chapter 10). Remove the driver's airbag as described in Section 26.

6 On early models, disconnect the wiring connectors from the switches, then undo the retaining screws and remove the assembly from the top of the steering column (see illustration). If an individual switch requires removing then undo the retaining screws, disconnect the wiring connector and slide the switch out from the mounting bracket (see illustrations).

7 On later models, disconnect the wiring connectors from the switches, then undo the

4.4 Release the retaining clip and withdraw the switch from the mounting bracket

4.6a To remove the complete combination switch assembly, disconnect the wiring connectors then undo the screws (arrowed)

4.6b Slacken the retaining screws (arrowed) . . .

4.6c . . . then slide the combination switch out of position and disconnect its wiring (shown with steering wheel removed)

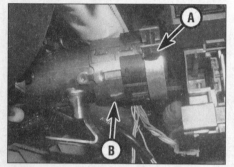

4.7 Slacken the clamp bolt (A) and withdraw the switch assembly, releasing it from locating lug (B)

4.10a If required, unclip the diagnostic socket cover . . .

4.10b . . . then undo the two retaining screws (arrowed) . . .

retaining clamp bolt and release the switch assembly from the top of the steering column **(see illustration)**.

8 Refitting is the reverse of removal, ensuring all wiring connectors are securely reconnected.

Facia switches

9 Lift the steering column adjustment lever up, then turn the three fasteners through 90° and lower the fusebox cover **(see illustration 3.2a)**.

10 Unclip the trim cover from the vehicle diagnostic socket, then slacken and remove the screws from the base of the switch panel **(see illustrations)**.

11 Withdraw the switch/diagnostic socket panel from the facia and disconnect its wiring connectors. Each individual switch can then be unclipped and removed from the mounting panel **(see illustration)**.

12 Refitting is the reverse of removal, noting the wiring connectors are fitted correctly.

Hazard warning light switch

13 Taking great care not to damage the switch or facia, gently prise the switch out of position and disconnect it from the wiring connector **(see illustrations)**.

14 Refitting is the reverse of removal.

Centre console switches

15 The switch panel can be unclipped out of position **(see illustration)**; to make access easier, the centre console assembly can be unbolted from the floor. See Chapter 11 for centre console removal and refitting details. Each individual switch can then be unclipped and removed from the panel.

4.11 . . . and remove the panel from the facia, disconnecting the wiring connectors

4.13a Carefully prise out the switch from the facia panel . . .

4.13b . . . and disconnect its wiring connectors

4.15 Unclip the switch the panel from the centre console

4.16a Carefully prise out the retaining screw cover . . .

4.16b . . . then undo the retaining screw

4.17a Carefully prise out the switch panel assembly . . .

4.17b . . . and disconnect its wiring block connector(s)

4.19a Carefully unclip the switch from the door grab handle . . .

4.19b . . . and disconnect its wiring block connector

Door mounted switches

Front

Note: *The switches cannot be removed separately and come as a complete assembly.*
16 Prise out the trim retaining screw cover from out of the door grab handle in the armrest. Undo the retaining screw **(see illustrations)**.
17 The switch panel assembly can then be carefully prised out of position and its wiring disconnected **(see illustrations)**.
18 Refitting is the reverse of removal.

Rear

19 Using a small screwdriver, carefully prise the switch from the top of the door grab handle, and disconnect the wiring **(see illustrations)**.

Overhead console switches

20 Unclip the cover from the rear of the overhead console **(see illustration)**.

21 Undo the two retaining screws and free the console from the roof lining. Disconnect the wiring connectors and remove the console from the vehicle **(see illustrations)**.

22 To remove the sunroof switch, slacken and remove the retaining screws and lift off the printed circuit board; the switch can then be slid out of position **(see illustrations)**. All

4.20 Unclip the cover from the overhead console . . .

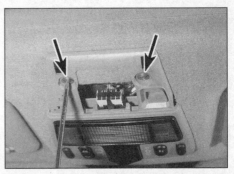

4.21a . . . and undo the retaining screws (arrowed) . . .

4.21b . . . then lower the console out and disconnect the wiring connectors

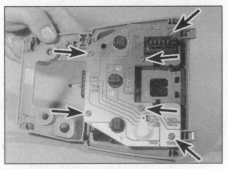

4.22a Undo the retaining screws and remove the printed circuit board . . .

4.22b . . . the switch can then be slid out of position

4.24 Carefully prise out the switch, and disconnect its wiring block connector(s)

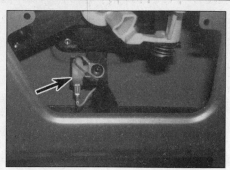

4.34 Luggage compartment light switch (arrowed) – Saloon models

the other switches are integral with the console and can only be renewed by renewing the complete console assembly.
23 Refitting is the reverse of removal ensuring that the wiring is correctly routed. Do not overtighten the circuit board screws, as the board is easily broken.

Seat switches

24 Carefully prise the switch out from the side of the seat **(see illustration)**, and disconnect it from the wiring connector(s).
25 Reconnect the wiring connector, and clip the switch back into position.

Stop-light switch

26 Refer to Chapter 9.

Handbrake warning switch

27 Remove the centre console as described in Chapter 11.
28 Disconnect the wiring connector from the warning light switch, then unclip the switch and remove it from the handbrake lever.
29 Refitting in the reverse of removal.

Courtesy light switch

Note: *On later models there are no switches fitted to the door pillars, the switching of the interior lights is controlled by the door locking units.*
30 Where fitted, open the door and remove the rubber cover from the switch. Release the retaining clips and carefully ease the switch out from the pillar, disconnecting its wiring connector as it becomes accessible. Tie a

piece of string to the wiring to prevent it falling back into the door pillar.
31 Refitting is a reverse of the removal procedure. Refit the rubber cover to the switch prior to clipping it into the door pillar.

Luggage area light switch

32 On Saloon models, open up the boot lid then remove the retaining clips and lift off the inner trim panel to gain access to the switch.
33 On Estate models, open up the tailgate then undo the retaining screws and remove the inner handle. On Family Estate models unclip the surround from the lock inner button, prise out the trim clips and remove the inner trim panel from the tailgate.
34 Undo the retaining screw and remove the switch, disconnecting it from the wiring connector **(see illustration)**.
35 Refitting is the reverse of removal.

Rain sensor switch

Note: *The rain sensor is part of the interior mirror housing. The mirror housing is a tight fit on the mounting bracket on the windscreen, it may be necessary to take the vehicle to a Peugeot Dealer to be removed as there is a possibility of the windscreen breaking on removal.*
36 Carefully unclip the rear view mirror housing from its mounting bracket on the inside of the windscreen.
37 Disconnect the wiring connector then carefully release the side retaining clips and remove the rain sensor from the windscreen.
Caution: Do not touch the rain sensor lens

or the windscreen glass in the area of the sensor. These areas must be kept spotlessly clean if the sensor is to function correctly.
38 Refitting is the reverse of removal, ensuring that the sensor and mirror are clipped securely in position.

Reversing light switch

Manual transmission models

39 Refer to Chapter 7A.

Automatic transmission models

40 Refer to Chapter 7B, Section 7 or 9.

Starter inhibitor switch

Automatic transmission models

41 Refer to Chapter 7B, Section 7 or 9.

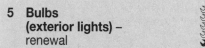

5 Bulbs (exterior lights) – renewal

General

1 Whenever a bulb is renewed, note the following points.
  a) Disconnect the battery negative lead before starting work.
  b) Remember that if the light has just been in use, the bulb may be extremely hot.
  c) Always check the bulb contacts and holder, ensuring that there is clean metal-to-metal contact between the bulb and its live(s) and earth. Clean off any corrosion or dirt before fitting a new bulb.
  d) Wherever bayonet-type bulbs are fitted ensure that the live contact(s) bear firmly against the bulb contact.
  e) Always ensure that the new bulb is of the correct rating and that it is completely clean before fitting it; this applies particularly to headlight/foglight bulbs (see below).

Headlight

2 Release the retaining clip and remove the access cover from the rear of the headlight unit **(see illustration)**.
3 Disconnect the wiring connector from the rear of the bulb, then unhook and release the ends of the bulb retaining clip and release the bulb from the rear of the light unit **(see illustration)**.
4 When handling the new bulb, use a tissue or clean cloth to avoid touching the glass with the fingers; moisture and grease from the skin can cause blackening and rapid failure of this type of bulb. If the glass is accidentally touched, wipe it clean using methylated spirit.
5 Install the new bulb, ensuring that its locating tabs are correctly located in the light cut-outs, and secure it in position with the retaining clip.
6 Reconnect the wiring connector and refit the access cover, making sure it is securely refitted.

5.2 Depress the retaining clip and remove the access cover from the rear of the headlight unit

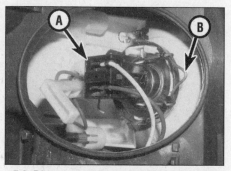

5.3 Disconnect the wiring connector (A) then release the retaining clip (B) and remove the bulb

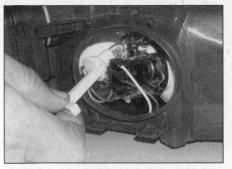

5.8 Twist the bulbholder to remove the sidelight bulb

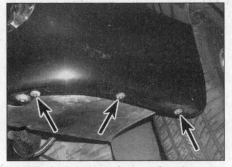

5.11 Undo the screws (arrowed) and remove the splash shield from beneath the foglight

5.12 Release the bulbholder from the rear of the foglight unit

Front sidelight

7 Depress the retaining clip and remove the access cover from the rear of the headlight unit **(see illustration 5.2)**.
8 Rotate the sidelight bulbholder and release it from the headlight unit **(see illustration)**. The bulb is of the capless (push-fit) type, and can be removed by simply pulling it out of the bulbholder.
9 Refitting is the reverse of the removal procedure, making sure the access cover is securely refitted.

Front foglight

10 To improve access, firmly apply the handbrake then jack up the front of the vehicle and support it on axle stands.
11 If necessary, undo the retaining screws and remove the plastic cover from beneath the foglight **(see illustration)**.

12 Disconnect the wiring connector and release the bulbholder from the foglight **(see illustration)**.
13 The bulb can then be removed by simply pulling it out of the bulbholder.
14 When handling the new bulb, use a tissue or clean cloth to avoid touching the glass with the fingers; moisture and grease from the skin can cause blackening and rapid failure of this type of bulb. If the glass is accidentally touched, wipe it clean using methylated spirit.
15 Install the new bulb, ensuring that it is correctly located in the bulbholder.
16 Clip the bulbholder back into position in the rear of the foglight and reconnect the wiring connector.
17 If removed, refit the plastic cover tightening its retaining screws securely. Where necessary, lower the vehicle to the ground.

Direction indicator

18 To improve access on the left-hand side, remove the protective cover from the battery.
19 Rotate the bulbholder anti-clockwise and remove it from the rear of the light unit. The bulb is a bayonet fit in the holder, and can be removed by pressing it and twisting in an anti-clockwise direction **(see illustration)**.
20 Refitting is a reverse of the removal procedure.

Direction indicator side repeater

21 Carefully unclip the light unit and withdraw it from the wing **(see illustration)**.
22 Twist the bulbholder anti-clockwise and remove it from the light. The bulb is of the capless (push-fit) type, and can be removed by simply pulling it out of the bulbholder **(see illustrations)**.
23 Refitting is a reversal of removal.

Rear light cluster

Saloon models

24 From inside the luggage compartment, remove the securing clips (or screws) and remove the rear trim panel. Release the retaining clips (pull out the centre pins then prise out the complete clip) and peel back the trim panel to gain access to the rear of the light assembly, it may also prove necessary to undo the retaining screw and remove the tie-down hook. On some models, if work is being carried out on the left-hand side it will also be necessary to unscrew the fastener and remove the storage compartment to gain the necessary clearance required **(see illustrations)**.

5.19 Removing the front direction indicator bulb

5.21 Carefully prise the side repeater light out from the wing . . .

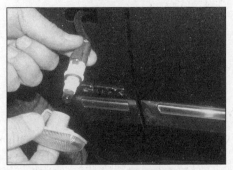

5.22a . . . twist the bulbholder . . .

5.22b . . . and pull out the capless bulb

5.24a On Saloon models, release the clips (or screws), and remove the rear trim panel from the luggage compartment

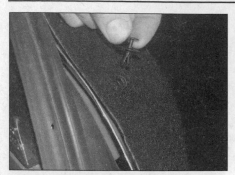

5.24b Release the retaining clips . . .

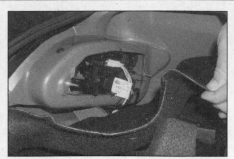

5.24c . . . and peel back the side trim panel to gain access to the rear light cluster

5.25 Depress the retaining clips and remove the bulbholder from the rear cluster . . .

5.26 . . . the relevant bulb can then be removed by pressing it in and turning anti-clockwise

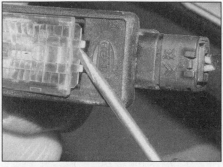

5.32a Carefully prise out the number plate light lens . . .

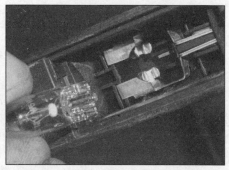

5.32b . . . and pull the bulb out from its holder (light unit removed for clarity)

25 Release the retaining clips and remove the bulbholder assembly from the rear of the light cluster **(see illustration)**.

26 All bulbs have bayonet fittings. The relevant bulb can be removed by pressing in and rotating anti-clockwise **(see illustration)**. Note that the stop/taillight bulb has offset pins to ensure it is fitted the correct way around.

27 Refitting is the reverse of the removal sequence.

Estate models

28 Remove the light unit as described in Section 7.

29 Release the retaining clips and remove the bulbholder from the rear of the light unit.

30 All bulbs have bayonet fittings. The relevant bulb can be removed by pressing in and rotating anti-clockwise. Note that the stop/taillight bulb has offset pins to ensure it is fitted the correct way around.

31 Refitting is the reverse of the removal sequence.

Number plate light

Saloon models

32 Using a small screwdriver carefully unclip the lens from the light unit. The bulb is of the capless (push-fit) type, and can be removed by simply pulling it out of the light unit **(see illustrations)**.

33 Refitting is the reverse of removal, ensuring that the lens is clipped securely in position.

Estate models

34 Open the tailgate, release the retaining clips and remove the tailgate trim panel.

35 Release the number plate light unit from inside the tailgate, then unclip lens from the light unit **(see illustrations)**.

36 The bulb is of the capless (push-fit) type,

and can be removed by simply pulling it out of the light unit.

37 Refitting is the reverse of removal. Making sure the lens is clipped into position securely.

High-level stop-light

38 Remove the light unit as described in Section 7, then remove the bulb/holder from the rear of the light unit.

39 Refitting is the reverse of the removal sequence.

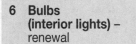

6 Bulbs (interior lights) – renewal

General

1 Refer to Section 5, paragraph 1.

Front courtesy and reading light

Note: *The overhead console may vary depending on model specification.*

With overhead console

2 Using a flat-bladed screwdriver, carefully unclip the light unit(s) from the overhead console **(see illustration)**. Each individual bulbholder can then be released from the light unit and the bulb removed.

3 On some models, the lens can be unclipped from the light unit assembly, then the bulb removed **(see illustrations)**.

4 Refitting is the reverse of removal.

Without overhead console

5 Using a small, flat-bladed screwdriver,

5.35a On Estate models, withdraw the number plate light from the tailgate . . .

5.35b . . . then unclip the lens and remove the bulb from the light unit

6.2 Carefully prise out the light unit from the overhead console

6.3a Carefully prise out the lens from the overhead console . . .

6.3b . . . then pull the relevant bulb out of position

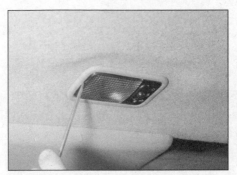

6.5 Carefully prise the courtesy light unit out from the headlining . . .

6.6a . . . then remove the bulbholder from the rear of the light . . .

6.6b . . . and pull out the bulb

carefully prise light unit assembly out of position (see illustration).

6 Twist the bulbholder anti-clockwise and remove it from the light. The bulb is of the capless (push-fit) type, and can be removed by simply pulling it out of the bulbholder (see illustrations).

7 Refitting is the reverse of removal.

Rear courtesy light

8 Refer to the information given above in paragraphs 5 to 7.

Luggage area light

9 Refer to the information given above in paragraphs 5 to 7.

Instrument illumination/warning lights

10 The instrument panel is a complete assembly and has no bulbs that can be renewed, the instrument panel is illuminated by soldered LEDs.

Door open warning light

11 Using a small, flat-bladed screwdriver, carefully prise the door open warning light unit assembly out of the door trim panel (see illustration).

12 Twist the bulbholder and remove it from the light unit (see illustration). The bulb is of the capless (push-fit) type, and can be removed by simply pulling it out of the bulbholder.

13 Refitting is the reverse of removal.

Glovebox illumination

14 Open up the glovebox, then using a small, flat-bladed screwdriver, carefully prise light unit assembly out of position. The bulb is of the capless (push-fit) type, and can be

removed by simply pulling it out of the bulbholder (see illustration).

Heater control illumination

Note: Depending on model specification, the heater control panel may be a complete assembly and have no bulbs that can be renewed. See your local Peugeot Dealer for more information.

15 Remove the heater control panel from the facia as described in Chapter 3, noting that it is not necessary to detach the control cables (where fitted).

16 Where possible, twist the relevant bulbholder anti-clockwise and remove it from the control unit.

17 The bulb is of the capless (push-fit) type, and can be removed by simply pulling it out of the bulbholder.

18 Refitting is the reverse of removal.

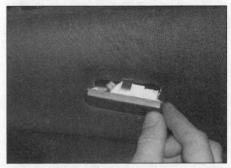

6.11 Carefully prise out the light unit from the door trim panel . . .

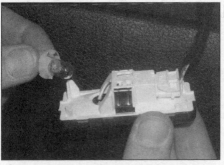

6.12 . . . then twist the bulbholder to remove it from the rear of the light unit

6.14 Carefully prise out the light unit and pull out the capless bulb

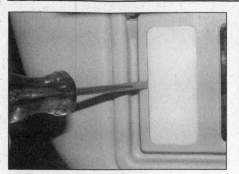

6.20a Carefully prise out the lens from the sun visor mirror light unit . . .

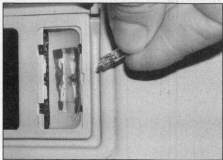

6.20b . . . and pull out the capless bulb

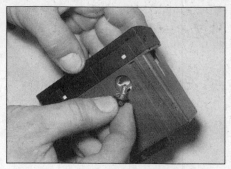

6.23 Where applicable, twist the bulb to remove it from the multi-function display unit

Clock illumination

19 The time clock is an operation of the multi-function display unit. Refer to the information given below in paragraphs 22 to 24 in this Section.

Sun visor illumination

20 Using a small, flat-bladed screwdriver, carefully prise the lens from the light unit. The bulb is of the capless (push-fit) type, and can be removed by simply pulling it out of the light unit (see illustrations).

21 Refitting is the reverse of removal.

Multi-function display

Note: *Depending on model specification, the multi-function display unit may be a complete*

unit and have no bulbs that can be renewed. See your local Peugeot Dealer for more information.

22 Remove the multi-function display as described in Section 11.

23 Where possible, twist the relevant bulbholder through 90° and remove it from the display (see illustration).

24 Refitting is the reverse of removal.

Switch illumination

25 All of the switches are fitted with illuminating bulbs; some are also fitted with a bulb to show when the circuit concerned is operating. On most switches, these bulbs are an integral part of the switch assembly, and cannot be obtained separately. Bulb renewal will therefore require the renewal of the complete switch assembly.

7 Exterior light units – removal and refitting

Note: *Disconnect the battery negative lead before removing any light unit, and reconnect the lead after refitting the light.*

Headlight

1 Open up the bonnet and remove the radiator grille panel as described in Chapter 11, Section 7.

2 Slacken and remove the headlight retaining bolts, there are three in total. To improve access to the outer retaining bolts, on the left-hand side, remove the protective cover from the battery and on the right-hand side, unscrew the filler neck from the washer bottle (see illustrations).

3 Disconnect the wiring as the headlight unit is manoeuvred out of position (see illustration).

4 On models equipped with a headlight levelling system, if necessary, remove the motor from the rear of the light unit by rotating it anti-clockwise and carefully unclipping its balljoint from the rear of the reflector assembly (see illustration).

5 When refitting the headlight levelling system, remove the cover from the rear of the light unit to gain access to the levelling mechanism for reconnecting the balljoint (see illustration).

7.2a Undo the two headlight retaining bolts (arrowed) . . .

7.2b . . . then the outer retaining bolt (arrowed) – left-hand headlamp

7.3 Manoeuvre the headlight unit out of position and disconnect the wiring connectors

7.4 Twist the headlight levelling motor anti-clockwise, then unclip the balljoint from the reflector assembly

7.5 Hold the reflector assembly back in position while refitting the levelling motor balljoint

7.8 Undo the three retaining bolts (arrowed) and remove the foglight from the bumper

7.9 The adjuster (arrowed) is on the rear of the foglight light unit

7.13 On Saloon models, disconnect the wiring connector(s) ...

6 Refitting is a direct reversal of the removal procedure. Lightly tighten the retaining bolts and check the alignment of the headlight with the bumper and bonnet. Once the light unit is correctly positioned, securely tighten the retaining bolts and check the headlight beam alignment using the information given in Section 8.

Front foglight

7 To improve access, it may be necessary to remove the front bumper as described in Chapter 11, Section 6.

8 Undo the three retaining bolts and remove the foglight from the front bumper **(see illustration)**.

9 Refitting is the reverse of removal. If necessary, adjust the foglight aim using the adjuster on the rear of the light unit **(see illustration)**.

Direction indicator side repeater

10 Unclip the rear of the light unit and withdraw it from the wing. Free the bulbholder by rotating it anti-clockwise, and remove the light unit from the vehicle. See Section 5 (bulb renewal) for illustrations.

11 Refitting is a reverse of the removal procedure.

Rear light cluster

Saloon models

12 From inside the luggage compartment, slacken and remove the retaining clips (or screws) and remove the rear trim panel. Release the retaining clips (pull out the centre pins then prise out the complete clip) and peel back the trim panel to gain access to the rear of the light assembly, it may also prove necessary to undo the retaining screw and

remove the tie-down hook. On some models, if work is being carried out on the left-hand side it will also be necessary to unscrew the fastener and remove the storage compartment to gain the necessary clearance required. See Section 5 (bulb renewal) for illustrations.

13 Depress the retaining clip(s) and disconnect the wiring connector(s) from the rear of the light cluster **(see illustration)**.

14 Slacken and remove the retaining nuts and unclip the light unit from the vehicle **(see illustrations)**.

15 Refitting is the reverse of removal, ensuring that the retaining nuts are securely tightened.

Rear wing light

Estate models

16 Remove the storage compartment cover from the luggage compartment, and open up the access cover in the compartment to reveal the light unit **(see illustration)**.

17 Depress the retaining clip and disconnect the wiring connector, then undo the retaining nut and remove the light unit from the wing **(see illustration)**.

18 Refitting is the reverse of removal, tightening the retaining nut securely.

Tailgate light unit

Estate models

19 Open up the tailgate and unclip the retaining nut covers from the end(s) of the tailgate trim panel **(see illustration)**.

7.14a ... then undo the retaining nuts (arrowed) ...

7.14b ... and remove the rear light unit

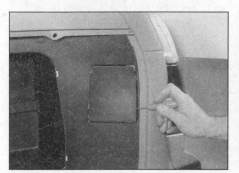

7.16 On Estate models, unclip the access cover ...

7.17 ... then disconnect the wiring connector. Unscrew the nut (arrowed) and remove the rear wing light unit

7.19 Unclip the retaining nut covers from the end of the trim panel ...

7.20a . . . undo the two retaining nuts . . .

7.20b . . . and disconnect the wiring connector

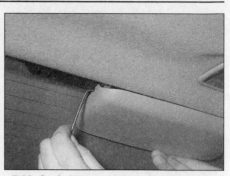

7.22 On Saloon models, using a hooked piece of welding rod, release the clips . . .

7.23 . . . then free the high-level stop-light from its guides and disconnect the wiring

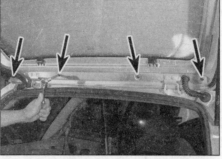

7.25 On Estate models undo the tailgate spoiler retaining screws (arrowed) . . .

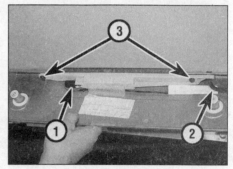

7.26 . . . then disconnect the wiring connector (1) and washer hose (2). Undo the retaining screws (3) and separate the high-level stop-light and spoiler

20 Undo the retaining nuts and release the light unit from the tailgate. Depress the retaining clip on the back of the light unit to disconnect the wiring connector **(see illustrations)**.

21 Refitting is the reverse of removal, tightening the retaining nuts securely. **Note:** *It may be necessary to remove the tailgate trim panel (as described in Chapter 11, Section 18). The wiring may not be long enough, to allow* the light unit to come away from the tailgate so as to be disconnected.

High-level stop-light

Saloon models

22 Using hooked pieces of welding rod, insert the rods into the cut-outs on each end of the light unit and release the retaining clips by pulling them downwards **(see illustration)**.
23 Slide the light unit backwards to free it from its guides and remove it from the vehicle, disconnecting the wiring connector as it becomes accessible **(see illustration)**.
24 Refitting is the reverse of removal.

Estate models

25 Open up the tailgate then slacken and remove the spoiler retaining screws from the top edge of the tailgate **(see illustration)**.
26 Release the spoiler then disconnect the wiring connector and washer hose and remove it from the tailgate. Undo the retaining screws and separate the stop-light and spoiler **(see illustration)**.
27 Refitting is the reverse of removal.

Number plate light

Saloon models

28 Carefully prise the light unit out from the bumper, disconnecting its wiring connector as it becomes accessible **(see illustration)**.
29 On refitting, reconnect the wiring connector and clip the light unit securely in position.

7.28 Carefully prise out the number plate light from the bumper and disconnect it from the wiring

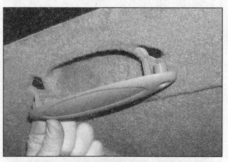

7.30a On Estate models, undo the retaining screws and remove the inner grab handle . . .

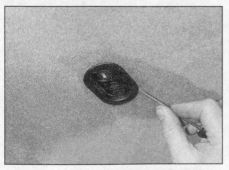

7.30b . . . unclip the surround from the lock inner button (where applicable) . . .

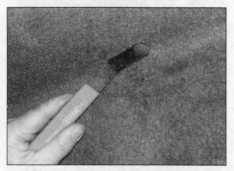

7.30c . . . then carefully prise out the securing clips, to release the trim panel

7.31 Disconnect the wiring connector and push the number plate light unit out of position

Estate models

30 Open up the tailgate then undo the retaining screws and remove the inner handle (on 7-seat models, unclip the surround from the lock inner button), then prise out the trim

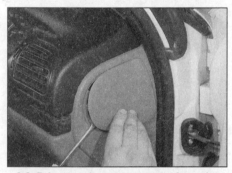

9.3 Prise out the access cover from the driver's end of the facia

8.2 Arrows show the location of the headlight adjusters

clips and remove the trim panel from the tailgate **(see illustrations)**.
31 Disconnect the wiring connector from the rear of the light unit and push the light out of position **(see illustration)**.
32 Refitting is the reverse of removal.

8 Headlight beam alignment – general information

Accurate adjustment of the headlight beam is only possible using optical beam setting equipment, and this work should therefore be carried out by a Peugeot dealer or suitably-equipped workshop.

For reference, the headlights can be adjusted by rotating the adjusters on the rear of the headlight unit. The outer screw adjusts the headlight beam vertical aim, and the inner

screw the headlight beam horizontal aim **(see illustration)**.

On models equipped with headlight levelling, ensure that the headlight beam adjuster switch is set to position 0 before the headlights are adjusted. On models not equipped with headlight levelling, ensure that the manual adjuster on the rear of each light unit is set to position 0 before adjustment.

9 Instrument panel – removal and refitting

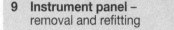

Removal

1 Disconnect the battery negative terminal.
2 Fully lower the steering column to improve access to the instrument panel.
3 Carefully prise out the access cover from the driver's end of the facia **(see illustration)**.
4 Slacken and remove the three retaining screws from the top of the instrument panel. Carefully unclip the shroud and remove it from the vehicle; the shroud can be pushed out, via the facia aperture **(see illustrations)**.
5 Unscrew the four instrument panel retaining screws. Insert a screwdriver between the top of the panel and the facia, and carefully lever the instrument panel out of position **(see illustration)**.
6 Withdraw the panel until the wiring connector is accessible, then release the retaining clips and disconnect the connector **(see illustrations)**. The instrument panel can then be removed from the vehicle.

9.4a Undo the retaining screws (arrowed) . . .

9.4b . . . then unclip the base of the shroud from the facia . . .

9.4c . . . and remove it from the vehicle

9.5 Undo the retaining screws (arrowed), and release the instrument panel from the facia

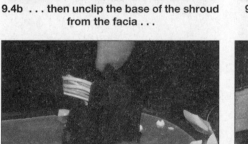

9.6a Release the securing clip . . .

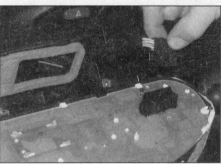

9.6b . . . and disconnect the instrument panel wiring connector

11.2 Carefully unclip the end covers from the multi-function display . . .

11.3 . . . undo the four retaining screws (arrowed) . . .

11.4 . . . release the securing clip and disconnect the wiring block connector

Refitting

7 Reconnect the wiring connector, securing it in position with the retaining clip, and refit the instrument panel back into position in the facia. Refit the panel retaining screws and tighten securely.
8 Clip the shroud back into position and securely tighten its retaining screws. Refit the cover to the end of the facia.
9 Reconnect the battery and check the operation of the panel warning lights to ensure that they are functioning correctly.

10 Instrument panel components – general information

The instrument panel is a complete assembly and has no components that can be renewed separately. Refer to your Peugeot dealer for the latest parts information; they will be able to advise you on the best course of action should the instrument(s) develop a fault.

11 Multi-function display – removal and refitting

Note: For setting the parameters on the display unit see your vehicle handbook.
1 The multi-function display unit has the following functions:
   a) Date.
   b) Time.
   c) Radio display.
   d) Trip computer*.
   e) Door, boot/tailgate and bonnet open warning.
   f) Ambient temperature (the °C symbol flashes when there's a risk of ice).
   g) Warning messages (eg, 'top up fuel tank') displayed for 10 seconds.
   h) Satellite navigation system (depending on vehicle specification).
* The trip computer is operated each time the button on the end of the wash/wipe stalk is pressed. Each time it is pressed the following data is displayed: date, fuel range, distance travelled, average fuel consumption, current fuel consumption and average speed. **Note:** To reset the display to zero, press the stalk for more than two seconds.

Removal

2 Taking great care not to damage either the unit or facia, carefully prise the end covers from the multi-function display unit **(see illustration)**.
3 Undo the retaining screws and remove the display unit from the facia panel **(see illustration)**.
4 Disconnect the wiring connector **(see illustration)**.

Refitting

5 Refitting is the reverse of removal.

12 Cigarette lighter – removal and refitting

Removal

1 Disconnect the battery negative terminal.

Manual transmission models

2 Unclip the gearchange lever gaiter from the centre console.
3 Reach in behind the cigarette lighter, then disconnect the wiring connector(s) and push the cigarette lighter out of position.

Automatic transmission models

4 Remove the centre console as described in Chapter 11. The cigarette lighter can then easily be pushed out of position.

14.5 Undo the three screws (arrowed) to remove the cover

Refitting

5 Refitting is a reversal of the removal procedure, ensuring all the wiring connectors are securely reconnected.

13 Clock – general information

The time clock is one of the operations of the multi-function display unit. Refer to the information given in Section 11 for the removal and refitting of the display unit.

14 Horn(s) – removal and refitting

Removal

Air horn

1 The air horn assembly (both the horn and compressor) are located behind the left-hand front wing.
2 To gain access to the assembly, firmly apply the handbrake then jack up the front of the vehicle and support it on axle stands.
3 Disconnect the wiring connector(s) then slacken and remove the horn and compressor mounting nuts and remove the assembly from the vehicle. The horn and compressor can then be separated.

Conventional horns

4 Models not fitted with an air horn are fitted with twin conventional horns. The horns are located behind the front bumper, one is fitted on the right-hand side and the other on the left-hand side.
5 To gain access to the assembly, firmly apply the handbrake then jack up the front of the vehicle and support it on axle stands. Undo the retaining screws, and free the wheelarch liner/cover from the underside of the bumper and wheelarch (as applicable) **(see illustration)**.
6 Disconnect the wiring connector(s) then slacken and remove the mounting nut(s) and remove the horn(s) from the vehicle **(see illustration)**.

14.6 Disconnect the wiring connector and undo the retaining nut (arrowed)

Refitting

7 Refitting is the reverse of removal.

15 Wiper arm – removal and refitting

Note: *The wiper arms are a very tight fit on the spindles, and it is likely that a puller will be needed to remove them safely, without damage.*

Removal

1 Operate the wiper motor then switch it off so that the wiper arm returns to the at-rest position.

2 Prise off the wiper arm retaining nut cover (where fitted) then slacken and remove the nut **(see illustration)**.

3 Lift the blade off the glass and pull the

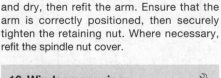

15.2 Unscrew the wiper arm retaining nut and remove the arm

wiper arm off the motor. Carefully lever the arm off the spindle using a large, flat-bladed screwdriver. If the arm is very tight, free it from the spindle using a suitable puller **(see illustration)**.

Refitting

4 Ensure that the wiper and spindle are clean and dry, then refit the arm. Ensure that the arm is correctly positioned, then securely tighten the retaining nut. Where necessary, refit the spindle nut cover.

16 Windscreen wiper motor and linkage – removal and refitting

Removal

1 Disconnect the battery negative terminal.

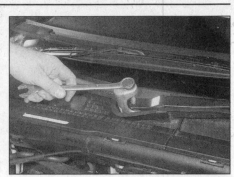

15.3 If the arm is a tight fit, a puller will be required to free it from the spindle

2 Remove the wiper arms as described in the previous Section.

3 Unscrew the retaining nut, then unclip and remove the left- and right-hand plastic inlet vent covers from the base of the windscreen **(see illustration)**.

4 Unclip the left- and right-hand inlet vent panels, and remove them from beneath the windscreen to gain access to the wiper motor **(see illustration)**.

5 Trace the wiring back from the wiper motor and disconnect it at the wiring connector **(see illustration)**.

6 Slacken and remove the wiper motor mounting nuts and bolt, and manoeuvre the wiper motor assembly out of position. Recover the spacers from the motor mounting rubbers **(see illustrations)**.

7 If necessary, mark the relative positions of the motor shaft and crank, then unscrew the retaining nut and washer and free the wiper

16.3 Unscrew the retaining nut and unclip the inlet vent covers . . .

16.4 . . . and vent panels to gain access to the wiper motor

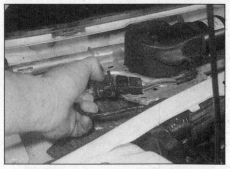

16.5 Depress the clip and disconnect the wiper motor wiring connector

16.6a Slacken and remove the mounting nuts and bolt (arrowed) . . .

16.6b . . . then manoeuvre the wiper motor out of position . . .

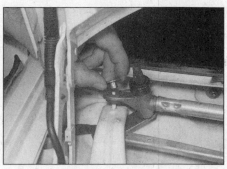

16.6c . . . and recover the spacers from the motor mounting rubbers

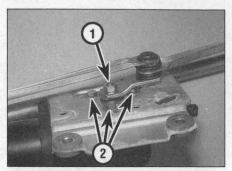

16.7 Wiper motor spindle nut (1) and mounting bolts (2)

17.4a On Estate models, slacken and remove the retaining nuts (arrowed) . . .

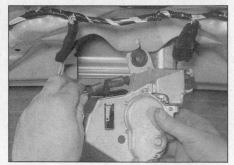

17.4b . . . then manoeuvre the motor out of position and disconnect the wiring . . .

17.4c . . . noting that it may first be necessary to slide off the spacer

linkage from the motor spindle. Unscrew the motor retaining bolts, and separate the motor and linkage **(see illustration)**.

Refitting

8 Refitting is the reverse of removal, ensuring all fasteners are securely tightened. Also ensure that the inlet vent panels are correctly clipped in position prior to refitting the wiper arms.

17 Rear screen/tailgate wiper motor – removal and refitting

Removal

1 Disconnect the battery negative terminal.
2 Remove the wiper arm as described in Section 15.

17.5 Remove the sealing grommet from the tailgate and examine it for signs of damage or deterioration

3 Open up the tailgate then prise out the retaining clips and remove the inner trim panel.
4 Slacken and remove the wiper motor retaining nuts and carefully manoeuvre the motor out of position, disconnecting its wiring connector as it becomes accessible **(see illustrations)**. **Note:** *It may be necessary to slide the spacer off the motor spindle to gain the necessary clearance required to withdraw the motor.*
5 Recover the spacers from the motor mounting rubbers and remove the rubber sealing grommet from the tailgate glass **(see illustration)**.

Refitting

6 Refitting is the reverse of removal. Prior to refitting, check the mounting rubbers, washers and sealing grommet (as applicable) for damage and renew if necessary.

18 Washer system components – removal and refitting

1 The washer reservoir is located behind the right-hand front wing. On Estate models, the reservoir also supplies the tailgate washer. On models equipped with headlight washers, the reservoir also supplies the headlight washer jets via an additional pump.

Washer system reservoir

2 Working in the engine compartment, remove the filler cap and unscrew the washer reservoir filler neck **(see illustration)**.
3 Firmly apply the handbrake then jack up the front of the vehicle and support it on axle stands. Remove the right-hand front roadwheel. Remove the retaining screws and fasteners, and peel back the wheelarch liner to reveal the reservoir.
4 If necessary, drain the reservoir by remove the rubber plug from the union on the reservoir base. Once all the fluid has drained, securely refit the plug.
5 Release the retaining clip(s) and disconnect the hose(s) from the washer pump union(s) (as applicable). Where there is more than one hose connection, make alignment marks to ensure that the hoses are correctly reconnected on refitting **(see illustration)**.
6 Disconnect the wiring connectors from the washer pump(s) and the fluid level sender unit.
7 Slacken and remove the retaining bolt from the top of the reservoir and remove it from the

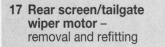

18.2 Unscrew and remove the filler neck from the washer reservoir

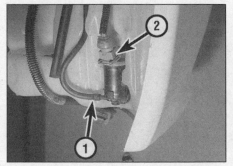

18.5 Washer pump hose (1) and wiring connector (2)

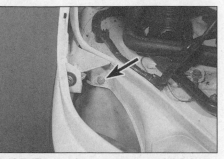

18.7 The washer reservoir retaining bolt (arrowed) is only easily accessible once the headlight is removed

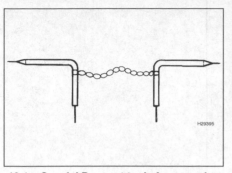

19.1a Special Peugeot tools for removing the radio/cassette player

19.1b Using two small Allen keys to release the radio/cassette

19.2 Slide out the radio/cassette unit and disconnect the wiring connectors (A) and aerial lead (B)

vehicle. **Note:** *Access to the bolt is very poor, and the bolt can only be easily reached if the headlight is removed* **(see illustration).**
8 Refitting is the reverse of removal, ensuring that the hose(s) are securely reconnected. Refill the reservoir and check for leakage.

Washer pump

9 Disconnect the wiring connector and washer hose(s) from the pump. Drain the fluid reservoir (see paragraphs 3 to 5).
10 Carefully ease the pump out from the reservoir, and recover its sealing grommet. Wash off any spilt fluid with cold water.
11 Refitting is the reverse of removal, using a new sealing grommet if the original one shows signs of damage or deterioration. Refill the reservoir, and check the pump grommet for leaks.

Washer reservoir level switch

12 Firmly apply the handbrake then jack up the front of the vehicle and support it on axle stands. Remove the right-hand front roadwheel. Remove the retaining screws and fasteners, and peel back the wheelarch liner to reveal the reservoir.
13 Disconnect the wiring connector from the level switch, and carefully ease the switch out from the reservoir. Recover the sealing grommet and wash off any spilt fluid with cold water.
14 Refitting is the reverse of removal, using a new sealing grommet if the original one shows signs of damage or deterioration.

Windscreen washer jets

15 Open up the bonnet to gain access to the windscreen washer jets. Disconnect the washer hoses from the relevant jet, then depress the retaining clips and carefully ease the jet away from the bonnet.
16 On refitting, securely connect the jet to the hose, and clip it into position in the bonnet. Check the operation of the jet. If necessary adjust the nozzles using a pin, aiming one nozzle to a point slightly above the centre of the swept area, and the other to slightly below the centre point to ensure complete coverage.

Tailgate washer jet

17 Open up the tailgate then undo the

retaining screws and free the spoiler from the upper edge of the tailgate **(see illustrations 7.25 and 7.26).**
18 Disconnect the washer hose then unclip the jet and remove it from the spoiler.
19 Refitting is the reverse of removal. If necessary adjust the nozzle using a pin.

Headlight washer jets

20 Remove the front bumper (Chapter 11).
21 Disconnect the washer hose then undo the retaining screws and remove the jet assembly from the bumper.
22 Refitting is the reverse of removal.

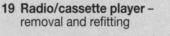

19 Radio/cassette player – removal and refitting

Note: *The following removal and refitting procedure is for the range of equipment fitted by Peugeot. Note that it is likely the special removal tools will be required to withdraw the audio unit from the facia – refer to your Peugeot dealer for further information.*

Removal

1 Insert the tools into the holes in each side of the unit to release the retaining clips **(see illustrations). Note:** *If the special tools are not available, it may be possible to release the clips using two lengths of welding rod.*
2 Carefully slide the audio unit out of position whilst ensuring that the wiring does not become trapped or caught. Disconnect the wiring connectors and aerial lead and remove

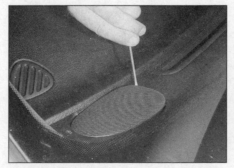

20.1 Carefully prise out the speaker from the top of the facia . . .

the unit from the vehicle **(see illustration).**
Note: *If there is insufficient wiring to allow the unit to be withdrawn, remove the ashtray and surround and remove it from centre console. Working inside the ashtray aperture, slacken and remove the retaining screws and remove centre console side panels (see Chapter 11) to allow access to the wiring from behind.*

Refitting

3 Refitting is the reverse of removal.

20 Loudspeakers – removal and refitting

Facia loudspeaker

1 Carefully prise the speaker out of position, taking great care not to damage the facia panel or speaker grille **(see illustration).**
2 Disconnect the wiring connector and remove the speaker from the vehicle **(see illustration).**
3 Refitting is the reverse of removal, ensuring the speaker is clipped securely in position.

Front door speaker

4 Carefully prise the speaker grille out of position, taking great care not to damage the door panel or speaker grille **(see illustration).**
5 Slacken and remove the retaining screws then remove the speaker from the door, disconnecting the wiring connector as it becomes accessible **(see illustrations).**
6 Refitting is the reverse of removal.

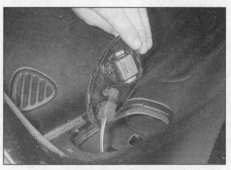

20.2 . . . and disconnect its wiring connector (viewed through windscreen)

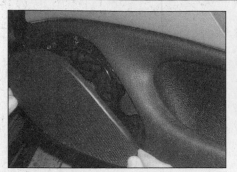

20.4 Carefully prise out the speaker grille from the door trim panel . . .

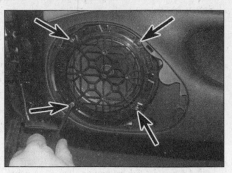

20.5a . . . then undo the retaining screws (arrowed) . . .

20.5b . . . and remove the speaker, disconnecting it from the wiring

20.7 On Saloon models, unscrew the retaining nuts from within the luggage compartment . . .

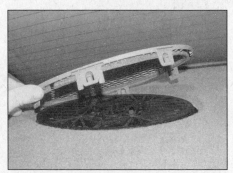

20.8a . . . then unclip the grille from the rear parcel shelf . . .

20.8b . . . and lift the rear speaker out of position

Rear speaker

Saloon models

7 From within the luggage compartment, unscrew the two plastic retaining nuts from the base of the speaker **(see illustration)**.

20.10 On Estate models, unclip the trim panel from the rear pillar to gain access to the rear speaker

8 From inside the vehicle, unclip the grille from the rear parcel shelf, then lift the speaker out of position, disconnecting its wiring as it becomes accessible **(see illustrations)**.
9 Refitting is the reverse of removal.

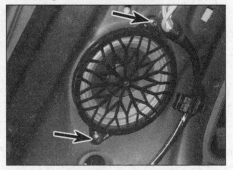
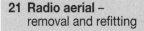

20.11a Undo the speaker retaining screws (arrowed) . . .

Estate models

10 Open up the tailgate. Peel the tailgate sealing strip away from the relevant rear pillar upper trim panel, then unclip the trim panel and remove it from the car **(see illustration)**.
11 Undo the retaining screws and remove the speaker, disconnecting its wiring connector as it becomes accessible **(see illustrations)**.
12 Refitting is the reverse of removal.

21 Radio aerial – removal and refitting

Removal

1 The aerial mast is a screw-fit in its base, and is easily removed.
2 To remove the complete aerial, remove the overhead console or courtesy light (as

20.11b . . . then remove the speaker and disconnect it from the wiring

21.2a Remove the insulating cap . . .

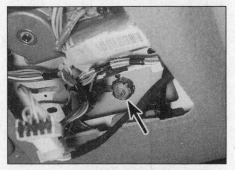

21.2b . . . to gain access to the aerial retaining nut (arrowed)

applicable – see Section 6) to gain access to the mounting nut. Remove the insulating cap then slacken and remove the aerial lead nut (see illustrations). Detach the aerial lead and lift the aerial off from the roof, noting its rubber seal.

Refitting

3 Refitting is the reverse of removal.

22 Cruise control system components – removal and refitting

1 The main components of the system are the electronic control unit (ECU), the vacuum pump, the solenoid valve, the actuator and the cable. The system is controlled by the switch on the steering column, and there are also switches on the brake and (where necessary) clutch pedals.

Removal

Electronic control unit (ECU)

2 The cruise control ECU is located behind the glovebox. Prior to removal, disconnect the battery negative terminal.
3 Remove the retaining clips and remove the undercover from beneath the passenger side of the facia (see illustration).
4 Disconnect the wiring connector(s) then undo the retaining nuts and remove the ECU from underneath the facia (see illustration).

Vacuum pump

5 The vacuum pump is situated in the engine compartment. Prior to removal, disconnect the battery negative terminal.
6 Disconnect the wiring connector and vacuum hose from the pump, then undo the retaining screws and remove the pump from its mounting bracket.

Solenoid valve

7 The solenoid valve is mounted onto the same bracket as the vacuum pump.
8 Disconnect the battery negative terminal, then disconnect the solenoid wiring connector and vacuum hose.
9 Undo the screws and remove the solenoid valve from the engine compartment.

Throttle actuator and cable

10 Unclip the cable from the throttle cam balljoint, then carefully prise off the retaining clip and free the outer cable from its mounting bracket.
11 Disconnect the vacuum hose from the actuator unit, then undo the retaining nut and remove the actuator and cable assembly from the engine compartment.
12 If necessary, remove the outer cable retaining clip and detach the cable and bracket from the actuator.

System operating switch

13 Refer to Section 4, paragraphs 2 to 7.

22.3 Remove the cover from below the glovebox . . .

Brake and clutch pedal switches

14 Refer to Chapter 9, Section 22.

Refitting

15 Refitting is the reverse of removal. On completion check the operation of the cruise control system.

23 Anti-theft alarm and engine immobiliser system – general information

Note: *This information is applicable only to the anti-theft alarm system fitted by Peugeot as standard equipment.*

General

1 Most models in the range are fitted with an anti-theft alarm system as standard equipment. The alarm is automatically armed and disarmed using the remote central locking transmitter (where applicable). In addition to the alarm function, the system also incorporates an engine immobiliser.

Anti-theft alarm system

2 Note that if the doors are operated using the key, the alarm will not be armed or disarmed (as applicable). If for some reason the remote central locking transmitter fails whilst the alarm is armed, the alarm can be disarmed using the key. To do this, open the door with the key, then enter the vehicle, noting that the alarm will sound as the door is opened, and switch on the ignition switch whilst depressing the small alarm button,

22.4 . . . and remove the ECU (arrowed)

located on the centre console. Note that the ignition switch must be turned on and the button depressed within 10 seconds of opening the door.
3 The alarm system has switches on the bonnet, tailgate and each of the doors. It also has ultrasonic sensing, which detects movement inside the vehicle, via sensors mounted on either side of the vehicle interior. If required, the ultrasonic sensing facility can be switched off, whilst retaining the switched side of the system. To switch off the ultrasonic sensing, with the ignition switch off, depress the alarm switch (located on the centre console) until the alarm indicator light is continuously lit. Now, when the doors are locked using the remote central locking transmitter, and the alarm is armed, only the switched side of the alarm system is operational (and the alarm indicator light will revert to its flashing mode). This facility is useful, as it allows you to leave the windows/sunroof open, and still arm the alarm. If the windows/sunroof are left open with the ultrasonic sensing not switched off, the alarm may be falsely triggered by a gust of wind.
4 To deactivate the complete alarm system, switch on the ignition switch and then depress the alarm switch on the centre console and hold for approximately two seconds. The alarm indicator light should then flash rapidly for three seconds, indicating the alarm is disarmed. To reactivate the system, simply lock then unlock the vehicle using the remote transmitter; the alarm will be functional again the next time the vehicle is locked with the remote control.
5 Should the alarm system become faulty, the vehicle should be taken to a Peugeot dealer for examination.

Coded engine immobiliser

⚠️ **Warning: Do not forget the immobiliser code – if the correct code cannot be entered, the engine management electronic control unit may have to be renewed.**

6 This device prevents the engine from being started unless a confidential code is keyed into the pad located in the driver's side facia lower panel. The immobiliser has two modes of operation – manual, where the owner must enter the code every time in order to enable the vehicle to be started, or automatic, where the system is automatically disarmed (for 1 minute only) using the remote central locking unit. The mode of operation can be chosen by the owner, and full details are given in the vehicle handbook. The owner can also change the code, if wished.
7 When the ignition is turned on, if the green light on the key pad is illuminated, the system is disabled and the engine can be started normally. If the red light is illuminated, the system is working (the engine cannot be started, and the alarm will sound if starting is attempted).

24.3a Insert two thin screwdrivers . . .

24.3b . . . and release the drive cable from the seat motor

24.4a Undo the retaining screws . . .

24.4b . . . and remove the seat motor(s)

24.5a Using a small screwdriver . . .

24.5b . . . remove the wiring connector insert . . .

8 Should the immobiliser system become faulty, the vehicle should be taken to a Peugeot dealer for examination.

Disconnecting the battery

9 Prior to disconnecting the battery, the alarm system must be deactivated as described in paragraph 4. Failure to deactivate the alarm will lead to the siren sounding when the battery is disconnected. Once the battery is reconnected, reactivate the alarm using the remote central locking unit.

24 Electric front seat components – removal and refitting

1 Renewal of the front seat heater pads should be entrusted to a Peugeot dealer. Renewal involves dismantling of the complex seat assembly and is especially difficult to achieve successfully especially if side airbags are fitted. In practice, it will be very difficult for the home mechanic to carry out the job without ruining the upholstery. For the removal and refitting of the operating switches see Section 4.

Removal

Seat motor

2 Remove the front seat as described in Chapter 11, Section 25.
3 Insert two thin screwdrivers into the drive cable end of the motor and release the drive cable from the motor (see illustrations).
4 Undo the retaining screws from each end of the seat motor, and remove the motor from the seat motor bracket (see illustrations).
5 Each individual seat motor wiring can be removed from the wiring block connector. Withdraw the wiring connector insert, then using a small screwdriver release the terminal(s) required (take note of the wiring location for refitting) (see illustrations).

Drive cable and gear mechanism

6 Remove the front seat as described in Chapter 11, Section 25.
7 Disconnect the drive cable from the seat motor as described in paragraph 3.
8 Depending on which gear mechanism requires removing, it will be necessary to unclip the back seat cover from under the seat base, carefully prise out the retaining clip from the rear of the seat frame, and carefully peel the seat cover away from the lower seat frame (see illustrations).
9 Undo the two retaining screws, and remove the gear mechanism from the seat frame (see illustration).
10 To remove the rear seat tilt gear mechanism, it will be necessary to remove the

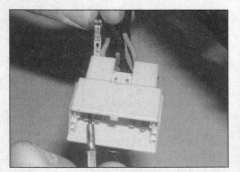

24.5c . . . and unclip the wiring terminal(s) required

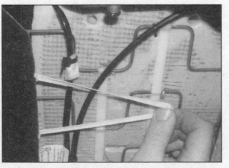

24.8a Unclip the seat cover from under the seat base . . .

24.8b . . . prise out the retaining clip . . .

24.8c . . . and peel the seat cover from the frame

24.9 Undo the two retaining screws (arrowed)

24.10a Release the C-clip (arrowed) . . .

C-clip from the splined driveshaft that connects the both sides of the seat back. Slide the splined shaft out of position then undo the retaining screws and remove the gear mechanism from the seat frame (see illustrations).

Refitting

11 Refitting is the reverse of removal. On completion check the operation of the seat motors.

25 Airbag system –
general information and precautions

Driver's and passenger airbags are fitted as standard to all the models in the range; side air bags are also fitted in the outer sides of the front seat backrests. The passenger airbag has a switch in the centre console which deactivates the airbag, so a child is able to sit in the front seat. Both driver's and passenger airbags have the word AIRBAG stamped on the airbag unit; the driver's is fitted to the centre of the steering wheel, and the passenger's is fitted to the top of the facia. The airbag system comprises of the airbag unit(s) (complete with gas generators), the control unit (with an integral impact sensor) and a warning light in the instrument panel.

The airbag system is triggered in the event of a heavy frontal impact above a predetermined force, depending on the point of impact. The airbags are inflated within milliseconds, and form a safety cushion between the driver and steering wheel, and the passenger and facia. This prevents contact between the upper body and wheel/facia, and therefore greatly reduces the risk of injury. The side airbags are designed to protect the head and thorax and adjust according to the seat position. The airbag then deflates almost immediately. The control unit also operates the front seat belt tensioner mechanisms at the same time as the airbag(s) (see Chapter 11, Section 26).

Every time the ignition is switched on, the airbag control unit performs a self-test. The self-test takes approximately 6 seconds and during this time the airbag warning light in the

24.10b . . . and slide the splined shaft (arrowed) out from the seat mechanism . . .

instrument panel is illuminated. After the self-test has been completed, the warning light should go out. If the warning light fails to come on, remains illuminated after the initial period, or comes on at any time when the vehicle is being driven, there is a fault in the airbag system. The vehicle should be taken to a Peugeot dealer for examination at the earliest possible opportunity.

⚠ **Warning: Before carrying out any operations on the airbag system, disconnect the battery negative terminal and wait at least two minutes. Remove the centre console (see Chapter 11) then release the retaining clip and disconnect the main wiring connector from the airbag control unit (see illustration 26.1a and 26.1b). When operations are complete, reconnect the control unit and refit the centre console. Make sure no one is inside the vehicle when the battery is reconnected then, with the driver's door open, switch the ignition on from outside the vehicle.**

⚠ **Warning: Note that the airbag(s) must not be subjected to temperatures in excess of 100°C. When the airbag is removed, ensure that it is stored the correct way up to prevent possible inflation.**

⚠ **Warning: Do not allow any solvents or cleaning agents to contact the airbag assemblies. They must be cleaned using only a damp cloth.**

⚠ **Warning: The airbags and control unit are both sensitive to impact. If either is dropped or damaged they should be renewed.**

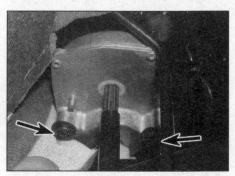

24.10c . . . then undo the two retaining screws (arrowed)

⚠ **Warning: Disconnect the airbag control unit wiring plug prior to using arc-welding equipment on the vehicle.**

26 Airbag system components –
removal and refitting

Note: Refer to the warnings in Section 25 before carrying out the following operations.
1 Disconnect the battery negative terminal, wait at least two minutes, then remove the centre console as described in Chapter 11. Release the retaining clip and disconnect the main wiring connector from the airbag control unit (see illustrations). This will disable the airbag system.

26.1a Release the retaining clip . . .

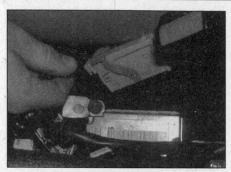

26.1b . . . and disconnect the airbag control unit wiring block connector

26.2a Carefully insert a screwdriver into the steering wheel to release the airbag retaining clip

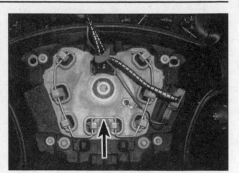

26.2b Airbag retaining clip, arrow shows the position of the screwdriver so as to release the airbag unit

26.3 Remove the driver's airbag unit from the steering wheel and disconnect its wiring connector

26.8 Passenger airbag unit retaining nuts (arrowed)

Driver's airbag

Removal

2 Insert a screwdriver into the hole in the lower part of the steering wheel, taking care not to damage any wiring. Push the screwdriver against the retaining spring in the steering wheel to release the airbag unit from the steering wheel **(see illustrations)**.

3 Carefully lift the airbag assembly away from the steering wheel and disconnect the wiring connectors from the rear of the unit **(see illustration)**. Note that the airbag must not be knocked or dropped, and should be stored the correct way up with its padded surface uppermost.

Refitting

4 Ensure that the wiring connectors are

securely reconnected. Firmly press the airbag unit centrally into place on the steering wheel, until it locks into position. Making sure the wires do not become trapped.

5 Reconnect the airbag control unit wiring connector then refit the centre console as described in Chapter 11.

6 Ensure no one is inside the vehicle and reconnect the battery. With the driver's door open, turn on the ignition switch and check the operation of the airbag warning light.

Passenger airbag

Removal

7 Remove the facia (see Chapter 11).

8 Slacken and remove the retaining nuts then release the airbag unit from its mountings and remove it from the facia **(see illustration)**.

Refitting

9 Manoeuvre the airbag into position, making sure it is correctly engaged with its mounting tangs, then refit the mounting nuts and tighten them securely.

10 Refit the facia as described in Chapter 11 and reconnect the battery (see paragraph 6).

Airbag control unit

Removal

11 With the wiring connector already disconnected (see paragraph 1), unscrew the retaining nuts and remove the control unit from under the centre console inside the vehicle **(see illustration)**.

Refitting

12 Refit the control unit, making sure the arrow on the top of the unit is pointing towards the front of the vehicle. Refit the mounting nuts and tighten them to the specified torque setting.

13 Reconnect the wiring connector and refit the centre console (see Chapter 11).

14 Ensure no one is inside the vehicle, then reconnect the battery. With the driver's door open, turn on the ignition switch and check the operation of the airbag warning light.

Airbag wiring contact unit

Note: *On later models, the airbag wiring contact unit is part of the steering column combination switches. Refer to Section 4 for the removal and refitting of the switch assembly.*

Removal

15 Remove the driver's airbag unit then remove the steering wheel as described in Chapter 10. Ensure that the front wheels are pointing in the straight-ahead position.

16 Undo the retaining screws securing the steering column lower shroud in position, then unclip and remove both the upper and lower shrouds from the column, disconnecting the cruise control and/or radio control switch wiring connector(s) (as applicable) **(see illustrations)**.

17 Trace the wiring back from the contact unit and disconnect it at the connector **(see illustration)**.

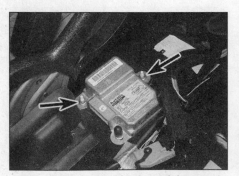

26.11 Airbag control unit retaining nuts (arrowed)

26.16a Undo the screws and remove the steering column lower shroud . . .

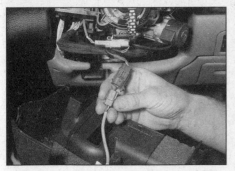

26.16b . . . disconnect the switch wiring connector(s)

26.17 Disconnect the contact unit wiring connector . . .

26.18a . . . then undo the retaining screws (arrowed) . . .

18 Slacken and remove the retaining screws and remove the contact unit from the top of the steering column **(see illustrations)**.

Refitting

19 Prior to refitting it is necessary to ensure that the contact unit is correctly centralised, with the arrow markings on the top of the unit correctly aligned, and that the front wheels are pointing in the straight-ahead position. If there is any doubt about the unit position, rotate the contact unit insert in a clockwise direction until resistance is felt. From this point, rotate the insert back through two to two-and-a-half rotations until the arrows on the top surface of the unit are correctly aligned; the wiring harness will be at the bottom **(see illustration)**. Do not rotate the unit from now on.

20 Slide the contact unit into position, making sure its wiring is correctly routed, and engage it with the switch housing column. Ensure that the contact ring is correctly

26.18b . . . and remove the unit from the top of the steering column

seated and securely tighten its retaining screws.

21 Reconnect the contact unit wiring connector, making sure it is correctly routed.

22 Reconnect the wiring connector(s) and refit the steering column shrouds. Ensure that

26.19 Prior to refitting the steering wheel, centralise the contact unit so that the index marks (arrowed) are aligned

the wiring is not trapped by the shrouds, then refit the retaining screws and tighten them securely.

23 Refit the steering wheel as described in Chapter 10, then refit the airbag unit as described in paragraphs 4 to 6.

Peugeot 406 wiring diagrams

Diagram 1

Key to symbols

Bulb	—⊗—	Item no.	**2**
Flashing bulb	—⊗—	Single speed pump/motor	(M)
Switch	—o̶ o—		
Multiple contact switch (ganged)		Twin speed pump/motor	(M)
Fuse/fusible link	F5	Gauge/meter	◉
		Earth point	—●⟂
Resistor	—▭—	Diode	—▷|—
Variable resistor	—▭—		
Variable resistor	—▱—	Light emitting diode (LED)	—▷|—
Wire splice, unspecified connector or soldered joint		Solenoid actuator	▨
Connecting wires		Heating element	⎍⎍

Wire identifier (MF15) and colour (green with yellow tracer) — ▬▬ MF15 (VJ) ▬▬

Screened cable

Dashed outline denotes part of a larger item, containing in this case an electronic or solid state device.

46Nr - 46 pin black connector
A4/C5/J3 - pin identification

Key to circuits

Diagram 1	Information for wiring diagrams.
Diagram 2	Engine cooling fans.
Diagram 3	Engine cooling fans.
Diagram 4	Engine cooling fans.
Diagram 5	Engine cooling fan, starting & charging & horn.
Diagram 6	Engine management (XU engines - Sagem SL96).
Diagram 7	Engine management (XU engines - Bosch MP7.3).
Diagram 8	Engine management (EW7/EW10 engines).
Diagram 9	Engine management (DW10 engines).
Diagram 10	Engine management (DW12 engines).
Diagram 11	Fuel additive injection, typical cruise control.
Diagram 12	Typical AL4 automatic transmission.
Diagram 13	Instrument cluster.
Diagram 14	Airbags & pretensioners, vehicle area network & diagnostic socket.
Diagram 15	Stop, reversing, dir. indicators & hazard lights.
Diagram 16	Foglights, side/tail lights, headlights & heater blower.
Diagram 17	Typical interior lighting, cigar lighter & electric mirrors.
Diagram 18	Heated screen/mirrors, wash/wipe, electric windows.
Diagram 19	Audio system & central locking.

Passenger fusebox

Fuse	Rating	Circuit protected
F1	Shunt	Seatbelt pretensioner, airbags
F2	5A	Air thermistor, ventilation controls
F3	10A	Stop lights, clutch pedal, instrument cluster, cruise control, passenger airbag disable
F4	5A	Ignition +ve for built-in systems interface
F5	-	Spare
F6	10A	Engine management ECU
F7	15A	Alarm
F8	10A	Display, interior light, memory seats, satellite navigation, luggage compartment light, alarm LED
F9	5A	Battery +ve for built-in systems interface
F10	15A	Audio system
F11	10A	LH stop light, high level stop light
F12	10A	RH stop light
F13	20A	Driver's electric window
F14	30A	Rear electric windows
F15	-	Battery +ve towing socket
F16	20A	Driver's electric seat, seat memory
F17	20A	Passenger's electric seat
F18	10A	Switch illumination
F19	10A	Rear foglights
F20	-	Spare
F21	-	Spare
F22	10A	Interior lighting, rain sensor, seat memory
F23	20A	Cigar lighter
F24	-	Spare
F25	20A	Front & rear wash/wipe
F26	-	Spare
F27	5A	Ignition +ve for built-in systems interface
F28	-	Spare
F29	10A	LH main beam headlight
F30	10A	RH main beam headlight, main beam warning light
F31	10A	LH dipped beam
F32	10A	RH dipped beam headlight, dipped beam warning light
F33	-	Spare
F34	10A	Front LH & rear RH side light
F35	10A	Front RH & rear LH side light, number plate lights, cruise control
F36	-	Spare
F37	-	Spare
F38	-	Spare
F39	-	Spare
F40	40A	Ventilation

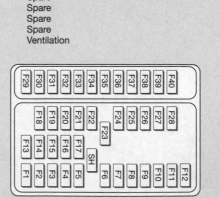

Earth locations

E1	Behind LH headlight	E10	LH 'C' pillar
E2	LH inner wing	E11	RH side of luggage compartment
E3	Front of engine	E12	LH front footwell
E4	LH front footwell	E13	Between front seats
E5	Behind RH headlight	E14	RH 'C' pillar
E6	Behind RH side of dash	E15	LH rear corner of luggage compartment
E7	Behind LH rear light unit	E16	Between front seats
E8	RH strut tower		
E9	LH front footwell		

H32608

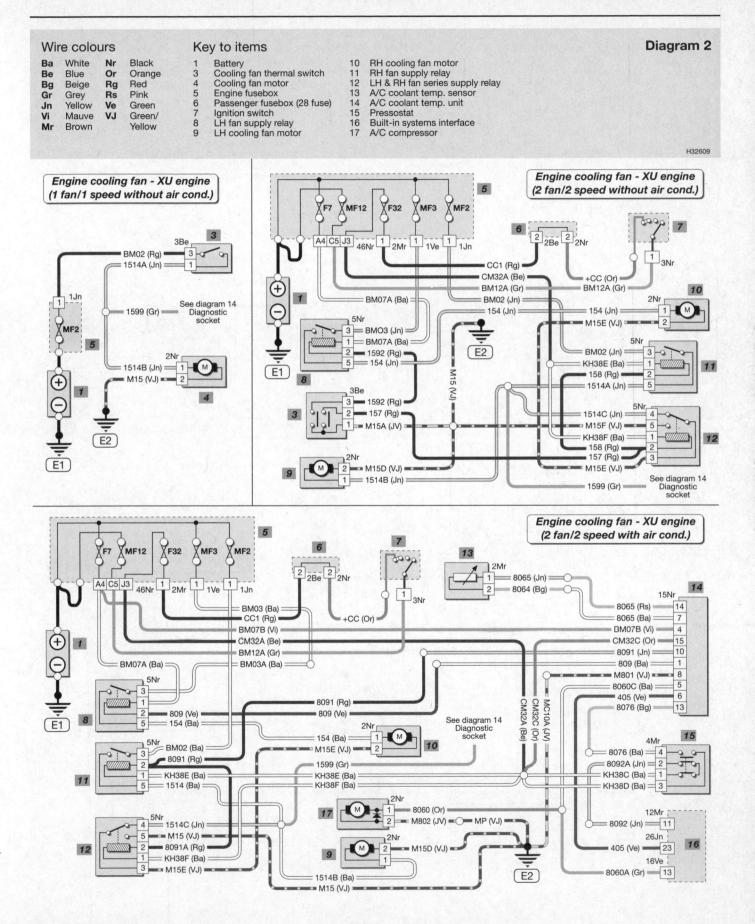

Wire colours

Ba	White	**Nr**	Black
Be	Blue	**Or**	Orange
Bg	Beige	**Rg**	Red
Gr	Grey	**Rs**	Pink
Jn	Yellow	**Ve**	Green
Vi	Mauve	**VJ**	Green/
Mr	Brown		Yellow

Key to items

1 Battery
3 Cooling fan thermal switch
4 Cooling fan motor
5 Engine fusebox
6 Passenger fusebox (28 fuse)
7 Ignition switch
8 LH fan supply relay
9 LH cooling fan motor
10 RH cooling fan motor
11 RH fan supply relay
12 LH & RH fan series supply relay
13 A/C coolant temp. sensor
14 A/C coolant temp. unit
15 Pressostat
16 Built-in systems interface
17 A/C compressor

Diagram 2

H32609

Engine cooling fan - XU engine (1 fan/1 speed without air cond.)

Engine cooling fan - XU engine (2 fan/2 speed without air cond.)

Engine cooling fan - XU engine (2 fan/2 speed with air cond.)

Wire colours

Ba	White	**Nr**	Black
Be	Blue	**Or**	Orange
Bg	Beige	**Rg**	Red
Gr	Grey	**Rs**	Pink
Jn	Yellow	**Ve**	Green
Vi	Mauve	**VJ**	Green/
Mr	Brown		Yellow

Key to items

1 Battery
4 Cooling fan motor
5 Engine fusebox
6 Passenger fusebox (28 fuse)
7 Ignition switch
15 Pressostat
16 Built-in systems interface
18 Engine management multifunction relay
19 Low speed fan relay
20 Twin speed resistor
21 Engine management control unit
22 Coolant temp. sensor
23 High speed fan relay
24 Cooling fan relay

Diagram 3

H32610

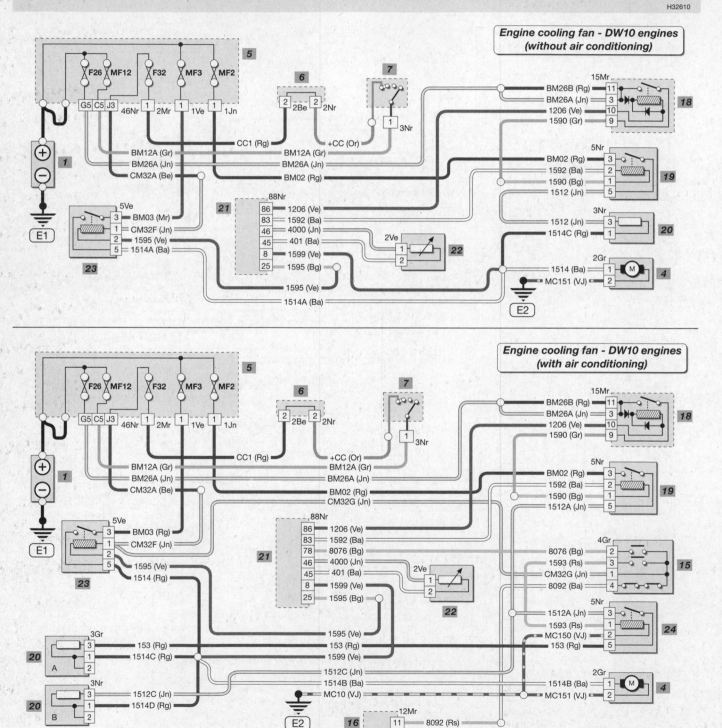

Engine cooling fan - DW10 engines (without air conditioning)

Engine cooling fan - DW10 engines (with air conditioning)

Wire colours

Ba	White	**Nr**	Black
Be	Blue	**Or**	Orange
Bg	Beige	**Rg**	Red
Gr	Grey	**Rs**	Pink
Jn	Yellow	**Ve**	Green
Vi	Mauve	**VJ**	Green/
Mr	Brown		Yellow

Key to items

1 Battery
4 Cooling fan motor
5 Engine fusebox
6 Passenger fusebox (28 fuse)
7 Ignition switch
15 Pressostat
16 Built-in systems interface
18 Engine management multifunction relay

19 Low speed fan relay
20 Twin speed resistor
21 Engine management control unit
22 Coolant temp. sensor
23 High speed fan relay
24 Cooling fan relay

Diagram 4

H32611

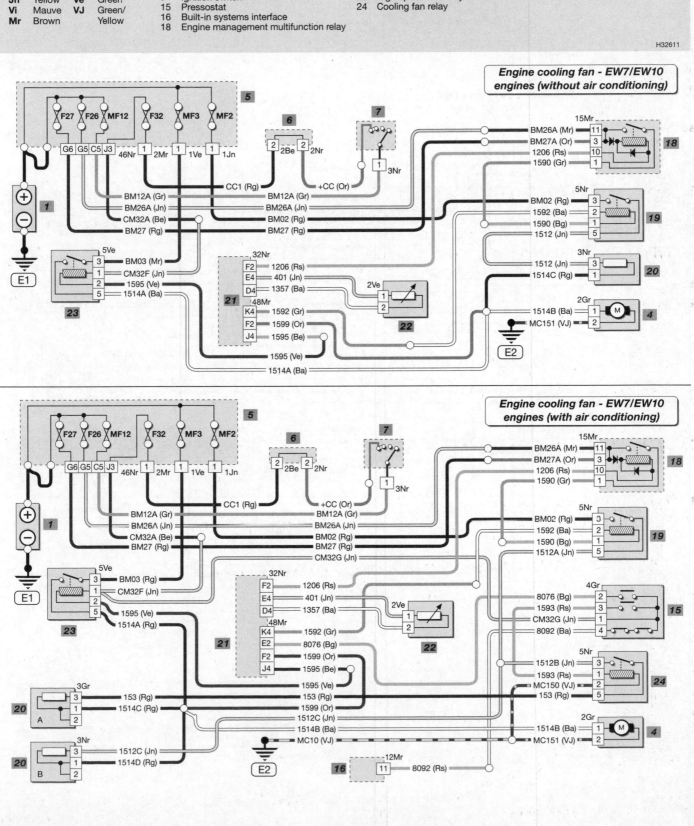

Engine cooling fan - EW7/EW10 engines (without air conditioning)

Engine cooling fan - EW7/EW10 engines (with air conditioning)

Wire colours				Key to items					
Ba	White	Nr	Black	1	Battery	19	Low speed fan relay	28	Horn (low tone)
Be	Blue	Or	Orange	4	Cooling fan motor (single)	20	Twin speed resistor	29	Horn (high tone)
Bg	Beige	Rg	Red	5	Engine fusebox	21	Engine management control unit	30	Starter motor
Gr	Grey	Rs	Pink		a = air horn compressor relay	22	Coolant temp. sensor	31	Alternator
Jn	Yellow	Ve	Green	6	Passenger fusebox (28 fuse)	23	High speed fan relay		
Vi	Mauve	VJ	Green/	7	Ignition switch	24	Cooling fan relay		
Mr	Brown		Yellow	15	Pressostat	27	Steering column assembly		
				16	Built-in systems interface		a = horn switch		
				18	Engine management multifunction relay				

Diagram 5

H32612

Engine cooling fan - DW12 engines

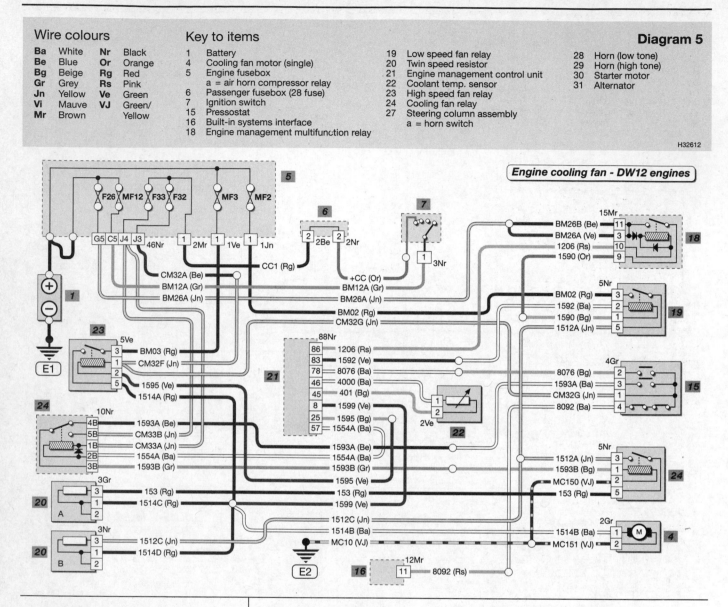

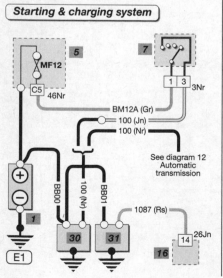

Starting & charging system

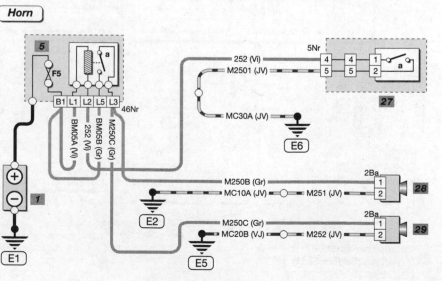

Horn

Wire colours

Ba	White	Nr	Black
Be	Blue	Or	Orange
Bg	Beige	Rg	Red
Gr	Grey	Rs	Pink
Jn	Yellow	Ve	Green
Vi	Mauve	VJ	Green/
Mr	Brown		Yellow

Key to items

1	Battery
5	Engine fusebox
6	Passenger fusebox (28 fuse)
7	Ignition switch
16	Built-in systems interface
18	Engine management multifunction relay
21	Engine management control unit
22	Coolant temp. sensor
32	Inertia switch
33	Fuel gauge sender/fuel pump
34	Canister purge solenoid
35	Vehicle speed sensor
36	Throttle housing heater
37	Engine speed sensor
38	Front oxygen sensor
39	Throttle position sensor
40	MAP sensor
41	Inlet air temp. sensor
42	Knock sensor
43	Idle regulator stepper motor
44	Fuel injector
45	Ignition coil
46	Spark plugs

Diagram 6

H32613

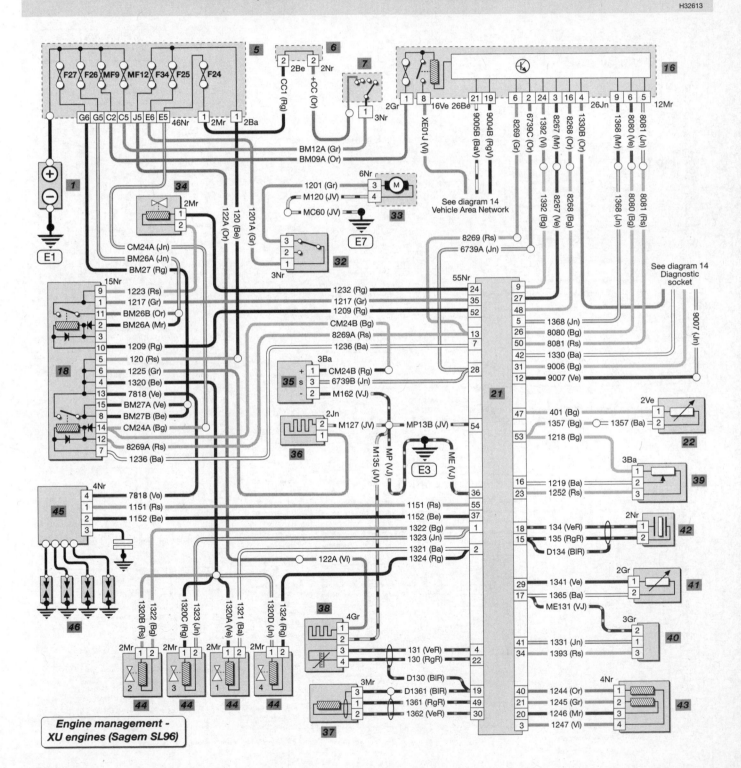

Engine management -
XU engines (Sagem SL96)

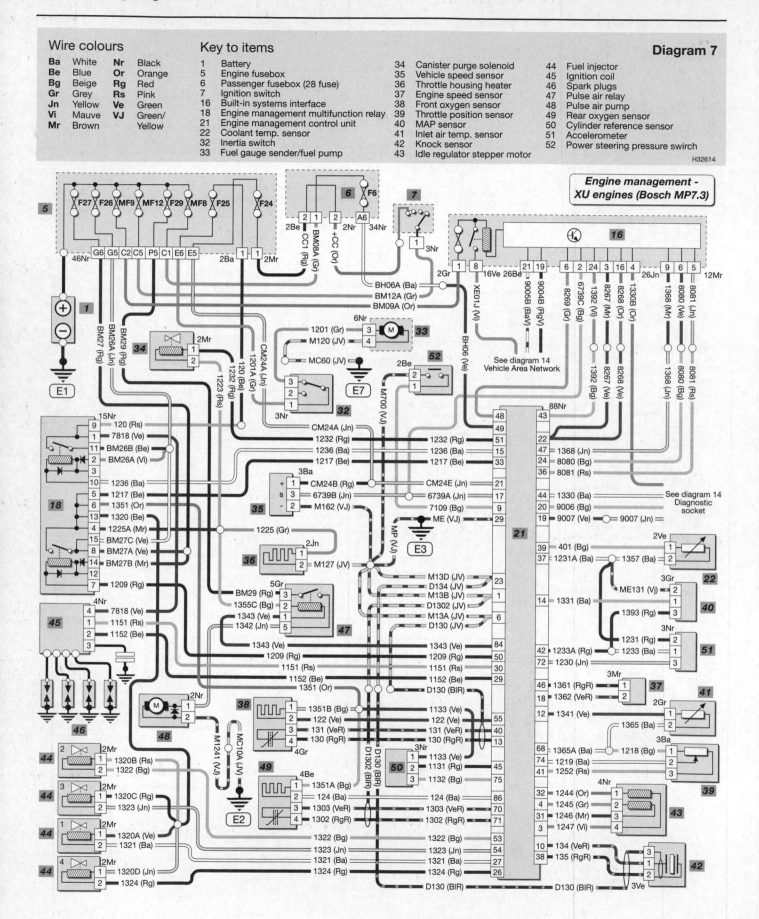

Wire colours

Ba	White	**Nr**	Black
Be	Blue	**Or**	Orange
Bg	Beige	**Rg**	Red
Gr	Grey	**Rs**	Pink
Jn	Yellow	**Ve**	Green
Vi	Mauve	**VJ**	Green/
Mr	Brown		Yellow

Key to items

1	Battery
5	Engine fusebox
6	Passenger fusebox (28 fuse)
7	Ignition switch
16	Built-in systems interface
18	Engine management multifunction relay
21	Engine management control unit
22	Coolant temp. sensor
32	Inertia switch
33	Fuel gauge sender/fuel pump
34	Canister purge solenoid
35	Vehicle speed sensor
36	Throttle housing heater
37	Engine speed sensor
38	Front oxygen sensor
39	Throttle position sensor
40	MAP sensor
41	Inlet air temp. sensor
42	Knock sensor
43	Idle regulator stepper motor
44	Fuel injector
45	Ignition coil
46	Spark plugs
47	Pulse air relay
48	Pulse air pump
49	Rear oxygen sensor
50	Cylinder reference sensor
51	Accelerometer
52	Power steering pressure swirch

Diagram 7

**Engine management –
XU engines (Bosch MP7.3)**

H32614

Wire colours

Ba	White	Nr	Black
Be	Blue	Or	Orange
Bg	Beige	Rg	Red
Gr	Grey	Rs	Pink
Jn	Yellow	Ve	Green
Vi	Mauve	VJ	Green/
Mr	Brown		Yellow

Key to items

1	Battery	33	Fuel gauge sender/fuel pump
5	Engine fusebox	34	Canister purge solenoid
	b = pulse air relay	35	Vehicle speed sensor
6	Passenger fusebox (28 fuse)	36	Throttle housing heater
7	Ignition switch	37	Engine speed sensor
16	Built-in systems interface	38	Front oxygen sensor
18	Engine management multifunction relay	39	Throttle position sensor
21	Engine management control unit	40	MAP sensor
22	Coolant temp. sensor	41	Inlet air temp. sensor
32	Inertia switch	42	Knock sensor

43	Idle regulator stepper motor
44	Fuel injector
45	Ignition coil
46	Spark plugs
48	Pulse air pump
49	Rear oxygen sensor
50	Cylinder reference sensor
52	Power steering pressure switch
55	EGR valve

Diagram 8

H32615

Engine management - EW7/EW10 engines

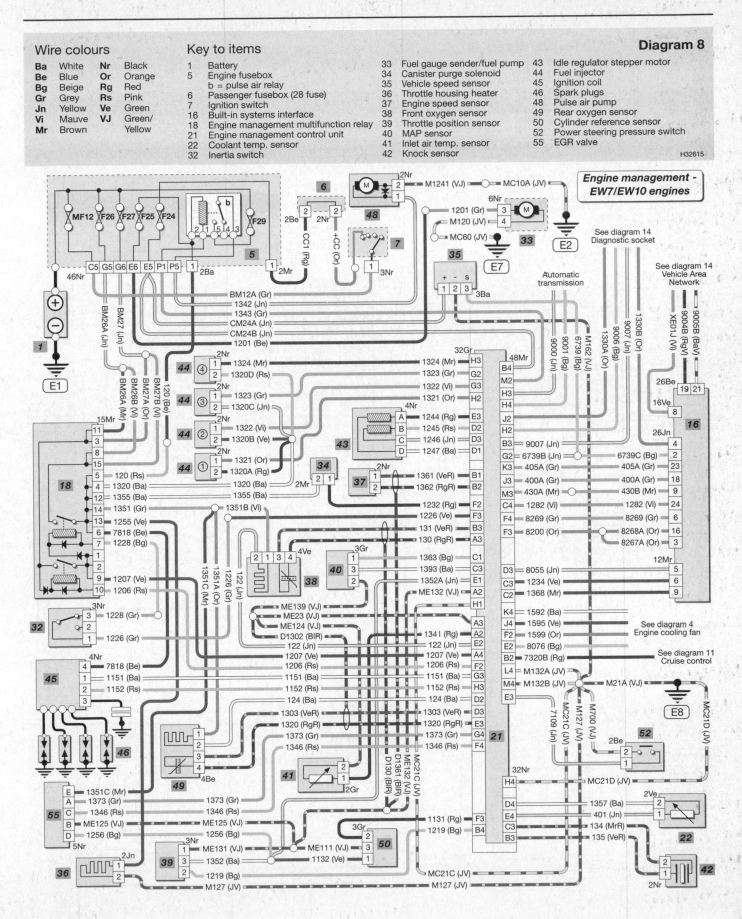

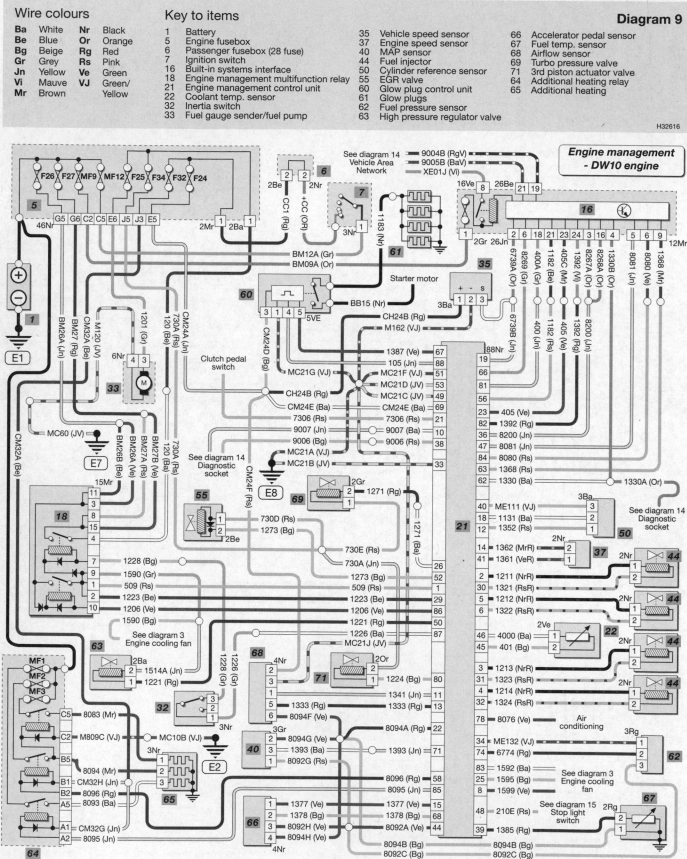

Diagram 9

Wire colours
Ba	White	Nr	Black
Be	Blue	Or	Orange
Bg	Beige	Rg	Red
Gr	Grey	Rs	Pink
Jn	Yellow	Ve	Green
Vi	Mauve	VJ	Green/Yellow
Mr	Brown		

Key to items
1 Battery
5 Engine fusebox
6 Passenger fusebox (28 fuse)
7 Ignition switch
16 Built-in systems interface
18 Engine management multifunction relay
21 Engine management control unit
22 Coolant temp. sensor
32 Inertia switch
33 Fuel gauge sender/fuel pump

35 Vehicle speed sensor
37 Engine speed sensor
40 MAP sensor
44 Fuel injector
50 Cylinder reference sensor
55 EGR valve
60 Glow plug control unit
61 Glow plugs
62 Fuel pressure sensor
63 High pressure regulator valve

66 Accelerator pedal sensor
67 Fuel temp. sensor
68 Airflow sensor
69 Turbo pressure valve
71 3rd piston actuator valve
64 Additional heating relay
65 Additional heating

Engine management - DW10 engine

H32616

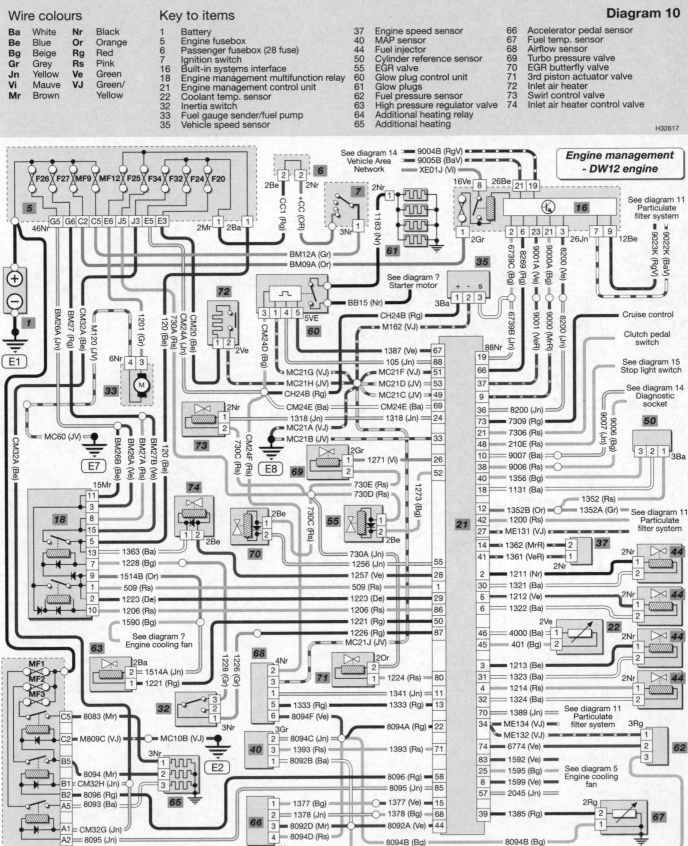

Wire colours

Ba	White	Nr	Black
Be	Blue	Or	Orange
Bg	Beige	Rg	Red
Gr	Grey	Rs	Pink
Jn	Yellow	Ve	Green
Vi	Mauve	VJ	Green/
Mr	Brown		Yellow

Key to items

1	Battery	37	Engine speed sensor	66	Accelerator pedal sensor
5	Engine fusebox	40	MAP sensor	67	Fuel temp. sensor
6	Passenger fusebox (28 fuse)	44	Fuel injector	68	Airflow sensor
7	Ignition switch	50	Cylinder reference sensor	69	Turbo pressure valve
16	Built-in systems interface	55	EGR valve	70	EGR butterfly valve
18	Engine management multifunction relay	60	Glow plug control unit	71	3rd piston actuator valve
21	Engine management control unit	61	Glow plugs	72	Inlet air heater
22	Coolant temp. sensor	62	Fuel pressure sensor	73	Swirl control valve
32	Inertia switch	63	High pressure regulator valve	74	Inlet air heater control valve
33	Fuel gauge sender/fuel pump	64	Additional heating relay		
35	Vehicle speed sensor	65	Additional heating		

Diagram 10

Engine management - DW12 engine

H32617

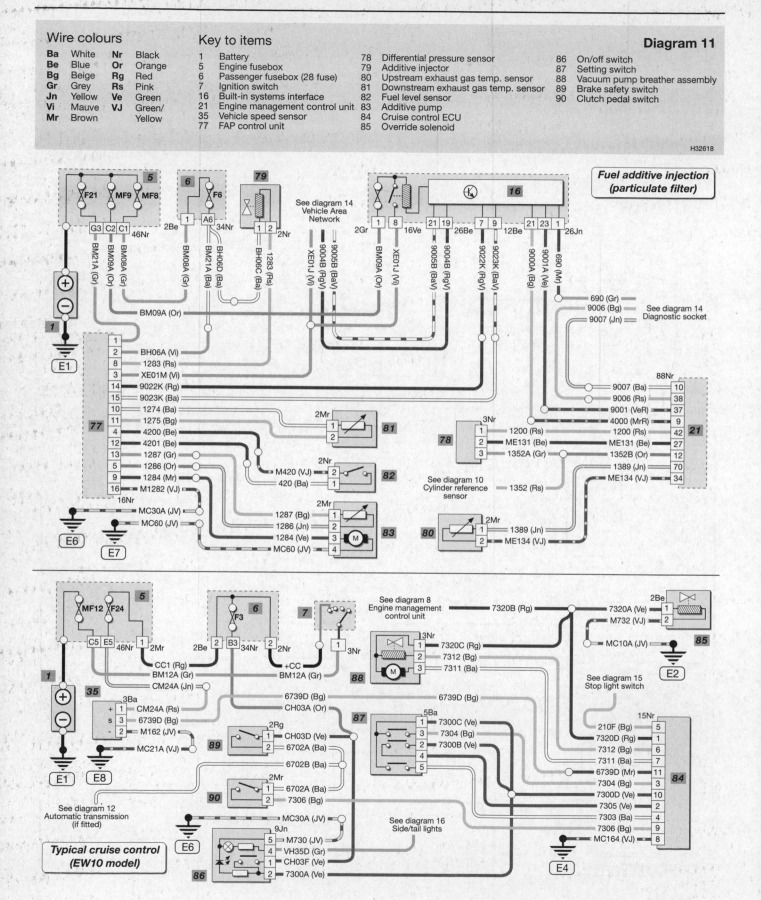

Wire colours

Ba	White	Nr	Black
Be	Blue	Or	Orange
Bg	Beige	Rg	Red
Gr	Grey	Rs	Pink
Jn	Yellow	Ve	Green
Vi	Mauve	VJ	Green/
Mr	Brown		Yellow

Key to items

1 Battery
5 Engine fusebox
6 Passenger fusebox (28 fuse)
7 Ignition switch
16 Built-in systems interface
21 Engine management control unit
35 Vehicle speed sensor
77 FAP control unit

78 Differential pressure sensor
79 Additive injector
80 Upstream exhaust gas temp. sensor
81 Downstream exhaust gas temp. sensor
82 Fuel level sensor
83 Additive pump
84 Cruise control ECU
85 Override solenoid

86 On/off switch
87 Setting switch
88 Vacuum pump breather assembly
89 Brake safety switch
90 Clutch pedal switch

Diagram 11

H32618

Fuel additive injection (particulate filter)

Typical cruise control (EW10 model)

Diagram 12

Wire colours

Ba	White	**Nr**	Black
Be	Blue	**Or**	Orange
Bg	Beige	**Rg**	Red
Gr	Grey	**Rs**	Pink
Jn	Yellow	**Ve**	Green
Vi	Mauve	**VJ**	Green/
Mr	Brown		Yellow

Key to items

1 Battery
5 Engine fusebox
  c = starter inhibitor relay
6 Passenger fusebox (28 fuse)
7 Ignition switch
16 Built-in systems interface
94 Transmission hydraulic block
95 Gear lever locking relay
96 Gear lever lock solenoid
97 Transmission mode switch
98 Selector lever illumination
99 Aurtomatic transmission control unit
100 Solenoid

H32619

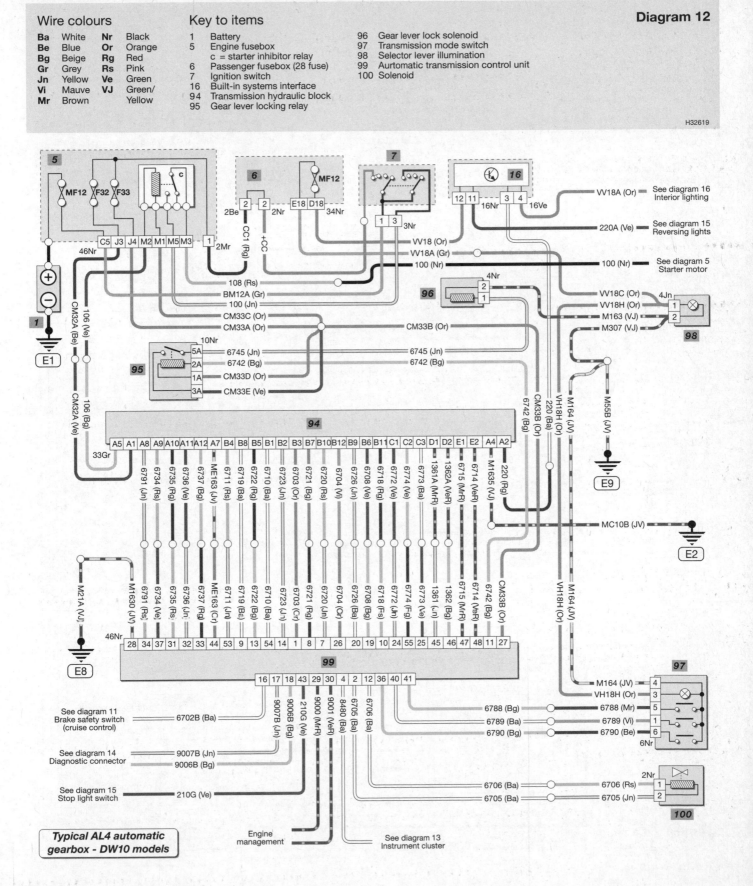

Typical AL4 automatic gearbox - DW10 models

Key to items

Diagram 13

1 = Battery
5 = Engine fusebox
6 = Passenger fusebox (28 fuse)
7 = Ignition switch
33 = Fuel gauge sender/fuel pump
102 = Instrument cluster
  a = Water in fuel warning light
  b = Airbag warning light
  c = Seatbelt warning light
  d = Fuel cap warning light
  e = Rear foglight warning light
  f = Pre-heat warning light
  g = Door ajar warning light
  h = Immobiliser warning light
  i = Handbrake/brake fluid warning light

102 = Instrument cluster cont.
  k = Engine management warning light
  l = Alternator warning light
  m = Low fuel warning light
  n = Stop warning light
  o = LH indicator warning light
  p = RH indicator warning light
  q = ABS warning light
  r = ESP warning light
  s = Particle filter warning light
  t = Instrument control unit
  u = Selection/program display
  v = Coolant temp. display
  w = Oil temp display
  x = LPG gauge

102 = Instrument cluster cont.
  y = Speedometer
  z = Tachometer
  a1 = Fuel gauge
  b1 = Oil level gauge
  c1 = Front foglight warning light
  d1 = Main beam warning light
  e1 = Dip beam warning light
  f1 = Side airbag warning light
  g1 = Low oil warning light
  h1 = LPG warning light
  i1 = low washer warning light
  j1 = Pad wear warning light
103 = Engine coolant level unit
104 = Water in fuel sensor

105 = Handbrake switch
106 = Low brake fluid switch
107 = Fuel cap switch
108 = Seatbelt switch
109 = Oil pressure switch
110 = Oil level sensor
111 = Oil temp. switch/oil temp. sensor
112 = Oil temp. sensor/oil level gauge sensor
113 = LH pad wear sensor
114 = RH pad wear sensor

H32620

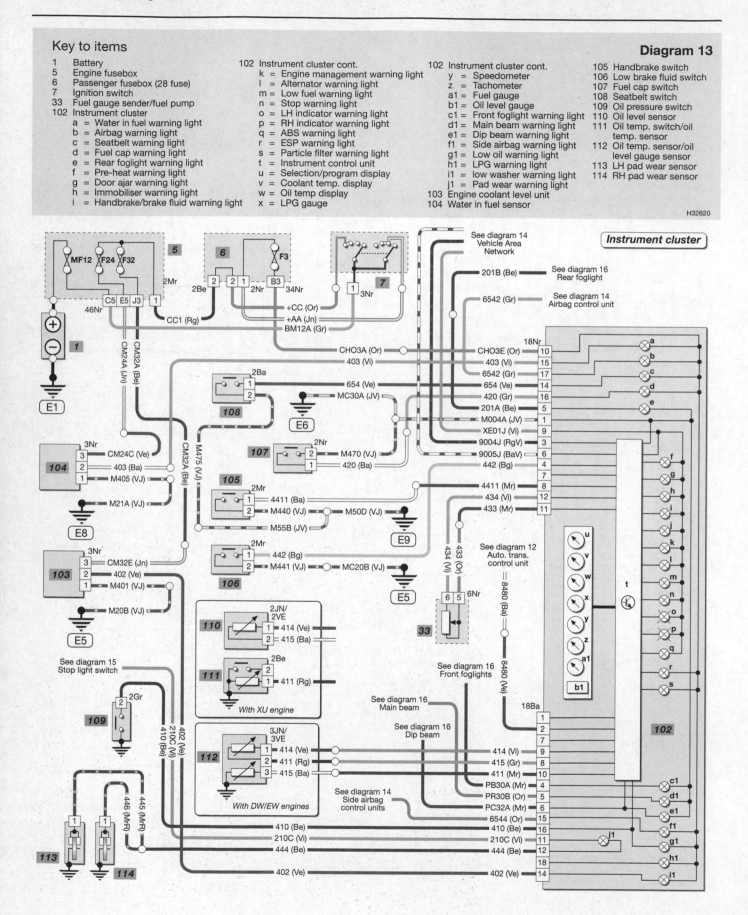

Wire colours

Ba	White	**Nr**	Black
Be	Blue	**Or**	Orange
Bg	Beige	**Rg**	Red
Gr	Grey	**Rs**	Pink
Jn	Yellow	**Ve**	Green
Vi	Mauve	**VJ**	Green/
Mr	Brown		Yellow

Key to items

1 Battery
5 Engine fusebox
6 Passenger fusebox (28 fuse)
7 Ignition switch
16 Built-in systems interface
102 Instrument cluster
118 Airbag control unit
119 LH side airbag control unit
120 RH side airbag control unit

121 LH side airbag control unit
122 LH side airbag
123 RH side airbag
124 Driver's airbag
125 Passenger's airbag
126 Passenger's airbag disable switch
127 Driver's seatbelt pretensioner
128 Passenger's seatbelt pretensioner
129 Transponder

130 Navigation control unit
131 Radio unit
132 CD player
133 Multifunction screen
134 Heater panel
135 Diagnostic connector

Diagram 14

H32621

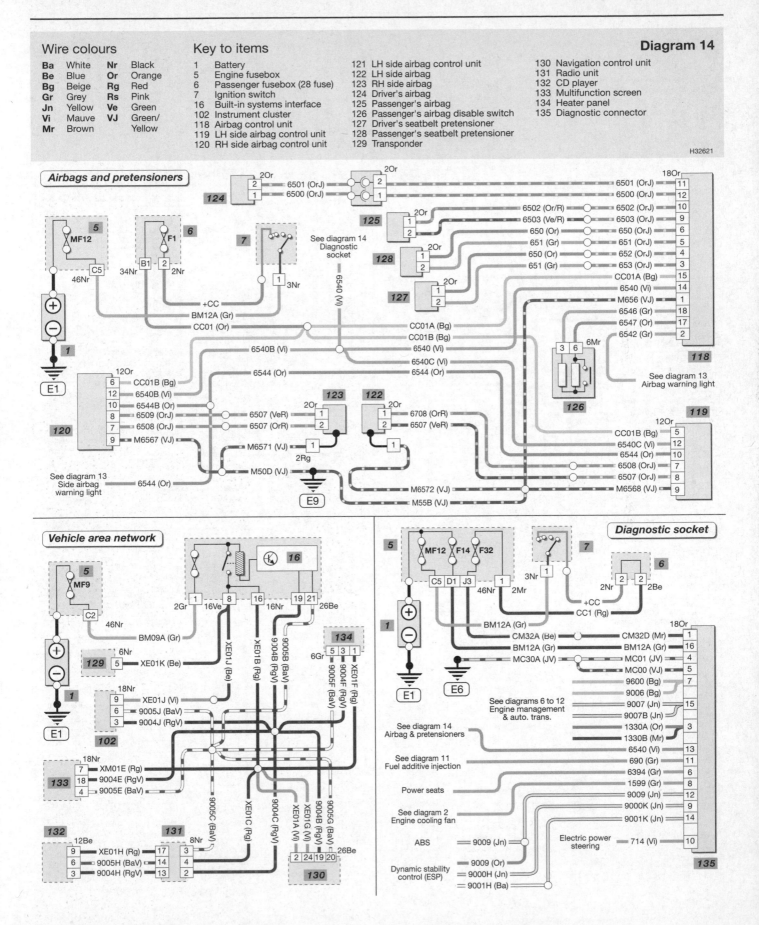

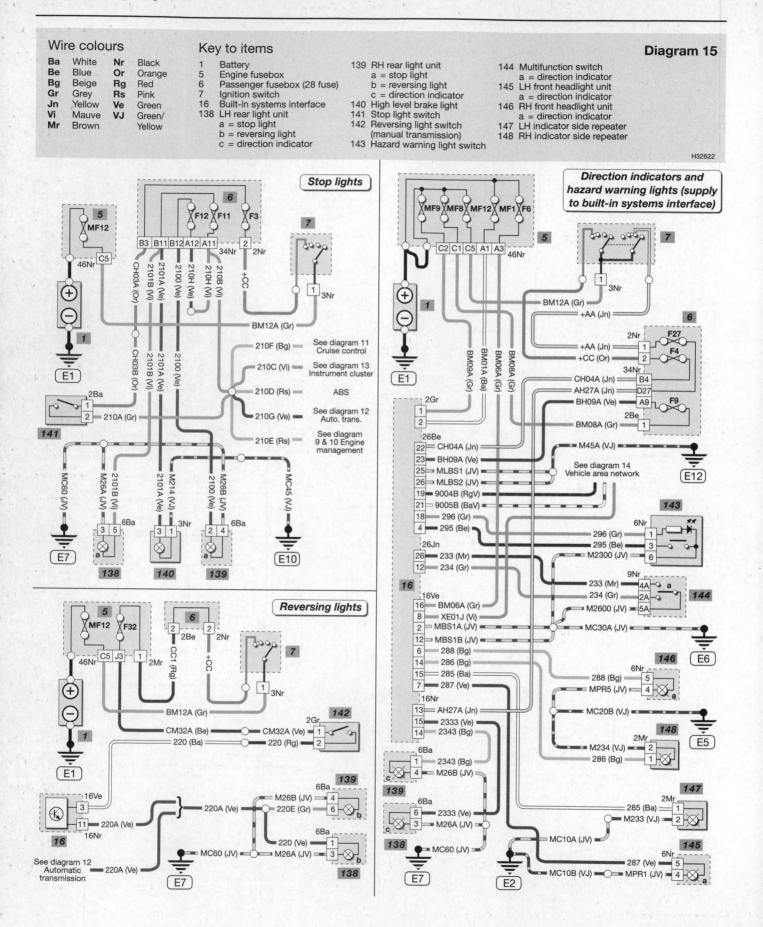

Wire colours

Ba	White	Nr	Black
Be	Blue	Or	Orange
Bg	Beige	Rg	Red
Gr	Grey	Rs	Pink
Jn	Yellow	Ve	Green
Vi	Mauve	VJ	Green/
Mr	Brown		Yellow

Key to items

1 Battery
5 Engine fusebox
6 Passenger fusebox (28 fuse)
7 Ignition switch
16 Built-in systems interface
138 LH rear light unit
  a = stop light
  b = reversing light
  c = direction indicator

139 RH rear light unit
  a = stop light
  b = reversing light
  c = direction indicator
140 High level brake light
141 Stop light switch
142 Reversing light switch
  (manual transmission)
143 Hazard warning light switch

144 Multifunction switch
  a = direction indicator
145 LH front headlight unit
  a = direction indicator
146 RH front headlight unit
  a = direction indicator
147 LH indicator side repeater
148 RH indicator side repeater

Diagram 15

H32622

Stop lights

Reversing lights

Direction indicators and hazard warning lights (supply to built-in systems interface)

Wire colours

Ba	White	Nr	Black
Be	Blue	Or	Orange
Bg	Beige	Rg	Red
Gr	Grey	Rs	Pink
Jn	Yellow	Ve	Green
Vi	Mauve	VJ	Green/
Mr	Brown		Yellow

Note:
Connector pin numbers may vary
for estate models (items 138 & 139).

Key to items

1	Battery
5	Engine fusebox
	c = front foglight relay
6	Passenger fusebox (28 fuse)
7	Ignition switch
16	Built-in systems interface
134	Heater panel
138	LH rear light unit
	d = foglight
	e = tail light
139	RH rear light unit
	d = foglight
	e = tail light

144	Multifunction switch cont.
	b = front/rear foglight
	c = side/headlight
	d = headlight dip/main
	e = headlight flasher
145	LH front headlight unit
	c = dipped beam
	d = main beam
146	RH front headlight unit
	c = dipped beam
	d = main beam
150	LH front foglight

151	RH front foglight
152	Passenger fusebox (12 fuse)
153	Number plate light
154	Passenger compartment air thermistor
155	Blower control module
156	Heater blower
157	Air inlet flap reduction motor

Diagram 16

H32623

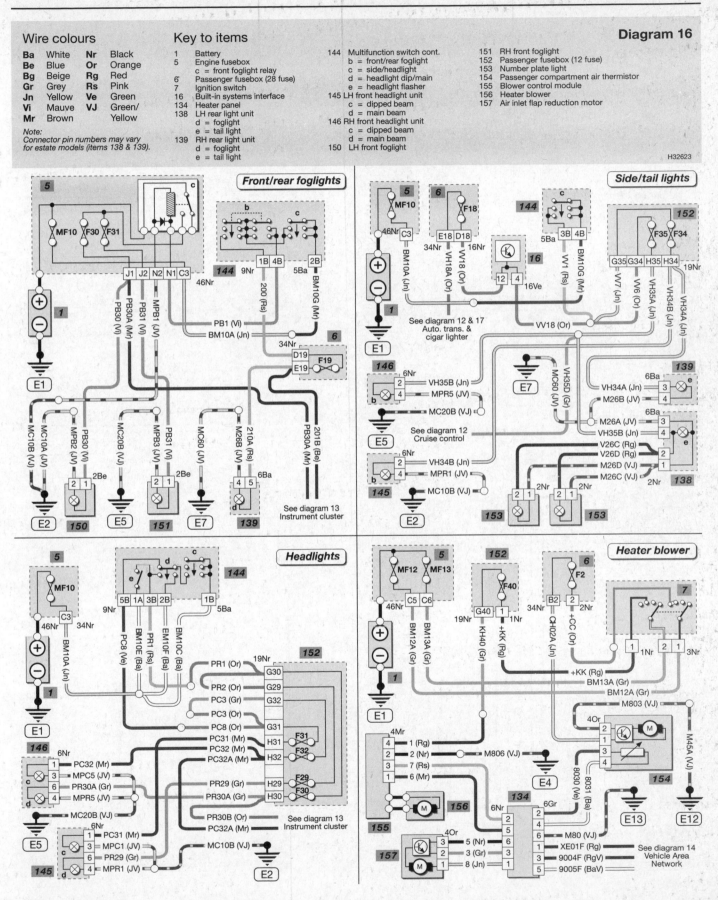

Front/rear foglights

Side/tail lights

Headlights

Heater blower

Wire colours

Ba	White	**Nr**	Black
Be	Blue	**Or**	Orange
Bg	Beige	**Rg**	Red
Gr	Grey	**Rs**	Pink
Jn	Yellow	**Ve**	Green
Vi	Mauve	**VJ**	Green/Yellow
Mr	Brown		

Key to items

1	Battery
5	Engine fusebox
6	Passenger fusebox (28 fuse)
7	Ignition switch
16	Built-in systems interface
160	Front courtesy light
161	Map reading light
162	LH vanity mirror light
163	RH vanity mirror light
164	Luggage compartment light
165	Luggage compartment light switch
166	Rear courtesy light
167	Glovebox light
168	Glovebox light switch
169	Door tread courtesy light
170	LH front door lock
171	LH rear door lock
172	RH front door lock
173	RH rear door lock
174	Cigar lighter
175	Ashtray light
176	Electric window/mirror switch
177	LH door mirror assembly
178	RH door mirror assembly

Diagram 17

H32624

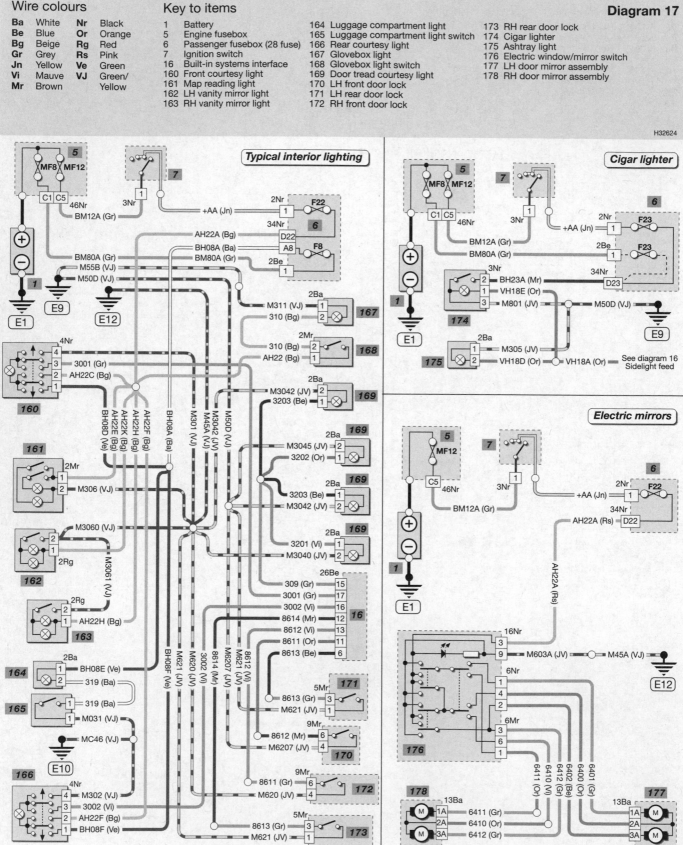

Typical interior lighting

Cigar lighter

Electric mirrors

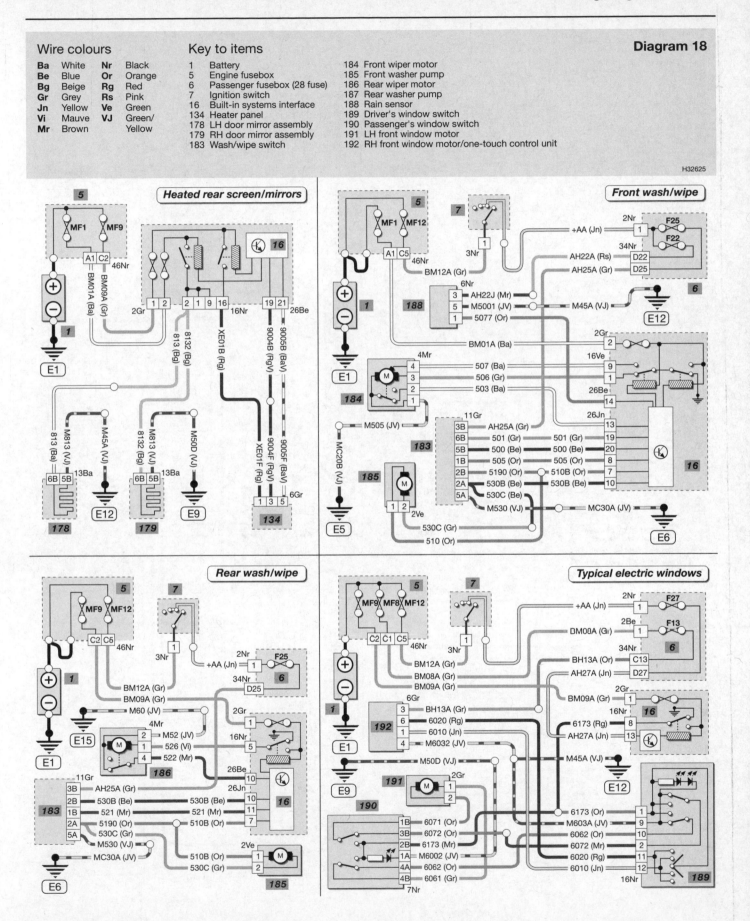

Wire colours

Ba	White	**Nr**	Black
Be	Blue	**Or**	Orange
Bg	Beige	**Rg**	Red
Gr	Grey	**Rs**	Pink
Jn	Yellow	**Ve**	Green
Vi	Mauve	**VJ**	Green/
Mr	Brown		Yellow

Key to items

1 Battery
5 Engine fusebox
6 Passenger fusebox (28 fuse)
7 Ignition switch
16 Built-in systems interface
134 Heater panel
178 LH door mirror assembly
179 RH door mirror assembly
183 Wash/wipe switch

184 Front wiper motor
185 Front washer pump
186 Rear wiper motor
187 Rear washer pump
188 Rain sensor
189 Driver's window switch
190 Passenger's window switch
191 LH front window motor
192 RH front window motor/one-touch control unit

Diagram 18

H32625

Heated rear screen/mirrors

Front wash/wipe

Rear wash/wipe

Typical electric windows

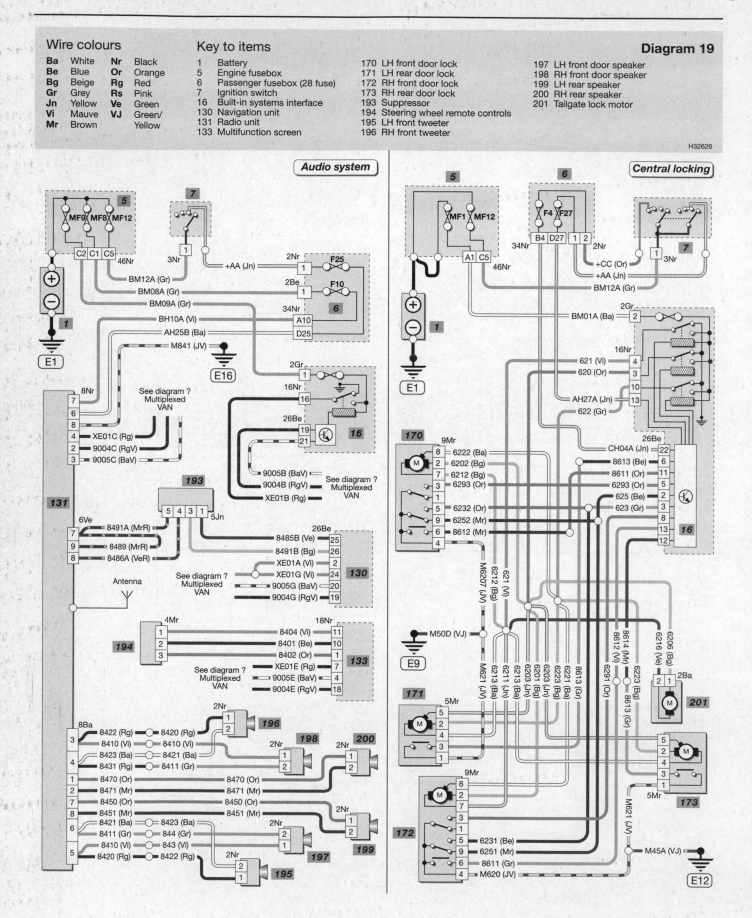

Wire colours

Ba	White	Nr	Black
Be	Blue	Or	Orange
Bg	Beige	Rg	Red
Gr	Grey	Rs	Pink
Jn	Yellow	Ve	Green
Vi	Mauve	VJ	Green/
Mr	Brown		Yellow

Key to items

1 Battery
5 Engine fusebox
6 Passenger fusebox (28 fuse)
7 Ignition switch
16 Built-in systems interface
130 Navigation unit
131 Radio unit
133 Multifunction screen

170 LH front door lock
171 LH rear door lock
172 RH front door lock
173 RH rear door lock
193 Suppressor
194 Steering wheel remote controls
195 LH front tweeter
196 RH front tweeter

197 LH front door speaker
198 RH front door speaker
199 LH rear speaker
200 RH rear speaker
201 Tailgate lock motor

Diagram 19

H32626

Audio system

Central locking

Dimensions and weights	**REF•1**	Disconnecting the battery	**REF•7**
Conversion factors	**REF•2**	Tools and working facilities	**REF•8**
Buying spare parts	**REF•3**	MOT test checks	**REF•10**
Vehicle identification numbers	**REF•4**	Fault finding	**REF•14**
General repair procedures	**REF•5**	Glossary of technical terms	**REF•25**
Jacking and vehicle support	**REF•6**	Index	**REF•30**

Dimensions and weights

Note: *All figures are approximate, and may vary according to model. Refer to manufacturer's data for exact figures.*

Dimensions

Overall length:
Saloon	4600 mm
Estate	4740 mm
Overall width (excluding mirrors)	1765 mm

Overall height (unladen):
Saloon	1415 mm
Estate	1505 mm
Wheelbase	2700 mm

Weights

Kerb weight*:

Saloon models:
1.8 litre petrol	1260 kg
2.0 litre petrol	1350 kg

2.0 litre diesel:
RHY models	1300 kg
RHZ models	1410 kg
2.2 litre diesel	1410 kg

Estate models:
1.8 litre petrol	1310 kg
2.0 litre petrol	1400 kg

2.0 litre diesel:
RHY models	1380 kg
HHZ models	1425 kg
2.2 litre diesel	1460 kg

Maximum gross vehicle weight*:

Saloon models:
1.8 litre petrol	1790 kg
2.0 litre petrol	1890 kg

2.0 litre diesel:
RHY models	1870 kg
RHZ models	1950 kg
2.2 litre diesel	1950 kg

Estate models:
1.8 litre petrol	1960 kg
2.0 litre petrol	2050 kg

2.0 litre diesel:
RHY models	2030 kg
RHZ models	2075 kg
2.2 litre diesel	2110 kg
Maximum towing weight (braked trailer)	1300 to 1500 kg
Maximum trailer nose weight	80 kg

* *For automatic transmission models add 20 kg*

Conversion factors

Length (distance)

Inches (in)	x 25.4	=	Millimetres (mm)	x 0.0394	= Inches (in)
Feet (ft)	x 0.305	=	Metres (m)	x 3.281	= Feet (ft)
Miles	x 1.609	=	Kilometres (km)	x 0.621	= Miles

Volume (capacity)

Cubic inches (cu in; in^3)	x 16.387	=	Cubic centimetres (cc; cm^3)	x 0.061	= Cubic inches (cu in; in^3)
Imperial pints (Imp pt)	x 0.568	=	Litres (l)	x 1.76	= Imperial pints (Imp pt)
Imperial quarts (Imp qt)	x 1.137	=	Litres (l)	x 0.88	= Imperial quarts (Imp qt)
Imperial quarts (Imp qt)	x 1.201	=	US quarts (US qt)	x 0.833	= Imperial quarts (Imp qt)
US quarts (US qt)	x 0.946	=	Litres (l)	x 1.057	= US quarts (US qt)
Imperial gallons (Imp gal)	x 4.546	=	Litres (l)	x 0.22	= Imperial gallons (Imp gal)
Imperial gallons (Imp gal)	x 1.201	=	US gallons (US gal)	x 0.833	= Imperial gallons (Imp gal)
US gallons (US gal)	x 3.785	=	Litres (l)	x 0.264	= US gallons (US gal)

Mass (weight)

Ounces (oz)	x 28.35	=	Grams (g)	x 0.035	= Ounces (oz)
Pounds (lb)	x 0.454	=	Kilograms (kg)	x 2.205	= Pounds (lb)

Force

Ounces-force (ozf; oz)	x 0.278	=	Newtons (N)	x 3.6	= Ounces-force (ozf; oz)
Pounds-force (lbf; lb)	x 4.448	=	Newtons (N)	x 0.225	= Pounds-force (lbf; lb)
Newtons (N)	x 0.1	=	Kilograms-force (kgf; kg)	x 9.81	= Newtons (N)

Pressure

Pounds-force per square inch (psi; lbf/in^2; lb/in^2)	x 0.070	=	Kilograms-force per square centimetre (kgf/cm^2; kg/cm^2)	x 14.223	= Pounds-force per square inch (psi; lbf/in^2; lb/in^2)
Pounds-force per square inch (psi; lbf/in^2; lb/in^2)	x 0.068	=	Atmospheres (atm)	x 14.696	= Pounds-force per square inch (psi; lbf/in^2; lb/in^2)
Pounds-force per square inch (psi; lbf/in^2; lb/in^2)	x 0.069	=	Bars	x 14.5	= Pounds-force per square inch (psi; lbf/in^2; lb/in^2)
Pounds-force per square inch (psi; lbf/in^2; lb/in^2)	x 6.895	=	Kilopascals (kPa)	x 0.145	= Pounds-force per square inch (psi; lbf/in^2; lb/in^2)
Kilopascals (kPa)	x 0.01	=	Kilograms-force per square centimetre (kgf/cm^2; kg/cm^2)	x 98.1	= Kilopascals (kPa)
Millibar (mbar)	x 100	=	Pascals (Pa)	x 0.01	= Millibar (mbar)
Millibar (mbar)	x 0.0145	=	Pounds-force per square inch (psi; lbf/in^2; lb/in^2)	x 68.947	= Millibar (mbar)
Millibar (mbar)	x 0.75	=	Millimetres of mercury (mmHg)	x 1.333	= Millibar (mbar)
Millibar (mbar)	x 0.401	=	Inches of water (inH$_2$O)	x 2.491	= Millibar (mbar)
Millimetres of mercury (mmHg)	x 0.535	=	Inches of water (inH$_2$O)	x 1.868	= Millimetres of mercury (mmHg)
Inches of water (inH$_2$O)	x 0.036	=	Pounds-force per square inch (psi; lbf/in^2; lb/in^2)	x 27.68	= Inches of water (inH$_2$O)

Torque (moment of force)

Pounds-force inches (lbf in; lb in)	x 1.152	=	Kilograms-force centimetre (kgf cm; kg cm)	x 0.868	= Pounds-force inches (lbf in; lb in)
Pounds-force inches (lbf in; lb in)	x 0.113	=	Newton metres (Nm)	x 8.85	= Pounds-force inches (lbf in; lb in)
Pounds-force inches (lbf in; lb in)	x 0.083	=	Pounds-force feet (lbf ft; lb ft)	x 12	= Pounds-force inches (lbf in; lb in)
Pounds-force feet (lbf ft; lb ft)	x 0.138	=	Kilograms-force metres (kgf m; kg m)	x 7.233	= Pounds-force feet (lbf ft; lb ft)
Pounds-force feet (lbf ft; lb ft)	x 1.356	=	Newton metres (Nm)	x 0.738	= Pounds-force feet (lbf ft; lb ft)
Newton metres (Nm)	x 0.102	=	Kilograms-force metres (kgf m; kg m)	x 9.804	= Newton metres (Nm)

Power

Horsepower (hp)	x 745.7	=	Watts (W)	x 0.0013	= Horsepower (hp)

Velocity (speed)

Miles per hour (miles/hr; mph)	x 1.609	=	Kilometres per hour (km/hr; kph)	x 0.621	= Miles per hour (miles/hr; mph)

Fuel consumption*

Miles per gallon, Imperial (mpg)	x 0.354	=	Kilometres per litre (km/l)	x 2.825	= Miles per gallon, Imperial (mpg)
Miles per gallon, US (mpg)	x 0.425	=	Kilometres per litre (km/l)	x 2.352	= Miles per gallon, US (mpg)

Temperature

Degrees Fahrenheit = (°C x 1.8) + 32   Degrees Celsius (Degrees Centigrade; °C) = (°F - 32) x 0.56

It is common practice to convert from miles per gallon (mpg) to litres/100 kilometres (l/100km), where mpg x l/100 km = 282

Spare parts are available from many sources, including maker's appointed garages, accessory shops, and motor factors. To be sure of obtaining the correct parts, it will sometimes be necessary to quote the vehicle identification number. If possible, it can also be useful to take the old parts along for positive identification. Items such as starter motors and alternators may be available under a service exchange scheme – any parts returned should be clean.

Our advice regarding spare parts is as follows.

Officially appointed garages

This is the best source of parts which are peculiar to your car, and which are not otherwise generally available (eg, badges, interior trim, certain body panels, etc). It is also the only place at which you should buy parts if the vehicle is still under warranty.

Accessory shops

These are very good places to buy materials and components needed for the maintenance of your car (oil, air and fuel filters, light bulbs, drivebelts, greases, brake pads, touch-up paint, etc). Components of this nature sold by a reputable shop are usually of the same standard as those used by the car manufacturer.

Besides components, these shops also sell tools and general accessories, usually have convenient opening hours, charge lower prices, and can often be found close to home. Some accessory shops have parts counters where components needed for almost any repair job can be purchased or ordered.

Motor factors

Good factors will stock the more important components which wear out comparatively quickly, and can sometimes supply individual components needed for the overhaul of a larger assembly (eg, brake seals and hydraulic parts, bearing shells, pistons, valves). They may also handle work such as cylinder block reboring, crankshaft regrinding, etc.

Tyre and exhaust specialists

These outlets may be independent, or members of a local or national chain. They frequently offer competitive prices when compared with a main dealer or local garage, but it will pay to obtain several quotes before making a decision. When researching prices, also be sure to ask what 'extras' may be added – for instance, fitting a new valve, balancing the wheel, and checking the tracking (front wheels) are all commonly charged on top of the price of a new tyre.

Other sources

Beware of parts or materials obtained from market stalls, car boot sales or similar outlets. Such items are not invariably sub-standard, but there is little chance of compensation if they do prove unsatisfactory. in the case of safety-critical components such as brake pads, there is the risk not only of financial loss, but also of an accident causing injury or death.

Second-hand components or assemblies obtained from a car breaker can be a good buy in some circumstances, but this sort of purchase is best made by the experienced DIY mechanic.

Modifications are a continuing and unpublicised process in vehicle manufacture, quite apart from major model changes. Spare parts manuals and lists are compiled upon a numerical basis, the individual vehicle identification numbers being essential to correct identification of the component concerned.

When ordering spare parts, always give as much information as possible. Quote the car model, year of manufacture and registration, chassis and engine numbers as appropriate.

The *Vehicle Identification Number (VIN)* plate is riveted to the right-hand end of the bonnet lock crossmember and is visible once the bonnet has been opened. The vehicle identification (chassis) number is also stamped onto the top of the right-hand side of the engine compartment bulkhead and is stamped on a plate attached to the top, left-hand end of the facia (visible through the windscreen) **(see illustrations)**. On certain models a *Homologation plate* is attached to the left-hand end of the bonnet locking crossmember.

The *engine number and code* can be found on the front of the cylinder block. On petrol engine models the number and code are stamped onto the cylinder block surface; on XU7JP4 engines it can be found at the bottom, left-hand corner of the block, and EW7 and EW10 engines it is situated just behind the power steering pump. On diesel engine models the engine number and code are stamped onto the lower part of the cylinder block surface, just to the left (as seen from the drivers seat) of the oil filter **(see illustrations)**.

The *paint code* is stamped onto the side of the left-hand front suspension strut mounting turret in the engine compartment.

The vehicle identification number (VIN) plate (arrowed) is riveted to the right-hand end of the bonnet lock crossmember

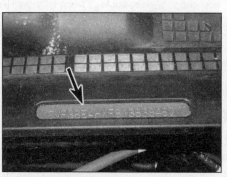

The chassis number (arrowed) is also stamped onto the top of the engine compartment bulkhead

The engine number and code can be found on the front of the cylinder block (arrowed) on 2.0 litre diesel engine . . .

. . . and on the front of the cylinder block (arrowed) on 2.2 litre diesel engines (starter motor removed for clarity)

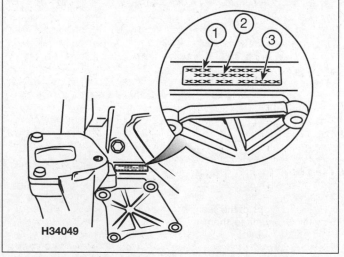

H34049

The engine number and code on the front of the cylinder block (EW7 and EW10 petrol engines)

1 Legislation type and Engine code
2 Component number
3 Serial number

Whenever servicing, repair or overhaul work is carried out on the car or its components, observe the following procedures and instructions. This will assist in carrying out the operation efficiently and to a professional standard of workmanship.

Joint mating faces and gaskets

When separating components at their mating faces, never insert screwdrivers or similar implements into the joint between the faces in order to prise them apart. This can cause severe damage which results in oil leaks, coolant leaks, etc upon reassembly. Separation is usually achieved by tapping along the joint with a soft-faced hammer in order to break the seal. However, note that this method may not be suitable where dowels are used for component location.

Where a gasket is used between the mating faces of two components, a new one must be fitted on reassembly; fit it dry unless otherwise stated in the repair procedure. Make sure that the mating faces are clean and dry, with all traces of old gasket removed. When cleaning a joint face, use a tool which is unlikely to score or damage the face, and remove any burrs or nicks with an oilstone or fine file.

Make sure that tapped holes are cleaned with a pipe cleaner, and keep them free of jointing compound, if this is being used, unless specifically instructed otherwise.

Ensure that all orifices, channels or pipes are clear, and blow through them, preferably using compressed air.

Oil seals

Oil seals can be removed by levering them out with a wide flat-bladed screwdriver or similar implement. Alternatively, a number of self-tapping screws may be screwed into the seal, and these used as a purchase for pliers or some similar device in order to pull the seal free.

Whenever an oil seal is removed from its working location, either individually or as part of an assembly, it should be renewed.

The very fine sealing lip of the seal is easily damaged, and will not seal if the surface it contacts is not completely clean and free from scratches, nicks or grooves. If the original sealing surface of the component cannot be restored, and the manufacturer has not made provision for slight relocation of the seal relative to the sealing surface, the component should be renewed.

Protect the lips of the seal from any surface which may damage them in the course of fitting. Use tape or a conical sleeve where possible. Lubricate the seal lips with oil before fitting and, on dual-lipped seals, fill the space between the lips with grease.

Unless otherwise stated, oil seals must be fitted with their sealing lips toward the lubricant to be sealed.

Use a tubular drift or block of wood of the appropriate size to install the seal and, if the seal housing is shouldered, drive the seal down to the shoulder. If the seal housing is unshouldered, the seal should be fitted with its face flush with the housing top face (unless otherwise instructed).

Screw threads and fastenings

Seized nuts, bolts and screws are quite a common occurrence where corrosion has set in, and the use of penetrating oil or releasing fluid will often overcome this problem if the offending item is soaked for a while before attempting to release it. The use of an impact driver may also provide a means of releasing such stubborn fastening devices, when used in conjunction with the appropriate screwdriver bit or socket. If none of these methods works, it may be necessary to resort to the careful application of heat, or the use of a hacksaw or nut splitter device.

Studs are usually removed by locking two nuts together on the threaded part, and then using a spanner on the lower nut to unscrew the stud. Studs or bolts which have broken off below the surface of the component in which they are mounted can sometimes be removed using a stud extractor. Always ensure that a blind tapped hole is completely free from oil, grease, water or other fluid before installing the bolt or stud. Failure to do this could cause the housing to crack due to the hydraulic action of the bolt or stud as it is screwed in.

When tightening a castellated nut to accept a split pin, tighten the nut to the specified torque, where applicable, and then tighten further to the next split pin hole. Never slacken the nut to align the split pin hole, unless stated in the repair procedure.

When checking or retightening a nut or bolt to a specified torque setting, slacken the nut or bolt by a quarter of a turn, and then retighten to the specified setting. However, this should not be attempted where angular tightening has been used.

For some screw fastenings, notably cylinder head bolts or nuts, torque wrench settings are no longer specified for the latter stages of tightening, "angle-tightening" being called up instead. Typically, a fairly low torque wrench setting will be applied to the bolts/nuts in the correct sequence, followed by one or more stages of tightening through specified angles.

Locknuts, locktabs and washers

Any fastening which will rotate against a component or housing during tightening should always have a washer between it and the relevant component or housing.

Spring or split washers should always be renewed when they are used to lock a critical component such as a big-end bearing retaining bolt or nut. Locktabs which are folded over to retain a nut or bolt should always be renewed.

Self-locking nuts can be re-used in non-critical areas, providing resistance can be felt when the locking portion passes over the bolt or stud thread. However, it should be noted that self-locking stiffnuts tend to lose their effectiveness after long periods of use, and should then be renewed as a matter of course.

Split pins must always be replaced with new ones of the correct size for the hole.

When thread-locking compound is found on the threads of a fastener which is to be re-used, it should be cleaned off with a wire brush and solvent, and fresh compound applied on reassembly.

Special tools

Some repair procedures in this manual entail the use of special tools such as a press, two or three-legged pullers, spring compressors, etc. Wherever possible, suitable readily-available alternatives to the manufacturer's special tools are described, and are shown in use. In some instances, where no alternative is possible, it has been necessary to resort to the use of a manufacturer's tool, and this has been done for reasons of safety as well as the efficient completion of the repair operation. Unless you are highly-skilled and have a thorough understanding of the procedures described, never attempt to bypass the use of any special tool when the procedure described specifies its use. Not only is there a very great risk of personal injury, but expensive damage could be caused to the components involved.

Environmental considerations

When disposing of used engine oil, brake fluid, antifreeze, etc, give due consideration to any detrimental environmental effects. Do not, for instance, pour any of the above liquids down drains into the general sewage system, or onto the ground to soak away. Many local council refuse tips provide a facility for waste oil disposal, as do some garages. If none of these facilities are available, consult your local Environmental Health Department, or the National Rivers Authority, for further advice.

With the universal tightening-up of legislation regarding the emission of environmentally-harmful substances from motor vehicles, most vehicles have tamperproof devices fitted to the main adjustment points of the fuel system. These devices are primarily designed to prevent unqualified persons from adjusting the fuel/air mixture, with the chance of a consequent increase in toxic emissions. If such devices are found during servicing or overhaul, they should, wherever possible, be renewed or refitted in accordance with the manufacturer's requirements or current legislation.

OIL CARE
FOLLOW THE CODE
OIL BANK LINE
0800 66 33 66
www.oilbankline.org.uk

Note: It is antisocial and illegal to dump oil down the drain. To find the location of your local oil recycling bank, call this number free.

The jack supplied with the vehicle tool kit should only be used for changing the roadwheels – see *Wheel changing* at the front of this manual. When carrying out any other kind of work, raise the vehicle using a hydraulic (or 'trolley') jack, and always supplement the jack with axle stands positioned under the vehicle jacking points.

To raise the front of the vehicle, position the jack head underneath the centre of the front suspension subframe. Lift the vehicle to the required height and support it on axle stands positioned underneath the vehicle jacking points on the sills **(see illustration)**.

To raise the rear of the vehicle, position the jack head underneath the rear suspension lower arm, directly beneath the coil spring. Lift the vehicle to the required height and support it on axle stands positioned underneath the vehicle jacking points on the sills **(see illustration)**.

The jack supplied with the vehicle locates with the jacking points on the sills. Ensure that the jack head is correctly engaged before attempting to raise the vehicle.

Never work under, around, or near a raised vehicle, unless it is adequately supported in at least two places.

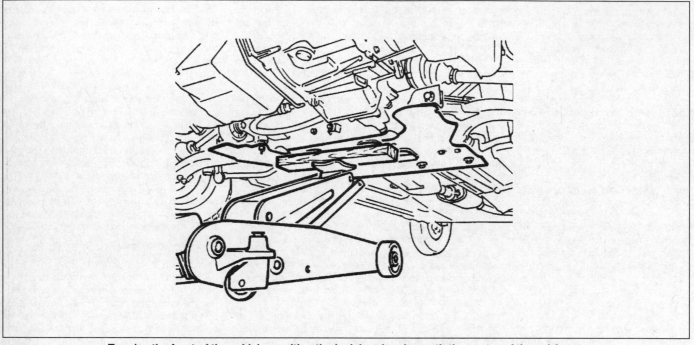

To raise the front of the vehicle, position the jack head underneath the centre of the subframe

Note the use of the block of wood placed on the jack head

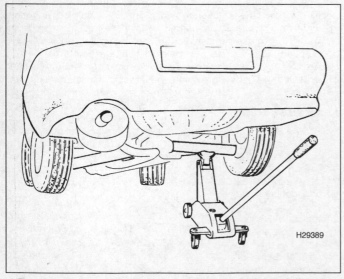

To raise the rear of the vehicle, position the jack head directly underneath one of the rear suspension lower arms

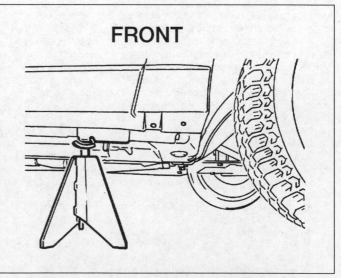

FRONT

Axle stands should be placed under the strengthened part of the sill (this is the jacking point when changing a wheel – see *Wheel changing* at the front of this manual)

1 Prior to disconnecting the battery, the alarm system must be deactivated as described in paragraph 2. Failure to deactivate the alarm will lead to the siren sounding when the battery is disconnected. Once the battery is reconnected, reactivate the alarm using the remote central locking unit.

2 To deactivate the complete alarm system, switch on the ignition switch and then depress the alarm switch on the centre console and hold for approximately two seconds. The alarm indicator light should then flash rapidly for three seconds, indicating the alarm is disarmed. To reactivate the system, simply lock then unlock the vehicle using the remote transmitter; the alarm will be functional again the next time the vehicle is locked with the remote control.

3 The battery is located on the front left-hand side of the engine compartment.

4 Lift off the battery cover then slacken the battery negative (earth) terminal connector (coloured green). Lift the terminal connector off the battery post.

5 The radio/cassette/CD player/autochanger unit fitted as standard equipment by Peugeot is equipped with an anti-theft system, to deter thieves. If the power source is disconnected, the radio/cassette will automatically recode itself as long as it is still fitted to the correct vehicle. If the unit is removed it will not operate in another vehicle.

Lift off the battery cover . . .

. . . then slacken the battery negative (earth) terminal connector (coloured green). Lift the terminal connector off the battery post

Introduction

A selection of good tools is a fundamental requirement for anyone contemplating the maintenance and repair of a motor vehicle. For the owner who does not possess any, their purchase will prove a considerable expense, offsetting some of the savings made by doing-it-yourself. However, provided that the tools purchased meet the relevant national safety standards and are of good quality, they will last for many years and prove an extremely worthwhile investment.

To help the average owner to decide which tools are needed to carry out the various tasks detailed in this manual, we have compiled three lists of tools under the following headings: *Maintenance and minor repair, Repair and overhaul,* and *Special.* Newcomers to practical mechanics should start off with the *Maintenance and minor repair* tool kit, and confine themselves to the simpler jobs around the vehicle. Then, as confidence and experience grow, more difficult tasks can be undertaken, with extra tools being purchased as, and when, they are needed. In this way, a *Maintenance and minor repair* tool kit can be built up into a *Repair and overhaul* tool kit over a considerable period of time, without any major cash outlays. The experienced do-it-yourselfer will have a tool kit good enough for most repair and overhaul procedures, and will add tools from the *Special* category when it is felt that the expense is justified by the amount of use to which these tools will be put.

Maintenance and minor repair tool kit

The tools given in this list should be considered as a minimum requirement if routine maintenance, servicing and minor repair operations are to be undertaken. We recommend the purchase of combination spanners (ring one end, open-ended the other); although more expensive than open-ended ones, they do give the advantages of both types of spanner.

- [ ] *Combination spanners:*
  Metric - 8 to 19 mm inclusive
- [ ] *Adjustable spanner - 35 mm jaw (approx.)*
- [ ] *Spark plug spanner (with rubber insert) - petrol models*
- [ ] *Spark plug gap adjustment tool - petrol models*
- [ ] *Set of feeler gauges*
- [ ] *Brake bleed nipple spanner*
- [ ] *Screwdrivers:*
  Flat blade - 100 mm long x 6 mm dia
  Cross blade - 100 mm long x 6 mm dia
  Torx - various sizes (not all vehicles)
- [ ] *Combination pliers*
- [ ] *Hacksaw (junior)*
- [ ] *Tyre pump*
- [ ] *Tyre pressure gauge*
- [ ] *Oil can*
- [ ] *Oil filter removal tool*
- [ ] *Fine emery cloth*
- [ ] *Wire brush (small)*
- [ ] *Funnel (medium size)*
- [ ] *Sump drain plug key (not all vehicles)*

Repair and overhaul tool kit

These tools are virtually essential for anyone undertaking any major repairs to a motor vehicle, and are additional to those given in the *Maintenance and minor repair* list. Included in this list is a comprehensive set of sockets. Although these are expensive, they will be found invaluable as they are so versatile - particularly if various drives are included in the set. We recommend the half-inch square-drive type, as this can be used with most proprietary torque wrenches.

The tools in this list will sometimes need to be supplemented by tools from the *Special* list:

- [ ] *Sockets (or box spanners) to cover range in previous list (including Torx sockets)*
- [ ] *Reversible ratchet drive (for use with sockets)*
- [ ] *Extension piece, 250 mm (for use with sockets)*
- [ ] *Universal joint (for use with sockets)*
- [ ] *Flexible handle or sliding T "breaker bar" (for use with sockets)*
- [ ] *Torque wrench (for use with sockets)*
- [ ] *Self-locking grips*
- [ ] *Ball pein hammer*
- [ ] *Soft-faced mallet (plastic or rubber)*
- [ ] *Screwdrivers:*
  Flat blade - long & sturdy, short (chubby), and narrow (electrician's) types
  Cross blade – long & sturdy, and short (chubby) types
- [ ] *Pliers:*
  Long-nosed
  Side cutters (electrician's)
  Circlip (internal and external)
- [ ] *Cold chisel - 25 mm*
- [ ] *Scriber*
- [ ] *Scraper*
- [ ] *Centre-punch*
- [ ] *Pin punch*
- [ ] *Hacksaw*
- [ ] *Brake hose clamp*
- [ ] *Brake/clutch bleeding kit*
- [ ] *Selection of twist drills*
- [ ] *Steel rule/straight-edge*
- [ ] *Allen keys (inc. splined/Torx type)*
- [ ] *Selection of files*
- [ ] *Wire brush*
- [ ] *Axle stands*
- [ ] *Jack (strong trolley or hydraulic type)*
- [ ] *Light with extension lead*
- [ ] *Universal electrical multi-meter*

Sockets and reversible ratchet drive

Brake bleeding kit

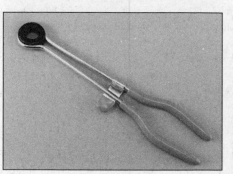

Torx key, socket and bit

Hose clamp

Angular-tightening gauge

Special tools

The tools in this list are those which are not used regularly, are expensive to buy, or which need to be used in accordance with their manufacturers' instructions. Unless relatively difficult mechanical jobs are undertaken frequently, it will not be economic to buy many of these tools. Where this is the case, you could consider clubbing together with friends (or joining a motorists' club) to make a joint purchase, or borrowing the tools against a deposit from a local garage or tool hire specialist. It is worth noting that many of the larger DIY superstores now carry a large range of special tools for hire at modest rates.

The following list contains only those tools and instruments freely available to the public, and not those special tools produced by the vehicle manufacturer specifically for its dealer network. You will find occasional references to these manufacturers' special tools in the text of this manual. Generally, an alternative method of doing the job without the vehicle manufacturers' special tool is given. However, sometimes there is no alternative to using them. Where this is the case and the relevant tool cannot be bought or borrowed, you will have to entrust the work to a dealer.

- ☐ Angular-tightening gauge
- ☐ Valve spring compressor
- ☐ Valve grinding tool
- ☐ Piston ring compressor
- ☐ Piston ring removal/installation tool
- ☐ Cylinder bore hone
- ☐ Balljoint separator
- ☐ Coil spring compressors (where applicable)
- ☐ Two/three-legged hub and bearing puller
- ☐ Impact screwdriver
- ☐ Micrometer and/or vernier calipers
- ☐ Dial gauge
- ☐ Stroboscopic timing light
- ☐ Dwell angle meter/tachometer
- ☐ Fault code reader
- ☐ Cylinder compression gauge
- ☐ Hand-operated vacuum pump and gauge
- ☐ Clutch plate alignment set
- ☐ Brake shoe steady spring cup removal tool
- ☐ Bush and bearing removal/installation set
- ☐ Stud extractors
- ☐ Tap and die set
- ☐ Lifting tackle
- ☐ Trolley jack

Buying tools

Reputable motor accessory shops and superstores often offer excellent quality tools at discount prices, so it pays to shop around.

Remember, you don't have to buy the most expensive items on the shelf, but it is always advisable to steer clear of the very cheap tools. Beware of 'bargains' offered on market stalls or at car boot sales. There are plenty of good tools around at reasonable prices, but always aim to purchase items which meet the relevant national safety standards. If in doubt, ask the proprietor or manager of the shop for advice before making a purchase.

Care and maintenance of tools

Having purchased a reasonable tool kit, it is necessary to keep the tools in a clean and serviceable condition. After use, always wipe off any dirt, grease and metal particles using a clean, dry cloth, before putting the tools away. Never leave them lying around after they have been used. A simple tool rack on the garage or workshop wall for items such as screwdrivers and pliers is a good idea. Store all normal spanners and sockets in a metal box. Any measuring instruments, gauges, meters, etc, must be carefully stored where they cannot be damaged or become rusty.

Take a little care when tools are used. Hammer heads inevitably become marked, and screwdrivers lose the keen edge on their blades from time to time. A little timely attention with emery cloth or a file will soon restore items like this to a good finish.

Working facilities

Not to be forgotten when discussing tools is the workshop itself. If anything more than routine maintenance is to be carried out, a suitable working area becomes essential.

It is appreciated that many an owner-mechanic is forced by circumstances to remove an engine or similar item without the benefit of a garage or workshop. Having done this, any repairs should always be done under the cover of a roof.

Wherever possible, any dismantling should be done on a clean, flat workbench or table at a suitable working height.

Any workbench needs a vice; one with a jaw opening of 100 mm is suitable for most jobs. As mentioned previously, some clean dry storage space is also required for tools, as well as for any lubricants, cleaning fluids, touch-up paints etc, which become necessary.

Another item which may be required, and which has a much more general usage, is an electric drill with a chuck capacity of at least 8 mm. This, together with a good range of twist drills, is virtually essential for fitting accessories.

Last, but not least, always keep a supply of old newspapers and clean, lint-free rags available, and try to keep any working area as clean as possible.

Micrometers

Dial test indicator ("dial gauge")

Strap wrench

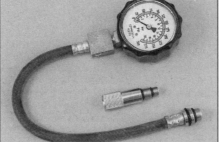

Compression tester

Fault code reader

This is a guide to getting your vehicle through the MOT test. Obviously it will not be possible to examine the vehicle to the same standard as the professional MOT tester. However, working through the following checks will enable you to identify any problem areas before submitting the vehicle for the test.

Where a testable component is in borderline condition, the tester has discretion in deciding whether to pass or fail it. The basis of such discretion is whether the tester would be happy for a close relative or friend to use the vehicle with the component in that condition. If the vehicle presented is clean and evidently well cared for, the tester may be more inclined to pass a borderline component than if the vehicle is scruffy and apparently neglected.

It has only been possible to summarise the test requirements here, based on the regulations in force at the time of printing. Test standards are becoming increasingly stringent, although there are some exemptions for older vehicles.

An assistant will be needed to help carry out some of these checks.

The checks have been sub-divided into four categories, as follows:

1 Checks carried out **FROM THE DRIVER'S SEAT**

2 Checks carried out **WITH THE VEHICLE ON THE GROUND**

3 Checks carried out **WITH THE VEHICLE RAISED AND THE WHEELS FREE TO TURN**

4 Checks carried out on **YOUR VEHICLE'S EXHAUST EMISSION SYSTEM**

---

1 Checks carried out **FROM THE DRIVER'S SEAT**

Handbrake

☐ Test the operation of the handbrake. Excessive travel (too many clicks) indicates incorrect brake or cable adjustment.
☐ Check that the handbrake cannot be released by tapping the lever sideways. Check the security of the lever mountings.

Footbrake

☐ Depress the brake pedal and check that it does not creep down to the floor, indicating a master cylinder fault. Release the pedal, wait a few seconds, then depress it again. If the pedal travels nearly to the floor before firm resistance is felt, brake adjustment or repair is necessary. If the pedal feels spongy, there is air in the hydraulic system which must be removed by bleeding.

☐ Check that the brake pedal is secure and in good condition. Check also for signs of fluid leaks on the pedal, floor or carpets, which would indicate failed seals in the brake master cylinder.
☐ Check the servo unit (when applicable) by operating the brake pedal several times, then keeping the pedal depressed and starting the engine. As the engine starts, the pedal will move down slightly. If not, the vacuum hose or the servo itself may be faulty.

Steering wheel and column

☐ Examine the steering wheel for fractures or looseness of the hub, spokes or rim.
☐ Move the steering wheel from side to side and then up and down. Check that the steering wheel is not loose on the column, indicating wear or a loose retaining nut. Continue moving the steering wheel as before, but also turn it slightly from left to right.
☐ Check that the steering wheel is not loose on the column, and that there is no abnormal

movement of the steering wheel, indicating wear in the column support bearings or couplings.

Windscreen, mirrors and sunvisor

☐ The windscreen must be free of cracks or other significant damage within the driver's field of view. (Small stone chips are acceptable.) Rear view mirrors must be secure, intact, and capable of being adjusted.

☐ The driver's sunvisor must be capable of being stored in the "up" position.

Seat belts and seats

Note: *The following checks are applicable to all seat belts, front and rear.*

☐ Examine the webbing of all the belts (including rear belts if fitted) for cuts, serious fraying or deterioration. Fasten and unfasten each belt to check the buckles. If applicable, check the retracting mechanism. Check the security of all seat belt mountings accessible from inside the vehicle.

☐ Seat belts with pre-tensioners, once activated, have a "flag" or similar showing on the seat belt stalk. This, in itself, is not a reason for test failure.

☐ The front seats themselves must be securely attached and the backrests must lock in the upright position.

Doors

☐ Both front doors must be able to be opened and closed from outside and inside, and must latch securely when closed.

2 Checks carried out WITH THE VEHICLE ON THE GROUND

Vehicle identification

☐ Number plates must be in good condition, secure and legible, with letters and numbers correctly spaced – spacing at (A) should be at least twice that at (B).

☐ The VIN plate and/or homologation plate must be legible.

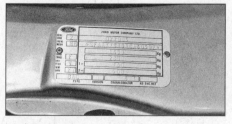

Electrical equipment

☐ Switch on the ignition and check the operation of the horn.

☐ Check the windscreen washers and wipers, examining the wiper blades; renew damaged or perished blades. Also check the operation of the stop-lights.

☐ Check the operation of the sidelights and number plate lights. The lenses and reflectors must be secure, clean and undamaged.

☐ Check the operation and alignment of the headlights. The headlight reflectors must not be tarnished and the lenses must be undamaged.

☐ Switch on the ignition and check the operation of the direction indicators (including the instrument panel tell-tale) and the hazard warning lights. Operation of the sidelights and stop-lights must not affect the indicators - if it does, the cause is usually a bad earth at the rear light cluster.

☐ Check the operation of the rear foglight(s), including the warning light on the instrument panel or in the switch.

☐ The ABS warning light must illuminate in accordance with the manufacturers' design. For most vehicles, the ABS warning light should illuminate when the ignition is switched on, and (if the system is operating properly) extinguish after a few seconds. Refer to the owner's handbook.

Footbrake

☐ Examine the master cylinder, brake pipes and servo unit for leaks, loose mountings, corrosion or other damage.

☐ The fluid reservoir must be secure and the fluid level must be between the upper (A) and lower (B) markings.

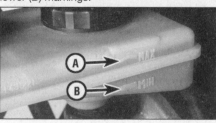

☐ Inspect both front brake flexible hoses for cracks or deterioration of the rubber. Turn the steering from lock to lock, and ensure that the hoses do not contact the wheel, tyre, or any part of the steering or suspension mechanism. With the brake pedal firmly depressed, check the hoses for bulges or leaks under pressure.

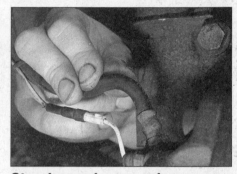

Steering and suspension

☐ Have your assistant turn the steering wheel from side to side slightly, up to the point where the steering gear just begins to transmit this movement to the roadwheels. Check for excessive free play between the steering wheel and the steering gear, indicating wear or insecurity of the steering column joints, the column-to-steering gear coupling, or the steering gear itself.

☐ Have your assistant turn the steering wheel more vigorously in each direction, so that the roadwheels just begin to turn. As this is done, examine all the steering joints, linkages, fittings and attachments. Renew any component that shows signs of wear or damage. On vehicles with power steering, check the security and condition of the steering pump, drivebelt and hoses.

☐ Check that the vehicle is standing level, and at approximately the correct ride height.

Shock absorbers

☐ Depress each corner of the vehicle in turn, then release it. The vehicle should rise and then settle in its normal position. If the vehicle continues to rise and fall, the shock absorber is defective. A shock absorber which has seized will also cause the vehicle to fail.

Exhaust system

☐ Start the engine. With your assistant holding a rag over the tailpipe, check the entire system for leaks. Repair or renew leaking sections.

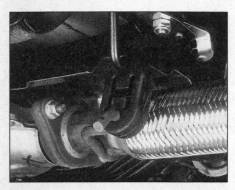

3 Checks carried out
WITH THE VEHICLE RAISED AND THE WHEELS FREE TO TURN

Jack up the front and rear of the vehicle, and securely support it on axle stands. Position the stands clear of the suspension assemblies. Ensure that the wheels are clear of the ground and that the steering can be turned from lock to lock.

Steering mechanism

☐ Have your assistant turn the steering from lock to lock. Check that the steering turns smoothly, and that no part of the steering mechanism, including a wheel or tyre, fouls any brake hose or pipe or any part of the body structure.

☐ Examine the steering rack rubber gaiters for damage or insecurity of the retaining clips. If power steering is fitted, check for signs of damage or leakage of the fluid hoses, pipes or connections. Also check for excessive stiffness or binding of the steering, a missing split pin or locking device, or severe corrosion of the body structure within 30 cm of any steering component attachment point.

Front and rear suspension and wheel bearings

☐ Starting at the front right-hand side, grasp the roadwheel at the 3 o'clock and 9 o'clock positions and rock gently but firmly. Check for free play or insecurity at the wheel bearings, suspension balljoints, or suspension mountings, pivots and attachments.

☐ Now grasp the wheel at the 12 o'clock and 6 o'clock positions and repeat the previous inspection. Spin the wheel, and check for roughness or tightness of the front wheel bearing.

☐ If excess free play is suspected at a component pivot point, this can be confirmed by using a large screwdriver or similar tool and levering between the mounting and the component attachment. This will confirm whether the wear is in the pivot bush, its retaining bolt, or in the mounting itself (the bolt holes can often become elongated).

☐ Carry out all the above checks at the other front wheel, and then at both rear wheels.

Springs and shock absorbers

☐ Examine the suspension struts (when applicable) for serious fluid leakage, corrosion, or damage to the casing. Also check the security of the mounting points.

☐ If coil springs are fitted, check that the spring ends locate in their seats, and that the spring is not corroded, cracked or broken.

☐ If leaf springs are fitted, check that all leaves are intact, that the axle is securely attached to each spring, and that there is no deterioration of the spring eye mountings, bushes, and shackles.

☐ The same general checks apply to vehicles fitted with other suspension types, such as torsion bars, hydraulic displacer units, etc. Ensure that all mountings and attachments are secure, that there are no signs of excessive wear, corrosion or damage, and (on hydraulic types) that there are no fluid leaks or damaged pipes.

☐ Inspect the shock absorbers for signs of serious fluid leakage. Check for wear of the mounting bushes or attachments, or damage to the body of the unit.

Driveshafts
(fwd vehicles only)

☐ Rotate each front wheel in turn and inspect the constant velocity joint gaiters for splits or damage. Also check that each driveshaft is straight and undamaged.

Braking system

☐ If possible without dismantling, check brake pad wear and disc condition. Ensure that the friction lining material has not worn excessively, (A) and that the discs are not fractured, pitted, scored or badly worn (B).

☐ Examine all the rigid brake pipes underneath the vehicle, and the flexible hose(s) at the rear. Look for corrosion, chafing or insecurity of the pipes, and for signs of bulging under pressure, chafing, splits or deterioration of the flexible hoses.

☐ Look for signs of fluid leaks at the brake calipers or on the brake backplates. Repair or renew leaking components.

☐ Slowly spin each wheel, while your assistant depresses and releases the footbrake. Ensure that each brake is operating and does not bind when the pedal is released.

□ Examine the handbrake mechanism, checking for frayed or broken cables, excessive corrosion, or wear or insecurity of the linkage. Check that the mechanism works on each relevant wheel, and releases fully, without binding.

□ It is not possible to test brake efficiency without special equipment, but a road test can be carried out later to check that the vehicle pulls up in a straight line.

Fuel and exhaust systems

□ Inspect the fuel tank (including the filler cap), fuel pipes, hoses and unions. All components must be secure and free from leaks.

□ Examine the exhaust system over its entire length, checking for any damaged, broken or missing mountings, security of the retaining clamps and rust or corrosion.

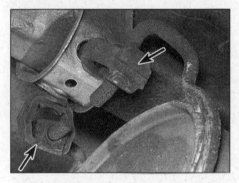

Wheels and tyres

□ Examine the sidewalls and tread area of each tyre in turn. Check for cuts, tears, lumps, bulges, separation of the tread, and exposure of the ply or cord due to wear or damage. Check that the tyre bead is correctly seated on the wheel rim, that the valve is sound and properly seated, and that the wheel is not distorted or damaged.

□ Check that the tyres are of the correct size for the vehicle, that they are of the same size and type on each axle, and that the pressures are correct.

□ Check the tyre tread depth. The legal minimum at the time of writing is 1.6 mm over at least three-quarters of the tread width. Abnormal tread wear may indicate incorrect front wheel alignment.

Body corrosion

□ Check the condition of the entire vehicle structure for signs of corrosion in load-bearing areas. (These include chassis box sections, side sills, cross-members, pillars, and all suspension, steering, braking system and seat belt mountings and anchorages.) Any corrosion which has seriously reduced the thickness of a load-bearing area is likely to cause the vehicle to fail. In this case professional repairs are likely to be needed.

□ Damage or corrosion which causes sharp or otherwise dangerous edges to be exposed will also cause the vehicle to fail.

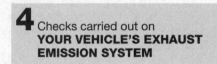

4 Checks carried out on **YOUR VEHICLE'S EXHAUST EMISSION SYSTEM**

Petrol models

□ Have the engine at normal operating temperature, and make sure that it is in good tune (ignition system in good order, air filter element clean, etc).

□ Before any measurements are carried out, raise the engine speed to around 2500 rpm, and hold it at this speed for 20 seconds. Allow the engine speed to return to idle, and watch for smoke emissions from the exhaust tailpipe. If the idle speed is obviously much too high, or if dense blue or clearly-visible black smoke comes from the tailpipe for more than 5 seconds, the vehicle will fail. As a rule of thumb, blue smoke signifies oil being burnt (engine wear) while black smoke signifies unburnt fuel (dirty air cleaner element, or other carburettor or fuel system fault).

□ An exhaust gas analyser capable of measuring carbon monoxide (CO) and hydrocarbons (HC) is now needed. If such an instrument cannot be hired or borrowed, a local garage may agree to perform the check for a small fee.

CO emissions (mixture)

□ At the time of writing, for vehicles first used between 1st August 1975 and 31st July 1986 (P to C registration), the CO level must not exceed 4.5% by volume. For vehicles first used between 1st August 1986 and 31st July 1992 (D to J registration), the CO level must not exceed 3.5% by volume. Vehicles first

used after 1st August 1992 (K registration) must conform to the manufacturer's specification. The MOT tester has access to a DOT database or emissions handbook, which lists the CO and HC limits for each make and model of vehicle. The CO level is measured with the engine at idle speed, and at "fast idle". The following limits are given as a general guide:

At idle speed -
    CO level no more than 0.5%
At "fast idle" (2500 to 3000 rpm) -
    CO level no more than 0.3%
    (Minimum oil temperature 60ºC)

□ If the CO level cannot be reduced far enough to pass the test (and the fuel and ignition systems are otherwise in good condition) then the carburettor is badly worn, or there is some problem in the fuel injection system or catalytic converter (as applicable).

HC emissions

□ With the CO within limits, HC emissions for vehicles first used between 1st August 1975 and 31st July 1992 (P to J registration) must not exceed 1200 ppm. Vehicles first used after 1st August 1992 (K registration) must conform to the manufacturer's specification. The MOT tester has access to a DOT database or emissions handbook, which lists the CO and HC limits for each make and model of vehicle. The HC level is measured with the engine at "fast idle". The following is given as a general guide:

At "fast idle" (2500 to 3000 rpm) -
    HC level no more than 200 ppm
    (Minimum oil temperature 60ºC)

□ Excessive HC emissions are caused by incomplete combustion, the causes of which can include oil being burnt, mechanical wear and ignition/fuel system malfunction.

Diesel models

□ The only emission test applicable to Diesel engines is the measuring of exhaust smoke density. The test involves accelerating the engine several times to its maximum unloaded speed.

Note: *It is of the utmost importance that the engine timing belt is in good condition before the test is carried out.*

□ The limits for Diesel engine exhaust smoke, introduced in September 1995 are:
Vehicles first used before 1st August 1979:
    Exempt from metered smoke testing, but must not emit "dense blue or clearly visible black smoke for a period of more than 5 seconds at idle" or "dense blue or clearly visible black smoke during acceleration which would obscure the view of other road users".
Non-turbocharged vehicles first used after 1st August 1979: 2.5m⁻¹
Turbocharged vehicles first used after 1st August 1979: 3.0m⁻¹

□ Excessive smoke can be caused by a dirty air cleaner element. Otherwise, professional advice may be needed to find the cause.

Engine

- [ ] Engine fails to rotate when attempting to start
- [ ] Engine rotates, but will not start
- [ ] Engine difficult to start when cold
- [ ] Engine difficult to start when hot
- [ ] Starter motor noisy or excessively-rough in engagement
- [ ] Engine starts, but stops immediately
- [ ] Engine idles erratically
- [ ] Engine misfires at idle speed
- [ ] Engine misfires throughout the driving speed range
- [ ] Engine hesitates on acceleration
- [ ] Engine stalls
- [ ] Engine lacks power
- [ ] Engine backfires
- [ ] Oil pressure warning light illuminated with engine running
- [ ] Engine runs-on after switching off
- [ ] Engine noises

Cooling system

- [ ] Overheating
- [ ] Overcooling
- [ ] External coolant leakage
- [ ] Internal coolant leakage
- [ ] Corrosion

Fuel and exhaust systems

- [ ] Excessive fuel consumption
- [ ] Fuel leakage and/or fuel odour
- [ ] Excessive noise or fumes from exhaust system

Clutch

- [ ] Pedal travels to floor – no pressure or very little resistance
- [ ] Clutch fails to disengage (unable to select gears)
- [ ] Clutch slips (engine speed increases, with no increase in vehicle speed)
- [ ] Judder as clutch is engaged
- [ ] Noise when depressing or releasing clutch pedal

Manual transmission

- [ ] Noisy in neutral with engine running
- [ ] Noisy in one particular gear
- [ ] Difficulty engaging gears
- [ ] Jumps out of gear
- [ ] Vibration
- [ ] Lubricant leaks

Automatic transmission

- [ ] Fluid leakage
- [ ] Transmission fluid brown, or has burned smell
- [ ] General gear selection problems
- [ ] Transmission will not downshift (kickdown) with accelerator pedal fully depressed
- [ ] Engine will not start in any gear, or starts in gears other than Park or Neutral
- [ ] Transmission slips, shifts roughly, is noisy, or has no drive in forward or reverse gears

Driveshafts

- [ ] Vibration when accelerating or decelerating
- [ ] Clicking or knocking noise on turns (at slow speed on full-lock)

Braking system

- [ ] Vehicle pulls to one side under braking
- [ ] Noise (grinding or high-pitched squeal) when brakes applied
- [ ] Excessive brake pedal travel
- [ ] Brake pedal feels spongy when depressed
- [ ] Excessive brake pedal effort required to stop vehicle
- [ ] Judder felt through brake pedal or steering wheel when braking
- [ ] Brakes binding
- [ ] Rear wheels locking under normal braking

Suspension and steering

- [ ] Vehicle pulls to one side
- [ ] Wheel wobble and vibration
- [ ] Excessive pitching and/or rolling around corners, or during braking
- [ ] Wandering or general instability
- [ ] Excessively-stiff steering
- [ ] Excessive play in steering
- [ ] Lack of power assistance
- [ ] Tyre wear excessive

Electrical system

- [ ] Battery will only hold a charge for a few days
- [ ] Ignition/no-charge warning light remains illuminated with engine running
- [ ] Ignition/no-charge warning light fails to come on
- [ ] Lights inoperative
- [ ] Instrument readings inaccurate or erratic
- [ ] Horn inoperative, or unsatisfactory in operation
- [ ] Windscreen wipers inoperative, or unsatisfactory in operation
- [ ] Windscreen washers inoperative, or unsatisfactory in operation
- [ ] Electric windows inoperative, or unsatisfactory in operation
- [ ] Central locking system inoperative, or unsatisfactory in operation

Introduction

The vehicle owner who does his or her own maintenance according to the recommended service schedules should not have to use this section of the manual very often. Modern component reliability is such that, provided those items subject to wear or deterioration are inspected or renewed at the specified intervals, sudden failure is comparatively rare. Faults do not usually just happen as a result of sudden failure, but develop over a period of time. Major mechanical failures in particular are usually preceded by characteristic symptoms over hundreds or even thousands of miles. Those components which do occasionally fail without warning are often small and easily carried in the vehicle.

With any fault-finding, the first step is to decide where to begin investigations. Sometimes this is obvious, but on other occasions, a little detective work will be necessary. The owner who makes half a dozen haphazard adjustments or replacements may be successful in curing a fault (or its symptoms), but will be none the wiser if the fault recurs, and ultimately may have spent more time and money than was necessary. A calm and logical approach will be found to be more satisfactory in the long run. Always take into account any warning signs or abnormalities that may have been noticed in the period preceding the fault – power loss, high or low gauge readings, unusual smells, etc – and remember that failure of components such as fuses or spark plugs may only be pointers to some underlying fault.

The pages which follow provide an easy-reference guide to the more common problems which may occur during the operation of the vehicle. These problems and their possible causes are grouped under headings denoting various components or systems, such as Engine, Cooling system, etc. The general Chapter which deals with the problem is also shown in brackets; refer to the relevant part of that Chapter for system-specific information. Whatever the fault, certain basic principles apply. These are as follows:

Verify the fault. This is simply a matter of being sure that you know what the symptoms are before starting work. This is particularly important if you are investigating a fault for someone else, who may not have described it very accurately.

Don't overlook the obvious. For example, if the vehicle won't start, is there fuel in the tank? (Don't take anyone else's word on this particular point, and don't trust the fuel gauge either!) If an electrical fault is indicated, look for loose or broken wires before digging out the test gear.

Cure the disease, not the symptom. Substituting a flat battery with a fully-charged one will get you off the hard shoulder, but if the underlying cause is not attended to, the new battery will go the same way. Similarly, changing oil-fouled spark plugs for a new set will get you moving again, but remember that the reason for the fouling (if it wasn't simply an incorrect grade of plug) will have to be established and corrected.

Don't take anything for granted. Particularly, don't forget that a 'new' component may itself be defective (especially if it's been rattling around in the boot for months), and don't leave components out of a fault diagnosis sequence just because they are new or recently-fitted. When you do finally diagnose a difficult fault, you'll probably realise that all the evidence was there from the start.

Engine

Engine fails to rotate when attempting to start

- [ ] Battery terminal connections loose or corroded (see *Weekly checks*)
- [ ] Battery discharged or faulty (Chapter 5)
- [ ] Broken, loose or disconnected wiring in the starting circuit (Chapter 5)
- [ ] Defective starter solenoid or switch (Chapter 5)
- [ ] Defective starter motor (Chapter 5)
- [ ] Starter pinion or flywheel ring gear teeth loose or broken (Chapters 2 and 5)
- [ ] Engine earth strap broken or disconnected (Chapter 5)

Engine rotates, but will not start

- [ ] Fuel tank empty
- [ ] Battery discharged (engine rotates slowly) (Chapter 5)
- [ ] Battery terminal connections loose or corroded (*Weekly checks*)
- [ ] Ignition components damp or damaged – petrol models (Chapters 1 and 5)
- [x] Broken, loose or disconnected wiring in the ignition circuit – petrol models (Chapters 1 and 5)
- [ ] Worn, faulty or incorrectly-gapped spark plugs – petrol models (Chapter 1)
- [ ] Preheating system faulty – diesel models (Chapter 5)
- [ ] Fuel injection system fault – petrol models (Chapter 4)
- [ ] Stop solenoid faulty – diesel models (Chapter 4)
- [ ] Air in fuel system – diesel models (Chapter 4)
- [ ] Major mechanical failure (eg camshaft drive) (Chapter 2)

Engine difficult to start when cold

- [ ] Battery discharged (Chapter 5)
- [ ] Battery terminal connections loose or corroded (see *Weekly checks*)
- [ ] Worn, faulty or incorrectly-gapped spark plugs – petrol models (Chapter 1)
- [ ] Preheating system faulty – diesel models (Chapter 5)
- [ ] Fuel injection system fault – petrol models (Chapter 4)
- [ ] Other ignition system fault – petrol models (Chapters 1 and 5)
- [ ] Low cylinder compressions (Chapter 2)

Engine difficult to start when hot

- [ ] Air filter element dirty or clogged (Chapter 1)
- [ ] Fuel injection system fault – petrol models (Chapter 4)
- [ ] Low cylinder compressions (Chapter 2)

Starter motor noisy or excessively-rough in engagement

- [ ] Starter pinion or flywheel ring gear teeth loose or broken (Chapters 2 and 5)
- [ ] Starter motor mounting bolts loose or missing (Chapter 5)
- [ ] Starter motor internal components worn or damaged (Chapter 5)

Engine starts, but stops immediately

- [ ] Loose or faulty electrical connections in the ignition circuit – petrol models (Chapters 1 and 5)
- [ ] Vacuum leak at the throttle body or inlet manifold – petrol models (Chapter 4)
- [ ] Blocked injector/fuel injection system fault – petrol models (Chapter 4)

Engine idles erratically

- [ ] Air filter element clogged (Chapter 1)
- [ ] Vacuum leak at the throttle body, inlet manifold or associated hoses – petrol models (Chapter 4)
- [ ] Worn, faulty or incorrectly-gapped spark plugs – petrol models (Chapter 1)
- [ ] Uneven or low cylinder compressions (Chapter 2)
- [ ] Camshaft lobes worn (Chapter 2)
- [ ] Timing belt incorrectly fitted (Chapter 2)
- [ ] Blocked injector/fuel injection system fault – petrol models (Chapter 4)
- [ ] Faulty injector(s) – diesel models (Chapter 4)

Engine misfires at idle speed

- [ ] Worn, faulty or incorrectly-gapped spark plugs – petrol models (Chapter 1)
- [ ] Faulty spark plug HT leads (where fitted) – petrol models (Chapter 1)
- [ ] Vacuum leak at the throttle body, inlet manifold or associated hoses – petrol models (Chapter 4)
- [ ] Blocked injector/fuel injection system fault – petrol models (Chapter 4)
- [ ] Faulty injector(s) – diesel models (Chapter 4)
- [ ] Distributor cap cracked or tracking internally – petrol models (where applicable) (Chapter 1).
- [ ] Uneven or low cylinder compressions (Chapter 2)
- [ ] Disconnected, leaking, or perished crankcase ventilation hoses (Chapter 4)

Engine misfires throughout the driving speed range

- [ ] Fuel filter choked (Chapter 1)
- [ ] Fuel pump faulty, or delivery pressure low (Chapter 4)
- [ ] Fuel tank vent blocked, or fuel pipes restricted (Chapter 4)
- [ ] Vacuum leak at the throttle body, inlet manifold or associated hoses – petrol models (Chapter 4)
- [ ] Worn, faulty or incorrectly-gapped spark plugs – petrol models (Chapter 1)
- [ ] Faulty spark plug HT leads (where fitted) – petrol models (Chapter 1)
- [ ] Faulty injector(s) – diesel models (Chapter 4)
- [ ] Distributor cap cracked or tracking internally – petrol models (where applicable) (Chapter 1)

Engine misfires throughout the driving speed range (continued)

- [ ] Faulty ignition coil – petrol models (Chapter 5)
- [ ] Uneven or low cylinder compressions (Chapter 2)
- [ ] Blocked injector/fuel injection system fault – petrol models (Chapter 4)

Engine hesitates on acceleration

- [ ] Worn, faulty or incorrectly-gapped spark plugs – petrol models (Chapter 1)
- [ ] Vacuum leak at the throttle body, inlet manifold or associated hoses (Chapter 4)
- [ ] Blocked injector/fuel injection system fault – petrol models (Chapter 4)
- [ ] Faulty injector(s) – diesel models (Chapter 4)

Engine (continued)

Engine stalls

- ☐ Vacuum leak at the throttle body, inlet manifold or associated hoses – petrol models (Chapter 4)
- ☐ Fuel filter choked (Chapter 1)
- ☐ Fuel pump faulty, or delivery pressure low – petrol models (Chapter 4)
- ☐ Fuel tank vent blocked, or fuel pipes restricted (Chapter 4)
- ☐ Blocked injector/fuel injection system fault – petrol models (Chapter 4)
- ☐ Faulty injector(s) – diesel models (Chapter 4)

Engine lacks power

- ☐ Timing belt incorrectly fitted (Chapter 2)
- ☐ Fuel filter choked (Chapter 1)
- ☐ Fuel pump faulty, or delivery pressure low (Chapter 4)
- ☐ Uneven or low cylinder compressions (Chapter 2)
- ☐ Worn, faulty or incorrectly-gapped spark plugs – petrol models (Chapter 1)
- ☐ Vacuum leak at the throttle body, inlet manifold or associated hoses – petrol models (Chapter 4)
- ☐ Blocked injector/fuel injection system fault – petrol models (Chapter 4)
- ☐ Faulty injector(s) – diesel models (Chapter 4)
- ☐ Injection pump timing incorrect – diesel models (Chapter 4)
- ☐ Brakes binding (Chapters 1 and 9)
- ☐ Clutch slipping (Chapter 6)

Engine backfires

- ☐ Timing belt incorrectly fitted (Chapter 2)
- ☐ Vacuum leak at the throttle body, inlet manifold or associated hoses – petrol models (Chapter 4)
- ☐ Blocked injector/fuel injection system fault – petrol models (Chapter 4)

Oil pressure warning light illuminated with engine running

- ☐ Low oil level, or incorrect oil grade (*Weekly checks*)
- ☐ Faulty oil pressure sensor (Chapter 5)
- ☐ Worn engine bearings and/or oil pump (Chapter 2)
- ☐ High engine operating temperature (Chapter 3)
- ☐ Oil pressure relief valve defective (Chapter 2)
- ☐ Oil pick-up strainer clogged (Chapter 2)

Engine runs-on after switching off

- ☐ Excessive carbon build-up in engine (Chapter 2)
- ☐ High engine operating temperature (Chapter 3)
- ☐ Fuel injection system fault – petrol models (Chapter 4)
- ☐ Faulty stop solenoid – diesel models (Chapter 4)

Engine noises

Pre-ignition (pinking) or knocking during acceleration or under load

- ☐ Ignition timing incorrect/ignition system fault – petrol models (Chapters 1 and 5)
- ☐ Incorrect grade of spark plug – petrol models (Chapter 1)
- ☐ Incorrect grade of fuel (Chapter 1)
- ☐ Vacuum leak at the throttle body, inlet manifold or associated hoses – petrol models (Chapter 4)
- ☐ Excessive carbon build-up in engine (Chapter 2)
- ☐ Blocked injector/fuel injection system fault – petrol models (Chapter 4)

Whistling or wheezing noises

- ☐ Leaking inlet manifold or throttle body gasket – petrol models (Chapter 4)
- ☐ Leaking exhaust manifold gasket or pipe-to-manifold joint (Chapter 4)
- ☐ Leaking vacuum hose (Chapters 4, 5 and 9)
- ☐ Blowing cylinder head gasket (Chapter 2)

Tapping or rattling noises

- ☐ Worn valve gear or camshaft (Chapter 2)
- ☐ Ancillary component fault (coolant pump, alternator, etc) (Chapters 3, 5, etc)

Knocking or thumping noises

- ☐ Worn big-end bearings (regular heavy knocking, perhaps less under load) (Chapter 2)
- ☐ Worn main bearings (rumbling and knocking, perhaps worsening under load) (Chapter 2)
- ☐ Piston slap (most noticeable when cold) (Chapter 2)
- ☐ Ancillary component fault (coolant pump, alternator, etc) (Chapters 3, 5, etc)

Cooling system

Overheating

☐ Insufficient coolant in system (*Weekly checks*)
☐ Thermostat faulty (Chapter 3)
☐ Radiator core blocked, or grille restricted (Chapter 3)
☐ Cooling fan faulty (Chapter 3)
☐ Inaccurate temperature gauge sender unit (Chapter 3)
☐ Airlock in cooling system (Chapter 3)
☐ Pressure cap faulty (Chapter 3)

Overcooling

☐ Thermostat faulty (Chapter 3)
☐ Inaccurate temperature gauge sender unit (Chapter 3)
☐ Cooling fan faulty (Chapter 3)

External coolant leakage

☐ Deteriorated or damaged hoses or hose clips (Chapter 1)
☐ Radiator core or heater matrix leaking (Chapter 3)
☐ Pressure cap faulty (Chapter 3)
☐ Coolant pump internal seal leaking (Chapter 3)
☐ Coolant pump-to-block seal leaking (Chapter 3)
☐ Boiling due to overheating (Chapter 3)
☐ Core plug leaking (Chapter 2)

Internal coolant leakage

☐ Leaking cylinder head gasket (Chapter 2)
☐ Cracked cylinder head or cylinder block (Chapter 2)

Corrosion

☐ Infrequent draining and flushing (Chapter 1)
☐ Incorrect coolant mixture or inappropriate coolant type (Chapter 1)

Fuel and exhaust systems

Excessive fuel consumption

☐ Air filter element dirty or clogged (Chapter 1)
☐ Fuel injection system fault – petrol models (Chapter 4)
☐ Faulty injector(s) – diesel models (Chapter 4)
☐ Ignition timing incorrect/ignition system fault – petrol models (Chapters 1 and 5)
☐ Tyres under-inflated (*Weekly checks*)

Fuel leakage and/or fuel odour

☐ Damaged or corroded fuel tank, pipes or connections (Chapter 4)

Excessive noise or fumes from exhaust system

☐ Leaking exhaust system or manifold joints (Chapters 1 and 4)
☐ Leaking, corroded or damaged silencers or pipe (Chapters 1 and 4)
☐ Broken mountings causing body or suspension contact (Chapter 1)

Clutch

Pedal travels to floor – no pressure or very little resistance

☐ Broken clutch cable/adjuster mechanism – cable-operated clutch (Chapter 6)
☐ Faulty hydraulic release system – hydraulically-operated clutch (Chapter 6)
☐ Broken clutch release bearing or fork (Chapter 6)
☐ Broken diaphragm spring in clutch pressure plate (Chapter 6)

Clutch fails to disengage (unable to select gears).

☐ Faulty clutch cable/adjuster mechanism – cable-operated clutch (Chapter 6)
☐ Faulty hydraulic release system – hydraulically-operated clutch (Chapter 6)
☐ Clutch disc sticking on gearbox input shaft splines (Chapter 6)
☐ Clutch disc sticking to flywheel or pressure plate (Chapter 6)
☐ Faulty pressure plate assembly (Chapter 6)
☐ Clutch release mechanism worn or incorrectly assembled (Chapter 6)

Clutch slips (engine speed increases, with no increase in vehicle speed)

☐ Faulty clutch cable/adjuster mechanism – cable-operated clutch (Chapter 6)
☐ Faulty hydraulic release system – hydraulically-operated clutch (Chapter 6)
☐ Clutch disc linings excessively worn (Chapter 6)
☐ Clutch disc linings contaminated with oil or grease (Chapter 6)
☐ Faulty pressure plate or weak diaphragm spring (Chapter 6)

Judder as clutch is engaged

☐ Clutch disc linings contaminated with oil or grease (Chapter 6)
☐ Clutch disc linings excessively worn (Chapter 6)
☐ Faulty or distorted pressure plate or diaphragm spring (Chapter 6).
☐ Worn or loose engine or gearbox mountings (Chapter 2)
☐ Clutch disc hub or gearbox input shaft splines worn (Chapter 6)

Noise when depressing or releasing clutch pedal

☐ Worn clutch release bearing (Chapter 6)
☐ Worn or dry clutch pedal bushes (Chapter 6)
☐ Faulty pressure plate assembly (Chapter 6)
☐ Pressure plate diaphragm spring broken (Chapter 6)
☐ Broken clutch disc cushioning springs (Chapter 6)

Manual transmission

Noisy in neutral with engine running

☐ Input shaft bearings worn (noise apparent with clutch pedal released, but not when depressed) (Chapter 7)*
☐ Clutch release bearing worn (noise apparent with clutch pedal depressed, possibly less when released) (Chapter 6)

Noisy in one particular gear

☐ Worn, damaged or chipped gear teeth (Chapter 7)*

Difficulty engaging gears

☐ Clutch fault (Chapter 6)
☐ Worn or damaged gearchange linkage/cable (Chapter 7)
☐ Incorrectly-adjusted gearchange linkage/cable (Chapter 7)
☐ Worn synchroniser units (Chapter 7)*

Jumps out of gear

☐ Worn or damaged gearchange linkage/cable (Chapter 7)
☐ Incorrectly-adjusted gearchange linkage/cable (Chapter 7)
☐ Worn synchroniser units (Chapter 7)*
☐ Worn selector forks (Chapter 7)*

Vibration

☐ Lack of oil (Chapter 1)
☐ Worn bearings (Chapter 7)*

Lubricant leaks

☐ Leaking differential output oil seal (Chapter 7)
☐ Leaking housing joint (Chapter 7)*
☐ Leaking input shaft oil seal (Chapter 7)*

*Although the corrective action necessary to remedy the symptoms described is beyond the scope of the home mechanic, the above information should be helpful in isolating the cause of the condition, so that the owner can communicate clearly with a professional mechanic.

Automatic transmission

Note: Due to the complexity of the automatic transmission, it is difficult for the home mechanic to properly diagnose and service this unit. For problems other than the following, the vehicle should be taken to a dealer service department or automatic transmission specialist. Do not be too hasty in removing the transmission if a fault is suspected, as most of the testing is carried out with the unit still fitted.

Fluid leakage

☐ Automatic transmission fluid is usually dark in colour. Fluid leaks should not be confused with engine oil, which can easily be blown onto the transmission by airflow.
☐ To determine the source of a leak, first remove all built-up dirt and grime from the transmission housing and surrounding areas using a degreasing agent, or by steam-cleaning. Drive the vehicle at low speed, so airflow will not blow the leak far from its source. Raise and support the vehicle, and determine where the leak is coming from. The following are common areas of leakage:

a) Oil pan (Chapter 1 and 7)
b) Dipstick tube (Chapter 1 and 7)
c) Transmission-to-fluid cooler unions (Chapter 7)

Transmission fluid brown, or has burned smell

☐ Transmission fluid level low (Chapter 1)

General gear selection problems

☐ Chapter 7B deals with checking the selector cable on automatic transmissions. The following are common problems which may be caused by a faulty cable:
a) Engine starting in gears other than Park or Neutral.
b) Indicator panel indicating a gear other than the one actually being used.
c) Vehicle moves when in Park or Neutral.
d) Poor gear shift quality or erratic gear changes.

Transmission will not downshift (kickdown) with accelerator pedal fully depressed

☐ Low transmission fluid level (Chapter 1)
☐ Incorrect selector cable adjustment (Chapter 7)

Engine will not start in any gear, or starts in gears other than Park or Neutral

☐ Incorrect starter/inhibitor (multi-function) switch adjustment (Chapter 7)
☐ Incorrect selector cable adjustment (Chapter 7)

Transmission slips, shifts roughly, is noisy, or has no drive in forward or reverse gears

☐ There are many probable causes for the above problems, but the home mechanic should be concerned with only one possibility – fluid level. Before taking the vehicle to a dealer or transmission specialist, check the fluid level and condition of the fluid as described in Chapter 1. Correct the fluid level as necessary, or change the fluid if needed. If the problem persists, professional help will be necessary.

Driveshafts

Vibration when accelerating or decelerating

- ☐ Worn inner constant velocity joint (Chapter 8)
- ☐ Bent or distorted driveshaft (Chapter 8)
- ☐ Worn intermediate bearing (Chapter 8)

Clicking or knocking noise on turns (at slow speed on full-lock)

- ☐ Worn outer constant velocity joint (Chapter 8)
- ☐ Lack of constant velocity joint lubricant, possibly due to damaged gaiter (Chapter 8)
- ☐ Worn intermediate bearing (Chapter 8)

Braking system

Note: *Before assuming that a brake problem exists, make sure that the tyres are in good condition and correctly inflated, that the front wheel alignment is correct, and that the vehicle is not loaded with weight in an unequal manner. Apart from checking the condition of all pipe and hose connections, any faults occurring on the anti-lock braking system should be referred to a Peugeot dealer for diagnosis.*

Vehicle pulls to one side under braking

- ☐ Worn, defective, damaged or contaminated brake pads/shoes on one side (Chapters 1 and 9)
- ☐ Seized or partially-seized brake caliper piston/wheel cylinder (Chapters 1 and 9)
- ☐ A mixture of brake pad/shoe lining materials fitted between sides (Chapters 1 and 9)
- ☐ Brake caliper/backplate mounting bolts loose (Chapter 9)
- ☐ Worn or damaged steering or suspension components (Chapters 1 and 10)

Noise (grinding or high-pitched squeal) when brakes applied

- ☐ Brake pad/shoe friction lining material worn down to metal backing (Chapters 1 and 9)
- ☐ Excessive corrosion of brake disc/drum (may be apparent after the vehicle has been standing for some time (Chapters 1 and 9)
- ☐ Foreign object (stone chipping, etc) trapped between brake disc and shield (Chapters 1 and 9)

Excessive brake pedal travel

- ☐ Faulty master cylinder (Chapter 9)
- ☐ Air in hydraulic system (Chapters 1 and 9)
- ☐ Faulty vacuum servo unit (Chapter 9)

Brake pedal feels spongy when depressed

- ☐ Air in hydraulic system (Chapters 1 and 9)
- ☐ Deteriorated flexible rubber brake hoses (Chapters 1 and 9)
- ☐ Master cylinder mounting nuts loose (Chapter 9)
- ☐ Faulty master cylinder (Chapter 9)

Excessive brake pedal effort required to stop vehicle

- ☐ Faulty vacuum servo unit (Chapter 9)
- ☐ Disconnected, damaged or insecure brake servo vacuum hose (Chapter 9)
- ☐ Primary or secondary hydraulic circuit failure (Chapter 9)
- ☐ Seized brake caliper/wheel cylinder piston (Chapter 9)
- ☐ Brake pads/shoes incorrectly fitted (Chapters 1 and 9)
- ☐ Incorrect grade of brake pads/shoes fitted (Chapters 1 and 9)
- ☐ Brake pad/shoe linings contaminated (Chapters 1 and 9)
- ☐ Faulty vacuum pump – diesel models (Chapter 9)

Judder felt through brake pedal or steering wheel when braking

- ☐ Excessive run-out or distortion of discs/drums (Chapters 1 and 9)
- ☐ Brake pad/shoe linings worn (Chapters 1 and 9)
- ☐ Brake caliper/backplate mounting bolts loose (Chapter 9)
- ☐ Wear in suspension or steering components or mountings (Chapters 1 and 10)

Brakes binding

- ☐ Seized brake caliper/wheel cylinder piston (Chapter 9)
- ☐ Incorrectly-adjusted handbrake mechanism (Chapter 9)
- ☐ Faulty master cylinder (Chapter 9)

Rear wheels locking under normal braking

- ☐ Rear brake pad/shoe linings contaminated (Chapters 1 and 9)
- ☐ Rear brake discs/drums warped (Chapters 1 and 9)

Suspension and steering

Note: *Before diagnosing suspension or steering faults, be sure the trouble is not due to tyre pressures, mixtures of tyre types, or binding brakes.*

Vehicle pulls to one side

- [ ] Defective tyre (*Weekly checks*)
- [ ] Excessive wear in suspension or steering components (Chapters 1 and 10)
- [ ] Incorrect front wheel alignment (Chapter 10)
- [ ] Accident damage to steering or suspension components (Chapter 1)

Wheel wobble and vibration

- [ ] Front roadwheels out of balance (vibration felt mainly through the steering wheel) (Chapters 1 and 10)
- [ ] Rear roadwheels out of balance (vibration felt throughout the vehicle) (Chapters 1 and 10)
- [ ] Roadwheels damaged or distorted (Chapters 1 and 10)
- [ ] Faulty or damaged tyre (*Weekly checks*)
- [ ] Worn steering or suspension joints, bushes or components (Chapters 1 and 10)
- [ ] Wheel bolts loose (Chapters 1 and 10)

Excessive pitching and/or rolling around corners, or during braking

- [ ] Defective shock absorbers (Chapters 1 and 10)
- [ ] Broken or weak spring and/or suspension component (Chapters 1 and 10)
- [ ] Worn or damaged anti-roll bar or mountings (Chapter 10)

Wandering or general instability

- [ ] Incorrect front wheel alignment (Chapter 10)
- [ ] Worn steering or suspension joints, bushes or components (Chapters 1 and 10)
- [ ] Roadwheels out of balance (Chapters 1 and 10)
- [ ] Faulty or damaged tyre (*Weekly checks*)
- [ ] Wheel bolts loose (Chapters 1 and 10)
- [ ] Defective shock absorbers (Chapters 1 and 10)

Excessively-stiff steering

- [ ] Seized steering linkage balljoint or suspension balljoint (Chapters 1 and 10)
- [ ] Broken or incorrectly-adjusted auxiliary drivebelt (Chapter 1)
- [ ] Incorrect front wheel alignment (Chapter 10)
- [ ] Steering gear damaged (Chapter 10)

Excessive play in steering

- [ ] Worn steering column/intermediate shaft joints (Chapter 10)
- [ ] Worn track rod balljoints (Chapters 1 and 10)
- [ ] Worn steering gear (Chapter 10)
- [ ] Worn steering or suspension joints, bushes or components (Chapters 1 and 10)

Lack of power assistance

- [ ] Broken or incorrectly-adjusted auxiliary drivebelt (Chapter 1)
- [ ] Incorrect power steering fluid level (*Weekly checks*)
- [ ] Restriction in power steering fluid hoses (Chapter 1)
- [ ] Faulty power steering pump (Chapter 10)
- [ ] Faulty steering gear (Chapter 10)

Tyre wear excessive

Tyres worn on inside or outside edges

- [ ] Tyres under-inflated (wear on both edges) (*Weekly checks*)
- [ ] Incorrect camber or castor angles (wear on one edge only) (Chapter 10)
- [ ] Worn steering or suspension joints, bushes or components (Chapters 1 and 10)
- [ ] Excessively-hard cornering
- [ ] Accident damage

Tyre treads exhibit feathered edges

- [ ] Incorrect toe setting (Chapter 10)

Tyres worn in centre of tread

- [ ] Tyres over-inflated (*Weekly checks*)

Tyres worn on inside and outside edges

- [ ] Tyres under-inflated (*Weekly checks*)

Tyres worn unevenly

- [ ] Tyres/wheels out of balance (Chapter 1)
- [ ] Excessive wheel or tyre run-out (Chapter 1)
- [ ] Worn shock absorbers (Chapters 1 and 10)
- [ ] Faulty tyre (*Weekly checks*)

Electrical system

Note: *For problems associated with the starting system, refer to the faults listed under 'Engine' earlier in this Section.*

Battery will only hold a charge for a few days

- [ ] Battery defective internally (Chapter 5)
- [ ] Battery terminal connections loose or corroded (*Weekly checks*)
- [ ] Auxiliary drivebelt worn or incorrectly adjusted (Chapter 1)
- [ ] Alternator not charging at correct output (Chapter 5)
- [ ] Alternator or voltage regulator faulty (Chapter 5)
- [ ] Short-circuit causing continual battery drain (Chapters 5 and 12)

Ignition/no-charge warning light remains illuminated with engine running

- [ ] Auxiliary drivebelt broken, worn, or incorrectly adjusted (Chapter 1)
- [ ] Alternator brushes worn, sticking, or dirty (Chapter 5)
- [ ] Alternator brush springs weak or broken (Chapter 5)
- [ ] Internal fault in alternator or voltage regulator (Chapter 5)
- [ ] Broken, disconnected, or loose wiring in charging circuit (Chapter 5)

Ignition/no-charge warning light fails to come on

- [ ] Warning light bulb blown (Chapter 12)
- [ ] Broken, disconnected, or loose wiring in warning light circuit (Chapter 12)
- [ ] Alternator faulty (Chapter 5)

Lights inoperative

- [ ] Bulb blown (Chapter 12)
- [ ] Corrosion of bulb or bulbholder contacts (Chapter 12)
- [ ] Blown fuse (Chapter 12)
- [ ] Faulty relay (Chapter 12)
- [ ] Broken, loose, or disconnected wiring (Chapter 12)
- [ ] Faulty switch (Chapter 12)

Instrument readings inaccurate or erratic

Instrument readings increase with engine speed

- [ ] Faulty voltage regulator (Chapter 12)

Fuel or temperature gauges give no reading

- [ ] Faulty gauge sender unit (Chapters 3 and 4)
- [ ] Wiring open-circuit (Chapter 12)
- [ ] Faulty gauge (Chapter 12)

Fuel or temperature gauges give continuous maximum reading

- [ ] Faulty gauge sender unit (Chapters 3 and 4)
- [ ] Wiring short-circuit (Chapter 12)
- [ ] Faulty gauge (Chapter 12)

Horn inoperative, or unsatisfactory in operation

Horn operates all the time

- [ ] Horn push either earthed or stuck down (Chapter 12)
- [ ] Horn cable-to-horn push earthed (Chapter 12)

Horn fails to operate

- [ ] Blown fuse (Chapter 12)
- [ ] Cable or cable connections loose, broken or disconnected (Chapter 12)
- [ ] Faulty horn (Chapter 12)

Horn emits intermittent or unsatisfactory sound

- [ ] Cable connections loose (Chapter 12)
- [ ] Horn mountings loose (Chapter 12)
- [ ] Faulty horn (Chapter 12)

Windscreen wipers inoperative, or unsatisfactory in operation

Wipers fail to operate, or operate very slowly

- [ ] Wiper blades stuck to screen, or linkage seized or binding (Chapters 1 and 12)
- [ ] Blown fuse (Chapter 12)
- [ ] Cable or cable connections loose or disconnected (Chapter 12)
- [ ] Faulty relay (Chapter 12)
- [ ] Faulty wiper motor (Chapter 12)

Wiper blades sweep over too large or too small an area of the glass

- [ ] Wiper arms incorrectly positioned on spindles (Chapter 1)
- [ ] Excessive wear of wiper linkage (Chapter 12)
- [ ] Wiper motor or linkage mountings loose or insecure (Chapter 12)

Wiper blades fail to clean the glass effectively

- [ ] Wiper blade rubbers worn or perished (*Weekly checks*)
- [ ] Wiper arm tension springs broken, or arm pivots seized (Chapter 12)
- [ ] Insufficient windscreen washer additive to adequately remove road film (*Weekly checks*)

Electrical system (continued)

Windscreen washers inoperative, or unsatisfactory in operation

One or more washer jets inoperative

- [ ] Blocked washer jet (Chapter 1)
- [ ] Disconnected, kinked or restricted fluid hose (Chapter 12)
- [ ] Insufficient fluid in washer reservoir (*Weekly checks*)

Washer pump fails to operate

- [ ] Broken or disconnected wiring or connections (Chapter 12)
- [ ] Blown fuse (Chapter 12)
- [ ] Faulty washer switch (Chapter 12)
- [ ] Faulty washer pump (Chapter 12)

Washer pump runs for some time before fluid is emitted from jets

- [ ] Faulty one-way valve in fluid supply hose (Chapter 12)

Electric windows inoperative, or unsatisfactory in operation

Window glass will only move in one direction

- [ ] Faulty switch (Chapter 12)

Window glass slow to move

- [ ] Regulator seized or damaged, or in need of lubrication (Chapter 11)
- [ ] Door internal components or trim fouling regulator (Chapter 11)
- [ ] Faulty motor (Chapter 11)

Window glass fails to move

- [ ] Blown fuse (Chapter 12)
- [ ] Faulty relay (Chapter 12)
- [ ] Broken or disconnected wiring or connections (Chapter 12)
- [ ] Faulty motor (Chapter 11)

Central locking system inoperative, or unsatisfactory in operation

Complete system failure

- [ ] Blown fuse (Chapter 12)
- [ ] Faulty relay (Chapter 12)
- [ ] Broken or disconnected wiring or connections (Chapter 12)
- [ ] Faulty motor (Chapter 11)

Latch locks but will not unlock, or unlocks but will not lock

- [ ] Faulty master switch (Chapter 12)
- [ ] Broken or disconnected latch operating rods or levers (Chapter 11)
- [ ] Faulty relay (Chapter 12)
- [ ] Faulty motor (Chapter 11)

One solenoid/motor fails to operate

- [ ] Broken or disconnected wiring or connections (Chapter 12)
- [ ] Faulty operating assembly (Chapter 11)
- [ ] Broken, binding or disconnected latch operating rods or levers (Chapter 11)
- [ ] Fault in door latch (Chapter 11)

A

ABS (Anti-lock brake system) A system, usually electronically controlled, that senses incipient wheel lockup during braking and relieves hydraulic pressure at wheels that are about to skid.

Air bag An inflatable bag hidden in the steering wheel (driver's side) or the dash or glovebox (passenger side). In a head-on collision, the bags inflate, preventing the driver and front passenger from being thrown forward into the steering wheel or windscreen.

Air cleaner A metal or plastic housing, containing a filter element, which removes dust and dirt from the air being drawn into the engine.

Air filter element The actual filter in an air cleaner system, usually manufactured from pleated paper and requiring renewal at regular intervals.

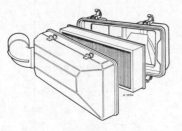

Air filter

Allen key A hexagonal wrench which fits into a recessed hexagonal hole.

Alligator clip A long-nosed spring-loaded metal clip with meshing teeth. Used to make temporary electrical connections.

Alternator A component in the electrical system which converts mechanical energy from a drivebelt into electrical energy to charge the battery and to operate the starting system, ignition system and electrical accessories.

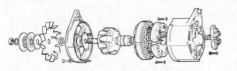

Alternator (exploded view)

Ampere (amp) A unit of measurement for the flow of electric current. One amp is the amount of current produced by one volt acting through a resistance of one ohm.

Anaerobic sealer A substance used to prevent bolts and screws from loosening. Anaerobic means that it does not require oxygen for activation. The Loctite brand is widely used.

Antifreeze A substance (usually ethylene glycol) mixed with water, and added to a vehicle's cooling system, to prevent freezing of the coolant in winter. Antifreeze also contains chemicals to inhibit corrosion and the formation of rust and other deposits that

would tend to clog the radiator and coolant passages and reduce cooling efficiency.

Anti-seize compound A coating that reduces the risk of seizing on fasteners that are subjected to high temperatures, such as exhaust manifold bolts and nuts.

Anti-seize compound

Asbestos A natural fibrous mineral with great heat resistance, commonly used in the composition of brake friction materials. Asbestos is a health hazard and the dust created by brake systems should never be inhaled or ingested.

Axle A shaft on which a wheel revolves, or which revolves with a wheel. Also, a solid beam that connects the two wheels at one end of the vehicle. An axle which also transmits power to the wheels is known as a live axle.

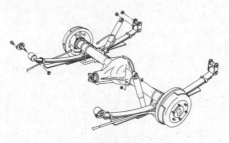

Axle assembly

Axleshaft A single rotating shaft, on either side of the differential, which delivers power from the final drive assembly to the drive wheels. Also called a driveshaft or a halfshaft.

B

Ball bearing An anti-friction bearing consisting of a hardened inner and outer race with hardened steel balls between two races.

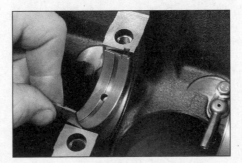

Bearing

Bearing The curved surface on a shaft or in a bore, or the part assembled into either, that permits relative motion between them with minimum wear and friction.

Big-end bearing The bearing in the end of the connecting rod that's attached to the crankshaft.

Bleed nipple A valve on a brake wheel cylinder, caliper or other hydraulic component that is opened to purge the hydraulic system of air. Also called a bleed screw.

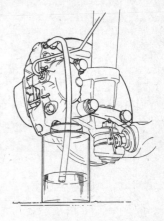

Brake bleeding

Brake bleeding Procedure for removing air from lines of a hydraulic brake system.

Brake disc The component of a disc brake that rotates with the wheels.

Brake drum The component of a drum brake that rotates with the wheels.

Brake linings The friction material which contacts the brake disc or drum to retard the vehicle's speed. The linings are bonded or riveted to the brake pads or shoes.

Brake pads The replaceable friction pads that pinch the brake disc when the brakes are applied. Brake pads consist of a friction material bonded or riveted to a rigid backing plate.

Brake shoe The crescent-shaped carrier to which the brake linings are mounted and which forces the lining against the rotating drum during braking.

Braking systems For more information on braking systems, consult the *Haynes Automotive Brake Manual*.

Breaker bar A long socket wrench handle providing greater leverage.

Bulkhead The insulated partition between the engine and the passenger compartment.

C

Caliper The non-rotating part of a disc-brake assembly that straddles the disc and carries the brake pads. The caliper also contains the hydraulic components that cause the pads to pinch the disc when the brakes are applied. A caliper is also a measuring tool that can be set to measure inside or outside dimensions of an object.

Camshaft A rotating shaft on which a series of cam lobes operate the valve mechanisms. The camshaft may be driven by gears, by sprockets and chain or by sprockets and a belt.

Canister A container in an evaporative emission control system; contains activated charcoal granules to trap vapours from the fuel system.

Canister

Carburettor A device which mixes fuel with air in the proper proportions to provide a desired power output from a spark ignition internal combustion engine.

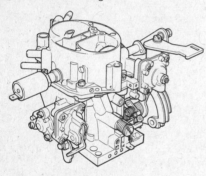

Carburettor

Castellated Resembling the parapets along the top of a castle wall. For example, a castellated balljoint stud nut.

Castellated nut

Castor In wheel alignment, the backward or forward tilt of the steering axis. Castor is positive when the steering axis is inclined rearward at the top.

Catalytic converter A silencer-like device in the exhaust system which converts certain pollutants in the exhaust gases into less harmful substances.

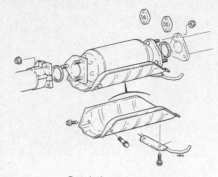

Catalytic converter

Circlip A ring-shaped clip used to prevent endwise movement of cylindrical parts and shafts. An internal circlip is installed in a groove in a housing; an external circlip fits into a groove on the outside of a cylindrical piece such as a shaft.

Clearance The amount of space between two parts. For example, between a piston and a cylinder, between a bearing and a journal, etc.

Coil spring A spiral of elastic steel found in various sizes throughout a vehicle, for example as a springing medium in the suspension and in the valve train.

Compression Reduction in volume, and increase in pressure and temperature, of a gas, caused by squeezing it into a smaller space.

Compression ratio The relationship between cylinder volume when the piston is at top dead centre and cylinder volume when the piston is at bottom dead centre.

Constant velocity (CV) joint A type of universal joint that cancels out vibrations caused by driving power being transmitted through an angle.

Core plug A disc or cup-shaped metal device inserted in a hole in a casting through which core was removed when the casting was formed. Also known as a freeze plug or expansion plug.

Crankcase The lower part of the engine block in which the crankshaft rotates.

Crankshaft The main rotating member, or shaft, running the length of the crankcase, with offset "throws" to which the connecting rods are attached.

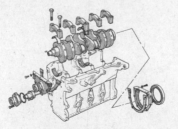

Crankshaft assembly

Crocodile clip See Alligator clip

D

Diagnostic code Code numbers obtained by accessing the diagnostic mode of an engine management computer. This code can be used to determine the area in the system where a malfunction may be located.

Disc brake A brake design incorporating a rotating disc onto which brake pads are squeezed. The resulting friction converts the energy of a moving vehicle into heat.

Double-overhead cam (DOHC) An engine that uses two overhead camshafts, usually one for the intake valves and one for the exhaust valves.

Drivebelt(s) The belt(s) used to drive accessories such as the alternator, water pump, power steering pump, air conditioning compressor, etc. off the crankshaft pulley.

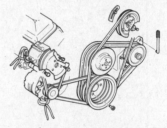

Accessory drivebelts

Driveshaft Any shaft used to transmit motion. Commonly used when referring to the axleshafts on a front wheel drive vehicle.

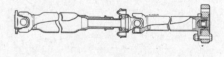

Driveshaft

Drum brake A type of brake using a drum-shaped metal cylinder attached to the inner surface of the wheel. When the brake pedal is pressed, curved brake shoes with friction linings press against the inside of the drum to slow or stop the vehicle.

Drum brake assembly

E

EGR valve A valve used to introduce exhaust gases into the intake air stream.

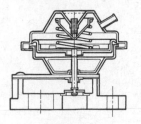

EGR valve

Electronic control unit (ECU) A computer which controls (for instance) ignition and fuel injection systems, or an anti-lock braking system. For more information refer to the *Haynes Automotive Electrical and Electronic Systems Manual.*

Electronic Fuel Injection (EFI) A computer controlled fuel system that distributes fuel through an injector located in each intake port of the engine.

Emergency brake A braking system, independent of the main hydraulic system, that can be used to slow or stop the vehicle if the primary brakes fail, or to hold the vehicle stationary even though the brake pedal isn't depressed. It usually consists of a hand lever that actuates either front or rear brakes mechanically through a series of cables and linkages. Also known as a handbrake or parking brake.

Endfloat The amount of lengthwise movement between two parts. As applied to a crankshaft, the distance that the crankshaft can move forward and back in the cylinder block.

Engine management system (EMS) A computer controlled system which manages the fuel injection and the ignition systems in an integrated fashion.

Exhaust manifold A part with several passages through which exhaust gases leave the engine combustion chambers and enter the exhaust pipe.

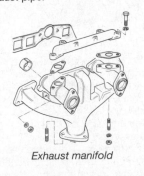

Exhaust manifold

F

Fan clutch A viscous (fluid) drive coupling device which permits variable engine fan speeds in relation to engine speeds.

Feeler blade A thin strip or blade of hardened steel, ground to an exact thickness, used to check or measure clearances between parts.

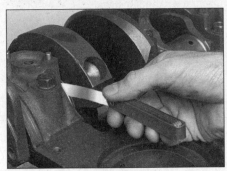

Feeler blade

Firing order The order in which the engine cylinders fire, or deliver their power strokes, beginning with the number one cylinder.

Flywheel A heavy spinning wheel in which energy is absorbed and stored by means of momentum. On cars, the flywheel is attached to the crankshaft to smooth out firing impulses.

Free play The amount of travel before any action takes place. The "looseness" in a linkage, or an assembly of parts, between the initial application of force and actual movement. For example, the distance the brake pedal moves before the pistons in the master cylinder are actuated.

Fuse An electrical device which protects a circuit against accidental overload. The typical fuse contains a soft piece of metal which is calibrated to melt at a predetermined current flow (expressed as amps) and break the circuit.

Fusible link A circuit protection device consisting of a conductor surrounded by heat-resistant insulation. The conductor is smaller than the wire it protects, so it acts as the weakest link in the circuit. Unlike a blown fuse, a failed fusible link must frequently be cut from the wire for replacement.

G

Gap The distance the spark must travel in jumping from the centre electrode to the side

Adjusting spark plug gap

electrode in a spark plug. Also refers to the spacing between the points in a contact breaker assembly in a conventional points-type ignition, or to the distance between the reluctor or rotor and the pickup coil in an electronic ignition.

Gasket Any thin, soft material - usually cork, cardboard, asbestos or soft metal - installed between two metal surfaces to ensure a good seal. For instance, the cylinder head gasket seals the joint between the block and the cylinder head.

Gasket

Gauge An instrument panel display used to monitor engine conditions. A gauge with a movable pointer on a dial or a fixed scale is an analogue gauge. A gauge with a numerical readout is called a digital gauge.

H

Halfshaft A rotating shaft that transmits power from the final drive unit to a drive wheel, usually when referring to a live rear axle.

Harmonic balancer A device designed to reduce torsion or twisting vibration in the crankshaft. May be incorporated in the crankshaft pulley. Also known as a vibration damper.

Hone An abrasive tool for correcting small irregularities or differences in diameter in an engine cylinder, brake cylinder, etc.

Hydraulic tappet A tappet that utilises hydraulic pressure from the engine's lubrication system to maintain zero clearance (constant contact with both camshaft and valve stem). Automatically adjusts to variation in valve stem length. Hydraulic tappets also reduce valve noise.

I

Ignition timing The moment at which the spark plug fires, usually expressed in the number of crankshaft degrees before the piston reaches the top of its stroke.

Inlet manifold A tube or housing with passages through which flows the air-fuel mixture (carburettor vehicles and vehicles with throttle body injection) or air only (port fuel-injected vehicles) to the port openings in the cylinder head.

J

Jump start Starting the engine of a vehicle with a discharged or weak battery by attaching jump leads from the weak battery to a charged or helper battery.

L

Load Sensing Proportioning Valve (LSPV) A brake hydraulic system control valve that works like a proportioning valve, but also takes into consideration the amount of weight carried by the rear axle.

Locknut A nut used to lock an adjustment nut, or other threaded component, in place. For example, a locknut is employed to keep the adjusting nut on the rocker arm in position.

Lockwasher A form of washer designed to prevent an attaching nut from working loose.

M

MacPherson strut A type of front suspension system devised by Earle MacPherson at Ford of England. In its original form, a simple lateral link with the anti-roll bar creates the lower control arm. A long strut - an integral coil spring and shock absorber - is mounted between the body and the steering knuckle. Many modern so-called MacPherson strut systems use a conventional lower A-arm and don't rely on the anti-roll bar for location.

Multimeter An electrical test instrument with the capability to measure voltage, current and resistance.

N

NOx Oxides of Nitrogen. A common toxic pollutant emitted by petrol and diesel engines at higher temperatures.

O

Ohm The unit of electrical resistance. One volt applied to a resistance of one ohm will produce a current of one amp.

Ohmmeter An instrument for measuring electrical resistance.

O-ring A type of sealing ring made of a special rubber-like material; in use, the O-ring is compressed into a groove to provide the sealing action.

O-ring

Overhead cam (ohc) engine An engine with the camshaft(s) located on top of the cylinder head(s).

Overhead valve (ohv) engine An engine with the valves located in the cylinder head, but with the camshaft located in the engine block.

Oxygen sensor A device installed in the engine exhaust manifold, which senses the oxygen content in the exhaust and converts this information into an electric current. Also called a Lambda sensor.

P

Phillips screw A type of screw head having a cross instead of a slot for a corresponding type of screwdriver.

Plastigage A thin strip of plastic thread, available in different sizes, used for measuring clearances. For example, a strip of Plastigage is laid across a bearing journal. The parts are assembled and dismantled; the width of the crushed strip indicates the clearance between journal and bearing.

Plastigage

Propeller shaft The long hollow tube with universal joints at both ends that carries power from the transmission to the differential on front-engined rear wheel drive vehicles.

Proportioning valve A hydraulic control valve which limits the amount of pressure to the rear brakes during panic stops to prevent wheel lock-up.

R

Rack-and-pinion steering A steering system with a pinion gear on the end of the steering shaft that mates with a rack (think of a geared wheel opened up and laid flat). When the steering wheel is turned, the pinion turns, moving the rack to the left or right. This movement is transmitted through the track rods to the steering arms at the wheels.

Radiator A liquid-to-air heat transfer device designed to reduce the temperature of the coolant in an internal combustion engine cooling system.

Refrigerant Any substance used as a heat transfer agent in an air-conditioning system. R-12 has been the principle refrigerant for many years; recently, however, manufacturers have begun using R-134a, a non-CFC substance that is considered less harmful to the ozone in the upper atmosphere.

Rocker arm

Rocker arm A lever arm that rocks on a shaft or pivots on a stud. In an overhead valve engine, the rocker arm converts the upward movement of the pushrod into a downward movement to open a valve.

Rotor In a distributor, the rotating device inside the cap that connects the centre electrode and the outer terminals as it turns, distributing the high voltage from the coil secondary winding to the proper spark plug. Also, that part of an alternator which rotates inside the stator. Also, the rotating assembly of a turbocharger, including the compressor wheel, shaft and turbine wheel.

Runout The amount of wobble (in-and-out movement) of a gear or wheel as it's rotated. The amount a shaft rotates "out-of-true." The out-of-round condition of a rotating part.

S

Sealant A liquid or paste used to prevent leakage at a joint. Sometimes used in conjunction with a gasket.

Sealed beam lamp An older headlight design which integrates the reflector, lens and filaments into a hermetically-sealed one-piece unit. When a filament burns out or the lens cracks, the entire unit is simply replaced.

Serpentine drivebelt A single, long, wide accessory drivebelt that's used on some newer vehicles to drive all the accessories, instead of a series of smaller, shorter belts. Serpentine drivebelts are usually tensioned by an automatic tensioner.

Serpentine drivebelt

Shim Thin spacer, commonly used to adjust the clearance or relative positions between two parts. For example, shims inserted into or under bucket tappets control valve clearances. Clearance is adjusted by changing the thickness of the shim.

Slide hammer A special puller that screws into or hooks onto a component such as a shaft or bearing; a heavy sliding handle on the shaft bottoms against the end of the shaft to knock the component free.

Sprocket A tooth or projection on the periphery of a wheel, shaped to engage with a chain or drivebelt. Commonly used to refer to the sprocket wheel itself.

Starter inhibitor switch On vehicles with an automatic transmission, a switch that prevents starting if the vehicle is not in Neutral or Park.

Strut See MacPherson strut.

T

Tappet A cylindrical component which transmits motion from the cam to the valve stem, either directly or via a pushrod and rocker arm. Also called a cam follower.

Thermostat A heat-controlled valve that regulates the flow of coolant between the cylinder block and the radiator, so maintaining optimum engine operating temperature. A thermostat is also used in some air cleaners in which the temperature is regulated.

Thrust bearing The bearing in the clutch assembly that is moved in to the release levers by clutch pedal action to disengage the clutch. Also referred to as a release bearing.

Timing belt A toothed belt which drives the camshaft. Serious engine damage may result if it breaks in service.

Timing chain A chain which drives the camshaft.

Toe-in The amount the front wheels are closer together at the front than at the rear. On rear wheel drive vehicles, a slight amount of toe-in is usually specified to keep the front wheels running parallel on the road by offsetting other forces that tend to spread the wheels apart.

Toe-out The amount the front wheels are closer together at the rear than at the front. On front wheel drive vehicles, a slight amount of toe-out is usually specified.

Tools For full information on choosing and using tools, refer to the *Haynes Automotive Tools Manual*.

Tracer A stripe of a second colour applied to a wire insulator to distinguish that wire from another one with the same colour insulator.

Tune-up A process of accurate and careful adjustments and parts replacement to obtain the best possible engine performance.

Turbocharger A centrifugal device, driven by exhaust gases, that pressurises the intake air. Normally used to increase the power output from a given engine displacement, but can also be used primarily to reduce exhaust emissions (as on VW's "Umwelt" Diesel engine).

U

Universal joint or U-joint A double-pivoted connection for transmitting power from a driving to a driven shaft through an angle. A U-joint consists of two Y-shaped yokes and a cross-shaped member called the spider.

V

Valve A device through which the flow of liquid, gas, vacuum, or loose material in bulk may be started, stopped, or regulated by a movable part that opens, shuts, or partially obstructs one or more ports or passageways. A valve is also the movable part of such a device.

Valve clearance The clearance between the valve tip (the end of the valve stem) and the rocker arm or tappet. The valve clearance is measured when the valve is closed.

Vernier caliper A precision measuring instrument that measures inside and outside dimensions. Not quite as accurate as a micrometer, but more convenient.

Viscosity The thickness of a liquid or its resistance to flow.

Volt A unit for expressing electrical "pressure" in a circuit. One volt that will produce a current of one ampere through a resistance of one ohm.

W

Welding Various processes used to join metal items by heating the areas to be joined to a molten state and fusing them together. For more information refer to the *Haynes Automotive Welding Manual*.

Wiring diagram A drawing portraying the components and wires in a vehicle's electrical system, using standardised symbols. For more information refer to the *Haynes Automotive Electrical and Electronic Systems Manual*.

Note: *References throughout this index are in the form* **"Chapter number"** • *"Page number"*

A

Accelerator cable
diesel engine – 4B•6
petrol engine – 4A•2
Accelerator pedal – 4A•3
Accelerator pedal position sensor
diesel engine – 4B•13
Accessory shops – REF•3
Accumulator rail
diesel engine – 4B•3, 4B•8
Acknowledgements – 0•6
Aerial – 12•18
Air conditioning system – 3•9, 3•10
refrigerant leaks
diesel engine – 1B•7
petrol engine – 1A•8
Air filter
diesel engine – 1B•13, 4B•5
petrol engine – 1A•13, 4A•2
Air injection valve
petrol engine – 4C•3
Air inlet sensor
diesel engine – 4B•4
Air mass meter
diesel engine – 4B•14
Air pressure sensor
Magneti Marelli system – 4A•13
Air pump
petrol engine – 4C•3
Air temperature sensor
Bosch Motronic and Sagem Lucas system – 4A•11
Magneti Marelli system – 4A•13
Airbags – 0•5, 12•21
Alarm system – 12•19
Alternator – 5A•3, 5A•4
Antifreeze – 0•13, 0•18
diesel engine – 1B•17
petrol engine – 1A•16
Anti-lock braking system (ABS) – 9•17, 9•18
Anti-roll bar – 10•7, 10•12, 10•13
Anti-theft alarm system – 12•19
Asbestos – 0•5
Automatic transmission – 2D•4, 2D•7, 7B•1 *et seq*
fault finding – REF•20
Automatic transmission fluid – 0•18, 7B•2
diesel engine – 1B•8
leaks
diesel engine – 1B•7
petrol engine – 1A•8
petrol engine – 1A•7
Auxiliary drivebelt – 5A•3
diesel engine – 1B•11
petrol engine – 1A•11

B

Badges – 11•20
Balance shaft housing – 2D•12
Battery – 0•5, 0•16, 5A•2, 12•20, REF•7
Big-end bearings – 2D•19, 2D•24
Bleeding
brakes – 9•2
clutch – 6•4
fuel system
diesel engine – 4B•4
power steering system – 10•17
Blower motor – 3•9
Body electrical system – 12•1 *et seq*
Bodywork and fittings – 11•1 *et seq*
corrosion – REF•11
Bonnet – 11•6, 11•7
Boot lid – 11•14, 11•15
Bosch Motronic fuel injection system – 4A•9
Brake fluid – 0•13, 0•18
diesel engine – 1B•15
leaks
diesel engine – 1B•7
petrol engine – 1A•8
petrol engine – 1A•15
Brake pedal switches
cruise control system – 12•19
Braking system – 9•1 *et seq*, REF•9, REF•10
diesel engine – 1B•11
fault finding – REF•21
petrol engine – 1A•11
Bulbs – 0•17, 12•6, 12•8
clock illumination – 12•10
courtesy and reading light – 12•8, 12•9
direction indicator – 12•7
door open warning light – 12•9
foglight – 12•7
glovebox illumination – 12•9
headlight – 12•6
heater control illumination – 12•9
high-level stop-light – 12•8
instrument illumination/warning lights – 12•9
luggage area light – 12•9
multi-function display – 12•10
number plate light – 12•8
rear light cluster – 12•7
sidelight – 12•7
sun visor illumination – 12•10
switch illumination – 12•10
Bumpers – 11•4
Burning – 0•5

C

Cables
  accelerator
    diesel engine – 4B•6
    petrol engine – 4A•2
  bonnet release – 11•7
  clutch – 6•2
  electric seats – 12•20
  folding seat – 11•21
  gearchange – 7A•3
  handbrake – 9•15
  heater/ventilation – 3•8
Calipers – 9•10, 9•11
Camshaft oil seals
  DW diesel engine – 2C•25
  EW petrol engine – 2B•11
  XU petrol engine – 2A•10
Camshaft position sensor
  diesel engine – 4B•13
  petrol engine – 4A•11
Camshaft sprocket
  DW diesel engine – 2C•11
  EW petrol engine – 2B•9, 2B•10
  XU petrol engine – 2A•9, 2A•10
Camshafts
  DW diesel engine – 2C•13
  EW petrol engine – 2B•11
  XU petrol engine – 2A•10
Carpets – 11•2, 11•24
Cassette player – 12•17
Catalytic converter – 4C•4
  diesel engine – 4B•17
  petrol engine – 4A•15
Central locking
  boot lid lock motor – 11•18
  door lock motor – 11•18
  electronic control units (ECU) – 11•18
  tailgate lock motor – 11•18
Centre console – 11•25
  switches – 12•4
Charcoal canister
  petrol engine – 4C•2
Charging – 5A•2, 5A•3
Cigarette lighter – 12•14
Clock – 12•14
  illumination bulbs – 12•10
Clutch – 6•1 *et seq*
  diesel engine – 1B•8
  fault finding – REF•19
  petrol engine – 1A•9
Clutch fluid – 0•13, 0•18
  leaks
    diesel engine – 1B•7
    petrol engine – 1A•8
Clutch pedal switches
  cruise control system – 12•19
Coil
  ignition – 5B•2
  spring – 10•10

Compression test
  DW diesel engine – 2C•4
  EW petrol engine – 2B•4
  XU petrol engine – 2A•3
Connecting rods – 2D•14, 2D•17, 2D•24
Console – 11•25
  switches – 12•4, 12•5
Contents – 0•2
Conversion factors – REF•2
Coolant – 0•13, 0•18
  diesel engine – 1B•16
  leaks
    diesel engine – 1B•7
    petrol engine – 1A•8
  petrol engine – 1A•15
Coolant pump – 3•7
  sprocket
    diesel engine – 2C•12
Cooling, heating and ventilation systems – 3•1 *et seq*
  fault finding – REF•18
Courtesy light
  bulbs – 12•8, 12•9
  switch – 12•6
Crankcase – 2D•16
Crankcase emission control – 4C•1
  diesel engine – 4C•3
  petrol engine – 4C•2
Crankshaft – 2D•14, 2D•18, 2D•21
Crankshaft (RPM) sensor
  petrol engine – 4A•12
Crankshaft oil seals
  DW diesel engine – 2C•25
  EW petrol engine – 2B•17
  XU petrol engine – 2A•14
Crankshaft pulley
  DW diesel engine – 2C•6
  EW petrol engine – 2B•6
  XU petrol engine – 2A•5
Crankshaft speed/position sensor
  diesel engine – 4B•12
Crankshaft sprocket
  DW diesel engine – 2C•11
  EW petrol engine – 2B•9, 2B•10
  XU petrol engine – 2A•9, 2A•10
Cruise control system
  brake and clutch pedal switches – 12•19
  electronic control unit (ECU) – 12•19
  operating switch – 12•19
  solenoid valve – 12•19
  throttle actuator and cable – 12•19
  vacuum pump – 12•19
Crushing – 0•5
Cylinder block – 2D•16
Cylinder head – 2D•8, 2D•10, 2D•11
  DW diesel engine – 2C•15
  EW petrol engine – 2B•12
  XU petrol engine – 2A•11
Cylinder head cover
  DW diesel engine – 2C•5
  EW petrol engine – 2B•5
  XU petrol engine – 2A•4

D

Dents in bodywork – 11•2
Depressurisation
  fuel injection system – 4A•7
Diesel engine in-car repair procedures – 2C•1 *et seq*
Diesel injection equipment – 0•5
Dimensions – REF•1
Direction indicator – 12•11
  bulbs – 12•7
Disconnecting the battery – 12•20, REF•7
Discs – 9•7, 9•8
Doors – 11•7, 11•8, 11•10, 11•12, 11•18, REF•9
  switches – 12•5
  warning light bulbs – 12•9
Drivebelt – 5A•3
  diesel engine – 1B•11
  petrol engine – 1A•11
Driveplate
  DW diesel engine – 2C•26
  EW petrol engine – 2B•18
  XU petrol engine – 2A•14
Driveshafts – 8•1 *et seq*, REF•10
  fault finding – REF•21
  gaiter
    diesel engine – 1B•9
    petrol engine – 1A•9
  oil seals – 7A•4
Drivetrain
  diesel engine – 1B•11
  petrol engine – 1A•11
Drums – 9•9
DW diesel engine in-car repair procedures – 2C•1 *et seq*

E

Earth fault – 12•2
ECU and sensors
  diesel engine – 4B•4
EGR valve
  diesel engine – 4C•3
Electric cooling fans – 3•6
Electric shock – 0•5
Electric windows – 11•18
Electrical equipment – REF•9
  diesel engine – 1B•11
  petrol engine – 1A•11
Electrical fault finding – 12•2, REF•23, REF•24
Electronic control system
  diesel engine – 4B•3, 4B•12
Electronic control unit (ECU)
  automatic transmission – 7B•5
  cruise control system – 12•19
  diesel engine – 4B•12
  ABS – 9•18
  petrol fuel injection – 4A•10
  central locking – 11•18
Emission control systems – 4C•1 *et seq*, REF•11
  diesel engine – 1B•15

Engine fault finding – REF•16, REF•17
Engine immobiliser – 12•19
Engine oil – 0•12, 0•18
  diesel engine – 1B•6
  leaks
    diesel engine – 1B•7
    petrol engine – 1A•8
  petrol engine – 1A•6
Engine removal and overhaul procedures – 2D•1 *et seq*
Environmental considerations – REF•5
Evaporative emission control
  petrol engine – 4C•1, 4C•2
EW series petrol engine in-car repair procedures – 2B•1 *et seq*
Exhaust emission control
  diesel engine – 4C•2, 4C•3
  petrol engine – 4C•1, 4C•2
Exhaust gas recirculation system
  diesel engine – 4C•2, 4C•3
Exhaust manifold
  diesel engine – 4B•15
  petrol engine – 4A•14
Exhaust specialists – REF•3
Exhaust system – REF•10, REF•11
  diesel engine – 4B•17
  petrol engine – 4A•15

F

Facia panel – 11•26
  switches – 12•4
Fans – 3•6
  sensor – 3•7
Fault finding – REF•14 *et seq*
  automatic transmission – REF•20
  braking system – REF•21
  clutch – REF•19
  cooling system – REF•18
  driveshafts – REF•21
  electrical system – 12•2, REF•23, REF•24
  engine – REF•16, REF•17
  fuel and exhaust systems – REF•18
  manual transmission – REF•20
  suspension and steering – REF•22
Filling – 11•3
Filter
  air
    diesel engine – 1B•13, 4B•5
    petrol engine – 1A•13, 4A•2
  fuel
    diesel engine – 1B•6, 1B•13
    petrol engine – 1A•14
  oil
    diesel engine – 1B•6
    petrol engine – 1A•6
  particulate emission
    diesel engine – 4C•2
  pollen
    diesel engine – 1B•10
    petrol engine – 1A•9

Fire – 0•5
Fluid cooler
automatic transmission – 7B•4
Flywheel
DW diesel engine – 2C•26
EW petrol engine – 2B•18
XU petrol engine – 2A•14
Foglight – 12•11
bulbs – 12•7
Footbrake – REF•8
Fuel additive system
diesel engine – 4C•3, 4C•4
Fuel and exhaust system –
petrol models – 4A•1 *et seq,* REF•11
Fuel and exhaust systems –
diesel models – 4B•1 *et seq,* REF•11
fault finding – REF•18
Fuel filter
diesel engine – 1B•13
petrol engine – 1A•14
Fuel filter water draining
diesel engine – 1B•6
Fuel gauge sender unit
diesel engine – 4B•7
petrol engine – 4A•8
Fuel injection systems – 4A•3
diesel engine – 4B•4
petrol engine – 4A•8
Fuel injectors
diesel engine – 4B•3, 4B•10
petrol engine – 4A•9, 4A•12
Fuel leaks
diesel engine – 1B•7
petrol engine – 1A•8
Fuel lift pump
diesel engine – 4B•3, 4B•6
Fuel pressure control valve
diesel engine – 4B•14
Fuel pressure regulator
Bosch Motronic and Sagem Lucas system – 4A•10
Magneti Marelli system – 4A•12
Fuel pressure sensor
diesel engine – 4B•3, 4B•14
Fuel pump
diesel engine – 4B•3, 4B•7
petrol engine – 4A•7
sprocket
diesel engine – 2C•12
Fuel rail
Bosch Motronic and Sagem Lucas system – 4A•9
Magneti Marelli system – 4A•12
Fuel tank – 4A•8
Fuel temperature sensor
diesel engine – 4B•13
Fume or gas intoxication – 0•5
Fuses – 0•17, 12•3

G

Gaiter
driveshaft
diesel engine – 1B•9
petrol engine – 1A•9
steering gear – 10•17
Garages – REF•3
Gashes in bodywork – 11•2
Gaskets – REF•5
Gearchange
cables – 7A•3
linkage – 7A•3
Glossary of technical terms – REF•25 *et seq*
Glovebox – 11•24
illumination bulbs – 12•9
Glow plugs – 5C•2
Grille – 11•6

H

Handbrake – 9•14, 9•15, REF•8
diesel engine – 1B•11
petrol engine – 1A•11
warning switch – 12•6
Handles
door – 11•10
Hazard warning light switch – 12•4
Headlight – 12•10
beam alignment – 12•13
bulbs – 12•6
washer jets – 12•17
Headlining – 11•25
Heat exchanger
diesel engine – 4C•3
Heat shield(s)
diesel engine – 4B•18
petrol engine – 4A•15
Heater – 3•8, 3•9
control illumination bulbs – 12•9
High-level stop-light – 12•12
bulbs – 12•8
High-pressure fuel pump
diesel engine – 4B•3, 4B•7
Hinge lubrication
diesel engine – 1B•10
petrol engine – 1A•10
Horn(s) – 12•14
Hoses
braking system – 9•4
cooling system – 3•3
Hub bearings – 10•3, 10•9
Hydraulic pipes and hoses – 9•4
Hydraulic tappets
DW diesel engine – 2C•13
EW petrol engine – 2B•11
XU petrol engine – 2A•10
Hydrofluoric acid – 0•5

I

Idle speed stepper motor
Bosch Motronic and Sagem Lucas system – 4A•11
Magneti Marelli system – 4A•13
Idler roller
diesel engine – 2C•12
Ignition switch – 10•15
Ignition system (petrol models) – 1A•13, 5B•1 *et seq*
Immobiliser system – 12•19
Indicator – 12•11
bulbs – 12•7
Injectors
diesel engine – 4B•3, 4B•10
petrol engine – 4A•9, 4A•12
Inlet air pressure sensor
Magneti Marelli system – 4A•13
Inlet air temperature sensor
Bosch Motronic and Sagem Lucas system – 4A•11
Magneti Marelli system – 4A•13
Inlet ducts
diesel engine – 4B•5
petrol engine – 4A•2
Inlet manifold
diesel engine – 4B•14
petrol engine – 4A•13
Inlet sensor
diesel engine – 4B•4
Input shaft oil seal
manual transmission – 7A•5
Input speed sensor
automatic transmission – 7B•5
Instrument panel – 12•13, 12•14
bulbs – 12•9
diesel engine – 1B•11
petrol engine – 1A•11
Intercooler
diesel engine – 4B•17
Intermediate bearing (driveshaft) – 8•5
Introduction – 0•6

J

Jacking and vehicle support – REF•6
Joint mating faces – REF•5
Jump starting – 0•8

K

Knock sensor – 5B•2

L

Lambda sensor
petrol engine – 4C•2
Leakdown tests
diesel engine – 2C•4
Leaks – 0•10
diesel engine – 1B•7
petrol engine – 1A•8
Locknuts, locktabs and washers – REF•5
Locks
bonnet – 11•7
boot lid – 11•15, 11•18
door – 11•10, 11•18
lubrication
diesel engine – 1B•10
petrol engine – 1A•10
steering column – 10•15
tailgate – 11•17, 11•18
Loudspeakers – 12•17
Lower arm – 10•6, 10•11
Lubricants and fluids – 0•18
Luggage area light bulbs – 12•9
switch – 12•6

M

Magneti Marelli system
petrol engine – 4A•12
Main bearings – 2D•19, 2D•21
Manifold absolute pressure sensor
Bosch Motronic and Sagem Lucas system – 4A•11
Manifolds
diesel engine – 4B•14, 4B•15
petrol engine – 4A•13, 4A•14
Manual transmission – 2D•4, 2D•5, 7A•1 *et seq*
fault finding – REF•20
oil – 7A•2
diesel engine – 1B•14
petrol engine – 1A•14
Master cylinder
brake – 9•12
clutch – 6•3
Matrix – 3•8
Mirrors – 11•18, REF•8
MOT test checks – REF•8 *et seq*
Motor factors – REF•3
Mountings
DW diesel engine – 2C•26
EW petrol engine – 2B•18
XU petrol engine – 2A•15
Multi-function display – 12•14
bulbs – 12•10
Multi-function switch
automatic transmission – 7B•5

N

Number plate light – 12•12
  bulbs – 12•8

O

Oil
  engine – 0•12, 0•18
    diesel engine – 1B•6
    petrol engine – 1A•6
  leaks
    diesel engine – 1B•7
    petrol engine – 1A•8
  manual transmission – 7A•2
    diesel engine – 1B•14
    petrol engine – 1A•14
Oil cooler
  DW diesel engine – 2C•25
  XU petrol engine – 2A•13
Oil filter
  diesel engine – 1B•6
  petrol engine – 1A•6
Oil level sensor – 5A•5
Oil pressure sensor
  automatic transmission – 7B•7
Oil pressure warning light switch – 5A•5
Oil pump
  DW diesel engine – 2C•24
  EW petrol engine – 2B•16
  XU petrol engine – 2A•13
Oil seals – REF•5
  camshaft
    DW diesel engine – 2C•25
    EW petrol engine – 2B•11
    XU petrol engine – 2A•10
  crankshaft
    DW diesel engine – 2C•25
    EW petrol engine – 2B•17
    XU petrol engine – 2A•14
  driveshaft – 7A•4
  input shaft
    manual transmission – 7A•5
  selector shaft
    automatic transmission – 7B•4
    manual transmission – 7A•5
Open circuit – 12•2
Outlet ducts
  diesel engine – 4B•5

Output speed sensor
  automatic transmission – 7B•5

P

Pads – 9•4, 9•5
  diesel engine – 1B•10
  petrol engine – 1A•10
Park Lock solenoid
  automatic transmission – 7B•6
Particulate emission system – 1B•15, 4C•2
  filter – 4B•18
Parts – REF•3
Pedals
  accelerator
    petrol engine – 4A•3
    diesel engine – 4B•13
  brake – 9•12
  clutch – 6•2
Petrol engine in-car repair procedures
  EW engine – 2B•1 *et seq*
  XU engine – 2A•1 *et seq*
Pipes and hoses – 9•4
Piston rings – 2D•20
Pistons – 2D•14, 2D•17, 2D•24
Plastic components – 11•3
Poisonous or irritant substances – 0•5
Pollen filter
  diesel engine – 1B•10
  petrol engine – 1A•9
Power steering fluid – 0•15, 0•18
  leaks
    diesel engine – 1B•7
    petrol engine – 1A•8
Power steering pump – 10•17
Preheating system (diesel models) – 5C•1 *et seq*
Pressure control valve
  diesel engine – 4B•3
Pressure-regulating valve
  braking system – 9•16
Priming fuel system
  diesel engine – 4B•4
Pulleys
  DW diesel engine – 2C•12
  EW petrol engine – 2B•9
  XU petrol engine – 2A•9, 2A•10
Puncture repair – 0•9
Purge valve renewal
  petrol engine – 4C•2

R

Radiator – 3•4
  flushing
    diesel engine – 1B•16
    petrol engine – 1A•16
  grille – 11•6
Radio aerial – 12•18
Radio/cassette player – 12•17
Rain sensor switch – 12•6
Reading light bulbs – 12•8, 12•9
Rear light cluster – 12•11
  bulbs – 12•7
Rear screen
  glass – 11•19
  wiper motor – 12•16
Rear wing light – 12•11
Refrigerant leaks
  diesel engine – 1B•7
  petrol engine – 1A•8
Regulator
  window – 11•12
Relays – 12•3
  Bosch Motronic and Sagem Lucas system – 4A•12
  Magneti Marelli system – 4A•13
Release mechanism
  clutch – 6•5
Repair procedures – REF•5
Respraying – 11•3
Reversing light switch
  manual transmission – 7A•5
Road test
  diesel engine – 1B•11
  petrol engine – 1A•11
Roadside repairs – 0•7 *et seq*
Rocker arms
  diesel engine – 2C•13
Routine maintenance & servicing – diesel models – 1B•1 *et seq*
Routine maintenance & servicing – petrol models – 1A•1 *et seq*
  bodywork and underframe – 11•1
  upholstery and carpets – 11•2
RPM sensor
  petrol engine – 4A•12
Rust holes in bodywork – 11•2

S

Safety first! – 0•5, 0•13, 0•15
Sagem Lucas fuel injection system
  petrol engine – 4A•9
Scalding – 0•5
Scratches in bodywork – 11•2
Screw threads and fastenings – REF•5
Seat belts – 11•21, 11•22
  switches – 12•6
Seats – 11•20, 12•20
Secondary air injection
  petrol engine – 4C•2, 4C•3

Selector cable
  automatic transmission – 7B•3
Selector lever position switch
  automatic transmission – 7B•6
Selector shaft oil seal
  automatic transmission – 7B•4
  manual transmission – 7A•5
Servo unit – 9•13
Shock absorbers – 10•9, REF•9, REF•10
  diesel engine – 1B•9
  petrol engine – 1A•10
Shoes – 9•6
Shoes
  diesel engine – 1B•15
  handbrake – 9•15
  petrol engine – 1A•14
Short circuit – 12•2
Sidelight bulbs – 12•7
Silencer
  petrol engine – 4A•15
Slave cylinder
  clutch – 6•3
Solenoid valve
  cruise control system – 12•19
Spare parts – REF•3
Spark plug
  petrol engine – 1A•12
Speed sensor
  diesel engine – 4B•14
  petrol engine – 4A•12
Speedometer drive
  automatic transmission – 7B•4
  manual transmission – 7A•6
Springs
  suspension – 10•10, REF•10
Sprockets
  DW diesel engine – 2C•11
  EW petrol engine – 2B•9
  XU petrol engine – 2A•9
Starter motor – 5A•4, 5A•5
Starting and charging systems – 5A•1 *et seq*
Start-up after overhaul – 2D•26
Steering angles – 10•18
Steering – 10•16, 10•17, REF•9, REF•10
  column – 10•13, 10•14, REF•8
    switches – 12•3
  diesel engine – 1B•9, 1B•11
  petrol engine – 1A•10, 1A•11
  wheel – 10•13, REF•8
Stop-light – 12•12
  bulbs – 12•8
  switch – 9•17
Strut
  boot lid – 11•15
  suspension – 10•4, 10•5
    diesel engine – 1B•9
    petrol engine – 1A•10
  tailgate – 11•16

Stub axle – 10•10
Subframe – 10•7
Sump
  DW diesel engine – 2C•23
  EW petrol engine – 2B•15
  XU petrol engine – 2A•12
Sun visor illumination bulbs – 12•10
Sunroof – 11•19
Suspension and steering – 10•1 *et seq,* REF•9, REF•10
  diesel engine – 1B•9, 1B•11
  fault finding – REF•22
  petrol engine – 1A•10, 1A•11
Switches – 12•3
  centre console – 12•4
  cooling system – 3•6
  courtesy light – 12•6
  cruise control system – 12•19
  door – 12•5
  facia – 12•4
  handbrake warning – 12•6
  hazard warning light – 12•4
  illumination – 12•10
  luggage area light – 12•6
  oil pressure warning light – 5A•5
  overhead console – 12•5
  rain sensor – 12•6
  reversing light
    manual transmission – 7A•5
  seat – 12•6
  selector lever position
    automatic transmission – 7B•6
  steering column – 12•3
  stop-light – 9•17
  washer reservoir level – 12•17
Swivel hub – 10•3

T

Tailgate – 11•16, 11•17
  light unit – 12•11
  washer jet – 12•17
  wiper motor – 12•16
Tailpipe
  diesel engine – 4B•18
Tappets
  DW diesel engine – 2C•13
  EW petrol engine – 2B•11
  XU petrol engine – 2A•10
Temperature gauge sender – 3•7
Temperature sensor – 3•6
  diesel engine – 4B•13
  Bosch Motronic and Sagem Lucas system – 4A•11
  Magneti Marelli system – 4A•13
Tensioner pulleys
  DW diesel engine – 2C•12
  EW petrol engine – 2B•10, 2B•11
  XU petrol engine – 2A•9, 2A•10

Thermostat – 3•5
Throttle actuator and cable
  cruise control system – 12•19
Throttle bodies
  diesel engine – 4B•14
Throttle housing heater
  Magneti Marelli system – 4A•13
Throttle housing
  petrol engine – 4A•9
Throttle potentiometer
  Bosch Motronic and Sagem Lucas system – 4A•10
  Magneti Marelli system – 4A•13
Timing belt covers
  DW diesel engine – 2C•7
  EW petrol engine – 2B•6
  XU petrol engine – 2A•5
Timing belt
  diesel engine – 1B•15, 2C•8
  EW petrol engine – 2B•7
  petrol engine – 1A•15
  XU petrol engine – 2A•5
Timing belt sprockets and tensioner
  DW diesel engine – 2C•11
  EW petrol engine – 2B•9
  XU petrol engine – 2A•9
Timing holes
  DW diesel engine – 2C•5
  EW petrol engine – 2B•4
  XU petrol engine – 2A•3
Timing
  ignition – 5B•2
Tools – REF•5, REF•8
Towing – 0•10
Track arm – 10•12
Track rod – 10•18
Trailing arm – 10•11
Transmission mountings
  DW diesel engine – 2C•26
  EW petrol engine – 2B•18
  XU petrol engine – 2A•15
Trim panels – 11•8, 11•19, 11•20, 11•24
Turbocharger
  diesel engine – 4B•4, 4B•5, 4B•16
Tyre – REF•11
  condition and pressure – 0•14
  pressures – 0•18
  specialists – REF•3

U

Underbonnet check points – 0•11
Underframe – 11•1
Under-panels – 11•19
Unleaded petrol – 4A•3
Upholstery – 11•2
Upper arm – 10•11

V

Vacuum hose leaks
  diesel engine – 1B•7
  petrol engine – 1A•9
Vacuum pump
  braking system – 9•19, 9•20
  cruise control system – 12•19
Vacuum servo unit – 9•13
Valve timing holes
  DW diesel engine – 2C•5
  EW petrol engine – 2B•4
  XU petrol engine – 2A•3
Valves – 2D•10
Vehicle identification numbers – REF•4, REF•9
Vehicle speed sensor
  diesel engine – 4B•14
  petrol engine – 4A•12
Vehicle support – REF•6
Ventilation system – 3•8

W

Warning light sender – 3•7
Warning lights bulbs – 12•9
Washer system – 12•16
  fluid – 0•15

Weekly checks – 0•11 *et seq*
Weights – REF•1
Wheels – REF•11
Wheel alignment – 10•18
Wheel bearings – 10•3, 10•9, REF•10
Wheel changing – 0•9
Wheel cylinder – 9•11
Wheel sensor – 9•19
Wheelarch liners – 11•19
Windows – 11•18, 11•19
  door – 11•12
Windscreen – 11•19, REF•8
  washer jets – 12•17
  wiper motor and linkage – 12•15
Wing light – 12•11
Wipers
  arm – 12•15
  blades – 0•16
Working facilities – REF•9
Wiring diagrams – 12•22 *et seq*

X

XU petrol engine in-car repair procedures – 2A•1 *et seq*

Haynes Manuals – The Complete UK Car List

Title	Book No.
ALFA ROMEO Alfasud/Sprint (74 - 88) up to F *	0292
Alfa Romeo Alfetta (73 - 87) up to E *	0531
AUDI 80, 90 & Coupe Petrol (79 - Nov 88) up to F	0605
Audi 80, 90 & Coupe Petrol (Oct 86 - 90) D to H	1491
Audi 100 & 200 Petrol (Oct 82 - 90) up to H	0907
Audi 100 & A6 Petrol & Diesel (May 91 - May 97) H to P	3504
Audi A3 Petrol & Diesel (96 - May 03) P to 03	4253
Audi A4 Petrol & Diesel (95 - 00) M to X	3575
Audi A4 Petrol & Diesel (01 - 04) X to 54	4609
AUSTIN A35 & A40 (56 - 67) up to F *	0118
Austin/MG/Rover Maestro 1.3 & 1.6 Petrol (83 - 95) up to M	0922
Austin/MG Metro (80 - May 90) up to G	0718
Austin/Rover Montego 1.3 & 1.6 Petrol (84 - 94) A to L	1066
Austin/MG/Rover Montego 2.0 Petrol (84 - 95) A to M	1067
Mini (59 - 69) up to H *	0527
Mini (69 - 01) up to X	0646
Austin/Rover 2.0 litre Diesel Engine (86 - 93) C to L	1857
Austin Healey 100/6 & 3000 (56 - 68) up to G *	0049
BEDFORD CF Petrol (69 - 87) up to E	0163
Bedford/Vauxhall Rascal & Suzuki Supercarry (86 - Oct 94) C to M	3015
BMW 316, 320 & 320i (4-cyl) (75 - Feb 83) up to Y *	0276
BMW 320, 320i, 323i & 325i (6-cyl) (Oct 77 - Sept 87) up to E	0815
BMW 3- & 5-Series Petrol (81 - 91) up to J	1948
BMW 3-Series Petrol (Apr 91 - 99) H to V	3210
BMW 3-Series Petrol (Sept 98 - 03) S to 53	4067
BMW 520i & 525e (Oct 81 - June 88) up to E	1560
BMW 525, 528 & 528i (73 - Sept 81) up to X *	0632
BMW 5-Series 6-cyl Petrol (April 96 - Aug 03) N to 03	4151
BMW 1500, 1502, 1600, 1602, 2000 & 2002 (59 - 77) up to S *	0240
CHRYSLER PT Cruiser Petrol (00 - 03) W to 53	4058
CITROËN 2CV, Ami & Dyane (67 - 90) up to H	0196
Citroën AX Petrol & Diesel (87 - 97) D to P	3014
Citroën Berlingo & Peugeot Partner Petrol & Diesel (96 - 05) P to 55	4281
Citroën BX Petrol (83 - 94) A to L	0908
Citroën C15 Van Petrol & Diesel (89 - Oct 98) F to S	3509
Citroën C3 Petrol & Diesel (02 - 05) 51 to 05	4197
Citroën CX Petrol (75 - 88) up to F	0528
Citroën Saxo Petrol & Diesel (96 - 04) N to 54	3506
Citroën Visa Petrol (79 - 88) up to F	0620
Citroën Xantia Petrol & Diesel (93 - 01) K to Y	3082
Citroën XM Petrol & Diesel (89 - 00) G to X	3451
Citroën Xsara Petrol & Diesel (97 - Sept 00) R to W	3751
Citroën Xsara Picasso Petrol & Diesel (00 - 02) W to 52	3944
Citroën ZX Diesel (91 - 98) J to S	1922
Citroën ZX Petrol (91 - 98) H to S	1881
Citroën 1.7 & 1.9 litre Diesel Engine (84 - 96) A to N	1379
FIAT 126 (73 - 87) up to E *	0305
Fiat 500 (57 - 73) up to M *	0090
Fiat Bravo & Brava Petrol (95 - 00) N to W	3572
Fiat Cinquecento (93 - 98) K to R	3501
Fiat Panda (81 - 95) up to M	0793
Fiat Punto Petrol & Diesel (94 - Oct 99) L to V	3251
Fiat Punto Petrol (Oct 99 - July 03) V to 03	4066
Fiat Regata Petrol (84 - 88) A to F	1167
Fiat Tipo Petrol (88 - 91) E to J	1625
Fiat Uno Petrol (83 - 95) up to M	0923
Fiat X1/9 (74 - 89) up to G *	0273
FORD Anglia (59 - 68) up to G *	0001
Ford Capri II (& III) 1.6 & 2.0 (74 - 87) up to E *	0283
Ford Capri II (& III) 2.8 & 3.0 V6 (74 - 87) up to E	1309

Title	Book No.
Ford Cortina Mk I & Corsair 1500 ('62 - '66) up to D*	0214
Ford Cortina Mk III 1300 & 1600 (70 - 76) up to P *	0070
Ford Escort Mk I 1100 & 1300 (68 - 74) up to N *	0171
Ford Escort Mk I Mexico, RS 1600 & RS 2000 (70 - 74) up to N *	0139
Ford Escort Mk II Mexico, RS 1800 & RS 2000 (75 - 80) up to W *	0735
Ford Escort (75 - Aug 80) up to V *	0280
Ford Escort Petrol (Sept 80 - Sept 90) up to H	0686
Ford Escort & Orion Petrol (Sept 90 - 00) H to X	1737
Ford Escort & Orion Diesel (Sept 90 - 00) H to X	4081
Ford Fiesta (76 - Aug 83) up to Y	0334
Ford Fiesta Petrol (Aug 83 - Feb 89) A to F	1030
Ford Fiesta Petrol (Feb 89 - Oct 95) F to N	1595
Ford Fiesta Petrol & Diesel (Oct 95 - Mar 02) N to 02	3397
Ford Fiesta Petrol & Diesel (Apr 02 - 05) 02 to 54	4170
Ford Focus Petrol & Diesel (98 - 01) S to Y	3759
Ford Focus Petrol & Diesel (Oct 01 - 05) 51 to 05	4167
Ford Galaxy Petrol & Diesel (95 - Aug 00) M to W	3984
Ford Granada Petrol (Sept 77 - Feb 85) up to B *	0481
Ford Granada & Scorpio Petrol (Mar 85 - 94) B to M	1245
Ford Ka (96 - 02) P to 52	3570
Ford Mondeo Petrol (93 - Sept 00) K to X	1923
Ford Mondeo Petrol & Diesel (Oct 00 - Jul 03) X to 03	3990
Ford Mondeo Petrol & Diesel (July 03 - 07) 03 to 56	4619
Ford Mondeo Diesel (93 - 96) L to N	3465
Ford Orion Petrol (83 - Sept 90) up to H	1009
Ford Sierra 4-cyl Petrol (82 - 93) up to K	0903
Ford Sierra V6 Petrol (82 - 91) up to J	0904
Ford Transit Petrol (Mk 2) (78 - Jan 86) up to C	0719
Ford Transit Petrol (Mk 3) (Feb 86 - 89) C to G	1468
Ford Transit Diesel (Feb 86 - 99) C to T	3019
Ford 1.6 & 1.8 litre Diesel Engine (84 - 96) A to N	1172
Ford 2.1, 2.3 & 2.5 litre Diesel Engine (77 - 90) up to H	1606
FREIGHT ROVER Sherpa Petrol (74 - 87) up to E	0463
HILLMAN Avenger (70 - 82) up to Y	0037
Hillman Imp (63 - 76) up to R *	0022
HONDA Civic (Feb 84 - Oct 87) A to E	1226
Honda Civic (Nov 91 - 96) J to N	3199
Honda Civic Petrol (Mar 95 - 00) M to X	4050
Honda Civic Petrol & Diesel (01 - 05) X to 55	4611
Honda Jazz (01 - Feb 08) 51 - 57	4735
HYUNDAI Pony (85 - 94) C to M	3398
JAGUAR E Type (61 - 72) up to L *	0140
Jaguar MkI & II, 240 & 340 (55 - 69) up to H *	0098
Jaguar XJ6, XJ & Sovereign; Daimler Sovereign (68 - Oct 86) up to D	0242
Jaguar XJ6 & Sovereign (Oct 86 - Sept 94) D to M	3261
Jaguar XJ12, XJS & Sovereign; Daimler Double Six (72 - 88) up to F	0478
JEEP Cherokee Petrol (93 - 96) K to N	1943
LADA 1200, 1300, 1500 & 1600 (74 - 91) up to J	0413
Lada Samara (87 - 91) D to J	1610
LAND ROVER 90, 110 & Defender Diesel (83 - 07) up to 56	3017
Land Rover Discovery Petrol & Diesel (89 - 98) G to S	3016
Land Rover Discovery Diesel (Nov 98 - Jul 04) S to 04	4606
Land Rover Freelander Petrol & Diesel (97 - Sept 03) R to 53	3929
Land Rover Freelander Petrol & Diesel (Oct 03 - Oct 06) 53 to 56	4623
Land Rover Series IIA & III Diesel (58 - 85) up to C	0529
Land Rover Series II, IIA & III 4-cyl Petrol (58 - 85) up to C	0314

Title	Book No.
MAZDA 323 (Mar 81 - Oct 89) up to G	1608
Mazda 323 (Oct 89 - 98) G to R	3455
Mazda 626 (May 83 - Sept 87) up to E	0929
Mazda B1600, B1800 & B2000 Pick-up Petrol (72 - 88) up to F	0267
Mazda RX-7 (79 - 85) up to C *	0460
MERCEDES-BENZ 190, 190E & 190D Petrol & Diesel (83 - 93) A to L	3450
Mercedes-Benz 200D, 240D, 240TD, 300D & 300TD 123 Series Diesel (Oct 76 - 85)	1114
Mercedes-Benz 250 & 280 (68 - 72) up to L *	0346
Mercedes-Benz 250 & 280 123 Series Petrol (Oct 76 - 84) up to B *	0677
Mercedes-Benz 124 Series Petrol & Diesel (85 - Aug 93) C to K	3253
Mercedes-Benz C-Class Petrol & Diesel (93 - Aug 00) L to W	3511
MGA (55 - 62) *	0475
MGB (62 - 80) up to W	0111
MG Midget & Austin-Healey Sprite (58 - 80) up to W *	0265
MINI Petrol (July 01 - 05) Y to 05	4273
MITSUBISHI Shogun & L200 Pick-Ups Petrol (83 - 94) up to M	1944
MORRIS Ital 1.3 (80 - 84) up to B	0705
Morris Minor 1000 (56 - 71) up to K	0024
NISSAN Almera Petrol (95 - Feb 00) N to V	4053
Nissan Almera & Tino Petrol (Feb 00 - 07) V to 56	4612
Nissan Bluebird (May 84 - Mar 86) A to C	1223
Nissan Bluebird Petrol (Mar 86 - 90) C to H	1473
Nissan Cherry (Sept 82 - 86) up to D	1031
Nissan Micra (83 - Jan 93) up to K	0931
Nissan Micra (93 - 02) K to 52	3254
Nissan Primera Petrol (90 - Aug 99) H to T	1851
Nissan Stanza (82 - 86) up to D	0824
Nissan Sunny Petrol (May 82 - Oct 86) up to D	0895
Nissan Sunny Petrol (Oct 86 - Mar 91) D to H	1378
Nissan Sunny Petrol (Apr 91 - 95) H to N	3219
OPEL Ascona & Manta (B Series) (Sept 75 - 88) up to F *	0316
Opel Ascona Petrol (81 - 88)	3215
Opel Astra Petrol (Oct 91 - Feb 98)	3156
Opel Corsa Petrol (83 - Mar 93)	3160
Opel Corsa Petrol (Mar 93 - 97)	3159
Opel Kadett Petrol (Nov 79 - Oct 84) up to B	0634
Opel Kadett Petrol (Oct 84 - Oct 91)	3196
Opel Omega & Senator Petrol (Nov 86 - 94)	3157
Opel Rekord Petrol (Feb 78 - Oct 86) up to D	0543
Opel Vectra Petrol (Oct 88 - Oct 95)	3158
PEUGEOT 106 Petrol & Diesel (91 - 04) J to 53	1882
Peugeot 205 Petrol (83 - 97) A to P	0932
Peugeot 206 Petrol & Diesel (98 - 01) S to X	3757
Peugeot 206 Petrol & Diesel (02 - 06) 51 to 06	4613
Peugeot 306 Petrol & Diesel (93 - 02) K to 02	3073
Peugeot 307 Petrol & Diesel (01 - 04) Y to 54	4147
Peugeot 309 Petrol (86 - 93) C to K	1266
Peugeot 405 Petrol (88 - 97) E to P	1559
Peugeot 405 Diesel (88 - 97) E to P	3198
Peugeot 406 Petrol & Diesel (96 - Mar 99) N to T	3394
Peugeot 406 Petrol & Diesel (Mar 99 - 02) T to 52	3982
Peugeot 505 Petrol (79 - 89) up to G	0762
Peugeot 1.7/1.8 & 1.9 litre Diesel Engine (82 - 96) up to N	0950
Peugeot 2.0, 2.1, 2.3 & 2.5 litre Diesel Engines (74 - 90) up to H	1607
PORSCHE 911 (65 - 85) up to C	0264

* Classic reprint

Title	Book No.
Porsche 924 & 924 Turbo (76 - 85) up to C	0397
PROTON (89 - 97) F to P	3255
RANGE ROVER V8 Petrol (70 - Oct 92) up to K	0606
RELIANT Robin & Kitten (73 - 83) up to A *	0436
RENAULT 4 (61 - 86) up to D *	0072
Renault 5 Petrol (Feb 85 - 96) B to N	1219
Renault 9 & 11 Petrol (82 - 89) up to F	0822
Renault 18 Petrol (79 - 86) up to D	0598
Renault 19 Petrol (89 - 96) F to N	1646
Renault 19 Diesel (89 - 96) F to N	1946
Renault 21 Petrol (86 - 94) C to M	1397
Renault 25 Petrol & Diesel (84 - 92) B to K	1228
Renault Clio Petrol (91 - May 98) H to R	1853
Renault Clio Diesel (91 - June 96) H to N	3031
Renault Clio Petrol & Diesel (May 98 - May 01) R to Y	3906
Renault Clio Petrol & Diesel (June 01 - '05) Y to 55	4168
Renault Espace Petrol & Diesel (85 - 96) C to N	3197
Renault Laguna Petrol & Diesel (94 - 00) L to W	3252
Renault Laguna Petrol & Diesel (Feb 01 - Feb 05) X to 54	4283
Renault Mégane & Scénic Petrol & Diesel (96 - 99) N to T	3395
Renault Mégane & Scénic Petrol & Diesel (Apr 99 - 02) T to 52	3916
Renault Megane Petrol & Diesel (Oct 02 - 05) 52 to 55	4284
Renault Scenic Petrol & Diesel (Sept 03 - 06) 53 to 06	4297
ROVER 213 & 216 (84 - 89) A to G	1116
Rover 214 & 414 Petrol (89 - 96) G to N	1689
Rover 216 & 416 Petrol (89 - 96) G to N	1830
Rover 211, 214, 216, 218 & 220 Petrol & Diesel (Dec 95 - 99) N to V	3399
Rover 25 & MG ZR Petrol & Diesel (Oct 99 - 04) V to 54	4145
Rover 414, 416 & 420 Petrol & Diesel (May 95 - 98) M to R	3453
Rover 45 / MG ZS Petrol & Diesel (99 - 05) V to 55	4384
Rover 618, 620 & 623 Petrol (93 - 97) K to P	3257
Rover 75 / MG ZT Petrol & Diesel (99 - 06) S to 06	4292
Rover 820, 825 & 827 Petrol (86 - 95) D to N	1380
Rover 3500 (76 - 87) up to E *	0365
Rover Metro, 111 & 114 Petrol (May 90 - 98) G to S	1711
SAAB 95 & 96 (66 - 76) up to R *	0198
Saab 90, 99 & 900 (79 - Oct 93) up to L	0765
Saab 900 (Oct 93 - 98) L to R	3512
Saab 9000 (4-cyl) (85 - 98) C to S	1686
Saab 9-3 Petrol & Diesel (98 - Aug 02) R to 02	4614
Saab 9-5 4-cyl Petrol (97 - 04) R to 54	4156
SEAT Ibiza & Cordoba Petrol & Diesel (Oct 93 - Oct 99) L to V	3571
Seat Ibiza & Malaga Petrol (85 - 92) B to K	1609
SKODA Estelle (77 - 89) up to G	0604
Skoda Fabia Petrol & Diesel (00 - 06) W to 06	4376
Skoda Favorit (89 - 96) F to N	1801
Skoda Felicia Petrol & Diesel (95 - 01) M to X	3505
Skoda Octavia Petrol & Diesel (98 - Apr 04) R to 04	4285
SUBARU 1600 & 1800 (Nov 79 - 90) up to H *	0995
SUNBEAM Alpine, Rapier & H120 (67 - 74) up to N *	0051
SUZUKI SJ Series, Samurai & Vitara (4-cyl) Petrol (82 - 97) up to P	1942
Suzuki Supercarry & Bedford/Vauxhall Rascal (86 - Oct 94) C to M	3015
TALBOT Alpine, Solara, Minx & Rapier (75 - 86) up to D	0337

Title	Book No.
Talbot Horizon Petrol (78 - 86) up to D	0473
Talbot Samba (82 - 86) up to D	0823
TOYOTA Avensis Petrol (98 - Jan 03) R to 52	4264
Toyota Carina E Petrol (May 92 - 97) J to P	3256
Toyota Corolla (80 - 85) up to C	0683
Toyota Corolla (Sept 83 - Sept 87) A to E	1024
Toyota Corolla (Sept 87 - Aug 92) E to K	1683
Toyota Corolla Petrol (Aug 92 - 97) K to P	3259
Toyota Corolla Petrol (July 97 - Feb 02) P to 51	4286
Toyota Hi-Ace & Hi-Lux Petrol (69 - Oct 83) up to A	0304
Toyota Yaris Petrol (99 - 05) T to 05	4265
TRIUMPH GT6 & Vitesse (62 - 74) up to N *	0112
Triumph Herald (59 - 71) up to K *	0010
Triumph Spitfire (62 - 81) up to X	0113
Triumph Stag (70 - 78) up to T *	0441
Triumph TR2, TR3, TR3A, TR4 & TR4A (52 - 67) up to F *	0028
Triumph TR5 & 6 (67 - 75) up to P *	0031
Triumph TR7 (75 - 82) up to Y *	0322
VAUXHALL Astra Petrol (80 - Oct 84) up to B	0635
Vauxhall Astra & Belmont Petrol (Oct 84 - Oct 91) B to J	1136
Vauxhall Astra Petrol (Oct 91 - Feb 98) J to R	1832
Vauxhall/Opel Astra & Zafira Petrol (Feb 98 - Apr 04) R to 04	3758
Vauxhall/Opel Astra & Zafira Diesel (Feb 98 - Apr 04) R to 04	3797
Vauxhall/Opel Astra Petrol (04 - 07) 04 - 07	4732
Vauxhall/Opel Astra Diesel (04 - 07) 04 - 07	4733
Vauxhall/Opel Calibra (90 - 98) G to S	3502
Vauxhall Carlton Petrol (Oct 78 - Oct 86) up to D	0480
Vauxhall Carlton & Senator Petrol (Nov 86 - 94) D to L	1469
Vauxhall Cavalier Petrol (81 - Oct 88) up to F	0812
Vauxhall Cavalier Petrol (Oct 88 - 95) F to N	1570
Vauxhall Chevette (75 - 84) up to B	0285
Vauxhall/Opel Corsa Diesel (Mar 93 - Oct 00) K to X	4087
Vauxhall Corsa Petrol (Mar 93 - 97) K to R	1985
Vauxhall/Opel Corsa Petrol (Apr 97 - Oct 00) P to X	3921
Vauxhall/Opel Corsa Petrol & Diesel (Oct 00 - Sept 03) X to 53	4079
Vauxhall/Opel Corsa Petrol & Diesel (Oct 03 - Aug 06) 53 to 06	4617
Vauxhall/Opel Frontera Petrol & Diesel (91 - Sept 98) J to S	3454
Vauxhall Nova Petrol (83 - 93) up to K	0909
Vauxhall/Opel Omega Petrol (94 - 99) L to T	3510
Vauxhall/Opel Vectra Petrol & Diesel (95 - Feb 99) N to S	3396
Vauxhall/Opel Vectra Petrol & Diesel (Mar 99 - May 02) T to 02	3930
Vauxhall/Opel Vectra Petrol & Diesel (June 02 - Sept 05) 02 to 55	4618
Vauxhall/Opel 1.5, 1.6 & 1.7 litre Diesel Engine (82 - 96) up to N	1222
VW 411 & 412 (68 - 75) up to P *	0091
VW Beetle 1200 (54 - 77) up to S	0036
VW Beetle 1300 & 1500 (65 - 75) up to P	0039
VW 1302 & 1302S (70 - 72) up to L *	0110
VW 1303, 1303S & GT (72 - 75) up to P	0159
VW Beetle Petrol & Diesel (Apr 99 - 01) T to 51	3798
VW Golf & Jetta Mk 1 Petrol 1.1 & 1.3 (74 - 84) up to A	0716
VW Golf, Jetta & Scirocco Mk 1 Petrol 1.5, 1.6 & 1.8 (74 - 84) up to A	0726

Title	Book No.
VW Golf & Jetta Mk 1 Diesel (78 - 84) up to A	0451
VW Golf & Jetta Mk 2 Petrol (Mar 84 - Feb 92) A to J	1081
VW Golf & Vento Petrol & Diesel (Feb 92 - Mar 98) J to R	3097
VW Golf & Bora Petrol & Diesel (April 98 - 00) R to X	3727
VW Golf & Bora 4-cyl Petrol & Diesel (01 - 03) X to 53	4169
VW Golf & Jetta Petrol & Diesel (04 - 07) 53 to 07	4610
VW LT Petrol Vans & Light Trucks (76 - 87) up to E	0637
VW Passat & Santana Petrol (Sept 81 - May 88) up to E	0814
VW Passat 4-cyl Petrol & Diesel (May 88 - 96) E to P	3498
VW Passat 4-cyl Petrol & Diesel (Dec 96 - Nov 00) P to X	3917
VW Passat Petrol & Diesel (Dec 00 - May 05) X to 05	4279
VW Polo & Derby (76 - Jan 82) up to X	0335
VW Polo (82 - Oct 90) up to H	0813
VW Polo Petrol (Nov 90 - Aug 94) H to L	3245
VW Polo Hatchback Petrol & Diesel (94 - 99) M to S	3500
VW Polo Hatchback Petrol (00 - Jan 02) V to 51	4150
VW Polo Petrol & Diesel (02 - May 05) 51 to 05	4608
VW Scirocco (82 - 90) up to H *	1224
VW Transporter 1600 (68 - 79) up to V	0082
VW Transporter 1700, 1800 & 2000 (72 - 79) up to V *	0226
VW Transporter (air-cooled) Petrol (79 - 82) up to Y *	0638
VW Transporter (water-cooled) Petrol (82 - 90) up to H	3452
VW Type 3 (63 - 73) up to M *	0084
VOLVO 120 & 130 Series (& P1800) (61 - 73) up to M *	0203
Volvo 142, 144 & 145 (66 - 74) up to N *	0129
Volvo 240 Series Petrol (74 - 93) up to K	0270
Volvo 262, 264 & 260/265 (75 - 85) up to C *	0400
Volvo 340, 343, 345 & 360 (76 - 91) up to J	0715
Volvo 440, 460 & 480 Petrol (87 - 97) D to P	1691
Volvo 740 & 760 Petrol (82 - 91) up to J	1258
Volvo 850 Petrol (92 - 96) J to P	3260
Volvo 940 petrol (90 - 98) H to R	3249
Volvo S40 & V40 Petrol (96 - Mar 04) N to 04	3569
Volvo S40 & V50 Petrol & Diesel (Mar 04 - Jun 07) 04 to 07	4731
Volvo S70, V70 & C70 Petrol (96 - 99) P to V	3573
Volvo V70 / S80 Petrol & Diesel (98 - 05) S to 55	4263

AUTOMOTIVE TECHBOOKS

Title	Book No.
Automotive Electrical and Electronic Systems Manual	3049
Automotive Gearbox Overhaul Manual	3473
Automotive Service Summaries Manual	3475
Automotive Timing Belts Manual – Austin/Rover	3549
Automotive Timing Belts Manual – Ford	3474
Automotive Timing Belts Manual – Peugeot/Citroën	3568
Automotive Timing Belts Manual – Vauxhall/Opel	3577

DIY MANUAL SERIES

Title	Book No.
The Haynes Air Conditioning Manual	4192
The Haynes Car Electrical Systems Manual	4251
The Haynes Manual on Bodywork	4198
The Haynes Manual on Brakes	4178
The Haynes Manual on Carburettors	4177
The Haynes Manual on Diesel Engines	4174
The Haynes Manual on Engine Management	4199
The Haynes Manual on Fault Codes	4175
The Haynes Manual on Practical Electrical Systems	4267
The Haynes Manual on Small Engines	4250
The Haynes Manual on Welding	4176

* Classic reprint

All the products featured on this page are available through most motor accessory shops, cycle shops and book stores. Our policy of continuous updating and development means that titles are being constantly added to the range. For up-to-date information on our complete list of titles, please telephone: (UK) +44 1963 442030 • (USA) +1 805 498 6703 • (Sweden) +46 18 124016 • (Australia) +61 3 9763 8100

CL23.12/07

Preserving Our Motoring Heritage

<
The Model J Duesenberg Derham Tourster. Only eight of these magnificent cars were ever built – this is the only example to be found outside the United States of America

Almost every car you've ever loved, loathed or desired is gathered under one roof at the Haynes Motor Museum. Over 300 immaculately presented cars and motorbikes represent every aspect of our motoring heritage, from elegant reminders of bygone days, such as the superb Model J Duesenberg to curiosities like the bug-eyed BMW Isetta. There are also many old friends and flames. Perhaps you remember the 1959 Ford Popular that you did your courting in? The magnificent 'Red Collection' is a spectacle of classic sports cars including AC, Alfa Romeo, Austin Healey, Ferrari, Lamborghini, Maserati, MG, Riley, Porsche and Triumph.

A Perfect Day Out

Each and every vehicle at the Haynes Motor Museum has played its part in the history and culture of Motoring. Today, they make a wonderful spectacle and a great day out for all the family. Bring the kids, bring Mum and Dad, but above all bring your camera to capture those golden memories for ever. You will also find an impressive array of motoring memorabilia, a comfortable 70 seat video cinema and one of the most extensive transport book shops in Britain. The Pit Stop Cafe serves everything from a cup of tea to wholesome, home-made meals or, if you prefer, you can enjoy the large picnic area nestled in the beautiful rural surroundings of Somerset.

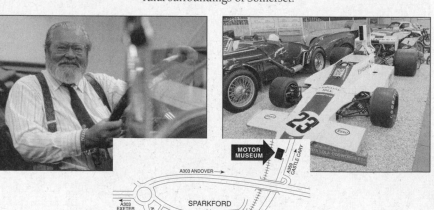

>
John Haynes O.B.E., Founder and Chairman of the museum at the wheel of a Haynes Light 12.

<
Graham Hill's Lola Cosworth Formula 1 car next to a 1934 Riley Sports.

The Museum is situated on the A359 Yeovil to Frome road at Sparkford, just off the A303 in Somerset. It is about 40 miles south of Bristol, and 25 minutes drive from the M5 intersection at Taunton.
Open 9.30am - 5.30pm (10.00am - 4.00pm Winter) 7 days a week, *except Christmas Day, Boxing Day and New Years Day*
Special rates available for schools, coach parties and outings Charitable Trust No. 292048